Contributions to Economics

AF904137

The series *Contributions to Economics* provides an outlet for innovative research in all areas of economics. Books published in the series are primarily monographs and multiple author works that present new research results on a clearly defined topic, but contributed volumes and conference proceedings are also considered. All books are published in print and ebook and disseminated and promoted globally. The series and the volumes published in it are indexed by Scopus and ISI (selected volumes).

László Mátyás

Central and Eastern European Economies and the War in Ukraine

Between a Rock and a Hard Place

Springer

Editor
László Mátyás
Department of Economics and Business
Central European University
Budapest, Hungary and Vienna, Austria

ISSN 1431-1933 ISSN 2197-7178 (electronic)
Contributions to Economics
ISBN 978-3-031-61560-3 ISBN 978-3-031-61561-0 (eBook)
https://doi.org/10.1007/978-3-031-61561-0

© The Editor(s) (if applicable) and The Author(s), under exclusive license to Springer Nature Switzerland AG 2024, corrected publication 2024
Chapter 2 "Economic Growth & Resilience" is licensed under the terms of the Creative Commons Attribution 4.0 International License (http://creativecommons.org/licenses/by/4.0/). For further details see license information in the chapter.
This work is subject to copyright. All rights are solely and exclusively licensed by the Publisher, whether the whole or part of the material is concerned, specifically the rights of translation, reprinting, reuse of illustrations, recitation, broadcasting, reproduction on microfilms or in any other physical way, and transmission or information storage and retrieval, electronic adaptation, computer software, or by similar or dissimilar methodology now known or hereafter developed.
The use of general descriptive names, registered names, trademarks, service marks, etc. in this publication does not imply, even in the absence of a specific statement, that such names are exempt from the relevant protective laws and regulations and therefore free for general use.
The publisher, the authors, and the editors are safe to assume that the advice and information in this book are believed to be true and accurate at the date of publication. Neither the publisher nor the authors or the editors give a warranty, expressed or implied, with respect to the material contained herein or for any errors or omissions that may have been made. The publisher remains neutral with regard to jurisdictional claims in published maps and institutional affiliations.

This Springer imprint is published by the registered company Springer Nature Switzerland AG
The registered company address is: Gewerbestrasse 11, 6330 Cham, Switzerland

If disposing of this product, please recycle the paper.

Preface

During the period after the great financial crisis before the Covid pandemic hit, according to most economic indicators, Central and Eastern European Countries (CEEC) experienced a steady catch up to the European Union's average. Although the Covid shock had an understandably negative effect on these emerging economies, overall, they have proved to be quite resilient, not underperforming more developed EU countries.[1]

Then, straight after Covid, Russia attacked Ukraine, and a second serious economic shock hit the region. As these countries are neighbouring the conflict zone, they were heavily affected by the events. The current volume explores the effects of the war on Central and Eastern European EU member states' economies and their likely economic outlook after the war. At the time of writing this volume, the war is still raging, with peace nowhere on the horizon; thus, all information and data available have to be taken with a pinch of salt. Nevertheless, the main economic facts, trends, and directions are already clearly visible, making an objective economic analysis feasible. This is also imperative, as decisions are being made that are likely to have a long-lasting effect on the region and Europe. Therefore, as far as possible, the studies are fact and data driven. As it is often the case, economics, policy, and politics are intrinsically intertwined. In editing this volume, however, we tried to focus solely on the economy, leaving aside the political side of events.

Chapter 1 of the volume deals with sanctions, i.e., measuring the extent the more than a dozen sanction packages imposed on Russia have affected CEEC. Surprisingly, it has been found that beyond energy supply and security, sanctions had some, but overall limited effects on these economies. Energy related effects, on the other hand, were mitigated by several factors, but mostly by flexible regimes in the form of exceptions granted to the hardest hit.

Chapter 2 looks at the overall macroeconomic picture of the CEE economies. Luckily, the early bleaker expectations were avoided, and the region appears quite resilient. The impact was mainly growth-related, in most countries taking the form

[1] For a detailed analysis, see Mátyás (ed): Emerging European Economies after the Pandemic, Springer, 2022. In fact, the current book should be considered as a follow-up of that volume.

of a short but seemingly transitory recession and inflation, which turned out to be somewhat larger and more persistent than in Western Europe. These effects, however, were uneven across the CEEC, depending mostly on the fiscal space available and other country specific factors.

Dramatic changes in energy markets, energy security and its deep and wide-ranging effect on the CEE economies have been among the most visible and discussed shocks of the war. Chapter 3 scrutinizes them, along with likely mitigating policy tools, such as supply diversification, increased energy efficiency, an appropriate legal framework, and proper targeted incentives.

Another highly tangible effect of the war on the economy and society has been the surge in inflation. Many countries have experienced the largest inflation spike for over a generation, which obviously affects the way societies perceive the war. Central banks swiftly responded with a steady rate increase, gradually taming the alarming trend, but killing growth, at least in the short term. Chapter 4 presents a detailed analysis of these events.

Aggravated by the current war, budgets and, more generally, fiscal space have been under considerable strain since the Covid pandemic. The consequences are serious, but the stance taken on them is country specific, as the fiscal conditions have been quite different across the CEEC. Moreover, since some effects manifest themselves with a considerable lag, it is extremely hard to obtain a clear picture. Definitive answers are even more difficult to give if we consider the hard-to-predict burdens of the eventual reconstruction of Ukraine's economy. Chapter 5 does navigate readers through the maze of sometimes contradictory and not always up to the minute data and information, providing an analysis of where we are and where we are heading to.

Chapter 6 deals with external balances. The two most relevant negative shocks in this area were the deterioration of the current account balances mostly due to the surge in energy prices and the tightening of the external financial conditions that lead to substantial capital outflows. The magnitude of these, however, varied with countries, depending mostly on policy preferences and regimes.

Chapter 7 shows that while global trade slowed substantially in 2022 and 2023, both exports to and imports from Ukraine to the CEEC increased. Exports to Russia have also increased due to the obvious price effects. Overall, the terms of trade have deteriorated for the region, but as energy prices have declined, some considerable improvement can be noted. However, FDI to and from Russia and Ukraine has been minuscule, which perhaps comes as a surprise. Since 2022, IT related FDI originating in Ukraine has had a measurable job creation effect in some CEE economies.

Chapter 8 deals with Europe's largest refugee crisis since World War II. Although data is highly unreliable, the numbers are staggering. This represents a veritable demographic catastrophe for Ukraine. On the other hand, perhaps surprisingly, due to the positive attitude of governments and welcoming populations, Europe and the region were able to deal with this exodus relatively smoothly. It is safe to say that, despite the early burden and costs, the inflow of refugees had a positive effect on the CEE economies. The eventual return-rate, however, is hard to fathom, and may have a profound effect on the eventual reconstruction of Ukraine.

Chapter 9 focuses on the life of refugees, their access to education and the labour market. Despite the lack of hard data, it is safe to say that although in the early days they expected a quick return home, after two years of war there is a significant shift in their intentions. Refugees need a transparent legal framework for the transition from temporary to permanent residency in order to avoid the 'inactivity trap'. It should also be considered that many of the refugees are women with children whose husbands stayed in Ukraine; beyond language proficiency, their participation in the labour market is conditioned by affordable housing, childcare, and schooling.

The last chapter in the volume is about the reconstruction of Ukraine. The task is gargantuan, as it involves not only the 'reconstruction' but also the modernization of the country. There are several major challenges, and the ways to deal with them are still to be worked out. Some of the most pressing questions are: How to finance reconstruction? How to deal with Ukraine's colossal demographic deficit? How to handle the 'rapprochement' and eventual long-term EU integration without seriously disrupting the internal EU market? At the same time, how to help other EU candidate countries so they should not feel disenfranchised by the help and support provided to Ukraine? The success of this decades long process will have profound and long-lasting consequences on Europe's future. Therefore, we should find procedures to carry out these tasks in ways acceptable to the people of Europe and Ukraine alike, on the one hand, and efficient and fully transparent on the other.

Overall, although this war has had a major impact on the CEE economies, some are much more affected than others, as can be seen throughout the chapters. Nevertheless most seem to have proved quite resilient. Also, this shock may have speeded up structural and policy reforms long overdue in some countries and may also promote green transition.

Let me remark that although there are certain overlaps between the chapters, the issues are always addressed from different perspectives and to different depths. Also, we know that some of our readers may only be interested in some of the topics, and this approach may help them understand the broader picture as well. Finally, it is worth mentioning that the manuscript was closed at the end of March 2024, data and events represent the best of our knowledge at this point in time.

Martin Luther King, Jr once said:
"The ultimate measure of a man is not where he stands in moments of comfort and convenience, but where he stands at times of challenge and controversy." Perhaps this is also true for countries.

Budapest and Vienna, March 2024 *László Mátyás*

Acknowledgements

We address our thanks to all those who have facilitated the birth of this volume: the contributors who produced quality work, despite pestering, frequent requests, and onerous instructions from the editor, and our publisher Springer Nature, who had the foresight to publish a collection of analyses about the economic effects of this terrible ongoing war.

Comments and remarks received during the writing and editing process acknowledged at the end of each chapter have substantially improved the quality of the book. Editorial assistance by Eszter Timár has added much to the quality of this volume, and support received from György Bőgel, Balázs Csontó, and Júlia Király during the editing process are also kindly acknowledged.

The final camera-ready copy of the volume has been prepared with LaTeX and Overleaf by the authors, the editor, and the tireless and always helpful contribution of Polad Gulushov and Kristóf Reizinger.

In memory of Robin Bellers, who lived and died for English language excellence.

Contents

List of Contributors

Volume Editor:
László Mátyás
Central European University, Budapest, Hungary, and Vienna, Austria, e-mail: matyas@ceu.edu

Contributors:
Péter Benczúr
European Commission, Joint Research Centre, Ispra, Italy, e-mail: peter.benczur@ec.europa.eu

Szilárd Benk
Corvinus University of Budapest, Budapest, Hungary, e-mail: szilard.benk@uni-corvinus.hu

György Bőgel
Central European University, Budapest, Hungary and Vienna, Austria, e-mail: bogelgy@ceu.edu

Jan Brzozowski
Jagiellonian University, Kraków, Poland, e-mail: jan.brzozowski@uj.edu.pl

Jiaqian Chen
International Monetary Fund, Washington, DC, e-mail: jchen@imf.org

Maxim Chupilkin
European Bank for Reconstruction and Development, London, UK and University of Oxford, Oxford, UK, e-mail: chupilkm@ebrd.com

Balázs Csontó
International Monetary Fund, Washington, DC, e-mail: bcsonto@imf.org

Karolina Czerska-Shaw
Jagiellonian University, Kraków, Poland, e-mail: karolina.czerska@uj.edu.pl

Maciej Duszczyk
University of Warsaw, Warsaw, Poland, e-mail: m.duszczyk@uw.edu.pl

Jakub Głowacki
Krakow University of Economics, Kraków, Poland, e-mail: glowackj@uek.krakow.pl

Anna Gomola
Krakow University of Economics, Kraków, Poland, e-mail: gomolaa@uek.krakow.pl

Martin Guzi
Masaryk University, Brno, Czech Republic and Central European Labour Studies Institute (CELSI), Bratislava, Slovakia, e-mail: Martin.Guzi@econ.muni.cz

Dóra Győrffy
Corvinus University of Budapest, Budapest, Hungary, e-mail: dora.gyorffy@uni-corvinus.hu

Péter Horváth
Corvinus University of Budapest, Budapest, Hungary, e-mail: peter.horvath16@stud.uni-corvinus.hu;

Peter Huber
WIFO, Austrian Institute of Economic Research, Vienna, Austria, e-mail: peter.huber@wifo.ac.at

Ulrike Huemer
WIFO, Austrian Institute of Economic Research, Vienna, Austria, e-mail: ulrike.huemer@wifo.ac.at

Júlia Király
International Business School, Budapest, Hungary, e-mail: jkiraly@ibs-b.hu

Zsóka Kóczán
European Bank for Reconstruction and Development, London, UK, e-mail: koczanz@ebrd.com

István Kónya
Corvinus University of Budapest and Centre for Economic and Regional Studies, Budapest, Hungary, e-mail: istvan.konya@uni-corvinus.hu

Artem Kochnev
WIIW, Vienna Institute for International Economic Studies, Vienna, Austria, e-mail: kochnev@wiiw.ac.at

Michal Król
Krakow University of Economics, Kraków, Poland, e-mail: krolm@uek.krakow.pl

Michael Landesmann
WIIW, Vienna Institute for International Economic Studies, Vienna, Austria, e-mail: landesmann@wiiw.ac.at

Csaba László
Corvinus University of Budapest, Department of Macrofinance, Budapest, Hungary, e-mail: csaba.laszlo@malcon.hu

Łukasz Mamica
Krakow University of Economics, Kraków, Poland, e-mail: mamical@uek.krakow.pl

Monika Mazur-Bubak
Krakow University of Economics, Kraków, Poland, e-mail: mazurm@uek.krakow.pl

Olga Pindyuk
WIIW, Vienna Institute for International Economic Studies, Vienna, Austria, e-mail: pindyuk@wiiw.ac.at

Norbert Szepesi
Ministry of Finance, Budapest, Hungary, e-mail: norbert.szepesi@pm.gov.hu

Katalin Tausz,
Eötvös Loránd University, Budapest, Hungary, e-mail: tauszkati@gmail.com

Maryna Tverdostup
WIIW, Vienna Institute for International Economic Studies, Vienna, Austria, e-mail: tverdostup@wiiw.ac.at

Marcela Veselková
Social Policy Institute, Ministry of Labour, Social Affairs and Family of the Slovak Republic, Bratislava, Slovakia, e-mail: Marcela.Veselkova@employment.gov.sk

Chapter 1
Economic Sanctions

Júlia Király and Dóra Győrffy

Abstract The chapter provides a brief overview of the concept, history, and effectiveness of sanctions, as well as a stocktaking of the sanctions against Russia and their potential impact on the Central and Eastern European economies (CEEE). Given the limited non-energy trade and financial ties with Russia, individual, trade, and financial sanctions are likely to have affected the CEEE only to a limited extent. Notwithstanding the heavy dependence of the region on imports of Russian commodities, the impact of energy-related sanctions was also mitigated by several factors. First, the sharp increase in coal, petroleum, and natural gas prices started before the war in Ukraine, and reversed in the second half of 2022 despite the ongoing announcements on sanctions. Second, in order to minimize disruptions to supply, sanctions related to oil included several exemptions for countries with limited alternative options. Third, against the backdrop of high dependence on Russian imports, no sanctions were introduced on natural gas. Nonetheless, the assessment of the impact of sanctions is a challenging task as it requires a distinction between the impact of the war and sanctions, and thus an understanding of a no-sanction counterfactual scenario under which there could still be major disruptions to supply, and shocks to prices given the elevated uncertainty caused by the war.

Júlia Király ✉
International Business School, Budapest, Hungary, e-mail: jkiraly@ibs-b.hu

Dóra Győrffy
Corvinus University of Budapest, Budapest, Hungary, e-mail: dora.gyorffy@uni-corvinus.hu

© The Author(s), under exclusive license to Springer Nature Switzerland AG 2024
L. Mátyás (ed.), *Central and Eastern European Economies and the War in Ukraine*,
Contributions to Economics, https://doi.org/10.1007/978-3-031-61561-0_1

1.1 Introduction

The Russian invasion of Ukraine was followed by an unprecedented number of sanctions in several areas, ranging from individual restrictions to trade and financial sanctions. As of February 2024, the European Union (EU) had imposed 13 comprehensive packages of sanctions since 23 February 2022, including a number of economic sanctions aimed "to impose severe consequences on Russia for its actions and to effectively thwart Russian abilities to continue the aggression" (European Council, 2024).

Throughout history, countries often resorted to sanctions in order to trigger a change in the target's behavior by weakening its economic base, with the ultimate objective of protecting national interests and - in the case of modern sanctions - international norms.[1] Given their potential to incur significant costs for the target country, sanctions were described by U.S. president Woodrow Wilson in 1919 as "something more tremendous than war", and "often referred to in English as 'the economic weapon'" at the time (Mulder, 2022). Notwithstanding the sizeable economic costs of sanctions, however, there is mixed evidence as to whether sanctions are successful at achieving the desired change in the target's behavior (Morgan, Syropoulos & Yotov, 2023). Moreover, the scope and duration of sanctions is often weakened by the sanctioning country's concerns over negative spillbacks to its economy.

Following a brief overview of the concept, history, and effectiveness of sanctions, the chapter takes stock of the sanctions imposed on Russia since the start of the war in Ukraine, as well as the potential implications for Central and Eastern European economies (CEEE), with a few caveats. First, the chapter does not aim to assess the effectiveness of sanctions. While the public debate often focuses on whether sanctions against Russia have 'worked', the discourse is sometimes misleading and/or premature. Specifically, the effectiveness of sanctions should be assessed against their stated objective, i.e., to "thwart Russian abilities to continue the aggression" in this case (European Council, 2024). As of late-2023, however, it is premature to assess whether the strategy of sanctioning countries would eventually achieve their goal. Second, the chapter focuses on the potential impact on the CEEE as opposed to the impact on Russia. While the weakening of the Russian economy as a result of the sanctions could also affect the CEEE indirectly, the limited non-energy trade and financial ties between most CEE countries and Russia suggest modest effects on the CEEE via this channel. Third, the quantification of the impact of sanctions on the CEEE is a challenging task as it would require a comparison with a no-sanction counterfactual scenario, i.e., a scenario under which no sanction had been imposed and there was a credible commitment to not impose any sanction on Russia following the invasion of Ukraine.[2] Even in the absence of sanctions, however, there could

[1] In the context of sanctions during the interwar period, Mulder (2022) argues that "in the eyes of many internationalists" sanctions "also had a moral and legal purpose: to punish the crime of aggression".

[2] The latter is key as an expectation of the introduction of sanctions could trigger movements in markets (e.g., commodity prices) even before the first mention, the official announcement, or the time when the sanction becomes effective.

be major disruptions to trade and supply chains and shocks to prices amid high uncertainty caused by the war. As such, the main objective of the chapter is to highlight potential channels through which sanctions could have affected the CEEE.[3]

Against this backdrop, the chapter provides an overview of the individual, trade, and financial sanctions imposed on Russia.[4] Restrictive measures on private individuals and entities took the form of travel bans and asset freezes, with no significant impact on the CEEE. Sanctions affecting the financial sector affected the region mostly through the exposure of these banks to the CEEE, though not to a significant extent. Although there were several restrictions on non-energy trade, including bans on exports and imports, most CEE countries had moderate trade relations with Russia.

Given the heavy reliance on imports from Russia, the main channel through which the CEEE have been affected is energy trade. One of the earliest energy-related measures announced by the EU was the ban on imports of Russian coal. Although coal prices increased sharply in the first half of 2022, the impact of sanctions on the CEEE was mitigated by several factors, including the relatively low reliance on solid fossil fuels in total energy supply, the fact that the increase in coal prices can only partially be attributed to sanctions, and the quick reversal of the spike in prices.

Shortly after the announced restrictions on coal, the EU also unveiled an eventual ban on imports of Russian petroleum products, followed by the intention to prohibit maritime transportation of Russian-origin oil above a certain price cap in the fall of 2022. Despite the high reliance on Russian oil of CEE countries, the economic impact of sanctions was mitigated by a number of factors. Specifically, the surge in oil prices started well before the war in Ukraine, and the sharp increase in the first half of 2022 reversed during the remainder of the year despite further sanction announcements. Also, in order to minimize disruptions to supply, the EU's sanctions included exemptions for landlocked countries with limited alternative options, as well as for countries with capacity constraints.

In light of the heavy dependence on imports of Russian natural gas and the limited access to alternative sources of gas, the EU did not impose any sanction on imports of Russian natural gas. Supply, however, was affected by several developments, including Russia' decision to require payments for gas to be made in rubles by 'unfriendly' countries (i.e., a 'counter-sanction'), the suspension of gas flows via certain pipelines, as well as the explosion of the Nord Stream pipelines. Nonetheless, most CEE countries adjusted to the shock relatively smoothly, including by securing alternative sources via new liquefied natural gas (LNG) terminals and interconnectors. Moreover, the mild winter in 2022 and lower industrial consumption mitigated demand for natural gas, thereby contributing to the adjustment. Similarly to coal and oil prices, the spike in natural gas prices reversed in the fall of 2022.

---

[3] The assessment of the impact of the war in Ukraine is more straightforward, as it does not necessitate a distinction between the war and sanctions in terms of their impact. For the implications of the war for energy and trade, see Chapter 3 and 7, respectively.

[4] Throughout the chapter, the focus is on sanctions imposed by the EU, as in general they are binding for the CEE countries. As highlighted later, however, there are several country-specific exemptions from these restrictions.

In the first part of the chapter, we provide a general overview of sanctions (Section 1.2), focusing on the concept behind them (Section 1.2.1), their history (Section 1.2.2), and effectiveness (Section 1.2.3). This is followed by the stocktaking of sanctions on Russia and implications for the CEEE (Section 1.3), covering individual restrictions (Section 1.3.1), energy trade (Section 1.3.2), non-energy trade (Section 1.3.3), and developments in the financial sector (Section 1.3.4). Finally, Section 1.4 concludes.

1.2 General Overview of Sanctions

1.2.1 The Concept of Economic Sanctions

Sanctions could be defined as "the constellation of laws, authorities, and obligations laid out in a piece of legislation, government decree, UN resolution, or similar document that restrict or prohibit what is normally permissible conduct and against which performance will be assessed and compliance judged", with the types of sanctions including diplomatic/political, military, technological, and economic (Nephew, 2018). Focusing on the latter, the classic work by Hufbauer, Schott, Elliott and Oegg (2007) defines economic sanctions as "the deliberate, government-inspired withdrawal, or threat of withdrawal, of customary trade or financial relations" to ensure changes "in the target state's political behavior". This definition contains the most important elements necessary to understand sanctions: the objective of sanctions, the sanctioning and the sanctioned entity, and the nature of sanctions.[5]

The overarching objective of modern sanctions is related to "the enforcement of norms and the international legal and economic imagination behind them", i.e., "to protect international norms" (Mulder, 2022). In order to achieve this, economic sanctions aim to ensure changes "in the target state's political behavior" (Hufbauer et al., 2007), by damaging "the target's ability to obtain and use economic resources" (Nephew, 2018).[6] An additional goal of inflicting punishment (Nephew, 2018) and retributing wrongful actions (Hufbauer & Jung, 2021) has also been emphasized in the literature. While this could be interpreted as a 'moral' consideration, it also aims to serve as a deterrent for other actors (Hufbauer & Jung, 2021). Finally, although technological sanctions form a different category, they also have economic implications in the long run, by impairing "the technological development of a country, either in specific ways [...] or more generally" (Nephew, 2018).

Historically, sanctions tended to be imposed by the international community such as the United Nations, but the identity of the sender has become increasingly

[5] As noted in the definition, sanctions can also take the form of a threat, which might bring about the desirable consequences (Bergeijk, 2021).

[6] In terms of the 'desired' change in behavior, Hufbauer et al. (2007) identify five goals: modest policy change, major policy change, regime change, disruption of military adventure, and the impairment of military potential.

heterogeneous over time (Bergeijk, 2021). While the U.S. had been the dominant sanctioning country until the turn of the century, China, the EU, and Russia have become increasingly active since then, and non-state actors have also started to push for sanctions (Hufbauer & Jung, 2021). The target of sanctions is usually a state, while sanctions against designated individuals or entities are relatively new, with the aim of targeting perpetrators of wrongful behaviour, thereby minimizing collateral damage (Hufbauer & Jung, 2021).

Economic sanctions primarily affect trade – typically in the form of restrictions on imports and/or exports –, and finance, including commercial finance, international aid, and development assistance, as well as access to target-country assets within the sender's control (Hufbauer et al., 2007). More recently, the array of sanctions has grown, including pressure on private companies' behaviour, cyber warfare, and private litigation (Hufbauer & Jung, 2021).

1.2.2 A Brief History of Economic Sanctions

Although the history of sanctions goes back to ancient Greece with Pericles's Megarian decree enacted in 432 BC, their extensive use as a method of coercion started only after World War 1 (WW1) (Hufbauer et al., 2007). By introducing the possibility of sanctions into Article 16 of the Covenant of the League of Nations, the designers of the post-WW1 world order aimed to transform the experience of economic blockade against the central powers into a peacetime coercion tool. Given the potentially devastating impact of a full economic blockade on the target state's civilian population, the original objective was to use economic sanctions as a threat rather than actual policy, which made sanctions a kind of predecessor for the post-World War 2 (WW2) nuclear deterrent (Mulder, 2022). Following a steady increase after WW2, the number of new sanctions increased sharply over the past two decades (Figure 1.1).

Over time, both the scope of sanctioning countries and the type of sanctions changed. During the Cold War, trade and arms sale sanctions proliferated initiated mainly by the U.S., which was the dominant sanctioning country as it unilaterally imposed one third of total sanctions and was also active in multiple sanctioning coalitions (Morgan et al., 2023). Following the end of the Cold War, sanctions remained a critical element of global governance, as they were still viewed as a cheaper and easier tool of international coercion than sending in armed forces (Karns & Mingst, 2010). Also, in order to avoid the high humanitarian costs of general sanctions, new methods of targeted or 'smart' sanctions (typically travel and financial) had been devised, which aim to punish specific individuals and groups (Morgan et al., 2023). Since the early-1990s, the increase in the number of sanctions was partly related to the EU and the UN becoming more active. In the second half of the 2010s, however, the U.S. intensified its sanctioning activity, accounting for more than 40 percent of global sanctions in 2019 (Felbermayr, Kirilakha, Syropoulos, Yalcin & Yotov, 2022). Finally, the reasons for sanctioning have also broadened over time,

Fig. 1.1: Global sanctions (number of new sanctions)
Data: Syropoulos, Felbermayr, Kirilakha, Yalcin and Yotov (2023), authors' calculations
Note: For previous versions of the database, see Felbermayr, Kirilakha, Syropoulos, Yalcin and Yotov (2020); Kirilakha, Felbermayr, Syropoulos, Yalcin and Yotov (2021).

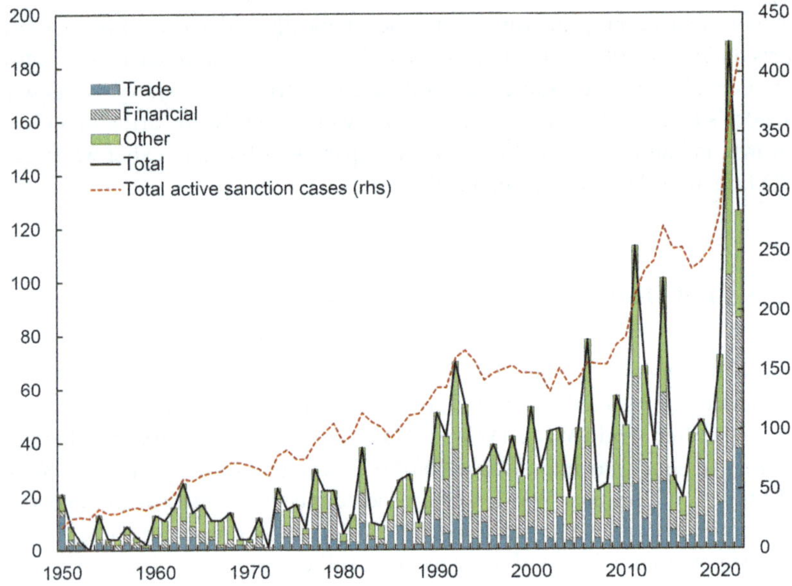

including not only aggression but also the restoration of democracy, fight against nuclear proliferation, terrorism, as well as human rights violations (Karns & Mingst, 2010).

1.2.3 The Effectiveness of Sanctions

Establishing whether sanctions are effective is a methodologically difficult endeavour. The objectives of sanctions are not always well-established, while the policy change following the introduction of sanctions could actually be the result of other factors. There are also cases when sanctioning does not take place as the threat of sanctions already induces policy change.

The pioneering research of Hufbauer et al. (2007) finds that only 34 percent of 174 post-WW1 sanctions can be considered at least partially successful. Those with modest goals such as the release of prisoners had a 51 percent success rate, while more ambitious objectives such as regime change or the disruption of military adventures were associated with a success rate of 31 and 21 percent, respectively. Focusing on the post-Cold War period and including threats along with actual sanctions, Schneider and Weber (2019) find a somewhat higher success rate of 57.5 percent.

While empirical findings largely depend on sample selection and model specification, the survey by Kaempfer and Lowenberg (2007) highlights a few factors that could increase the chances of sanctions' success, including political and economic weakness, a democratic political system in the target country, strong pre-sanction ties, as well as high costs for the target. At the same time, high costs for the sanctioning countries, assistance to the target by third countries, and the ambitiousness of the targeted policy change hinder success. These findings reinforce the importance of asymmetry in the working of sanctions – a lesson learnt from the interwar period (Mulder, 2022): sanctions imposed by large countries on small, dependent economies have the greatest chance to succeed, while large, less democratic countries with strong allies are less likely to be affected by sanctions.

In a recent survey of economic sanctions, Morgan et al. (2023) emphasize differences in methodologies across research disciplines: while economists evaluate the economic costs of sanctions, political scientists look for policy change as a measure of success. This difference strongly impacts the assessment of sanctions. Specifically, economists found a strong negative economic impact of sanctions on trade, foreign direct investment, growth, and poverty rates in the target state (Morgan et al., 2023). In contrast, political scientists found that the objectives of sanctions are met only in a fraction of cases, as economic hardship in the target state does not necessarily yield policy change (Morgan et al., 2023).

The effectiveness of sanctions largely depends on the process of implementation and enforcement. For example, finding the right type of sanctions, building a coalition of sanctioning countries, and discouraging sanction violations require strong sanctioning capacity, as well as careful planning and monitoring that cannot be done on an ad hoc basis (Early, 2021). There is also a need to convince the private sector to voluntarily comply with the sanctioning regime, especially in the case of extraterritorial sanction provisions (Early, 2021). The consideration of enforcement underscores the need that sanctioning be seen as a process, with each actor adapting to changing circumstances – the sender to enforce the sanction, and the target to neutralize them. This also highlights the importance of context, thereby making case study research indispensable in understanding and improving the mechanism of sanctions (Bergeijk, 2021).

Finally, the history of economic sanctions has also shown that sanctions have major unintended consequences. Focusing on the interwar period, Mulder (2022) notes that these limitations include not only the collateral damage to the civilian population but also the spread of policies that induced a growing fragmentation in the world economy. The interwar history of sanctions also showed that sanctions are effective when used against smaller states, and much less so against large, authoritarian powers.

1.3 Sanctions on Russia and Implications for the CEEE

The first international sanction targeting Russian individuals or entities since the Cold War was the Sergei Magnitsky Rule of Law Accountability Act in 2012, which allows visa restrictions and asset freezes on perpetrators of human rights violators (Aslund & Snegovaya, 2021). The occupation of Crimea and the Donbas in 2014 was followed by further sanctions, including the prohibition of business with occupied areas, and personal sanctions on individuals involved in the occupation and election interference. Aslund and Snegovaya (2021) argue that while sanctions did not lead to the withdrawal of Russian forces from the occupied territories, they are estimated to have lowered Russian GDP growth by around 2.5-3 percentage points per year.

In 2022, Russia was hit by an unprecedented number of sanctions. As President Putin signed decrees on the recognition of "the independence and sovereignty of the so-called Luhansk People's Republic (LNR) and Donetsk People's Republic (DNR) regions of Ukraine" and the ordering of Russian troops to the separatist territories on 21 February 2022, a series of sanctions was announced within three days, including an executive order by the U.S. administration banning investment and trade with these regions, travel bans, and asset freezes by the EU on five individuals, and the first major sanctions package by the EU (Bown, 2023). Following the invasion of Ukraine on 24 February 2022, further sanctions were introduced (Figure 1.2). As of February 2024, the European sanctions had been announced in 13 different packages between 23 February 2022 and 23 February 2024, with the stated objective being "to weaken Russia's economic base, depriving it of critical technologies and markets and significantly curtailing its ability to wage war" (European Council, 2023). The packages approved by the EU include several measures, including individual (asset freeze and travel bans) and economic (trade and financial) sanctions (Figure 1.2).

In the remainder of the section, we provide a brief overview of the individual and economic sanctions (energy trade, non-energy trade, and financial sector), as well as their potential impact on the CEEE.

1.3.1 Individuals and Entities

Individual sanctions, targeting those "responsible for supporting, financing or implementing actions which undermine the territorial integrity, sovereignty and independence of Ukraine or who benefit from these actions" in the form of travel bans and asset freezes, had been applied to more than 1,700 individuals and 400 entities (e.g., banks, firms in the defense sector and aviation), with €21.5 billion of assets frozen in the EU as of February 2024 (European Council, 2024).[7] The impact of the travel ban on tourism and the effect of asset freezes on the CEEE are likely to have been marginal. The extent, however, differs across countries. In Bulgaria, for

[7] For the latest list of individuals and entities subject to sanctions, see EUR-Lex (2024).

Fig. 1.2: New sanctions on Russia (number of sanctions)
Data: Bown (2023), authors' calculations
Note: Trade sanctions include restrictions on exports, imports, and trade support.

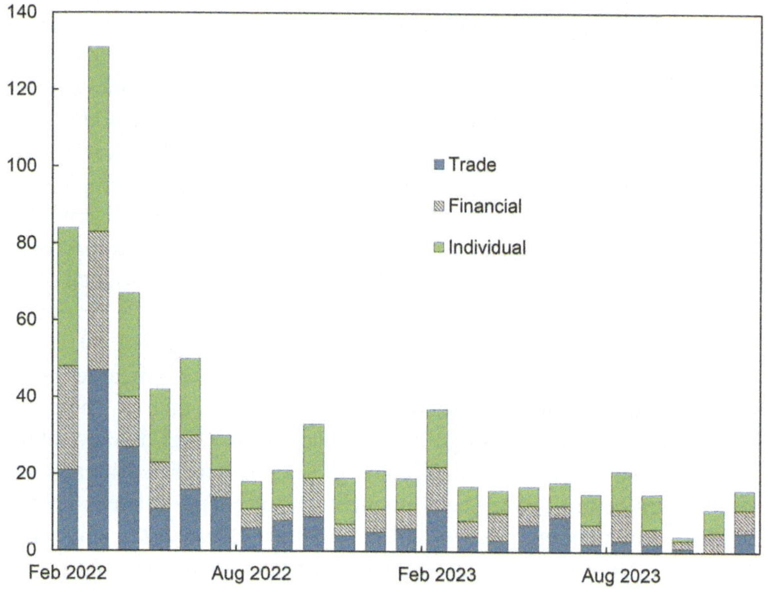

example, Russian visitors accounted for around 10 percent of tourist arrivals before the war (IMF, 2022a).

1.3.2 Energy Trade

Europe's heavy reliance on imports of Russian energy dates back to the post-WW2 period. Following the construction of the Druzhba (Friendship) pipeline, first oil reached Czechoslovakia, Hungary, and Poland in the early-1960s. Over the next two decades, the Bratstvo (Brotherhood) and the Yamal pipelines gave rise to the steady flow of Russian natural gas. As a result, Europe's pre-war trade ties with Russia had been dominated by energy-related products. In 2021, for example, mineral fuels constituted 62 percent of the EU's imports from Russia (European Commission, 2023).

Against this backdrop, energy-related sanctions were not imposed by the EU in the immediate aftermath of the Russian invasion of Ukraine.[8] Nonetheless, in early-March 2022, the EU announced ambitious plans to reduce its reliance on imports of Russian energy, as the Versailles Declaration aimed to – among others –

[8] In contrast, the U.S. announced a ban on imports of Russian coal, oil, and LNG on 8 March 2022.

"phase out our dependency on Russian gas, oil and coal imports as soon as possible" (European Commission, 2022). Specifically, the plans included an expedited reduction in reliance on fossil fuels and an increasing role for renewables, the diversification of supplies and routes, the development of a hydrogen market, the improvement of the interconnection of European gas and electricity networks, as well as the improvement of energy efficiency.

The adoption of the Versailles Declaration was followed by the introduction of a series of sanctions, albeit to a different extent across fossil fuels. In addition to bans on imports of certain Russian fossil fuels, the sanctions also included restrictions on exports and investments targeting the Russian energy sector. For example, the EU's 4th package, announced in March 2022, aimed to "prohibit new investments in the Russian energy sector, as well as a to introduce a comprehensive export restriction on equipment, technology and services for the energy industry" (Council of the EU, 2022g).

In the remainder of the section, we take stock of sanctions on coal, oil, and natural gas, as well as their impact on the CEEE. Notwithstanding the difficulties associated with the quantification of a no-sanction counterfactual scenario, energy-related sanctions did not seem to have a significant impact on the CEEE for several reasons. First, following a steady increase in 2021, energy prices skyrocketed after the Russian invasion of Ukraine but before the announcement of energy-related sanctions by the EU. Also, while energy price volatility remained elevated, the surge in prices proved temporary, with coal, gas, and oil prices returning to their pre-war level by the end of 2022. Second, there were no major supply disruptions, as (i) most countries succeeded in securing alternative routes or sources; (ii) countries having limited access to alternative energy sources and routes were exempted from sanctions, with the potential to even benefit from the discount on Russian energy in some cases; and (iii) there were no sanctions on natural gas, in which case the region had the largest dependence on Russian imports. Third, some sanctions, including those on exports of machinery and equipment or technology to Russia, would affect the capacity of the Russian energy sector only in the medium and long run, therefore there were no spillback effects on the CEEE in the short run.

1.3.2.1 Coal

The Russian invasion of Ukraine was followed by an announcement by the EU in April 2022 on banning imports of Russian coal as of August 2022, as part of the 5th package of sanctions (Council of the EU, 2022a). Against this backdrop, coal prices surged in the first half of 2022 (Figure 1.3). Rising prices, however, cannot fully be attributed to sanctions.

Indeed, coal prices increased sharply already in the second half of 2021 on the back of a shift in demand from gas towards coal triggered by the increase in natural gas prices and the post-pandemic recovery in demand, especially from China (International Energy Agency, 2022). Following a temporary drop in late-2021, coal prices rose further in early-2022, driven by concerns around natural gas supply due

Fig. 1.3: Coal and natural gas prices (USD)
Data: MarketWatch (2023); World Bank (2023), authors' calculations
Note: Coal prices are based on Coal (API2) CIF ARA (ARGUS-McCloskey) Continuous Contract. API2 is the benchmark price for coal imported by Europe. Coal and natural gas prices are expressed in terms of USD per ton and mmbtu, respectively.

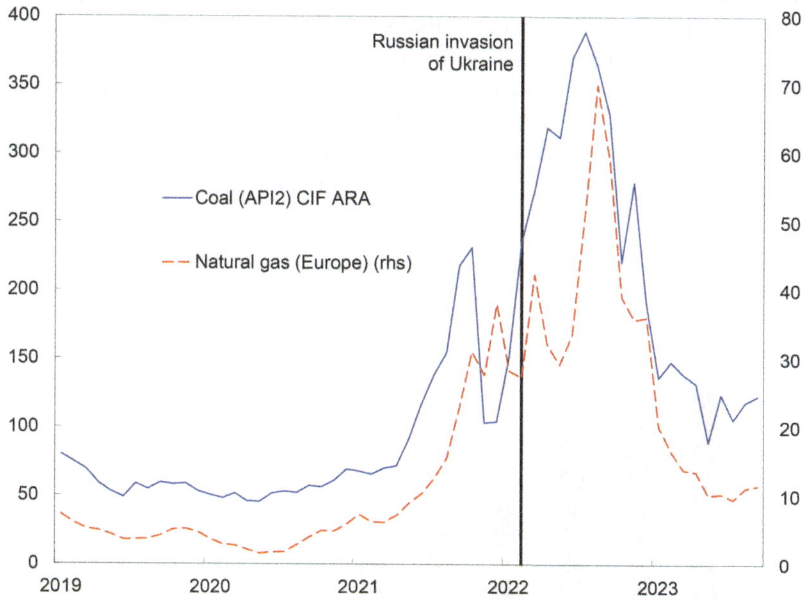

to tensions between Russia and Ukraine, and – reportedly – Covid-19-related staff shortages at the Russian railways used to transport coal (Bloomberg, 2022c). After the start of the war, coal prices skyrocketed, with API2 prices increasing by around 20 percent on the day of the invasion and doubling over the next few days, reaching a historic peak of USD458/t in early-March. In other words, the first wave of the surge in coal prices took place even before the announcement of sanctions on Russian coal.

Following some normalization throughout March with the end of the heating season, coal prices increased sharply again until mid-2022. First, as the sanctions announced by the U.S. and the EU led to uncertainty around coal supplies, countries explored alternative sources of coal. In the first half of 2022, for example, coal imports at Antwerp-Rotterdam-Amsterdam (ARA) increased by a third, partly thanks to increased coal from Australia, Colombia, and the U.S. (Bloomberg, 2022b). Second, given that the EU ban was to become effective only in August 2022, demand for Russian coal increased with the aim of increasing inventories. Third, the surge in natural gas prices was again associated with an increase in demand for coal.

The impact on coal prices, however, differed across different types of coal and proved transitory. Specifically, the shift in demand from Russian coal to other coal resulted in a significant discount on Russian coal prices. For example, "Russian coal at Baltic ports was sold at a 41 percent discount to ARA (Amsterdam Rotterdam Antwerp) prices in March, widening to a 67 percent discount in July" (International Energy Agency, 2022). Also, the surge in coal prices proved short-lived, with API2 prices decreasing to below USD200/t at the end of 2022 and below USD100/t in May 2023 (Figure 1.3). This could be related to several factors. For example, there was uncertainty around the execution of the ban by the EU. While sanctions were supposed to "prohibit EU operators from transferring coal and providing services – such as financing and insurance – to all shipments of such products originating in Russia", an EC guidance issued in September 2022 indicated that the transfer of goods, including coal, to countries outside the EU "should be allowed to combat food and energy insecurity around the world" (Bloomberg, 2022a). Also, as natural gas prices normalized, the need to substitute coal for natural gas also declined.

Fig. 1.4: Imports of solid fossil fuels, 2021 (percentage of total)
Data: Eurostat (2023f), authors' calculations

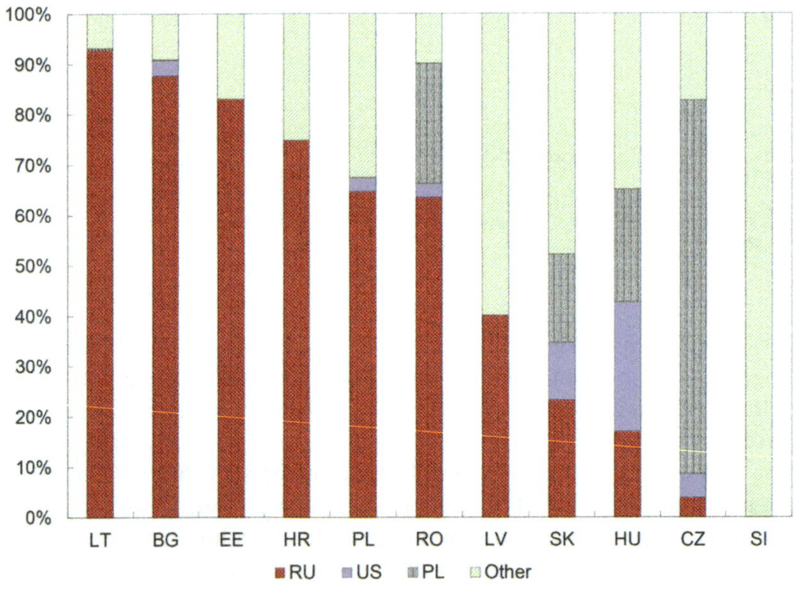

The impact of developments in the coal market on the CEEE was relatively modest. Although the source of imports of solid fossil fuels had been predominantly Russia in most CEE countries before the war (Figure 1.4), solid fossil fuels typically constituted a relatively modest share in total energy supply (Figure 1.5). A notable exception is Poland where coal played an important role. Nonetheless, Poland announced a unilateral ban on imports of Russian coal in April 2022 (i.e., before the EU ban became effective). Reportedly, this was followed by some coal shortages, prompting Poland to suspend the ban on the use of lignite for heating (Reuters, 2022b). In contrast, most CEE countries were less affected, given their low reliance on solid fossil fuels in total energy supply (e.g., Baltics, Croatia, Hungary, Romania).

Fig. 1.5: Total energy supply, 2021 (percentage of total)
Data: Eurostat (2023a), authors' calculations

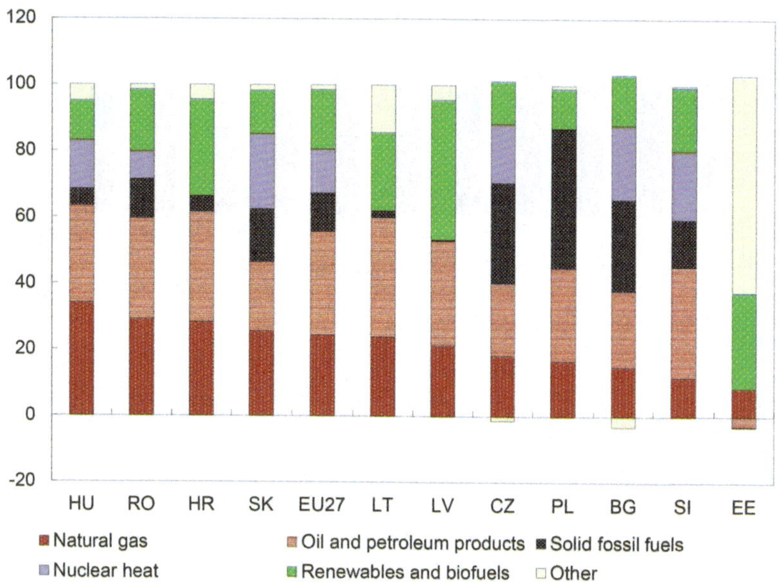

1.3.2.2 Oil

Shortly after the sanctions announced on Russian coal, the EU's 6th package, unveiled in late-May 2022, included an eventual ban on imports of Russian petroleum products (European Council, 2022). Compared with solid fossil fuels, the reliance of the CEEE on oil and petroleum products was much higher. Specifically, oil and petroleum constituted around 20-30 percent of total energy supply in most CEE countries (Figure 1.5). Moreover, it was almost entirely imported from abroad (Figure 1.6), with a relatively large reliance on Russian imports, albeit to a varying extent across the CEEE (Figure 1.7). For example, Russian imports amounted to around 60-75 percent of total imports in Lithuania, Poland, and Slovakia, and less than 10 percent in Bulgaria, Croatia, and Slovenia (Figure 1.7). Given the large overall reliance of the region on Russian oil, sanctions had the potential to affect the CEEE through higher prices and supply disruptions. The final impact, however, seemed rather limited for several reasons.

At the time of the announcement of the EU's 6th package, Brent oil price was USD126 up from USD101 on the day of the invasion (Figure 1.8). The surge in oil

Fig. 1.6: Total oil supply, 2021 (percentage of total)
Data: Eurostat (2023a), authors' calculations

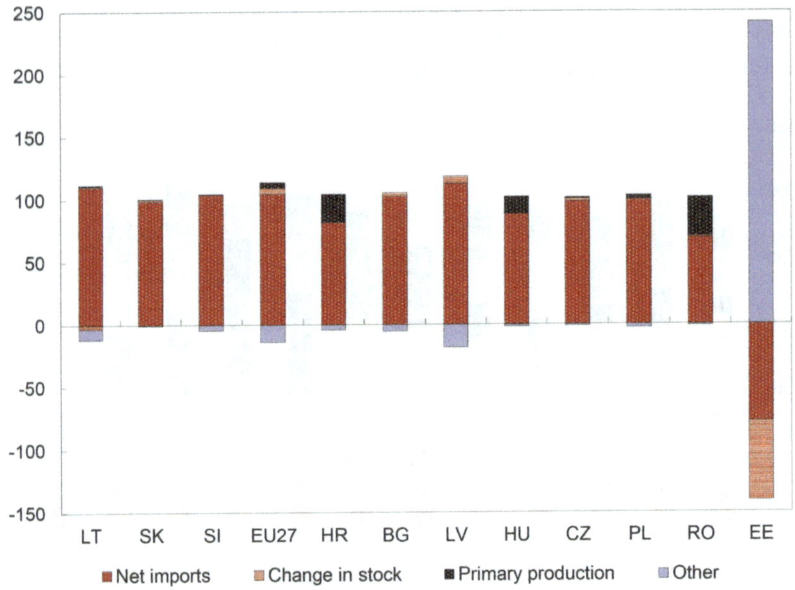

Fig. 1.7: Imports of oil and petroleum products, 2021 (percentage of total)
Data: Eurostat (2023e), authors' calculations

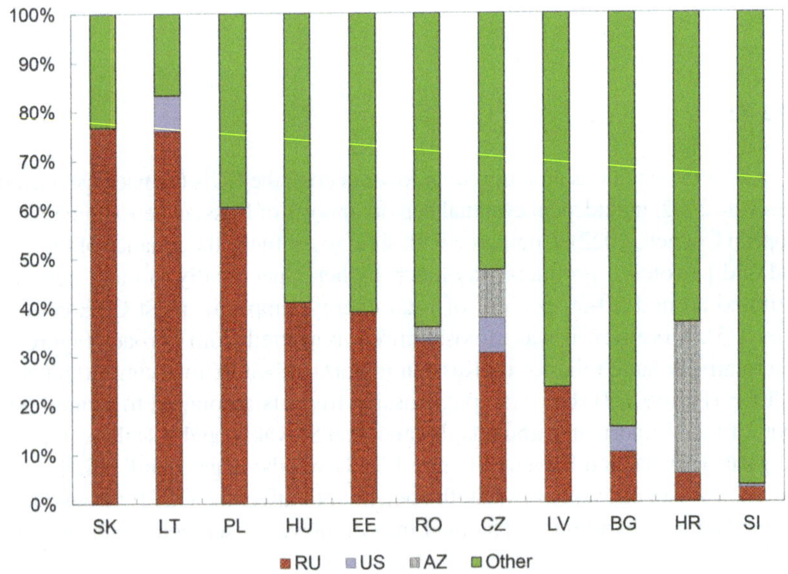

prices, however, started well before the war in Ukraine. Following the pandemic-related drop in oil prices to below USD10 in the spring of 2020, the gradual global economic recovery was associated with a steady increase in oil prices to close to USD80 by the end of 2021 and USD100 by the start of the war in late-February 2022. While sanctions on oil and petroleum were not announced by the EU until late-May, Brent prices reached a peak of USD138 two weeks after the start of the war on the back of concerns around supply disruptions. Notwithstanding high volatility and another spike in May and June 2022, the announcement of the EU's 6th sanctions package was followed by a gradual decline in oil prices throughout the second half of 2022.

Fig. 1.8: Crude oil prices (USD per barrel)
Data: World Bank (2023); Statista (2023), authors' calculations

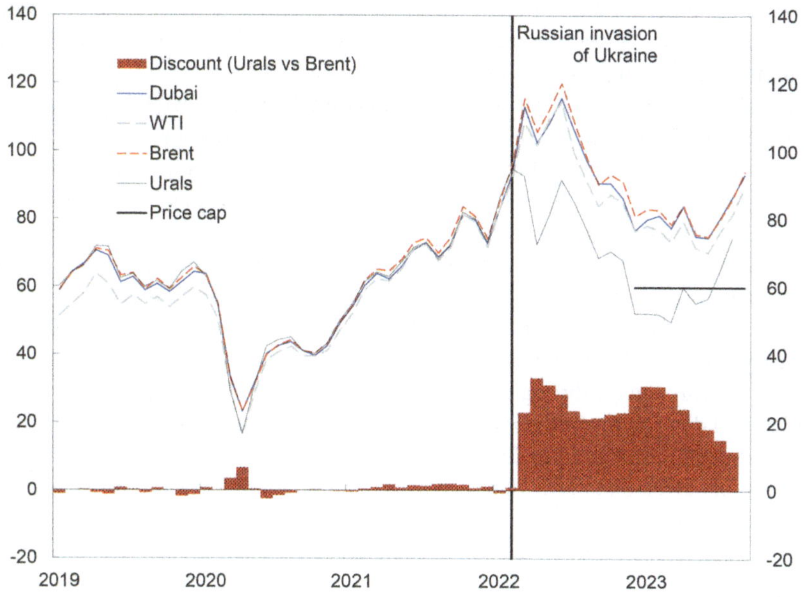

This gradual decline took place despite further announcements on sanctions in the fall of 2022. In early September, the G7 countries announced their intention to implement "a comprehensive prohibition of services which enable maritime transportation of Russian-origin crude oil and petroleum products globally" above a certain 'price cap', with the aim of "preventing Russia from profiting from its war of aggression, to supporting stability in global energy markets and to minimising negative economic spillovers" (HM Treasury, 2022). In October, the EU's 8th package adopted the price cap and further restrictions related to the "maritime transport" of Russian oil (from December 2022 and February 2023 in the case of crude oil and refined products, respectively) (Council of the EU, 2022b). By the time the European

Council agreed on the level of the crude oil price cap at USD60 per barrel in December 2022,[9] Urals was already trading below the cap (Figure 1.8).[10] Nonetheless, a decree signed by Russian President Putin in December banned Russian oil exports from February 2023 in the case of contracts complying with the price cap.

Why did oil prices decline continuously despite the introduction of new sanctions? First, prices overshot in the immediate aftermath of the invasion on account of concerns around supply disruptions. Significant disruptions, however, did not materialize as a few countries were exempted from the sanctions, the U.S. released oil from the Strategic Petroleum Reserve (Axios, 2022), and sanctions led to global trade diversion, thereby limiting the decrease in global supply. As regards the latter, Kilian and Patel (2023) note that "Russia was not only able to divert crude oil originally destined for Europe and its allies to countries not participating in the embargo but was able to raise its overall oil tanker export volume by as much as 40 percent", with China, India, and Turkey benefiting the most from the shift. Also, "the fact that the USD60 price cap on Russian crude [. . .] was too high to be binding undoubtedly helped reduce the frictions in the tanker market, as did India's decision to proceed without Western insurance and Russia's move to expand its own tanker fleet". Second, global demand decelerated in the second half of 2022 against the backdrop of higher commodity prices, tighter global financial conditions, and a slowdown in oil demand from China amid Covid-19-related lockdowns (on the latter, see U.S. Energy Information Administration, 2022). Indeed, Kilian and Patel (2023) argue that "the price of oil in 2022 was driven first and foremost by global demand".

In addition to higher prices, major supply disruptions could have affected CEE economies, especially those with a larger reliance on imports of Russian oil and limited alternative options. For example, landlocked countries such as Czechia, Hungary, and Slovakia had no direct access to maritime transport, leading to a high reliance on Russian oil through the Druzhba pipeline. In order to minimize the risk of potential disruptions in these countries, the EU's 6th sanctions package included specific exemptions, including for crude oil delivered by pipeline to Czechia, Hungary, and Slovakia given that they, "due to their geographic situation, suffer from a specific dependence on Russian supplies and have no viable alternative options" (European Council, 2024). Given their capacity constraints (e.g., in terms of refinery), Bulgaria and Croatia were also exempted in the case of seaborne crude oil and vacuum gas oil, respectively. In addition, the package also allowed for the possibility of "emergency measures" in the presence of "sudden interruptions of supply". Nonetheless, there were increasing efforts to reduce reliance on Russian oil. Czechia, for example, aimed for higher supply via the Transalpine Pipeline, connecting the country to Austria, Germany, and Italy (Upstream, 2023).

The possible impact of sanctions on the CEEE was also affected by the fragmentation of the oil market. While the pre-war period was characterized by the strong co-movement of and minor differences among different oil price benchmarks (Brent, Dubai, WTI, and Urals), the shift in demand from Russian to other oil was associated

[9] See Council of the EU (2022d).

[10] The EC also agreed on a price cap of USD45 and USD100 barrel on discount (fuel oil) and premium (diesel) petroleum products, respectively, in February 2023 (Council of the EU, 2023a).

with a discount on Urals prices (Figure 1.8). Specifically, Urals was trading at a discount relative to Brent in the range of USD20-30 in the second half of 2022. As a result, countries that continued to rely on imports of Russian oil (e.g., those that were exempted from the import ban) benefited from the discount on Urals. This, however, was sometimes offset by an increase in pipeline fees (Reuters, 2023a).

1.3.2.3 Natural Gas

Compared with coal and oil and petroleum products, the dependence on imports of Russian natural gas was significantly higher across Europe. Specifically, natural gas constituted around 10-35 percent of total energy supply in the CEEE (Figure 1.5). Moreover, countries relied primarily on imports to meet their gas demand needs (Figure 1.9), except for Romania given its large domestic gas production. Imports of natural gas were predominantly from Russia, with six CEE countries receiving at least around 70 percent of gas imports from Russia in 2021 (Figure 1.10). Also, the vulnerability of some CEE countries was exacerbated by the lack of access to alternative sources of gas, including pipelines to other gas exporting regions (Azerbaijan, North Africa, Norway) or LNG. A few exceptions included the Baltics, Croatia, and Poland (Figure 1.11). Taking into account country characteristics, Di Bella et al. (2022) estimate that the adjustment to a full shut-off of Russian natural gas would have taken place through a 10 percent demand compression, leading to an output loss in the range of 0.6-6.5 percent in the most vulnerable group of CEE countries (Czechia, Hungary, and Slovakia) given their high reliance on Russian imports and the limited availability of alternative routes. In Hungary, for example, non-Russian sources of gas were "limited by transmission capacity constraints (Croatia, Romania) and production constraints (Central Asian suppliers) (IMF, 2023a). In contrast, the potential loss of output was estimated in the range of 0.2-2.4 in the rest of the CEEE.

Against this backdrop, the EU did not impose any sanction on imports of Russian natural gas following the invasion of Ukraine (CNN, 2023; Politico, 2023). This also fits the historical pattern: Högselius (2013) notes that "military aggression mattered little for Western Europeans' preparedness to expand East-West energy relations". First, "Austrian minister of transportation Ludwig Weiss and Soviet gas minister Alexei Kortunov inaugurate[d] the Soviet-Austrian gas trade on September 1, 1968" ten days after the "Warsaw Pact forces had invaded Czechoslovakia" (Högselius, 2013). Second, negotiations for gas through the proposed Yamal pipeline started in the spring of 1980, i.e., a few months after the Soviet invasion of Afghanistan. Third, an agreement on the Nord Stream 2 pipelines was announced in June 2015, only a bit more than a year after the Russian annexation of Crimea (Reuters, 2015).

In the absence of sanctions on Russian gas imports by the EU, a full shut-off never happened. Imports of Russian gas, however, were disrupted by several developments. Following the decree by Russian President Putin in late-March 2022, which required payments for gas to be made in rubles by 'unfriendly' countries, Gazprom suspended exports of natural gas to Bulgaria and Poland in April given their refusal to pay in

Fig. 1.9: Total natural gas supply, 2021 (percentage of total)
Data: Eurostat (2023a), authors' calculations

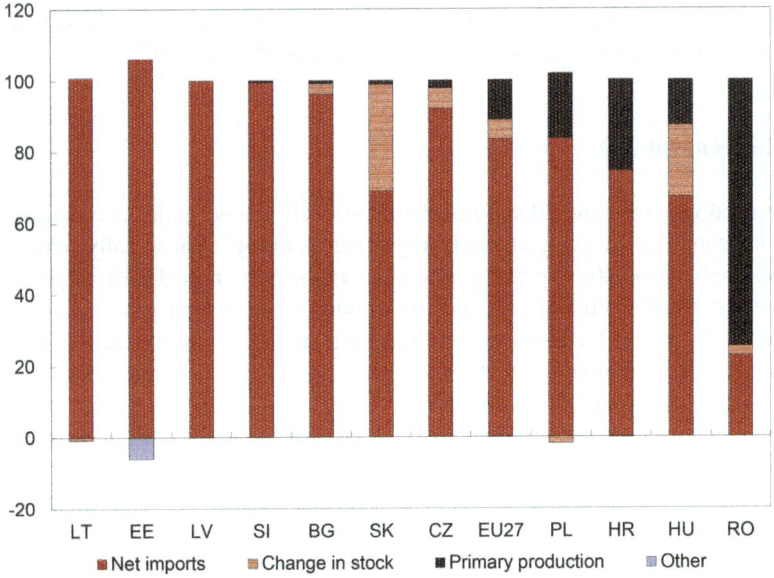

Fig. 1.10: Imports of natural gas, 2021 (percentage of total)
Data: Eurostat (2023d), authors' calculations

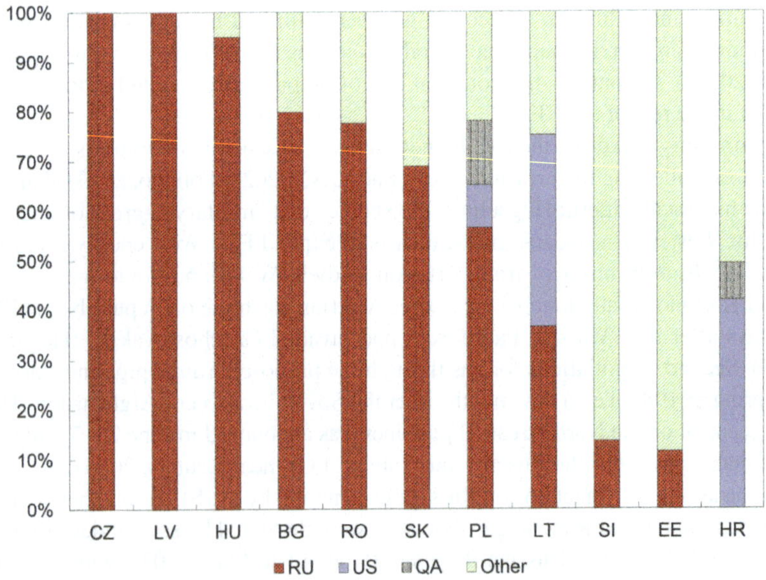

Fig. 1.11: Imports of liquified natural gas, 2021 (percentage of total)
Data: Eurostat (2023d), authors' calculations

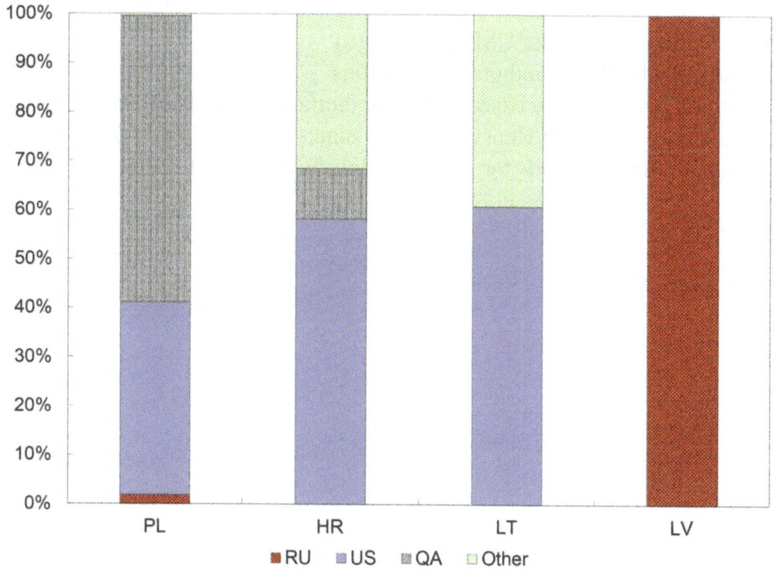

rubles (CNN, 2022b). This illustrates the importance of 'counter-sanctions' imposed by the sanctioned country on the sanctioning ones. Gazprom also suspended gas flows through the Yamal pipeline in May (CNN, 2022a), and then via Nord Stream in mid-2022, with the latter due to maintenance. Moreover, this was followed by the explosion of the Nord Stream pipelines in September 2022. Finally, Russia announced in September 2022 that it would not fully resume natural gas shipments to Europe until sanctions were lifted.

Notwithstanding the major disruptions to the supply of Russian gas, most CEE countries adjusted to the shock relatively smoothly. First, the Baltics and Poland made significant efforts to reduce their dependence on Russian gas following the Russian annexation of Crimea in 2014, including through new LNG terminals and a pipeline from Norway. Second, several countries succeeded in securing alternative routes or sources, including "LNGs and Azeri gas through existing infrastructure via Greece and Turkey" in Bulgaria (IMF, 2022a), as well as new interconnectors between Czechia and Germany (Reuters, 2022a), and Slovakia and Poland (European Climate, Infrastructure and Environment Executive Agency, 2022). Third, reportedly, gas continued to flow to Hungary, with Gazprom even considering "the possibility of supplying extra contractual volumes of natural gas to Hungary in 2023 and applying a deferred payment for these supplies" (Reuters, 2023b). Finally, demand for gas was relatively modest thanks to lower industrial consumption and the mild winter. As regards the latter, Neely and Dunn (2023) calculate that temperature in December

2022 and January 2023 was higher than the historical average in each CEE country's capital.

Fig. 1.12: Natural gas prices (USD per mmbtu)
Data: World Bank (2023), authors' calculations
Note: Natural gas prices are based on the Netherlands Title Transfer Facility (TTF) in Europe, the spot price at Henry Hub, Louisiana in the U.S., and the LNG import price in Japan. Mmbtu stands for metric million British thermal unit.

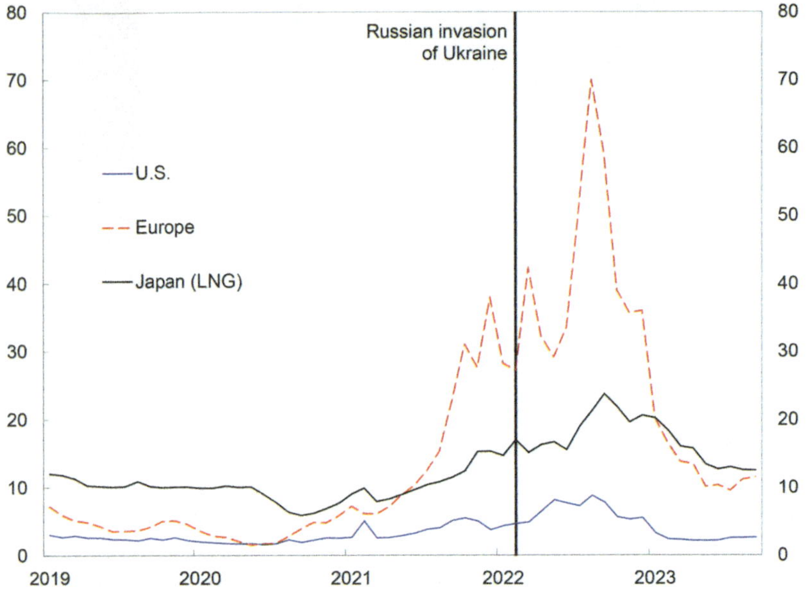

In addition to supply disruptions, the Russian invasion of Ukraine was also followed by skyrocketing gas prices even in the absence of sanctions in mid-2022 (Figure 1.12). As Blanchard and Pisani-Ferry (2022) argue, even without sanctions, Russia had a strong incentive to adjust its export policy with the aim of maximizing revenues in order to be able to finance the war. Indeed, as Russia changed its gas export strategy, gas prices started to increase sharply in 2021, and futures prices indicated an expected increase by close to 60 percent in 2022 even before the invasion (IMF, 2022c). Blanchard and Pisani-Ferry (2022) note that Russia would normally face an intertemporal trade-off given the low short-run and the high long-run elasticity of demand for natural gas: although it could maximize revenue by increasing prices in the short run, importing countries would then have an incentive to discover alternative sources, thereby lowering revenues in the long run. The war, however, altered this trade-off by creating an even greater need for higher revenues in the short run and lowering the prospects of future revenues in anticipation of potential sanctions and diversification attempts of importing countries.

Similarly to coal, oil, and petroleum prices, the sharp increase in gas prices was followed by a moderation to their pre-war level by the end of 2022. In other words, concerns around supply amid a series of disruptions caused 'only' heightened volatility and a temporary surge in prices in mid-2022.

1.3.3 Non-energy Trade

Restrictions on non-energy trade, including bans on exports and imports of certain goods and services, were part of the early response of the EU to the Russian invasion of Ukraine. The EU's 1st package, for example, already included "an import ban on goods from the non-government controlled areas of the Donetsk and Luhansk oblasts, restrictions on trade and investments related to certain economic sectors, a prohibition to supply tourism services, and an export ban for certain goods and technologies" (Council of the EU, 2022c). As part of the following packages, the export ban was gradually extended to cover further goods, including certain technology (e.g., quantum computers and advanced semiconductors), types of machinery and transportation equipment, aviation and space industry goods and technology (e.g., aircraft engines), maritime navigation goods and radio communication technology, several 'dual-use goods' (e.g., drones), luxury goods, and civilian firearms (European Council, 2024). Moreover, a ban on imports from Russia was introduced on several goods, including gold, cement, asphalt, wood, paper, synthetic rubber and plastics, seafood, liquor, cigarettes, and cosmetics (European Council, 2024).

In addition to restrictions on the trade of goods, some services were also sanctioned. Specifically, the EU's 6th sanctions package, announced in June 2022, included the prohibition of accounting (auditing, bookkeeping, tax consulting), public relations, and business and management consulting services (European Council, 2024; Council of the EU, 2022e). The prohibition was widened to include architectural and engineering services, IT consultancy services, and legal advisory services in October 2022 as part of the 8th package (Council of the EU, 2022b) and "the provision of EU advertising, market research and public opinion polling services, as well as product testing and technical inspection services" in December 2022 as part of the 9th package (Council of the EU, 2022h). Finally, a number of restrictions was introduced in the transport sector, including the prohibition of Russian "road transport operators from entering the EU, including for goods in transit", the ban of Russian carriers to have access to EU airports and overfly EU airspace, and the closure of EU ports to Russia's merchant fleet (European Council, 2024).[11]

The impact on the CEEE was mitigated by the low level of trade with Russia (Figure 1.13). Specifically, exports of goods to Russia amounted to less than 2 percent of GDP in the CEEE at the onset of the war, with the exception of the Baltics. Similarly,

[11] Nonetheless, there were a few exemptions. For example, the closure of ports "does not affect vessels carrying: energy; pharmaceutical, medical, agricultural and food products; humanitarian aid; nuclear fuel and other goods necessary for the functioning of civil nuclear capabilities; and coal" (European Council, 2024).

Fig. 1.13: Non-commodity trade, 2021 (percentage of GDP)
Data: Eurostat (2023b, 2023c), authors' calculations
Note: Non-commodity trade refers to trade excluding coal, lignite, crude petroleum, natural gas, coke, refined petroleum products, metal ores, and other mining and quarrying products. The share in total trade shows the sum of non-commodity exports and imports with Russia relative to the sum of total exports and imports.

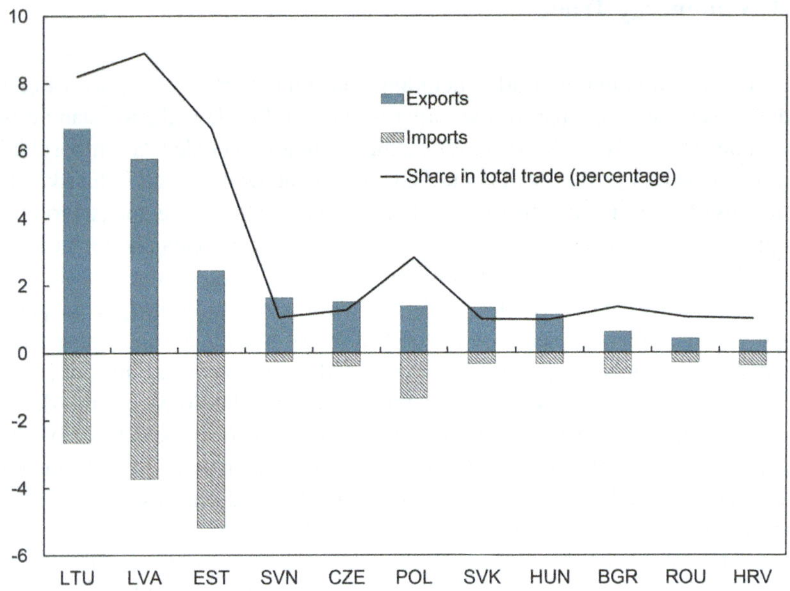

imports were less than 1 percent of GDP in most CEE countries. Trade ties were also negligible when expressed as a share of total trade, with the sum of exports to and imports from Russia constituting 1-3 percent of international trade. Moreover, certain goods were not sanctioned. Most notably, there were no restrictions related to food supplies and fertilizers in order to protect food security and affordability (European Council, 2024). Also, against the backdrop of the potential to cause supply chain disruptions, several critical raw materials were exempt from sanctions (Investigate Europe, 2023).[12] Finally, there were also signs of possible trade diversion, as the drop in exports to Russia was accompanied by a surge in exports to Central Asia in some countries (Brooks & Fortun, 2023).[13]

[12] In order to increase and diversify the supply of raw materials, the European Commission proposed a European critical raw materials act in 2023, identifying 34 critical raw materials (Council of the EU, 2023b).

[13] The authors, however, note that the results "should not be read as indicating an obvious violation of export controls" given that they analyzed aggregate-level export data.

1.3.4 Financial Sector

The EU's 3rd sanctions package, announced between 29 February and 2 March 2022, included the prohibition of "the provision of specialised financial messaging services, which are used to exchange financial data (SWIFT)" to seven Russian banks; investments, participation in, or contribution to projects co-financed by the Russian Direct Investment Fund; as well as the sale, supply, transfer, or export of "euro denominated banknotes to Russia or to any natural or legal person, entity or body in Russia, including the government and the Central Bank of Russia, or for use in Russia" (Council of the EU, 2022f). As a result of the exclusion of banks from SWIFT, Russian banks could not engage in international transactions via this messaging service. As part of the 6th package, announced on 3 June 2022, this was extended to three additional Russian financial institutions (Council of the EU, 2022e).

In addition to the exclusion from SWIFT, individual sanctions were also imposed on certain Russian banks, including Sberbank. Against this backdrop, Sberbank ceased its operations in the region, including via the sale of its units to Hrvatska Postanska Banka in Croatia and Nova Ljubljanska Banka in Slovenia, as well as the revoking of its license by the central bank in Hungary (S&P Global, 2023). As such, the share of domestic banks in the banking sector increased in the CEEE.

In general, the direct exposure of CEE banks was limited to Russia (see, for example, IMF, 2022a, 2022b, 2022d, 2022e, 2023b). In Romania, for example, "resident banks' exposure to domestic corporates with majority-Russian capital" was as low as 0.05 percent of their total exposure to non-financial corporates (IMF, 2022d). Similarly, the exposure of resident banks to Russian borrowers was less than 0.5 percent of total loans in Bulgaria (IMF, 2022a). In terms of the presence of CEE banks in Russia, OTP Bank of Hungary operates a subsidiary in Russia. The overall impact on the group of the subsidiary's deteriorating profitability following the start of the war in Ukraine, however, had been manageable as of late-2023. As noted by OTP Bank (2023), Russian assets and net loans amounted to 3.1 and 3.3 percent, respectively, of the consolidated total assets and loans at the end of 2022, and even "under an unexpected and extremely negative scenario of deconsolidating the Russian entity and writing down the outstanding gross intragroup exposure as well, the effect for the consolidated CET1 ratio would be -71 bps". Finally, an indirect impact could operate via the Russian exposure of parent banks to the extent they change the funding of their CEE subsidiaries. As of late-2023, however, there was no evidence of any significant impact.

A special case in point is the International Investment Bank (IIB), a Russian-controlled multilateral institution. Following the start of the war, Bulgaria, Czechia, Romania, and Slovakia quit the institution, while Hungary ended its membership after the sanctioning of top officials of IIB by the U.S. in April 2023 (Reuters, 2023c).[14] Given the limited operations of the IIB in the region, this did not have any major impact on the CEEE. Nonetheless, it could entail some costs for former member

[14] Poland quit the IIB in 2000, while the remaining CEE countries never became its members.

countries given the uncertainty around the recovery of their paid-in capital as of late-2023 (Direkt36, 2023).

1.4 Conclusions

Given the limited non-energy trade and financial ties with Russia, we argued that individual, trade, and financial sanctions are likely to have affected the CEEE only to a limited extent. Notwithstanding the heavy dependence of the region on imports of Russian commodities, the impact of energy-related sanctions was also mitigated by several factors. First, the sharp increase in coal, petroleum, and natural gas prices started before the war in Ukraine, and reversed in the second half of 2022 despite the ongoing announcements on sanctions. Second, in order to minimize disruptions to supply, sanctions related to oil included several exemptions for countries with limited alternative options. Third, against the backdrop of high dependence on Russian imports, no sanctions were introduced on natural gas. Nonetheless, we also highlighted that the assessment of the impact of sanctions is a challenging task as it would require an understanding of a no-sanction counterfactual scenario under which there could still be major disruptions to supply and shocks to prices in the context of elevated uncertainty caused by the war.

In terms of the design of sanctions, a key takeaway for policymakers is that flexibility in the form of exemptions for those with limited alternative options could minimize short-run disruptions and economic costs. The exemptions in the case of crude oil delivered by pipeline, for example, alleviated the pressure on Czechia, Hungary, and Slovakia. Similarly, costs can be mitigated by preemptive policies, such as measures aimed at diversifying supplies and this reducing the country's dependence on single-origin imports (e.g., the efforts of the Baltics and Poland to reduce their dependence on Russian gas following the Russian annexation of Crimea in 2014, including through new LNG terminals and a pipeline from Norway), as well as by a quick response to changing circumstances (e.g., LNG in Bulgaria, and new interconnectors between Czechia and Germany).

Acknowledgements We would like to thank Balázs Csontó for his constructive comments and suggestions, as well as his help with the data and literature. We would also like to thank László Jankovics, Tamás Pletser, and two anonymous referees for their valuable comments. The usual disclaimer applies.

References

Aslund, A. & Snegovaya, M. (2021). The Impact of Western Sanctions on Russia and How They Can Be Made Even More Effective. *Atlantic Council, May 3, 2021.*

Axios. (2022). *Biden ordering massive release of oil in bid to curb gas prices.* 31 March 2022, https://www.axios.com/2022/03/31/biden-strategic-petroleum-reserve-oil-release. (Accessed: 01-01-2024)

Bergeijk, P. A. v. (2021). Introduction to the Research Handbook on Economic Sanctions. *Chapter 1 In: Bergeijk, Peter A.G. van (ed.), Research Handbook on Economic Sanctions, Edward Elgar, Cheltenham and Northhampton.*

Blanchard, O. J. & Pisani-Ferry, J. (2022). Fiscal support and monetary vigilance: Economic policy implications of the Russia-Ukraine war for the European Union. *Peterson Institute for International Economics Policy Brief 22-5.* https://www.piie.com/publications/policy-briefs/fiscal-support-and-monetary-vigilance-economic-policy-implications.

Bloomberg. (2022a). *EU Guidance Weakens Bloc's Sanctions on Coal, Countries Warn.* 20 September 2022, https://www.bloomberg.com/news/articles/2022-09-20/eu-guidance-weakens-the-bloc-s-sanctions-on-coal-countries-warn. (Accessed: 11-10-2023)

Bloomberg. (2022b). *Europe Snaps Up Coal From Abroad to Fill Gap Left by Russia.* 5 July 2022, https://www.bloomberg.com/news/articles/2022-07-05/coal-imports-pour-into-energy-starved-europe-from-around-globe. (Accessed: 11-10-2023)

Bloomberg. (2022c). *Russian Coal Firm Asks Clients to Postpone Deliveries on Covid.* 23 February 2022, https://www.bloomberg.com/news/articles/2022-02-23/russian-coal-firm-asks-clients-to-postpone-deliveries-on-covid. (Accessed: 11-10-2023)

Bown, C. P. (2023). *Russia's war on Ukraine: A sanctions timeline.* https://www.piie.com/sites/default/files/documents/russia-sanction-timeline.xlsx. (Accessed: 01-01-2024)

Brooks, R. & Fortun, J. (2023). Global Macro Views - Trade Diversion around Russia Export Controls. *17 August 2023, Institute of International Finance.* https://www.iif.com/portals/0/Files/content/IIF081723_GMV.pdf?_cldee=SMY4-pf0nr5ydstQbgQ3JkOylL5fo16IKa8f4SigGfs&recipientid=contact-c8c50ae1e6f0e81180d102bfc0a80172-a7b460cc7dd84396a515610dbf05682a&utm_source=ClickDimensions&utm_medium=email&utm_campaign=Press%20Emails&esid=25cbdea6-f83c-ee11-bdf4-0022482d3cc4.

CNN. (2022a). *Europe is running out of time to find alternatives to Russian gas.* 12 May 2022, https://www.cnn.com/2022/05/12/energy/russian-gas-ukraine-europe/index.html. (Accessed: 11-10-2023)

CNN. (2022b). *Russia shuts off gas supplies to Poland and Bulgaria.* 27 April 2022, https://edition.cnn.com/2022/04/26/energy/poland-russia-gas/index.html. (Accessed: 11-10-2023)

CNN. (2023). *The West hasn't gone after Russia's nuclear energy. Here's why.* 7 March 2023, https://edition.cnn.com/2023/03/06/energy/russia-nuclear-industry-no-sanctions/index.html. (Accessed: 24-10-2023)

Council of the EU. (2022a). EU adopts fifth round of sanctions against Russia over its military aggression against Ukraine. *Press release, 8*

April 2022. https://www.consilium.europa.eu/en/press/press-releases/2022/04/08/eu-adopts-fifth-round-of-sanctions-against-russia-over-its-military-aggression-against-ukraine/.

Council of the EU. (2022b). EU adopts its latest package of sanctions against Russia over the illegal annexation of Ukraine's Donetsk, Luhansk, Zaporizhzhia and Kherson regions. *Press release, 6 October 2022*. https://www.consilium.europa.eu/en/press/press-releases/2022/10/06/eu-adopts-its-latest-package-of-sanctions-against-russia-over-the-illegal-annexation-of-ukraine-s-donetsk-luhansk-zaporizhzhia-and-kherson-regions/.

Council of the EU. (2022c). EU adopts package of sanctions in response to Russian recognition of the non-government controlled areas of the Donetsk and Luhansk oblasts of Ukraine and sending of troops into the region. *Press release, 23 February 2022*. https://www.consilium.europa.eu/en/press/press-releases/2022/02/23/russian-recognition-of-the-non-government-controlled-areas-of-the-donetsk-and-luhansk-oblasts-of-ukraine-as-independent-entities-eu-adopts-package-of-sanctions/.

Council of the EU. (2022d). Russian oil: EU agrees on level of price cap. *Press release, 3 December 2022*. https://www.consilium.europa.eu/en/press/press-releases/2022/12/03/russian-oil-eu-agrees-on-level-of-price-cap/.

Council of the EU. (2022e). Russia's aggression against Ukraine: EU adopts sixth package of sanctions. *Press release, 3 June 2022*. https://www.consilium.europa.eu/en/press/press-releases/2022/06/03/russia-s-aggression-against-ukraine-eu-adopts-sixth-package-of-sanctions/.

Council of the EU. (2022f). Russia's military aggression against Ukraine: EU bans certain Russian banks from SWIFT system and introduces further restrictions. *Press release, 2 March 2022*. https://www.consilium.europa.eu/en/press/press-releases/2022/03/02/russia-s-military-aggression-against-ukraine-eu-bans-certain-russian-banks-from-swift-system-and-introduces-further-restrictions/.

Council of the EU. (2022g). Russia's military aggression against Ukraine: fourth EU package of sectoral and individual measures. *Press release, 15 March 2022*. https://www.consilium.europa.eu/en/press/press-releases/2022/03/15/russia-s-military-aggression-against-ukraine-fourth-eu-package-of-sectoral-and-individual-measures/.

Council of the EU. (2022h). Russia's war of aggression against Ukraine: EU adopts 9th package of economic and individual sanctions. *Press release, 16 December 2022*. https://www.consilium.europa.eu/en/press/press-releases/2022/12/16/russia-s-war-of-aggression-against-ukraine-eu-adopts-9th-package-of-economic-and-individual-sanctions/.

Council of the EU. (2023a). EU agrees on level of price caps for Russian petroleum products. *Press release, 4 February 2023*. https://www.consilium.europa.eu/en/press/press-releases/2023/02/04/eu-agrees-on-level-of-price-caps-for-russian-petroleum-products/.

Council of the EU. (2023b). *Infographic - An EU critical raw materials act for the future of EU supply chains*. https://www.consilium.europa.eu/en/infographics/

critical-raw-materials/. (Accessed: 03-11-2023)

Di Bella, G., Flanagan, M. J., Foda, K., Maslova, S., Pienkowski, A., Stuermer, M. & Toscani, F. G. (2022). Natural Gas in Europe – The Potential Impact of Disruptions to Supply. *IMF Working Paper 22/145.*

Direkt36. (2023). *A magyarokra „nyomást kell gyakorolnunk" – kiszivárgott iratok tárják fel az orosz vezetésű budapesti bank megroppanását.* 13 March 2023, https://www.direkt36.hu/a-magyarokra-nyomast-kell-gyakorolnunk-kiszivargott-iratok-tarjak-fel-az-orosz-vezetesu-budapesti-bank-megroppanasat/. (Accessed: 09-11-2023)

Early, B. R. (2021). Making sanctions work: promoting compliance, punishing violations, and discouraging sanctions busting. *Chapter 8 In: Bergeijk, Peter A.G. van (ed.), Research Handbook on Economic Sanctions, Edward Elgar, Cheltenham and Northhampton.*

EUR-Lex. (2024). *Consolidated text: Council Regulation (EU) No 269/2014 of 17 March 2014 concerning restrictive measures in respect of actions undermining or threatening the territorial integrity, sovereignty and independence of Ukraine.* https://eur-lex.europa.eu/legal-content/EN/TXT/?uri=CELEX%3A02014R0269-20240223. (Accessed: 27-03-2024)

European Climate, Infrastructure and Environment Executive Agency. (2022). *CEF Energy: the Gas Interconnector Poland-Slovakia (GIPS) celebrates its opening.* 26 August 2022, https://cinea.ec.europa.eu/news-events/news/cef-energy-gas-interconnector-poland-slovakia-gips-celebrates-its-opening-2022-08-26_en. (Accessed: 11-10-2023)

European Commission. (2022). Informal meeting of the Heads of State or Government. Versailles Declaration. *Versailles, 11 March 2022.* https://www.consilium.europa.eu/media/54773/20220311-versailles-declaration-en.pdf.

European Commission. (2023). *Russia. EU trade relations with Russia. Facts, figures and latest developments.* https://policy.trade.ec.europa.eu/eu-trade-relationships-country-and-region/countries-and-regions/russia_en. (Accessed: 11-10-2023)

European Council. (2022). *Special meeting of the European Council, 30-31 May 2022.* https://www.consilium.europa.eu/en/meetings/european-council/2022/05/30-31/. (Accessed: 11-10-2023)

European Council. (2023). *EU response to Russia's invasion of Ukraine.* https://www.consilium.europa.eu/en/policies/eu-response-ukraine-invasion/. (Accessed: 09-07-2023)

European Council. (2024). *EU sanctions against Russia explained.* https://www.consilium.europa.eu/en/policies/sanctions/restrictive-measures-against-russia-over-ukraine/sanctions-against-russia-explained/. (Accessed: 23-02-2024)

Eurostat. (2023a). *Complete energy balances.* https://ec.europa.eu/eurostat/estat-navtree-portlet-prod/BulkDownloadListing?sort=1&downfile=data%2Fnrg_bal_c.tsv.gz. (Accessed: 15-04-2023)

Eurostat. (2023b). *EU trade since 2002 by CPA 2.1.* https://ec.europa.eu/eurostat/databrowser/view/ds-059268__custom_8094024/default/table. (Accessed: 25-

10-2023)

Eurostat. (2023c). *GDP and main components (output, expenditure and income).* https://ec.europa.eu/eurostat/estat-navtree-portlet-prod/BulkDownloadListing?sort=1&downfile=data%2Fnama_10_gdp.tsv.gz. (Accessed: 29-05-2023)

Eurostat. (2023d). *Imports of natural gas by partner country.* https://ec.europa.eu/eurostat/estat-navtree-portlet-prod/BulkDownloadListing?sort=1&downfile=data%2Fnrg_ti_gas.tsv.gz. (Accessed: 19-04-2023)

Eurostat. (2023e). *Imports of oil and petroleum products by partner country.* https://ec.europa.eu/eurostat/estat-navtree-portlet-prod/BulkDownloadListing?sort=1&downfile=data%2Fnrg_ti_oil.tsv.gz. (Accessed: 20-04-2023)

Eurostat. (2023f). *Imports of solid fossil fuels by partner country.* https://ec.europa.eu/eurostat/estat-navtree-portlet-prod/BulkDownloadListing?sort=1&downfile=data%2Fnrg_ti_sff.tsv.gz. (Accessed: 20-04-2023)

Felbermayr, G., Kirilakha, A., Syropoulos, C., Yalcin, E. & Yotov, Y. V. (2020). The global sanctions data base. *European Economic Review Vol. 129, October 2020.*

Felbermayr, G., Kirilakha, A., Syropoulos, C., Yalcin, E. & Yotov, Y. V. (2022). The 'Global Sanctions Data Base: Mapping international sanction policies from 1950-2019'. *Chapter 5 In: Garicano, Luis and Rohner, Dominic and di Mauro, Beatrice Weder (eds.), Global Economic Consequences of the War in Ukraine, Sanctions, Supply Chains and Sustainability, Centre for Economic Policy Research Press, London, UK.*

HM Treasury. (2022). G7 Finance Ministers statement on Russia's war of aggression against Ukraine. *G7 Finance Minister and Central Bank Governors' meeting on 02 September 2022.* https://www.gov.uk/government/news/g7-finance-ministers-statement-on-russias-war-of-aggression-against-ukraine.

Hufbauer, G. C. & Jung, E. (2021). Economic sanctions in the twenty-first century. *Chapter 2 In: Bergeijk, Peter A.G. van (ed.), Research Handbook on Economic Sanctions, Edward Elgar, Cheltenham and Northhampton.*

Hufbauer, G. C., Schott, J. J., Elliott, K. A. & Oegg, B. (2007). Economic Sanctions Reconsidered. *3rd Edition, Peterson Institute for International Economics, Washingon, D.C..*

Högselius, P. (2013). Red Gas – Russia and the Origins of European Energy Dependence. *Palgrave Macmillan Transnational History Series, New York, 2013.*

IMF. (2022a). Bulgaria 2022 Article IV Consultation — Press Release; and Staff Report for Bulgaria. *IMF Country Report No. 22/190, June 2022.*

IMF. (2022b). Czech Republic 2019 Article IV Consultation — Press Release; Staff Report; Supplementary Information; and Statement by the Executive Director for the Republic of Czech Republic. *IMF Country Report No. 22/23, January 2022.*

IMF. (2022c). Rising Caseloads, A Disrupted Recovery, and Higher Inflation. *World Economic Outlook Update, January 2022.*

IMF. (2022d). Romania 2022 Article IV Consultation — Press Release; Staff Report; and Statement by the Executive Director for Romania. *IMF Country Report No. 22/310, September 2022.*

IMF. (2022e). Slovak Republic 2022 Article IV Consultation — Press Release; and Staff Report. *IMF Country Report No. 22/202, June 2022.*

IMF. (2023a). Hungary 2022 Article IV Consultation — Press Release; Staff Report; and Statement by the Executive Director for Hungary. *IMF Country Report No. 23/70, February 2023.*

IMF. (2023b). Republic of Slovenia 2022 Article IV Consultation — Press Release; and Staff Report. *IMF Country Report No. 23/27, January 2023.*

International Energy Agency. (2022). Prices - Coal Market Update. *July 2022.* https://www.iea.org/reports/coal-market-update-july-2022/prices.

Investigate Europe. (2023). *Russia: Europe imports €13 billion of 'critical' metals in sanctions blindspot.* 24 October 2023, https://www.investigate-europe.eu/posts/russia-sanctions-europe-critical-raw-materials-imports. (Accessed: 03-11-2023)

Kaempfer, W. H. & Lowenberg, A. D. (2007). The Political Economy of Economic Sanctions. *Chapter 27 in: Sandler, T. and K. Hartley (eds), Handbook of Defense Economics Volume 2, Elsevier, Amsterdam, 2007.*

Karns, M. P. & Mingst, K. A. (2010). International Organizations: The Politics and Processes of Global Governance. *2nd Edition, Lynne Rienner, Boulder and London, 2010.*

Kilian, L. & Patel, K. (2023). Trade diversion has helped ease the impact of the embargo on Russian oil. *February 21, 2023, Federal Reserve Bank of Dallas.* https://www.dallasfed.org/research/economics/2023/0221.

Kirilakha, A., Felbermayr, G., Syropoulos, C., Yalcin, E. & Yotov, Y. V. (2021). The Global Sanctions Data Base (GSDB): an update that includes the years of the Trump presidency. *Chapter 4 In: Bergeijk, Peter A.G. van (ed.), Research Handbook on Economic Sanctions, Edward Elgar, Cheltenham and Northhampton.*

MarketWatch. (2023). *Coal (API2) CIF ARA (ARGUS-McCloskey) Continuous Contract.* https://www.marketwatch.com/investing/future/mtfc00/download-data?startDate=4/18/2021&endDate=05/18/2023. (Accessed: 01-06-2023)

Morgan, T. C., Syropoulos, C. & Yotov, Y. V. (2023). Economic Sanctions: Evolutions, Consequences, and Challenges. *Journal of Economic Perspectives, Vol. 37, No. 1, pp. 3-30..*

Mulder, N. (2022). The Economic Weapon: The Rise of Sanctions as a Tool of Modern War. *Yale University Press, New Haven and London, 2022.*

Neely, C. J. & Dunn, J. (2023). Reviewing the Impact of Energy Sanctions on Russia. *February 16, 2023, Federal Reserve Bank of St. Louis.* https://www.stlouisfed.org/en/on-the-economy/2023/feb/reviewing-impact-energy-sanctions-russia.

Nephew, R. (2018). The Art of Sanctions - A View from the Field. *Columbia University Press, New York, 2018.*

OTP Bank. (2023). *OTP Bank PLC - Integrated Annual Report 2022.* Budapest, 28 April 2023, https://www.otpgroup.info/static/sw/file/230428_Annual_report

.pdf. (Accessed: 03-11-2023)

Politico. (2023). *EU balks at adding Russian gas pipeline ban to sanctions package.* 16 May 2023, https://www.politico.eu/article/eu-balks-add-russia-natural-gas-pipeline-ban-sanctions-package-g7/. (Accessed: 24-10-2023)

Reuters. (2015). *Exclusive: Gazprom building global alliance with expanded Shell.* 19 June 2015, https://www.reuters.com/article/us-gazprom-shell-exclusive/exclusive-gazprom-building-global-alliance-with-expanded-shell-idUSKBN0OZ0IQ20150619. (Accessed: 11-10-2023)

Reuters. (2022a). *Czechs, Poles ask for EU funding for revived gas interconnector project.* 30 September 2022, https://www.reuters.com/markets/europe/czechs-poles-ask-eu-funding-revived-gas-interconnector-project-2022-09-30/. (Accessed: 11-10-2023)

Reuters. (2022b). *Poland allows use of brown coal to heat homes amid supply crisis.* 29 September 2022, https://www.reuters.com/business/energy/poland-allows-use-brown-coal-heat-homes-amid-supply-crisis-2022-09-29/#:~:text=Poland%20is%20heavily%20dependent%20on,provided%20by%20coal%2Dfired%20plants. (Accessed: 11-10-2023)

Reuters. (2023a). *Exclusive: Oil group MOL disputes hikes to pipeline fees through Ukraine, Croatia.* 28 April 2023, https://www.reuters.com/business/energy/oil-group-mol-disputes-hikes-pipeline-fees-through-ukraine-croatia-2023-04-28/. (Accessed: 27-10-2023)

Reuters. (2023b). *Hungary agrees on option for more Russian gas shipments, oil transit fees.* 11 April 2023, https://www.reuters.com/business/energy/hungary-agrees-option-more-russian-gas-shipments-oil-transit-fees-2023-04-11/. (Accessed: 11-10-2023)

Reuters. (2023c). *US places sanctions on officials of Intl Investment Bank in Budapest.* 12 April 2023, https://www.reuters.com/article/ukraine-russia-usa-controls/us-places-sanctions-on-officials-of-intl-investment-bank-in-budapest-idINL8N36F44M. (Accessed: 25-10-2023)

Schneider, G. & Weber, P. M. (2019). Biased, But Surprisingly Effective: Economic Coercion after the Cold War. *CESifo Forum, Vol. 20, No. 4, pp. 9-13..*

S&P Global. (2023). *Russia-Ukraine war splinters Europe's banking industry.* 22 February 2023, https://www.spglobal.com/marketintelligence/en/news-insights/latest-news-headlines/russia-ukraine-war-splinters-europe-s-banking-industry-74075106. (Accessed: 25-10-2023)

Statista. (2023). *Average monthly price of Urals crude oil.* https://www.statista.com/statistics/1112243/urals-crude-oil-price/. (Accessed: 01-06-2023)

Syropoulos, C., Felbermayr, G., Kirilakha, A., Yalcin, E. & Yotov, Y. V. (2023). The global sanctions data base–Release 3: COVID-19, Russia, and multilateral sanctions. *Special Issue Paper, Review of International Economics, 21 June 2023.* (Accessed: 25-10-2023)

Upstream. (2023). *Russian oil lure: Hungary and Czech Republic take opposite directions.* 11 May 2023, https://www.upstreamonline.com/production/russian-oil-lure-hungary-and-czech-republic-take-opposite-directions/2-1-1449968. (Accessed: 11-10-2023)

U.S. Energy Information Administration. (2022). Short-Term Energy Outlook. *December 2022.* https://www.eia.gov/outlooks/steo/archives/dec22.pdf.

World Bank. (2023). *Commodity Markets - "Pink Sheet" Data - Monthly prices.* https://thedocs.worldbank.org/en/doc/5d903e848db1d1b83e0ec8f744e55570-0350012021/related/CMO-Historical-Data-Monthly.xlsx. (Accessed: 01-06-2023)

Chapter 2
Economic Growth & Resilience

Péter Benczúr and István Kónya

Abstract This chapter looks at the overall macroeconomic and social situation of the CEEE at the onset of Russia's aggression on Ukraine and over the consecutive 18 months. Given its close proximity to the Covid-19 crisis, we interpret these shocks together as a twin crisis and draw parallels with the 2008-12 Global Financial Crisis (GFC). Unlike during the GFC, most of the CEEE seems to have recovered from the first phase (the Covid-19 shock) quickly. Under the surface, one can nevertheless discover important vulnerabilities and imbalances, in energy prices and supply security, the build-up of inflationary pressures and a decreased fiscal space. Though the status of the resilience capacities of the CEEE in early 2022 was still better than before the GFC, it was somewhat weaker than before the Covid-19 shock. Moreover, through their fossil energy imports, the CEEE had a substantial direct exposure to Russia. At the onset of the Ukraine shock, there were widespread fears of catastrophic consequences for industry, households in the winter, and further massive increases in energy prices. Such doomsday scenarios did not materialise, as European countries reacted more flexibly to both the quantity and price shock than anticipated. While in the majority of the CEEE the Ukrainian war lead to either a recession or a slowdown of the recovery from Covid, the recession is fairly shallow and seems to be mostly transitory. Overall, the main consequence of the war seems to be inflation, with a heterogeneous impact on the population. This may increase social pressures further, and coupled with increased societal polarisation, it may jeopardise the green transition. Finally, the war will have important geopolitical repercussions. With stronger geoeconomic and geopolitical competition, globalisation patterns may

The original version of this chapter was previously published without open access. A correction to this chapter is available at https://doi.org/10.1007/978-3-031-61561-0_11.

Péter Benczúr ✉
European Commission, Joint Research Centre, Ispra, Italy, e-mail: peter.benczur@ec.europa.eu

István Kónya
Corvinus University of Budapest and Centre for Economic and Regional Studies, Budapest, Hungary
e-mail: istvan.konya@uni-corvinus.hu

The opinions expressed are those of the authors only and should not be considered as representative of the European Commission's official position.

© European Commission 2024, corrected publication 2024

L. Mátyás (ed.), *Central and Eastern European Economies and the War in Ukraine*,
Contributions to Economics, https://doi.org/10.1007/978-3-031-61561-0_2

change, which will surely affect the CEEE that are highly integrated into the world economy.

2.1 Introduction

The economic shock of the Russian aggression of Ukraine (which was in fact preceded by already creeping energy prices) hit all countries of the world as they were only recovering from the previous shock, the socio-economic consequences of the Covid-19 pandemic. Having close ties to Russia, especially in terms of energy imports, EU countries and the CEEE even more, had to face a particularly severe challenge.

At a first look, the situation may resemble the EU's double dip crisis of 2008-12 (the global financial crisis, GFC), where the originally global financial crisis evolved into an EU specific sovereign debt crisis. Looking more closely, however, one finds that the CEEE's Covid-19 economic shock was substantially smaller and less long-lasting than the onset of the 2008 GFC. As predicted already in the summer of 2021 (see Figure 1.16 of Benczúr & Kónya, 2022, Chapter 1 in Matyas, 2022), most economic indicators had returned to their 2019 pre-crisis values before the second shock hit (i.e., by 2021-22). This was not the case in the GFC. It rarely happened that variables had recovered by the time the second wave hit: they may have started to recover but then the second wave caused a further decline (a double dip), or the second wave hit while conditions were still deteriorating due to the first wave.

Tables 2.1 and 2.2 show the maximum impact (drop or peak) and the speed of recovery (the number of years after which a variable has returned to its pre-crisis value) for three major economic and five important social variables, and their combined overall behaviour (Section 2.4 will present more detailed dynamics of some of these variables).

The tables show that the biggest GDP drop in the GFC was larger than in the Covid-19 shock, with the exception of Bulgaria, Czechia, Austria and Poland. The speed of recovery (the number of years after which GDP has returned to its pre-crisis value) was even more clearly slower in the GFC than after Covid-19. The same statements remain true also for household gross disposable income and employment – one can even add that most countries managed to avoid any drop of household income.

In the social domain, the impact of the GFC was quantitatively smaller than in the economic domain, but recovery was often rather slow. Income inequality and unmet health needs did not show a visible crisis impact under the GFC. The social impact of the Covid-19 shock was rather contained, though the annual figures often hide a marked within-year impact and recovery. Though it was often feared, neither inequality nor poverty have increased substantially, pointing to good crisis management and overall resilience.

Apart from the exception of some countries and variables, it seems as if the CEEE have recovered from the Covid-19 shock. Looking deeper, however, one can discover important additional vulnerabilities in the context of energy and food prices and

Table 2.1: Impact and recovery: economic and social variables
Data (in order of appearance): Eurostat (2023k), Eurostat (2023u), Eurostat (2023d), Eurostat (2023aa), Eurostat (2023n), Eurostat (2023s), authors' calculations
(1) N indicates that the variable has not yet returned to its pre-crisis level, while .. indicates a missing value
(2) Imp. indicates the maximum impact during 2008-12 and 2020-21. A worsening is indicated by a negative value for GDP, household gross disposable income, employment, and a positive value for all the social variables. Rec. is the number of years after which a variable has returned to its pre-crisis value.
(3) GDP is chain linked volumes, in national currency. HH GDI is Gross Disposable Income of households in real terms per capita. Employment is total employment from 20 to 64 years (Eurostat, 2023d for the GFC, Eurostat, 2023aa for the Covid period). Inequality is the income quintile share ratio (S80/S20). Poverty is people at risk of poverty or social exclusion.
(4) The drop for household income in Slovakia happened only in 2011-14.

	GDP				HH GDI				Employment				Inequality				Poverty			
	GFC		Covid		GFC		Covid		GFC		Covid		GFC		Covid		GFC		Covid	
	Imp.	Rec.	Imp.	Rec.	Imp.	Rec.	Imp.	Rec.	Imp.	Rec.	Imp.	Rec.	Imp.	Rec.	Imp.	Rec.	Imp.	Rec.	Imp.	Rec.
EU	-4.3	6	-5.6	3	-2.3	8	0.1	0	-1.9	8	-1.0	2	0.0	0	0.0	0	1.4	9	0.6	N
AT	-3.8	3	-6.5	3	-2.3	N	-3.1	N	-0.4	2	-2.0	3	0.1	3	-0.1	0	-1.4	0	0.8	N
BG	-3.3	3	-4.0	2	3.1	0	..	..	-7.8	9	-1.6	3	0.0	0	-0.1	0	4.5	6	0.4	2
CZ	-4.7	6	-5.5	3	0.1	0	-0.6	2	-2.0	5	-0.6	3	0.1	5	0.1	N	0.1	5	-0.6	0
EE	-14.6	6	-1.0	2	-12.4	7	2.4	0	-10.3	9	-1.4	3	0.4	N	0.0	0	1.6	N	-0.9	0
HR	-10.5	10	-8.5	2	-9.4	9	-0.1	2	-6.8	10	0.2	0	0.0	4	0.0	3	1.5	5	0.1	3
LV	-18.1	9	-2.3	2	-18.7	7	2.5	0	-11.1	10	-2.0	N	0.1	2	0.1	3	5.9	6	-0.6	0
LT	-14.8	6	0.0	2	-10.8	5	7.3	0	-7.7	7	-1.5	3	1.2	3	-0.3	0	5.7	6	-1.0	0
HU	-6.6	6	-4.5	2	-4.3	6	-0.4	2	-1.6	4	-0.1	2	0.4	N	-0.1	0	5.3	9	-0.6	0
PO	2.8	0	-2.0	2	4.6	0	1.0	0	-0.7	6	0.4	0	-0.1	0	-0.3	0	-2.7	0	-0.9	0
RO	-9.2	6	-3.7	2	-7.8	7	1.6	0	-0.9	4	0.1	0	-0.4	0	0.1	3	-1.0	0	-0.5	0
SI	-8.0	9	-4.2	2	-6.3	9	3.7	0	-4.7	9	-1.1	2	0.1	12	-0.1	0	1.1	7	0.6	2
SK	-5.5	2	-3.3	2	-0.4	3	0.6	0	-4.2	8	-1.0	3	0.5	10	-0.1	0	0.0	4	0.8	N

supply security. Equally importantly, the seemingly quick and successful recovery from the previous shock did put a significant burden on policies and (fiscal) policy space and has created new imbalances.

The Russian aggression in Ukraine has also led to important geopolitical turbulences and consequences, with many EU countries reconsidering their energy supply partners and overall energy mix. This has further accelerated the already ongoing green (and other) transitions, which were also emphasised in the resilience arm of the Next Generation EU program (European Commission, 2020a), RePowerEU (European Commission, 2022b) in particular.

This chapter sets out to provide a deeper look at the pre-crisis situation in the CEEE, covering also the aftermath of the Covid-19 shock and how it phased into the

Table 2.2: Impact and recovery: economic and social variables cont.
Data (in order of appearance): Eurostat (2023bb, 2023p, 2023v), authors' calculations
(1) N indicates that the variable has not yet returned to its pre-crisis level, while .. indicates a missing value
(2) Imp. indicates the maximum impact during 2008-12 and 2020-21. A worsening is indicated by a negative value for the overall economic effect, and a positive value for all the social variables. Rec. is the number of years after which a variable has returned to its pre-crisis value.
(3) NEET is young people neither in employment nor in education and training, in the age group of 15-29 years. Long-term unemployment refers to a duration of at least 12 months, in the age group 15-74. Unmet health needs is self-reported, covering the reasons of too expensive, too far to travel or waiting list, in the population of 16 years or over. The impact of the overall measures is the unweighted average of the corresponding economic and social variables' impact, while the recovery time is the median value.
(4) The long-term unemployment series starts only in 2009, hence the corresponding GFC measures use this as the last pre-crisis year.

	NEET				Long-term unempl.				Unmet health needs				Economic: overall				Social: overall			
	GFC		Covid		GFC		Covid		GFC		Covid		GFC		Covid		GFC		Covid	
	Imp.	Rec.	Imp.	Rec.	Imp.	Rec.	Imp.	Rec.	Imp.	Rec.	Imp.	Rec.	Imp.	Rec.	Imp.	Rec.	Imp.	Rec.	Imp.	Rec.
EU	0.7	10	0.3	3	1.8	9	0.1	3	0.8	8	0.3	N	-2.8	8	-2.2	2	0.9	9	0.3	3
AT	0.2	7	0.3	N	0.1	10	0.6	3	-0.1	0	0.0	0	-2.1	3	-3.8	3	-0.2	3	0.3	3
BG	1.5	10	0.3	3	3.8	10	-0.2	0	-4.8	0	0.0	0	-2.7	3	-2.8	2.5	1.0	6	0.1	0
CZ	0.5	9	0.3	N	1.0	7	0.2	3	0.4	8	-0.1	0	-2.2	5	-2.2	3	0.4	7	0.0	3
EE	1.6	11	0.3	3	3.8	5	0.7	N	1.0	N	-2.5	0	-12.5	7	0.0	2	1.7	N	-0.5	0
HR	1.6	N	0.2	3	5.1	8	0.4	3	0.0	0	0.3	3	-8.9	10	-2.8	2	1.6	5	0.2	3
LV	1.7	8	0.4	N	4.8	6	-0.3	0	6.2	7	1.0	2	-16.0	9	-0.6	2	3.7	6	0.1	2
LT	1.2	7	0.5	N	4.7	7	0.7	N	-2.6	0	1.0	N	-11.1	6	1.9	2	2.1	6	0.2	N
HU	0.7	7	0.4	2	1.3	5	0.2	N	-0.5	0	0.1	N	-4.2	6	-1.7	2	1.4	7	0.0	2
PO	0.7	10	0.3	3	1.6	7	0.2	N	3.0	9	-1.5	0	2.2	0	-0.2	0	0.5	7	-0.4	0
RO	1.5	N	0.8	N	1.1	8	0.0	0	1.1	5	-0.2	0	-6.0	6	-0.7	0	0.5	5	0.0	0
SI	1.0	13	0.1	2	2.5	13	0.0	0	0.0	0	1.9	N	-6.3	9	-0.5	2	0.9	12	0.5	2
SK	0.9	10	0.2	2	3.3	8	0.0	0	0.9	N	0.5	N	-3.3	3	-1.2	2	1.1	10	0.3	2

second, more severe economic shock around early 2022. As such, it also serves as a general introduction to most of the consecutive chapters, which explore the events, developments, and policy reactions in more depth. Our analysis here intentionally proceeds in a rather parallel fashion to Benczúr and Kónya (2022) (Chapter 1 of Matyas, 2022). We first look at the status and vulnerability of these economies as they have just emerged from the pandemic shock (Section 2.2): what was their overall economic stance and did they have more or less imbalances than before the previous crisis? The section also looks at exposure to Russia and Ukraine. Section 2.3 continues with a quick look at how the resilience capacities of CEEE weathered the Covid-19 shock. Section 2.4 analyses the immediate dynamics of the 2022 shock, performing also a comparison of the 2008-12 and the combined 2020- dual crises. Section 2.5 takes an early look at the broader social consequences. Section 2.6 presents a tentative outlook, identifying inflation as the most serious negative legacy of the situation. Finally, Section 2.7 draws some lessons and conclusions for broad economic policies.

2.2 Economic Stance, Imbalances, and Exposure

The Covid epidemic proved to be a large but transitory shock for the CEEE. In hindsight, as documented in the previous section, the region weathered the crisis surprisingly well, considering GDP and the main labour market indicators. While inflation and public debt rose significantly (see also Chapters 4 and 5), there was hope towards the end of 2021 that these imbalances would be gradually resolved over the coming years. While not entirely unexpected, the 2022 February decision of Vladimir Putin, the president of Russia, to attack Ukraine upended these optimistic expectations. In this part we look at key indicators about the region's general economic stance at the onset of the war, focusing on continued imbalances and the remaining space for economic policy options after just reemerging from the Covid years.

Figure 2.1 presents GDP growth and inflation (measured by the HICP) in 2021Q1 and 2022Q2, relative to the same period of the previous year. The differences are striking. Between 2020Q1-2021Q1 GDP growth was low or negative in most countries, and inflation was mostly subdued. A year later, between 2021Q1 and 2022Q1, both GDP growth and inflation increased significantly. Interestingly, while in the first period there was a clear inflationary difference between countries with floating currencies (Czechia, Hungary, Poland and Romania) and countries linked to the Euro, by the second period the distinction disappears. Broad inflationary pressures were evident in the whole CEEE group already before the war broke out.

Other measures of imbalances are shown on Figure 2.2, which contain snapshots of the trade balance and budget balance in 2021Q1 and 2022Q1, as above. During the Covid period, economic contraction led to mostly positive trade balances, which by early 2021 turned to deficits, sometimes significant ones (Slovakia, Latvia and Hungary). The fiscal stance, however, improved as countries started to unwind the large stimulus packages as economies recovered. In two countries, Hungary and Romania, budget deficits were still uncomfortably large, due to idiosyncratic reasons (elections in Hungary and sustained overheating already before Covid in Romania).

Fiscal consolidation was dictated by the significant growth in public debt between 2019-2021, as shown in Figure 2.3. While not especially large compared to other European countries, the US and Japan[1], public debt increased between 2019-2021 by around 10 percentage points across the CEEE. In Croatia, Slovenia and Hungary already high values – above the Maastricht criterion of 60% – grew significantly. In the Baltic countries, Czechia and Bulgaria, fiscal space remained considerable at the

[1] Public debt as a share of GDP was 117.3% in France, 144.2% in the US, and 254.5% in Japan (source: OECD).

Fig. 2.1: GDP growth and inflation
Data: Eurostat (2023j, 2023l), authors' calculations.
(1) Growth rates (in percentages) relative to the same quarter of the previous year.
(2) GDP: chain-linked volume. Inflation: harmonised index of consumer prices.

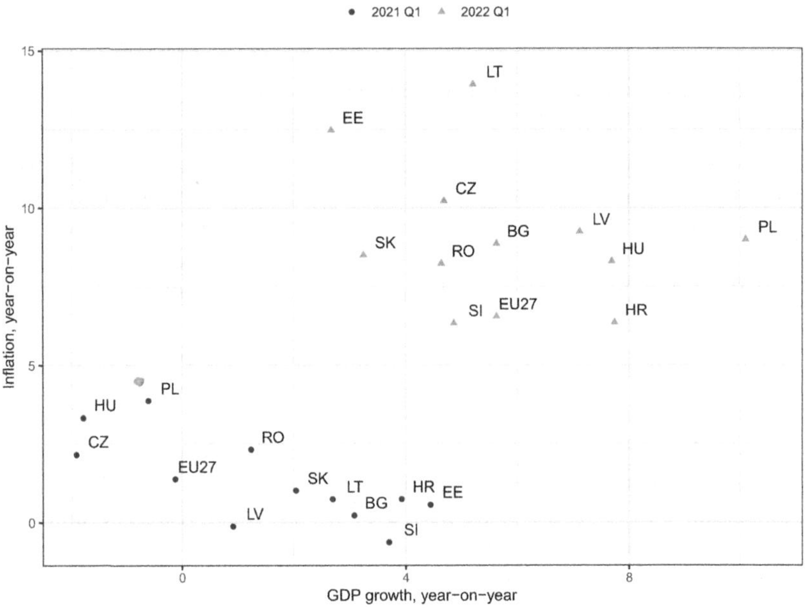

onset of the war, with some room for manoeuvre in case of Romania, Poland and Slovakia as well. With rising interest rates, however, economies would have to be much more cautious in taking on additional debt (see also Chapters 4 and 5).

As a concise summary of the overall imbalances of the CEEE, we utilise one of the tools that were created after the GFC for identifying macroeconomic imbalances: the Macroeconomic Imbalance Procedure (MIP) Scoreboard of the European Commission's Alert Mechanism Report (AMR, European Commission, 2023). Looking at 14 core macroeconomic variables in the internal, external, and labour market domains, every annual AMR presents flags for each variable that exceeds a pre-agreed limit (in some cases, there are both upper and lower limits). Though the tool was put to work in 2013 first, one can look at earlier values of the corresponding time series and

Fig. 2.2: Trade balance and budget deficit
Data: Eurostat (2023j, 2023t), authors' calculations.
(1) Trade balance: %GDP. Budget balance: general government, %GDP.
(2) Data are seasonally adjusted.

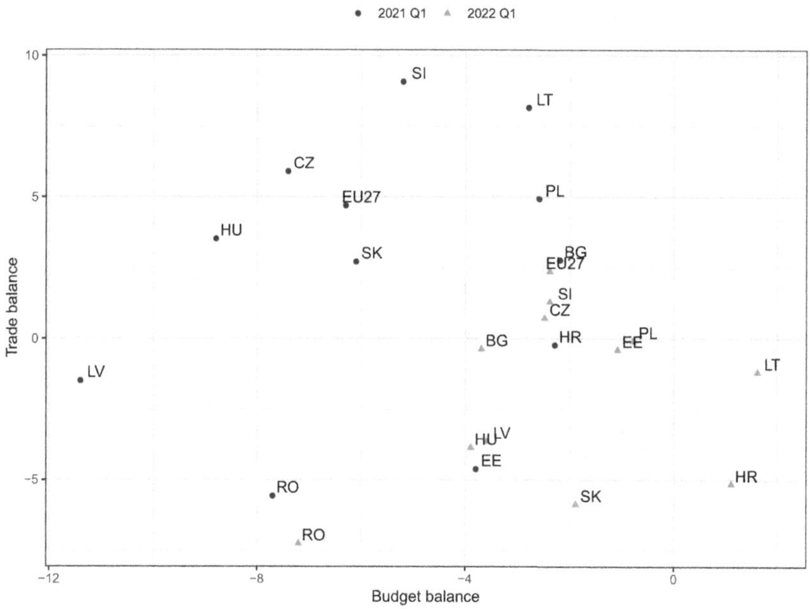

apply the same limits to them.[2] Figure 2.4 thus presents the number of flags for the overall EU, Austria, and all the CEEE in 2007, 2019 and 2022.

The figure reveals that EU countries typically faced much more imbalances before the GFC than before the Covid-2019 shock or at the onset of the aggression in Ukraine. This was not the case for Austria, Czechia, and the EU as a whole. Interestingly, the economic impact of the GFC and the Covid shock on these three entities (see the overall economic impact column in Figure 2.1) was rather similar, while for all other countries the Covid impact was substantially smaller.

The comparison of the EU as a whole and the per country average underlines that many problems of the GFC were due to cross-country heterogeneity, and not overall imbalances. This was no longer the case in 2019 and even less in 2022, pointing to the more common nature of these two shocks.

[2] For some of the variables (those in the employment domain that are based on the EU Labour Force Survey microdata), the current official series of Eurostat do not go back to 2007. This is due to the fact that there was a major revision of the corresponding methodology (see sections 3 and 4 of Eurostat, 2023g), and data were often back-casted only until 2009. In these cases we used the old and discontinued series for 2007 (Eurostat, 2023z for unemployment and youth unemployment, Eurostat, 2023m for the economic activity rate and Eurostat, 2023x for long-term unemployment) but applied the same MIP limits.

Fig. 2.3: Increase in gross public debt, 2019-2121
Data: Eurostat (2023b), authors' calculations.

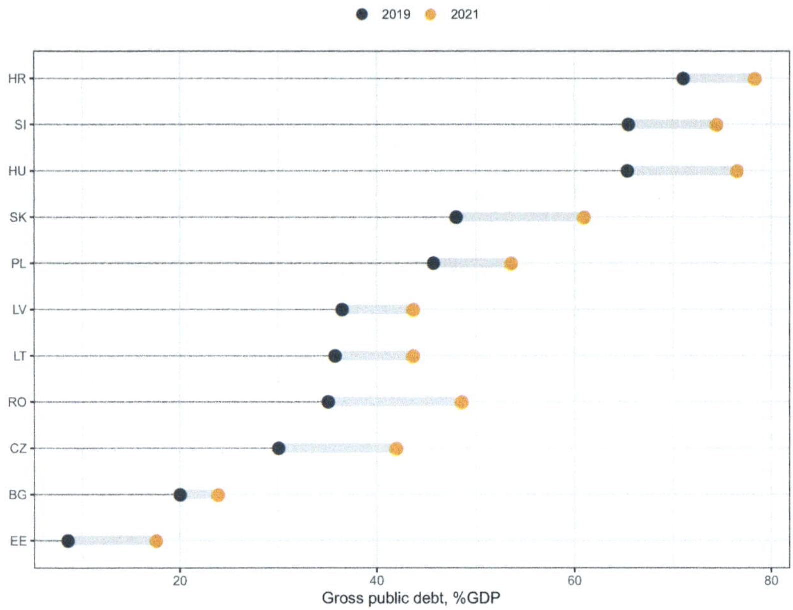

Croatia, Romania, Slovenia and Slovakia still faced three flags in 2019, and Hungary four. The situation deteriorated slightly by 2022, with Latvia, Hungary and Slovakia showing four flags. For the two latter countries, the Alert Mechanism Report[3] prescribed an in-depth review in 2024 to assess the causes and consequences of their macroeconomic imbalances. In terms of country averages, both EU countries and CEEE had slightly more imbalances in 2022 than in 2019; with the CEEE having slightly less imbalances than the EU in both years. Chapter 6 digs deeper into the external dimension of imbalances and their sustainability; while Chapter 9 looks into labour markets.

We now turn to the extent of direct and indirect exposure of the CEEE to the Ukraine war. Chapters 1,3 and 7 present detailed overviews and further analyses of trade patterns between the CEEE, Russia and Ukraine; here we refer to them only as potential sources of exposure and vulnerabilities. Import and export shares in the region of Belarus, Russia and Ukraine were relatively low even before the war. For exports, only Latvia and Lithuania had values above 5% (17% and 13%, respectively). For imports, exposure was somewhat larger, but with the exception of Latvia, import shares of the three countries were below or just above 10%. The reason for higher

[3] See: https://economy-finance.ec.europa.eu/economic-and-fiscal-governance/macroeconomic-imbalance-procedure/alert-mechanism-report_en.

Fig. 2.4: Number of MIP flags in 2007, 2019 and 2022
Data: European Commission (2023); Eurostat (2023z, 2023m, 2023x)

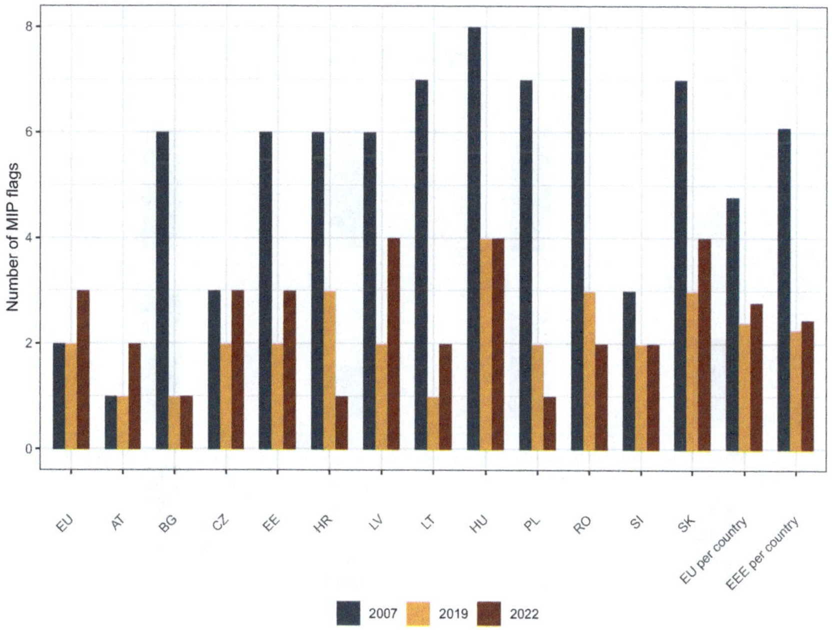

import dependency is obvious: many of the CEEE relied to a significant extent on Russian oil and natural gas to power their economies.

Figure 2.5 plots the share of total and Russian imports in oil and natural gas used in 2019 (note that for Austria, Russian gas imports data are missing). There are various important lessons one can learn from the figure. First, with the exception of Romania (and partially Croatia and Poland), the rest of the CEEE relied almost completely on imported oil and gas. In case of natural gas, Russia was the exclusive or dominant source, with the exceptions of Latvia and Slovenia. In case of oil, imports are more diverse, but even here Russia was the most important source for the majority of the countries.

Import dependence matters mostly when (i) countries are particularly energy intensive, and (ii) their energy needs are covered by fossil fuels (mostly oil and gas). Figure 2.6 shows that the region made significant progress on only one front between 2007 (just before the start of the global financial crisis) and 2019 (just before the Covid crisis). Energy intensity of GDP declined for all countries, the most for those who were very energy intensive in 2007 (Estonia, Bulgaria and Czechia). By 2019, the CEEE were somewhat, but not dramatically more energy intensive than Austria.

The share of oil and gas used in gross available energy, however, remained roughly the same as it was in 2007. This, no doubt, was at least partly the result of low prices throughout the 2010s, and the general view that notwithstanding other frictions,

Fig. 2.5: Oil and natural gas dependency on Russia (2019)
Data: Eurostat (2023w, 2023q, 2023r), authors' calculations.
(1) Share of imported natural gas and oil in total usage, all sources and Russia.

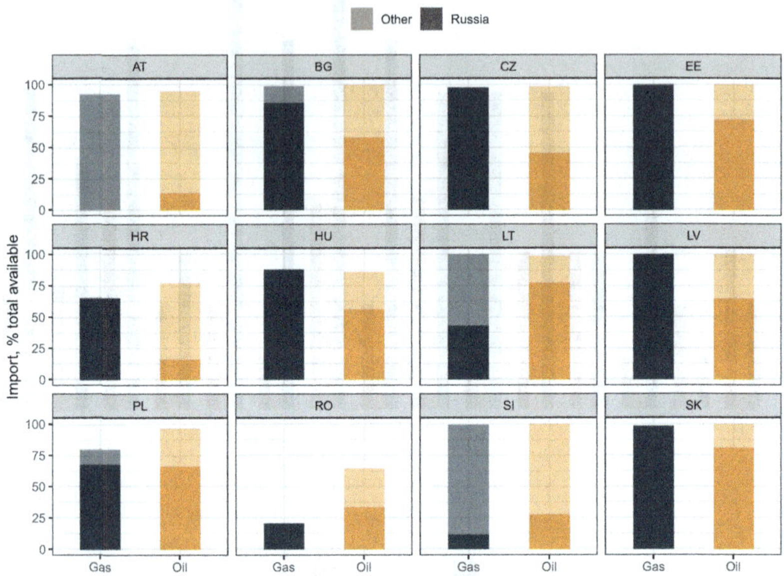

Russia was a reliable source of fossil fuels. Overall, we conclude that the CEEE's main direct exposure was via its import reliance on Russian oil and gas. For the former, alternatives were available, but in case of natural gas, many countries in the region relied almost completely on Russian supply. Chapter 3 offers a more in-depth discussion and analysis.

To summarise, at the onset of the Ukrainian war the CEEE had just rebounded from the Covid crisis. Recent GDP growth had been strong, but signs of overheating – mostly manifesting as increasing inflation – and some macroeconomic imbalances were present. Fiscal consolidation started in most countries, along with monetary tightening to get inflation under control. While overall trade with the three countries involved in the war was modest, much of the energy needs of the CEEE were covered by Russian imports. Two risks were associated with this exposure. First, an abrupt halt of Russian imports of natural gas (and to a lesser extent, oil) were thought to lead to catastrophic consequences for industry, and households in the winter. Second, disruptions to the oil and gas markets were expected to lead to much higher prices, exacerbating the inflation problem. We return to these risk scenarios and their eventual unfolding in Section 2.4.1.

Fig. 2.6: Energy intensity and composition
Data: Eurostat (2023w, 2023f), authors' calculations.
(1) Energy intensity of GDP in purchasing power standards (PPS). Unit: kilograms of oil equivalent (KGOE) per thousand euro.
(2) GAE: Gross Abailable Energy.

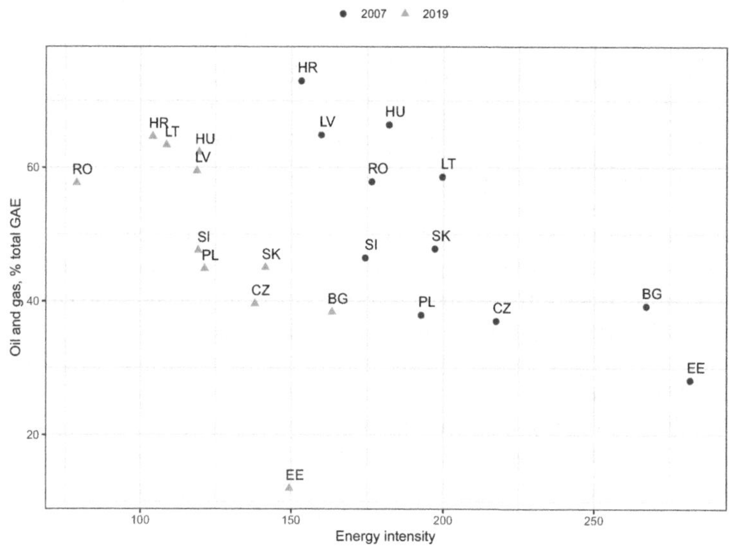

2.3 The Status of Resilience Capacities

Already since the GFC, but particularly after the Covid-19 shock, economic policies have started to emphasise the need not only to reduce vulnerabilities but to identify the necessary capacities of resilience, crucial for coping with shocks, transitions and various other challenges (Manca, Benczur & Giovannini, 2017 and European Commission, 2020c). Relative to its relatively narrow original interpretation as the capacity to absorb and recover from shocks,[4] the current focus includes aspects beyond recovery: to 'bounce forward' from shocks and to manage successfully the ongoing digital and sustainability transitions (Giovannini, Benczur, Campolongo, Cariboni & Manca, 2020). This has been more than reinforced by the Recovery and Resilience Facility (European Commission, 2020b) of the Next Generation EU program (European Commission, 2020a), which channelled funds to enhance the green and digital transitions.

[4] See European Central Bank (2016); International Monetary Fund (2016); OECD (2016); European Commission (2017).

As discussed in Benczúr and Kónya (2022) (Chapter 1 of Matyas, 2022), the CEEE were in a good overall resilience status[5] before the Covid-19 crisis. Indeed, we have seen in the introduction that the implied economic disturbance was relatively short lived. At the same time, the crisis did leave some longer-lasting effects of global supply chain disruptions, and its management have used up some of the buffers of governments (by accumulating debt, for example) and households (by decumulating savings).

The economic shock of the Russian aggression of Ukraine, in particular the hike in energy prices, also highlighted the need to accelerate the energy transition, to diversify energy supplies, and to manage the overall green and digital transitions in a reinforced and more strategic fashion. These again point to the importance of similar resilience characteristics.

Tables 2.3, 2.4, and 2.5 look at a similar set of resilience characteristics as in Benczúr and Kónya (2022) (Chapter 1 of Matyas, 2022). The employed economic and institutional variables are based on Alessi et al. (2020) (characteristics 1, 3-5 in Table 2.3), World Bank (2019) (characteristics 2 in Table 2.3 and characteristics 4 in Table 2.4, and Jolles, Meyermans and Vasicek (2018) (characteristics 1-4 in Table 2.4). Relative to our previous analysis, some of the variables had to be dropped or adjusted.[6] The variables for household finances and social cohesion (Table 2.5) also had to be adjusted slightly, as we had no post-Covid values for the liquid savings of households, the ability to go back to normal, and voluntary work. Finally, we have added two new indicators, the role of uncertainty in long-term investment decisions and societal polarisation, which reveal additional important developments around the Covid-19 shock.

Relative to the GFC, most CEEE had significantly better resilience characteristics both at the onset of the Covid-19 and the Russian aggression crises. In line with this, they weathered the economic shock of Covid-19 rather well (see Tables 2.1 and 2.2). The declines were smaller in GDP (except for Bulgaria, Czechia and Poland), household income (except for Czechia) and employment. Social consequences also stayed fairly contained. However, the resilience picture changes when we compare the pre-Covid period with 2021. From the nine characteristics considered, Hungary and Poland show only one and three improvements (government efficiency for Hungary, expenditures on social protection, active labour market policies and the net international investment position for Poland). There is a noticeable worsening for almost all of the CEEE in the growth of the unit labour cost (driven by labour shortages and the reemergence of inflation), the growth of financial sector liabilities (the only exception is Estonia), regulatory quality and the role of business regulations

[5] Benczúr and Kónya (2022) (Chapter 1 of Matyas, 2022) offers an overview and discussion of the measurement of resilience, which the interested reader can consult. In brief, we look at various resilience characteristics, i.e., variables that are shown to be a good ex ante predictor of crisis performance (Alessi et al., 2020).

[6] In particular, there was no post-Covid value for the OECD's product market regulation indicator (OECD, n.d.). The World Bank's Doing Business Index (World Bank, 2021) has been discontinued, which was the source of the efficiency of resolving insolvencies. We have replaced these two with the European Investment Bank's indicator on the impact of business regulations on long-term investment decisions European Investment Bank (2023), which however only started in 2016.

Table 2.3: Resilience characteristics: economic variables
Data (in order of appearance): Eurostat (2023cc), European Commission (2024a), Eurostat (2023dd), Eurostat (2024a), Eurostat (2024b)
(1) Expenditures on category 2-7 LMP per person wanting to work.
(2) Improvement means a decline.

	EU	AT	BG	EE	CZ	HR	LV	LT	HU	PL	RO	SI	SK
Expenditures on social protection (% of GDP)													
2005-07	18.0	19.8	10.5	12.0	9.3	13.7	8.6	10.7	17.0	16.5	10.0	17.0	13.4
2017-19	19.3	20.3	11.9	12.4	12.8	14.0	11.8	12.9	13.2	16.4	11.7	16.7	14.4
2021	20.5	21.9	13.4	13.6	13.5	14.1	13.8	14.3	13.1	17.3	13.4	17.9	16.2
Active labour market policies (ALMP, (1))													
2005-07	1787	1938	340	385	84		160	503	548	416	138	483	250
2017-19	1932	2983	497	2233	1351	1082	339	1057	3100	1230	141	857	830
2021	2534	3565	3859	2354	1832	2164	306	1805	1790	3463	225	1105	649
Unit labour cost (nominal, 3-year change, (2))													
2005-07		2.8	12.3	3.5	21.8	6.9	46.0	20.5	13.2	-0.7	38.3	7.3	7.6
2017-19		5.0	18.9	11.1	14.1	-0.4	14.7	16.4	11.0	6.2	23.4	5.8	11.1
2021		9.9	16.4	13.9	10.7	8.1	14.3	19.2	12.9	12.1	10.9	12.8	12.5
Net international investment position (% of GDP)													
2005-07		-12.7	-58.6	-29.0	-75.9	-75.1	-62.6	-50.6	-94.3	-45.3	-37.5	-17.7	-60.6
2017-19		8.2	-36.7	-23.0	-28.4	-55.3	-45.4	-30.3	-51.6	-54.6	-44.9	-19.8	-67.7
2021		15.6	-18.6	-14.5	-13.4	-32.5	-27.3	-7.4	-52.2	-39.8	-47.0	-7.7	-60.5
Financial sector liabilities (annual percentage growth, (2))													
2005-07	13.1	14.7	30.5	10.2	22.8	21.8	41.6	38.6	25.5	20.3	38.5	19.9	12.3
2017-19	3.3	2.3	6.3	12.1	10.2	5.2	2.4	9.4	6.9	4.0	7.3	6.4	10.9
2021	8.8	8.2	9.6	7.8	18.5	11.7	13.3	22.6	16.5	12.3	14.3	14.1	23.7

in long-term investment decisions. On the positive side, important policy levers have stayed strong, like social protection expenditures (except for Hungary) and active labour market policies (except for Latvia, Hungary and Slovakia). The net international investment position did not deteriorate substantially in any of the CEEE.

It is interesting to observe that uncertainty was already an important concern for investment decisions before the Covid-19 shock (last variable in Table 2.4). Its importance grew further by 2021, and even further by 2022 (except for Latvia). Given the continued war and other global and geopolitical challenges, this is likely to remain a major concern.

Table 2.4: Resilience characteristics: institutions and overall
Data (in order of appearance): World Bank (2023), World Bank (2023), World Bank (2023), European Investment Bank (2023), European Investment Bank (2023).
(1) A scale from -2.5 (weak) to 2.5 (strong).
(2) The share of respondents who indicated the factor as a major or minor obstacle. Improvement means a decline.
(3) The number of improvements in the five variables in Table 2.3 and the first four in this table.

	EU	AT	BG	EE	CZ	HR	LV	LT	HU	PL	RO	SI	SK
	Government effectiveness (1)												
2005-07		1.79	-0.04	0.95	1.03	0.49	0.54	0.71	0.76	0.38	-0.28	0.91	0.80
2017-19		1.47	0.13	0.97	1.12	0.50	0.98	0.99	0.46	0.54	-0.16	1.08	0.60
2021		1.53	-0.17	1.07	1.35	0.55	0.83	1.02	0.60	0.25	-0.16	1.14	0.49
	Regulatory quality (1)												
2005-07		1.65	0.64	1.09	1.29	0.42	0.92	0.97	1.15	0.76	0.40	0.83	1.06
2017-19		1.47	0.60	1.24	1.59	0.45	1.15	1.13	0.60	0.90	0.43	0.73	0.87
2021		1.34	0.43	1.34	1.55	0.49	1.22	1.27	0.49	0.83	0.29	0.82	0.87
	Control of corruption (1)												
2005-07		1.94	-0.11	0.38	0.99	0.08	0.35	0.19	0.62	0.26	-0.23	0.98	0.37
2017-19		1.53	-0.19	0.54	1.40	0.05	0.43	0.55	0.06	0.64	-0.20	0.83	0.17
2021		1.24	-0.26	0.62	1.51	0.04	0.72	0.82	0.01	0.55	-0.06	0.69	0.21
	Factors impacting long-term investment: business regulations, (2)												
2017-19	0.63	0.70	0.59	0.70	0.42	0.78	0.56	0.81	0.32	0.73	0.65	0.59	0.78
2021	0.65	0.68	0.60	0.66	0.33	0.81	0.63	0.86	0.36	0.74	0.61	0.59	0.77
	Factors impacting long-term investment: uncertainty, (2)												
2017-19	0.69	0.59	0.74	0.79	0.66	0.80	0.72	0.93	0.54	0.83	0.77	0.67	0.77
2021	0.73	0.72	0.77	0.80	0.66	0.82	0.83	0.94	0.68	0.87	0.80	0.79	0.81
2022	0.78	0.77	0.85	0.86	0.79	0.86	0.76	0.96	0.71	0.93	0.87	0.85	0.84
	Number of improvements (3)												
from GFC to Covid		4	5	6	8	7	8	8	4	5	7	4	3
From GFC to UA		4	4	7	8	6	8	8	4	6	6	5	3
From Covid to UA		5	4	8	7	5	5	6	1	3	5	5	4

Table 2.5: Resilience characteristics: household finances and social cohesion
Data (in order of appearance): Eurostat (2023ee), Eurostat (2023ff), European Social Survey, Eurobarometer (various issues), v2cacamps_osp of Varieties of Democracy (2022).
(1) Self-assessment. (2) Self-reported arrears in mortgage or rent, utility bills or hire purchase. (3) European Social Survey, answers 7-10 to the question "Most people can be trusted or you can't be too careful". (4) Average of the share of people who tend to trust the national legal system,the national government, and the national parliament. (5) Is society polarised into antagonistic, political camps? On a scale from 0 (not at all) to 4 (yes, to a large extent). (6) The number of improvements in the four variables.

	EU	AT	BG	EE	CZ	HR	LV	LT	HU	PL	RO	SI	SK
	Inability to face unexpected difficulties (1)												
2005-07	35.2	27.3	77.6	40.6	28.0		67.0	55.1	58.9	58.0	46.2	42.6	50.6
2017-19	32.4	19.7	40.6	24.5	34.1	53.6	55.0	48.7	32.6	31.9	47.6	34.4	32.0
2021	30.2	18.6	36.4	18.1	27.1	46.5	41.7	36.4	34.8	24.5	47.3	24.6	27.0
	Arrears (2)												
2005-07	10.0	3.6	25.1	8.3	7.9	0.0	16.4	15.1	17.8	22.4	10.7	14.5	9.7
2017-19	8.8	5.0	31.5	3.0	7.9	18.7	12.6	9.1	13.2	8.5	16.4	13.7	9.2
2021	8.9	4.8	20.4	2.4	5.7	16.6	7.2	6.6	11.2	7.0	9.4	9.0	6.3
	Trust in people (3)												
2006-08	0.25	0.31	0.14	0.30	0.34	0.19	0.21		0.18	0.17		0.21	0.19
2018	0.28	0.39	0.12	0.31	0.38	0.19	0.21	0.25	0.28	0.18		0.24	0.19
2020	0.27		0.15	0.37	0.40	0.24		0.30	0.27			0.27	0.20
	Trust in institutions (4)												
2005-07	0.41	0.59	0.18	0.26	0.51	0.21	0.27	0.22	0.36	0.19	0.27	0.35	0.30
2017-19	0.37	0.59	0.21	0.31	0.53	0.18	0.28	0.33	0.47	0.32	0.28	0.24	0.28
2021	0.39	0.55	0.20	0.34	0.52	0.22	0.30	0.37	0.47	0.30	0.37	0.26	0.24
2023	0.37	0.51	0.16	0.38	0.43	0.29	0.33	0.31	0.44	0.33	0.30	0.27	0.24
	Polarisation (5)												
2005-07	1.16	2.06	0.99	0.65	1.46	2.47	0.32	0.20	2.57	3.22	2.52	2.88	1.49
2017-19	1.74	2.19	1.70	1.06	1.63	2.65	0.26	0.42	3.85	3.93	2.47	2.93	1.96
2021	2.64	2.46	2.86	2.06	2.35	2.82	1.00	1.34	3.85	3.98	3.04	3.98	2.18
2022	2.35	2.46	3.05	1.81	2.01	2.82	1.20	1.55	3.88	3.98	3.23	3.98	2.44
	Number of improvements (6)												
from GFC to Covid	3	2	2	4	2	0	5	4	4	4	2	3	2
From GFC to UA	3	1	4	4	4	2	3	4	4	3	2	3	3
From Covid to UA	2	2	3	4	3	4	3	4	1	2	3	4	3

Switching to household finances and social cohesion (Table 2.5), these factors mostly confirm the overall good level of resilience capacities of the CEEE. When comparing the pre-GFC and pre-Covid periods, five of the countries had only two or less improvements (Bulgaria, Czechia, Croatia, Romania and Slovakia). The situation had improved by the end of 2021: relative to the GFC, all but Croatia and Romania had registered an improvement in more than half of the indicators. When looking at the impact of the Covid-19 crisis (last line of the table), only Hungary and Poland show a small number of improvements.

Household finances had improved (or at least had not deteriorated) overall, the only exception being a slight increase in the inability to face unexpected difficulties in Hungary. At the same time, trust and social cohesion show a more mixed picture. Trust in people and institutions had registered relatively small improvements. Polarisation, on the other hand, had increased in all of the CEEE (also in Austria and the EU overall), with two slight reversals by 2022 in Estonia and Czechia). There had been a noticeable jump by 2021 in Bulgaria, Romania, and Slovakia (in the case of the latter, from an already high level). In Hungary, polarisation was medium-high (a value of 2) in 2000. It increased substantially in 2006 and then further in 2010, in line with domestic political developments. In a somewhat parallel fashion, Poland had an even higher value (2.5) in 2000, which increased gradually until 2007, reversed in 2008-10, and increased further in 2011 and 2016.

To sum up, most CEEE had better resilience characteristics at the onset of the Covid-19 and the Russian aggression crises than before the GFC. The resilience picture of 2021 compares less favourably to the pre-Covid period. Together with inflation pressures, the buildup of some imbalances, and an uncertain economic environment, these may foreshadow a less quick recovery from the current shock than what happened after Covid-19. In terms of household finances and social cohesion factors, the CEEE situation is relatively good, though increasing levels of political polarisation may represent a major future challenge.

2.4 The Shock and its Aftermath

In this section we discuss the two main components of the shock that hit the CEEE in conjunction with the war: energy prices and refugees. While both are analysed in more detail in Chapters 3 and 8 respectively, we provide a first overview and discuss their macroeconomic consequences. We also show how the current twin crises – the Covid epidemic and the Ukrainian war as the first and second phases – compare to the earlier global financial crisis (followed by the European sovereign debt crisis as its second phase). We already presented some comparison points in the Introduction, and here we show additional details for the two main macroeconomic indicators, GDP and inflation.

2.4.1 Energy Prices, GDP, and Inflation

The main shock that hit the region (and Europe in general) was the spike in energy prices, driven by oil and natural gas imported from Russia. As we saw earlier, Figure 2.5 shows the exposure of the CEEE to imports in their overall use of oil and natural gas (measured by Gross Available Energy, GAE), and the share of Russia in total imports in 2019. Overall, the region was heavily dependent on Russian imports, especially for natural gas. Romania is the only significant producer of oil and gas, with most other countries relying overwhelmingly on imported hydrocarbons. For the landlocked economies of Czechia, Hungary and Slovakia, Russian gas remains the only feasible alternative in the short run. There is somewhat more flexibility in importing oil, but as the figure shows, Russian supply was crucial for most countries.

Fig. 2.7: Oil and natural gas prices in Europe
Data: FRED (2023b, 2023a), authors' calculations.

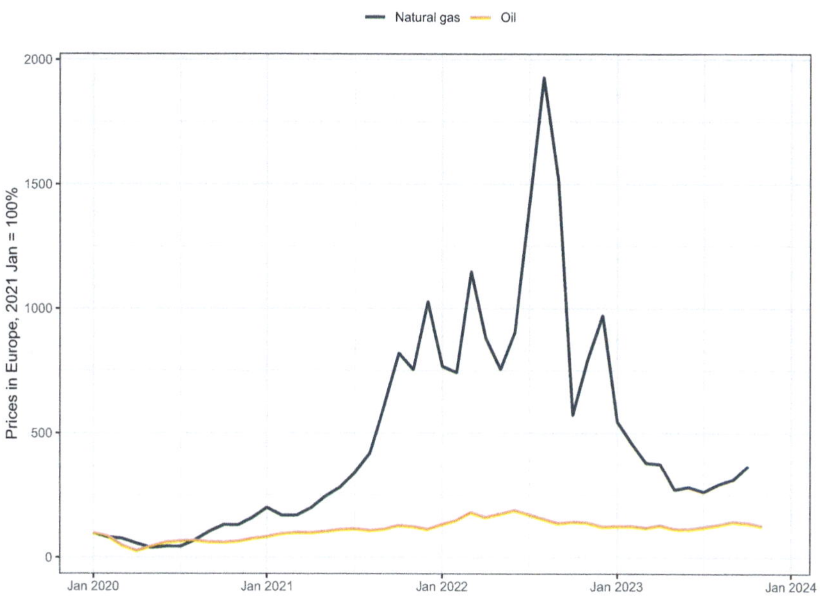

Figure 2.7 plots the evolution of oil and natural gas spot prices in Europe, normalising both to equal 100% in January 2020. Both prices started rising well before the war broke out. As Russian supply was strategically cut from the summer of 2021, natural gas prices in particular rose tenfold by early 2022. At their peak, the European spot gas price was almost 20 times above its level just before the Covid crisis broke out. While oil and gas are both significantly cheaper in 2023 than in 2022, prices are still significantly higher than in 2020. This prolonged and large

terms-of-trade shock was the most important and immediate consequence of the war for the CEEE (see also Chapter 7).

To provide some context, we first show a comparison of the two main macroeconomic indicators, real GDP and inflation, between the current dual crisis and the previous financial crisis. Figure 2.8 plots the evolution of real GDP from the end of 2019 until the first quarter of 2023 (for the current crises) and from the middle of 2008 until the end of 2013 (the financial crisis).

Skyrocketing prices reflected not only immediate shortages, but also fears that European economies would suffer catastrophic losses as oil and gas supplies dwindle. In hindsight, expectations of large-scale shutdowns of industry and freezing households proved to be exaggerated. European countries reacted more flexibly to both the quantity and price shock than anticipated (Moll, Benjamin and Schularick, Moritz and Zachmann, Georg, 2023). While in the majority of the CEEE the Ukrainian war led to either a recession or a slowdown of the recovery from Covid, the recession is fairly shallow and with the exceptions of Estonia, Hungary and Latvia it also seems to be highly transitory.

Fig. 2.8: The evolution of GDP during the two twin crises
Data: Eurostat (2023j), authors' calculations.
(1) Chain linked real GDP, 2008Q1 = 100% (bottom) and 2019Q4 = 100% (top).

The figure also vividly shows how different the two crises are. During the financial crisis and its aftermath, the recession was much more prolonged. The Covid recession was typically deeper, but economies rebounded much faster and much stronger. There are three interesting exceptions: Czechia, Poland and Slovakia, where – except for the first wave of the Covid recession – GDP paths are remarkably similar across the two episodes. For Poland, this is explained by the fact that it was the only country to avoid a recession during the financial crisis. The behaviour of the other two countries during the Covid epidemic is less obvious, although they too weathered the financial crisis relatively well.

Differences between the two crises episodes are even more pronounced in case of inflation. As Figure 2.9 shows, since 2021 inflation has risen dramatically throughout the region, while the GFC was characterised by low and and quite stable inflation. In most countries, price pressures started in the second phase of the current crisis, in 2021, after the initial shock of the Covid epidemic was over. This was due to supply bottlenecks and the effects of monetary and fiscal policy used to counter the effects of the Covid recession. There are, however, significant differences across countries in both the size of the inflation rise, and in the role of energy (and food) in the increase.

Fig. 2.9: Inflation
Data: Eurostat (2023l), authors' calculations.
(1) Inflation rate, HICP.

Inflation rose the most in the three Baltic countries and Hungary, and the least in the countries that are either in the Eurozone or use currencies that are pegged (Bulgaria) or tightly managed (Romania). In case of the Baltics, which are the most exposed to Russian energy and trade (see also Figure 2.5), oil and gas prices contributed significantly to the rise in consumer prices . In Hungary, which partly capped household energy prices (Sgaravatti, Tagliapietra, Trasi & Zachmann, 2023), inflation rose despite this policy to the highest and most persistent level in the CEEE. When we remove both energy and food prices from the household basket, Hungarian inflation is clearly the highest in the region. At least part of the explanation lies in the large fiscal expansion (due to parliamentary elections) in the second half of 2021 (see Figure 2.2). As Figure 2.10 shows, another reason for high Hungarian inflation is the significant depreciation of the forint, even compared to the other floating currencies in the region.

Fig. 2.10: Exchange rates in countries with floating currencies
Data: Eurostat (2023h), authors' calculations.

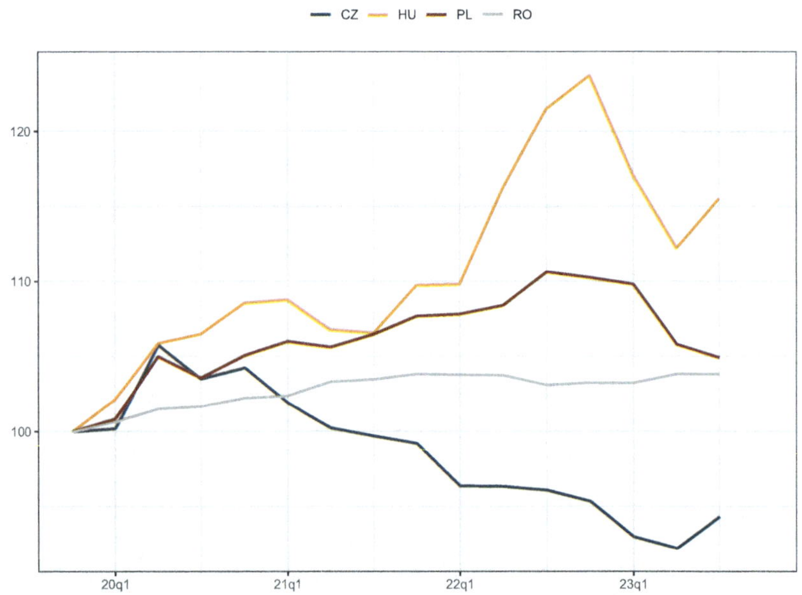

Overall, the main impact of the war seems to be on inflation, with a much smaller and mostly transitory decline in economic activity. It is as yet too early to say how persistent inflation will remain. Decreasing energy prices and monetary tightening are contributing to declining inflation across the region, but the pace and magnitude varies significantly. Also, inflation may have had a heterogeneous impact on the population, as different income groups faced differential exposure to food and energy price hikes. We return to this issue in Section 2.5.

2.4.2 Terms-of-trade and Real Incomes

As we saw earlier, while the overall trade exposure of the CEEE to Russia (and Belarus and Ukraine) is moderate to small, the spike in oil and gas prices was still a major shock to the region. We also saw that the shock had a modest effect on GDP. In this section we take another look at the real impact of the energy price rise, utilising an alternative measure of wellbeing.[7] The crucial concept in this section is the terms-of-trade (TOT), the relative price of a country's exports in terms of its imports.

Fig. 2.11: Terms-of-trade in the CEEE
Data: Eurostat (2023j), authors' calculations.
(1) Terms-of-trade: export price deflator divided by the import price deflator.

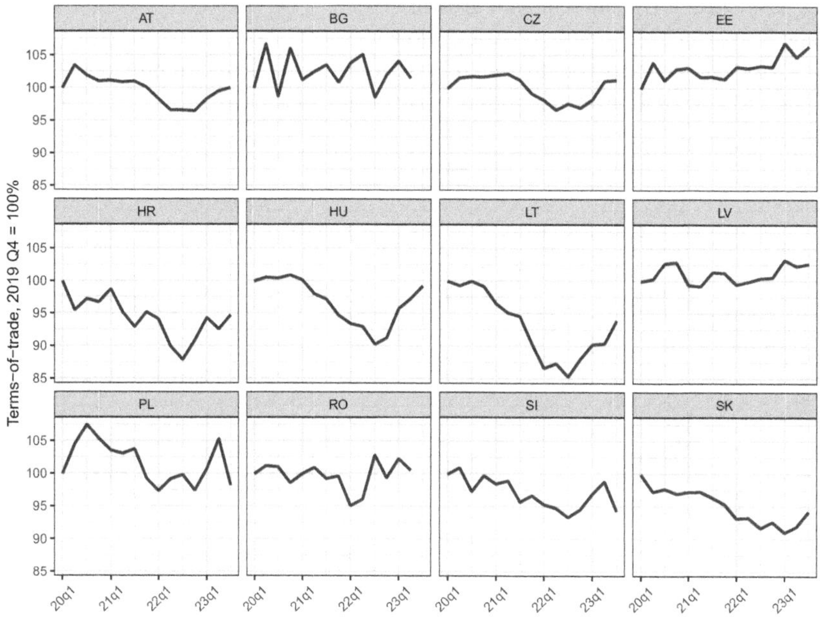

Figure 2.11 plots the evolution of this variable from the beginning of 2020. There are two interesting observations evident from the figure. First, in Austria, Czechia, Croatia, Hungary, Latvia, Poland, Slovenia and Slovakia there was a significant worsening of the TOT already in 2021. Second, the impact of the energy price rise during the early phases of the war was not particularly pronounced, and quickly reversed (with the exception of Slovakia). This means that while the terms-of-trade decline had been large and lasting, it was not strictly driven by the war itself.

[7] The discussion relies heavily on Oblath (2019), who did the analysis for Hungary.

To gain more insight into the effects of the TOT decline, we introduce an alternative measure of welfare to GDP, Gross Domestic Income (GDI). Much less reported, GDI is also part of the European system of national accounts, and can be fairly easily calculated from data on GDP, imports and exports, and the terms-of-trade. The main difference between real GDP and real GDI is that the latter corrects for changes in the terms-of-trade. The reason for this correction is that real GDP records only changes in the *volumes* of exports and imports, but ignores relative *price* changes. As a measure of welfare, this can be misleading. Suppose that between two periods, export volumes do not change, but imports become more expensive relative to exports. This leaves real GDP unchanged, but clearly the overall purchasing power of domestic income falls, since the same export volume is sufficient to buy fewer imported goods and services. Since this was clearly the case for the CEEE since 2021, it is instructive to look at real GDI as well, which corrects real GDP for the TOT change.[8]

Fig. 2.12: Real GDP and real GDI growth
Data: Eurostat (2023j), authors' calculations.
(1) Real GDP: chained growth rate, relative to the same period of previous year.
(2) RGDI: real GDP growth adjusted for terms-of-trade changes.

Figure 2.12 shows the quarterly changes in RGDP and RGDI for each country, relative to the same period in the previous year. Not surprisingly, in the countries where the terms-of-trade declined the most, the purchasing power of produced

[8] For details on the calculations, see Oblath (2019) or Reinsdorf (2010).

output also suffered. In Latvia, for example, RGDI growth was significantly negative throughout 2022, while RGDP growth remained positive until the second half of the year. In Hungary there is also a stark difference between volume changes (positive and high until mid 2022), and RGDI (much smaller since 2021 and negative already in mid 2022). Slovakia and Czechia show similar patterns. This is important not only because of welfare changes (of which RGDI is an improved measure), but also because RGDI paints a better picture of domestic income developments than RGDP. As Oblath (2019) shows, the TOT correction exposes the extent of Hungarian fiscal expansion in 2021 even more starkly. Terms-of-trade shocks do not necessarily lead to deteriorating trade balances, if the country in question cuts back on imports and/or increases exports to pay for the rising prices of the former. In Hungary, however, this adjustment mechanism was delayed by fiscal policy until 2023, due to the parliamentary elections in 2022.

2.4.3 The Labour Market

Fig. 2.13: Adult refugees from Ukraine at the end of 2022
Data: Eurostat (2023c, 2023a), authors' calculations.
(1) Refugees: quarterly means of monthly values.

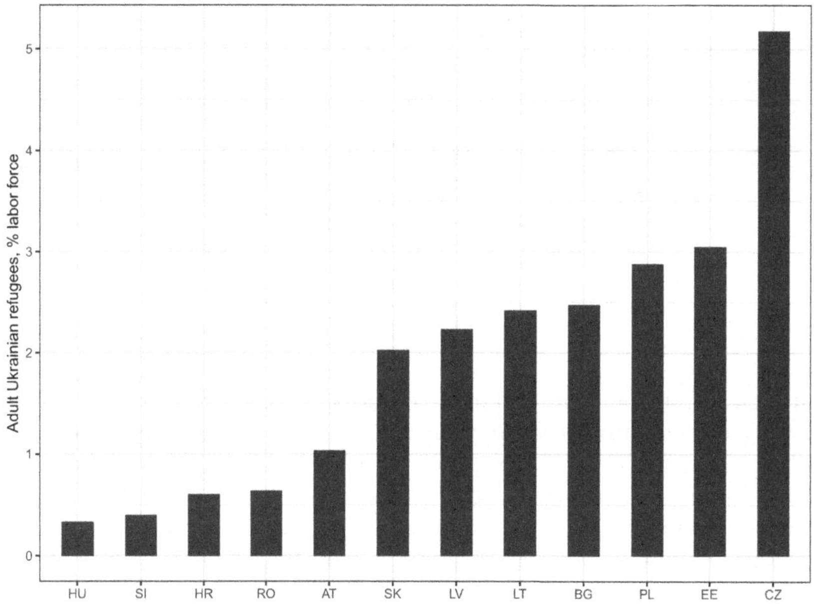

The second shock of the war in the CEEE was the large number of refugees fleeing Ukraine and arriving in the various countries of the European Union (Chapter 8 offers a deeper look and analysis). The number of refugees varies greatly across the CEEE, with some countries – notably Poland, but also some others – taking a large share. Figure 2.13 shows the stock of *adult* Ukrainian refugees at the end of 2022 (note that many who initially arrived in CEEE countries later left for Western Europe). The chart shows refugee numbers as a percentage of the labour force.

Fig. 2.14: Labour market tightness
Data: Eurostat (2023y, 2023o), authors' calculations.
(1) Unemployment rate: quarterly means of monthly values.
(2) Tightness: ratio of vacancy rate to unemployment rate.

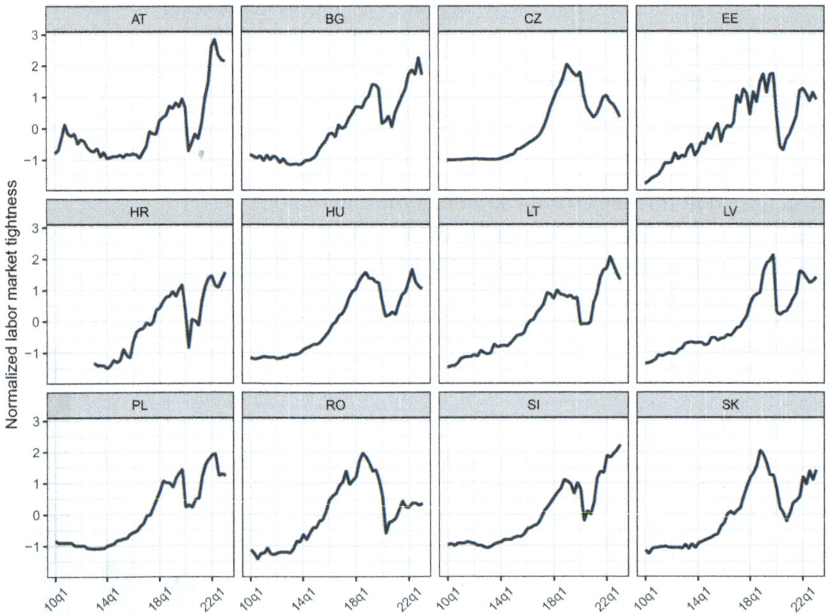

It is clear from the figure that in the majority of the CEEE Ukrainian refugees could potentially contribute significantly to labour supply (see Chapter 9 for a more detailed analysis). In Czechia, they amount to more than 5% of the labour force, with Poland, Bulgaria, the three Baltic economies and Slovakia following (Poland has the highest absolute numbers). It is yet unclear whether the refugees will remain in these countries, or return to Ukraine once the war ends. Providing employment to such numbers depends on the current stance of the labour market, which is depicted in Figure 2.14. Labour market tightness is defined as the vacancy rate (the ratio of open job vacancies to overall jobs) divided by the unemployment rate. Since individual countries have systematically different values (reflecting country-specific institutional and measurement issues), we normalise the indicator by subtracting the sample mean and then by dividing with the sample standard deviation.

Vacancy data starts in 2010, which was just after the global financial crisis, with an accordingly weak labour market. Tightness then rose significantly across the region, reaching its peak in 2019. The Covid crisis led to a sharp drop, although the trough was in most cases still well above the 2010 value. As for GDP, the Covid crisis proved to be short-lived also on the labour market, and tightness rebounded quickly, reaching in some cases even higher levels than before the recession. The war led to small drops in about half of the countries, but overall labour markets remained very tight. We can conclude that allowing Ukrainian refugees to work would contribute significantly to an easing of labour market shortages in many countries of the region. More details are provided in Chapter 9.

2.4.4 Policy Response and Adjustment

Fig. 2.15: Imports from Russia, Belarus and Ukraine
Data: Eurostat (2023i), authors' calculations.
(1) Total imports from Belarus (BY), Russia (RU) and Ukraine (UA), % total imports.

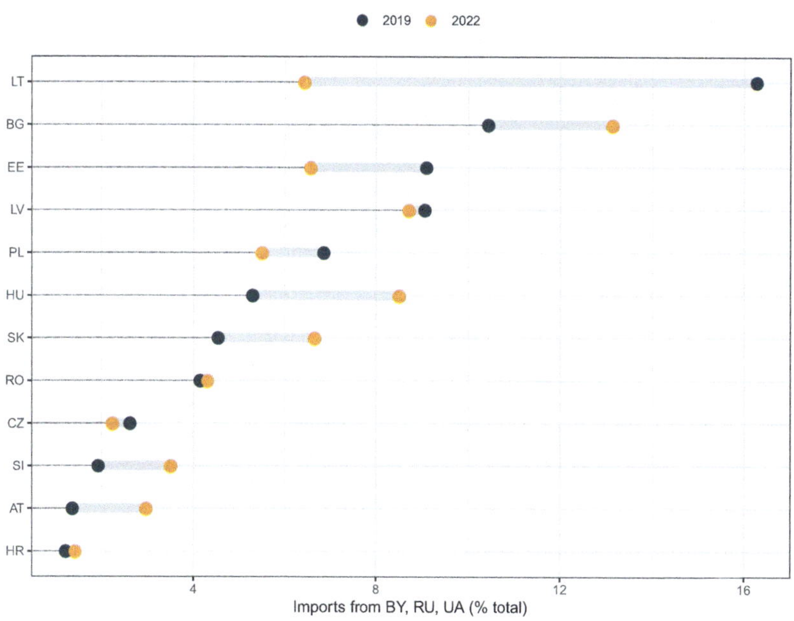

After describing the main shocks leading up to and during the war, we finish this section with a discussion of how economies adjusted. We already discussed some aspects of this, but it is worth looking at additional indicators. In particular, we look at two main channels of adjustment: first, the trade exposure to Russia, Belarus and Ukraine; and second, the reaction to inflation.

Figure 2.15 shows how import shares (measured at current prices) of Ukraine, Belarus and Russia in the total imports of the CEEE changed between 2019 (the year before Covid) and 2022. There are two broad country groups evident from the figure. Some economies, chiefly the Baltics and Czechia, successfully diversified their imports and saw a declining share, even taking the energy price spike into account. The declines are highly pronounced for Latvia and Estonia, while in the other two countries the volume decrease was almost balanced by the price rise. In the other countries the import share of the three countries rose, likely due to the price effect. For Bulgaria, Hungary and Slovakia in particular, the lack of alternatives, especially for natural gas, means that at least in the short run adjustment is difficult (see also Figure 2.5). The fall of energy prices by 2023, however, will likely show declining import shares also in these economies, once data is available.

Fig. 2.16: Interest rates
Data: OECD (2023b); Eurostat (2023e), authors' calculations.
(1) Yield: EMU convergence criteria long rates.
(2) 3-months rates: money market rates.

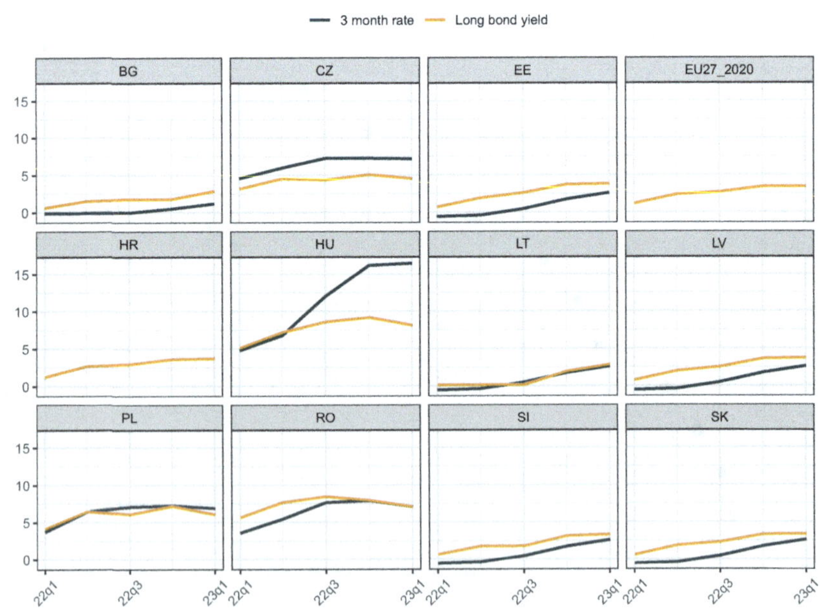

Apart from energy security and affordability, the other key challenge remains inflation. We showed earlier that it is high, although declining throughout the region, with some countries – Hungary in particular – facing significant challenges to again reach price stability in line with their inflation goals. We also showed that out of the four economies with floating currencies, the problems of Hungary (and to a lesser extent, Poland) are exacerbated by depreciating currencies. To briefly illustrate how monetary policy responded to inflation, and what challenges this poses to fiscal policy, Figure 2.16 plots the short-run money market rates and the long-run government bond yields in the CEEE.

In countries that are in the Eurozone the short-run rate tracks the ECB policy rate very closely, which is rising, but still remains modest in international comparison. In late 2023, its deposit rate is 4%, while the comparable rate is 5.50% in the USA and 5.25% in the UK. Long yields have tracked the short rates closely, with marginal differences across the countries. In Bulgaria, with its currency board arrangement, we see very similar developments. Considering current inflation rates, Eurozone monetary policy remains fairly loose, but inflation expectations remain mostly anchored.

Czechia, Hungary, Poland and Romania are the economies with floating currencies and independent monetary policies. Recalling Figure 2.9, we saw that their inflation performance was largely comparable to the Eurozone countries, with Hungary being a notable exception. The cost of this, however, was higher interest rates, both in the short run and in the long run. Comparing Czechia, Poland and Romania to the Eurozone countries, the short-run gap at the beginning of 2023 is about 4 percentage points. Looking at Figure 2.8, the impact of significantly higher interest rates is not yet evident in the GDP numbers, but monetary policy operates with long and varying lags. Also, in these countries long bond yields are also high, indicating that inflation expectations may not be suitably anchored. As inflation is falling, it will be an important task for central banks to strengthen and reestablish credibility.

Hungary is an outlier even in the second group of countries. As we saw earlier, its inflation performance has been the worst in the whole CEEE. Reacting partly to inflation, and partly to the depreciation of the forint, the central bank raised interest rates to levels not seen since the mid 1990s. This has managed to stabilise the currency, but at the cost of slowing down real activity. The long yield is also the highest compared to the other floaters, indicating the doubts of financial markets about a quick and credible disinflation. Moreover, while higher rates put a bigger burden on debt financing in all countries, this is particularly acute in Hungary, which faces the unenviable choice between significant fiscal consolidation on the one hand, and an implicit default via high inflation on the other.

2.5 Social Impact: a Preliminary Look

Unavoidable statistical lags in the collection of important social and distributional data make it difficult to provide a timely assessment of the enfolding social impact of the crisis. This is particularly true about indicators that are based on the EU-SILC microdata:[9] though the outcome of the 2022 fieldwork is already released, its income variables typically refer to the previous calendar year. Nevertheless, apart from the poverty and income inequality variables, the most relevant social data are already available at least for 2022.

As a starting point, we look at the recently proposed Social Convergence Framework (SCF) of the European Union, laid out in the European Commission (2024b) and detailed in the Council of the European Union (2023). Using a set of 16 indicators, the SCF assigns flags if a given indicator of a country points to a combination of low and non-improving situation.[10] Table 2.6 indicates the number of new flags in the areas of equal opportunities, fair working conditions, and social protection and inclusion (see Table 2.7 for the specific variables in each group).

Table 2.6 reveals that social conditions have started to deteriorate in many of the CEEE, especially in Bulgaria and Estonia, with 6 and 4 new flags. Most of these fall into the area of social protection and inclusion (poverty), and income inequality. Using flash estimates for income inequality and monetary poverty (Eurostat, 2023gg), one finds that the poverty-related flags would apply also with estimated 2022 income, while inequality may decline. Overall, the number of new flags in social protection and inclusion is noticeably higher among the CEEE than the EU average. Not surprisingly, five out of the seven EU countries that were selected for a deeper analysis in the Social Convergence Framework are from the CEEE[11] (indicated by bold in the table).

Table 2.7 digs more into the specific indicators, but to save space, presents only the CEEE aggregate numbers for current and new flags. As also seen in Benczúr and Kónya (2022), the CEEE in general face more social issues than most other EU countries. This is particularly true about digital skills, income inequality, and social protection and inclusion in general. These preexisting problems deteriorated further in 2022, particularly for poverty and the ability of social transfers to reduce poverty. On the other hand, the CEEE performance in employment is fairly good.

The noticeable deterioration of social conditions (especially poverty) already indicates that the shock may affect groups of the population differently. This is hardly surprising, given that a major part of the shock was an increase in energy and food prices, which started already around August 2021. This potential for a social deterioration was noticed early on, and has led to important government interventions to cushion the effect. There were however visible differences in the degree of targeting these interventions to specific vulnerable groups and businesses. Such differences can have a major influence on the overall fiscal costs and social impact of such measures (see, for example, Varga, Roeger & in 't Veld, 2022 for a model-based assessment).

To overcome statistical lags, policy analyses (like European Commission, 2022a) turned to studies that tried to nowcast the social impact. This typically meant to see how higher prices increase the cost of living using previous household budget data (using the EU Household Budget Survey, EU-HBS). In one of the earliest such studies, Menyhert (2022) used August 2022 inflation data and the 2015 wave of

[9] European Union Statistics on Income and Living Conditions.

[10] See Annex 6 of European Commission (2024b).

[11] The other two are Italy and Spain.

Table 2.6: Social impact of the shock
Data: European Commission (2024b) Annex 9
(1) The cells indicate the number of new flags in the Social Convergence Framework (European Commission, 2024b) in 2024 (2022 data, though often referring to the income year of 2021).
(2) The EU number is the average across all Member States.
(3) See Table 2.7 for the variables in each of the areas.
(4) Using flash estimates for inequality and more recent data for digital skills (Eurostat, 2023hh), Bulgaria and Estonia would no longer have a new flag in the equal opportunities area, while Latvia and Romania would.

	EU	AT	BG	CZ	EE	HR	LV	LT	HU	PL	RO	SI	SK
Equal opportunities	0.37	0	1	1	1	0	0	0	0	0	0	0	0
Fair working conditions	0.19	0	0	1	0	0	0	0	0	0	1	0	0
Social protection and inclusion	1.07	1	5	0	3	1	1	2	2	0	1	1	2
Total	1.63	1	**6**	2	**4**	1	1	**2**	**2**	0	**2**	1	2

the EU-HBS to assess the increase in living costs by households. The author finds that the price increases between August 2021 and 2022 led to an 11.1% increase in living costs on average across the EU. The increase was the largest among the CEEE, especially in the Baltic states (with the maximum of 27.57% in Estonia). The impact was broadly similar across the population, though the gap in the living cost increase between the top and bottom income quintiles reached 3-5% in countries like Estonia, Italy or Latvia.

The increase in the costs of living was also predicted to translate into increases in material and social deprivation, and similar measures like energy or transport poverty. Menyhert (2022) found that material and social deprivation may increase by 2 percentage points in the EU on average (with the largest predicted impact in Slovakia at 5.3 percentage points). In a parallel analysis, Fulvimari, Temursho, Vaitkeviciute and Weitzel (2023) predict a massive increase in the population share of households who spend more than 10% of their budget on energy (from 26.9% to 43.4% at the EU level) and who spend more than 6% on private transport fuel (from 37% to 47.2% at the EU level).[12]

[12] The changes refer to the time period from August 2021 to January 2023. It is important to note that there is an ongoing discussion about the measurement of energy poverty, as it is a culturally sensitive multi-dimensional phenomenon (Thomson, Bouzarovski & Snell, 2017). For a recent review, see for example Menyhert (2023).

Table 2.7: Main areas of social issues in the CEEE
Data: European Commission (2024b) Annex 9
(1) The cells indicate the number of flags and new flags in 2022 (2024 edition of the Joint Employment Report).

	2022 flags	new flags in 2022
Equal opportunities		
Early leavers from education and training	3	0
Individuals' level of digital skills	6	0
Young NEET rate	3	1
Gender employment gap	2	0
Income quintile ratio	5	2
Fair working conditions		
Employment rate	1	0
Unemployment rate	0	0
Long-term unemployment rate	2	1
GDHI per capita growth	0	0
Social protection and inclusion		
At-risk-of-poverty or social exclusion rate	6	5
At-risk-of-poverty or social exclusion rate for children	3	2
Impact of social transfers on poverty reduction	7	4
Disability employment gap	7	3
Housing cost overburden	2	2
Children aged less than 3 years in formal childcare	7	0
Self-reported unmet need for medical care	4	3

2.6 Outlook and Possible Paths

At the time of writing, the main legacy of the Covid aftermath and the Ukrainian war is high inflation, while GDP growth seems to be only mildly affected. The policy response to high inflation, however, will have an impact on the real economy as well. In this subsection we compare earlier and currently available forecasts from the OECD Economic Outlook to show how the region is expected to cope in the near future.

Besides the data, we present three forecasts, that were published in 2021 December, 2022 June, and 2023 June. The first is the last one made before the Ukrainian war, relying on data until mid-2021. The second, while not actually including data from 2022, was published after the war broke out, incorporating some of its effects into

Fig. 2.17: GDP forecasts
Data: OECD (2023a, 2022, 2021), authors' calculations.

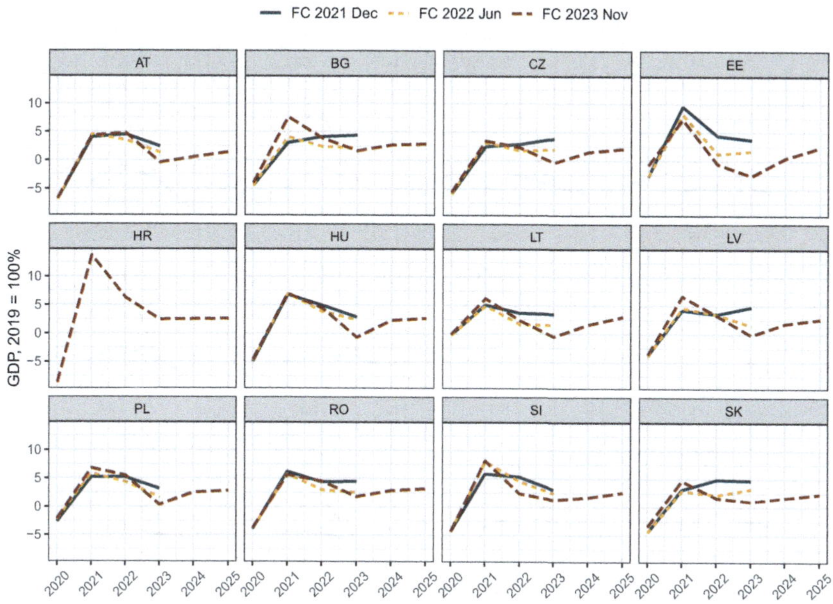

the forecast. Finally, the last and current round is based on data until 2023, with the knowledge of which immediate risks did or did not materialise during the first phase of the conflict. Data are available at the annual frequency, hence the occasionally large differences between forecast rounds.

Figure 2.17 shows the data and forecasts for GDP. Comparing the 2021 and 2022 projections, the latter shows the expected impact of the war. In most cases (except for Slovenia), we see a lower GDP path in the later forecast. In retrospect, this has held up remarkably well, with the available data and the new, 2023 forecast tracking the 2022 paths quite closely. The major exception is Bulgaria, where 2021 turned up to be a much better year than even the 2022 projection nowcasted. In Slovakia, the revision was also dramatic, but even with the faster rebound after Covid the post-2022 path seems to track well with the 2022 forecast. Overall, the OECD projects continued economic growth in 2023 and 2024 across the region. The effect of the war led to lower growth rates for the majority of the CEEE, but recessions for the most part are not expected (with the exceptions of Estonia and Hungary).

As we discussed repeatedly, inflation (Figure 2.18) has proved to be a surprise compared to the 2021 December forecast. In most countries, it has proved to be higher and more persistent than the 2022 projections (Poland and Slovakia are exceptions). This is reflected in the projected evolution of long bond yields (Figure 2.19), which

Fig. 2.18: Inflation forecasts
Data: OECD (2023a, 2022, 2021), authors' calculations.

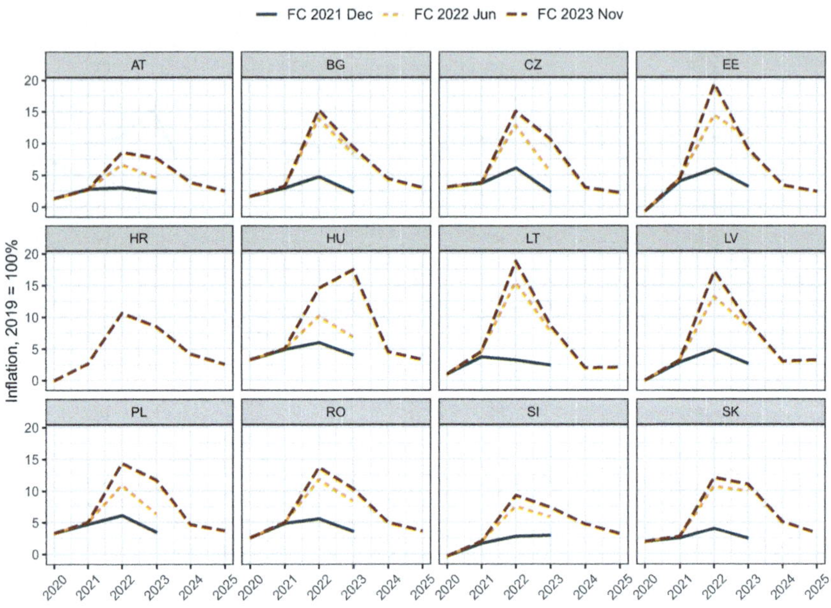

are in the last forecast almost universally above the 2022 projections. Inflation is now the main economic challenge for the CEEE in the near future.

Fig. 2.19: Forecast for interest rates
Data: OECD (2023a, 2022, 2021), authors' calculations.

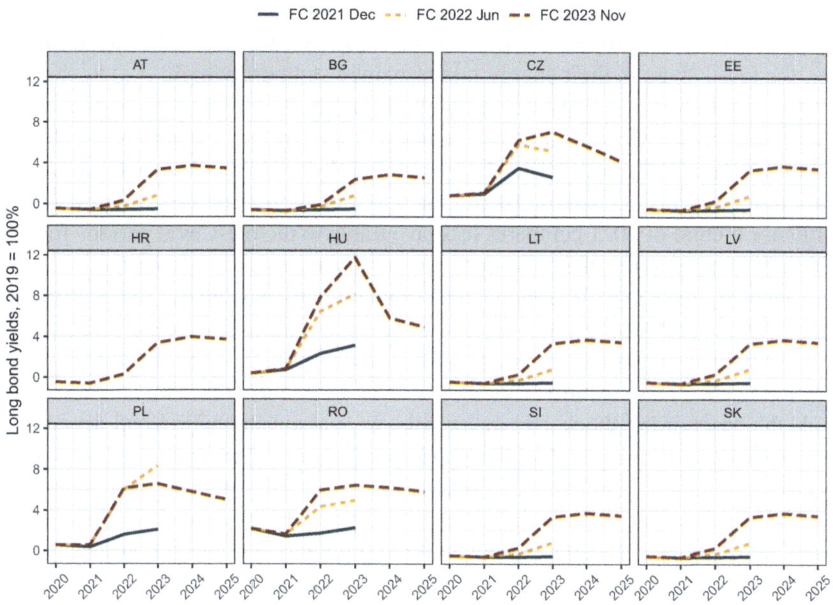

2.7 Lessons and Recommendations

The current economic crisis, caused by Russia's aggression on Ukraine, has followed a previous major crisis episode, the Covid-19 pandemic. As such, there is a strong parallel with the EU's two-phase crisis in 2008-12, when the originally global financial crisis evolved into an EU specific sovereign debt crisis.

Unlike during the GFC, the CEEE seems to have recovered from the first phase of the current crisis (the Covid-19 shock) quickly, with minor exceptions of a few countries and variables. Looking deeper, however, one can discover important additional vulnerabilities in the context of energy and food prices and supply security. Equally importantly, the seemingly quick and successful recovery from the previous shock did put a significant burden on policies and (fiscal) policy space and has created new imbalances. Broad inflationary pressures were evident in the whole CEEE group already before the war broke out. While inflation and public debt rose significantly, there was hope towards the end of 2021 that these imbalances would be gradually resolved over the coming years. The attack on Ukraine upended these optimistic expectations.

The most important source of economic exposure to the war was due to fossil energy import dependency. With the exception of Romania (and partially Croatia and

Poland), the rest of the CEEE relied almost completely on imported oil and gas . In case of natural gas, Russia was the exclusive or dominant source, with the exceptions of Latvia and Slovenia. In case of oil, imports are more diverse, but even here Russia was the most important source for the majority of the countries. Though there was a significant reduction in the energy intensity of the CEEE in the decade before the war, the fossil share in their energy mix remained stubbornly high.

As a final element to understand how prepared the CEEE were to face a next economic shock, we looked at the status of their coping capacities (resilience). Relative to the GFC, most CEEE had significantly better resilience characteristics both at the onset of the Covid-19 and the Russian aggression crises. However, the resilience picture of 2021 compares less favourably to the pre-Covid period. Together with inflation pressures, the buildup of some imbalances, and an uncertain economic environment, these may foreshadow a less quick recovery from the shock of the war than after Covid-19. In terms of household finances and social cohesion factors, the CEEE situation is relatively good, though increasing levels of political polarisation may represent a major future challenge.

At the onset of the shock, two major risks were associated with fossil dependence on Russia. First, an abrupt halt of Russian imports of natural gas (and to a lesser extent, oil) were thought to lead to catastrophic consequences for industry, and households in the winter. Second, disruptions to the oil and gas markets were expected to lead to much higher prices, exacerbating the inflation problem. In hindsight, expectations of large-scale shutdowns of industry and freezing households proved to be exaggerated. European countries reacted more flexibly to both the quantity and price shock than anticipated. While in the majority of the CEEE the Ukrainian war led to either a recession or a slowdown of the recovery from Covid, the recession is fairly shallow, and with the exceptions of Estonia, Hungary and Latvia, it also seems to be highly transitory. The picture nevertheless changes noticeably when one looks at real Gross Domestic Income, which accounts better for changes in the terms of trade (like the case of an energy price shock for importers).

Overall, the main impact of the war seems to be on inflation, with a much smaller and mostly transitory decline in economic activity. It is as yet too early to say how persistent inflation will remain. Decreasing energy prices and monetary tightening are contributing to declining inflation across the region, but the pace and magnitude varies significantly. Also, inflation may have had a heterogeneous impact on the population, as different income groups faced differential exposure to food and energy price hikes.

References

Alessi, L., Benczur, P., Campolongo, F., Cariboni, J., Manca, A. R., Menyhert, B. & Pagano, A. (2020). The resilience of EU member states to the financial and economic crisis. *Social Indicators Research*, *148*, 569-598.

Benczúr, P. & Kónya, I. (2022). Convergence to the centre. In L. Mátyás (Ed.),

Emerging European Economies after the Pandemic: Stuck in the Middle Income Trap? (pp. 1–51). Cham: Springer International Publishing. Retrieved from https://doi.org/10.1007/978-3-030-93963-2_1 doi: 10.1007/978-3-030-93963-2_1

Council of the European Union. (2023). *Introduction of a Social Convergence Framework in the European Semester* (Tech. Rep.). Council of the European Union. Retrieved from https://data.consilium.europa.eu/doc/document/ST-9481-2023-ADD-1/en/pdf

European Central Bank. (2016). Increasing resilience and long-term growth: the importance of sound institutions and economic structures for euro area countries and EMU. *Economic Bulletin.*

European Commission. (2017). *Economic resilience in EMU, thematic discussions on growth and jobs, note for the Eurogroup* (Tech. Rep.). Brussels: European Commission.

European Commission. (2020a). *Europe's moment: Repair and prepare for the next generation* (Tech. Rep.). European Commission. Retrieved from https://ec.europa.eu/commission/presscorner/detail/en/ip_20_940

European Commission. (2020b). *Recovery plan for Europe* (Tech. Rep.). European Commission. Retrieved from https://ec.europa.eu/info/strategy/recovery-plan-europe_en

European Commission. (2020c). *Strategic Foresight Report – Charting the course towards a more resilient Europe* (Tech. Rep.). European Commission. Retrieved from https://ec.europa.eu/info/strategy/strategic-planning/strategic-foresight/2020-strategic-foresight-report_en

European Commission. (2022a). *European economic forecast: autumn 2022.* https://data.europa.eu/doi/10.2765/785228.

European Commission. (2022b). *REPowerEU: Affordable, secure and sustainable energy for Europe* (Tech. Rep.). European Commission. Retrieved from https://commission.europa.eu/strategy-and-policy/priorities-2019-2024/european-green-deal/repowereu-affordable-secure-and-sustainable-energy-europe_en

European Commission. (2023). *Alert Mechanism Report 2024, Statistical Annex.* https://commission.europa.eu/publications/2024-european-semester-alert-mechanism-report_en.

European Commission. (2024a). *LMP expenditures.* https://webgate.ec.europa.eu/empl/redisstat/databrowser/view/LMP_IND_EXP/default/table?lang=en&category=lmp_indic. (Accessed: 20-01-2024)

European Commission. (2024b). *Proposal for a Joint Employment Report 2024.* https://op.europa.eu/en/publication-detail/-/publication/93b9c730-8da5-11ee-8aa6-01aa75ed71a1/language-en.

European Investment Bank. (2023). *EIB Investment Survey (EIBIS).* https://data.eib.org/eibis/download. (Accessed: 01-08-2023)

Eurostat. (2023a). *Beneficiaries of temporary protection at the end of the month by citizenship, age and sex – monthly data.* https://ec.europa.eu/eurostat/databrowser/view/MIGR_ASYTPSM/default/table?category=migr.migr_asy.migr_asytp. (Accessed: 12-07-2023)

Eurostat. (2023b). *Debt by currency of issue.* https://ec.europa.eu/eurostat/databrowser/view/GOV_10DD_DCUR/default/table?lang=en&category=gov.gov_gfs10.gov_10dd.gov_10dd_sgd. (Accessed: 12-07-2023)
Eurostat. (2023c). *Employment and activity by sex and age - quarterly data.* https://ec.europa.eu/eurostat/databrowser/product/page/LFSI_EMP_Q. (Accessed: 12-07-2023)
Eurostat. (2023d). *Employment rate by sex.* https://ec.europa.eu/eurostat/databrowser/view/TESEM010/default/table. (Accessed: 11-09-2023)
Eurostat. (2023e). *EMU convergence criterion series - quarterly data.* https://ec.europa.eu/eurostat/databrowser/product/page/irt_lt_mcby_q. (Accessed: 12-07-2023)
Eurostat. (2023f). *Energy intensity.* https://ec.europa.eu/eurostat/databrowser/product/page/nrg_ind_ei. (Accessed: 12-07-2023)
Eurostat. (2023g). *EU labour force survey.* https://ec.europa.eu/eurostat/statistics-explained/index.php?title=EU_labour_force_survey. (Accessed: 06-12-2023)
Eurostat. (2023h). *Euro/ECU exchange rates - quarterly data.* https://ec.europa.eu/eurostat/databrowser/view/ERT_BIL_EUR_Q/default/table?lang=en&category=ert.ert_bil.ert_bil_eur. (Accessed: 12-07-2023)
Eurostat. (2023i). *EU trade since 1999 by SITC.* https://ec.europa.eu/eurostat/databrowser/view/DS-018995__custom_7450834/default/table?lang=en. (Accessed: 12-07-2023)
Eurostat. (2023j). *GDP and main components (output, expenditure and income).* https://ec.europa.eu/eurostat/databrowser/view/namq_10_gdp/default/table?lang=en. (Accessed: 12-07-2023)
Eurostat. (2023k). *Gross domestic product (GDP) at market prices.* https://ec.europa.eu/eurostat/databrowser/view/TIPSAU10/default/table. (Accessed: 11-09-2023)
Eurostat. (2023l). *HICP - monthly data (index).* https://ec.europa.eu/eurostat/databrowser/view/PRC_HICP_MIDX/default/table?lang=en. (Accessed: 12-07-2023)
Eurostat. (2023m). *Inactive population as a percentage of the total population, by sex and age.* https://ec.europa.eu/eurostat/databrowser/view/lfsa_ipga/default/table?lang=en. (Accessed: 06-12-2023)
Eurostat. (2023n). *Income quintile share ratio (S80/S20) by sex.* https://ec.europa.eu/eurostat/databrowser/view/TESSI180/default/table. (Accessed: 14-07-2023)
Eurostat. (2023o). *Job vacancy statistics by NACE Rev. 2 activity - quarterly data (from 2001 onwards).* https://ec.europa.eu/eurostat/databrowser/view/jvs_q_nace2/default/table?lang=en. (Accessed: 12-07-2023)
Eurostat. (2023p). *Long-term unemployment rate by sex.* https://ec.europa.eu/eurostat/databrowser/view/TESEM130/default/table. (Accessed: 25-06-2023)
Eurostat. (2023q). *Natural gas import dependency by country of origin.* https://ec.europa.eu/eurostat/databrowser/view/nrg_ind_idogas/default/table?lang=en. (Accessed: 12-07-2023)
Eurostat. (2023r). *Oil and petroleum products import dependency by country of origin.* https://ec.europa.eu/eurostat/databrowser/view/NRG_IND_IDOOIL/default/

table?lang=en&category=nrg.nrg_quant.nrg_quanta.nrg_ind.nrg_ind_. (Accessed: 12-07-2023)

Eurostat. (2023s). *People at risk of poverty or social exclusion by sex.* https://ec.europa.eu/eurostat/databrowser/view/TEPSR_LM410/default/table. (Accessed: 25-06-2023)

Eurostat. (2023t). *Quarterly non-financial accounts for general government.* https://ec.europa.eu/eurostat/databrowser/view/gov_10q_ggnfa/default/table. (Accessed: 12-07-2023)

Eurostat. (2023u). *The real gross disposable income of households per capita.* https://ec.europa.eu/eurostat/databrowser/view/TEPSR_WC310/default/table. (Accessed: 17-07-2023)

Eurostat. (2023v). *Self-reported unmet needs for medical examination by sex, age, main reason declared and income quintile.* https://ec.europa.eu/eurostat/databrowser/view/HLTH_SILC_08/default/table. (Accessed: 11-07-2023)

Eurostat. (2023w). *Simplified energy balances.* https://ec.europa.eu/eurostat/databrowser/view/NRG_BAL_S/default/table?lang=en. (Accessed: 12-07-2023)

Eurostat. (2023x). *Unemployment by sex, age and duration of unemployment.* https://ec.europa.eu/eurostat/databrowser/view/lfsa_ugad/default/table?lang=en. (Accessed: 06-12-2023)

Eurostat. (2023y). *Unemployment by sex and age – monthly data.* https://ec.europa.eu/eurostat/databrowser/view/UNE_RT_M/default/table?lang=en. (Accessed: 12-07-2023)

Eurostat. (2023z). *Unemployment rates by sex, age and citizenship.* https://ec.europa.eu/eurostat/databrowser/view/lfsa_urgan/default/table?lang=en. (Accessed: 06-12-2023)

Eurostat. (2023aa). *Employment rates by sex, age and citizenship.* https://ec.europa.eu/eurostat/databrowser/view/LFSA_ERGAN/default/table. (Accessed: 11-09-2023)

Eurostat. (2023bb). *Young people neither in employment nor in education and training by sex.* https://ec.europa.eu/eurostat/databrowser/view/TESEM150/default/table. (Accessed: 13-07-2023)

Eurostat. (2023cc). *General government expenditure by function (cofog).* https://ec.europa.eu/eurostat/databrowser/view/gov_10a_exp/default/table?lang=en. (Accessed: 25-06-2023)

Eurostat. (2023dd). *Nominal unit labour cost - 3 years % change.* https://ec.europa.eu/eurostat/databrowser/view/tipslm10/default/table?lang=en. (Accessed: 25-06-2023)

Eurostat. (2023ee). *Inability to face unexpected financial expenses - EU-SILC survey.* https://ec.europa.eu/eurostat/databrowser/view/ilc_mdes04/default/table?lang=en. (Accessed: 17-07-2023)

Eurostat. (2023ff). *Arrears (mortgage or rent, utility bills or hire purchase) from 2003 onwards - EU-SILC survey.* https://ec.europa.eu/eurostat/databrowser/view/ilc_mdes05/default/table?lang=en. (Accessed: 01-08-2023)

Eurostat. (2023gg). *Experimental statistics: income inequality and poverty indicators.*

https://ec.europa.eu/eurostat/documents/7894008/8256843/Main_tables_FE_2022.xlsx/b76f409f-1177-1506-e759-c20afe87a379?t=1689327475300. (Accessed: 01-02-2024)

Eurostat. (2023hh). *Individuals who have basic or above basic overall digital skills by sex.* https://ec.europa.eu/eurostat/databrowser/view/tepsr_sp410/default/table?lang=en&category=tepsr.tepsr_eo.tepsr_eo_hi. (Accessed: 01-02-2024)

Eurostat. (2024a). *Net international investment position - annual data.* https://ec.europa.eu/eurostat/databrowser/view/tipsii10/default/table?lang=en. (Accessed: 20-01-2024)

Eurostat. (2024b). *Total financial sector liabilities, non-consolidated - annual data.* https://ec.europa.eu/eurostat/databrowser/view/tipsfs10/default/table?lang=en. (Accessed: 25-01-2024)

FRED. (2023a). *Crude Oil Prices: Brent - Europe.* https://fred.stlouisfed.org/series/DCOILBRENTEU. (Accessed: 12-07-2023)

FRED. (2023b). *Global price of Natural gas, EU.* https://fred.stlouisfed.org/series/PNGASEUUSDM. (Accessed: 12-07-2023)

Fulvimari, A., Temursho, U., Vaitkeviciute, A. & Weitzel, M. (2023). *Economic and distributional effects of higher energy prices on households in the EU* (Fair Transition Working Papers No. May 2023). European Commission.

Giovannini, E., Benczur, P., Campolongo, F., Cariboni, J. & Manca, A. R. (2020). *Time for transformative resilience: the Covid-19 emergency* (Tech. Rep.). Ispra: JRC Science for Policy Report, JRC120489.

International Monetary Fund. (2016). *A macroeconomic perspective on resilience* (Tech. Rep.). Washington DC: International Monetary Fund.

Jolles, M., Meyermans, E. & Vasicek, B. (2018). Determinants of economic resilience in the euro area: an empirical assessment of policy levers. In *Quarterly report on the euro area, volume 17, no 3.* European Commission.

Manca, A. R., Benczur, P. & Giovannini, E. (2017). *Building a scientific narrative towards a more resilient EU society* (Tech. Rep.). Ispra: JRC Science for Policy Report, JRC106265.

Matyas, L. (Ed.). (2022). *Emerging European Economies after the Pandemic Stuck in the Middle Income Trap?* Washington, D.C.: Springer, Contributions to Economics.

Menyhert, B. (2022). *The effect of rising energy and consumer prices on household finances, poverty and social exclusion in the EU* (JRC Technical Reports No. JRC130650). Luxembourg: European Commission Joint Research Centre.

Menyhert, B. (2023). *Energy poverty – New insights and analysis for improved measurement and policy* (JRC Technical Reports No. JRC133804). Luxembourg: European Commission Joint Research Centre.

Moll, Benjamin and Schularick, Moritz and Zachmann, Georg. (2023). *The power of substitution: The Great German Gas debate in retrospect.* (Tech. Rep.). BPEA Conference Draft. Retrieved from https://www.brookings.edu/articles/the-power-of-substitution-the-great-german-gas-debate-in-retrospect/

Oblath, G. (2019). Külkereskedelmi cserearány-változások és hatásuk a bruttó hazai reáljövedelemre, a belföldi felhasználásra és a jövedelmi felzárkózásra.

Külgazdaság, *63*, 3-41.
OECD. (n.d.). *Indicators of product market regulation, previous PMR vintages.*
OECD. (2016). *G20 policy paper on economic resilience and structural policies'* (Tech. Rep.). Paris: Author.
OECD. (2021). *Economic Outlook No 110 - December 2021.* https://stats.oecd.org/. (Accessed: 12-07-2023)
OECD. (2022). *Economic Outlook No 111 - June 2022.* https://stats.oecd.org/. (Accessed: 12-07-2023)
OECD. (2023a). *Economic Outlook No 114 - November 2023.* https://stats.oecd.org/. (Accessed: 12-07-2023)
OECD. (2023b). *Monthly Monetary and Financial Statistics (MEI).* https://stats.oecd.org/. (Accessed: 12-07-2023)
Reinsdorf, M. B. (2010). Terms of trade effects: Theory and measurement. *Review of Income and Wealth*, *56*, S177-S205.
Sgaravatti, G., Tagliapietra, S., Trasi, C. & Zachmann, G. (2023). *National fiscal policy responses to the energy crisis.* Bruegel Datasets https://www.bruegel.org/dataset/national-policies-shield-consumers-rising-energy-prices. (Accessed: 01-02-2024)
Thomson, H., Bouzarovski, S. & Snell, C. (2017). Rethinking the measurement of energy poverty in Europe: A critical analysis of indicators and data. *Indoor and Built Environment*, *26(7)*.
Varga, J., Roeger, W. & in 't Veld, J. (2022). E-quest: A multisector dynamic general equilibrium model with energy and a model-based assessment to reach the eu climate targets. *Economic Modelling*, *114*, 105911. Retrieved from https://www.sciencedirect.com/science/article/pii/S0264999322001572 doi: https://doi.org/10.1016/j.econmod.2022.105911
Varieties of Democracy. (2022). *The V-Dem Dataset.* https://v-dem.net/data/the-v-dem-dataset/. (Accessed: 29-03-2022)
World Bank. (2019). *Including institutions: boosting resilience in Europe* (Tech. Rep.). Washington DC: World Bank.
World Bank. (2021). *Doing business legacy.* https://www.worldbank.org/en/businessready/doing-business-legacy. (Accessed: 31-01-2024)
World Bank. (2023). *Worldwide Governance Indicators (WGI).* https://info.worldbank.org/governance/wgi/. (Accessed: 01-08-2023)

Open Access This chapter is licensed under the terms of the Creative Commons Attribution 4.0 International License (http://creativecommons.org/licenses/by/4.0/), which permits use, sharing, adaptation, distribution and reproduction in any medium or format, as long as you give appropriate credit to the original author(s) and the source, provide a link to the Creative Commons license and indicate if changes were made.

The images or other third party material in this chapter are included in the chapter's Creative Commons license, unless indicated otherwise in a credit line to the material. If material is not included in the chapter's Creative Commons license and your intended use is not permitted by statutory regulation or exceeds the permitted use, you will need to obtain permission directly from the copyright holder.

Chapter 3
Energy Markets: Current Situation and Possibilities for Stabilisation

Jakub Głowacki, Anna Gomola, Michał Król, Łukasz Mamica, and Monika Mazur-Bubak

Abstract The chapter outlines the consequences of Russia's attack on Ukraine in February 2022 on the energy market with a focus on Central and Eastern European countries. The influence of energy prices on the competitiveness of the economy is illustrated with examples from chemicals and chemical products manufacturing, as well as paper and paper products manufacturing. Additionally, the chapter discusses the characteristics of changes occurring as part of the transition towards renewable energy sources and their participation in the energy mixes of Central and Eastern European countries. The chapter also reviews actions aimed at mitigating the consequences of the increase in energy prices, with particular reference to the solutions in Poland.

3.1 Introduction

The Russian invasion of Ukraine in February 2022 triggered a chain of consequences for Europe's energy security and widely understood energy politics. The energy crisis compromised the competitiveness of energy-intensive industries on the global market. Above all, the steep increase in gas prices led to worse economic indicators in countries where gas was dominant in the energy mix (such as Germany and

Łukasz Mamica ✉
Krakow University of Economics, Kraków, Poland, e-mail: mamical@uek.krakow.pl

Jakub Głowacki
Krakow University of Economics, Kraków, Poland, e-mail: glowackj@uek.krakow.pl

Anna Gomola
Krakow University of Economics, Kraków, Poland, e-mail: gomolaa@uek.krakow.pl

Michal Król
Krakow University of Economics, Kraków, Poland, e-mail: krolm@uek.krakow.pl

Monika Mazur-Bubak
Krakow University of Economics, Kraków, Poland, e-mail: mazurm@uek.krakow.pl

© The Author(s), under exclusive license to Springer Nature Switzerland AG 2024

L. Mátyás (ed.), *Central and Eastern European Economies and the War in Ukraine*, Contributions to Economics, https://doi.org/10.1007/978-3-031-61561-0_3

Italy). The influence of energy prices on the economy's competitiveness is illustrated with chemical and chemical products manufacturing and paper and paper product manufacturing. This comparative analysis comprises data on the EU level, focusing on Poland and the Czech Republic, i.e., two neighbouring countries characterised by different energy mixes (coal-based power in Poland and nuclear power in Czech Republic).

The chapter will also discuss the changes occurring as part of the transition towards renewable energy sources and the participation thereof in the energy mixes of Central and Eastern European Countries (CEEC), with a particular emphasis on developments in the sector in 2022, in the aftermath of the war.

Compared to other countries in the region, the need for prompt independence from the Russian fossil fuels supply, following the war outbreak in Ukraine posed a comparatively minor challenge for Poland and the Czech Republic. This was due to their high levels of energy security: Poland mines its own coal and has sufficient gas resources to cover a third of its requirements; the Czech Republic, on the other hand, relies predominantly on nuclear power and has its coal reserves.

The subsequent parts of this chapter review the actions aimed at mitigating the consequences of the increase in energy prices. To offer a historical context, the authors discuss strategies applied during the fuel crisis of the 1970s and compare them with the gas crisis in 2022. A particular emphasis is placed on the systemic actions in Poland, i.e., programmes such as 'Clean Air' (with a budget of 23.7 billion euro), 'My Heat' (offering subsidies for the installation of heat pumps in new single-family houses) and 'My Electricity' (designed to support individual PV micro-installations). The chapter concludes with a presentation of the concept of energy insecurity. In addition to its theoretical dimension, the authors discuss how the situation of people unable to heat their homes changed between 2022 and the preceding year, before the Russian invasion of Ukraine.

3.2 Changes in the Pricing of Energy Supplies

Russia's aggression in Ukraine, which started in February 2022, triggered a steep increase in energy prices in European markets. In the second half of 2022, gas prices for EU household consumers were, on average, 79.5% higher than in the preceding year (Figure 3.1). The highest increase was recorded in Latvia (256.5%) and the Netherlands (208.9%); the lowest – was in Slovakia (17.8%) and Hungary (14.6%). In Poland, gas prices for household consumers increased by 44.5%.

Fig. 3.1: Gas prices for household consumers: bi-annual data (2018 to 2023) in EU 27 (average) and Poland in EUR per kilowatt-hour.
Data: Eurostat (2023d), authors' calculations.

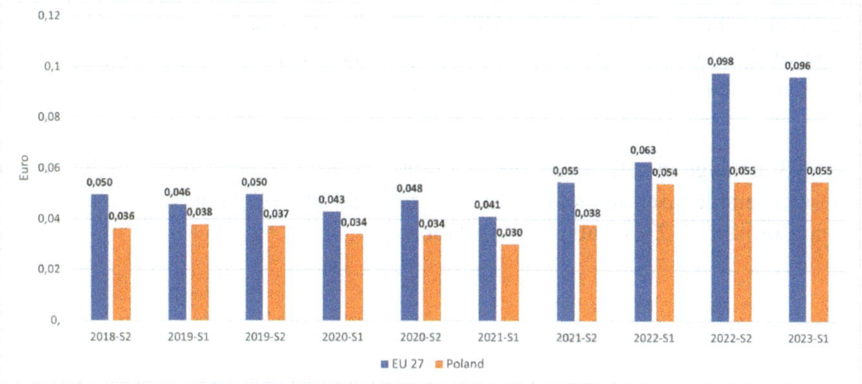

Within a year of the outbreak of the war, gas prices for non-household consumers increased by 105.8% in the entire EU and by 137% in Poland (in comparison to prices in the second half of 2021). The steepest increase was recorded in Romania (241.3%) and Hungary (224.5%). The disproportion in Hungary between the increase in prices for household consumers and for other users is particularly noteworthy (14.6% vs 224.5%). France and Ireland, on the other hand, experienced the lowest rate increase for non-household consumers – 53.7% and 50%, respectively.

Fig. 3.2: Gas prices for non-household consumers: bi-annual data (2018 to 2023) for EU 27 and Poland in EUR per kilowatt-hour.
Data: Eurostat (2023e), authors' calculations.

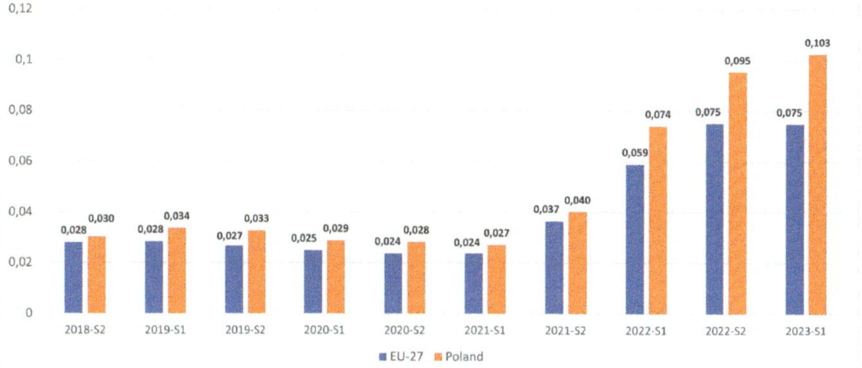

Compared to the same period the preceding year, in the first half of 2023, gas prices for non-household consumers increased by 26.9% on average in the EU (Figure 3.3). Nonetheless, the disproportion between particular countries was notable, with Hungary and Slovakia experiencing an increase (85.3% in the former and 66.4% in the latter), while in Denmark and Lithuania, prices dropped (by 40.6% and 27.4% respectively). In Poland, gas prices for non-household consumers increased by 38.6% in the analysed period.

Fig. 3.3: Change in natural gas prices for non-household consumers, including all non-recoverable taxes and levies, from the first half of 2022 to the first half of 2023. Data: Eurostat (2023e), authors' calculations.

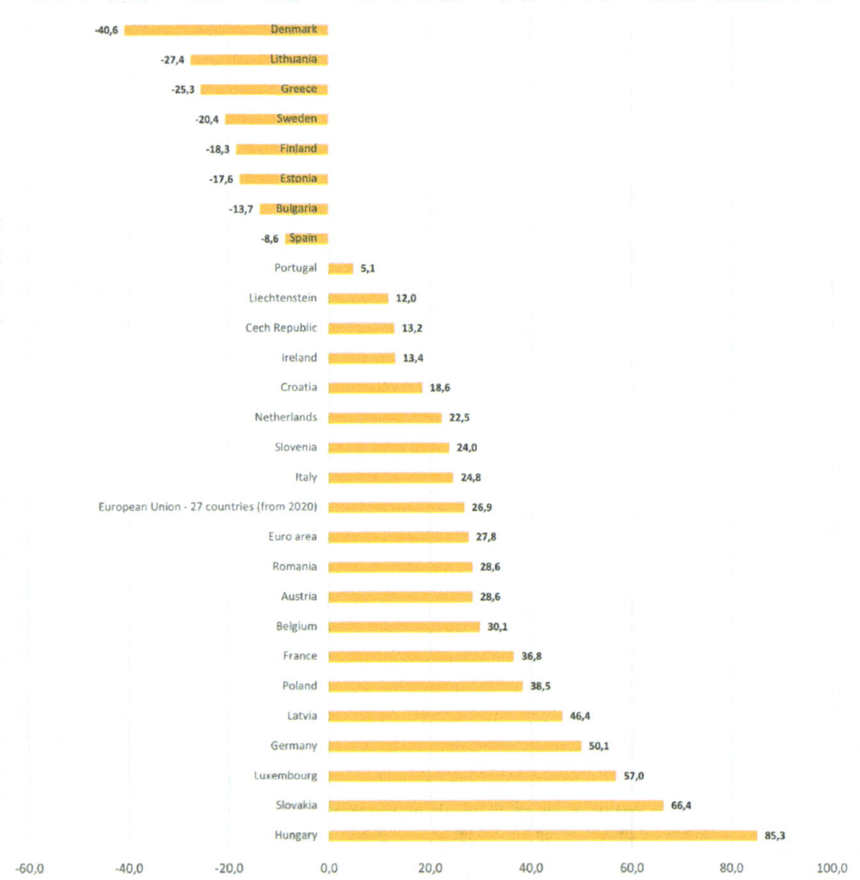

In the second half of 2022, electricity prices for household consumers in the EU were 58.5% higher on average than during the preceding year (Figure 3.4). As in other cases, the dynamics of change varied with individual countries. The steepest increase was recorded in Greece (186.9%) and Denmark (144.8%); in Hungary and Bulgaria, on the other hand, the increase amounted to 8.1% and 5.2%, respectively. The surge in household energy prices continued into 2023: Compared to the same period a year earlier, the analysis of the data from the first half of 2023 showcases a price increase of 102.8% in the Netherlands and 99.3% in Lithuania. Six countries, however, recorded a decrease in electricity prices for household consumers in that period, ranging from 0.2% in Poland and 1.4% in Sweden to as much as 34.8% in Greece and 40.5% in Spain.

Fig. 3.4: Electricity prices for household consumers: bi-annual data (2018 to 2023) in EU 27 and Poland in EUR per kilowatt-hour.
Data: Eurostat (2023b), authors' calculations.

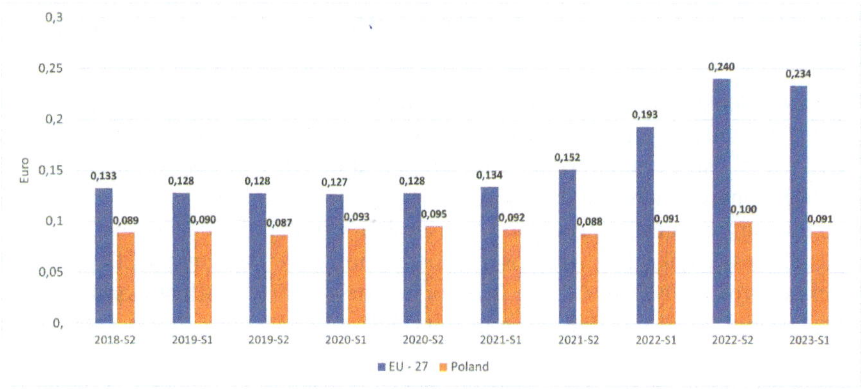

Fig. 3.5: Electricity prices for non-household consumers: bi-annual data 2007–2023.
Data: Eurostat (2023c), authors' calculations.

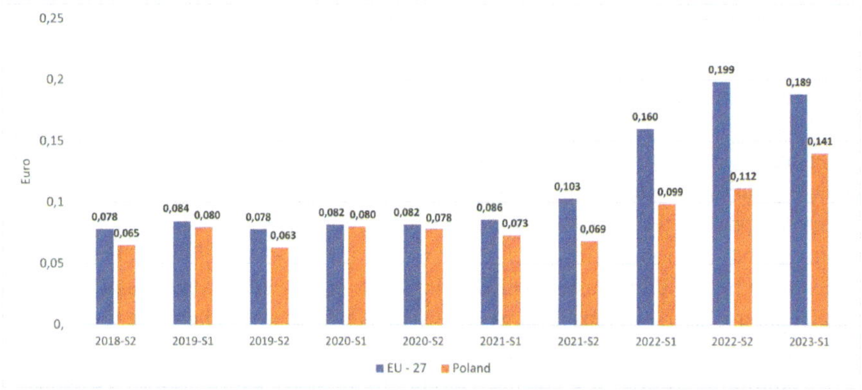

The average increase in electricity prices for non-household consumers in the EU between the second half of 2021 and the corresponding period in 2022 was higher than that for household consumers, reaching 92.6% (Figure 3.5). The countries that recorded the highest increase in this regard were Romania (200.4%), Lithuania (154.6%), and the Czech Republic (133.3%). The lowest increase rates were recorded in France (52.7%) and Finland (44.3%). In Poland, the increase rate oscillated around 62.8%, i.e., 49% higher than prices for household consumers. In the first half of 2023, the highest increase rates in comparison to the same period in 2022 were noted in France (109,9%), Luxembourg (101.4%) and Croatia (97.2%). The steepest decrease rates (above 30%) were recorded in Bulgaria (33.5%), Greece (34.8%) and Spain (38.7%).

3.3 The Impact of Energy Prices on Energy-Intensive Industries

Energy is considered the driving force of the economy, playing a key role in every aspect of it and impacting on economic growth (Ayres & Warr, 2005; Stern & Kander, 2012). It is also essential to the production and delivery of almost all goods and services. Energy-intensive industries are the following: the steel sector, extraction and mining, chemical industry, and industrial processing of products such as paper and cellulose (Makridou, Andriosopoulos, Doumpos & Zopounidis, 2016). These branches profoundly influence the shape of industrial policy, which also encompasses the principles of sustainable development (Dolfsma & Mamica, 2020). Companies representing energy-intensive industries are particularly vulnerable to increases in energy pricing, as energy costs constitute the main component of their cost structures. Moreover, fluctuations in the prices of energy and its resources affect not only operational costs but may also lead to a decrease in a company's competitiveness in the international market.

The ongoing energy crisis resulted in a negative supply shock, which, in turn, took its toll on the economy in the entire EU — particularly on energy-intensive industries. Given that there are no forecasts prognoses of significant decreases in energy prices in the upcoming years, we should by all means develop solutions to enable Central European companies to maintain their competitiveness on the international market. According to Eurostat data, overall employment and industrial production in the EU in 2022 exceeded the 2021 levels despite the rapid growth in energy prices. However, the situation, is different in energy-intensive sectors, which constitute a vital component of the EU economy. As stated above, the energy crisis compromised competitiveness of the energy-intensive industries in the context of the global economy. Moreover, these industries also face additional challenges inherent in its pursuit of sustainable development, energy effectiveness and reduction in greenhouse gas emissions. Energy-intensive industries are, in fact, key to achieving climate neutrality in the EU by 2050.

A country's energy mix strongly affects its industrial production. The energy mixes of the countries most affected by the crisis, i.e., Germany and Italy, are based on natural gas. The market production dynamics of the German chemical industry decreased by 14% within a single year. However, the same sector in Poland recorded a positive dynamic of 3.5% (Eurostat, 2024).

This section discusses the situation in the selected energy-intensive sectors in the EU (aggregated approach), and more specifically in Poland and the Czech Republic. The choice is not accidental: Poland and the Czech Republic are small, open economies, but their means of securing energy broadly differ. While Poland resorts primarily to coal, the Czech Republic relies mainly on nuclear energy. The analysis of the situation in energy-intensive sectors will focus on the manufacturing of chemicals and chemical products as well as that of paper and paper products. Each of these requires a particular proportion of raw materials to produce goods. The chemical industry uses natural gas, solar energy, and oil and petroleum products. In the paper industry, on the other hand, the operation of the production machinery requires a large quantity of electricity; the central part is consumed during the paper web drying process. The analyses are based on the monthly data for the overall market production in the selected sectors, covering the period between January 2001 and August 2023.

Fig. 3.6: The dynamics of market production for the manufacturing of paper and paper products in the EU between 2001 and 2023
Data: (Eurostat, 2024), authors' calculations.

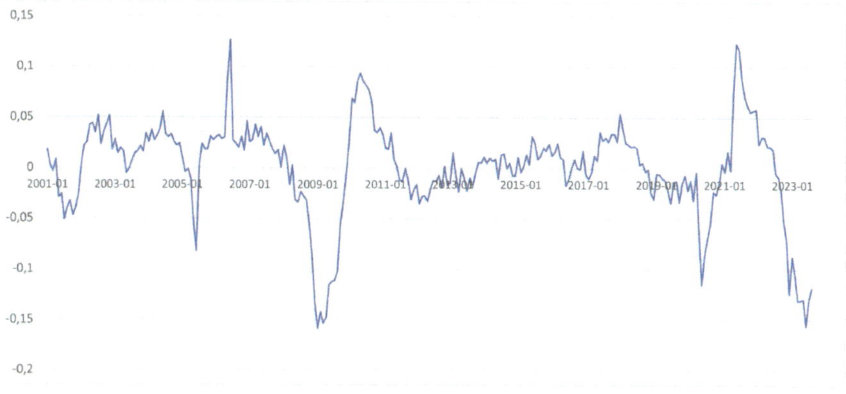

As illustrated by Figures 3.6 and 3.7, both the chemical and paper production sectors have recently experienced the lowest average value of market production dynamics since the 2008 crisis, when the entire continent was struck by recession. Moreover, the situation of energy-intensive industries in 2023 was, in fact, worse than during the Covid-19 pandemic.

As illustrated by Figures 3.8 and 3.9, the chemical industry in both Poland and the Czech Republic has had the lowest market production dynamics since the 2008 recession. Moreover, Poland is shown to have lower production dynamics than the

Fig. 3.7: The dynamics of market production for the manufacturing of chemicals and chemical products in the EU between 2001 and 2023
Data: (Eurostat, 2024) authors' calculations.

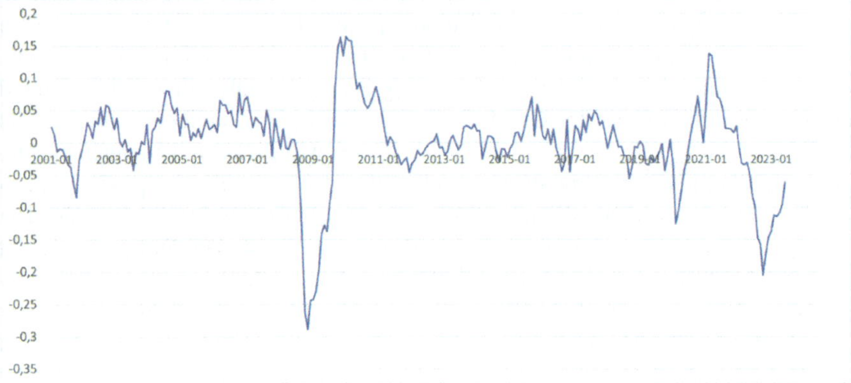

Fig. 3.8: The dynamics of market production for manufacturing of chemicals and chemical products in the Czech Republic between 2001 and 2023
Data: (Eurostat, 2024), authors' calculations.

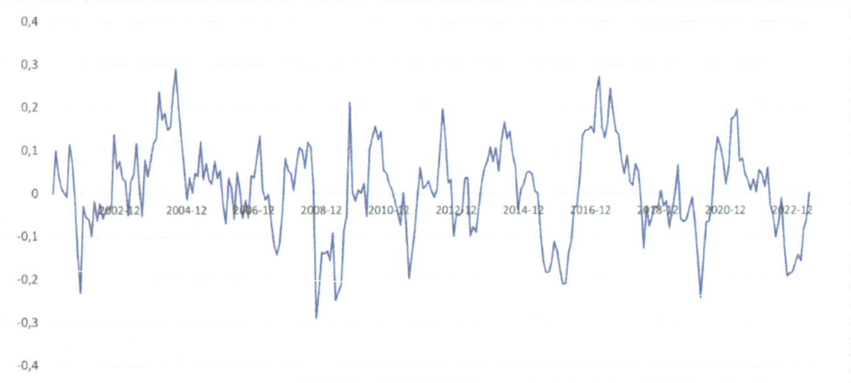

Czech Republic – this is directly linked to its energy mix, which is less optimal than that of its neighbour.

As shown in Figures 3.10 and 3.11, the paper and paper products industries in both Poland and the Czech Republic have recently recorded the lowest value of market production dynamics since the 2008 recession in Europe. Similarly to the chemical sector, Poland's paper and paper products industry is characterised by lower production dynamics than the Czech Republic, which is linked to its suboptimal energy mix.

During the crisis period, EU countries experienced large fluctuations in energy prices. Therefore, their governments ought to respond by designing solutions and

Fig. 3.9: The dynamics of market production for manufacturing of chemicals and chemical products in Poland between 2001 and 2023
Data: (Eurostat, 2024), authors' calculations.

Fig. 3.10: The dynamics of market production for the manufacturing of paper and paper products in the Czech Republic between 2001 and 2023
Data: (Eurostat, 2024), authors' calculations.

mechanisms to support energy-intensive industries in the EU. In doing so, the governments should arrive at a common solution applicable to all EU countries. The solution, however, should not be based on unconditional energy subsidies for energy-intensive industries, as this would be a costly fiscal measure.

Fig. 3.11: The dynamics of market production for the manufacturing of paper and paper products in Poland between 2001 and 2023
Data: (Eurostat, 2024), authors' calculations.

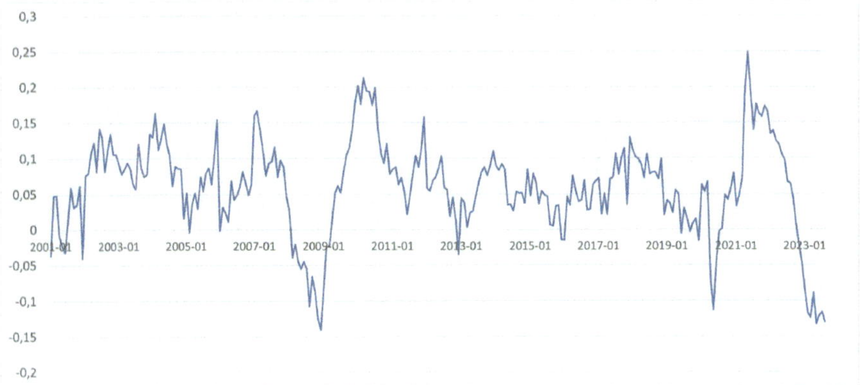

3.4 The Role of Renewable Energy Resources in Shaping Energy Security in Selected Central-Eastern European Countries

Regarding energy transformation, the countries of Central-Eastern Europe (CEE) are characterised by a certain 'delay' compared to their more developed Western neighbours. The roots of this disparity are easily traced back to their earlier economic systems, in which energy was obtained mainly from solid fuels (Pakulska, 2021). Solid fuels indeed continue to play a significant role in the energy structures of CEE countries, especially Poland, Slovakia, the Czech Republic, Bulgaria and Hungary.

In Poland, the energy sector is still predominantly based on the combustion of lignite and hard coal (Marks-Bielska, Bielski, Pik & Kurowska, 2020). For many years, the Polish government strongly supported the coal industry, which was directly reflected in its reluctance to commit to decarbonisation. The interests of the coal regime are protected by a network of connections between the Polish government and coal-mining companies, many of which are owned by the state (Brauers & Oei, 2020). As coal has been in use in Poland for over a century (Kochanek, 2021), it remains a powerful barrier to a larger scale implementation of renewable energy. This, in turn, leads to further consequences, e.g. the deterioration of air quality (Król & Gomola, 2022). The Polish 'carbon culture' stands strong not only due to the reluctance to challenge the current state of affairs, but also because of the fear of changes that would require a large-scale transformation of infrastructure (Juszczyk & Shakeel, 2020). It should also be emphasised that Poland continues to be one of the global leaders in hard coal and lignite mining (Kochanek, 2021). In the EU, Poland is the leader in hard coal mining and ranks second in terms of lignite mining (Brauers & Oei, 2020).

In 2022, the consumption of hard coal in the EU totalled 160 million tonnes, marking an 11% decrease compared to 2019 (Eurostat, 2023). Hard coal continues to be traded and consumed by all EU countries excluding Malta. In 2022, Poland and Germany were its largest consumers, contributing 38% and 25%, respectively, to the EU's overall hard coal consumption. Together, these two nations accounted for nearly two-thirds of the total consumption, with Italy, the Netherlands, France, Spain and the Czech Republic following suit (Eurostat, 2023). Six countries within the EU dominate the consumption of brown coal, accounting for 97% of the total usage. Among them, Germany takes the lead with 46%, followed by Poland at 19%. Other significant consumers include the Czech Republic (11%), Bulgaria (10%), Romania (6%) and Greece (5%). These nations collectively comprise the overwhelming majority of brown coal consumption in the EU (Eurostat, 2022).

It is necessary to emphasise that Poland and the Czech Republic had already had high levels of energy security before the outbreak of war. Poland's energy independence is indeed secured by the large proportion of coal in its energy mix; it is, moreover, capable of covering a third of its gas requirements with its own production (Jonek-Kowalska, 2022). Similarly, the Czech Republic has the capacity to cover all its energy requirements with coal; added to that, the large share of nuclear energy in the country's mix strongly contributes to its energy independence (Jonek-Kowalska, 2022). In this case the Czech Republic has implemented additional measures to reduce its reliance on Russia in the nuclear power industry. This includes opting to change the supplier of nuclear fuel for the Temelín Nuclear Power Plant and reclaiming ownership of the vital Czech nuclear company Škoda JS from an entity associated with the Kremlin (Dębiec, 2023). In contrast, Slovakia, having suspended its hard coal mining activity, imports all its coal supplies from Russia and Ukraine. In Hungary, natural gas remains the principal source of energy, although, its domestic gas production is continuously decreasing, currently amounting to 2 billion m^3 each year. This amount covers about a fifth of the country's overall gas requirements; the remainder is imported mainly from Russia (Kochanek, 2021). Nevertheless, the problem of dependency on Russian imports did not pertain only to the CEEC – it indeed affected the EU in its entirety. Examining product categories in 2021, energy emerged as the EU's primary import from Russia, constituting 62% of the EU's imports from Russia that year and amounting to €99 billion (Eurostat, 2022b).

Researchers point to nuclear energy as indispensable in eliminating solid fuels (Brook et al., 2014). Yet, as of now, only a few CEEC have tapped into the potential of their own nuclear energy: Bulgaria, the Czech Republic, Hungary, Romania, Slovakia and Slovenia (IRENA, 2023). However, considering long-term energy security and climate goals, it appears necessary to accelerate the investment in renewable energy sources: in the OECD countries, the energy security risk is decreased by wind power, hydroelectricity and overall renewable energy sources (Cergibozan, 2022). These sources have the potential to cover two thirds of global energy requirements and thus contribute to reducing the emission of greenhouse gases, which is crucial for the goals of limiting the increase in global temperature to 2 degrees by 2050 (Gielen et al., 2019) and abandoning fossil fuels, as stated in the final agreement of COP28 in Dubai.

Table 3.1: Total installed renewable energy capacity in MW (2015–2022)
Data: based on IRENA (2023)

Country / year	2015	2016	2017	2018	2019	2020	2021	2022	Change (%) 2015-2022	Capacity increase
Bulgaria	4136	4145	4289	4316	4319	4364	4532	5205	26%	1069
Croatia	2713	2793	2916	2979	3068	3255	3490	3593	32%	880
Czech Republic	4214	4212	4278	4271	4373	4451	4552	4934	17%	720
Estonia	594	607	615	609	716	829	1012	1178	98%	584
Hungary	1077	1048	1224	1630	2288	3024	3906	3926	265%	2849
Latvia	1782	1778	1796	1779	1826	1826	1823	1965	10%	183
Lithuania	693	768	787	836	859	937	1159	1617	133%	924
Poland	6919	7881	7982	8301	9361	12275	16457	21242	207%	14323
Romania	11212	11162	11145	11169	11169	11121	11120	11141	-1%	-71
Slovakia	2384	2397	2385	2330	2431	2377	2406	2406	1%	23
Slovenia	1419	1409	1479	1474	1512	1612	1704	1878	32%	459

Table 3.1 presents the levels of installed renewable energy capacity in eleven CEEC between 2015 and 2022. The choice of 2015 as the starting point stems from the fact that one year prior, in 2014, Russia annexed Crimea. That turn of events should have alerted country leaders that a future cooperation in the energy market between their respective states and Russia might be threatened -- and thus, they should have taken action to make their economies independent from external supply. Considerable investments in renewable energy sources were made by Poland, where between 2015 and 2022 installed renewable power increased by 14.323 MW i.e., by 207%. The decisive factor behind this steep growth was the interest of individual consumers in solar energy (Igliński et al., 2023). Nonetheless, when analysing this type of data, it should be noted that energy consumption significantly differs between countries; hence, for the purpose of comparative analysis, we ought to look primarily at the percentage changes rather than the values of installed capacity. To offer an example, according to the International Energy Agency, in 2021, Poland consumed 171.3 TWh of electric energy, and Estonia – only 9.4 TWh (IEA, 2022). Yet, this is due to the fact that Poland's population is substantially larger. The upward trend is observed in each analysed country aside from Romania. Percentage values demonstrate that the country which did most in terms of renewable investments was Hungary, where, over seven years, the installed capacity was increased by 265%. Poland comes second with a 207% increase, followed by Lithuania, where renewable capacity grew by 133% in the analysed period.

Each country uses different renewable energy technologies, as illustrated by Table 3.3. Croatia, Latvia, Romania, Bulgaria, Slovakia and Slovenia are characterised by the prevalence of installed hydropower (percentage-wise in comparison to other types of installed power in a given country). Poland, the Czech Republic, Hungary and Estonia, on the other hand, source most of their renewable energy from solar

Table 3.2: Renewable energy technologies in 2022 (installed capacities in %)
Data: based on IRENA (2023)

Country / year	Hydropower	Wind	Solar	Biogas	Solid biofuels	Geothermal	Renewable municipal waste
Bulgaria	48,1%	13,5%	37,4%	0,6%	0,3%	-	-
Croatia	61,2%	29%	5,1%	1,6%	2,7%	0,3%	-
Czech Republic	22,6%	6,9%	53,2%	7,5%	9,2%	-	0,6%
Estonia	0,8%	26,7%	45,4%	0,9%	18,8%	-	7,2%
Hungary	1,5%	8,3%	76,1%	2,2%	11,2%	0,1%	0,7%
Latvia	81,8%	6,9%	2,9%	2,9%	5,5%	-	-
Lithuania	7,2%	50,3%	35,1%	2,3%	3,8%	-	1,2%
Poland	4,6%	37,6%	52,6%	1,2%	3,8%	-	0,2%
Romania	59%	27,1%	12,7%	0,3%	1%	-	-
Slovakia	67,1%	0,2%	22,3%	3,4%	6,8%	-	0,2%
Slovenia	62,5%	0,2%	33,7%	1,6%	2,1%*	-	-

power, and the major part of Lithuania's installed power is wind technology. It is worth noting that some CEEC utilise solid biofuels – especially Estonia (18.8%), Hungary (11.2%) and the Czech Republic (9,2%). 7.2% of Estonia's installed power is renewable municipal waste. Nevertheless, the CEEC (such as Poland) which are largely founded on unstable wind and solar power are likely to encounter an array of challenges not long from now (Pakulska, 2021); this is why it is necessary to devise strategies of balancing future domestic energy production when solid fuels will no longer be an option.

The CEEC are yet to face a lengthy process of energy transformation – one that will require new investments in domestic energy technologies, developing production infrastructure for renewable energy, and expanding information and communication technology. These ought to be financially supplemented by investments in electronic waste management – proportionately to the growing share of renewable energy in the energy structure (Pakulska, 2021). In the CEEC long-term actions to support the development of renewable energy sources paired with nuclear power might be decisive in achieving energy security, ensuring low price levels and, thus, improving the livelihood of disadvantaged citizens while contributing to attaining ambitious climate goals.

3.5 Instruments to Mitigate the Consequences of Energy Crises

3.5.1 The Consequences of the Energy Crises

An economic crisis will likely have far-reaching ramifications affecting various social, economic and political aspects. Typical economic repercussions include higher energy prices, limited supply, changes in the labour market, and decreased economic growth (Hauser, Schönheit, Scharf, Anke & Möst, 2021; Hutter & Weber, 2022; Simionescu, Radulescu, Balsalobre-Lorente & Cifuentes-Faura, 2023; Nosova, 2022; Kennedy, 2022). Utilising data from several sectors of the German economy to assess the short-term consequences of an energy crisis, Hauser et al. (2020) found that energy crises had already deeply affected industrial production in the short term. Even though the sales of energy-intensive sectors could improve their situation immediately after the Russian aggression on Ukraine, the decrease in production will result in further future damage. Sectors such as steel, chemicals or glass are usually at the beginning of production chains, which implies their macroeconomic impact. Furthermore, an energy crisis is likely to inflict social and environmental consequences, including increased pollution and deeper energy poverty (Halkos & Gkampoura, 2021; L. Mamica, Glowacki & Makiela, 2021; Karpinska et al., 2021). At this point, explaining the importance of energy poverty would be worth explaining. However, there is no single, universally accepted definition of this concept. In developing countries, energy poverty tends to be perceived in terms of access to more sophisticated sources of energy than the burning of solid fuels by households (Sadath & Acharya, 2017). A different approach assumes that energy poverty occurs when fuel costs to maintain satisfactory heating conditions exceed 10% of income (Boardman, 1991).

On the other hand, energy crises may prompt some positive changes in the economy, such as new priorities in energy policy and the development of new technologies (Arner, Barberis & Buckley, 2015; Mårald, 2010; Passarelli, Bongiorno, Cucino & Cariola, 2023; Zemtsov, 2020).

3.5.2 Similarities to the Oil Crisis of the 1970s

Schramm (2023) identifies similarities between the oil crisis in the 1970s and the recent gas crisis in 2022. The 1970s crisis was the sum of complex factors affecting the global oil market. In October 1973, the Yom Kippur War — also known as the 'Oil War' -- broke out. It was a military conflict between Israel and a coalition of Arab countries, especially Egypt and Syria, that began on the holiday of Yom Kippur on October 6th, 1973. As a retort against the US and other countries for their support of Israel, the Arab countries introduced an embargo on oil supply to the US, Canada, the Netherlands, the UK and Denmark, among others. As a result, oil prices on the global market soared drastically. Many countries resorted to improving their energy effectiveness to mitigate the crisis, promoting energy saving and seeking alternative energy sources. Reforms were introduced to reduce their dependence on oil imports.

Two powerful impulses drove the gas crisis of 2022. Firstly, the economies of individual countries were visibly recovering after the Covid period and, thus, in need of energy resources. Following the pandemic, gas was at record low prices, and as the dynamic of economic growth rose, so did the pressure to increase the prices of energy resources. At the same time, Russia strove to limit the supply, which contributed to higher prices. The second impulse for a rapid price increase was the Russian aggression in Ukraine, as it compromised Russia's position at the international level and jeopardised the credibility of Gazprom as a partner. The limited availability of natural gas in Europe and many countries' long-standing dependence on Russian gas spurred the price increase further.

Table 3.3: Comparison between the 1973 and 2022 crises
Data: Based on Schramm (2023)

	Oil crisis of 1973	Gas crisis of 2022
Conditions and their observed explanatory values	Functional pressures are intense due to the 'weakest link' problem and deficiencies of previously existing domestic capacities. Political impulses: weak due to the asymmetry in the repercussions of the crisis, which resulted in different countries having different 'external' options and lacking regional political leadership.	Functional pressures are intense due to the 'weakest link' problem and deficiencies of previously existing domestic capacities. Political impulses: weak due to the asymmetry in the repercussions of the crisis, stemming from the lack of energy solidarity in Europe and the lack of regional political leadership.
Repercussions of the crisis	There are no efforts to build a supranational potential (inefficient actions of the Commission about the oil division mechanism and joint negotiations with third parties). Weak energy policy afflicting everyone (higher prices for every customer, unequal access to energy resources). Partial disintegration of Europe (trade barriers between Member States).	There are no efforts to build a supranational potential (joint energy purchase remains voluntary). Insufficient supranational regulations (mandatory energy saving remains at a small scale). Standard suboptimal policy (higher prices for every customer, unequal access to energy resources). The primacy of domestic actions (energy purchase, subsidies for companies).

As demonstrated in Table 3.3, the fuel crisis in the 1970s and the gas crisis of 2022 were similar in their course and consequences. Both crises were characterised by functional solid pressures, which stemmed from weak political impulses. What needed to be improved was strong leadership on the supranational scale and the energy necessary for solidarity to be more consistent. As a result, the repercussions of higher energy prices afflicted all groups of customers, including individual households. On the other hand, the commercial sector was subsidised in some countries, which disrupted the principle of competition and, eventually, deepened the stratification between wealthy and disadvantaged countries.

3.5.3 Instruments for Mitigating the Crisis: the Example of Poland

Over the last few years, Poland has introduced governmental and municipal tools to decrease household energy use. Thermo-modernisation programmes are widespread, with the governmental initiative 'Clean Air' 1 on the cutting edge. It is coordinated by the National Fund for Environmental Protection and Water Management together with the Ministry of Climate and Environment. Its primary purposes are to improve the energy efficiency of buildings across Poland (with a particular focus on single-family houses), help beneficiaries and their families to attain energy security and decrease heating bills.

Before 2029, 103 billion PLN (23.7 billion EUR) will be dedicated to the programme. Of this, 63.3 billion PLN (14.6 billion EUR) will be subsidies, and the remaining 39.7 billion PLN (9.1 billion EUR) will cover loans with a preferential interest rate. The programme aims to improve air quality and reduce the emission of greenhouse gases by modernising heat generators and improving energy efficiency in residential buildings. Its objectives include insulating and increasing the heat efficiency of about 4 million houses, thermal modernisation, and replacing about 3 million obsolete out-of-class furnaces (which massively contribute to pollution) with, e.g. low-emission boilers or heat pumps. The programme's beneficiaries are individuals who own or co-own single-family houses or apartments in single-family buildings with a separate land and mortgage register. The programme is also dedicated to individuals who have obtained permission to begin constructing a new single-family house, but before the house enters into service. The programme's priority is to support the most disadvantaged families; therefore, the subsidy amount depends on the income, and the calculation method was drawn from an earlier governmental programme for family support: 'Family 500+.' The current subsidy cap is a yearly income per household below 135,000 PLN (31,000 EUR), regardless of its sources. The EU funds, emission charges, own resources of voivodeship-level Funds for Environmental Protection and Water Management, thermo-modernisation relief, and the Thermo-Modernisation Fund finance the programme. About 83% of Polish municipalities participate in the programme.

A further example is the 'My Heat' programme, which offers subsidies for heat pumps in new single-family houses. Their owners can apply for funding to purchase and install a pump. The programme's goal is propelling the development of individual heating systems and pro-consumer energetics in the area of air, water and ground source heat pumps in new single-family houses; it also aims at increasing the share of the renewable energy sources in the final energy consumption. Consequently, the programme is designed to curtail emissions from the attempts to heat single-family houses with ineffective means of utilising fossil fuels. The funding within the framework of the 'My Heat' programme is available to owners and co-owners of new single-family houses. To qualify, the building ought to achieve a higher energy standard. The maximum amounts of funding are 7,000 PLN (1,600 EUR) for an air-to-air or air-to-water heat pump and 21,000 PLN (4,800 EUR) for a ground source pump.

Another governmental programme is ‘My Electricity’ supporting individual PV micro-installations. Its goal is to bolster energy production via PV installations (and, in consequence, expand the share of renewable energy sources in the final energy consumption), increase the individual consumption of generated electricity by storing it in electrical or thermal energy storages, and to improve the effectiveness of energy management. The funding is available for installations between 2 and 10 kW of installed power, and its maximum amount is 20,500 PLN (4,700 EUR), half of the qualified cost, of which 4,000 PLN (920 EUR) is the subsidy for just the PV installation. Additional funding will be available for the installation’s supplementary components and energy storage. In 2022, there were over 866,000 PV micro-installations in Poland, and 1.5% of the overall electricity generated originated from PV.

The ‘Warm Apartment’ programme aims to improve energy efficiency in multi-apartment residential buildings. It enables apartment owners to apply for funding in their respective municipalities. It is designed to support the purchase and installation of modern, efficient heating systems, replacing ineffective, solid fuel-based heat sources. After successfully installing a new system, the beneficiaries are eligible for additional funding to replace outdated, poorly insulated window joinery with new, draft-proof equivalent, effectively keeping the heat inside. ‘Warm Apartment’ is a supplementary programme, and the principle underlying its implementation is its combination with thermal modernisation and improving energy effectiveness.

The primary purpose of the ‘Warm Apartment’ programme is to improve air quality and reduce greenhouse gas emissions as a result of replacing ineffective heat sources with new technologies and improving energy efficiency in more than 80,000 residential units in multi-apartment buildings. The programme also supports the installation of central heating, domestic hot water, mechanical ventilation with heating recovery, as well as the installation and operation of gas-fired condensing boilers, higher-standard wood pellet boilers (i.e., fuelled by low-ash granulate manufactured from wood waste and compressed under high pressure, such as sawdust, shavings or chips), electric heating, air to water and air to air heat pumps, as well as access to a shared, efficient heat source. The programme’s primary beneficiaries are municipalities, which receive appropriate funding from the voivodeship-level Funds for Environmental Protection and Water Management. Then, the municipalities set the deadlines for submitting the final beneficiaries’ applications, that is, individual residents of a given municipality who are legal owners or have limited property rights of a residential unit in a multifamily building. Having accepted and evaluated the applications, the municipalities sign grant agreements with the beneficiaries. The average subsidy per residential unit is conditioned on the beneficiary’s income and falls between 15,000 and 39,999 PLN (3,400–9,200 EUR).

3.5.4 Energy Insecurity

The security of energy supply has long been deemed essential in developing countries. The interrelation between energy supply security and a state's developmental prospects became notably evident in the wake of the fuel crises, such as the oil crisis of the 1970s, which led to a rapid increase in inflation and inhibited development processes (Le & Park, 2021), making researchers aware of the robust relationship between a stable energy supply and the correct functioning of states in both the economic and military spheres. Currently, reflecting on political security without referring to a state's energy security is quite difficult. The definitions and terms characteristic of this domain pertain either to the question of internal security and living conditions (Boateng, Balogun, Dada & Armah, 2020; Hernández, 2015;Hernández, 2016; Hernández & Siegel, 2019), or to geopolitical relations – that is, on the level of the state's energy system (Chester, 2010; Sovacool, 2016). An important perspective is perceiving access to energy as a stipulation for human development based on addressing widely understood human needs. As early as the 1980s, this topic was discussed by Schumacher, who argued that energy access is fundamental to all human activity because it constitutes a prerequisite for all wares and, thus, it is an essential ingredient of life, like air, water and the soil (Auty, 2007, Ouedraogo, 2013; Schumacher & Kirk, 1982).

On the other hand, it has been emphasised since the 1980s that developed countries consume energy that exceeds the level necessary to achieve maximum prosperity. This, in turn, significantly contributes to the deterioration of the state of the natural environment (Dietz, Rosa & York, 2009; Goldemberg, 1990; Rao & Min, 2018).

At present, it is implausible to discuss energy security or the lack thereof in any other way than in the context of sustainable development. This notion is directly addressed by the seventh goal of the UN Development Programme: 'Affordable and Clean Energy' (United Nations, 2022). This goal should be considered one of the leading challenges for the globalised world economy. Following World War II, it was agreed that the economic interdependence between states offered the best means for political stabilisation and conflict prevention. The post-war period saw a considerable population growth – and with it came increased energy requirements. Currently, about 15–20 countries are exporting energy and supplying oil and gas to the rest of the world. The remaining countries are forced to rely on imports to maintain their energy capacity (Le & Park, 2021).

The 2008 recession, the COVID-19 pandemic and Russia's invasion of Ukraine unmasked the global energy system's vulnerability to economic and political crises. It is worth considering the vast research analysing the harmful consequences of the economic development that is contingent on using the country's natural resources, in particular sectors such as mining and forestry. The analyses demonstrate that in countries relying on their natural resources, these unfavourable consequences are correlated to lower economic development levels than in other countries. Moreover, the populations of such countries tend to more frequently experience problems related to the health sector. It has been observed that these countries are likely to form authoritarian governments (Auty, 2007;Bulte & Damania, 2008; James & Aadland,

2011; Sachs & Warner, 2001), which led them to coin the term for this problem: 'the curse of natural resources' (Dauvin & Guerreiro, 2017). The contingency of an economy on natural resources is linked to an array of anomalous phenomena hindering development, such as an excessive focus on unstable and unsustainable mining or the tendency to resort to the so-called 'energy blackmail' – inflicting pressure on trade partners by threatening to cut down on the supply (Freudenburg, 1992; Freudenburg & Gramling, 1998).

The concept of energy insecurity on the household level, i.e., about the situation of individual citizens, was preceded by research on extreme cases of energy deficit. The idea of 'energy poverty' was applied to analyse the situation of people trying to secure the necessary amounts of energy at a reasonable price. Numerous studies deploying various methods have been dedicated to describing and quantifying the scale of energy poverty. They incorporated, e.g. calculations based on the share of energy-related expenses in individual incomes and the ratio of income to the amount of energy-related expenses (Meyer, Laurence, Bart, Middlemiss & Maréchal, 2018; Moore, 2012). Some studies have identified instances of excessive undercutting of energy consumption to keep the bills down, thus pointing to the phenomenon of hidden energy poverty (Cong, Nock, Qiu & Xing, 2022).

These studies were then expanded and modified to introduce the concept of energy insecurity. It is generally agreed that this concept is more comprehensive than energy poverty due to its definition of the inability to sufficiently meet basic energy needs on the household level (Hernández, 2016). Owed to its broad character, the concept of energy insecurity applies to issues related to energy prices, availability (infrastructure), required amounts, the proximity (or the lack thereof) of its source, reliability and 'cleanness.' The concept also encompasses the utility of the available energy and the broad consequences of its deficits, both temporary and long-term (Boateng et al., 2020; Hernández, 2016; Hernández & Siegel, 2019; Cook et al., 2008; Wilkinson et al., 2009). Initially, it was formulated based on the research concerning food security in developing countries (Cook et al., 2008); however, the concept of energy security ought to be perceived as particularly closely related to the actual living conditions of individuals, regardless of the terminology classifying countries as 'developed' or 'developing.' The characteristic specificity of the field is patent, for instance, in the so-called 'heat or eat dilemma' (Bhattacharya, DeLeire, Haider & Currie, 2003; Frank et al., 2006; Nord & Kantor, 2006). Another crucial aspect is the emphasis on access to 'clean' – that is, renewable – energy sources. Boateng argues that access to clean energy is critical to achieving sustainable development and alleviating the disproportionate susceptibility to diseases among the most vulnerable women, children and infants (Boateng et al., 2020). Researchers agree that the concept of energy insecurity incorporates various aspects characteristic of the sustainable development goals (UNEP, 2015) and, as such, it contributes to the seventh goal of the UN Development Programme, i.e., 'Affordable and Clean Energy'(United Nations, 2022).

The concept of energy insecurity is founded on premises about societal and environmental justice, emphasising fair distribution not only about income but also about energy access. As noted by Swope and Hernández, low-income citizens are likely to experience difficulties covering their energy bills while living in energy-inefficient houses cumbersome to heat (Hernández, 2016; Hernández & Siegel, 2019).The experience of energy insecurity among some US citizens is closely related to their socioeconomic status; also leading to the deterioration of their wellbeing, afflicting their physical and mental health alike (Hernández, 2016). Similarly, studies conducted in France also point to a correlation between access to energy and citizens' health (Lacroix & Chaton, 2015; Lacroix & Jusot, 2014). Research has uncovered lower self-esteem among people experiencing energy deficits, with the most frequent health issues being problems related to sleep, exacerbation of asthma, worse mood, or even depression (Hernández, 2016; Hernández & Siegel, 2019; Lacroix & Chaton, 2015; Meyer et al., 2018; Sovacool, 2016). Some studies reveal further dramatic consequences of the deficits, pointing to increased mortality in the winter months in Europe (Healy, 2003).

Currently, affordable access to renewable energy (or, at least, 'clean' energy) required to heat and light the living space and to be able to cook ought to be considered a prerequisite for a safe and dignified existence. The research cited from the US and Europe testifies to the fact that the lack of energy security compromises people's ability to meet basic human needs: energy insecurity not only deprives people of adequate shelter but also negatively affects other areas of their lives, such as nutrition, education, employment opportunities and health (Nussbaum, 2004).

Table 3.4: The inability to keep houses adequately warm in selected CEEC between 2021 and 2022
Data: Eurostat (2022c)

Country / year	**2021**	**2022**	**2022 vs. 2021**
Bulgaria	23.7%	22.5%	-1.20%
Croatia	5.7%	7%	1.30%
Czech Republic	2.2%	2.9%	0.70%
Estonia	2%	3.4%	1.40%
Hungary	5.4%	4.7%	-0.70%
Latvia	4.9%	7.1%	2.20%
Lithuania	22.5%	17.5%	-5.00%
Poland	3.2%	4.9%	1.70%
Romania	10.1%	15.2%	5.10%
Slovakia	5.8%	7.1%	1.30%
Slovenia	1.7%	2.6%	0.90%

Between 2021 and 2022, the percentage of people unable to sufficiently heat their houses in the CEEC increased, on average, by 0.7% (Table 3.4). The worst decline was reported in Romania and Latvia, where the numbers rose by 5.1% and

2.2%, respectively, in the analysed period. Poland noted a 1.7% increase; however, in Lithuania, Bulgaria and Hungary, the number of people struggling with energy insecurity decreased by 5%, 1.2% and 0.7%, respectively. It must be emphasised that these values are contingent on the diverse activities in energy subsidies, such as financial shields or grants, offered by governments in each of those countries.

3.5.5 Policy Implications

The mitigation of the consequences of an energy crisis in the CEEC can encompass a variety of instruments and activities aimed at improving energy security, increasing energy efficiency, diversifying energy sources, or bolstering the resilience of energy systems against potential threats.

The primary defence mechanism against an energy crisis is the diversification of energy sources – notably, the development of renewable energy sources (Makiela, Mazur & Glowacki, 2022). Technologies sourcing solar energy, hydropower or biomass can contribute to the reduction of the dependency on a single type of fuel. Another crucial component is launching and running programmes aimed at improving energy efficiency in individual households, industry, construction, and the public sector by decreasing energy demand (Economidou et al., 2020).

A significant challenge is the necessity for a stable legal framework, including regulations that encourage investments in renewable energy sources that would be both pro-consumer and attractive to commercial investors. This type of legal framework would significantly contribute to the development of the energy sector (Kampas, Rozakis, Faber & Mamica, 2021). Additional funding for energy-related projects would also be beneficial in this context: governmental programmes supporting investment in new energy sources and modernising the infrastructure accelerate the energy transformation processes in economies relying on traditional energy sources. In the CEEC, it is furthermore crucial to decrease low emissions. Research shows consumers are willing to pay more if that means transitioning to renewable energy sources (Ł. Mamica, 2021).

The final link, albeit no less important, is education and the popularisation of energy-related topics. Raising awareness of energy efficiency and the benefits of using renewable energy sources can influence consumer habits (Szczygieł & Śliwa, 2023), and this, in turn, reduces pressure on fossil fuels-induced global warming. The declarations made at the COP28 in Dubai demonstrate no long-term alternative to decarbonisation. What is also important is that a reduction in purchasing energy supplies from Russia will compromise Moscow's capacity to conduct aggressive politics of territorial expansion.

3.6 Conclusion

The Russian invasion of Ukraine in 2022 led to significant destabilisation of energy markets in Europe. Particularly high increases were seen in gas prices. This has resulted in a worsening of the competitiveness of energy-intensive industries in Europe. The protective shields aimed at offsetting some of the price increases for a selected group of consumers had significant budgetary costs. The subsequent stabilisation of energy carrier prices, especially natural gas, allows for a slightly more optimistic outlook on the economic development of Europe than in the first half of 2022. At the same time, new energy supply channels bypassing Russia have been established, especially through the expansion of the infrastructure for receiving liquefied natural gas delivered by sea. High energy prices also led to an increase in the level of energy poverty throughout the CEEC. A more effective solution is, however, to reduce the energy intensity of households, through building insulation for example, rather than subsidising energy prices. The latter is only a temporary solution. Moreover, it does not provide additional benefits associated with achieving emission reduction targets and mitigating the negative consequences of climate change.

References

Arner, D. W., Barberis, J. & Buckley, R. P. (2015). The evolution of Fintech: A new post-crisis paradigm. *Geo. J. Int'l L.*, *47*, 1271.

Auty, R. M. (2007). Natural resources, capital accumulation and the resource curse. *Ecological Economics*, *61*(4), 627–634.

Ayres, R. U. & Warr, B. (2005). Accounting for growth: the role of physical work. *Structural Change and Economic Dynamics*, *16*(2), 181–209.

Bhattacharya, J., DeLeire, T., Haider, S. & Currie, J. (2003). Heat or eat? Cold-weather shocks and nutrition in poor American families. *American Journal of Public Health*, *93*(7), 1149–1154.

Boardman, B. (1991). Fuel poverty: from cold homes to affordable warmth. *(No Title)*.

Boateng, G. O., Balogun, M. R., Dada, F. O. & Armah, F. A. (2020). Household energy insecurity: dimensions and consequences for women, infants and children in low-and middle-income countries. *Social Science & Medicine*, *258*, 113068.

Brauers, H. & Oei, P.-Y. (2020). The political economy of coal in Poland: Drivers and barriers for a shift away from fossil fuels. *Energy Policy*, *144*, 111621.

Brook, B. W., Alonso, A., Meneley, D. A., Misak, J., Blees, T. & van Erp, J. B. (2014). Why nuclear energy is sustainable and has to be part of the energy mix. *Sustainable Materials and Technologies*, *1*, 8–16.

Bulte, E. & Damania, R. (2008). Resources for sale: Corruption, democracy and the natural resource curse. *The BE Journal of Economic Analysis & Policy*, *8*(1).

Cergibozan, R. (2022). Renewable energy sources as a solution for energy security risk: Empirical evidence from OECD countries. *Renewable Energy*, *183*,

617–626.

Chester, L. (2010). Conceptualising energy security and making explicit its polysemic nature. *Energy Policy*, *38*(2), 887–895.

Cong, S., Nock, D., Qiu, Y. L. & Xing, B. (2022). Unveiling hidden energy poverty using the energy equity gap. *Nature Communications*, *13*(1), 2456.

Cook, J. T., Frank, D. A., Casey, P. H., Rose-Jacobs, R., Black, M. M., Chilton, M., ... others (2008). A brief indicator of household energy security: associations with food security, child health, and child development in US infants and toddlers. *Pediatrics*, *122*(4), e867–e875.

Dauvin, M. & Guerreiro, D. (2017). The paradox of plenty: a meta-analysis. *World Development*, *94*, 212–231.

Dietz, T., Rosa, E. A. & York, R. (2009). Environmentally efficient well-being: Rethinking sustainability as the relationship between human well-being and environmental impacts. *Human Ecology Review*, 114–123.

Dolfsma, W. & Mamica, Ł. (2020). Industrial policy—an institutional economic framework for assessment. *Journal of Economic Issues*, *54*(2), 349–355.

Dębiec, K. (2023). *The Czech nuclear showdown enters the final straight.* Retrieved 25.02.24, from https://www.osw.waw.pl/en/publikacje/osw-commentary/2023-03-17/czech-nuclear-showdown-enters-final-straight

Economidou, M., Todeschi, V., Bertoldi, P., D'Agostino, D., Zangheri, P. & Castellazzi, L. (2020). Review of 50 years of EU energy efficiency policies for buildings. *Energy and Buildings*, *225*, 110322.

Eurostat. (2022). *Coal production and consumption see rebound in 2021.* Retrieved 7/10/2023, from https://ec.europa.eu/eurostat/web/products-eurostat-news/-/ddn-20220502-2

Eurostat. (2022b). *Energy represented 62% of EU imports from Russia.* Retrieved 17/10/2023, from https://ec.europa.eu/eurostat/web/products-eurostat-news/-/ddn-20220307-1

Eurostat. (2022c). *Inability to keep home adequately warm - EU-SILC survey.* Retrieved 17/10/2023, from https://ec.europa.eu/eurostat/databrowser/view/ilc_mdes01/default/table?lang=en

Eurostat. (2023). *Coal production and consumption up in 2022.* Retrieved 11/10/2023, from https://ec.europa.eu/eurostat/web/products-eurostat-news/w/ddn-20230622-2

Eurostat. (2023b). *Electricity prices for household consumers - bi-annual data (from 2007 onwards).* Retrieved 17/10/2023, from https://ec.europa.eu/eurostat/databrowser/view/nrg_pc_204/default/table?lang=en

Eurostat. (2023c). *Electricity prices for non-household consumers - bi-annual data (from 2007 onwards).* Retrieved 17/10/2023, from https://ec.europa.eu/eurostat/databrowser/view/nrg_pc_205/default/table?lang=en

Eurostat. (2023d). *Gas prices for household consumers - bi-annual data (from 2007 onwards).* Retrieved 15/09/2023, from https://ec.europa.eu/eurostat/databrowser/view/nrg_pc_202/default/table?lang=en

Eurostat. (2023e). *Gas prices for non-household consumers - bi-annual data (from 2007 onwards).* Retrieved 17/10/2023, from https://ec.europa.eu/eurostat/

databrowser/view/NRG_PC_203/default/table?lang=en

Eurostat. (2024). *Production in industry - monthly data.* Retrieved 16.02.2024, from https://ec.europa.eu/eurostat/databrowser/view/sts_inpr_m/default/table ?lang=en&category=sts.sts_ind.sts_ind_prod

Frank, D. A., Neault, N. B., Skalicky, A., Cook, J. T., Wilson, J. D., Levenson, S., ... others (2006). Heat or eat: the Low Income Home Energy Assistance Program and nutritional and health risks among children less than 3 years of age. *Pediatrics*, *118*(5), e1293–e1302.

Freudenburg, W. R. (1992). Addictive economies: extractive industries and vulnerable localities in a changing world economy 1. *Rural Sociology*, *57*(3), 305–332.

Freudenburg, W. R. & Gramling, R. (1998). Linked to what? Economic linkages in an extractive economy. *Society & Natural Resources*, *11*(6), 569–586.

Gielen, D., Boshell, F., Saygin, D., Bazilian, M. D., Wagner, N. & Gorini, R. (2019). The role of renewable energy in the global energy transformation. *Energy Strategy Reviews*, *24*, 38–50.

Goldemberg, J. (1990). One kilowatt per capita. *Bulletin of the Atomic Scientists*, *46*(1), 13.

Halkos, G. E. & Gkampoura, E.-C. (2021). Evaluating the effect of economic crisis on energy poverty in europe. *Renewable and Sustainable Energy Reviews*, *144*, 110981.

Hauser, P., Anke, C.-P., López, J. G., Möst, D., Scharf, H., Schönheit, D. & Schreiber, S. (2020). The impact of the COVID-19 crisis on energy prices in comparison to the 2008 financial crisis. In *Iaee energy forum/covid-19 issue.*

Hauser, P., Schönheit, D., Scharf, H., Anke, C.-P. & Möst, D. (2021). Covid-19's impact on European power sectors: an econometric analysis. *Energies*, *14*(6), 1639.

Healy, J. D. (2003). Excess winter mortality in Europe: a cross country analysis identifying key risk factors. *Journal of Epidemiology & Community Health*, *57*(10), 784–789.

Hernández, D. (2015). Sacrifice along the energy continuum: a call for energy justice. *Environmental Justice*, *8*(4), 151–156.

Hernández, D. (2016). Understanding 'energy insecurity'and why it matters to health. *Social Science & Medicine*, *167*, 1–10.

Hernández, D. & Siegel, E. (2019). Energy insecurity and its ill health effects: a community perspective on the energy-health nexus in New York City. *Energy Research & Social Science*, *47*, 78–83.

Hutter, C. & Weber, E. (2022). *Russia-ukraine war: Short-run production and labour market effects of the energy crisis* (Tech. Rep.). Germany: IAB-Discussion Paper.

IEA. (2022). *Energy Statistics Data Browser.* Retrieved from https://www.iea.org/data-and-statistics/data-tools/energy-statistics-data-browser?country=WORLD&fuel=Energy%20supply&indicator=TESbySource

Igliński, B., Piechota, G., Kiełkowska, U., Kujawski, W., Pietrzak, M. B. & Skrzatek, M. (2023). The assessment of solar photovoltaic in Poland: the photovoltaics potential, perspectives and development. *Clean Technologies and Environmental*

Policy, *25*(1), 281–298.
IRENA. (2023). *Renewable energy statistics 2023*. Abu Dhabi.
James, A. & Aadland, D. (2011). The curse of natural resources: An empirical investigation of US counties. *Resource and Energy Economics*, *33*(2), 440–453.
Jonek-Kowalska, I. (2022). Multi-criteria evaluation of the effectiveness of energy policy in Central and Eastern European countries in a long-term perspective. *Energy Strategy Reviews*, *44*, 100973.
Juszczyk, O. & Shakeel, S. R. (2020). Comparative Analysis of Barriers for Renewable Energy Technologies Diffusion in Finland and Poland. In *Advances in human factors, business management and leadership: Proceedings of the ahfe 2020 virtual conferences on human factors, business management and society, and human factors in management and leadership, july 16-20, 2020, usa* (pp. 269–275).
Kampas, A., Rozakis, S., Faber, A. & Mamica, Ł. (2021). Assessing the green growth trajectory through resource and impact decoupling indices: the case of Poland. *Polish J. Environ. Stud*, *30*, 2573–2587.
Karpinska, L. et al. (2021). Faces of Poverty: Who Are the Energy Poor in Poland? *Zarządzanie Publiczne*(57), 23–39.
Kennedy, M. D. (2022). Violence and Truth in 2022's Epoch End: COVID-19 and Russia's Invasion of Ukraine in the World Historical Context. *Journal of Public Governance*, *61*(3).
Kochanek, E. (2021). The energy transition in the Visegrad group countries. *Energies*, *14*(8), 2212.
Król, M. & Gomola, A. (2022). How to Reduce Low-Stack Emissions? An Assessment of the Willingness of Residents of Single-Family Houses to Replace Fossil Fuel Heating Systems. *Journal of Public Governance*, *60*(2), 48–63.
Lacroix, E. & Chaton, C. (2015). Fuel poverty as a major determinant of perceived health: the case of France. *Public Health*, *129*(5), 517–524.
Lacroix, E. & Jusot, F. (2014). Fuel poverty is it harmful for health? Evidence from French health survey data. In *Journées des économistes de la santé français (jesf)* (p. 19).
Le, T.-H. & Park, D. (2021). What drives energy insecurity across the world? A panel data analysis. *Energy Research & Social Science*, *77*, 102093.
Makiela, K., Mazur, B. & Glowacki, J. (2022). The impact of renewable energy supply on economic growth and productivity. *Energies*, *15*(13), 4808.
Makridou, G., Andriosopoulos, K., Doumpos, M. & Zopounidis, C. (2016). Measuring the efficiency of energy-intensive industries across European countries. *Energy Policy*, *88*, 573–583.
Mamica, Ł. (2021). Willingness to pay for the renewable energy sources of the residents of Kraków and their perception of the actions aimed at reducing the level of environmental pollution. *Polityka Energetyczna*, *24*.
Mamica, L., Glowacki, J. & Makiela, K. (2021). Determinants of the energy poverty of Polish students during the COVID-19 pandemic. *Energies*, *14*(11), 3233.
Mårald, E. (2010). Methanol as future fuel: efforts to develop alternative fuels in Sweden after the Oil Crisis. *History and Technology*, *26*(4), 335–357.

Marks-Bielska, R., Bielski, S., Pik, K. & Kurowska, K. (2020). The importance of renewable energy sources in Poland's energy mix. *Energies*, *13*(18), 4624.

Meyer, S., Laurence, H., Bart, D., Middlemiss, L. & Maréchal, K. (2018). Capturing the multifaceted nature of energy poverty: Lessons from Belgium. *Energy Research & Social Science*, *40*, 273–283.

Moore, R. (2012). Definitions of fuel poverty: Implications for policy. *Energy Policy*, *49*, 19–26.

Nord, M. & Kantor, L. S. (2006). Seasonal variation in food insecurity is associated with heating and cooling costs among low-income elderly americans. *The Journal of Nutrition*, *136*(11), 2939–2944.

Nosova, O. (2022). Transformational Change: Challenges and Development Prospects. The Case of Ukraine. *Social Entrepreneurship Review*, *1*, 7–16.

Nussbaum, M. C. (2004). Beyond the social contract: capabilities and global justice. An Olaf Palme lecture, delivered in Oxford on 19 June 2003. *Oxford Development Studies*, *32*(1), 3–18.

Ouedraogo, N. S. (2013). Energy consumption and human development: Evidence from a panel cointegration and error correction model. *Energy*, *63*, 28–41.

Pakulska, T. (2021). Green energy in central and eastern European (CEE) countries: New challenges on the path to sustainable development. *Energies*, *14*(4), 884.

Passarelli, M., Bongiorno, G., Cucino, V. & Cariola, A. (2023). Adopting new technologies during the crisis: An empirical analysis of agricultural sector. *Technological Forecasting and Social Change*, *186*, 122106.

Rao, N. D. & Min, J. (2018). Decent living standards: material prerequisites for human wellbeing. *Social Indicators Research*, *138*, 225–244.

Sachs, J. D. & Warner, A. M. (2001). The curse of natural resources. *European Economic Review*, *45*(4-6), 827–838.

Sadath, A. C. & Acharya, R. H. (2017). Assessing the extent and intensity of energy poverty using Multidimensional Energy Poverty Index: Empirical evidence from households in India. *Energy Policy*, *102*, 540–550.

Schramm, L. (2023). Some differences, many similarities: comparing Europe's responses to the 1973 oil crisis and the 2022 gas crisis. *European Political Science Review*, 1–16.

Schumacher, E. F. & Kirk, G. (1982). Schumacher on energy: Speeches and writings of EF Schumacher. *(No Title)*.

Simionescu, M., Radulescu, M., Balsalobre-Lorente, D. & Cifuentes-Faura, J. (2023). Pollution, political instabilities and electricity price in the cee countries during the war time. *Journal of Environmental Management*, *343*, 118206.

Sovacool, B. K. (2016). Differing cultures of energy security: An international comparison of public perceptions. *Renewable and Sustainable Energy Reviews*, *55*, 811–822.

Stern, D. I. & Kander, A. (2012). The role of energy in the industrial revolution and modern economic growth. *The Energy Journal*, *33*(3).

Szczygieł, E. & Śliwa, R. (2023). Social economy entities as a place to develop green skills–research findings. *Social Entrepreneurship Review*, *1*, 44–56.

UNEP. (2015). Time for global action.

United Nations. (2022). *Sustainable Development Goals.* Retrieved 05.12.2023, from https://sdgs.un.org/goals/goal7.

Wilkinson, P., Smith, K. R., Davies, M., Adair, H., Armstrong, B. G., Barrett, M., ... others (2009). Public health benefits of strategies to reduce greenhouse-gas emissions: household energy. *The Lancet*, *374*(9705), 1917–1929.

Zemtsov, S. (2020). New technologies, potential unemployment and 'nescience economy'during and after the 2020 economic crisis. *Regional Science Policy & Practice*, *12*(4), 723–743.

Chapter 4
Inflation Shock and Monetary Policy

Szilárd Benk, Péter Horváth and Norbert Szepesi

Abstract The war in Ukraine triggered the most substantial surge in inflation rates in decades, posing a formidable challenge for the central banks of Central and Eastern Europe (CEE) to curb inflation without compromising the ongoing post-Covid recovery. This chapter provides a brief discussion of the factors contributing to the inflationary pressure and evaluates the monetary policy responses in the region. The root cause of the inflationary pressure lies primarily in supply-side shocks disrupting international trade channels as a consequence of the war. Countries with loose monetary conditions witnessed the most pronounced spike in inflation rates in the aftermath of the war. Despite these challenges, central banks responded promptly, implementing aggressive interest rate hikes, keeping monetary conditions tight throughout 2022 and well after inflation rates began to decrease in 2023.

Szilárd Benk ✉
Corvinus University, Budapest, Hungary, e-mail: szilard.benk@uni-corvinus.hu

Péter Horváth
Corvinus University, Budapest, Hungary, e-mail: peter.horvath16@stud.uni-corvinus.hu;

Norbert Szepesi
Ministry of Finance, Budapest, Hungary, e-mail: norbert.szepesi@pm.gov.hu
The views expressed in the chapter are those of the author and do not necessarily represent the views of the Hungarian Ministry of Finance.

© The Author(s), under exclusive license to Springer Nature Switzerland AG 2024
L. Mátyás (ed.), *Central and Eastern European Economies and the War in Ukraine*,
Contributions to Economics, https://doi.org/10.1007/978-3-031-61561-0_4

4.1 Introduction

The conflict in Ukraine, unfolding against the backdrop of a fragile geoeconomic landscape, sent shockwaves through the global economy. As highlighted by Caldara, Conlisk, Iacoviello and Penn (2022), the geopolitical tensions and uncertainty stemming from the war resulted in a contraction of global output by approximately 1.5 percent, accompanied by a substantial increase in inflation rates, averaging nearly 1.3 percentage points of excess inflation. Echoing similar sentiments, Liadze, Macchiarelli, Mortimer-Lee and Sanchez Juanino (2023) estimate that the war may have contributed to an excess inflationary pressure of about 2 percentage points on a global scale.

As the geographically closest countries to the conflict zone, the nations in the Central and Eastern European (CEE) region find themselves particularly vulnerable to the shocks emanating from the war in Ukraine and the subsequent imposition of sanctions. This manifests in the form of excess inflationary pressure pushing up rates to multi-decade highs and supply-side contractions leading to a reduction in output. The task of monetary authorities in the region is not only to curb inflation and restore price stability but also to navigate this process cautiously, ensuring that their measures do not harm the already fragile growth potentials. The region's central banks have responded with aggressive interest rate hikes, effectively taming the rapidly rising inflation rates. Despite economic growth falling below pre-pandemic levels, the prospect of a 'soft landing' remains attainable for the region (IMF, 2023a).

In Section 4.2 we provide a short summary of the inflation developments and their determinants following the Covid crisis, factors that shaped the economies of CEE countries before the onset of war-related shocks.

In Section 4.3, the examination delves into the processes underlying the inflation shock, identifying demand-side and supply-side shocks in 4.3.1 over time, decomposing the evolution of the headline inflation rate into its sub-components in 4.3.2, and exploring factors such as wage dynamics and exchange rates in 4.3.3 and 4.3.4 respectively.

Subsequently, in Section 4.4 the assessment of monetary policy in the region is conducted, with 4.4.1 describing interest rate hikes, 4.4.2 discussing policy stance through the scope of real interest rates and their deviation from the equilibrium, and 4.4.3 briefly examining the possibility of a soft landing.

Finally, in Section 4.5 a comprehensive evaluation of our findings is presented.

4.2 Background: The Aftermath of the Covid Crisis

The period leading up to the pandemic was marked by relatively stable inflation developments in the CEE countries, although inflation exceeded the target in some of the non-euro area inflation-targeting countries. Concurrently, the monetary policy stance was characterized by low interest rates, with real rates predominantly in negative territory.

The impact of the Covid-19 shocks on economic activity and financial markets prompted aggressive monetary policy responses, such as policy rate cuts, foreign exchange intervention, liquidity operations, lending programs, and asset purchases, both within the CEE region and globally. Conventional easing measures were constrained by low interest rates and global financial conditions, leading to an increasing implementation of unconventional measures in many countries. Variations in monetary policy responses among countries were influenced by several factors, including differences in the policy framework and scope. The significant policy accommodation in response to Covid-19, including the use of unconventional tools, ultimately aided in mitigating the economic harm. These actions have been extensively documented by Király, Csontó, Jankovics and Mérő (2022) for the CEE countries.

The economic recovery from the pandemic saw a growing inflationary trend on a global scale. Inflation not only reemerged after more than a decade of unusually low and stable inflation following the Global Financial Crisis, but it also caught many off guard. The drivers of this new inflation surge are concisely summarized by Agarwal and Kimball (2022), who identified five key factors: Firstly, supply chain bottlenecks that initially arose from lockdowns and mobility restrictions, leading to disruptions in supply chains. Subsequently, this was exacerbated by the strong overall demand stemming from the economic recovery. Secondly, a shift in spending patterns and a change in demand from services to goods. Thirdly, an aggregate stimulus in the form of substantial fiscal measures combined with monetary easing. Fourthly, a shock to labor supply, with labor supply participation remaining below pre-pandemic levels in several countries. Finally, supply shocks to energy and food.

Energy, commodity, and food prices, however, proved to be complex contributors to inflation. The sharp increase in energy prices in 2021 can be attributed to a multitude of factors, such as the robust recovery of global demand, production cuts implemented by OPEC and non-OPEC countries, geopolitical tensions, and natural disasters. Moreover, the shift toward renewable energy sources led to reduced investments in fossil fuel extraction, constraining production and further escalating the cost of fossil fuels, ultimately resulting in multi-year highs for oil and gas prices. This mismatch between supply and demand led to a significant upsurge in energy prices, which subsequently affected general consumer prices.

The outbreak of the war in Ukraine has triggered another wave of inflation shocks. As both Russia and Ukraine are significant exporters of major commodities, the disruptions brought about by the war and subsequent sanctions have led to steep increases in global prices, particularly for oil and natural gas. Global food prices have also surged due to the fact that Ukraine and Russia combined account for 30 percent of global wheat exports. Additionally, regional agricultural prices have been affected by the sharp rise in the cost of agricultural fertilizers, an energy-intensive product heavily exported by Ukraine.

4.3 The Inflation Shock and Drivers of Inflation

Figure 4.1 illustrates the differing regional inflation dynamics across CEE countries during the 2020s. Inflation rates in the CEE countries peaked from the second half of 2022 to the early months of 2023. Slovenia exhibited the most modest peak inflation rate, standing at merely 11.7%. Notably, Slovenia was the first country in the region to stem the rise in inflation rates, achieving this milestone in July 2022. In contrast, Hungary experienced the steepest inflation rate, recording 26.2% in January 2023. Meanwhile, Serbia endured the most prolonged period of inflationary pressure, with rates only beginning to recede after March 2023. We list the dates when headline inflation peaked along with the respective inflation rates for each country in Table 4.1.

Fig. 4.1: Out of sync inflation dynamics
Data: Eurostat (2023d), authors' calculations

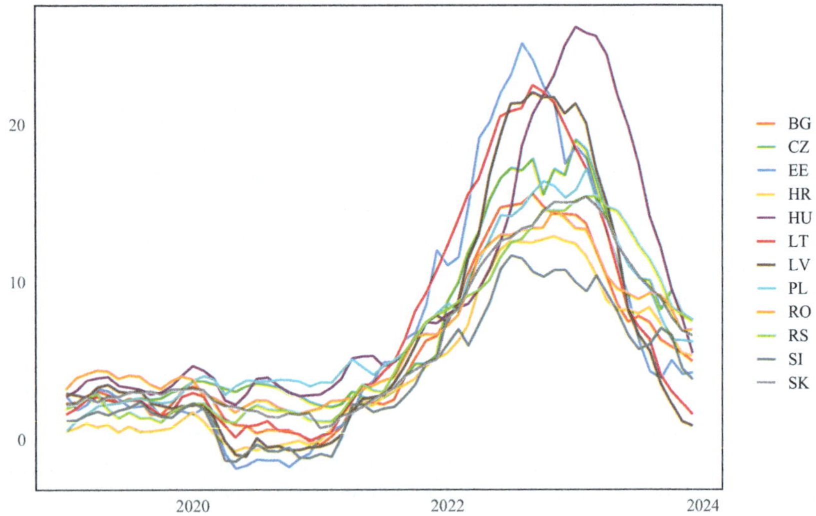

Table 4.1: Peak Inflation Rates
Data Eurostat (2023d), authors' calculations

Country	Month of Reaching Peak	Peak Inflation Rate
Hungary	2023-01	26.2%
Estonia	2022-08	25.2%
Lithuania	2022-09	22.5%
Latvia	2022-09	22.0%
Czechia	2023-01	19.1%
Poland	2023-02	17.2%
Bulgaria	2022-09	15.6%
Serbia	2023-03	15.5%
Slovakia	2023-02	15.4%
Romania	2022-11	14.6%
Croatia	2022-11	13.0%
Slovenia	2022-07	11.7%

The severity of the inflationary pressure induced by the war shock appears to be more country-specific, showing little correlation with the time it took to curb inflation rates. Not only did the timing and magnitude of peaks differ, but Figure 4.1 also illustrates regional inflation dynamics varying across countries during the 2020s. This variation can be attributed to several factors. For instance, in many economies, the demand contraction of the Covid shock was severe enough to induce deflation throughout 2020 and early 2021, particularly in Estonia, Latvia, and Slovenia, while some economies maintained positive inflation rates throughout the pandemic. Another factor disrupting the synchrony of inflation rates is policy actions taken to alleviate the welfare effect of rapid inflation on households. Examples include the price caps implemented in Hungary or Croatia, which delayed the inflation surge.

In the following subsections we delve into the factors influencing the evolution of inflation rates in the region. We explore the influence of supply-side and demand-side factors on the inflation process within the countries of the CEE region. Subsequently, in the next section, we evaluate the monetary policy actions taken to curb the process of rapidly rising prices.

4.3.1 The Inflation Shock

Emerging markets in Europe are notably sensitive to global factors. For example, fluctuations in commodity or energy prices have the potential to cascade through the economy, resulting in an unprecedented surge in domestic inflation. Recognizing this vulnerability is crucial, emphasizing the need for policy responses to mitigate risks and safeguard economic stability, given the interconnected nature of these markets with the global economic landscape.

After the economic upswing of the 2010s, the outbreak of the coronavirus pandemic brought the economies to a sudden stop across Europe. Stringent health regulations prompted the implementation of travel restrictions, assembly bans, and measures to minimize interpersonal contact. This resulted in a significant contraction in economic activity, particularly in services such as international and domestic tourism, global transportation, and entertainment, weakening the domestic demand at the same time. Asymmetries within the global economy were also exacerbated by factors constraining the supply side.

In the aftermath of the deep economic downturn, government interventions and a pickup in activity have led to a recovery on the demand side, however, in many cases, the supply side has struggled to meet the revived demand. One illustrative example is the surge in demand for electronic devices during the pandemic, which exceeded global chip manufacturing capacity. This led to an increase in waiting times for chips to be incorporated into semi-finished products, which particularly affected the automotive industry, a key sector in the CEE region. The surge in demand coupled with constrained supply dynamics has led to an inflationary trend, causing an increase in prices across various sectors.

In the second half of 2021, global economies encountered an upswing in commodity and energy prices, departing from a previously stable low level. The outbreak of the war in February 2022 further intensified this trend, causing a substantial rise in commodity and energy prices, thereby upsetting the basic structure of economies. The countries in the CEE region became particularly vulnerable to the consequences of rising commodity and energy prices.

Using a Structural Vector Autoregression (SVAR) model to isolate demand and supply-side shocks is an effective approach to conducting a historical decomposition analysis of the effects of these factors on inflation. This model allows for a thorough examination of the individual contributions of demand and supply shocks to inflation dynamics, spanning from the onset of the pandemic to the aftermath of the energy price hike. By disentangling demand and supply shocks, the SVAR model provides valuable insights into the factors driving inflation during this pivotal period.

The vector autoregressive (VAR) process serves as a statistical model designed to capture dynamic correlations among vectors of variables. In this method, vectors containing variables are regressed on their lagged values, offering insights into the temporal relationships and interdependencies among the variables over time.

However, in the SVAR setup, exogenous shocks in the economic context are distinctly separated from the residuals, ensuring they are orthogonal and hence uncorrelated. This characteristic facilitates the identification of exogenous structural shocks such as demand and supply. Consequently, the effects of these identified shocks can therefore be examined separately using the SVAR model.

The process is illustrated by the following structural form equation based on Kim and Mehrotra (2017):

$$B_0 y_t = B_1 y_{t-1} + \ldots + B_p y_{t-p} + e_t. \tag{4.1}$$

In this equation, y_t represents the $n \times 1$ vector of endogenous variables at time t, where n is the number of endogenous variables, and e_t is the $n \times 1$ vector of structural disturbances. B_p are the $n \times n$structural parameter matrices and p denotes the number of lags. B_0 is an invertible matrix that facilitates the modeling of simultaneous relationships among the endogenous variables within the system.

Based on this, the estimated reduced form model is expressed as follows:

$$y_t = A_1 y_{t-1} + \ldots + A_p y_{t-p} + u_t. \tag{4.2}$$

In this equation, the matrices A_p are $n \times n$ coefficient matrices, and u_t represents an error term with a covariance matrix $\sum_u$. The relationship between the reduced form and the structural form is delineated by $A_i = B_0^{-1} B_i$ for $i = 1 \ldots p$, where A_i is the i-th lag coefficient matrix in the reduced form, and $u_t = B_0^{-1} e_t$. This latter expression establishes a connection between the errors of the reduced form and the structural shocks.

The parameters of the structural equation can be obtained from the reduced form equation in several ways, with the Cholesky decomposition standing out as a widely embraced identification constraint. The Cholesky decomposition proves effective by enabling the estimation of structural parameters through the imposition of simultaneous zero constraints on the variance-covariance matrices of the residual components within the reduced form. This approach is widely used due to its ability to provide a clear and interpretable framework for assigning causality among variables, fostering a more meaningful economic interpretation of the estimated structural parameters (Sims, 1980).

The historical decomposition in SVAR is a valuable retrospective tool for understanding how different shocks influenced economic variables over time. This method breaks down the historical development of shocks including those from the demand and supply sides in our case, offering a clearer understanding of their specific impact on observed outcomes. The idea is that all the time series in a VAR can be fully decomposed into the contributions of the various shocks and an exogenous-baseline component. By summing up these contributions and the baseline at any point in time 't', the original time series can be reconstructed, providing a detailed view of the evolving factors that shaped economic dynamics over the analysed period. To perform historical decomposition, we followed the insights of Burbidge and Harrison (1985) and Mumtaz and Rummel (2015).

The endogenous variables under consideration are the real GDP and the consumer price index, both recorded as quarterly data spanning from 2010Q1 to 2023Q3. To capture distinct effects in individual countries, VAR models were separately estimated. To mitigate unit root presence, we applied logarithmic transformations and first differences to each variable. Given the quarterly nature of the data, a lag of 4 quarters was chosen in each case, balancing the need for adequate lag structure against the risk of overfitting. The selection of an optimal model specification is crucial to avoid overfitting, where excessive explanatory variables may cause the model to fit noise, compromising estimation accuracy. Striking the right balance involves including sufficient lags to address autocorrelation concerns while avoiding an excess that could lead to overfitting. As the recursive structure requires an ordering of the two variables, we performed the Cholesky-ordering of real GDP followed by CPI in every case.

Following our estimation, we provide a historical decomposition of consumer prices in the CEE region, offering insights into the contributions of supply and demand shocks to price dynamics during specific periods. Our findings indicate that following the outbreak of the pandemic, demand-side factors played a predominant role in shaping price dynamics, with the collapsing demand generating notable deflationary pressures. On the other hand, post-2021, with the resurgence of domestic demand and persisting supply-side bottlenecks, supply-side factors emerged as the primary contributors to the observed increase in consumer prices.

Fig. 4.2: Historical decomposition of supply and demand shocks - Bulgaria, Croatia, Czechia and Estonia
Data: Eurostat (2023b); IMF (2023b), authors' calculations
Note: The solid lines represent the inflation shocks retrieved from the residuals of the SVAR models. The bars represent the share of supply-side and demand-side shocks.

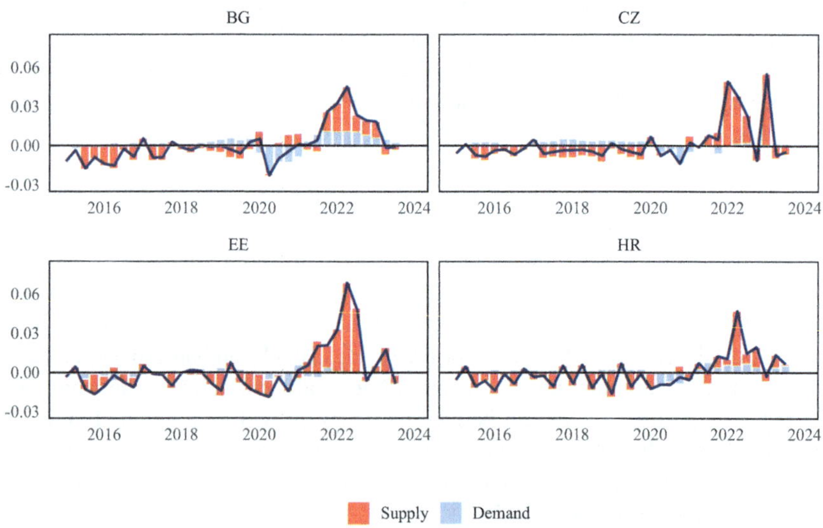

As depicted in Figure 4.2, a temporary decline in consumer prices occurred across most countries in 2020. While demand-side factors predominantly influenced this decline, supply-side factors also played a role in several countries. Nonetheless, it can be declared that, mainly, the demand-side factors were the primary drivers of consumer price dynamics in the CEE region during 2020.

Fig 4.2 Cont.: Historical decomposition of supply and demand shocks - Hungary, Latvia, Lithuania and Poland
Data: Eurostat (2023b); IMF (2023b), authors' calculations
Note: The solid lines represent the inflation shocks retrieved from the residuals of the SVAR models. The bars represent the share of supply-side and demand-side shocks.

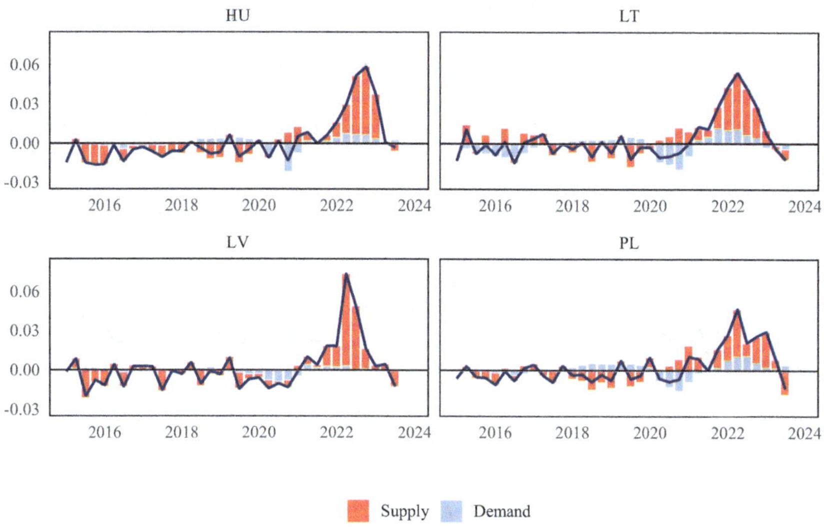

By the end of 2020, the demand side experienced a recovery, largely attributed to active governmental support and the easing of stringent epidemical regulations. However, from 2021 onwards, supply-side constraints were the main factors that fuelled the rise in consumer prices across the countries under review. Production-side bottlenecks, such as challenges in global logistics networks, escalated container shipping costs, and increased raw material and energy prices, have likely also contributed to this upswing, as well as the drought experienced over the summer of 2022 in some European countries. In addition to supply-side factors certain countries including Bulgaria, Croatia, Hungary, Latvia, Poland, and Slovenia, have also experienced the influence of demand-side factors fuelling consumer prices. In many cases, this influence was driven by substantial fiscal stimulus, materialised in rising trends in consumption and investment.

Consumer prices were already on the ascent throughout 2021 across all countries in the CEE region, but based on quarter-on-quarter data, in most cases, the peak occurred in 2022 or early 2023. By 2023, the regional pattern had undergone a shift. Many countries experienced a normalization of consumer prices; in some cases, prices even started to decline, while in others, prices continued to rise, albeit at a slower pace. The drivers behind price dynamics in 2023 also varied across the region. In certain cases, such as Czechia, Lithuania, Poland, and Slovakia, the supply side emerged as the primary driver steering the normalization in prices. While in other countries, like Estonia and Latvia, the demand side also played a role. Furthermore, in places like Croatia or Slovenia, both the supply and demand sides contributed to the further increase in consumer price levels in 2023.

Fig 4.2 Cont.: Historical decomposition of supply and demand shocks - Romania, Serbia, Slovakia, Slovenia
Data: Eurostat (2023b); IMF (2023b), authors' calculations
Note: The solid lines represent the inflation shocks retrieved from the residuals of the SVAR models. The bars represent the share of supply-side and demand-side shocks

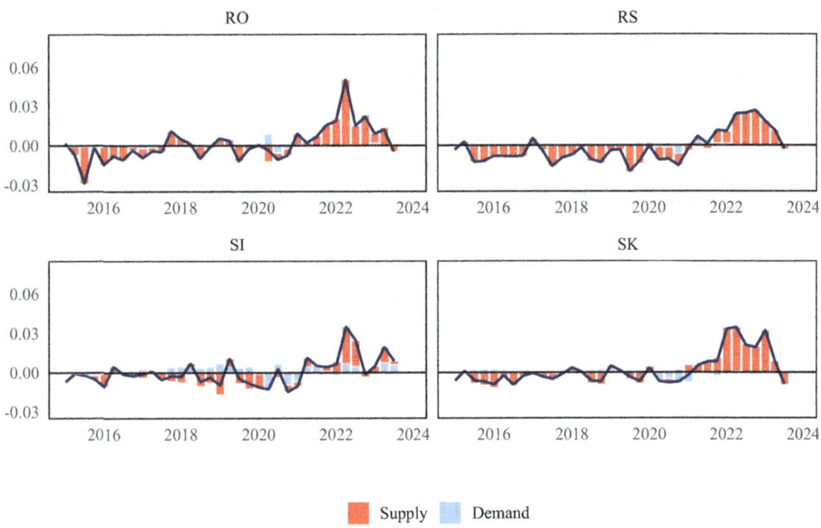

4.3.2 Decomposition of Inflation Rates

Following up on our analysis, we examine the decomposition of headline inflation rates to further uncover factors behind the series of supply shocks observed from 2022. We decompose the evolution of the headline inflation process to illustrate the contributions from core inflation, food, and energy inflationary processes. This analysis provides insights into the extent to which countries in the region were exposed to the impact of the energy shortage resulting from sanctions on Russia, as well as the constraints on access to affordable agricultural imports due to trade disruptions caused by the war. To conduct this analysis, we employ a simple panel regression with country and year-fixed effects.[1] We estimate the equation

[1] Our sample for the estimation runs from January 1996 to December 2023 in an unbalanced panel.

$$CPI_{i,t} = \beta_1 CORE_{i,t} + \beta_2 FOOD_{i,t} + \beta_3 ENERGY_{i,t} + \delta_i + \gamma_t + \epsilon_{i,t}, \quad (4.3)$$

where δ_i are country fixed effects, γ_t are annual fixed effects and β_j are the weights of each component in the headline inflation rate.

Using the regression coefficients from our estimation, we calculate the share of core, food, and energy inflation in the headline rate, and plot them from 2019 to the end of our sample. This can be seen in Figure 4.3.

Fig. 4.3: Contribution of core inflation, food, and energy prices to headline inflation rates - Bulgaria, Croatia, Czechia and Estonia
Data: Eurostat (2023d), authors' calculations
Note: The solid lines are the headline HICP inflation rates for each respective country, and the colored bars indicate the share of each component accounted for within headline inflation.

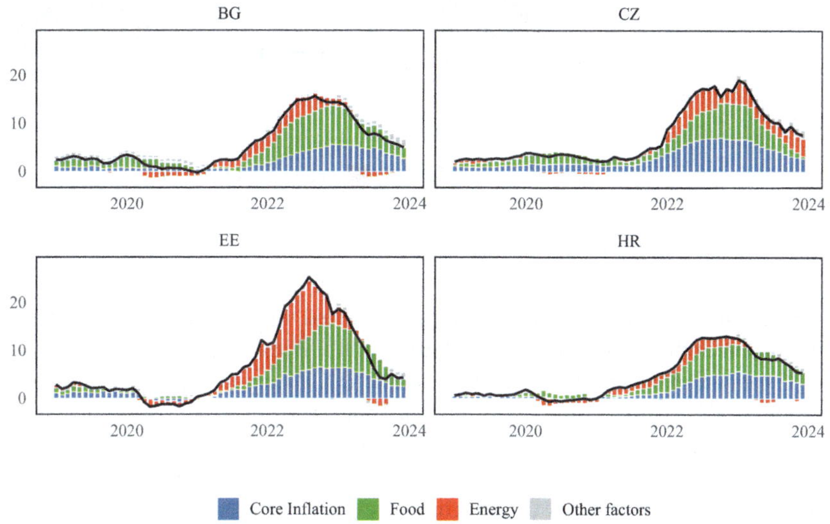

During the period preceding the war, inflation rates remained relatively low and stable from 2019 to 2020. However, a discernible inflationary pressure began to accumulate, possibly attributable to the demand-pull effect resulting from the easing of lockdowns and the excess demand generated by pandemic-related relief measures. Across the majority of countries in the region (e.g., Croatia, Czechia, Hungary, Lithuania, Poland, Romania, Serbia, and Slovakia), this trend is unsurprisingly driven by an upward-sloping trajectory in core and food inflation rates. Notably, in

Fig 4.3 Cont.: Contribution of core inflation, food, and energy prices to headline inflation rates - Hungary, Latvia, Lithuania and Poland
Data: Eurostat (2023d), authors' calculations
Note: The solid lines are the headline HICP inflation rates for each respective country, and the colored bars indicate the share of each component accounted for within headline inflation.

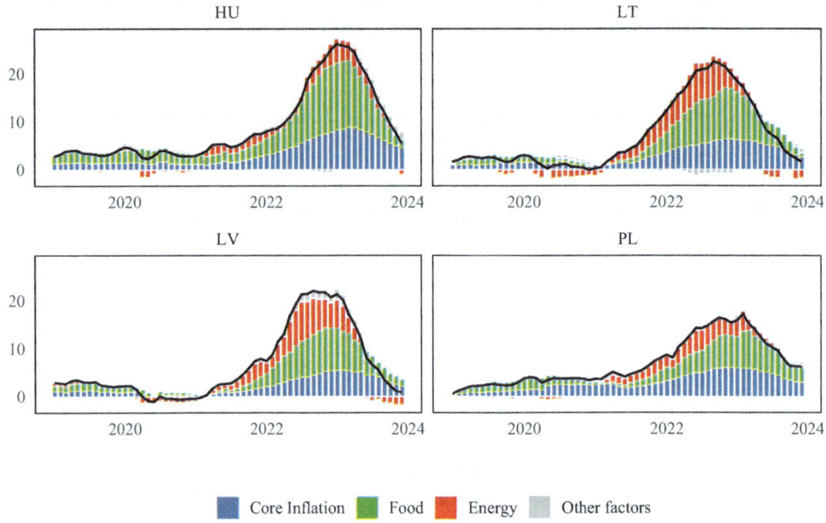

some countries, energy prices have already started to constitute a more substantial proportion in the composition of the headline HICP inflation rate.

The share of energy prices in the headline HICP remained negligible across our sample in the years leading up to the war shock. However, following the shock, it significantly increased in proportion, likely a consequence of the EU's sanction policy severing the region from Russian fossil fuel supplies (see Chapter 1). It is crucial to note that our estimates reflect the direct impact of energy prices on the headline HICP, encompassing for example elevated heating and automotive transportation costs for consumers. This, however, underestimates the true impact of the energy shortage on inflation rates, as it should have a substantial indirect effect on the prices of other goods due to increased producer prices. This indirect impact can be observed to some extent in core inflation rates, which also exhibit an upward-sloping trend following February 2022, most prominently in Hungary.

Food prices experienced a drastic increase as a consequence of the war shock, emerging as the largest contributor to headline inflation rates in the subsequent months. Preceding the outbreak of the war, food prices already accounted for a substantial proportion of the headline HICP, with their evolution closely mirroring that of the core inflation rate, both maintaining relatively low and stable trajectories.

Fig 4.3 Cont.: Contribution of core inflation, food, and energy prices to headline inflation rates - Romania, Serbia, Slovakia, Slovenia
Data: Eurostat (2023d), authors' calculations
Note: The solid lines are the headline HICP inflation rates for each respective country, and the colored bars indicate the share of each component accounted for within headline inflation.

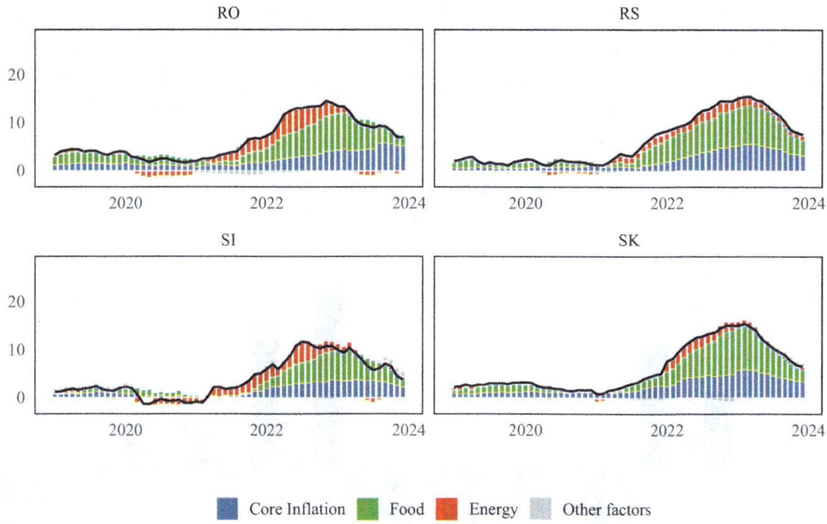

The disruption of trade induced by the war and subsequent sanction policies resulted in a notably steeper upward-sloping trend in food prices. By the end of our sample (November/December 2023), the excess inflationary pressure stemming from the shortage of cheap agricultural goods had mostly subsided. However, its impact appears to be more persistent than the direct effect of the energy crisis.

4.3.3 Wages and Inflation

Beyond dissecting the inflation rate into its sub-components, additional factors hold significance in the context of inflation. Real wages, tracking the changes in the purchasing power of consumers adjusted for inflation, play a crucial role. If real wages fall behind inflation, there is a risk of a decline in the standard of living for workers. Conversely, the evolution of real wages has implications for firms as well. When nominal wages grow faster than the inflation rate, it can contribute to excess inflationary pressure–a phenomenon known as wage-push inflation. In such instances, businesses face escalating labor costs, further driving up prices and creating a price-wage spiral effect.

To track changes in wages, we construct a real wage index from 2001 using quarterly industry aggregates sourced from Eurostat. The process involves three main steps. Firstly, we compute the total nominal wage volume of sectors B-N and determine hourly average wages in current price Euros based on employment statistics. Secondly, we adjust these figures using the implied GDP deflator, calculated as the ratio of nominal to real GDP. Finally, we calculate the change in real wages compared to the annual average of 2021, providing a basis for assessing wage fluctuations during the war in comparison to pre-shock levels. The results of these calculations are presented in Figure 4.4 below.

Fig. 4.4: Change in real wages compared to pre-war levels
Data: Eurostat (2023c, 2023a, 2023b), authors' calculation

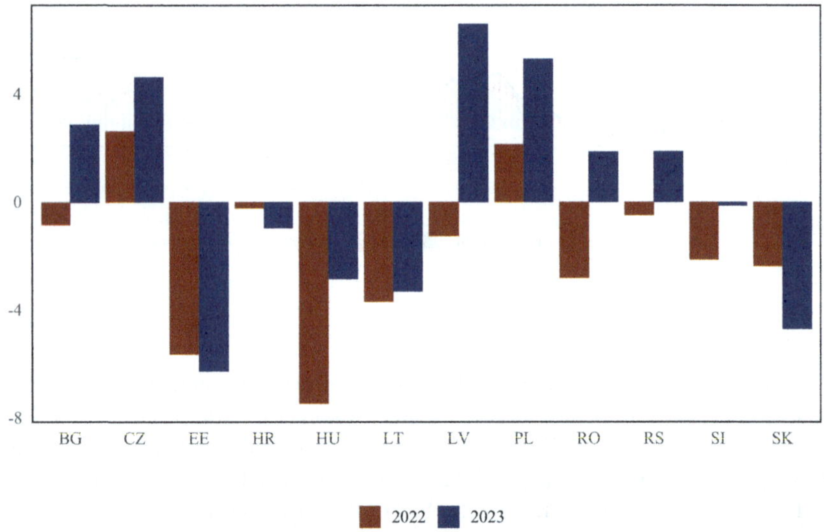

The data presented in Figure 4.4 suggests a lack of substantial evidence supporting significant wage-push inflationary pressure. By the end of our sample, noticeable real wage growth is apparent in countries like Bulgaria, Czechia, Latvia, Poland, Romania, and Serbia. However, this upward trend in wage growth only gained momentum following the inflationary pressure starting to ease in 2023. Only Czechia and Poland experienced positive real wage growth in 2022. In the rest of the CEE countries, wage growth barely outpaced or even lagged behind rising prices. Estonia, Hungary, Lithuania, and Slovakia experienced the least alignment with inflationary pressure in terms of wage growth. Hungary, having faced the steepest inflation rates in the region, witnessed the largest contraction in real wages. However, labor markets in Hungary seem to have rebounded, as the decline in real wages is far less substantial in 2023 than it was in the previous year. On the other hand, labor markets in Estonia and Slovakia seem to struggle despite encountering more modest inflationary pressure, as real wages are on the decline in 2023 as well. The labor market of Lithuania seems to stagnate around -4 percent real wage growth both in 2022 and 2023. In Slovenia's case, despite relatively early and low-rate inflation curbing in the region, the labor market contraction was relatively large, and wages did not yet manage to outpace inflation in 2023.

4.3.4 Exchange Rates and Inflation

Another important factor in the evolution of inflation rates is the external balance. Given that the region is comprised of small open economies, the prices of internationally traded goods have significance for their price levels. Exchange rates play a pivotal role in this context, influencing the cost of imports and exports. Fluctuations in exchange rates can directly impact the prices of goods traded globally, affecting the inflation dynamics of these economies. Exchange rates, in turn, are determined by various factors, such as interest rates, economic fundamentals, or political and market sentiments. For instance, raising interest rates–as seen across the board from regional central banks–appreciates the domestic currency. This makes the price of imports relatively cheaper, however at the cost of shrinking exports, overall resulting in a demand contraction.

Countries engage in bilateral trade with numerous foreign economies, utilizing various currencies. An invaluable tool for gauging the impact of exchange rate movements is a composite indicator, such as the real and nominal effective exchange rates (REER and NEER), published by the Bank for International Settlements (BIS). These BIS indicators offer a more comprehensive perspective by considering a basket of currencies. This approach takes into account the multilateral aspects of trade and minimizes the distortionary effects of individual currency fluctuations. The inclusion of inflation differentials in the REER further refines the analysis, allowing for a more accurate evaluation of the real purchasing power of these small open economies in response to changing exchange rates. Overall these indices are a valuable tool in assessing the external vulnerability of these countries. In Figure 4.5, we show how real and nominal exchange rates changed over time, compared to their pre-inflation shock levels observed in January of 2022.

Fig. 4.5: Change in effective exchange rates compared to pre-war levels
Data: BIS (2023), authors' calculation

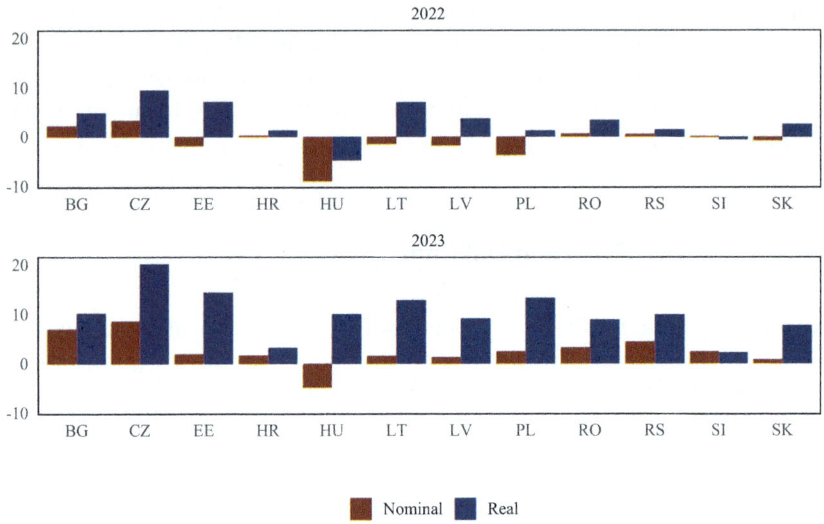

Over the long run, we observe a widespread appreciation in exchange rates, likely reflecting the impact of aggressive interest rate hikes taking effect [2]. However, the transmission in 2022 seems more moderate, with a number of countries showing depreciation in their exchange rates. The degree of depreciation (or appreciation) in these effective exchange rates, to some extent, indicates the susceptibility of countries to external shocks. The widespread real appreciation can be attributed to the inflation adjustment in the construction of the index. The largest depreciation could be observed in Hungary, indicating the most significant exposure to being cut off from the Russian energy supply.

4.4 Monetary Policy Stance

Monetary authorities in the region were quick to respond to the surge in inflation rates and implemented aggressive interest rate hikes as depicted in Figure 4.6. In response to rapidly escalating prices, the cummulative change in interest rates over the span of 2022 and 2023 ranged from 3.2 percentage points in Czechia to 9.3 percentage points in Hungary.

Prior to delving further into the analysis of interest rates, it is important to define the metrics we use for measuring interest rates movement. Our primary focus is

[2] Monetary policy actions and changes in interest rates are illustrated in the following section.

on tracking the changes in policy rates as closely as possible in each country. This is straightforward for Bulgaria, Czechia, Hungary, Poland, Romania, and Serbia, as they operate with independent currencies, affording them full monetary policy independence. While the definitions of policy rates may vary to some extent among these countries, each case typically involves a short-term interest rate. We source the policy rates of these countries from the International Financial Statistics database of the International Monetary Fund.

In the case of CEE countries that have joined the Eurozone, interest rates have been governed by the European Central Bank (ECB) since their accession. To effectively monitor short-term interest rate changes influenced by shifts in policy rates, both preceding and following Eurozone entry, we use 3-month interbank interest rates for these countries, data which is published by the OECD. Consequently, interest rates in these countries increased by a total of 4.5 percentage points, aligning with the policy set by the ECB.

4.4.1 Nominal Rates before and during the War

In order to have a baseline understanding of the severity of the inflation shock and subsequent aggressive policy action, we calculate the total change in interest rates from the start of the war in February 2022 to the end of our sample in December 2023. We show this cumulative change in Figure 4.6.

Fig. 4.6: Cumulative change in interest rates from the onset of the war
Data: IMF (2023a); OECD (2023), authors' calculations

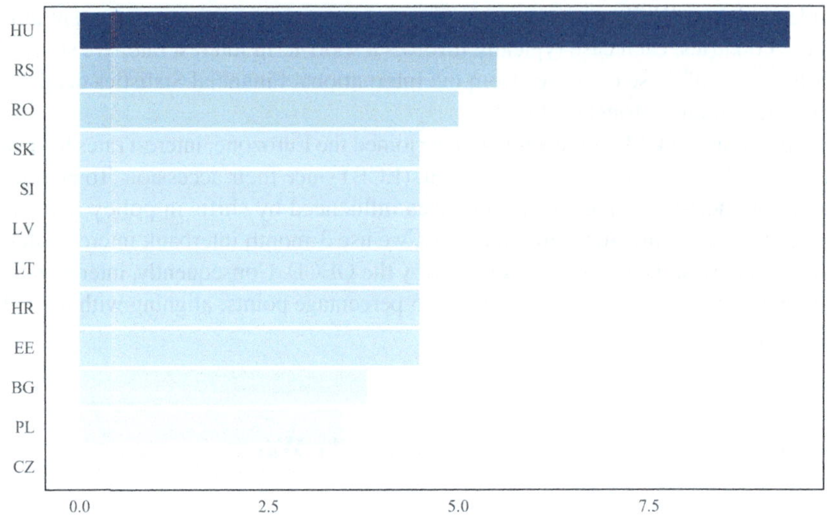

The most modest increases in policy rates were observed in Bulgaria, Poland, and Czechia. In Bulgaria, the slight uptick in the policy rate by 3.8 percentage points can be attributed to the influence of the currency board and its fixed exchange regime. Notably, Bulgaria's policy rate only began experiencing incremental adjustments in the latter months of 2022. Apart from Bulgaria, the Central Bank of Serbia commenced its policy rate increases relatively late compared to other regional central banks, initiating the process in April 2020. Since then, the policy rate has been raised to 6.5 percent. Before raising the policy rate, the Central Bank of Serbia employed monetary tightening by withdrawing liquidity from the markets through repo auctions (NBS, 2022).

The Central Bank of Poland initiated incremental interest rate hikes in 2021, before the onset of the war, aiming to temper excess demand following the easing of pandemic-related restrictions. Consequently, the policy rate in Poland reached 2.25 percent in January 2022 and was gradually raised further to 6.75 percent. However, with inflation steadily cooling off, the Central Bank of Poland shifted its stance and commenced interest rate reductions in the fourth quarter of 2023, currently standing at 5.75 percent.

Preceding the war shock, central banks in the region proactively implemented measures to tighten monetary conditions, aiming to mitigate excess demand resulting from the relaxation of lockdown measures and pandemic-related government relief programs. As seen in Poland, raising the policy rate could be observed in Czechia, Hungary, and Romania as well. In line with Polish monetary policy, Romania initiated its policy rate increase in October 2021. Starting from 1.25 percent, the Central Bank of Romania raised interest rates in three steps by 75 basis points leading up to the war shock. Subsequently, the Romanian policy rate was incrementally raised to 7 percent by January 2023.

The central banks of Czechia and Hungary were the first to implement tighter interest rate conditions, beginning in June 2021. However, in the months following the war shock, the trajectories of interest and inflation rates diverged for these two countries. In Czechia, the central bank aggressively raised the policy rate steeply from near zero to 3.75 percent by January 2022. Consequently, monetary conditions in the country were relatively tight compared to other regional counterparts at the onset of the war. As such, attributed to the already tight policy conditions pursued by their central bank, Czechia experienced the smallest increase in its policy rate in the months following the war shock.

Hungary, facing the steepest inflation rates in the region, adopted an exceptionally tight interest rate policy, as depicted in the graph above. Leading up to the war, the central bank incrementally raised rates from a relatively low 0.6 percent to 2.9 percent by January 2022. However, unlike the Czech case, the relatively tight pre-war monetary policy proved insufficient to halt the rapidly rising inflation. Consequently, the Central Bank of Hungary had to implement more aggressive interest rate hikes, resulting in a steeper upward trend in interest rates. This led to the highest interest rate in the region, reaching 13 percent by September 2022, a level maintained for a full calendar year. The tight monetary conditions managed to steer inflation on a downward trajectory, and consequently, starting from October 2023, Hungary, alongside Poland, initiated a phase of easing interest rates.

4.4.2 Equilibrium Real Rates and Policy Stance

While the assessment of policy rates has clear implications for policy stance and the severity of the inflation shock, thus far we have only described changes in nominal interest rates. However, the evaluation of real interest rates provides a more comprehensive understanding of interest rate policies, taking into account inflation adjustments. Moreover, determining an optimum level for real interest rates can vary not only across countries but also over time. We extend this section by assessing policy stance through real interest rates and examining their deviation from equilibrium real rates.

First, for our analysis, we define real interest rates approximating the Fisher (1930) equation as

$$r_t = i_t - \pi_{t+1}, \tag{4.4}$$

where r_t is the real rate, i_t is the nominal rate and $\pi_(t+1)$ is the one month ahead year-on-year inflation rate.[3]

Determining the equilibrium level of the real interest rate can be approached by various methodologies as shown in Ruch (2021). While multivariate approaches, such as Dynamic Stochastic General Equilibrium models or Time-Varying-Parameter Vector Autoregressions incorporating multiple economic factors and sophisticated frameworks are arguably more comprehensive, however, they can be computationally intensive. To maintain streamlined, parsimonious, and feasible estimations with the available data, we opt for estimating the equilibrium real rate as the trend component extracted from a univariate model.

A widely used method for estimating the long-run trend and cycle components of time series is the Hodrick-Prescott (HP) filter, as proposed by Hodrick and Prescott (1997). While the HP filter has faced criticism over the years for potential spurious dynamics, unreliability in estimates at the boundaries, and arbitrary parametrization, several papers, including works by Nelson and Nelson and Plosser (1982), Harvey and Jaeger (1993), Cogley and Nason (2013), and more recently Hamilton (2018), have raised concerns. Despite these criticisms, the HP filter remains a valuable tool in academia and policymaking, with no clearly superior alternative identified. Notably, authors such as Drehmann and Yetman (2018) and Moura (2022) actively advocate for its continued use.

While acknowledging the potential drawbacks of the methodology, we choose to base our equilibrium estimates on the HP filter. To address some of its limitations, we adopt a real-time (one-sided) HP filter approach for estimating the long-run real interest rate trend (equilibrium real interest rate) in each country. An illustrative advantage of the real-time estimation approach over the full sample (two-sided) method is evident when considering, for instance, the estimation of the equilibrium real rate for January 2022. The two-sided approach utilizes data beyond January 2022 — information not available at the time of the estimate — while the one-sided HP filter relies only on data available up to each given time period t. This approach, to some extent, helps mitigate spurious dynamics introduced by the two-sided estimate and aligns with the perspective of policy authorities, capturing the equilibrium real rate measurement from their contemporaneous vantage point. These estimated equilibrium real rates can be seen in Figure 4.7.

[3] Traditionally, real rates can be calculated by subtracting current-period expected inflation from the nominal interest rate. To some extent, this might over or undershoot our approximation of the real rate by a small margin, depending on the volatility of inflation. However, due to a lack of access to expected inflation rates, our approximation using one-month ahead inflation is the closest possible with the available data.

Fig. 4.7: Historical equilibrium real rates
Data: Eurostat (2023d); IMF (2023a); OECD (2023), authors' calculations

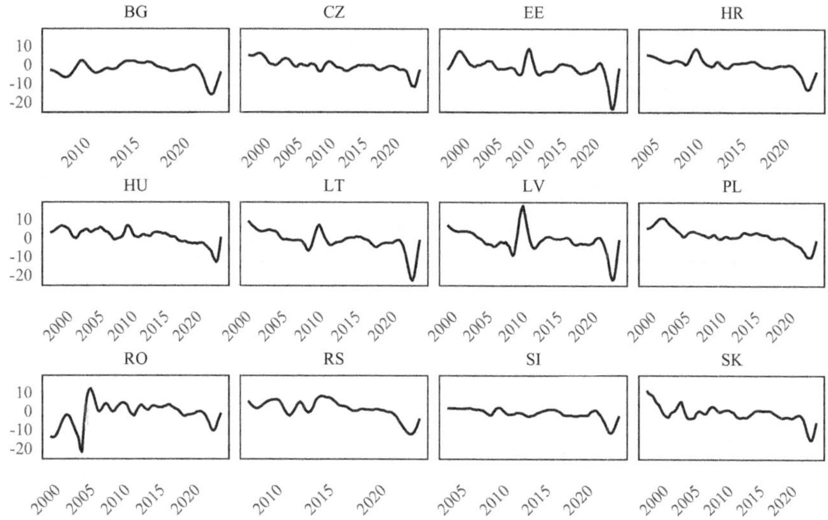

Historically, equilibrium real rates have followed relatively similar trajectories across these countries. Before the Global Financial Crisis (GFC), natural rates were generally positive but exhibited downward-sloping trends. During the GFC, real rates necessary for economic stabilization saw substantial jumps, reaching, in some cases, above 10 percent (e.g., in Latvia or Romania). The post-GFC era was characterized by near-zero or often negative equilibrium real rates until the onset of the Covid-19 pandemic. The pandemic-induced recession led to a further drop in real rates to stabilize the economies. Across all countries in the CEE region, the equilibrium real rate fell below -10 percent by the start of the war. Following the war shock, significant real rate adjustments were required to curb inflation, resulting in steep upward-sloping trends in the natural rates.

To assess the stance of policymakers, we plot the difference between the equilibrium real rates seen in Figure 4.7 and actual real rates calculated by Equation 4.4. We plot these real interest rate gaps from 2020 in Figure 4.8.

These real interest rate gaps serve as indicators of policy stance. A negative gap suggests that the interest rates set by the central bank are lower than what would be required to achieve the equilibrium rate. In such instances, monetary policy is geared towards boosting aggregate demand to promote growth. Conversely, a positive gap indicates that monetary conditions are tighter than necessary to reach the equilibrium real rate. In this scenario, monetary policy aims to contract demand to curb inflation. Given that interest rates are set by the ECB in Eurozone countries, in their cases, we can interpret these results as how fit the ECB's interest rate policy is for each country.

Fig. 4.8: Deviation from the natural real rates from 2021
Data: Eurostat (2023d); IMF (2023a); OECD (2023), authors' calculations

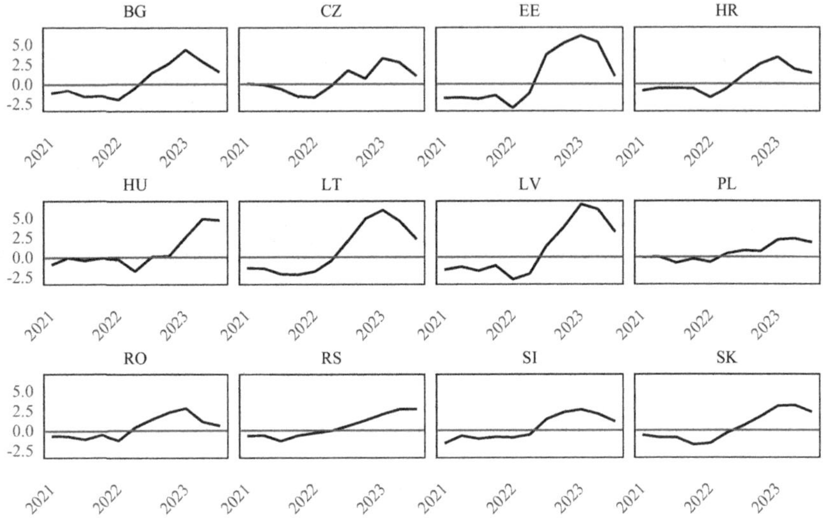

Prior to the initiation of the war, we observed negative interest rate gaps, aligning with the objectives of monetary authorities to stimulate economic recovery after the adverse effects of the pandemic. Notably, the policy stance preceding the war shock appears to significantly influence the pace at which inflation rates were rising, as illustrated in Section 4.3.

Countries with independent monetary policies, including Hungary, Poland, Romania, and Serbia, adopted a relatively cautious approach, maintaining real interest rates close to the equilibrium. An exception within this group was Bulgaria, where the interest rate gap reached nearly -2.5 percentage points, leading to a swift surge in inflation rates following the onset of the war. A similarly sharp upward trajectory in inflation rates was observed in Czechia. In the early months of 2021, the Czech real rate aligned with the equilibrium. However, with a modest increase in inflation by the end of the year, the interest rate gap widened, and prices surged rapidly as the war broke out. In Hungary, while the real rate closely followed its equilibrium in 2021, monetary conditions could only be considered tight from the latter half of 2022, the latest in the region, despite substantial rate hikes. Regarding policy stance, the National Bank of Poland appeared to be the most cautious, maintaining the lowest positive interest rate gap in the region. This strategy proved effective for the Polish economy, as inflation remained relatively moderate by regional standards, well within single digits by the end of our sample.

Similar patterns emerge in Eurozone member countries. Monetary conditions in Estonia, Latvia, and Lithuania proved to be relatively loose before the outbreak of the war in Ukraine, leading to a sharp upward trend in inflation rates during the early months of 2022. The policy stance dictated by the ECB exhibits heterogeneity for its regional member countries. While in the former three countries, the real rate gap was large and negative, Slovenia, and to a slightly lesser extent Slovakia, maintained real rates that were nearly aligned with the equilibrium, resulting in more moderate inflation rates following the war shock.

4.4.3 Achieving a Soft Landing

As highlighted in the preceding sections, the region has witnessed a decline in inflation rates, attributed to the successful implementation of rate hikes and a sustained tight policy stance over 2023. However, the achievement of this objective prompts consideration of the 'costs' involved in effectively curbing inflation. As indicated by the data presented in Table 4.2,[4] the region, which swiftly recovered in 2021 post the coronavirus pandemic, now faces diminishing growth prospects. While most nations in the region concluded 2022 with positive growth rates, the outlook for 2023 appears challenging.

Table 4.2: GDP growth, annual average
Data: Eurostat (2023b), authors' calculations

Country	2020	2021	2022	2023
Bulgaria	-4%	7.1%	4.2%	1.7%
Croatia	-8.2%	13.3%	6.4%	2.2%
Czechia	-5.5%	3.5%	2.4%	-0.4%
Estonia	-0.7%	7.4%	-0.5%	-3.2%
Hungary	-4.7%	7%	4.6%	-0.9%
Latvia	-3.5%	6.4%	3.5%	-0.4%
Lithuania	0.1%	6.2%	2.5%	-0.4%
Poland	-2%	6.8%	5.5%	0.2%
Romania	-3.5%	5.7%	4.6%	1.8%
Serbia	-0.9%	7.7%	2.6%	1.9%
Slovakia	-3.3%	4.8%	1.8%	0.9%
Slovenia	-5%	8.4%	2.9%	1.3%

[4] The '2023' column denotes the mean Real GDP for the first three quarters compared to the previous year.

Is a 'soft landing' still within reach? The gradual decline in inflation rates suggests some leeway for easing the current tight policy stances and considering gradual interest rate cuts, as seen in Hungary and Poland. Nevertheless, it is anticipated that interest rates will remain elevated throughout 2024. The prevailing concern is that the inflation risk associated with easing interest rates outweighs the potential benefits of stimulating growth. Consequently, the economic stagnation experienced in 2023 may persist into the following year in line with IMF (2023b) estimates.

4.5 Conclusions

The 2020s has been a unique period due to two unprecedented tail-risk events: first, a global pandemic, and subsequently, Russia's invasion of Ukraine. These events can be primarily interpreted as supply-side shocks, creating challenging tradeoff situations for policymakers without straightforward solutions. As a result, this period will provide a wealth of lessons for the future regarding the implementation of monetary policy, although some lessons are yet to be fully realized.

The post-Covid period witnessed the emergence of a new inflationary trend following more than a decade of low inflation. This trend coincided with a rapid recovery of activity, broad monetary stimuli, a loose policy stance, and negative equilibrium real rates. This was compounded by an energy price shock and the supply-side disruptions resulting from the war in Ukraine, driving inflation rates across the region. The subsequent sharp increase in energy and food prices fueled a new wave of inflation, with equilibrium rates reverting sharply in 2022 and 2023. The looser policy stance further intensified the impact of the inflation shock, resulting in a moderate slowdown in economic activity and effective stagnation in most CEE economies in 2023.

The aggressive rate hikes and swift adjustments in policy stance in response to the war shock led to real interest rates reaching up to 5 percentage points above equilibrium levels. Despite historically high interest rates and the gradual increase in equilibrium rates, monetary policy conditions remained tight in most countries. While this approach gradually led to moderating inflation, it also resulted in stagnation in 2023 and a weak growth outlook for 2024.

In conclusion, the aftermath of the war in Ukraine has posed significant challenges for monetary policy, highlighting the complex interplay between inflation management and economic growth. The aggressive rate hikes and adjustments in policy stance have gradually contributed to achieving price stability and near-target inflation. However, the tradeoff of stagnation in 2023 and a weak growth outlook for 2024 underscores the delicate balance between inflation management and sustainable economic recovery. As the process continues into 2024, policymakers need to navigate this balance adeptly, aiming to mitigate the impact of supply shocks on inflation while fostering robust economic growth in the region.

The unique experiences and responses to the inflation shock resulting from the war in Ukraine will serve as valuable insights for policymakers, economic analysts, and economic forecasters too, emphasizing the ongoing learning process in adapting to unprecedented global events and their impact on regional economic dynamics.

References

Agarwal, R. & Kimball, M. (2022). *The Future of Inflation, Part I: Will Inflation Remain High?* International Monetary Fund.

BIS. (2023). *Effective exchange rate indices - monthly data.* https://www.bis.org/statistics/eer/broad.xlsxn. (Accessed: 30-01-2024)

Burbidge, J. & Harrison, A. (1985). An historical decomposition of the great depression to determine the role of money. *Journal of Monetary Economics, 16*(1), 45–54.

Caldara, D., Conlisk, S., Iacoviello, M. & Penn, M. (2022). *The effect of the war in Ukraine on global activity and inflation.* https://ideas.repec.org/p/fip/fedgfn/2022-05-27-2.html. FED Notes, 2022-05-27-2.

Cogley, T. & Nason, J. M. (2013). Effects of the Hodrick-Prescott filter on trend and difference stationary time series Implications for business cycle research: Journal of Economic Dynamics and Control 19 (1-2), January-February 1995, pp. 253–278. In *Real business cycles* (pp. 626–651). Routledge.

Drehmann, M. & Yetman, J. (2018). *Why you should use the Hodrick-Prescott filter–at least to generate credit gaps.* https://www.bis.org/publ/work744.htm. BIS Working Paper, No 744.

Eurostat. (2023a). *Employment A*10 industry breakdowns - quarterly data.* https://ec.europa.eu/eurostat/databrowser/bookmark/3832a71b-d1c5-4a71-a39f-160e96a61e61?lang=en. (Accessed: 30-01-2024)

Eurostat. (2023b). *GDP and main components (output, expenditure and income) - quarterly data.* https://ec.europa.eu/eurostat/databrowser/bookmark/e1913e8e-4bfd-4ebf-9746-63d90115fff6?lang=en. (Accessed: 30-01-2024)

Eurostat. (2023c). *Gross value added and income A*10 industry breakdowns - quarterly data.* https://ec.europa.eu/eurostat/databrowser/bookmark/c07c07b5-15a0-46f8-a703-9ff773f45457?lang=en. (Accessed: 30-01-2024)

Eurostat. (2023d). *Harmonized Index of Consumer Prices (HICP) - monthly data.* https://ec.europa.eu/eurostat/databrowser/bookmark/32e7a918-c349-423b-bbc7-c41840ad819f?lang=en. (Accessed: 30-01-2024)

Fisher, I. (1930). The theory of interest. *New York, 43*, 1–19.

Hamilton, J. D. (2018). Why you should never use the Hodrick-Prescott filter. *Review of Economics and Statistics, 100*(5), 831–843.

Harvey, A. C. & Jaeger, A. (1993). Detrending, stylized facts and the business cycle. *Journal of applied econometrics, 8*(3), 231–247.

Hodrick, R. J. & Prescott, E. C. (1997). Postwar US business cycles: an empirical investigation. *Journal of Money, credit, and Banking*, 1–16.

IMF. (2023a). *International Financial Statistics: Monetary and Financial Accounts, Interest Rates, Central Bank Policy Rates, Monetary Policy-Related Interest*

Rate, Percent per Annum - monthly data. https://data.imf.org/?sk=0d9837b9-981f-4934-a2f7-3e24688d4b72&hide_uv=1. (Accessed: 30-01-2024)

IMF. (2023b). *International Financial Statistics: Prices, Consumer Price Index, All items, Index - monthly data.* https://data.imf.org/?sk=8db7bf83-9e18-4c20-b817-680aea53e13a&hide_uv=1. (Accessed: 30-01-2024)

IMF. (2023a). Regional Economic Outlook: Europe - Restoring Price Stability and Securing Strong and Green Growth. *November 2023.*

IMF. (2023b). World economic outlook: Navigating global divergences. *October 2023.*

Kim, S. & Mehrotra, A. (2017). Managing price and financial stability objectives in inflation targeting economies in Asia and the Pacific. *Journal of Financial Stability*, *29*, 106–116.

Király, J., Csontó, B., Jankovics, L. & Mérő, K. (2022). Monetary, macroprudential, and fiscal policy. In L. Mátyás (Ed.), *Emerging European Economies after the Pandemic: Stuck in the Middle Income Trap?* (pp. 255–324). Springer International Publishing. Retrieved from https://doi.org/10.1007/978-3-030-93963-2_6

Liadze, I., Macchiarelli, C., Mortimer-Lee, P. & Sanchez Juanino, P. (2023). Economic costs of the Russia-Ukraine war. *The World Economy*, *46*(4), 874–886.

Moura, A. (2022). *Why you should never use the Hodrick-Prescott filter: Comment.* https://www.nber.org/papers/w23429. NBER, Working Paper No 23429.

Mumtaz, H. & Rummel, O. (2015). Centre For Central Banking Studies. *Economic Modelling and Forecasting-Recent Developments in Structural VAR Modelling, Bank of England.*

NBS. (2022). *Annual Monetary Policy Report 2022.* https://www.nbs.rs/en/drugi-nivo-navigacije/publikacije-i-istrazivanja/IMP/. National Bank of Serbia.

Nelson, C. R. & Plosser, C. R. (1982). Trends and random walks in macroeconmic time series: some evidence and implications. *Journal of monetary economics*, *10*(2), 139–162.

OECD. (2023). *Monetary and Financial Statistics (MEI): Interest rates, Short-term interest rates, Per cent per annum - monthly data.* https://sdmx.oecd.org/public/rest/data/OECD.SDD.STES,DSD_STES@DF_FINMARK,4.0/HRV+SVN+SVK+POL+LTU+LVA+EST+CZE+HUN.M.IR3TIB.PA.....?startPeriod=1950-01. (Accessed: 30-01-2024)

Ruch, F. U. (2021). *Neutral real interest rates in inflation targeting emerging and developing economies.* https://elibrary.worldbank.org/doi/abs/10.1596/1813-9450-9711. World Bank, Washington, DC.

Sims, C. A. (1980). Macroeconomics and reality. *Econometrica: Journal of the Econometric Society*, 1–48.

Chapter 5
Fiscal Policy Developments

Csaba László

Abstract The chapter examines the impact of the war on the fiscal policies of the Central and Eastern European countries, its impact on indebtedness, public deficits, and on the financing conditions of the state. It gives a detailed overview of changes in risk perceptions over the medium and long term. Of particular importance is the effect of the global increase in inflation on fiscal developments, the adjustment measures taken by the countries under review and the analysis of the expenditure structure over the period. The analysis also identifies long-term fiscal risks and possible policy actions to further improve the resilience and adaptability of fiscal policy in the event of drastic external shocks.

5.1 Introduction

In addition to human suffering and global political and economic consequences, the Russian aggression against Ukraine immediately raised the question of how it will affect the fiscal policies of the countries of the region. Fiscal consolidation of economies that were just beginning to recover from the Covid epidemic in 2020 had barely begun. After the Covid outbreak, when it became clear that many of the economies would face unprecedented and unforeseen shutdowns, the EU Commission suspended the enforcement of fiscal rules. To mitigate the extent of the expected economic downturn, the 'escape clause', developed for such occasions, was naturally activated.

The initial idea was that, if the Covid epidemic could be properly managed in health and economic policy terms, fiscal rules would be suspended until the end of 2022. In its detailed forecast for autumn 2021, the EU Commission projected a picture of a consolidating fiscal policy (European Commission, 2021). The Commission

Csaba László ✉
Corvinus University of Budapest, Department of Macrofinance, Budapest, Hungary, e-mail: csaba.laszlo@malcon.hu

© The Author(s), under exclusive license to Springer Nature Switzerland AG 2024
L. Mátyás (ed.), *Central and Eastern European Economies and the War in Ukraine*, Contributions to Economics, https://doi.org/10.1007/978-3-031-61561-0_5

forecast an improving fiscal balance at the EU level. "The aggregate budget deficit in the EU is forecast to halve to around 3.5% of GDP in 2022 and decrease to 2.2% in 2023. The unwinding of the emergency support measures and the operation of the automatic stabilisers, as the economic recovery continues, are set to support the improvement in the budget balance" (European Commission, 2021, p. 34).

The Commission's autumn 2021 forecast also projected a clear improvement in the fiscal situation for the countries in the region. All, except Poland, were projected to have declining budget deficits in 2022 and further deficit reduction in 2023 (see Table 5.1). However, the improving fiscal balance did not yet imply a return to the lower pre-Covid deficit levels of 2019, i.e., fiscal consolidation in 2021 did not seem to have fully overcome the effects of the Covid epidemic.

Table 5.1: Net lending (+) or net borrowing (-), general government
Source: European Commission (2021, p. 171)

Year	2019	2020	2021	2022	2023
			Forecast	Forecast	Forecast
European Union	-0,5	-6,9	-6,6	-3,6	-2,3
Euro area	-0,6	-7,2	-7,1	-3,9	-2,4
Bulgaria	2,1	-4,0	-3,6	-2,8	-2,1
Czechia	0,3	-5,6	-7,0	-4,3	-3,9
Estonia	0,1	-5,6	-3,1	-2,5	-2,2
Croatia	0,3	-7,4	-4,1	-2,9	-2,1
Latvia	-0,6	-4,5	-9,5	-4,2	-2,0
Lithuania	0,5	-7,2	-4,1	-3,1	-1,1
Hungary	-2,1	-8,0	-7,5	-5,7	-3,8
Poland	-0,7	-7,1	-3,3	-1,8	-2,1
Romania	-4,4	-9,4	-8,0	-6,9	-6,3
Slovenia	0,4	-7,7	-7,2	-5,2	-4,4
Slovakia	-1,3	-5,5	-7,3	-4,2	-3,2

The vulnerabilities and risks of fiscal policy, as pointed out by Király, Csontó, Jankovics and Mérő (2022) had not disappeared. The uncertainties surrounding the economic recovery had also prompted caution in the EU and national economic policy and fiscal policymakers. The era of low interest rates was far from over. The ECB, which is the key determinant of interest rates in Europe, only started to raise its key interest rate in July 2022 after the first inflationary risks emerged and only reached the 4.5% level in several steps by September 2023 (main refinancing operations, ECB, 2024). In 2022, in economic growth, a more moderate continuation of the rapid rebound in 2021 was expected following the Covid downturn. In 2023, the

Commission expected a moderate but still strong growth for the year. A decline in growth prospects was not expected in countries where post-epidemic growth did not reach extreme levels. In 2022, countries where the Covid downturn had been lower than average and, therefore, the rebound was more moderate, were expected to see a slight acceleration in growth in 2022 (Bulgaria, Czechia, Latvia, and Poland, Table 5.2).

Table 5.2: Gross domestic product, volume (percentage change on previous year) Source: European Commission (2021, p. 154)

Year	2019	2020	2021	2022	2023
			Forecast	Forecast	Forecast
European Union	1.8	-5.9	5.0	4.3	2.5
Euro area	1.6	-6.4	5.0	4.3	2.4
Bulgaria	4.0	-4.4	3.8	4.1	3.5
Czechia	3.0	-5.8	3.0	4.4	3.2
Estonia	4.1	-3.9	9.0	3.7	3.5
Croatia	3.5	-8.1	8.1	5.6	3.4
Latvia	2.5	-3.6	4.7	5.0	4.0
Lithuania	4.6	-0.1	5.0	3.6	3.4
Hungary	4.6	-4.7	7.4	5.4	3.2
Poland	4.7	-2.5	4.9	5.2	4.4
Romania	4.2	-3.9	7.0	5.1	5.2
Slovenia	3.3	-4.2	6.4	4.2	3.5
Slovakia	4.2	-3.9	7.0	5.1	5.2

The relatively favourable growth outlook and the still low interest rate environment may explain why, in contrast to the relatively low deficits in 2019, no further significant deficit reduction was expected in 2022 and 2023. In this respect, the EU fiscal rules were not a major disciplining force even for the euro area region countries. The low level of interest rates and the expected favourable GDP growth sent a message to the countries of the region that debt levels would not increase dangerously even in the face of a temporarily higher budget deficit. While the Commission's projection for the EU and the euro area as a whole was for a decline in debt (Table 5.3), the largest declines in the debt-to-GDP ratio in the region of around 5 percentage points were expected in Croatia and Poland, while the Czech Republic and Romania were expected to see debts rise by around 4 percentage points over two years between 2021 and 2023. In Romania, this was due to an exceptionally high budget deficit of over 6%, while in the Czech Republic slightly below-average growth in the region and specific factors may have resulted in a higher increase in debt. In the other countries, a difference of 1-2% (+-) was expected. All these developments could have provided a good basis for launching a more sustained fiscal consolidation. This could be in line with a new framework for fiscal rules as well even if it was not yet fully developed.

Table 5.3: Gross debt, general government (as a percentage of GDP)
Source: European Commission (2021, p. 154)

Year	2019	2020	2021	2022	2023
			Forecast	Forecast	Forecast
European Union	78.8	91.8	92.1	90.0	89.1
Euro area	85.5	99.3	100.0	97.9	97.0
Bulgaria	20.0	24.7	26.7	26.7	26.8
Czechia	30.0	37.7	42.4	44.3	46.3
Estonia	8.6	19.0	18.4	20.4	21.4
Croatia	71.1	87.3	82.3	79.2	77.9
Latvia	36.7	43.2	48.2	50.7	49.8
Lithuania	35.9	46.6	45.3	44.1	46.0
Hungary	65.5	80.1	79.2	77.2	76.4
Poland	45.6	57.4	54.7	51.0	49.5
Romania	35.3	47.4	49.3	51.8	53.2
Slovenia	65.6	79.8	77.7	76.4	76.0
Slovakia	48.1	59.7	61.8	60.0	59.1

5.2 The Known Unknown has Occurred

Although various military and intelligence sources had been warning of the possibility of a Russian attack for months, the possible direct economic, political, and fiscal consequences of the outbreak of the war were not anticipated in the countries neighbouring the belligerents. For strategic reasons, Poland in particular had previously taken steps to establish a greater degree of energy sovereignty, but in the case of Germany, for example, the Nord Stream 2 pipeline was placed into operation only weeks or months earlier. Energy vulnerability was lowest in Poland and the Czech Republic (see Chapter 3). However, the Czech Republic regarding crude oil import was heavily exposed to Russia.

In general, however, the outbreak and protraction of the war took the region by surprise, and no one was prepared for it in terms of economic and fiscal policy. The situation was aggravated by the fact that, like the Covid epidemic, this conflict had been unprecedented for at least six or seven decades. Although there were military conflicts with serious consequences for the parties involved during the Cold War and after 1990 (e.g., the ex-Yugoslav war, in Crimea, and Eastern Ukraine), their scale and economic impact were not comparable to the global and regional impact of the war that started in February 2022. After the first weeks and months of the Russian invasion, the chances of a possible Russian blitzkrieg victory were quickly diminished by the strength of the Ukrainian resistance, reinforced by Western assistance. In any case, the world had to be prepared for a protracted war and its consequences.

5.3 Immediate Effects

In the first weeks and months of the outbreak of the war, it was not yet possible to clearly assess how the medium and long-term fiscal situation in the region would be affected by Russian aggression. Despite the fact that most countries in the region were also NATO members, the initial post-shock analyses did not rule out the possibility of a spill-over of the war into the region, with obvious unmeasurable fiscal implications. After the Western world's pro-Ukrainian stance and NATO's clear joint action, immediate escalation of the war did not seem realistic. In fiscal terms, other factors therefore came to the fore in the short term:

- The cost of caring for millions of refugees who left Ukraine in a short time (see Chapters 8 and 9).
- It was clear from the outset that in order to counterbalance Russia's numerical and resource superiority, Ukraine would need continued external (US and EU) assistance, the burden of which would surely affect the countries in the region.
- The expected problems in Russian energy supply threatened in several ways the public finances of countries in the region. The possible effects were not clear at the outset. In the last decades, all serious international conflicts involving major players in the global energy market almost always drastically increased energy prices. The situation has been exacerbated by the fact that Russia has been a major direct supplier of energy (mainly oil, gas, and nuclear fuel) to a significant number of countries in the region (see Chapter3).
- The experience of supply chain disruptions during Covid was still fresh, but land transport north of the Black Sea was made impossible for some time. In particular, the risk of immediate disruptions to energy supplies seemed alarming. In addition, it was very soon seen that the Western world would be forced to adopt a completely new approach to Russia. Instead of the relatively mild sanctions that had previously been imposed without any significant impact on the functioning of the Russian economy, a much broader and mutually more far-reaching sanctions process was launched (see a detailed analysis in Chapter 1).
- Russia and Ukraine had played a major role in world trade in food before the war broke out. In several North African countries (e.g., Egypt), imports from Russia and Ukraine contributed to feeding the population. Given that a significant part of the commercial transport used to take place via the Black Sea, which had become

a war zone, supply chains in this sector were also disrupted. Replacing maritime transport with land transport was almost unfeasible in the short term but also in the longer term it seemed to be difficult, both in terms of capacity and cost.

These factors, combined with other, initially invisible macroeconomic effects, determined the fiscal impact of the war on the countries of the region. As with all analyses of this type, it is difficult to separate the effects of the Russia-Ukraine war from other global economic developments. By 2023, however, other developments had made further major global impact on the region (the Israeli-Palestinian conflict that flared up in autumn 2023, the ongoing US-China tensions, etc.). Less than two weeks after the Russian aggression, one of the first estimates suggested huge numbers on the EU level. "A rough, back-of-the-envelope assessment of the corresponding short-term direct budgetary cost for the EU and its members could sum up to:

- An additional EUR 50 billion to contain the domestic price consequences of an aggravated supply shock;
- EUR 75 billion on energy independence;
- EUR 30 billion on refugees and humanitarian assistance;
- EUR 20 billion on security and defence in 2022, and twice as much in 2023.

All in all, total discretionary spending and tax cuts could represent EUR 175 billion or about 1.25% of the GDP in 2022. Further expenditures are called for in the medium term, especially on energy security and defence. They could represent at least half a percent of GDP per year (Pisani-Ferry, 2022)." Pisani-Ferry also suggested that the refugee, energy security, and partly the defense efforts should be administered and financed by the EU budget level.

5.4 Main Macroeconomic Impacts

The key macroeconomic factors triggered by the war in the region's fiscal situation included a surge in energy and food prices, which was decisive in pushing inflation to unprecedented levels both globally and regionally. Central bankers perceived inflationary risks already in late 2021 and early 2022, and the dilemma of anti-inflationary decisions was exacerbated by the outbreak of war (Prohorovs, 2022). In 2022, however, as it can be seen in Chapter 4, inflation reached double digits everywhere except Slovenia (9.3%), and reached or exceeded 15% in the Baltic countries, the Czech Republic, and Hungary (Table 5.4).

Inflation in 2022, mainly triggered by external shocks, also had a significant impact on fiscal policy. The impact of inflation on the fiscal stance is far from clear. According to the European Commission's Autumn Forecast 2023 (European Commission, 2023e, p. 45), one-off windfall revenues significantly increased fiscal revenues in 2020-2022. Much will depend on the prevalence of legally binding or politically unavoidable indexations of expenditure items.

The budgetary impact of inflation in 2022 was also difficult to estimate in advance because every country had already had formally adopted budgets months before the outbreak of the war, with fixed revenue and expenditure allocations. Revenue surges due to inflation are certainly less problematic for public finances, but for discretionary spending much depends on how rigid they are.

Table 5.4: Harmonised index of consumer prices (percentage change on preceding year)
Source: European Commission (2023d)

	2015-19	2020	2021	2022	2023
	Average				Forecast
EU	1.0	0.7	2.9	9.2	6.5
Euro area	1.0	0.3	2.6	8.4	5.6
Bulgaria	0.8	1.2	2.8	13.0	8.8
Czechia	1.6	3.3	3.3	14.8	12.2
Estonia	2.0	-0.6	4.5	19.4	9.4
Croatia	0.6	0.0	2.7	10.7	8.1
Latvia	1.7	0.1	3.2	17.2	9.6
Lithuania	1.7	1.1	4.6	18.9	8.8
Hungary	1.8	3.4	5.2	15.3	17.2
Poland	0.8	3.7	5.2	13.2	11.1
Romania	1.5	2.3	4.1	12.0	9.8
Slovenia	0.9	-0.3	2.0	9.3	7.5
Slovakia	1.2	2.0	2.8	12.1	10.8

In general, the debt ratio (public debt/GDP) is driven by the growth of GDP, the interest rate paid on government debt, and the general government primary balance.[1] The public discourse often focuses on the relationship between the first two drivers, r-g, as it largely determines the fiscal policy space.[2] Specifically, if the economy grows faster than the interest rate paid on debt (i.e., r-g is negative), the debt ratio is set to decline or, to put it differently, the stabilization of the debt ratio would necessitate a lower primary budget balance. Relatedly, a good summary is given by Blanchard, Leandro and Zettelmeyer: "[T]he debt ratio in the future depends on the initial debt ratio, current and future interest and growth rates, and current and future primary balances. Governments have limited control over r and g. The safe rate is under the control of the central bank, dependent on macroeconomic objectives.

[1] In addition, public debt is also affected by the valuation of FX-denominated debt on the back of changes in the exchange rate and one-off items.

[2] r is the interest rate on debt, while g is the GDP growth rate (with r and g either both nominal or both real).

Potential growth is hard to affect, structural reforms often have uncertain effects. Thus, the policy focus is on the primary balance, current and prospective, what it needs to be, and whether it can be achieved" (Blanchard et al., 2021, p. 4).

Due to this link, the usual fiscal policy wisdom is focused on the expected interest rate environment and potential GDP growth. The lower the interest rates and the higher the GDP growth, the larger room fiscal policy has to maneuver. In this aspect, the pre-Covid external environment characterized by low interest rates and high economic growth was favorable for fiscal policy decision makers.

In the 2010s, volumes were written about the era of zero, negative interest rates, and the fact that inflation was no longer a concern. As a consequence, government bond yields in the region fell to unprecedented levels. Ten-year yields in some CEE countries of the euro area were sometimes negative in 2019-2020 (Estonia, Latvia, Slovenia, and Slovakia). Even Hungary, with the highest debt in the region at the time, saw government bond yields fall to levels unprecedented for decades: below 2% by the end of 2019. Romania, with the highest yields, saw ten-year government bond yields fall below 3% in 2020 (Table 5.5).

Extremely low financing costs may encourage increased borrowing not only in the business sector, including the real estate sector, among others. There is also a moral hazard for the state in that if there is virtually no cost of financing public debt, the state can spend more freely and has less need to monitor the size of the budget deficit. The example of Japan, the world leader in public debt, has shown for decades that with the minimum interest rates, that have been the norm there for decades, a debt/GDP level of over 200% can be maintained without any problem. This approach was also supported by the modern monetary theory, where the limit to 'justified' fiscal spending should be only the potential for runaway inflation. This approach was highly popular with politicians who wanted to get rid of traditional fiscal constraints and were eager to spend as much as possible.

In this respect, the war of 2022 brought a moment of truth for the whole world. The surge in inflation outlined above forced the world's central banks to raise interest rates to unprecedented levels, with a concomitant surge in market interest rates. In fact, the rise in government market yields and other market rates began even before the ECB first raised interest rates in July 2022 (Table 5.5). In the four such countries in the region that had not yet joined the euro area, sovereign yields had already started to rise in the last quarter of 2021, months before the outbreak of the war (Czech Republic, Poland, Hungary, and Romania).

From the beginning of 2022, the rise in yields accelerated across the region. The four aforementioned countries also had the highest yield growth thereafter. These countries were probably the most affected by the yield surge due to market uncertainty, and yield spreads reached 500-600 basis points across the region. Non-euro zone countries are unable to enjoy the euro zone lower interest rate environment, supported by the strong euro zone economies, mostly Germany. During times of stress on the financial markets, these connections became more emphasized. For these countries, a decline in yields of 150-250 basis points started already from the middle of 2023, and the previously familiar 200-300 basis point spread between the lowest and highest yields in the region was restored. However, the return to extremely low funding costs has not yet occurred.

Table 5.5: EMU convergence criterion bond yields
Source: Eurostat Data Browser (2024a)

	2019-Q1	2019-Q2	2019-Q3	2019-Q4	2020-Q1	2020-Q2	2020-Q3	2020-Q4	2021-Q1	2021-Q2
European Union 27	1.19	0.93	0.34	0.43	0.42	0.49	0.26	0.08	0.20	0.43
Euro area	0.93	0.63	0.04	0.14	0.11	0.25	-0.01	-0.19	-0.07	0.16
Bulgaria	0.69	0.43	0.38	0.22	0.14	0.36	0.32	0.20	0.16	0.14
Czechia	1.81	1.75	1.20	1.43	1.46	1.02	0.93	1.11	1.55	1.76
Estonia	:	:	:	:	:	0.14	0.02	-0.13	-0.08	0.13
Croatia	2.20	1.62	0.79	0.53	0.71	1.04	0.87	0.71	0.54	0.50
Latvia	0.82	0.47	-0.01	0.09	0.00	0.19	-0.19	-0.26	-0.25	-0.04
Lithuania	0.31	0.31	0.31	0.31	0.31	0.26	0.16	0.16	0.16	0.16
Hungary	2.85	3.02	2.06	1.93	2.22	2.22	2.27	2.19	2.44	2.83
Poland	2.74	2.61	2.03	2.01	2.03	1.37	1.33	1.25	1.34	1.72
Romania	4.76	4.81	4.25	4.34	4.29	4.42	3.77	3.09	2.78	2.99
Slovenia	0.84	0.36	-0.08	-0.03	0.05	0.48	-0.03	-0.18	-0.04	0.13
Slovakia	0.78	0.42	-0.22	0.01	0.06	0.43	-0.22	-0.42	-0.22	0.01

	2021-Q3	2021-Q4	2022-Q1	2022-Q2	2022-Q3	2022-Q4	2023-Q1	2023-Q2	2023-Q3	2023-Q4
European Union 27	0.32	0.63	1.21	2.43	2.74	3.46	3.46	3.46	3.58	3.54
Euro area	0.00	0.18	0.68	1.77	2.12	2.89	3.03	3.07	3.24	3.21
Bulgaria	0.14	0.31	0.76	1.67	1.85	1.85	2.93	4.03	4.03	4.02
Czechia	1.79	2.53	3.23	4.58	4.41	5.11	4.58	4.50	4.30	4.37
Estonia	0.05	0.16	0.77	1.96	2.66	3.76	3.86	3.92	4.16	3.66
Croatia	0.42	0.34	1.34	2.81	2.99	3.65	3.76	3.72	3.87	3.83
Latvia	0.04	0.24	0.79	2.04	2.57	3.68	3.76	3.83	3.85	3.87
Lithuania	0.16	0.16	0.16	0.16	0.16	1.97	2.88	2.88	2.88	2.88
Hungary	2.92	4.06	5.16	7.24	8.64	9.23	8.18	7.78	7.20	6.90
Poland	1.69	3.03	4.26	6.58	6.15	7.22	6.11	5.97	5.60	5.53
Romania	3.65	5.08	5.72	7.73	8.49	7.98	7.12	6.47	6.67	6.58
Slovenia	0.03	0.16	0.71	1.82	1.84	3.20	3.39	3.29	3.45	3.49
Slovakia	-0.15	0.04	0.65	1.93	2.35	3.37	3.41	3.62	3.80	3.77

From an economic policy perspective, another important risk area of war impact is foreign trade, where some markets have been lost, and the region's countries have seen a drastic shift in foreign trade away from Russia, while energy and food market tensions have also seriously affected the region's countries (for more details, see Chapter 7 and the study of Almazán-Gómez, Llano, Pérez & Rauhut, 2023). Despite initial fears, foreign trade did not collapse anywhere in 2022 (Table 5.6). Export growth rates fell sharply in Estonia, and Slovakia saw export growth rates fall by less than 70%.

Table 5.6: Exports of goods and services volume (percentage change on preceding year)
Source: European Commission (2023d, p. 192)

	2015-19	2020	2021	2022	2023
	Average				Forecast
EU	4.60	-8.50	11.00	7.40	0.40
Euro area	4.40	-9.00	11.20	7.20	0.20
Bulgaria	5.30	-10.40	11.20	11.60	-0.80
Czechia	4.50	-8.00	6.90	7.20	2.50
Estonia	3.20	-5.50	22.10	3.00	-3.60
Croatia	6.90	-23.20	32.70	27.00	-0.40
Latvia	3.80	0.40	9.00	10.30	-3.20
Lithuania	7.50	0.20	17.00	12.20	-4.40
Hungary	5.60	-6.10	8.30	12.60	0.50
Poland	7.30	-1.10	12.30	6.70	-1.50
Romania	7.80	-9.50	12.60	9.60	1.30
Slovenia	6.50	-8.50	14.50	7.20	-0.80
Slovakia	4.20	-6.30	10.50	3.00	-1.20

In the case of imports, however, differences between countries in the region were more pronounced, especially for energy imports (Table 5.7). In Bulgaria, Croatia, and Hungary, import growth even increased, while elsewhere import growth fell to 10% or well below. Given that with a few exceptions (e.g., Romania and Poland), they rely heavily on imports for energy supply, it is not surprising that despite the war in the vicinity, imports continued to increase in the countries of the region.

The current account balance is one of the main elements of the external balance, especially for smaller open economies (all CEE countries except Poland) that have their own currency. It is an indicator that investors watch with a keen eye. Table 5.8 shows that during the first year of war, Slovenia, which had always been in surplus, also ran a deficit, but the Visegrad countries and Romania saw a very significant increase in their deficits - due in large part to the dramatic rise in energy costs (see Chapter 3).

Table 5.7: Imports of goods and services volume (percentage change on preceding year
Source: (European Commission, 2023d, p. 193)

	2015-19	2020	2021	2022	2023
	Average				Forecast
EU	5.30	-7.90	9.60	8.00	-0.60
Euro area	5.20	-8.60	9.00	7.90	-0.30
Bulgaria	5.60	-4.30	10.70	15.00	-4.90
Czechia	4.60	-8.20	13.30	6.30	-0.50
Estonia	3.60	1.30	23.20	3.20	-7.00
Croatia	7.70	-12.30	17.30	26.50	-5.60
Latvia	4.40	-1.10	15.10	11.10	-1.10
Lithuania	7.30	-4.30	19.90	12.40	-6.00
Hungary	6.50	-3.90	7.30	11.60	-6.00
Poland	6.80	-2.40	16.10	6.80	-6.60
Romania	10.70	-5.20	14.80	9.90	2.00
Slovenia	6.60	-9.10	17.80	9.00	-4.20
Slovakia	4.90	-8.10	11.70	4.20	-6.00

A sharp jump in the current account deficit could signal the risk of twin deficits, often feared from a fiscal policy perspective.[3] For most countries in the region, the alarming twin deficit risk is certain to be met in 2022. The varying magnitude of the threat relative to GDP also made the size of the threat different, but there were countries (e.g., Hungary) where the size exceeded 8% of GDP. From a fiscal policy point of view, twin deficits may also pose a serious threat to financial stability because one of the traditional ways of dealing with tensions arising from external imbalances (sharp exchange rate depreciation, dangerous falls in foreign exchange reserves, surges in inflation, social tensions, etc.), which markets expect, is fiscal stabilisation in the form of austerity and/or tax increases. It is therefore easy for fiscal policy to find itself in a situation where regardless of the overall state of the economy it is forced to pursue a pro-cyclical approach that reinforces recessionary conditions, even when counter-cyclical fiscal policy is needed to boost aggregate demand.

It is a positive development in this respect that by 2023 the international energy and food markets had stabilised to the extent that the energy import bill of all CEE

[3] In a theoretical model, if the household and financial and non-financial sector has a zero balance, the external sector balance is the same as the fiscal sector balance. Thus, the fiscal sector has a serious effect on external balances. In the case of high external deficits, the frequent approach is to improve the fiscal balance.

countries had decreased significantly, with a positive impact on the current account balance.

Table 5.8: Current-account balance (as a percentage of GDP)
Source: European Commission (2023d, p. 194)

	2015-2019	2020	2021	2022	2023
	Average				Forecast
EU	3.10	2.40	3.30	0.90	2.50
Euro area	3.40	2.30	3.60	1.00	2.50
Bulgaria	2.90	0.00	-1.70	-1.40	0.70
Czechia	-0.50	0.70	-2.30	-4.70	-0.30
Estonia	1.70	-2.00	-2.70	-3.30	0.60
Croatia	2.30	-1.10	0.80	-2.90	2.40
Latvia	0.30	2.60	-4.20	-4.80	-4.20
Lithuania	0.20	7.30	1.10	-5.50	0.30
Hungary	1.30	-1.00	-4.10	-8.20	0.90
Poland	-1.20	2.30	-1.30	-2.60	1.20
Romania	-2.70	-6.80	-7.50	-9.30	-7.30
Slovakia	-1.50	-0.10	-3.90	-7.50	-2.10
Slovenia	5.40	7.40	3.50	-0.80	3.70

For a long time, the impact on the region's economic growth after the outbreak of the war could not be estimated. The most extreme ideas were published, but most estimates expected GDP to shrink (Prohorovs, 2022; Smit et al., 2022; Liadze, Macchiarelli, Mortimer-Lee & Sanchez Juanino, 2023; Pisani-Ferry, 2022). One single day after the outbreak of the war, Nouriel Roubini sent the following warning signal to world decision-makers: "It is tempting to think that the war in Ukraine will have only a minor economic and financial impact globally, given that Russia represents merely 3% of the world economy. But policymakers and financial analysts need to avoid such wishful thinking." Moreover, Roubini (2022) clearly predicted the risk of a stagflationary recession, which in hindsight clearly did not happen. Nevertheless, he was right that the economic consequences were much greater than the role of the two countries concerned in the world economy.

The McKinsey authors predicted a recession in the US and Europe less than a month after the outbreak of the war (Smit et al., 2022). Table 5.9 shows that, unlike in the Covid epidemic, the CEE countries did not fall into recession (for a detailed analysis, see Chapter 2).

One of the most alarming fears was the impact of sanctions on economic growth and the fiscal situation. Chapter 1 shows that the outcome was more moderate than expected – mostly due to higher-than-expected adaptation and frequent exceptions. Further on, however, this region saw the highest energy vulnerability but, due to the high adaptability of prices and volumes, the energy market turmoil had less effects on the macroeconomic and fiscal situation (see Chapters 2 and 3).

By 2022, most CEE countries were returning to pre-Covid growth levels, with the negative effects of the war likely to have been partly offset by a return to normal post-Covid growth trends. For economic growth, however, a much more nuanced picture emerges when looking at the near-final 2023 data (Table 5.9). Although inflation had fallen significantly in most countries, and energy prices had also fallen, the adverse international environment led to a significant decline in economic growth in CEE countries, with five countries even slipping into recession (the Baltic States, the Czech Republic, and Hungary).

Growth in all other countries had also slowed down significantly. This is not surprising given that growth in the EU as a whole and in the euro area had fallen from 3.4% to just 0.5%. The wave of central bank interest rate hikes in 2022 certainly played a decisive role in this slowdown and recessionary process, affecting growth across Europe. Once the inflation threat was deemed to be serious, all European central banks started to raise interest rates in a desperate rush, regardless of short-term reduction in growth prospects and the increase in interest expenditure for public finances.

5.5 Key Developments in Fiscal Policy

A major difficulty in assessing fiscal policy in the region is that only with considerable delay are comparable statistics available. At the time of conducting this research, the detailed expenditure structure for 2022 is not yet available.

5.5.1 Revenues

During the Covid years (2020-2021), the government revenue/GDP ratio was certainly more stable than the expenditure/GDP ratio.

In 2020, overall revenues at the EU level as a share of GDP remained unchanged compared to 2015-2019 and increased by only 0.1% despite a 5.6% fall in the EU's overall economic output in 2020 and a 6% economic growth in 2021 as a result of the economic rebound after the Covid epidemic (Table 5.10).

The stability of revenues, which was also observed in the countries of the region, is attributed to the following factors. In modern tax systems, a significant share of revenues is in some way linked to the overall performance of the economy. Sales taxes vary essentially according to retail sales, while income taxes are adjusted to

Table 5.9: Gross domestic product, volume (percentage change on preceding year)
Source: European Commission (2023d, p. 170)

	2015-19	2020	2021	2022	2023
	Average				Forecast
EU	2.20	-5.60	6.00	3.40	0.60
Euro area	2.00	-6.10	5.90	3.40	0.60
Bulgaria	3.20	-4.00	7.70	3.90	2.00
Czechia	3.90	-5.50	3.60	2.40	-0.40
Estonia	3.70	-1.00	7.20	-0.50	-2.60
Croatia	3.10	-8.60	13.80	6.30	2.60
Latvia	2.80	-3.50	6.70	3.40	-0.20
Lithuania	3.50	0.00	6.30	2.40	-0.40
Hungary	4.10	-4.50	7.10	4.60	-0.70
Poland	4.60	-2.00	6.90	5.30	0.40
Romania	4.80	-3.70	5.70	4.60	2.20
Slovenia	3.60	-4.20	8.20	2.50	1.30
Slovakia	3.30	-3.30	4.80	1.80	1.30

corporate and household incomes. Other revenues, such as the wage bill (social security contributions), also largely move in line with wages. This is one of the reasons why government revenue is often mentioned as a prominent macroeconomic automatic stabiliser.

The ratio of property taxes to GDP in the EU, which is completely independent of the performance of the economy, averages only around 2%, and this average is exceeded only by data from three or four Western European countries - France, Belgium, Greece, and Spain (European Commission, 2023b, p. 71).

After the outbreak of the war in 2022, the CEE countries' revenue-to-GDP ratios showed shifts within 1% point. i.e., no significant shifts in revenues. This may have been due to the fact that the usual tax legislation each year is adopted before the start of the year, and no major tax changes are introduced during the year, except for example for Covid. Further on, the 2023 revenue/GDP ratios that were forecast are not showing drastic changes either.

5.5.2 Expenditures

In contrast to revenues, expenditures as a share of GDP could show larger fluctuations under potentially extreme economic conditions (Table 5.11). Major economic shocks

Table 5.10: Total revenue, general government (as a percentage of GDP)
Source: European Commission (2023d, p. 186)

	2015-2019	2020	2021	2022	2023
	Average				Forecast
EU	46.10	46.10	46.60	46.30	45.70
Euro area	46.30	46.40	47.00	46.90	46.20
Bulgaria	37.40	37.70	37.70	38.50	37.60
Czechia	41.00	41.50	41.40	41.40	41.90
Estonia	39.10	39.40	39.40	38.80	39.80
Croatia	45.10	46.70	46.10	45.00	45.30
Latvia	37.80	38.00	37.50	35.80	37.60
Lithuania	34.60	36.20	36.30	35.70	36.50
Hungary	45.10	43.90	41.20	42.60	42.30
Poland	40.10	41.30	42.30	40.20	41.50
Romania	32.50	32.50	32.90	33.70	33.50
Slovenia	44.50	43.70	44.90	44.10	44.10
Slovakia	39.90	39.40	40.20	40.20	42.10

during the year are much more difficult to track in legal and political terms in an already adopted budget. For example, in the Covid year, already 'set in stone' spending commitments could not be used to justify a government backtracking, which could lead to a major increase in spending/GDP. No government would reverse a pension or family support increase already introduced at the start of the year. But a year-over-year inflation shock in the opposite direction may not necessarily be followed by a fall in spending, which in turn could lead to a larger fall in expenditure/GDP.

In addition, discretionary spending policy may certainly make a significant impact on fiscal policy, but the later in the year the measures are introduced, the smaller the impact within that year. At the outbreak of the war, there was an almost immediate surplus demand for spending to cater for Ukrainian refugees, especially in countries bordering Ukraine.

They had to reinforce border defences and defence capabilities in the countries geographically closest to the war as quickly as possible, incurring immediate costs in 2022. Notwithstanding the demands for increased defence spending in NATO pushed by the US, the outbreak of the war soon forced the most affected CEE countries to rethink their defence capabilities. In Western Europe, Germany was perhaps the most visible in announcing defence budget increases. In the region, the Baltic countries, Poland, Slovakia, Hungary, Romania, and Bulgaria gave the natural response of

Table 5.11: Total general government expenditure (as a percentage of GDP)
Source: European Commission (2023d, p. 186)

	2015-2019 Average	2020	2021	2022	2023 Forecast
EU	47.10	52.80	51.30	49.60	48.90
Euro area	47.40	53.50	52.20	50.50	49.40
Bulgaria	36.60	41.50	41.70	41.40	40.60
Czechia	40.50	47.20	46.50	44.60	45.60
Estonia	39.30	44.90	41.90	39.80	42.70
Croatia	45.90	54.00	48.60	44.90	45.50
Latvia	38.40	42.50	44.70	40.40	40.80
Lithuania	34.30	42.70	37.40	36.40	38.10
Hungary	47.20	51.40	48.40	48.80	48.10
Poland	41.60	48.20	44.10	43.90	47.30
Romania	35.10	41.80	40.00	40.00	39.80
Slovenia	45.20	51.40	49.50	47.20	47.90
Slovakia	41.60	44.70	45.30	42.30	47.80

rethinking their defence strategy. However, in the short term, the extra budgetary commitments of major developments could not yet materialise.

The decision to procure a major weapons system can take up to one or two years to complete, but the physical delivery and actual expenditure itself may take several years. In the short term, therefore, these extra-large expenditures will only show up in budgets years later. From a long-term fiscal point of view, it must also be considered that the new weapons systems will entail additional substantial operating and maintenance costs.

The largest impact shock in 2022 was a single sharp rise in the price of energy prices. Under normal market economy conditions, the energy market usually operates according to normal market supply and demand rules, which does not mean that there are no different support schemes or favourable tax solutions for social groups, companies, or sectors based on need. However, the burden of normal market price fluctuations is not normally borne by the state.

The energy price shock of 2022 affected a large part of society and energy-intensive sectors to such an extent that public intervention was unavoidable. Almost all EU member states introduced various support schemes. And in many places, extra taxes were imposed to cover the extra costs, which hit the extra profits of some of the companies in the energy sector.

It caused the opposite effect that by 2022 expenditure on Covid protection fell significantly in the region. In most countries, the ratio of epidemic-related funding to GDP fell by two or three percentage points. Fortunately, by 2022, the direct burden of the epidemic had already been reduced, and other aid and compensation schemes had largely been phased out - certainly due to the emergence of war-related demands. This reduction certainly increased the room for manoeuvre for fiscal policy in 2022 on the expenditure side.

Despite extra war-related expenditure, expenditure/GDP fell by two to four percentage points in most EU and CEE countries. The exceptions were Hungary (0.4%), Poland (−0.2%), Romania (0%), and Bulgaria (-0.3%). Despite the fact that these countries border the war-affected countries, albeit in the case of Bulgaria only across the sea, they have one more feature in common that may explain the looser spending in 2022. Hungary held elections in 2022, Poland in 2023, Bulgaria has held continuous parliamentary elections, and Romania has continued government uncertainty. In Hungary and Poland, additional election-type spending has clearly emerged (see Table 5.11).

To sum up: Even in the year when the war broke out, the general government expenditure-to-GDP ratio in most CEE countries declined by two or three percentage points partly due to the surprise inflation. Even in the four countries listed as exceptions, other domestic policy factors may explain the deviation from the general trend.

According to the European Commission Autumn Forecast (2023d), in 2023 the expenditure level to GDP shows larger differences in the region although, except for Bulgaria (−0.8%), Hungary (−0.7%), and Romania (−0.2%), all other CEE countries experienced an expenditure increase. This could be mostly the consequence of lower inflation and weaker economic performance in most countries. This may have been the reverse of the effect compared to 2022. The budgets were planned and approved based on a higher inflation rate and economic growth forecast, therefore, the expenditures were later mostly inflexible when the deviation from the original macroeconomic estimates turned out.

In the case of the two largest expenditures increase, the general elections may have played a role in Poland (+3.4%) and Slovakia (+5.5%).

5.5.3 War-related Expenditure

All countries have some system in place to compensate for energy price increases, which have been noted several times before as a major macroeconomic shock (Table 5.12). Probably due to time pressure and administrative difficulties, most countries used non-targeted support schemes. The exceptions were Romania and Slovenia, where the share of targeted and non-targeted aid was almost equal.

To alleviate expenditure obligations, some countries introduced a tax on extra profits of energy sector companies in 2022 in four countries, but by 2023 this tax had become even more popular and was already applied in six countries. The net impact of fiscal schemes to manage the energy price boom thus affected the budget by 1-1.5 percentage points of GDP on average. With the exception of the Czech Republic, the net fiscal burden decreased in all countries due to the energy price decrease already observed in 2023.

Table 5.12: Energy support measures (level; % of GDP)
Source: European Commission (2023a, p. 55)

	1. Untargeted		2. Untargeted		3. Windfall revenues from energy sector		Net budgetary impact (1+2-3)	
	2022	2023	2022	2023	2022	2023	2022	2023
European Union - 27	0.40	0.30	1.10	1.00	0.20	0.20	1.20	1.10
Euro area	0.40	0.40	1.10	1.00	0.20	0.20	1.30	1.20
Bulgaria	0.00	0.00	3.40	1.00	1.90	0.20	1.50	0.80
Czechia	0.20	0.10	0.50	1.70	0.00	0.50	0.70	1.30
Estonia	0.10	0.00	0.70	0.30	0.00	0.00	0.80	0.30
Croatia	0.30	0.20	1.20	1.30	0.00	0.00	1.60	1.50
Latvia	0.50	0.10	0.90	0.80	0.00	0.00	1.50	1.00
Lithuania	0.00	0.00	1.30	0.70	0.00	0.00	1.30	0.70
Hungary	0.10	0.00	1.30	2.00	0.30	0.90	1.00	1.20
Poland	0.10	0.20	1.80	2.40	0.00	0.90	1.90	1.70
Romania	0.80	0.60	0.70	0.30	1.10	0.60	0.40	0.30
Slovenia	0.60	0.10	0.50	0.80	0.00	0.00	1.00	0.90
Slovakia	0.20	0.00	0.30	2.40	0.40	0.40	0.20	2.00

In recent years, the rise in energy prices due to the war has pushed EU countries to a wide variety of discretionary tax measures on energy-related taxes, rather than an emphasis on green considerations. Table 5.13 shows that at the EU level as a whole, from the beginning of 2020 to the end of 2023, there were a number of tax cuts, as well as a number of tax hikes, and in many cases levels remained stable. This shows that there are significant moves regarding energy taxation but there are no clear trends towards either tax increases or tax cuts.

Almost the day after the outbreak of the war, it was clear that there would be a large wave of refugees from Ukraine, with the short-term impact borne by the countries bordering Ukraine, while in the long term, the final host countries having to face an extra budgetary burden. In addition, the civil sector certainly took on a substantial cost, which is certainly not visible in budgetary statistics.

Table 5.13: Number of decreased, unchanged and increased energy excise tax rates in the EU and average unweighted change in %. January 1st, 2023 relative to January 1st, 2020
Source: European Commission (2023b, p. 118)
Notes: Tiered systems are not included

	Decrease	Unchanged	Increase
Gas Oil Propellant (EUR/l)	16	9	2
Gas Oil Heating Business (EUR/l)	9	10	8
Petrol (Unleaded) (EUR/l)	11	12	4
Electricity Business (EUR/MWh)	9	14	4
Electricity Non- Business (EUR/MWh)	10	13	4
Gas Business (EUR/MWh)	5	14	8
Gas Non-Business (EUR/MWh)	5	13	9

Contrary to preliminary fears, though not negligible, these expenditures remained at or below 0.5% of GDP, except in Estonia (see Table 5.14). They are also noticeable mainly in the countries bordering Ukraine and in the Czech Republic. And despite the fact that the end of the war is still not in sight, the magnitude of the amount is decreasing, while in Poland, which is the largest host country, it has also fallen from 0.5% in the first year to only 0.2% of GDP. This forecast of the Commission shows that a good number of refugees have moved on to other Western European or non-European countries or have been able to integrate quickly to a level where they need less state support.

In addressing the fiscal policy challenges of 2022, the scope for reducing the health and economic impact of the Covid epidemic through vaccination and other measures was increased by the fact that it was winding down and the associated expenditure could be substantially reduced (Table 5.15). This resulted in savings of two to three percentage points of GDP, except in a few countries where the share of Covid-related budget expenditure was already low (e.g., Croatia and Lithuania). In all countries, the share of expenditure related to the epidemic had decreased significantly by 2022, and in four countries it had virtually been eliminated (Estonia, the Czech Republic, Croatia, and Romania).

5.5.4 Fiscal Governance

After the Russian aggression, it was clear that not only at the national government level but also at the EU level there were huge new tasks to be delivered. Refugee, energy security, even European defence cooperation should be coordinated and financed at

Table 5.14: Budgetary costs to shelter and integrate people fleeing the war in Ukraine (level; % of GDP)
Source: European Commission (2023a, p. 56)

	2022	2023	2024
European Union - 27	0.1	0.1	0.1
Euro area	0.1	0.1	0.1
Bulgaria	0.1	0.2	0.2
Czechia	0.3	0.2	0.1
Estonia	0.6	0.8	0.7
Croatia	0.1	0.1	0.1
Latvia	0.3	0.3	0.3
Lithuania	0.2	0.3	0.3
Hungary	0.1	0.1	0.0
Poland	0.5	0.2	0.2
Romania	0.0	0.0	0.0
Slovenia	0.1	0.1	0.1
Slovakia	0.1	0.1	0.1

the EU level. More recently, Kelemen and Kathleen (2022) have traced the 'highly imbalanced' institutional development of the EU – strong on regulatory authority but weak on fiscal, coercive, or administrative capacity – to the predominance of economic motives and the weakness of security considerations in the history of integration (Kelemen & Kathleen, 2022). Will the Russian attack on Ukraine trigger a re-balancing? Will it result in a build-up of supranational core state powers that the EU has been lacking so far (Genschel, Leek & Weyns, 2023, p. 3)? The answer has been negative so far. No more supranational power concentration can be observed in Brussels.

But the EU Commission and the member states cooperated unexpectedly successfully on uncharted waters in 2022-2023 concerning the consequences of the war: supporting Ukraine's defence efforts, dealing with the refugees, organizing a long list of sanctions packages, focusing on energy security, etc. But the fiscal management of these tasks is of a different nature. Only weeks after the Russian aggression, President Macron suggested a new "Recovery Fund-style borrowing scheme" like the earlier Covid initiation to finance the new expenditure requirements (Mathieu & Oliver, 2022). This suggestion was not accepted.

Another serious obstacle regarding more fiscal decision making in the case of joint EU spending is that most of these decisions require unanimous voting; even one member state can block 26 other states' shared proposals. The heated debates of 26 member states and the vetoing Hungarian government in December 2023 about

Table 5.15: Pandemic-related emergency support (level; % of GDP, Covid-19 temporary emergency measures)
Source: European Commission (2023a, p. 56)

	2020	2021	2022
European Union - 27	3.30	3.10	0.70
Euro area	3.30	3.30	0.70
Bulgaria	2.80	3.70	1.00
Czechia	2.90	2.00	0.10
Estonia	1.10	2.30	0.00
Croatia	2.20	1.30	0.10
Latvia	2.70	5.00	1.20
Lithuania	1.50	0.60	0.40
Hungary	3.90	1.90	0.10
Poland	4.50	2.40	0.70
Romania	1.60	0.80	0.00
Slovenia	4.80	4.10	1.00
Slovakia	2.30	3.20	0.80

the new support packages to Ukraine have demonstrated that this may happen any time. Later, in February 2024, a compromise resolved this veto but the blocking opportunity is open for any government in any fiscal decision making in the future. To change this set of rules would require an EU treaty modification, which would not be an easy ride either.

Though fiscal rules were still suspended, behind the scenes in academia, national, and supranational government institutions, serious debates were conducted about the future of fiscal rules at the EU level. As a result of the long-running discussions, it became obvious that the fiscal rules, to be relaunched in 2023 or 2024, would have to be based on a set of new rules. The huge number of studies contained evolving suggestions, modelling the different scenarios.[4] A number of suggestions emerged from the debate, but it was clear from the outset that the conditions for the euro area accession would remain part of the framework. The 60% debt and 3% deficit rules may not be realistic goals for some EU countries not even in the medium term, but even if the 3% rule is respected, fiscal policy in many countries may still be pro-cyclical depending on the economic situation.

[4] See Arnold et al. (2022), Blanchard et al. (2021), Carnot and De Castro (2015), Davoodi et al. (2022), European Fiscal Board (2023), Larch, Busse, Gabrijelcic, Jankovics and Malzubris (2022), Radu (2023), and Wyplosz (2013).

5.5.5 General Government Deficit, Interest Rates, Primary Balance

As a result of the revenue and expenditure developments summarised above, in 2022 the general government deficit-to-GDP ratio fell everywhere in the EU, including the region, meaning that the first year of war did not have a huge fiscal impact leading to an increase in the deficit (Table 5.16). Reaching a declining deficit trajectory may have been due to the fact that all the countries experienced a large deficit increase in 2020 as a consequence of Covid and that, although deficit reduction started in most countries in 2021, fiscal consolidation was continued. The only exception was Poland, where the general government deficit increased to 3.7% in 2022.

According to the European Commission Autumn Forecast, in 2023 there were more differences in the region. Only four countries remained equal or below the 3% deficit threshold (Bulgaria, Estonia, Croatia, and Lithuania). Poland (−5.8%) and Slovakia (−5.7%), which held general elections in 2023, significantly raised their deficit, and according to the latest governmental reports, Hungary increased somewhat its deficit, which was already over 6.2%. All other countries showed slight changes regarding their deficit.

Table 5.16: Net lending (+) or net borrowing (-), general government (as a percentage of GDP)
Source: European Commission (2023d, p. 187)

	2015-2019 Average	2020	2021	2022	2023 Forecast
EU	-1.0	-6.7	-4.7	-3.3	-3.2
Euro area	-1.1	-7.1	-5.2	-3.6	-3.2
Bulgaria	0.8	-3.8	-4.0	-2.9	-3.0
Czechia	0.6	-5.8	-5.1	-3.2	-3.8
Estonia	-0.2	-5.4	-2.5	-1.0	-2.9
Croatia	-0.7	-7.3	-2.5	0.1	-0.1
Latvia	-0.6	-4.5	-7.2	-4.6	-3.2
Lithuania	0.3	-6.5	-1.1	-0.7	-1.6
Hungary	-2.1	-7.6	-7.2	-6.2	-5.8
Poland	-1.5	-6.9	-1.8	-3.7	-5.8
Romania	-2.6	-9.3	-7.2	-6.3	-6.3
Slovenia	-0.7	-7.6	-4.6	-3.0	-3.7
Slovakia	-1.7	-5.4	-5.2	-2.0	-5.7

Interest rate developments in 2022 still only moderately reflect the onset of inflation and the parallel rise in interest rates. The low level of interest rates as a share of GDP also reflects lower indebtedness in the region than the EU average. During periods of minimal or even zero interest rates, most countries sought to increase the maturity structure of their debt. This was a realistic option, especially for countries that have entered the euro area, as these countries have experienced interest rate convergence with the euro area. This process is further facilitated by the fact that the ECB purchases only government securities of euro area countries in its special open market operations (European Commission, 2022, p. 49-50, European Commission, 2023c, p. 34).

In a particularly tense international financial situation, non-euro area countries would also benefit greatly from ECB purchases of government securities, but the ECB is also likely to want to strengthen the willingness to enter the euro area by buying only euro area government debt in open market operations.

The scale of interest costs and spreads over the benchmarks are, by definition, determined by the level of debt. This is the reason why the interest burden in the Baltic countries and Bulgaria is negligible at less than 0.5% of GDP. On the other hand, the highest interest burden above the EU average (2.8% interest expenditure/GDP) is observed in Hungary, the only country in the region with a debt-to-GDP ratio that reached 80% during the Covid epidemic. The other countries with debt levels between 40% and 70% have an interest expenditure of around 1.5% of GDP (Table 5.17).

The 2023 developments are alarming due to the danger of high inflation, high market interest rates, and high indebtedness. In the case of Hungary, the interest expenditure which was around 2% right before Covid and in 2022 stood at only 2.8%, with a huge jump reached the 4.4% level compared to GDP, thereby reducing fiscal policy freedom. Poland showed a smaller but noticeable increase from 1.5% to 2.1%. Most other countries have experienced only a slight increase due to their small debt/GDP ratio and good ratings.

There are no significant shifts in the primary balance compared to the overall balance, given that the interest balance hardly changed in 2022 (Table 5.18). The only country where the primary deficit increased was Poland.

Nevertheless, the primary balance is in deficit everywhere, except Croatia, which was about to join the euro area in 2023, where fiscal policy had obviously done its utmost to meet the Maastricht criteria. However, compared to the 2015-2019 average, this is a clear sign of fiscal loosening, as almost all the countries had primary surpluses at the time.

In 2023, Croatia remained the only country with a primary surplus. Hungary tried to offset the interest expenditures increase with primary balance improvement. The other country with a smaller primary deficit was Latvia (2.5%). All the other countries remained roughly at the 2022 levels (Bulgaria, Czechia, and Romania) or increased their primary deficit.

In all the countries, the structural balance during Covid was substantially smaller than the overall deficit due to the economic impact of the epidemic (Table 5.19). With

Table 5.17: Interest expenditure, general government (as a percentage of GDP)
Source: European Commission (2023d, p. 187)

	2015-2019 Average	2020	2021	2022	2023 Forecast
EU	1.90	1.40	1.40	1.60	1.70
Euro area	2.00	1.50	1.50	1.70	1.70
Bulgaria	0.80	0.50	0.50	0.40	0.50
Czechia	0.80	0.80	0.80	1.10	1.30
Estonia	0.00	0.10	0.10	0.10	0.50
Croatia	2.70	2.00	1.50	1.40	1.20
Latvia	0.90	0.60	0.50	0.40	0.70
Lithuania	1.10	0.70	0.40	0.40	0.50
Hungary	2.70	2.30	2.30	2.80	4.40
Poland	1.60	1.30	1.10	1.50	2.10
Romania	1.20	1.40	1.50	1.50	1.60
Slovenia	2.50	1.60	1.20	1.10	1.30
Slovakia	1.50	1.20	1.10	1.00	1.00

the end of the epidemic and the normalisation of economic conditions, the gap in 2020 narrowed significantly.[5]

One year later, most CEE countries had the same structural deficit. It increased significantly only in one country from 2.2% to 5.6%, Slovakia and three countries could reduce the structural deficit (Latvia, Hungary, and Slovenia).

5.5.6 Public Debt

As a result of the fiscal policy developments outlined above, all countries, except the Czech Republic and Estonia, saw their debt levels fall in 2022 (Table 5.20). Nevertheless, there is still no cause for particular concern in the case of Estonia, which has the lowest debt level in the EU, the only country with a debt level below 20%. The Czech Republic's debt levels are still well below 50%.

[5] In recent years, there have been serious debates on the measurement methodology of structural and cyclically-adjusted public finance indicators, the uncertainties in the calculations and the extent of ex-post data revisions. For the indicators that underpin fiscal policy, these transparency problems have also called into question the seriousness of fiscal rules. It is probably due to all these problems that the new fiscal rules from 2024 onwards focus mainly on expenditure growth and abandon the previous cyclically adjusted indicators.

Table 5.18: Primary balance, general government (as a percentage of GDP)
Source: European Commission (2023d, p. 188.)
Note: Net lending/borrowing excluding interest expenditures

	2015-2019	2020	2021	2022	2023
	Average				Forecast
EU	0.90	-5.30	-3.40	-1.70	-1.50
Euro area	0.90	-5.50	-3.80	-1.90	-1.50
Bulgaria	1.60	-3.30	-3.50	-2.50	-2.50
Czechia	1.40	-5.00	-4.30	-2.10	-2.40
Estonia	-0.20	-5.40	-2.40	-0.90	-2.40
Croatia	2.00	-5.30	-1.00	1.50	1.00
Latvia	0.30	-3.80	-6.70	-4.20	-2.50
Lithuania	1.40	-5.80	-0.70	-0.30	-1.10
Hungary	0.70	-5.20	-4.90	-3.40	-1.40
Poland	0.10	-5.60	-0.70	-2.10	-3.80
Romania	-1.30	-7.80	-5.70	-4.80	-4.60
Slovenia	1.80	-6.10	-3.40	-1.90	-2.50
Slovakia	-0.20	-4.20	-4.10	-1.00	-4.70

For the region as a whole, even the most indebted Hungary and Slovenia, with their debt levels above 70% in 2022, had debt-to-GDP ratios below the EU average. Croatia, which achieved the fastest debt reduction, reduced its debt-to-GDP ratio from 87% to 68% in two years. Only these three countries are above the 60% Maastricht debt limit.

This favourable indebtedness of CEE countries is partly a consequence of the more prudent fiscal policies of recent decades, but it was certainly also influenced by the level of EU support after EU accession. Also, as relatively new members, the moral hazard of "it's OK to go bankrupt because 'Brussels' and 'Frankfurt' will bail us out" may have been less present in fiscal policy. This moral hazard difference would be very difficult to prove because we will not easily find hard evidence for example from Greece, Portugal, or Italy showing that their high indebtedness is a consequence of rational expectations of a 100% easy bailout from Brussels and Frankfurt. A bailout is never easy. There are always fiscal and political consequences. By 2023, Croatia was probably reaching the 60% indebtedness threshold with a significant indebtedness reduction continuation. Otherwise, all the other countries kept their 2022 public debt/GDP ratio, which means they could not proceed with the previous year's reduction.

Table 5.19: Structural budget balance, general government (as a percentage of potential GDP)
Source: European Commission (2023d, p. 189)

	2015-2019 Average	2020	2021	2022	2023 Forecast
EU	:	-3.60	-4.10	-3.70	-3.10
Euro area	:	-3.70	-4.50	-4.00	-3.20
Bulgaria	0.90	-2.30	-4.00	-3.30	-3.20
Czechia	0.00	-4.20	-4.80	-3.10	-2.90
Estonia	-0.60	-4.30	-4.30	-0.60	-0.70
Croatia	-0.90	-3.30	-2.90	-1.10	-1.00
Latvia	-1.40	-3.10	-7.20	-5.00	-2.70
Lithuania	-0.70	-6.40	-1.90	-1.10	-0.60
Hungary	-3.10	-5.90	-6.80	-6.60	-4.80
Poland	-1.80	-5.80	-2.40	-4.70	-5.30
Romania	-2.40	-7.40	-6.20	-5.90	-5.70
Slovenia	-0.60	-6.40	-6.10	-4.50	-3.70
Slovakia	-1.90	-4.30	-5.30	-2.20	-5.60

5.5.7 Fiscal Sustainability Risk

Each year, the European Commission's DG ECFIN produces a risk report on the sustainability of member states' fiscal policies. This comprehensive, detailed analysis assesses the fiscal risks of member states in the short, medium, and long term and rates their situation over different time horizons. The report therefore sends an important signal to governments, market participants, and the general public about the risks to be expected in each member state. The last such report was published in April 2023, already indicating whether and how the war had affected the fiscal risks of the region's member countries (European Commission, 2023c).

The summary in Table 5.21 shows the ratings for different time horizons. In the short term, for a one-year time horizon, the analysis rates the risk to fiscal sustainability as low for all countries in the region, similar to the one-year horizon in the previous report. These favourable ratings should not be surprising given that all countries in the region have lower indebtedness than the EU average, no country has financing issues, and the major international credit rating agencies have only marginally downgraded the long-term ratings of a few countries (Table 5.22). Thus, the negative effects of the war have not increased the short-term fiscal risks in the region. It is worth noting that the low-risk rating applies to all EU countries in the

Table 5.20: Gross debt, general government (as a percentage of GDP)
Source: European Commission (2023d, p. 190)

	2015-2019 Average	2020	2021	2022	2023 Forecast
EU	83.50	91.70	88.90	84.80	83.10
Euro area	90.00	99.10	96.50	92.50	90.40
Bulgaria	24.50	24.60	23.90	22.60	23.50
Czechia	34.50	37.70	42.00	44.20	44.70
Estonia	9.20	18.60	17.80	18.50	19.20
Croatia	76.60	86.80	78.10	68.20	60.80
Latvia	38.00	42.20	44.00	41.00	41.70
Lithuania	38.20	46.20	43.40	38.10	37.30
Hungary	71.40	79.30	76.70	73.90	69.90
Poland	50.20	57.20	53.60	49.30	50.90
Romania	36.10	46.80	48.50	47.20	47.90
Slovenia	74.20	79.60	74.40	72.30	69.30
Slovakia	50.60	58.90	61.10	57.80	56.70

2023 report and that Cyprus and Greece, which were rated as high-risk a year earlier, are now rated as low-risk (European Commission, 2023c, p. 16).

The picture is much more mixed for the medium-term assessment. Based on the 2023 report, two countries saw their risk assessment worsen, and three had improved. Romania and Slovenia moved from high risk to medium risk, while Bulgaria moved from medium to low risk, mainly due to an improving fiscal situation. Poland moved from low to medium risk, while Hungary moved down one category to high risk. For both countries, the worsening is explained by worse fiscal conditions, poorer economic growth prospects, and less favourable financing conditions (European Commission, 2023c, p. 14).

Four countries are rated low (Bulgaria, Estonia, Latvia, and Lithuania) Four countries are also rated as medium risk (Czechia, Poland, Romania, and Slovenia) mainly due to their increasing indebtedness. Three countries have a high risk (Croatia, Hungary, and Slovakia) mainly due to their higher indebtedness and their higher exposure to possible adverse changes in external conditions. It is surprising that Croatia's rating had not improved, despite the fact that its debt-to-GDP ratio declined by nearly 20% points between 2020 and 2022 and was projected by the European Commission to reach a debt-to-GDP ratio of 60.8% in 2023, with a further decline of 7.4% points (Table 5.20). For the long-term risk rating, only the Baltic countries received a low rating. Five countries were rated medium (Bulgaria, Czechia, Croatia,

Table 5.21: Fiscal sustainability risk classification by member states
Source: European Commission (2023c, p. 16)
Note: when different, the risk classification from the FSR 2021 is shown in brackets

	Overall short-term risk	Overall medium-term risk	Overall long-term risk
Bulgaria	Low	Low (Medium)	Medium
Czechia	Low	Medium	Medium (High)
Croatia	Low	High	Medium
Estonia	Low	Low	Low
Hungary	Low	High (Medium)	High
Latvia	Low	Low	Low
Lithuania	Low	Low	Low
Poland	Low	Medium (Low)	Medium
Romania	Low	Medium (High)	Medium
Slovenia	Low	Medium (High)	High
Slovakia	Low	High	High

Poland, and Romania) with one change. Czechia improved one category mainly due to its more favourable initial fiscal position. Three countries had the worst rating, i.e., high risk, mainly due to the fiscal risks of ageing (Hungary, Slovenia, and Slovakia; European Commission, 2023c, p. 13).

5.6 Long-term Credit Ratings

Although this has no direct impact on the fiscal situation, the way major credit rating agencies (notably Moody's and S&P) assess a country's long-term foreign currency sovereign risks in the case of debt issued in foreign currency is an important indicator of international perceptions of fiscal risk and, therefore, influences interest rates to be paid. Particularly in a tense international environment such as the war in the neighbourhood of the countries of the region, investors are particularly sensitive to changes in the risk of sovereign foreign currency debt. The severely misrated assets before the outbreak of the 2008 financial crisis led many, and in my opinion rightly so, to questioning the professional competence of rating agencies, but to this day these ratings still serve as a guide for investment professionals. Table 5.22 shows that the countries in the region are clearly in the investment grade category according to both Moody's and S&P. Czechia, the Baltic countries, Poland, Slovenia, and Slovakia are in the favourable rating categories starting with A, which clearly provides an already relatively low risk rating and continued favourable access to international financial markets.

Moody's did not change its rating for any country in a year before December 2022, except for Croatia, which was apparently upgraded by two notches to investment grade in view of its entry into the euro zone in January 2023. Of the others, Czechia and Slovakia received warnings in the form of negative outlooks, a harbinger of a possible downgrading, but Slovakia was not downgraded until March 2024, and Czechia has since regained a stable outlook with unchanged ratings (Moody's, 2024a, Moody's, 2024b).

In 2022, S&P upgraded the ratings of two countries. Bulgaria moved up one notch and, unsurprisingly for the reasons mentioned above, Croatia was upgraded by two notches. Three countries, on the other hand, received a negative outlook. Lithuania and Slovakia were rated as A+, while Hungary was rated as BBB. More than a year later, only Hungary has been downgraded to BBB-. Slovakia has regained its stable outlook with the A+ rating, while Lithuania continues to maintain its A+ rating with a negative outlook (S&P, 2024).

5.7 Eurosystem Financing Assistance

Euro area member countries have the opportunity through the ECB to facilitate the financing of public debt and improve market access. In 2021-2022, the Baltic countries, Slovakia, and Slovenia, members of the Euro area, could take advantage of this opportunity (Table 5.23). Through the Eurosystem, the ECB covered 24-72% of the total financing needs in 2021 by purchasing bonds of the respective countries. When assessing the impact of the war, an interesting aspect to consider is how the expected ECB bond purchases of these five countries in 2021 were fulfilled in 2022.

Table 5.23 shows that in 2022 all five countries experienced lower than expected ECB bond buying. In Estonia and Slovakia, the ECB's bond buying rate was below 10% of the Gross Financing Needs (GFN). For Lithuania and Slovakia, the ECB's bond purchase rate is much lower than initially expected. Only for Latvia were ECB bond purchases around 30% of the total GFN, as initially estimated.

Beyond this, however, a further question can be raised. The credit ratings, market access, and interest rate conditions of the euro area countries in the region are clearly more favourable than those of the countries with their own currency and very close to the average of the euro area countries (Table 5.5). In times of tightening market conditions, it would therefore be of much greater help, stability, and confidence to non-euro area countries if they could participate in the Eurosystem. Obviously, a number of technical issues would need to be resolved to create such a possibility. For example, should the ECB be able to buy non-euro-denominated government bonds of member states, or should it only be able to buy euro-denominated government bonds? Participation in the Eurosystem could also be one of many other incentives to join the euro area. A counterargument could be that non-euro area countries are already subject to looser fiscal rules and that ECB assistance might increase the risk of moral hazard in fiscal policy.

Table 5.22: Long-term foreign currency sovereign ratings
Source: European Commission (2022, p. 53) for November 2021, European Commission (2023c, p. 37) for December 2022

(at 2 November 2021)						
	Moody's			S&P		
	Rating	Since	Outlook	Rating	Since	Outlook
Bulgaria	Baa1	09.10.2020	STABLE	BBB-	29.11.2019	STABLE
Czechia	Aa3	04.10.2019	STABLE	AA-	24.08.2011	STABLE
Estonia	A1	23.04.2009	STABLE	AA-	13.01.2012	POS
Croatia	Ba1	13.11.2020	STABLE	BBB-	22.03.2019	STABLE
Latvia	A3	13.02.2015	STABLE	A+	21.02.2020	STABLE
Lithuania	A2	12.02.2021	STABLE	A+	21.02.2020	STABLE
Hungary	Baa2	24.09.2021	STABLE	BBB	15.02.2019	STABLE
Poland	A2	12.11.2002	STABLE	A-	12.10.2018	STABLE
Romania	Baa3	06.10.2006	STABLE	BBB-	16.05.2014	STABLE
Slovenia	A3	02.10.2020	STABLE	AA-	14.06.2019	STABLE
Slovakia	A2	13.02.2012	STABLE	A+	31.07.2015	STABLE
(at 9 December 2022)						
	Moody's			S&P		
	Rating	Since	Outlook	Rating	Since	Outlook
Bulgaria	Baa1	09.10.2020	STABLE	BBB	29.05.2020	STABLE
Czechia	Aa3	05.08.2022	NEG	AA-	24.08.2011	STABLE
Estonia	A1	31.03.2010	STABLE	AA-	31.03.2022	STABLE
Croatia	Baa2	15.07.2022	STABLE	BBB+	14.07.2022	STABLE
Latvia	A3	13.02.2015	STABLE	A+	21.02.2020	STABLE
Lithuania	A2	12.02.2021	STABLE	A+	02.12.2022	NEG
Hungary	Baa2	24.09.2021	STABLE	BBB	12.08.2022	NEG
Poland	A2	12.05.2017	STABLE	A-	12.10.2018	STABLE
Romania	Baa3	18.10.2021	STABLE	BBB-	16.04.2021	STABLE
Slovenia	A3	02.10.2020	STABLE	AA-	14.06.2019	STABLE
Slovakia	A2	05.08.2022	NEG	A+	20.05.2022	NEG

Table 5.23: Government GFN and possible total acquisitions of sovereign bonds by the Eurosystem - 2021 and 2022 estimates
Note: The cut-off dates for this table are 16 December 2021 (2021, 2022 forecasts) and 21 December 2022 (2022, 2023 forecasts)
A: GFNs, EUR bn
B: Public sector asset purchases under APP and PEPP, EUR bn
C: Public sector asset purchases under APP and PEPP, % of GFNs 2021
D: GFNs, EUR bn
E: Expected public sector asset purchases under APP and PEPP, EUR bn
F: Expected Public sector asset purchases under APP and PEPP, % of GFNs 2022
G: GFNs, EUR bn
H: Public sector asset purchases under APP and PEPP, EUR bn
I: Public sector asset purchases under APP and PEPP, % of GFNs 2021
J: GFNs, EUR bn

	2021	2021	2021	2022	2022	2022	2022	2022	2022	2023
				Forecast	Forecast	Forecast	Fact	Fact	Fact	Forecast
	A	B	C	D	E	F	G	H	I	J
Estonia	0.7	0.2	24	1.3	0.9	67	1.7	0	2.2	1.3
Latvia	4.1	1.3	31	3.8	1.2	32	2.1	0.6	30.4	2.4
Lithuania	3.4	1.8	51	3.0	1.8	61	3.2	0.6	17	.6 7
Slovenia	7.8	4.3	55	7.7	1.5	20	8.4	0.7	8.3	8.9
Slovakia	6.9	5.0	72	6.5	3.7	56	4.6	1.7	36.2	7.4

5.8 Public Debt Financing

The Gross Financing Needs (GFN) data show precisely that the region's lower indebtedness compared to the EU as a whole is naturally reflected in lower annual gross financing needs. The annual public debt financing needs for the EU as a whole in 2021-2022 will be 18-20% of GDP, which is lower than the annual financing needs of all CEEC (Table 5.24). Due to soaring deficits under Covid, in 2020 the GFN was above 10% in all but two countries (Bulgaria and Latvia) and above 20% of GDP in three countries (Croatia, Hungary, and Slovenia). By 2021, the GFN had fallen below 20% in all CEEC. The rule of thumb is also evident in the region that if there is no dramatic difference in maturity structure, the level of public debt largely determines the annual GFN. Accordingly, the highest GFN above 10% is found in the most indebted countries in 2021-2022 for Croatia, Hungary, Romania, and Slovenia while Poland is just below 10%.

Looking at the impact of the war, in contrast to Covid, where GFN increased dramatically across the region, there is no significant increase in 2022, and GFN in many countries had decreased further. In the Baltic countries, Bulgaria, and Slovakia GFN is below 5%, while Poland and Slovenia show a slight increase. These developments also reflect the trend already described that in 2022 there was no jump in either the budget deficit or the indebtedness in the region. The Commission's Spring 2023 forecast did not predict any dangerous trends for the GFN for 2023-2024.

Table 5.24: Gross financing needs (GFN) (% of GDP, 2019-2024)
Source: European Commission (2023c, p. 31)

	2019	2020	2021	2022	2023	2024 Forecast
EU	12.7	22.1	18.6	17.1	16.9	16.7
EA	13.7	23.3	20.3	18.5	18.4	18.2
BG	0.5	5.5	3.2	3.5	4.0	5.1
CZ	5.3	10.7	10.9	9.2	8.6	7.5
EE	1.3	10.5	2.8	4.6	3.5	5.1
HR	14.0	21.4	13.2	10.6	12.2	13.6
LV	4.5	9.1	10.0	5.6	6.0	4.5
LT	6.1	15.3	6.0	4.8	9.6	4.4
HU	18.1	27.0	17.1	15.6	13.6	14.4
PL	4.6	15.6	7.6	9.8	11.2	10.2
RO	7.6	15.7	10.6	10.8	9.5	9.8
SI	6.9	20.8	13.5	14.2	14.1	12.5
SK	3.7	14.2	8.0	4.3	6.1	5.5

The annual deficit and the ratio of debt maturing in a given year may also be important factors in further assessing the GFN (Tables 5.25-5.26). The popular day-to-day assessment of fiscal policy is focusing on the fiscal deficit; however refinancing the maturing debt could pose a much more dangerous risk to the state's fiscal sustainability. Unsurprisingly, the ratio of maturing debt to GDP is also below the EU and euro area average in all CEEC. There was only one country with a notable increase of 2% of GDP (Croatia).

Besides maturing debt, the maturity structure is the best indicator of stable, sustainable financing of public debt in the long run (Table 5.27). At the peak of the financial crisis in 2009, only the Czech Republic and Slovenia had an average maturity structure (6.2 and 5.9 years, respectively) above the EU average (simple). The remaining maturity (securities) in all Eurozone countries in the region was above 8 years in 2021-2022 and in all non-eurozone countries below the EU average (7.9 years). These data are perhaps the best reflection of the positive impact of euro area membership on the financing conditions of public debt and the reduced vulnerability of the euro area countries in the region. Despite tensions in the financial markets in the year of the war, the maturity structure became even more favourable by September

Table 5.25: Gross Financing Needs by Components (% of GDP), 2021 estimates, by country
Source: European Commission (2022, p. 48)
Note: GFN estimates/forecasts are calculated as the sum of the budgetary deficit, redemption of main debt instruments (securities and loan principal repayments), as well as stock- flow adjustments

	Budget deficit	Maturing debt	Stock Flow Adjustment	GFN
EU-27	6.6	12.4	-0.2	18.8
Euro area	7.1	13.6	-0.2	20.6
Bulgaria	3.6	0.6	0.2	4.5
Czechia	7.0	3.9	0.3	11.2
Estonia	3.1	0.9	-1.6	2.5
Croatia	4.1	9.3	-0.4	13.0
Latvia	9.5	4.5	-1.2	12.8
Lithuania	4.1	3.6	-1.3	6.3
Hungary	7.5	12.2	0.6	20.3
Poland	3.3	5.2	-1.2	7.3
Romania	8.0	3.9	-1.6	10.3
Slovenia	7.2	11.4	-3.3	15.3
Slovakia	7.3	2.0	-2.1	7.2

2022; with the exception of Bulgaria, i.e., no adverse developments in this respect in 2022.

Finally, some factors relevant to long-term financing vulnerability are examined, based on Table 5.28 (the underlying data are only available for 2021). The ratio of short-term debt to total debt is usually examined first, although in this respect a relatively high ratio of short-term debt to an otherwise very low level of debt may be misleading. This is exactly the case for Estonia, where the country had the highest ratio of short-term debt to total debt at 8.6% in 2021. Given that Estonia's total debt was less than 20% in 2021, the ratio of short-term debt to GDP was roughly 1.5% of GDP. Similarly, Croatia, Hungary, and Romania had a moderate vulnerability with short-term debt ratios of 5-6% of total debt. These ratios support the classification cited above: all the countries in the region received a low-risk rating in the Commission's 2023 short term assessment.

Another risk factor that is often examined is the share of foreign debt in total debt. Given that all the debt of the euro-area member states in the euro area is denominated in euros, the proportion of foreign currency debt in these countries can be considered zero. Croatia's (70.7%) and Bulgaria's (74.6%) exceptionally high foreign debt ratios should also be of less concern. Since the compilation of these statistics, Croatia

Table 5.26: Gross financing needs by components (% of GDP, 2022 estimates)
Source: European Commission (2023c, p. 33)

		Components		
	Total	Budget deficit	Maturing debt	Stock Flow Adjustment
EU	17	3,4	13,7	0
Euro area	18,6	3,5	15	0,1
Bulgaria	3,5	3,4	1,7	-1,6
Czechia	9,2	4,3	3,7	1,2
Estonia	4,6	2,3	1,3	1
Croatia	10,6	1,6	11,2	-2,1
Latvia	5,6	7,1	1,8	-3,3
Lithuania	4,8	1,9	3,4	-0,5
Hungary	15,6	6,3	8,7	0,6
Poland	9,8	4,8	4,9	0
Romania	10,8	6,6	4,9	-0,7
Slovenia	14,2	3,6	10,1	0,6
Slovakia	4,3	4,2	1,7	-1,6

Table 5.27: Average residual maturity of debt (general government)
Source: European Commission (2023c, p. 80)

	Debt securities					All debt (Oct. 2022)
	Dec.09	Dec.20	Dec.21	Sep. 2022.	Diff. 2022-2009	
Bulgaria	4,3	6,2	8,4	7,4	3,1	8,1
Czechia	6,2	6,0	5,9	6,4	0,2	6,1
Estonia						8,0
Croatia		7,6	7,9	8,2		6,0
Latvia	3,7	9,9	8,8	8,9	5,2	8,1
Lithuania		6,2	9,0	9,3		9,5
Hungary	4,1	3,7	5,6	6,9	2,8	5,9
Poland	5,3	4,8	4,4	4,4	-0,9	4,4
Romania	2,3	6,9	7,4	7,4	5,1	7,4
Slovenia	5,9	9,4	8,8	9,7	3,8	9,8
Slovakia	4,5	8,6	8,3	8,5	4,1	8,5
EU Average	5,4	7,0	7,6	7,9	2,5 (7,9)	8.5(simple)

has entered the euro zone and the risk of foreign currency indebtedness has been eliminated accordingly. Bulgaria is also in the final stages of the euro accession process and plans to enter the euro zone in 2025 (Krassen, Nikolov, 2024). Even if entry is delayed by one or two years, the euro-denominated debt for Bulgaria will no longer be a risk factor, which is a minimal risk in view of the fact that the debt-to-GDP ratio is below 25% anyway (Table 5.20). Among non-euro area member states, Romania has a foreign currency denominated debt ratio of over 50%, which in the event of an unexpected, drastic devaluation would significantly increase indebtedness and pose a serious financing risk. Hungary and Poland, on the other hand, have an external foreign currency debt of 20-25%, which can be considered moderate, given the economic openness of the two countries and their significant foreign trade.

The third factor is the proportion of public debt financed by non-residents. Indeed, from a risk perspective, it may be a problem if there is a high level of foreign currency debt, much of which is held by foreign investors. But here again, we should distinguish the situation in the euro area member states, where the national approach is less prevalent in the single European capital markets. Investors distinguish between euro investments mainly on the basis of interest rate conditions, given past experience and the euro zone safety net. Since Greece, which has experienced debt levels above 200%, has not gone bankrupt, the countries of the region with much lower debt levels and more stable fiscal policies are low risk.

A greater concern may be the financing of countries with their own currency by foreigners, assuming that foreigners are the most 'hysterical' investors and the easiest to flee a country's sovereign debt market in times of financial stress. Just as a parenthetical note, we have already seen domestic investors panicking in a country and line up outside bank branch offices, triggering a sovereign default. For countries that have not joined the euro zone, the share of non-residents in public debt is 30-50%, but this is more a sign of foreign investor confidence, due to integrated European financial markets and liberalised regulation than representing a real risk until a combination of a possible serious deterioration in external balance and irresponsible fiscal policy undermines confidence in the country.

5.9 Expenditure Structure

One of the most important measures of the impact of the war may be whether structural changes were needed on the expenditure side of fiscal policy. A few days before the present study was finalised in March 2024, Eurostat published details of the 2022 expenditure data. We will refer to these data in the remainder of this section (Eurostat Data Browser, 2024b).

There have been no significant shifts in the size of total expenditure except in Croatia, where the expenditure-to-GDP ratio fell by more than 9% points between 2020 and 2022, which was necessary to turn the deficit of more than 7% into a budget surplus by 2022.

Table 5.28: Government debt structure (2021) as shares of total debt (%)
Source: European Commission (2023c, p. 136)

	Short-term public debt (original maturity)	Public debt held in foreign currency	Public debt held by non-residents
Bulgaria	0.1	74.6	46.1
Czechia	2.6	7.7	29.7
Estonia	8.6	0.0	69.7
Croatia	5.7	70.7	34.0
Latvia	3.1	0.0	63.9
Lithuania	0.0	0.0	64.7
Hungary	5.9	22.6	31.7
Poland	1.2	22.7	33.1
Romania	5.1	53.3	49.2
Slovenia	2.1	0.1	55.2
Slovakia	3.6	0.0	49.6

There were no major shifts in general public services, except in Bulgaria and Croatia, where there was a 1.3 and 0.9% point drop in GDP, respectively. The refugee crisis and economic assistance to Ukraine in the aftermath of the war seem to have had little impact on national budgets. Even in the EU as a whole, foreign economic aid was only 0.3% of GDP and remained stable in 2022. And in CEEC, there was virtually no meaningful spending of any size on this expenditure item. In the aftermath of the war, serious reflection began almost from the first weeks about the way to strengthen the defence capabilities of the EU as a whole and of individual member states. The argument presented earlier that a major arms build-up can only be achieved over a longer period of time is confirmed by the 2022 figures. At the EU level, there was no increase in this area in 2022, but even in the region, only four countries (Estonia, Lithuania, Hungary, and Slovakia) saw an increase in defence spending, although the largest increase did not exceed 0.3% of GDP (Hungary). However, an important fact for the fiscal policy space for the future is that no country except the Baltic countries has a defence spending ratio above 2% of GDP, which seems to indicate that in the coming years the changed strategic situation and the much stronger US push to reach the 2% minimum will in any case lead to further spending increases in this area.

In the area of public order and safety, there was no substantial movement in 2022. There is already a wide variation in support for economic areas between CEEC. Estonia spends only 4.7% of its GDP on this area, while Hungary more than doubles its GDP to 10.7%. However, in terms of the impact of the war, it is worth looking at the breakdown because, unsurprisingly, fuel and energy has seen a significant increase in spending in most countries in the region. With the exception of Czechia, Slovakia, and Poland, all experienced significant increases ranging from 0.7% to 2.1%

of GDP. The largest increase was observed in Hungary, with 2.9% of GDP being spent by general government on this item. These figures confirm that most countries have tried to mitigate the severe impact of the sharp increase in energy prices. Despite the growing importance of environmental spending over the last 10-15 years, with numerous strategies and regulations implemented, spending on the environment is still below 1% of GDP across the EU. In the region, spending on the environment is lower than this, and in 2022 this low percentage was further reduced by 0.1% of GDP. There was no significant shift in housing benefit expenditure in 2022.

Health expenditures are not directly related to the war and may be more related to the end of the Covid epidemic. Health spending also fell marginally at the EU level by 0.3% of GDP, but in the region as a whole, with the exception of Bulgaria, health spending as a share of GDP fell by a larger ratio than this. The decline is particularly large in Latvia and Hungary (-1.5% and -1.3%): they have reduced their health expenditure by a total of 2 percentage points compared to 2020. However, it should also be noted that they had the largest increase during the Covid pandemic, and that this reduction is roughly back to the pre-Covid situation.

There have been no major shifts in the areas of recreation, culture, sport, and education. In social assistance, the bulk of which is made up of fixed transfers, spending as a share of GDP also fell by 0.3% at the EU level. The region has an inherently lower social expenditure ratio, but the Baltic countries, Croatia (-1%), and Poland have significantly reduced their social spending. A good part of this reduction was concentrated in pension type benefits at a rate of 0.5-0.6% of GDP (Estonia, Croatia, Poland, and Slovakia). Probably in these countries there is no preliminary fixed indexation mechanism for pensions to be compensated in the case of a surprise inflation during the year.

5.10 Long-term Fiscal Risks

Based on the experience of 2022-2023, there could be a serious risk of another significant increase in energy prices at any time. Of the expenditure changes described in the previous sub-chapter, the increase in energy expenditure was the most spectacular. This also highlights the risk that, although the energy industry is a fundamentally market-driven economic sector, it is an important national strategic issue and is so sensitive for households and businesses that fiscal policy cannot avert the need for additional spending in such an extreme situation. Moreover, experience shows that the required rapidity of the response may lead to significant additional expenditure in the short term, while the room for manoeuvre for fiscal policy is very limited over this time horizon, and it is difficult to find a counterbalance in the form of tax increases or expenditure cuts.

Developments in the financial markets in 2022-2023 showed that the period of negative, extremely low interest rates had ended for an unpredictable period. The previous state of grace may have sent the dangerous message to fiscal policymakers that spending could be unlimited, as the cost of additional debt was almost minimal.

While the EU and national fiscal rules limit this approach, in the Covid period, extremely high budget deficits and low interest rates coexisted hand in hand. Later, however, the traditional correlation was restored. Inflation started to pick up and central banks were forced to raise interest rates to previously unanticipated levels. As a result, government bond market interest rates also started to rise and some countries already experienced dramatically higher interest expenditure. Although market interest rates had not returned to their pre-2022 low levels, by 2023 the situation had been somewhat normalised. However, events in 2022-2023 show that, especially in countries where the debt-to-GDP ratio is already in the 60-75% range, fiscal policy should aim for further debt reduction.

While the increase in defence spending in 2022 is barely detectable, it is almost certain that in the coming years there will be major increases in this area. The share of defence spending in budget expenditure will almost certainly increase for most CEEC (Astrov et al., 2022, p. 374). While spending will be delayed, together with the substantial operating costs, it could make an impact on fiscal policy space for decades.

Although not directly related to the war, in the coming decades the additional expenditure associated with the climate crisis and the expenditure-increasing effects of ageing populations will also reduce the room for manoeuvring for fiscal policy. The European Commission's 2022 report specifically points out that countries in the CEE region are particularly vulnerable to the effects of the climate crisis (European Commission, 2022, p. 171).

An additional risk factor could be the share of Ukrainian reconstruction costs (see Chapter 10) to be allocated to CEEC. The third study on this subject, led by the World Bank, puts the expected cost of reconstruction at nearly USD 500 billion (The World Bank, 2024).

Given that the continuation of the war is increasing these costs day by day and that the end of the war is not in sight, these costs will certainly continue to increase. In the short term (1-1.5 years), reconstruction costs are certainly not expected to show up in the budget even if the war was to end within weeks. It would certainly take longer to spread the financing burden, to raise funds, to plan, to prepare, to select suppliers, and to start the actual work. Astrov et al. (2022, p. 367) suggest that Ukraine should have access to EU funds in the same way as if it was a full member. This proposal has several risks. In EU budgetary matters, even one country may have veto power, which proved to be a problem in December 2023, when Hungary vetoed the EUR 50 billion aid package for Ukraine (Hungary withdrew its veto in February 2024). The normal EU budget allocation is also perhaps the most contentious among member states. It is not necessarily expected that when such large sums are involved, and the pockets of previously net beneficiary member states are affected, this bargaining process will be an easy ride.

In addition, several issues are still unclear concerning the USD 500 billion. The most important ones: How much will non-EU countries contribute? How much of the burden will fall on businesses? What can Ukraine contribute from its own resources? How much can be financed from seized Russian assets? So far, the bulk of the vital financial and military support has been provided by European institutions, the US, and major Western European countries (UK, Germany, Denmark, and Norway). The Baltic countries, Poland, Czechia, and Slovakia have also provided substantial support in relation to their own economic strength, but the bulk of the resources has not come from CEEC (Statista, 2024).

In subsequent resource allocation debates, countries in the region may argue that they were already more affected by the economic consequences of the war because of their geographical proximity.

Over the past two years, EU institutions have provided more than 80 billion euros for Ukraine's defence and economic efforts (Statista, 2024). If either the war or reconstruction takes a similar toll on the EU budget in the longer term, there may sooner or later be a serious rethinking of resource allocation. In this case, if net contributors are unwilling to take on more of the burden, countries in the region could find themselves with less EU funding. It would be very difficult to restructure the current resource allocation for the 2021-2027 period, but in the next financial period EU funds could be reallocated from the catching up CEE countries.

EU funds improve the budgetary situation both directly and indirectly. This was clearly the case for the Hungarian economic policy and fiscal effects in 2007-2013, as shown in a 2017 study by KPMG-GKI (KPMG-GKI, 2017). A significant reduction in EU funding would therefore also pose a serious challenge for fiscal policy makers in CEEC.

5.11 Conclusion and Policy Recommendations

Despite the warning signs, no one was prepared for the unexpected outbreak of the Russian-Ukrainian war in February 2022. Weeks or months of the outbreak of the war, it was impossible to assess the expected economic consequences and their impact on the fiscal situation.

Contrary to initial expectations, direct macroeconomic effects were more moderate. In 2022, economic growth declined compared to the rapid post-Covid bounce-back but was broadly in line with an average year of growth in almost all CEEC. Amplifying the effects of the previous loose fiscal and monetary policy under Covid, a sharp surge in energy and food prices led to an unprecedented rise in inflation and interest rates. Primarily due to the soaring energy bill, external balances also deteriorated dangerously in many countries. Indirectly, all these factors had already significantly reduced growth by 2023 and pushed the most affected countries into recession. In addition to direct effects, in several areas the war also had indirect effects on the fiscal situation.

The impact of the war on budget revenues was moderate. Expenditure tended to decline relative to GDP, contrary to possible preliminary expectations. The largest direct expenditure increase was to cushion the impact of energy price increases, but the impact of rising market interest rates on government interest expenditure is already clearly visible, especially in 2023. It appears that the expenditure savings enabled by the Covid epidemic, which was fortunately already receding in 2022, have been used to offset these surpluses. However, the direct and almost immediate expenditure-increasing effect of the energy price hike has made it even clearer that the energy policies of the countries in the region need to accelerate the shift away from Russian sources, diversify energy supplies, and switch to green energy, whose prices are much less exposed to international conflicts. Contrary to preliminary expectations, even the budgets of the most directly affected countries have not been hit by the cost of caring for refugees from Ukraine, and in some countries defence spending has barely increased.

Due to the suspension of the EU's fiscal rules in 2020, in 2022-2023 only national fiscal rules and common sense limited the room for fiscal policy spending. In 2022-2023, fiscal policy in some countries made noticeable use of this opportunity for electoral spending (Poland, Hungary, and Slovakia).

Despite the war, the budget deficit showed a marked downward trend in 2022. However, in 2023 the trend is no longer consistent in the region. Most countries, however, still had public deficits above 3%, which, under the old/new fiscal rules that will come into force again in 2024, foreshadows the launch of the Excessive Deficit Procedure (EDP) for them in 2024. This, in turn, is likely to lead to faster fiscal consolidation given that under the EDP procedure, the countries concerned will generally face a 50-150 basis point higher financing cost (Kalan, Popescu & Reynaud, 2018, p. 17).

The more moderate direct impact of the war is reflected in the fact that debt levels in the region actually declined in 2022 and did not show any appreciable increase in 2023, despite interest rate hikes and weaker economic growth.

Nevertheless, there are instructive developments in the financing conditions. Although the debt-to-GDP ratios in the countries of the region are all below the EU average, and only four countries are above 60%, it cannot be argued that there are no financing and interest rate risks in the most indebted countries. It is clear that countries that have already entered the euro area can finance themselves at lower interest rates over longer maturities, have better credit ratings, and do not run foreign exchange risks. These positive effects also improve the financing conditions for the business sector, improving growth prospects. On top of this, they can also take advantage of the ECB's special government bond purchase facilities, which further reduces their funding risk and increases the confidence the market placed in them. By contrast, without the environment provided by the ECB, member states that have not yet joined the euro area are much more vulnerable. Against this background, from a fiscal risk perspective, it would clearly be in the interest of all CEEC to join the euro area.[6]

Paradoxically, in a situation of market stress, it is precisely those euro area countries that are much less in need of help that the ECB helps. It is for these exact reasons, however, that a possibility could be developed to allow non-euro area member states to benefit from ECB assistance in times of international financial market stresses that are clearly independent of the economic policies of the member states concerned. The 2022-2023 period could be a good example, when the energy price boom and

---

[6] Naturally, the decision to enter the euro area can be considered within a much broader framework. Here we have only explored aspects of the risk of fiscal financing. Other factors could well make a very clear case against joining.

the international market interest rate hikes were not due to irresponsible economic policies of individual countries. In this case, the Eurosystem could also be used by countries that have not yet joined the euro area. This option could increase the financial stability of the EU as a whole, without creating an additional burden at the EU or ECB level, but its mere existence would increase the financial stability of the countries concerned and the confidence placed in them.

Contrary to initial fears, the war did not shatter the fiscal situation of the CEEC, nor did it create unmanageable financing tensions, but it did pose a serious challenge to fiscal policymakers. Adjustments were needed in a number of areas. It is not yet safe to sit back and assume that no problems are to be expected. The war is still going on and it is impossible to predict what dangers we may still face. Following the principles of fiscal prudence will certainly help whatever challenges a fiscal decision-maker may face.

Acknowledgements In memory of József Thuma.

References

Almazán-Gómez, M. Á., Llano, C., Pérez, J. & Rauhut, D. (2023). Socioeconomic impacts of Russian invasion of Ukraine: A multiregional assessment for Europe. *Journal of Regional Science*. Retrieved from https://doi.org/10.1111/jors.12676

Arnold, N. G., Balakrishnan, R., Barkbu, B. B., Davoodi, H. R., Lagerborg, A., Lam, W. R., . . . Roehler, C. (2022). *Reforming the EU fiscal framework: Strengthening the fiscal rules and institutions*. International Monetary Fund.

Astrov, V., Ghodsi, M., Grieveson, R., Holzner, M., Kochnev, A., Landesmann, M., . . . Bykova, A. (2022). Russia's invasion of Ukraine: assessment of the humanitarian, economic, and fnancial impact in the short and medium term. *International Economics and Economic*, *19*, 331-381. Retrieved from https://link.springer.com/article/10.1007/s10368-022-00546-5

Blanchard, O., Leandro, A. & Zettelmeyer, J. (2021). Redesigning EU fiscal rules: From rules to standards. *Economic Policy*, *36*(106), 195–236.

Carnot, N. & De Castro, F. (2015). *The discretionary fiscal effort: an assessment of fiscal policy and its output effect.* European Commision. Retrieved from https://ec.europa.eu/economy_finance/publications/economic_paper/2015/pdf/ecp543_en.pdf

Davoodi, H., Elger, P., Fotiou, A., Garcia-Macia, M. D., Han, X., Lagerborg, A., . . . Medas, P. A. (2022). *Fiscal rules and fiscal councils: Recent trends and performance during the covid-19 pandemic* (Working Paper). Washington, D.C.: International Monetary Fund. https://www.imf.org/en/Publications/WP/Issues/2022/01/21/Fiscal-Rules-and-Fiscal-Councils-512128.

ECB. (2024, Jan). *Key ECB interest rates.* Retrieved from https://www.ecb.europa.eu/stats/policy_and_exchange_rates/key_ecb_interest_rates/html/index.en.html

European Commission. (2021). *European Economic Forecast.* https://economy-finance.ec.europa.eu/document/download/5dc6af22-3724-4767-a142-93d6aaca8255_en?filename=ip160_en.pdf. The European Commission.

European Commission. (2022). *Fiscal Sustainability Report 2021.* https://economy-finance.ec.europa.eu/document/download/3ce5dd16-d909-4a21-870a-aa3b1e893580_en?filename=dp171_en_vol1.pdf. The European Commission.

European Commission. (2023a). *The 2023 Stability & Convergence Programmes.* https://economy-finance.ec.europa.eu/document/download/93afdd65-d376-4a8d-bf0f-a12264709814_en?filename=ip253_en.pdf. The European Commission.

European Commission. (2023b). *Annual Report on Taxation 2023.* https://taxation-customs.ec.europa.eu/document/download/283669ce-33aa-49dc-ba2e-fd8d669a4482_en?filename=ART%20-%20Report%202023_Digital%20Version_1.pdf. The European Commission.

European Commission. (2023c). *Debt Sustainability Monitor 2022.* https://economy-finance.ec.europa.eu/document/download/efcd41eb-16dd-4fac-bb9e-d01456b1ef6a_en?filename=ip199_en_UPD.pdf. The European Commission.

European Commission. (2023d). *European Economic Forecast.* https://economy-finance.ec.europa.eu/document/download/4139ef72-9eb3-4fad-a116-ee87979f4d35_en?filename=ip258_en.pdf. The European Commission.

European Commission. (2023e). *European Economic Forecast, Autumn 2023.* https://economy-finance.ec.europa.eu/document/download/4139ef72-9eb3-4fad-a116-ee87979f4d35_en?filename=ip258_en.pdf. The European Commission Institutional Paper 258.

European Fiscal Board. (2023). *Annual Report 2023.* https://commission.europa.eu/document/download/59a7ea98-4501-4a5f-8705-b12562daf726_en?filename=EFB-2023-Annual-Report_final_en.pdf. The European Commission.

Eurostat Data Browser. (2024a). *EMU convergence criterion series - quarterly data.* Retrieved from https://ec.europa.eu/eurostat/databrowser/view/irt_lt_mcby_q__custom_10239161/default/table?lang=en (Accessed: 05-03-2024)

Eurostat Data Browser. (2024b). *General government expenditure by function (COFOG).* Retrieved from https://ec.europa.eu/eurostat/databrowser/view/gov_10a_exp__custom_10280251/default/table?lang=en (Accessed: 07-03-2024)

Genschel, P., Leek, L. & Weyns, J. (2023). War and integration. The Russian attack on Ukraine and the institutional development of the EU. *Journal of European Integration*, *45*(3), 343–360.

Kalan, F. D., Popescu, M. A. & Reynaud, J. (2018). *Thou shalt not breach: the impact on sovereign spreads of noncomplying with the EU fiscal rules.* International Monetary Fund.

Kelemen, R. D. & Kathleen, R. M. (2022). State-Building and the European Union:

Markets, War, and Europe's Uneven Political Development. *Comparative Political Studies*, *55*(6), 963–991.

Király, J., Csontó, B., Jankovics, L. & Mérő, K. (2022). Monetary, macroprudential, and fiscal policy. In *Emerging European Economies after the Pandemic: Stuck in the Middle Income Trap?* (pp. 255–324). Springer. https://link.springer.com/book/10.1007/978-3-030-93963-2.

KPMG-GKI. (2017). *A magyarországi európai uniós források felhasználásának és hatásainak elemzése a 2007-2013-as programozási időszak vonatkozásában Makrogazdasági elemzések összefoglalása.* Retrieved from https://archive.palyazat.gov.hu//magyarorszagi_europai_unios_forrasok_elemzese#

Krassen, Nikolov. (2024). *Bulgaria has real chance of entering eurozone in 2025.* Retrieved from https://www.euractiv.com/section/politics/news/bulgaria-has-real-chance-of-entering-eurozone-in-2025/ (Accessed: 07-03-2024)

Larch, M., Busse, M., Gabrijelcic, M., Jankovics, L. & Malzubris, J. (2022). Assessment of the EU's fiscal framework and the way forward: Persisting tensions between risk reduction and risk sharing. *Bruges European Economic Research Papers*(42).

Liadze, I., Macchiarelli, C., Mortimer-Lee, P. & Sanchez Juanino, P. (2023). Economic costs of the Russia-Ukraine war. *The World Economy*, *46*(4), 874–886.

Mathieu, P. & Oliver, N. (2022). *France plants seed for joint EU borrowing scheme to absorb sanctions effects.* https://www.euractiv.com/section/economy-jobs/news/france-plants-seed-for-joint-eu-borrowing-scheme-to-absorb-sanctions-effects/. Euroactive.

Moody's. (2024a). *Moody's Research.* Retrieved from https://www.moodys.com/credit-ratings/Czech-Republic-Government-of-credit-rating-218505?cy=can (Accessed: 10-03-2024)

Moody's. (2024b). *Moody's Research.* Retrieved from https://www.moodys.com/credit-ratings/Slovakia-Government-of-credit-rating-600011880?lang=en&cy=can (Accessed: 10-03-2024)

Pisani-Ferry, J. (2022). The economic policy consequences of the war. *Bruegel-Blogs*.

Prohorovs, A. (2022). Russia's war in Ukraine: Consequences for European countries' businesses and economies. *Journal of Risk and Financial Management*, *15*(7), 295.

Radu, D. (2023). *Domestic Medium-Term Budgetary Frameworks in the EU: Fit for Purpose and for the Future?* (Tech. Rep.). Brussels: Directorate General Economic and Financial Affairs (DG ECFIN), European .... https://economy-finance.ec.europa.eu/document/download/8973cfb2-be92-41a3-a252-5209f0161a3a_en?filename=dp189_en.pdf.

Roubini, N. (2022, Mar). *Russia's war and the global economy.* Retrieved from https://www.project-syndicate.org/onpoint/russias-war-and-the-global-economy-by-nouriel-roubini-2022-02

Smit, S., Hirt, M., Buehler, K., White, O., Greenberg, E., Mysore, M., ... Chewning, E. (2022). *War in Ukraine: Lives and livelihoods, lost and disrupted.* McKinsey & Company. Retrieved from https://www.mckinsey.com/capabilities/strategy-and-corporate-finance/

our-insights/war-in-ukraine-lives-and-livelihoods-lost-and-disrupted

S&P. (2024). *S&P Sovereign Ratings History.* Retrieved from https://www.spglobal.com/ratings/en/research/articles/231207-sovereign-ratings-history-12938172 (Accessed: 10-03-2024)

Statista. (2024). *Total bilateral aid commitments to Ukraine between January 24, 2022 and January 15, 2024, by donor and type.* Retrieved from https://www.statista.com/statistics/1303432/total-bilateral-aid-to-ukraine/ (Accessed: 10-03-2024)

The World Bank. (2024). *UKRAINE Third Rapid Damage and Needs Assessment (RDNA3) February 2022 – December 2023.* Retrieved from https://documents1.worldbank.org/curated/en/099021324115085807/pdf/P1801741bea12c012189ca16d95d8c2556a.pdf (Accessed: 10-03-2024)

Wyplosz, C. (2013). *Europe's quest for fiscal discipline - European Commission, Economic Paper 498.* Retrieved from https://ec.europa.eu/economy_finance/publications/economic_paper/2013/pdf/ecp498_en.pdf

Chapter 6
External Balances

Balázs Csontó and Jiaqian Chen

Abstract Following a stocktaking of the evolution of external balances between the Global Financial Crisis (GFC) and the war in Ukraine in the Central and Eastern European economies (CEEE), highlighting the large improvement in external flow and stock vulnerabilities, the chapter provides an overview of the impact of the external shocks stemming from the war in Ukraine on external balances in the region. First, the negative terms-of-trade shock stemming from surging energy prices led to a large deterioration in the current account balance in most CEE countries. Second, the tightening of external financial conditions was associated with capital outflows. The adjustment to the combined shock differed across CEE countries reflecting several factors, including differences in their monetary policy regime (members of the euro area and others) and policy preferences (degree of exchange rate flexibility in non-euro area countries), as well as their exposure to commodity prices. Going forward, the pre-war current account surpluses are unlikely to return in the medium term as the external position will be affected by population aging and investment needs related to economic convergence and digital and climate transition. Against this backdrop, fiscal and structural policies could help unlock investments, while the impact on the external position could be mitigated through the use of EU funds. Also, in order to maintain resilience to external shocks, it remains important to have adequate external buffers and conduct sound macroeconomic policies, especially for CEE countries that are not members of the euro area.

Balázs Csontó ✉
International Monetary Fund, Washington, DC, e-mail: bcsonto@imf.org
The views expressed in this paper are those of the author and do not necessarily represent the views of the IMF, its Executive Board, or IMF management.

Jiaqian Chen
International Monetary Fund, Washington, DC, e-mail: jchen@imf.org
The views expressed in this paper are those of the author and do not necessarily represent the views of the IMF, its Executive Board, or IMF management.

© The Author(s), under exclusive license to Springer Nature Switzerland AG 2024
L. Mátyás (ed.), *Central and Eastern European Economies and the War in Ukraine*, Contributions to Economics, https://doi.org/10.1007/978-3-031-61561-0_6

6.1 Introduction

The external position of the Central and Eastern European economies (CEEE) was affected by several global and domestic developments during the decades before the start of the war in Ukraine. Following the turbulent transition period in the early-1990s, most CEE countries embarked on a convergence path in the mid-1990s, characterized by rising trade, increasing integration into supply chains and international financial markets, and large foreign investments (IMF, 2010b). In the mid-2000s, against the backdrop of surging capital inflows on the back of both global and CEE-specific factors (e.g., EU membership), growth became increasingly driven by domestic demand, thereby giving rise to the emergence of elevated current account deficits and a sharp increase in external liabilities. In the wake of the Global Financial Crisis (GFC), the sudden stop in capital flows forced a large and prolonged adjustment in external balances, with the current account balance switching to surplus in several CEE countries in the 2010s, reflecting the combination of structural and cyclical factors. While the adjustment in the external position was needed to reduce vulnerabilities, there were some concerns around the impact of the decline in investments on potential growth. CNB Governor Miroslav Singer, for example, compared this to "a company with a perfect cash flow because of a lack of investment into research and development or new machinery" (E15, 2014).

The series of external shocks during the past two decades also highlighted the importance of sound policies and solid fundamentals. In the context of the GFC, Belka (2009) notes that "it is clear that at least some countries were not 'innocent bystanders' but that domestic policies had made them more vulnerable than others". Indeed, the post-GFC decline in external vulnerabilities, partly driven by the conduct of increasingly prudent fiscal policy, enhanced the resilience of CEE countries to external shocks, including the Taper Tantrum in 2013, the emerging market (EM) sell-off in 2018, or the pandemic shock in 2020. Also, six CEE countries are already members of the euro area, thereby benefiting from the safe haven status of the euro.

Nonetheless, the war in Ukraine affected the external position of the CEE countries via several channels. Most importantly, the surge in commodity prices implied a major negative terms-of-trade shock for the CEEE. In addition, the tightening of external financial conditions also affected the CEEE, including through increasing risk aversion in the immediate aftermath of the Russian invasion of Ukraine and monetary policy tightening in major advanced economies in response to the inflationary pressure in the remainder of 2022. Finally, in light of these shocks and elevated uncertainty around potential supply disruptions and the economic outlook, external demand also weakened.

Given the impact of surging commodity prices on imports, current account balances deteriorated significantly throughout the region, with the re-emergence of elevated deficits in some CEE countries following an extended period of modest deficits and surpluses. Higher energy prices also had a negative impact on corporate profitability and – combined with sharply increasing food prices – on households' net savings that was only partially offset by an improved fiscal balance in most CEE countries.

In light of the tightening of external financial conditions, most countries recorded portfolio outflows after the start of the war in Ukraine. At the same time, resilient foreign direct investment (FDI) inflows and stable or even increasing other investment flows provided support to the balance of payments in 2022. Nonetheless, the combined terms-of-trade and financial shock exerted a depreciation pressure on the currencies of inflation-targeting CEE countries (Czechia, Hungary, Poland, and Romania), triggering different responses across countries, including policy rate hikes and foreign exchange (FX) interventions. In addition to policy response, the impact of the negative external shock on the exchange rate was also mitigated by strong inflows of EU funds in some countries.

Specifically, the adjustment to the external shocks took place mostly through currency depreciation and policy rate hikes in Hungary and Poland. At the same time, the stability of the exchange rate was supported by the tightening cycle and foreign exchange (FX) interventions in Czechia and Romania, with the sizeable FX sales facilitated by the extraordinarily high level of reserves in the former.

Although current account balances improved in the CEEE on the back of lower commodity prices in 2023, the current account surpluses recorded during the pre-war decade are unlikely to return over the medium term. In addition to 'old' investment needs in the context of economic convergence, the external position will be affected by 'new' spending needs, including those related to climate and digital transformation. Moreover, CEE countries are facing significant challenges stemming from population aging that is exacerbated by net emigration in some cases. The re-emergence of current account deficits, however, is not a problem per se. To the extent the deficit reflects productive investments, it is a 'necessary' by-product in the context of economic convergence, and climate and digital transition.

Against this backdrop, structural policies could support investments needed to reinforce the convergence process and support the green and digital agenda, while fiscal policy should create space for investments in infrastructure and human capital, as well as incentives to foster the economic transformation. Also, the use of EU funds could mitigate the impact of high investment needs on the external position. Moreover, following the post-GFC improvement in external balances and reduction in external vulnerabilities, CEE countries weathered several external shocks well, highlighting the importance of strong fundamentals. Therefore, they should preserve and/or enhance their resilience to external shocks. This, however, also depends on policy frameworks. With six CEE countries already benefiting from the safe haven status of the euro and Bulgaria in the ERM-II, it remains important for inflation-targeting CEE countries to maintain an adequate level of FX reserves and keep external vulnerabilities contained via the conduct of sound macroeconomic policies while limiting the use of FX interventions to avoid a disorderly adjustment in the exchange rate.

In the first part of the chapter, we take stock of developments in the external position of the CEE countries during the pre-war period (Section 6.2), including the large post-GFC improvement in current account balances and its drivers from the perspective of trade and income (Section 6.2.1), the savings-investment gap (Section 6.2.2), its financing and implications for the net international investment position (NIIP) (Section 6.2.3), the evolution of real and nominal exchange rates (Section 6.2.4), and whether the external position was 'excessive' or in line with the 'equilibrium level'(Section 6.2.5). In the second part of the chapter, we provide an overview of the impact of external shocks stemming from the war in Ukraine (Section 6.3), including the change in the current account balance in light of the terms-of-trade shock (Section 6.3.1), the evolution of savings and investments (Section 6.3.2), capital flows against the backdrop of the tightening of external financial conditions (Section 6.3.3), as well as the exchange rate adjustment and the policy response to the external shocks (Section 6.3.4). Finally, Section 6.4 concludes.

6.2 External (Im)Balances Before the Start of the War in Ukraine

6.2.1 From Current Account Deficits to Surpluses

In general, the period between the GFC and the war in Ukraine was characterized by a large improvement in external positions compared with the pre-GFC external imbalances in most CEE countries. On average, the current account deficit was 0.1 percent of GDP between 2010 and 2021 down from 9.1 percent of GDP between 2004 and 2008 in the CEEE (Figure 6.1). Moreover, several CEE countries recorded current account surpluses during this period.

Notwithstanding differences across countries, the improvement in the current account balance in the wake of the GFC reflected the correction of previous imbalances. In countries with a pre-GFC boom in domestic demand fueled by capital inflows, the sudden stop in capital flows was associated by a sharp correction in economic activity and external balances. In the Baltics, for example, the cumulative improvement in the current account balance in 2009-10 was around 20 percent of GDP, with the large current account deficit turning into a surplus in 2009. Similarly, current account deficits contracted sharply in Hungary, Romania, Slovakia, and Slovenia. In countries with a sharp adjustment, the main driver tended to be the trade balance as imports collapsed (Figure 6.2). Indeed, Lane and Milesi-Ferretti (2011) note that the adjustment relied more on expenditure reduction than expenditure switching.

Against the backdrop of the rebalancing of growth from domestic demand to exports, there were modest deficits in most CEE countries and an increasing prevalence of deficits turning into surpluses (e.g., the Baltics and Hungary in 2010, Bulgaria and Croatia in 2011, Slovakia and Slovenia in 2012) between 2010 and 2012. Until the mid-2010s, domestic demand strengthened gradually on the back of improving private sector balance sheets and supportive policy measures in some cases, albeit with some setbacks (e.g., recession in Czechia and Slovenia in 2012-13 and Hungary in 2012 amid the euro area debt crisis). This, however, was coupled with continued strong export performance, supported by integration into German supply chains (e.g., Hungary, Slovakia), as well as idiosyncratic factors such as the positive impact of internal devaluation on competitiveness in the Baltics (IMF, 2010a). In addition to the trade balance, the primary and the secondary income balances also contributed to the improvement in the current account balance via several channels, including the

Fig. 6.1: Current account balance (percentage of GDP)
Data: Eurostat (2023a, 2023d), authors' calculations

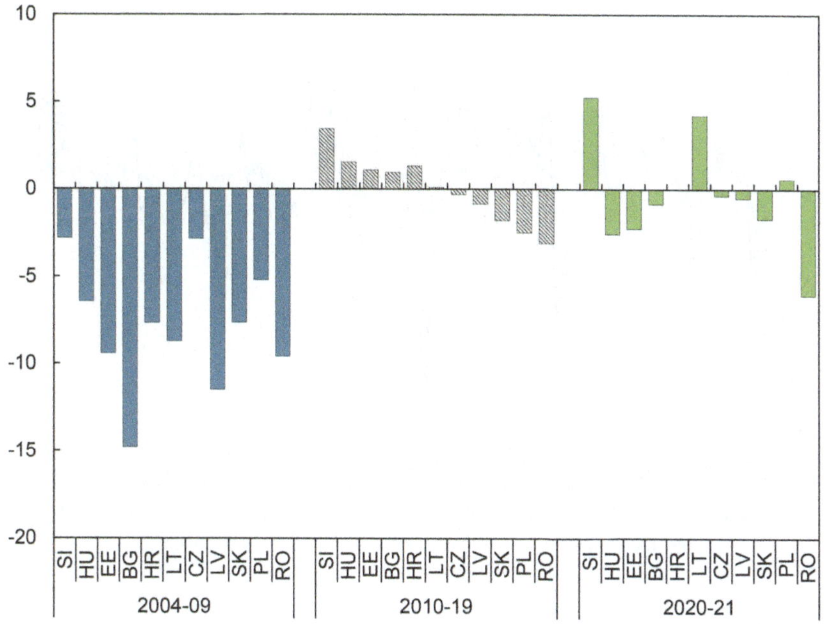

combination of low interest rates and declining external debt, lower profitability of foreign companies amid the ongoing recovery[1], and an increase in the absorption of EU funds (Figure 6.2).[2]

By the mid-2010s, the recovery from the GFC resumed, with output gaps closing throughout the region and current account balances peaking in most CEE countries. Between 2013 and 2019, Bulgaria, Croatia, Czechia, Estonia, Lithuania, Hungary, and Slovenia recorded current account surpluses for at least five out of seven years. This, combined with capital account surpluses, implied that most CEE countries had a positive net lending position vis-à-vis the rest of the world during this period.[3] Notwithstanding the recovery in imports against the backdrop of the strengthening of domestic demand (IMF, 2016a), the trade balance continued to have a strong contribution to improved current account balances, including on the back of an improvement in terms of trade due to the oil price shock in 2015 and a number of

[1] In some cases, the profitability of foreign firms was also affected by one-off factors. In Latvia, for example, the write-off of losses by foreign banks improved the income balance by around 6 percent of GDP in 2009 (IMF, 2010c).

[2] As they were only partially recorded in the current account, EU funds also contributed to an improvement in the capital account balance.

[3] The net lending position is the sum of the current and the capital account balances, with the latter dominated by EU funds in the CEEE.

Fig. 6.2: Net lending/borrowing: components, 2004-2021 (percentage of GDP)
Data: Eurostat (2023a, 2023d), authors' calculations

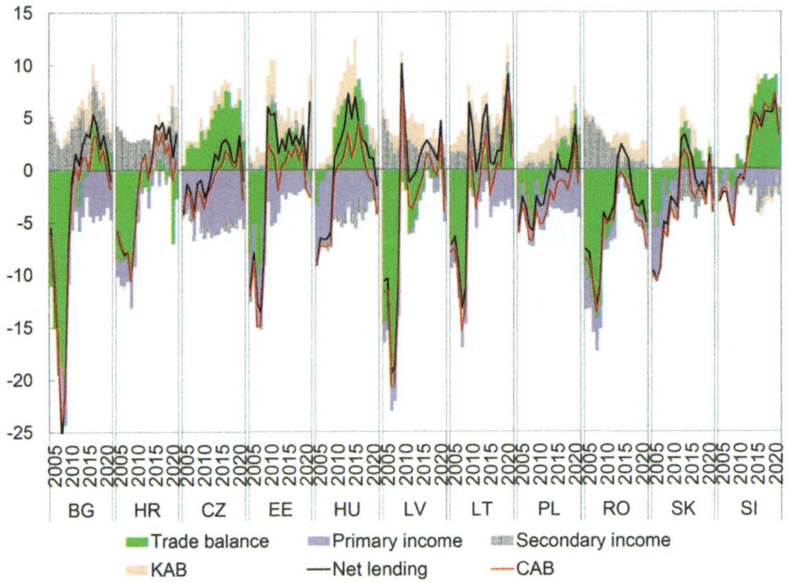

idiosyncratic factors.[4] At the same time, the income balance showed large variation across countries: while low interest rates and declining external debt helped keep interest payments contained and the secondary income balance continued to benefit from remittances and EU funds[5], the stronger cyclical position was associated with higher profitability of foreign companies.[6]

In the late-2010s, there were divergent developments in the region, with the current account balance stabilizing or improving in a few CEE countries (Croatia, Estonia, Lithuania, Poland, Slovenia), and gradually deteriorating in others (Czechia, Hungary,

[4] Among others, country-specific factors included the 2013 EU accession in Croatia (IMF, 2018b), strong services exports supported by reforms (e.g., the digitalization of government services) in Estonia (IMF, 2021d), the positive impact on exports of investments in the transport sector in Lithuania (IMF, 2019f), and strong integration into German supply chains in Slovakia and Slovenia (IMF, 2016d, 2017e).

[5] The latter, however, affected the capital account balance to an even larger extent in most countries, amounting to 2-3 percent of GDP in the mid-2010s.

[6] The primary income balance was also affected by one-off factors in a few countries. In Croatia, for example, the current account balance improved by 2 percent of GDP due to the one-off decline in profits of foreign-owned firms on the back of the conversion of Swiss franc loans in 2015 (IMF, 2016c), and was was boosted by one-off provisions of banks for losses related to the bankruptcy of Agrokor in 2017 (IMF, 2019d). Also, the current account balance was supported by the accounting of 'superdividends' in Estonia. Specifically, the profit repatriation of foreign firms in the form of 'discrete superdividend payments every few years' was recorded as negative FDI instead of an outflow in the current account, with its impact estimated at 2 percent of GDP in 2014 (IMF, 2015c).

Latvia, Romania, Slovakia). In Hungary and Romania, for example, the deterioration was close to 5 percent of GDP relative to its peak. In general, the deterioration was largely driven by increasing domestic demand on the back of pro-cyclical fiscal policy and tight labor markets, with signs of overheating in a few cases (IMF, 2019c). In addition, export performance was constrained by weaker external demand affecting vehicle production (e.g., Slovakia, IMF, 2019c) or the REER appreciation eroding competitiveness (Romania, IMF, 2019g).

In the early-2020s, the pandemic shock also led to divergent changes in the CEE countries. In 2020, the current account balance improved in six CEE countries, largely driven by the lower profit of foreign firms, falling consumption, and declining oil prices. This, however, was more than offset in five countries by the impact on exports of the decline in external demand and disruptions to supply chains. On average, the current account surplus reached its highest level since the GFC in the CEEE. As the recovery unfolded in 2021, current account balances deteriorated throughout the region, except for Croatia, with the average current account balance switching to the highest deficit since 2011.

6.2.2 Moderate Investments after the pre-GFC Boom

Compared with the pre-GFC period, the improvement in the external position in the 2010s took place against the backdrop of lower investments and higher savings across the region, with the former being the main driver (Figure 6.3). On average, the investment-to-GDP ratio declined by close to 7 percentage points during 2010-19 compared with the period of 2004-08, with the decline being the sharpest in countries that 'overinvested' before the GFC (IMF, 2015b).[7] In Latvia, for example, it fell from 37 percent of GDP between 2004-08 to 23 percent of GDP between 2010-19. In addition to lower investments, the post-GFC improvement in the external position was also driven by higher savings in some countries. In Bulgaria and Hungary, for example, savings increased by more than 5 percent of GDP during the post-GFC decade relative to the pre-GFC period. Notwithstanding differences across countries, the increase in the saving-investment gap was largely related to the private sector, especially non-financial corporations (Figure 6.4). These general developments in savings and investments in the 2010s, however, masked different trends in the early- and the late-2010s.

[7] Before the GFC, Estonia and Latvia recorded the highest investment rates in the region, exceeding 40 percent of GDP at their peak. Although Czechia and Slovenia also recorded sizeable investments, this was largely financed by domestic savings, thereby containing the current account deficit. While Hungary and Poland had the lowest investment rates, the low level of domestic savings contributed to elevated current account deficits in the former. There were also large differences across CEE countries in terms of sectoral positions. In Bulgaria, Estonia, Latvia, and Romania, elevated current account deficits were largely driven by the net borrowing position of households and non-financial corporations. In Croatia, Czechia, Hungary, Slovakia, and Slovenia, the current account deficit was largely related to net borrowing by non-financial corporations and the government, albeit to a different extent across countries.

Fig. 6.3: Savings and investments, 2004-2021 (percentage of GDP)
Data: Eurostat (2023a, 2023d), authors' calculations

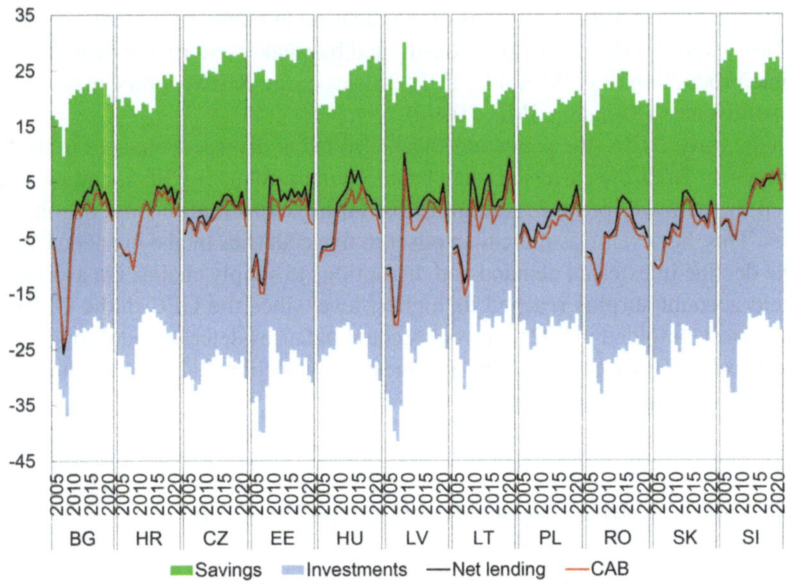

The relatively low level of investments during the 2010s reflected both cyclical and structural factors. In the aftermath of the GFC, the decline in investments was driven by bank deleveraging, the repair of private sector balance sheets, and uncertainty around the economic outlook. In addition to crisis legacies, investments were also affected by a structural shift in trend growth in the first half and middle of the 2010s. During this period, investments are estimated to have undershot the 'historical benchmark' (i.e., the level "consistent with the capital accumulation path of selected advanced European economies during 1951-2011 that has proven to be sustainable"), therefore higher investments seemed necessary to "get back on the fast convergence path" (IMF, 2016b).[8] In the second half of the 2010s, investments increased sharply in a few countries, partly related to the pick-up in the disbursement of EU funds.[9] This, however, was followed by a temporary decline in investments amid the pandemic-driven lockdown and uncertainty around the economic outlook in 2020.

Compared with the pre-GFC period, the savings rate also increased in several countries. In Bulgaria, Hungary, and Romania, for example, the savings-to-GDP

[8] At the same time, investments were broadly in line with the 'golden rule' defined as "a lower bound to which an investment rate in a country would eventually converge as it approaches its own steady state level underpinned by its deep structural characteristics and exogenous parameters" (IMF, 2016b).

[9] Croatia, for example, recorded an increase in investments from around 18 to 22 percent of GDP between the early- and late-2010s, partly related to Croatia's EU accession in 2013.

ratio increased by 6-7 percentage points by the mid-2010s relative to the pre-GFC period. In the second half of the 2010s, the savings rate stabilized in most CEE countries, with the notable exception of Croatia and Romania. In Croatia, the savings rate increased sharply in the second half of the 2010s, contributing to the current account surplus. In contrast, Romania witnessed a sharp decline in savings in the late-2010s, with a deterioration of the current account balance. In the early stage of the pandemic, savings remained broadly stable on average in the region, notwithstanding differences across countries. This was followed by decreasing savings across the region as consumption recovered.

From the perspective of sectoral positions, in the first half of the 2010s, non-financial corporations became net savers amid post-GFC deleveraging in most CEE countries, except for Czechia (and Estonia for a few years). Households also improved their net savings position in most countries on the back of suppressed consumption (IMF, 2016b). In comparison with other EU countries, however, the savings rate of households continued to be relatively low due to the higher share of consumption in household income and lower labor income share (IMF, 2016b). Similarly to the private sector, the public sector's net savings position also improved in most countries during this period, reflecting fiscal consolidation efforts, including the unwinding of counter-cyclical fiscal policy during the GFC.[10] In the second half of the 2010s, however, fiscal positions deteriorated across the region, as the loosening of fiscal policy was only partially offset by the cyclical upswing. Also, the net savings position of non-financial corporations worsened slightly as investment activity strengthened. During the first year of the pandemic, the large improvement in the net savings position of households and non-financial corporations was partially offset by the deterioration in the fiscal balance. Against the backdrop of the ensuing recovery in 2021, the net savings position of non-financial corporations and households fell but remained above the historical average in the case of the latter. This was partially offset by the declining, albeit still elevated, deficit of the general government.

6.2.3 Declining Overall External Vulnerabilities

Between the GFC and the war in Ukraine, the flip side of the improvement in the current account balance was the adjustment in capital inflows, albeit to a different

[10] In Slovenia, the one-off large deterioration related to the bank crisis in 2013 was followed by a continuous improvement until 2019.

Fig. 6.4: Net lending/borrowing by sectors, 2004-2021 (percentage of GDP)
Data: Eurostat (2023f, 2023d), authors' calculations

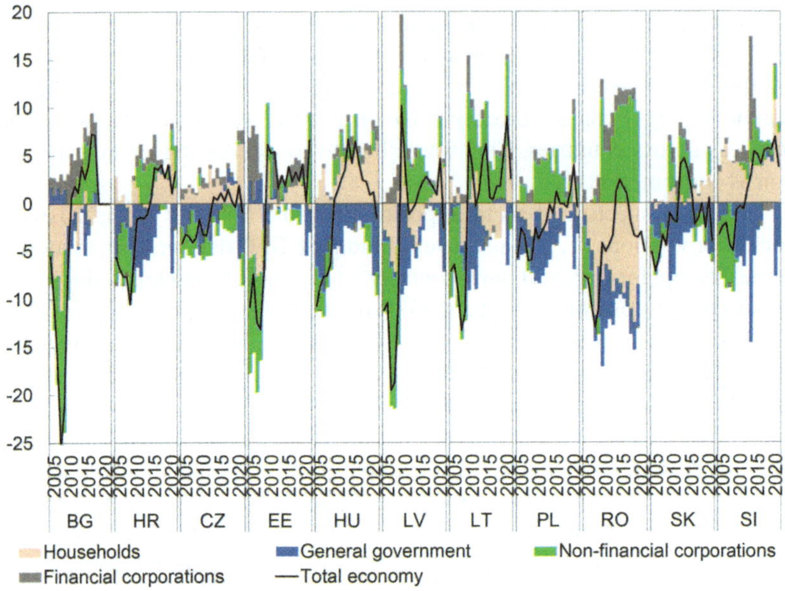

extent across countries and types of capital flows.[11] To some extent, this reflected a global phenomenon. Lane and Milesi-Ferretti (2018) note that the growth in cross-border positions relative to world GDP came to a halt after the GFC. They also highlight that in addition to the lower level of capital flows, their composition changed, with a reduction in cross-border banking given the shrinking balance sheets of many international banks, partially offset by rising portfolio flows on the back of increasing international bond issuances.[12]

[11] This followed the extraordinary surge in capital inflows before the GFC, supported by abundant global liquidity and low interest rates in advanced economies (IMF, 2010a), as well as CEE-specific factors such as good prospects associated with "new Europe" following the accession of the EU, progress on reform implementation, and accommodative domestic macro policies (Bakker & Gulde, 2010). Against this backdrop, emerging Europe recorded even higher capital inflows than most other EM regions (Abiad, Leigh & Mody, 2007). Bakker and Gulde (2010) point out that the size of cumulative capital inflows between 2003 and 2007, ranging from 33 percent of GDP in Czechia to 192 percent of GDP in Bulgaria, exceeded those before the Asian crisis. Abiad et al. (2007) also note that the flow of capital from the old to the new EU member states provided a counterexample to the global anomaly of 'uphill' flows from poor to rich countries known as the Lucas paradox (Lucas, 1990).

[12] In the early-2010s, a few CEE countries also relied on official financing from the European Commission and the IMF. Hungary and Latvia were the first CEE countries to enter a program with the IMF and the EU in November and December 2008, respectively. Shortly thereafter, Romania also entered into an agreement in May 2009 that was followed by two consecutive arrangements until 2015.

On the back of the changing pattern of capital flows and robust economic growth, there was a continuous improvement in the net international investment position (NIIP) relative to GDP in the 2010s (Figure 6.6). On average, net international investment liabilities decreased by 35 percent of GDP to 37 percent of GDP in the CEEE between 2009 and 2019, with the improvement close to 70 percent of GDP in Bulgaria and Hungary.[13] In general, this was primarily driven by a decline in other investment liabilities, reflecting the correction of pre-GFC imbalances, especially in the banking sector, as well as an increase in official reserve assets across the CEEE.

In most countries, the net FDI position remained broadly stable in the 2010s (Figure 6.6). Given the high degree of uncertainty around the region's outlook, FDI investors took a wait-and-see approach in the early-2010s, leading to moderate flows compared with the pre-GFC period (IMF, 2011).[14] Nonetheless, net FDI flows remained positive in the 2010s. In addition to cost competitiveness that made the region more attractive to foreign investors, Jirasavetakul and Rahman (2018) emphasize the role of the quality of labor and the provision of financial incentives, including tax holidays, investment credit and allowances, as well as VAT exemptions for imports, property assistance, guaranteed cheap finance, and training of labor. They also note that the composition of FDI inflows changed, with inflows into services shifting from the financial sector towards trade, transport and communications. Jirasavetakul and Rahman (2018) also highlight an increase in outward FDI in some CEE countries, especially Czechia and Hungary, potentially attributed to the "industrial upgrading by companies headquartered in these countries who are outsourcing parts of production to pursue cost efficiency" ('flying geese syndrome'), and/or "transitory capital from a third country that simply passes through" a CEE intermediary.

Net portfolio liabilities showed different patterns across countries, recording an increase in a few CEE countries (Croatia, Czechia, Romania) and a decrease elsewhere (Hungary). In general, portfolio flows continued to be largely driven by global factors, with strong capital inflows in the region throughout the decade amid abundant global liquidity and the search-for-yield environment. This, however, was interrupted several times by external shocks such as the euro area crisis in 2010-12, the Taper Tantrum in 2013, the EM market sell-off in 2018, or the Covid-19 pandemic in 2020, leading to temporary outflows (Figure 6.5). The pandemic, for example, was characterized by "an unprecedented sharp reversal of portfolio flows" (IMF, 2020), with portfolio bond

---

[13] In contrast, the pre-GFC period was characterized by the buildup of sizeable stock vulnerabilities. Between 2004 and 2009, the NIIP deteriorated by close to 30 percentage points to around 70 percent of GDP on average in the CEEE. While foreign liabilities were predominantly FDI liabilities in most CEE countries, there were also sizeable other investment liabilities in countries with large foreign bank funding (the Baltics, Croatia, Hungary, Romania, Slovenia), and non-trivial portfolio liabilities in Hungary and Poland.

[14] The high pre-GFC level of FDI inflows was the result of several factors. For example, Bruno, Campos, Estrin and Tian (2016) estimate that the EU membership boosted FDI inflows by 14-38 percent. Jirasavetakul and Rahman (2018) note that foreign investors were aiming to exploit lower wages in the manufacturing sector, as well as to access new markets, especially in the services sector. An example for the former is the sub-group of CEE countries (e.g., Hungary, Slovakia) where the integration into the German supply chain, especially in the automotive sector, resulted in the more balanced distribution of FDI between tradable and nontradable sectors.

and equity outflows reaching USD 4.7 billion and USD 0.4 billion, respectively, in the CEEE in March 2020 (EPFR, 2023). These episodes also highlighted the importance of country-specific fundamentals as investors tended to differentiate across countries. In addition to external financial conditions, other factors also played a role in driving portfolio flows. In Hungary, for example, capital outflows reflected the deliberate reduction in external debt, with bond repayments exceeding new issuances in the mid-2010s.

Fig. 6.5: Bond and equity flows in the CEEE, 2010-2021 (monthly, millions of USD)
Data: EPFR (2023), authors' calculations

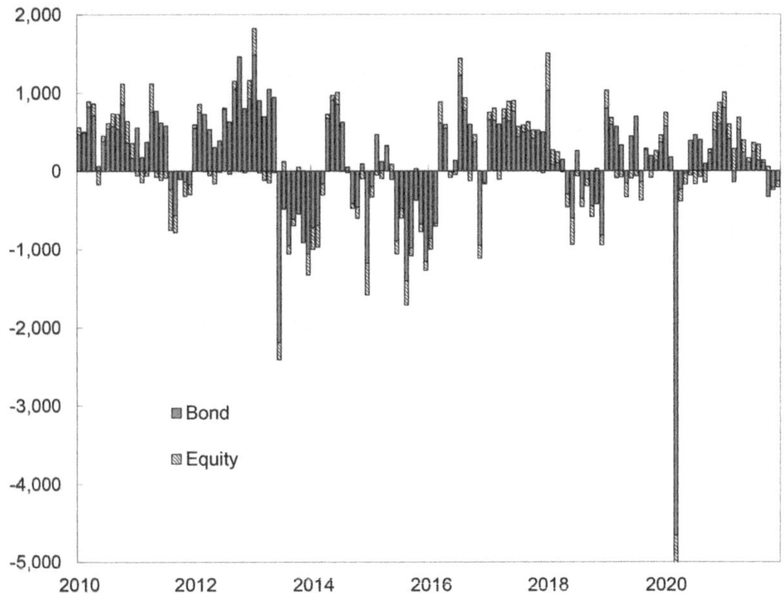

The decline in other investment liabilities reflected the sharp reversal in other investment flows in the context of the correction of significant pre-GFC imbalances. Specifically, annual net outflows exceeded 3 percent of GDP in the first half of the 2010s following an average annual inflow of close to 7 percent of GDP between 2004 and 2008. The largest reversal took place in countries with the highest pre-GFC reliance on bank funding (IMF, 2010b),[15] with more than half of the increase in

[15] Before the GFC, the credit and asset price boom was fueled by surging capital inflows in the banking sector in a few countries (IMF, 2010a). In the Baltics, for example, domestic banks, with significant financing from their Nordic parents in the aftermath of the EU membership, fueled the credit boom and economic overheating, especially in Estonia and Latvia (Purfield & Rosenberg, 2010). In addition to the pace of credit growth, another source of vulnerability emerged in the form of FX borrowing by unhedged households and firms throughout the region, except for Czechia, Poland, and Slovakia. Rosenberg and Tirpák (2008) find that borrowing in FX was primarily driven by interest rate differential and the size of external financing in the banking sector.

foreign funding-to-GDP ratio during 2003-08 unwound in two waves during 2008-12 in the broader region (IMF, 2013).[16] Between September 2008 (i.e., the collapse of Lehman Brothers) and mid-2010, the financing of regional banks by their Western parents dried up, especially in countries with a foreign-financed credit-driven growth model before the GFC (e.g., the Baltics). Nonetheless, the decline in foreign financing was mitigated by international coordination, including the Vienna Initiative aiming to "prevent a large-scale and uncoordinated withdrawal of cross-border bank groups from the region" and "Ensure that parent bank groups maintain their exposures and recapitalise their subsidiaries in emerging Europe".(Vienna Initiative, 2022a) Second, there was pressure on bank funding in mid-2011 amid the euro area crisis and the tightening of regulatory standards (e.g., Basel III) (Impavido, Rudolph & Ruggerone, 2013). Against the backdrop of a significant decline in funding, exceeding 10 percent of GDP in Estonia, Hungary, and Slovenia, the Vienna Initiative was renewed in January 2012 (IMF, 2013; Vienna Initiative, 2022b).[17] During the remainder of the decade, other investment flows normalized but remained below the pre-GFC level.

Fig. 6.6: Net international investment position: components, 2004-2021 (percentage of GDP)
Data: Eurostat (2023e, 2023d); Milesi-Ferretti (2022), authors' calculations

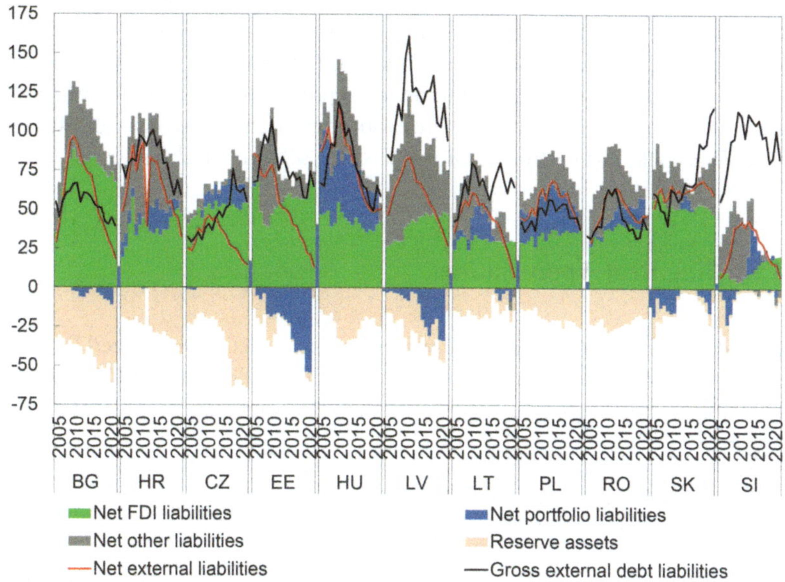

[16] Vogel and Winkler (2016) find that a higher foreign bank presence was associated with more stable cross-border bank flows.

[17] In addition to external developments, some idiosyncratic factors also contributed to outflows. In Hungary, for example, the conversion of CHF-loans led to a decline in banks' foreign liabilities and FX reserves.

In the 2010s, the increase in international reserves was supported by several factors, including the improvement in the current account balance, the favorable external environment, and the increasing absorption of EU funds.[18] In addition to general developments, it is worth highlighting the case of Czechia. In order to prevent an excessive appreciation of the koruna and the deepening of deflation in the face of hitting the 'technical zero', the CNB operated an exchange rate floor (CKZ/EUR of 27) between November 2013 and April 2017.[19] Against this backdrop, reserves increased by 40 percent of GDP between 2009 and 2019, exceeding 300 percent of the IMF's reserve adequacy (ARA) metric well above the adequate range of 100-150 percent (Figure 6.7). During the pandemic, the allocation of Special Drawing Rights (SDRs) by the IMF provided a further boost to reserves in August 2021 throughout the region (IMF, 2021). In Czechia, for example, the allocation of SDR2.09 billion increased reserves by 1.1 percent of GDP or 0.2 month of imports (IMF, 2022b). Following the post-GFC decade of improved external positions, reserves were within the adequate range according to the ARA metric at the start of the war in Ukraine, leaving the non-euro area CEE countries more resilient to the shock than at the onset of the GFC (Figure 6.7).

The large improvement in the current account balance, the decline in net external liabilities, and the increase in international reserves implied a reduction in overall external vulnerabilities in the CEEE (Figure 6.8).[20] At the same time, gross stock vulnerabilities increased in some countries, including a sharp increase in gross external liabilities in most countries and gross external debt in a few countries, especially starting in the late-2010s.[21] This could increase the region's exposure to external shocks, as gross flows tend to be more pro-cyclical than net flows, making them a better indicator of financial vulnerabilities (Lane & Milesi-Ferretti, 2007; Forbes & Warnock, 2011; Broner, Didier, Erce & Schmukler, 2013).

6.2.4 Stalling Real Appreciation

The period between the GFC and the war in Ukraine was characterized by broadly stable real exchange rates across CEE countries, following the pre-GFC period of steady real appreciation (Figure 6.9).[22] Although the combination of elevated current

[18] When discussing reserves, we focus on non-euro area CEE countries.

[19] As argued by Lízal and Schwarz (2013), "foreign exchange interventions represent a meaningful monetary policy tool for small open economies not facing serious liquidity problems" when facing the zero lower bound.

[20] Ahuja, Syed and Wiseman (2017) and the IMF (2021b) show that vulnerability to sudden stops is indicated by the current account balance, the degree of real effective exchange rate (REER) misalignment, the level of external debt (especially private debt) relative to exports, and reserves.

[21] In Hungary, gross external debt unadjusted for special purpose entities (SPEs) is significantly higher. This, however, distorts the picture as SPEs "typically perform a financial intermediary function" instead of real economic activity in the country (Koroknai & Lénárt-Odorán, 2011).

[22] Unless otherwise indicated, the chapter discusses real exchange rates based on consumer price indices (CPI).

Fig. 6.7: International reserves, 2004-2021 (percentage of ARA metric)
Data: IMF (2023b)
Note: The Assessing Reserve Adequacy (ARA) metric compares the level of reserves to a set of indicators, including short-term debt, medium- and long-term debt and equity liabilities, broad money, and export earnings (IMF, 2015a).

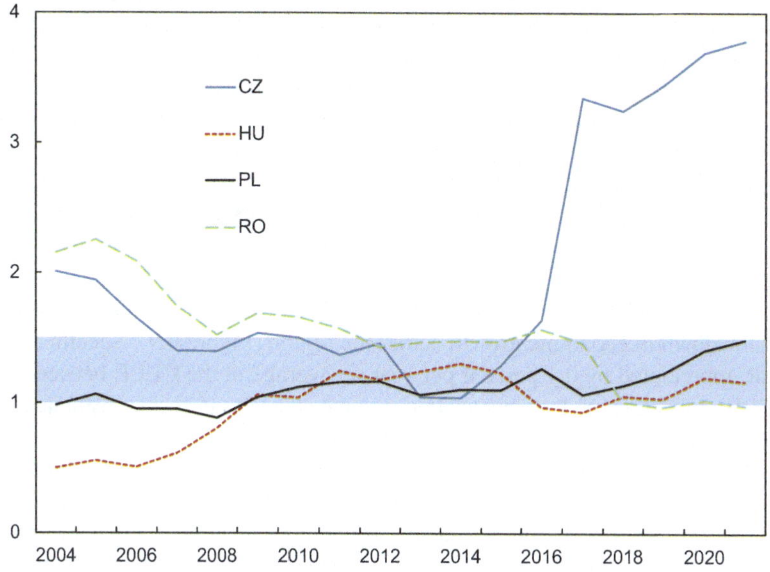

Fig. 6.8: External vulnerabilities in the CEEE (average)
Data: Eurostat (2023a, 2023e); Milesi-Ferretti (2022); Eurostat (2023d); IMF (2023b), authors' calculations

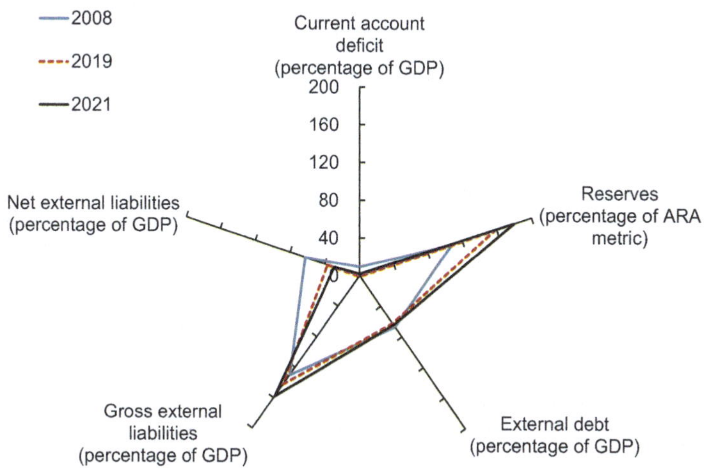

account deficits and real appreciation before the GFC, and modest current account balances and broadly stable real exchange rate during the pre-war period might suggest a causal relationship, with real appreciation causing a loss of external competitiveness, the picture is not so straightforward in catching-up economies: to the extent real appreciation is driven by higher productivity growth, it does not lead to a loss of competitiveness and thus a deterioration in the external balance. Specifically, as productivity gains lead to increasing real wages in the tradable sector and – assuming labor market mobility – in the nontradable sector, the relative price of nontradables increases and the price level converges to that in countries with higher productivity (Balassa-Samuelson hypothesis). This price convergence implies real appreciation via nominal appreciation and/or higher inflation. To explain the sharp appreciation of the real exchange rate during the pre-GFC period, a wide strand of papers focuses on the Balassa-Samuelson effect, finding evidence of productivity-driven real appreciation.[23] Nonetheless, there were also signs of excessive movements in the real exchange rate in a few cases.[24]

During the 2010s, real exchange rates were broadly stable against the backdrop of a slowdown in economic growth across the region (Figure 6.9). Specifically, the REER appreciated by 0.1 percent per year on average in the CEEE between 2010 and 2019, reflecting modest appreciation in some countries (Czechia, Estonia, Latvia, Lithuania, Slovakia, and Slovenia) and depreciation in others (Bulgaria, Croatia, Hungary, Poland, and Romania).[25] Żuk, Polgar, Savelin, del Hoyo and König (2018) show that convergence towards the EU average decelerated in the aftermath of the GFC, mostly due to slowing total factor productivity growth. In the context of the productivity puzzle, Gabrisch (2019) finds that slower productivity growth in the

[23] Several papers find evidence of such productivity-driven increase in the relative price of nontradables and the appreciation of the real exchange rate in the 1990s, notwithstanding differences in terms of the magnitude of the impact across papers (De Broeck & Sløk, 2001; Égert, Drine, Lommatzsch & Rault, 2003). Égert, Halpern and MacDonald (2005) also show that in addition to the Balassa-Samuelson effect, regulated price hikes and an inappropriate adjustment for the improving quality of products also contributed to the appreciation of the real exchange rate. Encompassing the period between the mid-1990s and early-2008, Mihaljek and Klau (2008) estimate that the Balassa-Samuelson effect contributed about 1.2 percentage point on average to inflation differential between CEEE and the euro area, ranging from 0.03 in Bulgaria to 4.6 percentage points in Lithuania. They also show that compared with the 1990s, the Balassa-Samuelson effect declined during 2002-2008 in Bulgaria, Croatia, Hungary, Latvia, and Slovakia, while it increased in Czechia, Estonia, Lithuania, Poland, and Slovenia.

[24] For example, imbalances were larger in countries with exchange rate pegs, namely the Baltics and Bulgaria (IMF, 2011), as they had less instruments to stop the credit boom. The IMF (2011) highlights the vicious circle of high wage growth and inflation amid economic overheating leading to decreasing real interest rates, thereby further boosting credit demand, as well as deteriorating tradable competitiveness. In the Baltics, this is also well-reflected in the significant appreciation of the REER based on unit labor costs (ULC) well exceeding the appreciation of the CPI-based REER, especially in Latvia (Figure 6.9). At the same time, floaters could use nominal appreciation to tighten monetary conditions, thereby keeping inflation low and real interest rates high.

[25] Overall, the ULC-based REER was also broadly stable in the CEEE, with an average annual appreciation of 1 percent during this period (Figure 6.9). This reflects appreciation of around 2-4 percent in the Baltics and Bulgaria, some modest strengthening in Czechia, Romania, and Slovakia, and depreciation in Croatia, Hungary, Poland, and Slovenia.

Fig. 6.9: Real effective exchange rates (annualized change, percentage)
Data: Eurostat (2024b, 2024a, 2024c), authors' calculations
Note: CPI and ULC refer to consumer price index and unit labor costs, respectively.

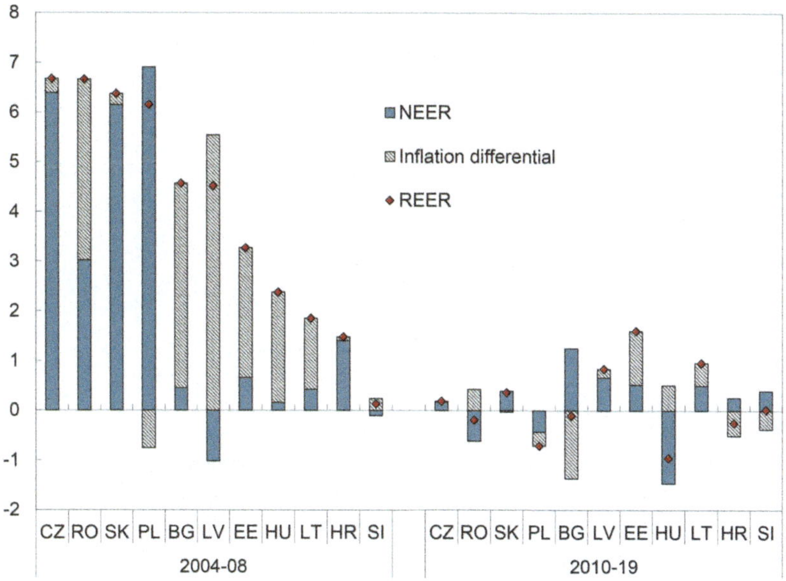

region was due to weaker external and domestic demand as opposed to "adverse technological progress".

In addition to the magnitude of changes in the real exchange rate, CEE countries also differed in terms of the relative importance of changes in the nominal exchange rate and inflation differential (Figure 6.9). Before the GFC, the real appreciation took the form of high inflation differential in countries with pegs (the Baltics, Bulgaria) and bands (Hungary), while there was a bigger reliance on nominal appreciation in others (Croatia, Czechia, Poland, Slovakia). In contrast, in addition to the broadly stable real exchange rate, the post-GFC was characterized by moderate inflation across CEE countries. Against this backdrop, there was no clear trend in the nominal exchange rate either. Hungary and Romania, however, provide an exception, as the exchange rate vis-à-vis the euro depreciated steadily throughout the decade (Figure 6.10). In the former, this was also coupled with the largest real depreciation in the region (Figure 6.9).

Among others, differences in the relative importance of inflation differential and changes in nominal exchange rates reflected the choice of the exchange rate regime. Specifically, following Slovakia and Slovenia, the Baltics also joined the euro area in the first half of the 2010s.[26] Similarly, Bulgaria was operating an exchange rate peg in

[26] Estonia, Latvia, and Lithuania adopted the euro in 2011, 2014, and 2015, respectively.

Fig. 6.10: Bilateral nominal exchange rates, 2004-2021 (cumulative change, percentage)
Data: Eurostat (2023c)

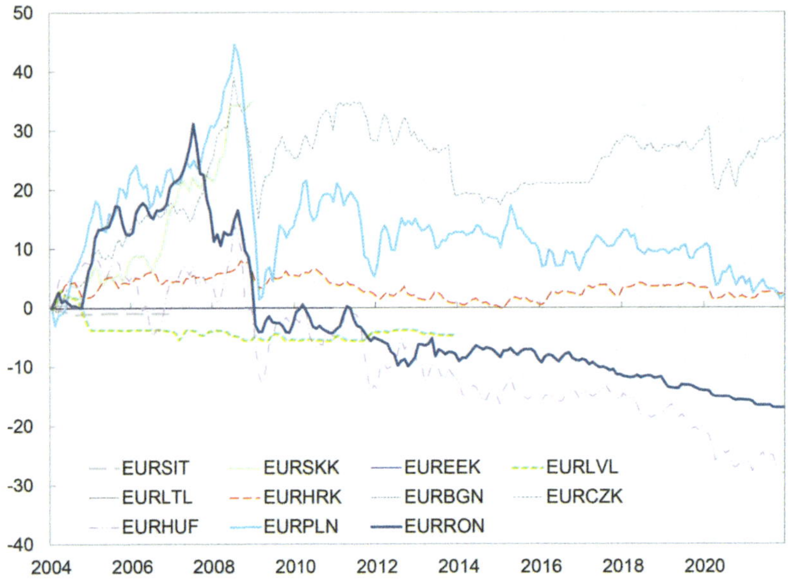

the form of currency board,[27] and Croatia used the exchange rate of the kuna vis-à-vis the euro as the nominal anchor for monetary policy.[28] Even across inflation-targeting CEE countries (Czechia, Hungary, Romania, Poland), there were differences in terms of the de facto exchange rate regime (IMF, 2023). In Hungary and Poland, the de facto exchange rate regime had been classified as a (free) floating arrangement since the GFC. At the same time, the floating regime was temporarily replaced by an exchange rate floor between 2013 and 2016 in Czechia,[29] and by a crawl-like system in 2016 and a stabilized arrangement in 2018 in Romania.[30]

The exchange rate regime affected the ability of CEE countries to respond to external shocks. In inflation-targeting CEE countries, FX intervention generally aimed at preventing disorderly market conditions during episodes of major external shocks, such as the Taper Tantrum in 2013 or the general EM sell-off in 2018. In addition,

---

[27] Bulgaria formally entered the ERM-II mechanism in July 2020.

[28] While the de jure arrangement was managed floating without a predetermined path, the classification of the de facto regime was switching between soft pegs (crawl-like, stabilized), and the residual category of other managed arrangements in the 2010s. Croatia entered the ERM-II mechanism in July 2020.

[29] The de facto regime was classified as other managed and stabilized arrangements during this period by IMF (2023b).

[30] Habermeier, Kokenyne, Veyrune and Anderson (2009) provide an overview of the classification of exchange rate arrangements.

changes in the policy rate were sometimes partly motivated by the evolution of the exchange rate. In Hungary and Poland, for example, the central bank emphasized the role of the pass-through of currency depreciation into inflation behind the policy rate hikes in 2011 and 2012.[31]

6.2.5 External Position: Excessive or Not?

In light of the large improvement in current account balances and the decline in the NIIP, was the external position of CEE countries excessive or not before the war in Ukraine? As Allen et al. (2023) note, "there are good reasons for countries to run current account surpluses or deficits, such as to smooth out the effects of temporary shocks, to save and accumulate assets to cover retirement needs, or to allow capital to flow to where it is scarcer and can have a higher rate of return". Standard theory predicts that in the absence of restrictions on trade and capital flows, capital should flow from richer to poorer countries as the marginal product of capital is higher in the capital-scarce poorer country.[32]. As such, the deficit of the current account could actually indicate the strength of the catching-up economy – that the country is undertaking investments during the convergence process. Similarly, the surplus of the current account might be a welcome development but could also be the result of insufficient investments. As noted by the IMF (2021g) for Poland, for example, the current account "surplus is deemed excessive given that income convergence is incomplete". In other words, neither the pre-GFC current account deficits nor the pre-war surpluses in the CEEE constitute a problem per se.

How can the 'appropriate' level of the current account balance be determined? A rule of thumb was provided by Lawrence Summers who famously argued in the aftermath of the Mexican crisis that "it is unlikely that any country can, over a long period of time, borrow more than 5 percent of its GNP annually unless it is growing at a very rapid rate" (Summers, 1996). Based on this 'rule', most CEE countries ran potentially unsustainable current account deficits before the GFC, while there was no reason for major concern during the period between the GFC and the war in Ukraine.

From the perspective of sustainability, the current account balance can be considered sustainable if it is consistent with a non-increasing ratio of net international investment liabilities to GDP.[33] Based on the evolution of NIIP, this implies unsustainable external positions before the GFC and sustainable positions after the GFC

[31] In November 2011 the MNB noted that "the depreciation of the forint in recent months is a threat to meeting the 3 per cent inflation target" (MNB, 2011), while in May 2012 the NBP explained that "elevated inflation will be driven by the previously observed weakening of the zloty and high commodity prices" (NBP, 2012).

[32] Lucas (1990) argues that "new investment will occur only in the poorer economy, and this will continue to be true until capital-labor ratios, and hence wages and capital returns, are equalized".

[33] In theory, the concept of solvency implies that "any path of the current account such that the infinite sum of all current accounts is equal to the initial foreign debt of the country is consistent with solvency" (Roubini & Wachtel, 1998).

throughout the region. A less stringent criterion is to run a current account balance that is consistent with a non-increasing external debt-to-GDP ratio, thereby taking into account both the level of the current account and the composition of its financing. This would imply that there is no reason for concern as long as the current account deficit is financed through non-debt generating capital inflows (e.g., FDI).

Another concept considers the equilibrium level of the current account balance on the basis of the drivers of savings and investments (see, for example, Chinn and Prasad (2003); Phillips et al. (2013); Coutinho, Turrini and Zeugner (2018); Cubeddu et al. (2019)), including cyclical factors (e.g., business cycle, commodity prices), macroeconomic and structural fundamentals (e.g., capital-labor ratio, NIIP position, demographics), and policies (e.g., fiscal policy) (Cubeddu et al., 2019). Based on the estimated relationship between the current account balance and its drivers, its excessive nature can be assessed by comparing its cyclically-adjusted level with the level of the current account balance consistent with medium-term fundamentals and desirable policies.

Despite the sharp improvement in the current account balance after the GFC, there was no sign of major overshooting in the CEEE during the first half of the 2010s.[34] In most CEE countries, external positions were assessed to be broadly in line with the level implied by medium-term fundamentals and policies. In other words, the significant post-GFC improvement in current account balances was broadly in line with cyclical developments, as well as changes in macroeconomic fundamentals and policies.

First, the improvement in the external position was largely driven by the cyclical downturn after the GFC. As discussed in Sections 6.2.1 and 6.2.2, this period was characterized by muted domestic demand amid the repair of private sector balance sheets and declining foreign bank funding, with the output gap staying negative until the mid-2010s. As the output gap then closed, its negative impact on the external position was offset by a positive terms-of-trade shock thanks to the sharp fall in oil prices in 2015-16 (see, for example, IMF, 2018a, 2017b, 2017c, 2017e).

Second, macroeconomic fundamentals also contributed to the improvement. As discussed in Section 6.2.2, in addition to the cyclical component, the decline in investment rates also reflected “a perceived structural shift in trend growth" (IMF, 2016b).[35] Moreover, the improvement in the NIIP also contributed to the higher current account balance as lower net external liabilities, coupled with low global interest rates, were associated with lower interest payments and profit of foreign investors, thereby improving the income balance.

---

[34] This is based on the IMF’s external balance assessments conducted as part of the regular Article IV consultations.

[35] Estimating two benchmarks for the speed of capital accumulation, the IMF (2016b) finds that both the ‘golden rule’ (a model-based steady-state rate) and the ‘historical benchmark’ (“an investment rate consistent with stylized transition dynamics derived from the historical experience of other European countries that have achieved convergence to present-day euro area income levels”) fell after the GFC.

Third, the current account balance improved on the back of stronger fiscal positions.[36] As a result of the sizeable fiscal consolidation efforts, the structural fiscal balance, i.e., the fiscal balance adjusted for cyclical effects and one-off factors, improved continuously in the first half of the 2010s throughout the region.[37]

In the second half of the 2010s, the deterioration in external balances partly reflected changes in the business cycle, including signs of overheating in a few countries. For example, the output gap is estimated to have exceeded 4 percent in Czechia, Hungary, and Romania (European Commission, 2023a).[38] The cyclical uptick also affected fiscal balances. Although fiscal policy became looser, as reflected in widening structural deficits in a few CEE countries (especially in Hungary and Romania), headline fiscal balances were supported by strong economic activity. Against this backdrop, the cyclical contribution to the current account balance turned negative. In Romania, for example, the business cycle was estimated to have worsened the current account balance by 0.6 percent of GDP in 2019 (IMF, 2019g). This was largely related to expansionary fiscal policy, with the current account balance moving closely together with the structural fiscal balance in the second half of the 2010s (Norton & Zhao, 2022). Notwithstanding the smaller positive output gap in Bulgaria, the cyclical contribution was estimated to have reached 3 percent of GDP in 2017 accounting for a temporary drop in public investment and strong tourism-related exports due to "political uncertainties in some traditional tourism destinations" (IMF, 2018a).

In addition to cyclical developments, however, there were increasing signs of excessive changes in the external position. In Bulgaria, Czechia, Estonia, Hungary, Latvia, Lithuania, and Slovenia, the external position was assessed to be stronger than the level implied by fundamentals in the late-2010s.[39] The reason for (moderately)

[36] There is a large literature on the relationship between fiscal and current account balances (see, for example, Gagnon, 2017). If Ricardian equivalence holds, changes in the fiscal balance would be offset by changes in the private sector's consumption and investment decisions, thereby having only a limited impact on the current account balance. The literature, however, finds a positive relationship between current account and fiscal balances. For example, Cubeddu et al. (2019) estimate that a 1 percentage point change in the fiscal stance is associated with a 0.33 percentage point deterioration in the current account balance. Moreover, fiscal policy could also have supply-side impact on the economy.

[37] This followed the worsening of the fiscal balance at the peak of the GFC in each CEE country, except for Hungary where fiscal policy acted in a pro-cyclical way given the lack of space following large pre-GFC fiscal imbalances.

[38] In the late-2010s, however, economic activity weakened in advanced Europe on the back of several factors "such as the tighter EU emission standards, a shift in preferences from diesel toward gasoline and other alternative fuel vehicles, and weakening global demand, especially from China" (IMF, 2019c). Nonetheless, the IMF (2019c) point out anecdotal evidence that vehicle production in the CEE countries was resilient thanks to robust demand for the types of cars (e.g., SUVs) produced in the region.

[39] Similarly, Kuziemska-Pawlak and Mućk (2019) estimate the current account balance to be higher than the level explained by medium- to long-term fundamentals in each CEE country, except for Lithuania, Romania, and Slovakia. They also note that Hungary is estimated to have the highest positive deviation from the structural level. Finally, in terms of the sign of the balance, they estimate that the 'structural' current account for 2016 was positive for Czechia, Estonia, Lithuania, and zero or slightly negative for other CEE countries.

stronger external positions, however, differed across countries, including a moderately undervalued exchange rate, strong fiscal position, and precautionary savings by households in the late-2010s in Czechia (IMF, 2019a); policy gaps, in particular a relatively tight fiscal policy, with no clear indication of undervaluation in the mid-2010s in Estonia (IMF, 2017a); weak private sector credit and the undervalued currency in Hungary (IMF, 2019b); low public health expenditure and credit growth offset by higher fiscal deficit in Latvia (IMF, 2019e); relatively strong fiscal policy (i.e., looser-than-desired fiscal policy in the rest of the world) in Lithuania (IMF, 2018d); and fiscal policy closer to its desired level than in trading partners, undervalued currency, and weak private sector credit in Slovenia (IMF, 2017d). In contrast, there were signs of modest overvaluation in Croatia in the mid-2010s, contributing to the relatively weak current account balance. Similarly, Romania also had a weak external position in the late-2010s (IMF, 2021i).

During the pandemic, the external position was largely affected by cyclical developments such as the lockdown, the temporary closing of borders, disruptions to supply chains, specific import needs related to the pandemic, the commodity price shock, and an extraordinarily high degree of uncertainty. As such, the contribution to the current account balance of Covid-19 related developments was estimated at -1.4 percent of GDP in Hungary (IMF, 2021c) and -1.6 percent of GDP in Poland (IMF, 2021g) in 2020, and -1.2 percent of GDP in Czechia in 2021 (IMF, 2022b).

There were also signs of excessive balances. Specifically, the external position was assessed to be stronger than the level implied by fundamentals and desired policies in Bulgaria, Estonia, Hungary, Latvia, Lithuania, Poland, and Slovenia. The strong position was driven by several factors. For example, the relatively tight fiscal policy (i.e., not as loose as in the rest of the world) and low health spending supported the current account balance in a few countries, including Bulgaria, Estonia, Latvia, and Lithuania (IMF, 2021a, 2021d, 2021e, 2021f). Moreover, the strong external position was also related to the undervaluation of the real exchange rate in Bulgaria, Estonia, Hungary, Poland, and Slovenia (IMF, 2021a, 2021d, 2021c, 2022c, 2021h). Also, there were some country-specific sectors such as weak private sector credit in Hungary or "structural impediments encouraging both higher savings and lower investment" in Bulgaria (IMF, 2021c, 2021a). At the same time, there were signs of the external position being weaker than the level implied by medium-term fundamentals and policies in Romania, largely owing to an overvaluation of the real exchange rate in the context of expansionary fiscal policy (IMF, 2021i; Norton & Zhao, 2022).

6.3 External Adjustment in the Wake of the War in Ukraine

The world economy witnessed several important shocks in 2022, all of which had significant impact on the CEE countries' external positions. In the aftermath of Russia's invasion of Ukraine, commodity prices soared amid concerns about a shortfall in global supplies from Russia and Ukraine, and trade disruptions caused by the war itself. Brent oil price exceeded USD 120 dollar per barrel in June 2022, before starting to decline in the second half of 2022 as demand growth from major economies, such as China, slowed and trade diversion enabled a steady supply of Russian crude oil to the global market. European gas prices had risen to a stratospheric level amid supply disruptions but subsequently declined, owing to substitution efforts and an exceptionally mild winter that reduced demand. Food prices also began to fall around the same period as supply and demand reacted to higher prices, including through the reopening of the Black Sea corridor, increased wheat production in Europe and India, and lower demand for price-elastic items. Despite the decline since mid-year, average commodity prices in 2022 were higher than those in 2021 and well above their pre-pandemic levels.

In addition to the terms-of-trade shock, the tightening of external financial conditions also affected the CEE economies, including via increasing risk aversion in the immediate aftermath of the Russian invasion of Ukraine and monetary policy tightening in major advanced economies thereafter. Specifically, soaring commodity prices prompted central banks to tighten monetary policy to fight the rapidly accelerating inflation, notably in the U.S. that contributed to the appreciation of the U.S. dollar in 2022. Moreover, in light of the commodity price shock, the tightening of financial conditions, and elevated uncertainty, external demand also weakened, with global growth decelerating from 6.3 percent in 2021 to 3.5 percent in 2022 (IMF, 2023).

6.3.1 Current Account Balances and the Terms-of-Trade Shock

With the exception of Bulgaria, the current account balance deteriorated significantly in each CEE country between 2021 and 2022, with the worsening averaging 2.7 percent of GDP and ranging from 0.6 percent of GDP in Estonia to 6.6 percent of GDP in Lithuania (Figure 6.11). Following the pre-war decade characterized by surpluses and modest deficits, each CEE country recorded a deficit, with the deficit close to or exceeding 5 percent of GDP in five out of 11 CEE countries. In Hungary, Slovakia, and Romania, for example, the deficit was in the range of 7-9 percent of GDP, respectively. Moreover, the current account balance was much lower than the level projected before the start of the war across CEE countries, except for Bulgaria, reflecting the unanticipated effect of the war (Figure 6.12). Before the war, four CEE countries were actually expected to record a current account surplus in 2022.

The deterioration in the current account balance was primarily driven by the trade balance (Figure 6.11).[40] Specifically, the sharp increase in commodity prices was associated with a surge in imports[41], while exports were affected by slowing global demand.[42] The worsening of the goods balance was only partially offset by

[40] For a detailed account of the impact of the war on external trade, see Chapter 7.

[41] In Poland, imports were also boosted by the positive impact on domestic demand of consumption by refugees (IMF, 2023e).

[42] Exports were also constrained by the restrictions introduced on exports to Russia. The impact on exports, however, was mitigated by several factors (see Chapter 1 on sanctions).

Fig. 6.11: Current account balance, 2021-2022 (percentage of GDP)
Data: Eurostat (2023a, 2023d), authors' calculations

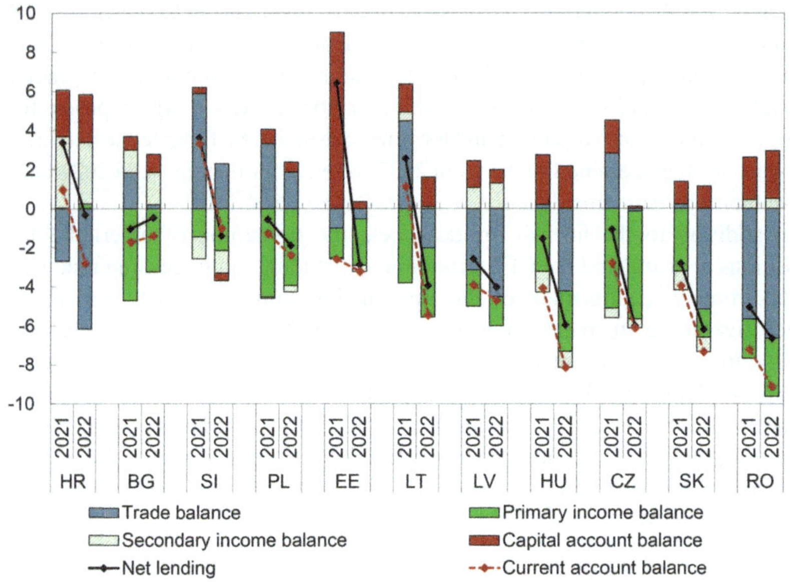

the strong performance of services in some countries, including Croatia, Estonia, Hungary, Latvia, Lithuania, and Poland (IMF, 2023a, 2023b, 2023b, 2023c, 2023d, 2023e). On average, the trade balance worsened by close to 3 percent of GDP in 2022, ranging from 1 percent of GDP in Romania to 6.5 percent of GDP in Lithuania.[43] Nonetheless, Bulgaria, Poland, and Slovenia continued to record a trade surplus. In general, changes in the primary and the secondary income balance were relatively modest on the back of offsetting factors such as increasing interest payments due to higher interest rates and declining declining FDI-related income outflows in the context of worsening profitability in some cases. In terms of the magnitude of changes, a major exception was Bulgaria and Slovakia where the primary income balance improved by 1.5 and 1.8 percent of GDP, respectively.[44]

[43] In Estonia, it improved by 0.5 percent of GDP.

[44] In Bulgaria, the primary income balance improved on the back of lower outflows related to equity income under FDI "probably due to the banking sector", as some restrictions on dividend payments and banks' foreign exposures were still in place in early-2022 (BNB, 2023). Similarly, the improvement in the primary income balance was related to declining outflows of dividends and reinvested earnings under FDI in Slovakia (NBS, 2023).

Fig. 6.12: Current account balance, 2022 (percentage of GDP)
Data: IMF (2022, 2023), authors' calculations

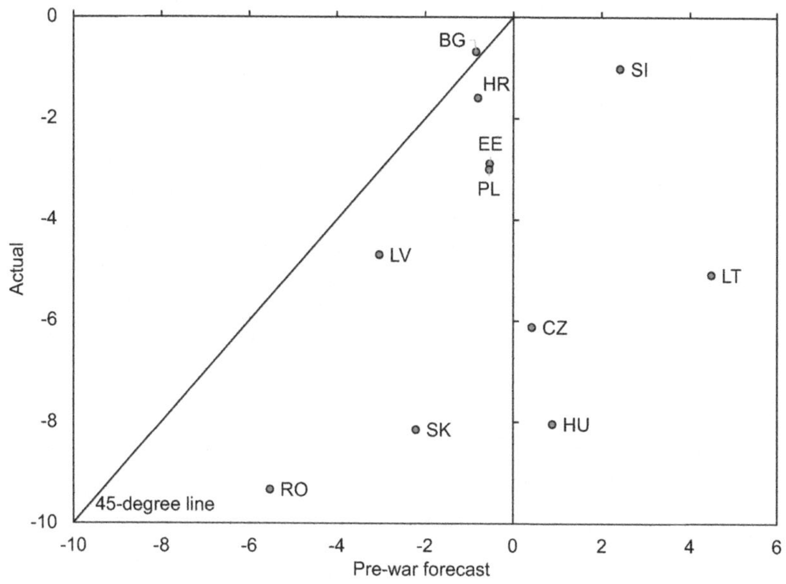

6.3.2 Declining Private Savings amid High Inflation

In 2022, the current account balance deteriorated against the backdrop of the combination of an increase in investment and a decrease in savings in most CEE countries (Figure 6.13). In general, this reflected robust private investments and resilient public investment supported by EU funds amid improved fiscal balances. Moreover, private savings were negatively affected by the sharp increase in energy prices throughout the region.

In most CEE countries, the deterioration in the external position reflected an improvement in the fiscal balance that was more than offset by the worsening of the private sector's net lending position (Figure 6.14). Indeed, the 'normalization' of fiscal policy following the large stimulus during Covid-19 implied a decrease in fiscal deficits in most CEE countries in 2022. At the same time, as surging energy prices had a negative impact on corporate profits and private investment remained strong, the net lending position of non-financial corporations declined. In a few cases (Croatia, Slovenia), the net lending position actually switched into a net borrowing position between 2021 and 2022. Similarly, households' net lending position was impaired by high inflation in the context of rising energy and food prices across CEE countries.

Fig. 6.13: Savings and investments: contribution to the change in the current account balance between 2021 and 2022 (percentage of GDP)
Data: IMF (2023), authors' calculations

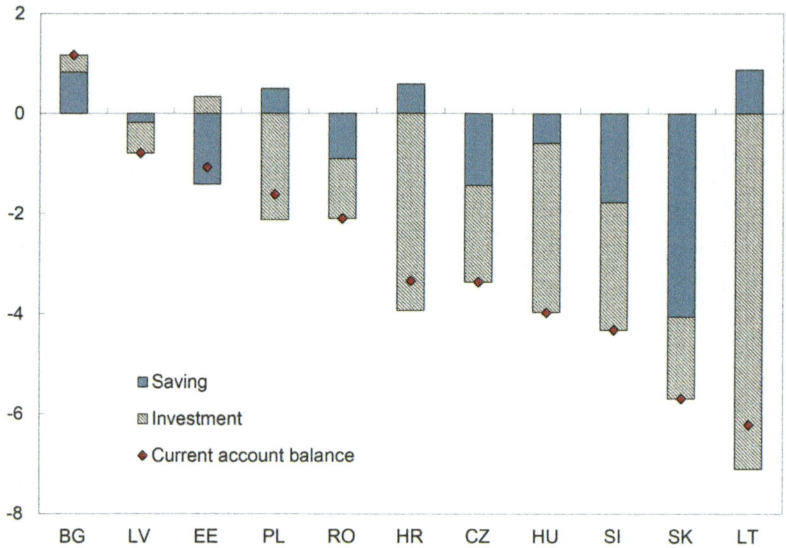

Fig. 6.14: Net lending/borrowing by sector, 2021-2022 (percentage of GDP)
Data: Eurostat (2023f, 2023d), authors' calculations

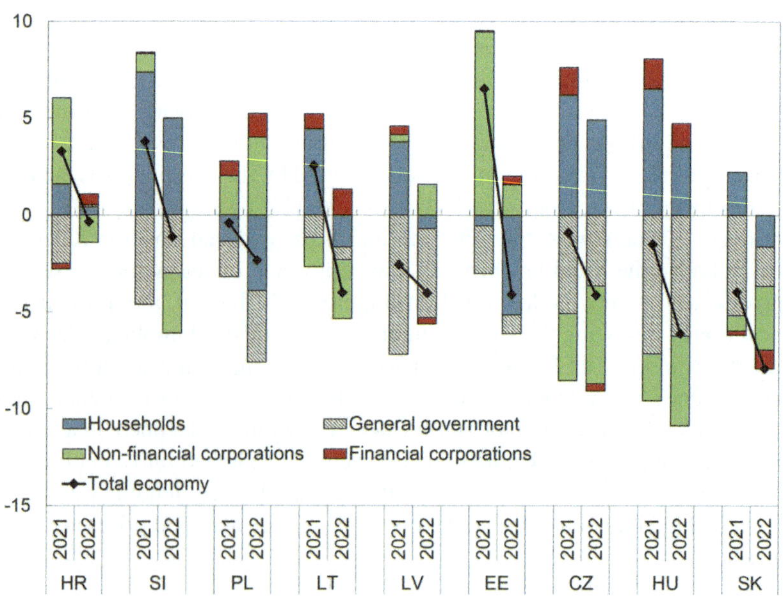

6.3.3 Capital Flows and Tighter External Financial Conditions

In addition to the terms-of-trade shock leading to a sharp deterioration in the current account balance, heightened risk aversion at the start of the war in Ukraine and the tightening of global financial conditions exerted pressure on capital inflows as well. As a result, cumulative bond outflows amounted to around USD2 billion between March and June 2022 in the CEEE (Figure 6.15). Although there was some normalization in the remainder of the year, the majority of CEE countries recorded negative net portfolio flows in 2022 (Figure 6.16). This is consistent with the pattern observed in other EMs against the backdrop of monetary policy tightening in advanced economies (IMF (2023a)).

Fig. 6.15: Bond and equity flows in the CEEE, 2022-2023 (monthly, millions of USD)
Data: EPFR (2023), authors' calculations

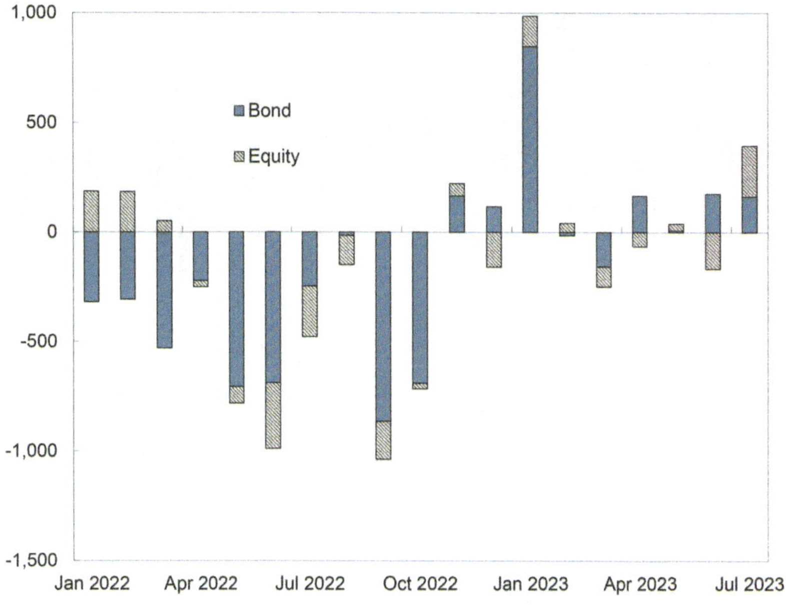

In line with their historical behavior, net FDI inflows were robust throughout the region. In Romania, for example, net FDI inflows reached historic high despite the lifting of restrictions on dividend payments introduced during the pandemic by the supervisory authority (NBR, 2023). Similarly, other investment flows remained positive and even increased in a few countries, thereby providing support to the balance of payments. This also fits the global pattern that other investment inflows to EMs, and in particular global banking flows, were broadly positive in 2022.

Notwithstanding the use of FX reserves in the context of disorderly market conditions at the start of the war in Ukraine (Section 6.3.4), most CEE countries recorded a modest increase in reserves in 2022, reflecting inflows of EU funds or the issuance of FX bonds (see, for example, IMF, 2023b, 2023e). A major exception was Czechia where the extraordinarily high level of reserves allowed for a cumulative intervention of EUR26 billion between May and September 2022 (CNB, 2023). Nonetheless, reserves stood at 366 percent of the ARA metric in Czechia at the end of 2022, well above the adequate range of 100-150 percent. Other inflation-targeting CEE countries also recorded reserves within the range, with Poland at the higher end (146 percent), and Hungary (110 percent) and Romania (100 percent) closer to the lower end of the range (IMF, 2023b).

Fig. 6.16: Financial account balance, 2021-2022 (percentage of GDP)
Data: Eurostat (2023a, 2023d), authors' calculations

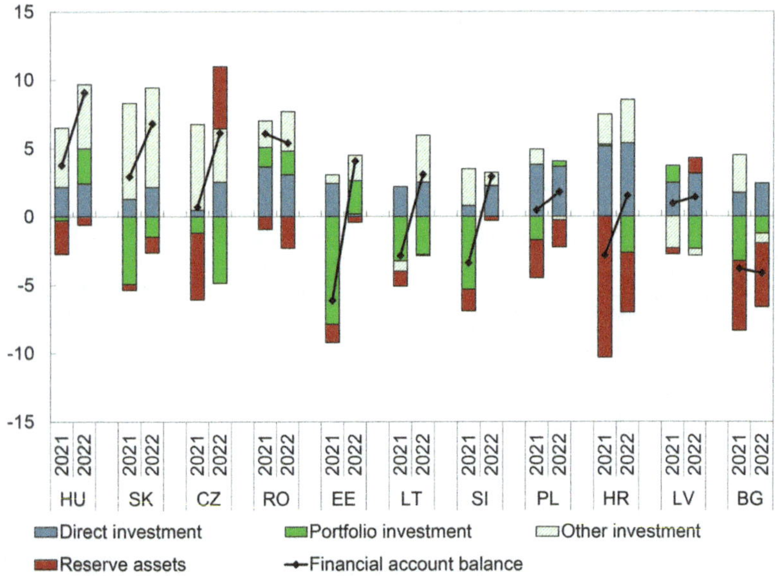

Despite the deterioration in current account balances, many CEE countries saw their NIIP improved in 2022 relative to 2021 (Figure 6.17), with much of the improvement driven by the increase in nominal GDP and revaluation effects on external debt in the context of rising yields (see, for example, IMF, 2023a, 2023b). In general, high inflation had a large contribution to reducing global net creditor and debtor positions relative to GDP by raising nominal GDP (Milesi-Ferretti, Gian Maria, 2023). As a result, external stock vulnerabilities of CEE countries remained contained in 2022, with net external liabilities significantly below their pre-GFC level (Figure 6.17).

Fig. 6.17: Net international investment position (percentage of GDP)
Data: IMF (2023), authors' calculations

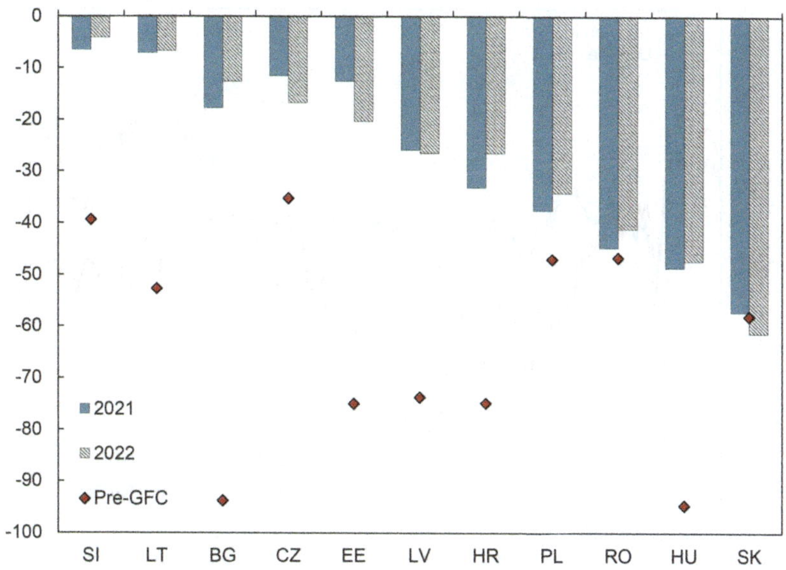

6.3.4 Policy Response to External Pressure

Notwithstanding the pressure on the currencies of inflation-targeting CEE countries stemming from the real and financial shocks, they showed different patterns. Specifically, the Romanian leu remained stable vis-à-vis the euro throughout 2022, while the Czech koruna, the Hungarian forint, and the Polish zloty depreciated by 5-7 percent in the immediate aftermath of the start of the war. During the remainder of the year, however, the performance of these currencies also differed remarkably. In March 2022, the koruna was already stronger than at the start of the war, and recorded a steady appreciation path between the fall of 2022 and the spring of 2023. While the zloty also rebounded quickly, it remained highly volatile in the remainder of 2022, with the exchange rate returning to its pre-war level only in 2023. The forint depreciated continuously until the fall, with the cumulative weakening reaching close to 15 percent against the euro, that was followed by a partial correction over the next few months. Despite the volatile external environment, all inflation-targeting CEE currencies were stronger as of early-November 2023 compared to the level just before the war in February 2022, with the exception of the Hungarian forint. In order to understand the drivers of cross-country differences, we turn to the policy response to the external pressure.

Although the depreciation of CEE currencies in the immediate aftermath of the start of the war indicates the presence of external pressure, the realized change in

Fig. 6.18: Bilateral nominal exchange rates, 2022-2023 (Jan 3, 2022=100)
Data: Eurostat (2023b), authors' calculations

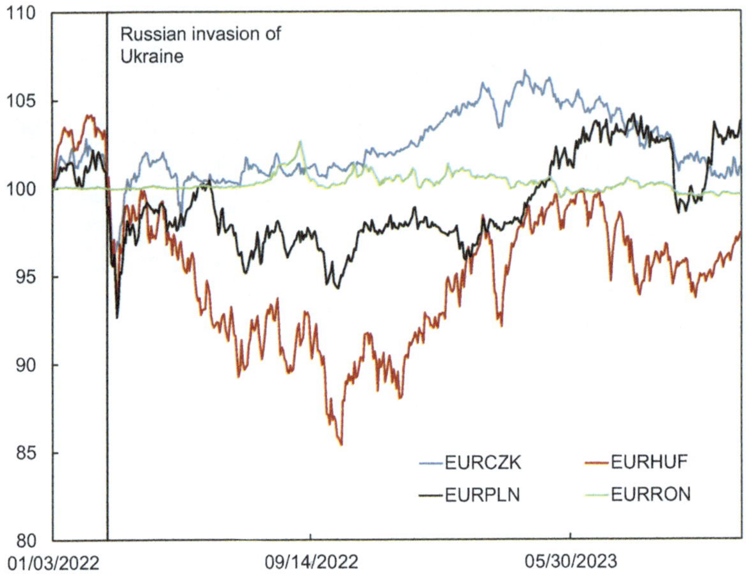

exchange rates may only be a partial measure of external pressure, as economies can resort to FX intervention or interest rate changes to cushion such pressure. Figure 6.19 plots the Exchange Market Pressure (EMP) index and its components for 2022, incorporating both realized exchange rate movement and policy intervention (purchases and sales of FX reserves and policy rate changes) by central banks.[45] As such, the index could provide an indication of both the magnitude of external pressure and the response to this pressure across countries.[46] The EMP index was the highest in Romania, potentially reflecting pre-war vulnerabilities, including signs of overheating, currency overvaluation, and a relatively weak external position (Section 6.2.5). At the same time, the EMP index was relatively modest in Poland and the EA-member CEE countries.

There were also differences in terms of the response to the pressure in 2022 (Figure 6.19). Most non-euro area CEE countries resorted to the combination of policy rate hikes, FX interventions, and exchange rate flexibility, albeit to a different extent across countries. In the case of interest rate decisions, however, it is not straightforward to attribute the policy decision to the external pressure as opposed to the acceleration in inflation. An exception is the extraordinary meeting of the

[45] The EMP index is based on Goldberg and Krogstrup (2023). The index, defined as the weighted and scaled sum of exchange rate depreciation, foreign exchange intervention, and policy rate changes, combines pressures observed in exchange rate adjustments with model-based estimates of incipient pressures that are absorbed by FX interventions and policy rate adjustments.

[46] For a comprehensive overview of monetary policy response to the external shock, see Chapter 4.

Fig. 6.19: Exchange market pressure
Data: Adler, Chang, Mano and Shao (2021); Goldberg and Krogstrup (2023); IMF (2023a), authors' calculations
Note: Positive values correspond to exchange market pressure that would depreciate the nominal exchange rate. A country's total exchange market pressure in 2022 is the sum of scaled and weighted observed FX interventions, short-term interest rate changes, and nominal exchange rate movements. Values of FX interventions and interest rate changes are expressed in terms of counterfactual exchange rate adjustments that would have occurred if no FX intervention or policy rate changes had been conducted. FX interventions are spot interventions from an updated data set of Adler et al. (2021).

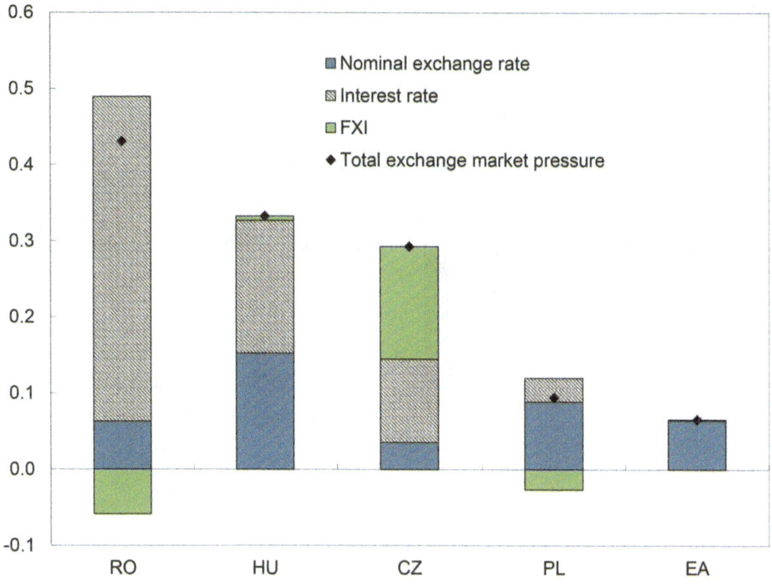

Monetary Policy Committee (MPC) of the central bank of Hungary raising the O/N collateralised lending rate by 950 basis points in mid-October 2022 amid pressure on the currency (MNB, 2023b). In addition to policy rate changes, most countries also intervened in FX markets. For example, the Czech koruna was supported by FX interventions facilitated by the extraordinarily high level of FX reserves (see Section 6.2.3), the "calming effect on domestic entities and the majority of foreign investors" of high reserves, and the positive interest rate differential following policy rate hikes (CNB, 2023). The CNB (2023) also noted that the less than full reliance on exchange rate adjustment was motivated by the "fear that a weaker koruna could boost already high inflation". The central bank of Poland also intervened in FX markets in March 2022 to mitigate the depreciation of the zloty (IMF, 2023e). While the central bank of Hungary did not comment explicitly on FX interventions, it noted its readiness "to intervene in a decisive manner using every instrument in its monetary policy toolkit, if necessary" (MNB, 2023a). In light of differences in the magnitude of the pressure and the policy response in the form of rate hikes and FX interventions, CEE countries differed in terms of the degree of exchange rate flexibility. While the exchange rate was broadly stable in Czechia and Romania in 2022, Hungary and Poland relied more on currency depreciation.

Fig. 6.20: Real effective exchange rates, 2022-2023 (cumulative change, percentage)
Data: Eurostat (2024b, 2024a), authors' calculations

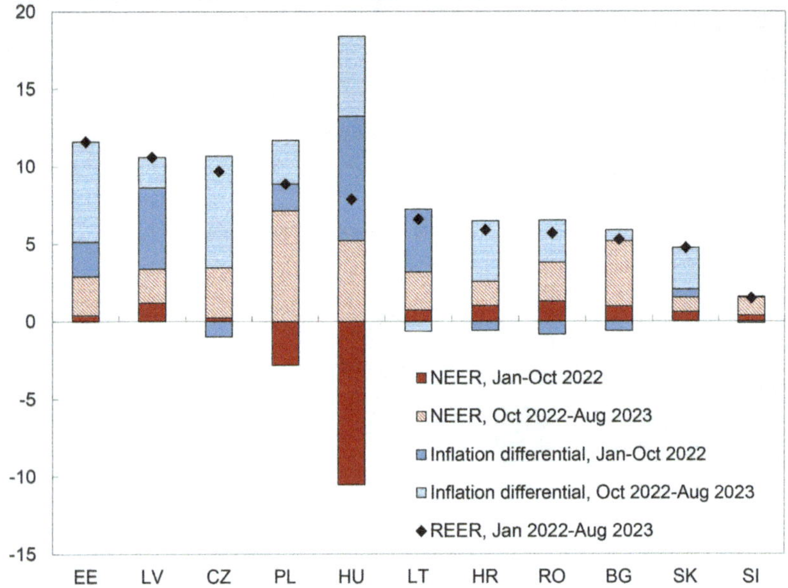

Following the start of the war in Ukraine, real exchange rates also underwent a major adjustment in the CEEE. Between early-2022 and late-2023, the REER strengthened in each CEE country, albeit to a different extent and in a different composition in terms of the relative importance of nominal exchange rates and inflation differential (Figure 6.20). Between January and October 2022, the nominal effective exchange rate (NEER) was broadly stable, with the exception of Hungary and Poland. At the same time, higher inflation relative to trading partners drove the appreciation of the REER in the Baltics and partially offset nominal depreciation in Hungary and Poland. Between late-2022 and late-2023, the REER appreciation was driven by the combination of NEER appreciation and inflation differential in most CEE countries. In Hungary and Poland, the rebound of the currency was associated with a relatively large contribution of the NEER appreciation to changes in the REER during this period. At the same time, the strengthening of the NEER was modest in a few countries (Croatia, Slovakia, Slovenia).

6.4 Conclusions

Following a decade of current account surpluses and modest deficits in the CEEE, the war in Ukraine was characterized by the re-emergence of (sizeable) deficits in most countries in the region. As this was largely driven by the temporary impact of the terms-of-trade shock, the worsening of balances was expected to reverse on the back of lower energy prices in 2023, with most CEE countries recording modest deficit or surplus (Figure 6.21). The current account surpluses recorded during the post-GFC decade, however, are unlikely to return over the medium term. Indeed, the current account 'norm' of most CEE countries was estimated to be in the negative territory in 2022 (Figure 6.21).[47] The 'normalization' of current account deficits is related to several factors. In addition to investments needed for most CEE countries to reinforce their convergence to the rest of the EU, public finances and the external position will be affected by further spending needs, including those related to climate and digital transformation. The EU's 'Fit for 55' package, for example, aims to reduce net greenhouse emissions by 57 percent by 2030 compared to 1990, including through investment in renewables, energy efficiency, and clean transport (European Commission, 2023b). In order to achieve the ultimate objective of climate neutrality by 2050, additional annual investments of around 2 percent of GDP are needed (Wolff, Tagliapietra & Lenaerts, 2023). Against the backdrop of the uncertainty around energy supply caused by the war in Ukraine and a "double urgency to transform Europe's energy system", the EU presented the REPowerEU Plan in mid-2022, necessitating an additional investment of €210 billion by 2027 (European Commission, 2022b).

[47] Allen et al. (2023) define the norm as "the benchmark levels consistent with the underlying macroeconomic and structural fundamentals at their actual values and with medium-term policies deemed desirable or appropriate by staff, once temporary and cyclical factors are excluded". For the latest assessment of the norm in the EEE, see IMF (2022a) for Bulgaria, IMF (2023a) for Croatia, IMF (2022b) for Czechia, IMF (2023b) for Estonia, IMF (2023b) for Hungary, IMF (2023c) for Latvia, IMF (2023d) for Lithuania, IMF (2023e) for Poland, IMF (2022d) for Romania, IMF (2022e) for Slovakia, and IMF (2023f) for Slovenia.

Fig. 6.21: Current account balance: actual, norm, and projection (percentage of GDP)
Data: IMF (2023); IMF (2023f, 2023a, 2023b, 2023e, 2023c, 2023d, 2022b, 2023b), authors' calculations

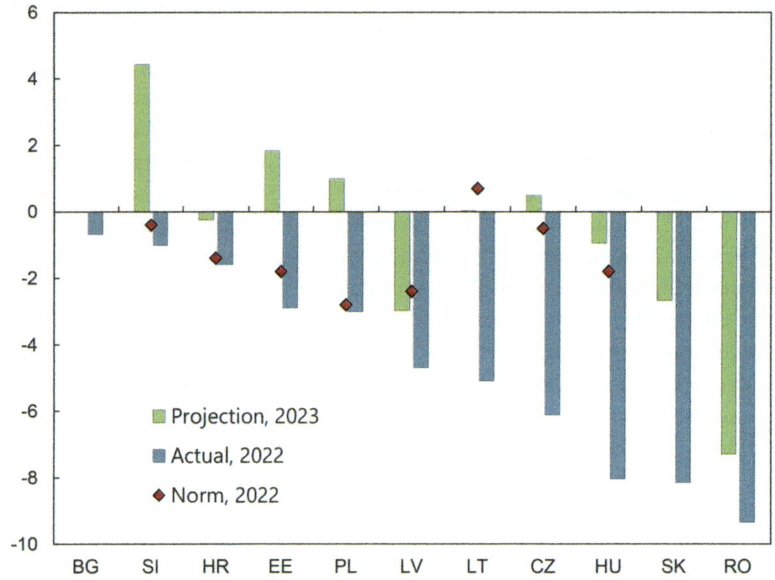

CEE countries are also facing significant challenges stemming from population aging. In addition, adverse demographic trends have been exacerbated by net emigration, thereby contributing to the increase in old-age dependency in many countries (IMF, 2016b). Specifically, the median old-age dependency ratio, defined as the ratio of population aged 30-64 years to population aged 65 and above, increased from 33 percent in 2004 to 42 percent in 2021 and is expected to rise even further to 51 percent by 2030 (United Nations, 2022). Population aging could affect the external position via several channels. Cubeddu et al. (2019) distinguished between a static and a dynamic effect: countries with a high share of young or elderly tend to dissave, while countries save more when the life expectancy of prime-aged savers increases. Overall, Ca'Zorzi, Chudik and Dieppe (2009) note that a higher share of dependent population is expected to be associated with a lower level of savings and a lower current account balance. In Estonia, for example, the declining and aging population is estimated to be a main driver of the current account deficit over the medium term (IMF, 2018c).

As discussed in Section 6.2.5, however, the deficit of the current account is not a problem per se. Therefore, CEE countries should pursue policies that support investments needed to resume the convergence process and to facilitate the green and digital transformation. For example, structural policies could contribute to unlocking investments, by removing labor market barriers, reducing the regulatory burden, and improving the business climate. Also, fiscal policy should create enough space for investments in infrastructure and human capital, as well as incentives to foster the economic transformation. At the same time, the implementation of a growth-friendly fiscal consolidation would help avoid excessive current deficits in CEE countries where the looser fiscal stance contributed to the worsening of the external position during the pandemic and the war in Ukraine. Finally, in countries with signs of currency overvaluation and/or loss of cost competitiveness, greater exchange rate flexibility and the alignment of wage dynamics with productivity growth would help lower the risk of the emergence of external imbalances.

In order to mitigate the pressure on the external position arising from high investment needs, CEE countries should also enhance their capacity to absorb EU funds, as well as ensure the effective use of these funds. Specifically, as part of NextGenerationEU, the EU's Recovery and Resilience Facility (RRF) "offers grants and loans to support reforms and investments in the EU Member States for a total of €723.8 billion in current prices" of which €338 billion and up to €385.8 billion are to be provided in the form of grants and loans, respectively (European Commission, 2022a). Poland's recovery and resilience plan, for example, includes RRF funding of €22.5 billion in grants and €11.5 billion in loans, with 42.7 and 21.3 percent of the plan supporting the green and the digital transition, respectively (European Commission, 2023c). Also, in Czechia, the investment gap of the green transition is expected to be covered by "the RRF and other structural EU funds" and revenues from the EU ETS (IMF, 2022b).

In addition to structural changes, CEE countries also remain exposed to temporary external shocks, including those related to commodity prices and shifts in global market sentiment. First, swings in commodity prices have had a large impact on the external position of CEE countries, as demonstrated by the sharp fall in prices in the mid-2010s or the surge at the start of the war in Ukraine. Going forward, oil and gas price volatility could be heightened by the climate transition. As estimated by Boer, Pescatori and Stuermer (2023), oil prices could decline to around USD 25 per barrel in 2030 if emission reduction is driven by demand-side policies, but increase to above USD 130 per barrel on the back of supply-side policies aimed at reducing production. This highlights the uncertainty around the evolution of commodity prices amid the climate transition, with major implications for the external position of both commodity exporters and importers. Second, given their integration into international financial markets, CEE countries also remain exposed to changes in global financial conditions, with the size of pressure differing across CEE countries depending on the strength of their fundamentals and their policy frameworks.

Against this backdrop, CEE countries should preserve and/or enhance their resilience to external shocks. Specifically, the REPowerEU Plan aims to enhance energy security, including by lowering the dependence on energy imports. The execution of such investments would thus increase the resilience to terms-of-trade shocks. Moreover, given that markets differentiate across countries during periods of the tightening of global financial conditions, the pressure on the balance of payments is mitigated by the conduct of sound policies and strong fundamentals. The exposure of CEE countries to such shocks also differs given the differences in their monetary policy frameworks. Specifically, six countries are already members of the euro area, thereby benefiting from the safe haven status of the euro during heightened volatility in international financial markets. Moreover, the remaining CEE countries have no opt-out right, therefore they are also supposed to join the euro area eventually. In fact, Bulgaria already entered the ERM-II mechanism in mid-2020. In the meantime, it remains important for inflation-targeting CEE countries (Czechia, Hungary, Poland, Romania) to maintain an adequate level of FX reserves and keep external vulnerabilities contained in order to strengthen their resilience to shocks. Also, when facing temporary external shocks, they can use FX intervention to avoid a disorderly adjustment in the exchange rate.

Acknowledgements We would like to thank Shakill Hassan, Anna Ilyina, Júlia Király, Florian Misch, Marco Rodriguez, Yorbol Yakhshilikov, and Zeine Zeidane for their valuable comments and support. The usual disclaimer applies.

References

Abiad, A. G., Leigh, D. & Mody, A. (2007). International Finance and Income Convergence: Europe is Different. *IMF Working Paper 07/64.*

Adlèr, G., Chang, K. S., Mano, R. & Shao, Y. (2021). Foreign Exchange Intervention: A Dataset of Public Data and Proxies. *IMF Working Paper 2021/47.*

Ahuja, A., Syed, M. & Wiseman, K. (2017). Assessing Country Risk — Selected Approaches — Reference Note. *Technical Notes and Manuals, Strategy, Policy, and Review Department, International Monetry Fund.*

Allen, C., Casas, C., Ganelli, G., Juvenal, L., Leigh, D., Rabanal, P., ... Jalles, J. T. (2023). 2022 Update of the External Balance Assessment Methodology. *IMF Working Paper 23/47.*

Bakker, B. B. & Gulde, A.-M. (2010). The Credit Boom in the EU New Member States: Bad Luck or Bad Policies? *IMF Working Paper 10/130.*

Belka, M. (2009). The impact of the crisis on new EU member states – Role and Contribution of the Fund in the Crisis. *Keynote remarks by Marek Belka, Director, European Department, Brussels, December 2, 2009.* https://www.imf.org/en/News/Articles/2015/09/28/04/53/sp120209.

BNB. (2023). *Economic Review 1/2023.* Bulgarian National Bank, 2023, https://www.bnb.bg/bnbweb/groups/public/documents/bnb_publication/pub_ec_r_2023_01_en.pdf. (Accessed: 04-12-2023)

Boer, L., Pescatori, A. & Stuermer, M. (2023). Not All Energy Transitions Are Alike: Disentangling the Effects of Demandand Supply-Side Policies on Future Oil Prices. *IMF Working Paper 23/160.*

Broner, F., Didier, T., Erce, A. & Schmukler, S. L. (2013). Gross capital flows: Dynamics and crises. *Journal of Monetary Economics 60 (2013): 113-133.*

Bruno, R., Campos, N., Estrin, S. & Tian, M. (2016). Foreign Direct Investment and the Relationship Between the United Kingdom and the European Union. *CEP Discussion Paper No 1453, October 2016.*

Ca'Zorzi, M., Chudik, A. & Dieppe, A. (2009). Current Account Benchmarks for Central and Eastern Europe: A Desperate Search? *ECB Working Paper Series No 995 / January 2009.*

Chinn, M. & Prasad, E. (2003). Medium-Term Determinants of Current Accounts in Industrial and Developing Countries: An Empirical Exploration. *Journal of International Economics, Vol 59, No 1, pp 47–76.*

CNB. (2023). Balance of Payments Report - 2022. *June 2023, Czech National Bank.*

Coutinho, L., Turrini, A. & Zeugner, S. (2018). Methodologies for the Assessment of Current Account Benchmarks. *IMF Working Paper 19/65.*

Cubeddu, L., Krogstrup, S., Adler, G., Rabanal, P., Dao, M. C., Hannan, S. A., . . . Wang, Z. (2019). The External Balance Assessment Methodology: 2018 Update. *IMF Working Paper 19/65.*

De Broeck, M. & Sløk, T. (2001). Interpreting Real Exchange Rate Movements in Transition Countries. *IMF Working Paper 01/56.*

E15. (2014). *Miroslav Singer: Our rising savings are not 'normal'.* 8 September 2014, https://www.e15.cz/e15-weekly/miroslav-singer-our-rising-savings-are-not-normal-1116753. (Accessed: 11-10-2023)

EPFR. (2023). *Bond flows, monthly.* https://epfr.com/. (Accessed: 05-09-2023)

European Commission. (2022a). NextGenerationEU. *https://commission.europa.eu/strategy-and-policy/eu-budget/eu-borrower-investor-relations/nextgenerationeu_en.* (Accessed: 30-10-2023)

European Commission. (2022b). REPowerEU: A plan to rapidly reduce dependence on Russian fossil fuels and fast forward the green transition. *Press release, 18 May 2022.* https://ec.europa.eu/commission/presscorner/detail/en/ip_22_3131.

European Commission. (2023a). *AMECO Database.* https://dashboard.tech.ec.europa.eu/qs_digit_dashboard_mt/public/sense/app/667e9fba-eea7-4d17-abf0-ef20f6994336/sheet/f38b3b42-402c-44a8-9264-9d422233add2/state/analysis/. (Accessed: 13-07-2023)

European Commission. (2023b). Commission welcomes completion of key 'Fit for 55' legislation, putting EU on track to exceed 2030 targets. *Press release, 9 October 2023.* https://ec.europa.eu/commission/presscorner/detail/en/ip_23_4754.

European Commission. (2023c). Poland's recovery and resilience plan. *https://commission.europa.eu/business-economy-euro/economic-recovery/recovery-and-resilience-facility/country-pages/polands-recovery-and-resilience-plan_en.* (Accessed: 30-10-2023)

Eurostat. (2023a). *Balance of payments by country - annual data (BPM6).* https://ec.europa.eu/eurostat/estat-navtree-portlet-prod/BulkDownloadListing?sort=1&downfile=data%2Fbop_c6_a.tsv.gz. (Accessed: 04-12-2023)

Eurostat. (2023b). *Euro/ECU exchange rates - daily data.* https://ec.europa.eu/eurostat/databrowser/view/ert_bil_eur_d__custom_8447483/default/table?lang=en. (Accessed: 12-11-2023)

Eurostat. (2023c). *Former euro area national currencies vs. euro/ECU - monthly data.* https://ec.europa.eu/eurostat/databrowser/view/ERT_H_EUR_M__custom_6550738/default/table. (Accessed: 14-06-2023)

Eurostat. (2023d). *GDP and main components (output, expenditure and income).* https://ec.europa.eu/eurostat/estat-navtree-portlet-prod/BulkDownloadListing?sort=1&downfile=data%2Fnama_10_gdp.tsv.gz. (Accessed: 04-12-2023)

Eurostat. (2023e). *International investment position - quarterly and annual data (BPM6).* https://ec.europa.eu/eurostat/estat-navtree-portlet-prod/BulkDownloadListing?sort=1&downfile=data%2Fbop_iip6_q.tsv.gz. (Accessed: 04-12-2023)

Eurostat. (2023f). *Net lending (+) /net borrowing (-), by subsector.* https://ec.europa.eu/eurostat/estat-navtree-portlet-prod/BulkDownloadListing?sort=1&downfile=data%2Ftipsnf10.tsv.gz. (Accessed: 04-12-2023)

Eurostat. (2024a). *Industrial countries' effective exchange rates - monthly data - Nominal effective exchange rate - 37 trading partners (industrial countries).* https://ec.europa.eu/eurostat/databrowser/view/ERT_EFF_IC_M__custom_10046832/default/table?lang=en. (Accessed: 23-02-2023)

Eurostat. (2024b). *Industrial countries' effective exchange rates - monthly data - Real effective exchange rate - 37 trading partners (industrial countries).* https://ec.europa.eu/eurostat/databrowser/view/ERT_EFF_IC_M__custom_10046832/default/table?lang=en. (Accessed: 23-02-2024)

Eurostat. (2024c). *Industrial countries' effective exchange rates - quarterly data - Real effective exchange rate (deflator: unit labour costs in the total economy - 37 trading partners - industrial countries).* https://ec.europa.eu/eurostat/databrowser/view/ert_eff_ic_q__custom_10042459/default/table. (Accessed: 23-02-2024)

Forbes, K. J. & Warnock, F. E. (2011). Capital Flow Waves: Surges, Stops, Flight, and Retrenchment. *NBER Working Paper 17351.*

Gabrisch, H. (2019). The productivity puzzle and the Kaldor-Verdoorn law: the case of Central and Eastern Europe. *NBP Working Paper No. 318.*

Gagnon, J. E. (2017). Do Governments Drive Global Trade Imbalances? *Peterson Institute for International Economics Working Paper 17-15.*

Goldberg, L. S. & Krogstrup, S. (2023). International Capital Flow Pressures and Global Factors. *NBER Working Paper 30887.*

Habermeier, K., Kokenyne, A., Veyrune, R. & Anderson, H. (2009). Revised System for the Classification of Exchange Rate Arrangements. *IMF Working Paper 09/211.*

IMF. (2010a). Emerging Europe and the Global Crisis: Lessons from the Boom and Bust. *Chapter 3 in IMF, 2010, Regional Economic Outlook: Europe – Building Confidence, October 2010.*

IMF. (2010b). Managing Capital Flows. *Chapter 2 in IMF, 2010, Regional Economic Outlook: Europe – Fostering Sustainability, May 2010.*

IMF. (2010c). Republic of Latvia 2010 Article IV Consultation. *IMF Country Report No. 10/356, December 2010.*

IMF. (2011). Emerging Europe: Underwriting a Solid Recovery. *Chapter 2 in IMF, 2011, Regional Economic Outlook: Europe – Strengthening the Recovery, May*

2011.

IMF. (2013). Regional Economic Issues: Central, Eastern, and Southeastern Europe – Financing Future Growth: The Evolving Role of Banking Systems in CESEE. *April 2013.*

IMF. (2015a). Assessing Reserve Adequacy - Specific Proposals. *April 2015, IMF.*

IMF. (2015b). Regional Economic Issues: Central, Eastern, and Southeastern Europe – Mind the Credit Gap. *May 2015.*

IMF. (2015c). Republic of Estonia 2015 Article IV Consultation — Press Release; Staff Report; and Informational Annex. *IMF Country Report No. 15/336, December 2015.*

IMF. (2016a). Regional Economic Issues: Central, Eastern, and Southeastern Europe – Effective Government for Stronger Growth. *November 2016.*

IMF. (2016b). Regional Economic Issues: Central, Eastern, and Southeastern Europe – How to Get Back on the Fast Track. *May 2016.*

IMF. (2016c). Republic of Croatia 2016 Article IV Consultation — Press Release; Staff Report; and Statement by the Executive Director for the Republic of Croatia. *IMF Country Report No. 16/187, June 2016.*

IMF. (2016d). Republic of Slovenia 2016 Article IV Consultation — Press Release and Staff Report for the Republic of Slovenia. *IMF Country Report No. 16/121, May 2016.*

IMF. (2017a). Republic of Estonia 2016 Article IV Consultation — Press Release; Staff Report; and Statement by the Executive Director for the Republic of Estonia. *IMF Country Report No. 17/9, January 2017.*

IMF. (2017b). Republic of Lithuania 2017 Article IV Consultation — Press Release and Staff Report. *IMF Country Report No. 17/177, June 2017.*

IMF. (2017c). Republic of Poland 2017 Article IV Consultation — Press Release; Staff Report; and Statement by the Executive Director for Republic of Poland. *IMF Country Report No. 17/220, July 2017.*

IMF. (2017d). Republic of Slovenia 2017 Article IV Consultation — Press Release; Staff Report; and Statement by the Executive Director for the Republic of Slovenia. *IMF Country Report No. 17/125, May 2017.*

IMF. (2017e). Slovak Republic 2017 Article IV Consultation — Press Release; Staff Report; and Informational Annex for Slovak Republic. *IMF Country Report No. 17/71, March 2017.*

IMF. (2018a). Bulgaria 2017 Article IV Consultation — Press Release; Staff Report; and Statement by the Executive Director for Bulgaria. *IMF Country Report No. 18/46, February 2018.*

IMF. (2018b). Republic of Croatia 2017 Article IV Consultation — Press Release; Staff Report; and Statement by the Executive Director for the Republic of Croatia. *IMF Country Report No. 18/5, January 2018.*

IMF. (2018c). Republic of Estonia 2018 Article IV Consultation — Press Release; and Staff Report. *IMF Country Report No. 18/125, May 2018.*

IMF. (2018d). Republic of Lithuania 2018 Article IV Consultation — Press Release; Staff Report; and Statement by the Executive Director for the Republic of Lithuania. *IMF Country Report No. 18/185, June 2018.*

IMF. (2019a). Czech Republic 2019 Article IV Consultation — Press Release and Staff Report. *IMF Country Report No. 19/160, June 2019.*

IMF. (2019b). Hungary 2019 Article IV Consultation — Press Release; Staff Report; and Statement by the Executive Director for Hungary. *IMF Country Report No. 19/357, December 2019.*

IMF. (2019c). Regional Economic Outlook: Europe – Facing Spillovers from Trade and Manufacturing. *November 2019.*

IMF. (2019d). Republic of Croatia 2018 Article IV Consultation — Press Release; Staff Report; and Statement by the Executive Director for the Republic of Croatia. *IMF Country Report No. 19/46, February 2019.*

IMF. (2019e). Republic of Latvia 2019 Article IV Consultation — Press Release; and Staff Report. *IMF Country Report No. 19/264, August 2019.*

IMF. (2019f). Republic of Lithuania 2019 Article IV Consultation — Press Release; Staff Report. *IMF Country Report No. 19/252, July 2019.*

IMF. (2019g). Romania 2019 Article IV Consultation — Press Release; Staff Report; Staff Supplement; and Statement by the Executive Director for Romania. *IMF Country Report No. 19/278, August 2019.*

IMF. (2020). Emerging and Frontier Markets: Managing Volatile Portfolio Flows. *Chapter 3 In: IMF, 2020, Global Financial Stability Report, April 2020.*

IMF. (2021). 2021 General SDR Allocation. *https://www.imf.org/en/Topics/special-drawing-right/2021-SDR-Allocation*. (Accessed: 03-11-2023)

IMF. (2021a). Bulgaria 2020 Article IV Consultation — Press Release; Staff Report; and Statement by the Executive Director for Bulgaria. *IMF Country Report No. 21/27, February 2021.*

IMF. (2021b). How to Assess Country Risk: The Vulnerability Exercise Approach Using Machine Learning. *Technical Notes and Manuals 01/03, Strategy, Policy, and Review Department, International Monetary Fund.*

IMF. (2021c). Hungary 2021 Article IV Consultation — Press Release; Staff Report. *IMF Country Report No. 21/135, June 2021.*

IMF. (2021d). Republic of Estonia 2021 Article IV Consultation — Press Release; and Staff Report. *IMF Country Report No. 21/160, July 2021.*

IMF. (2021e). Republic of Latvia 2021 Article IV Consultation — Press Release; Staff Report; and Statement by the Executive Director for the Republic of Latvia. *IMF Country Report No. 21/194, September 2021.*

IMF. (2021f). Republic of Lithuania 2021 Article IV Consultation — Press Release; Staff Report. *IMF Country Report No. 21/192, September 2021.*

IMF. (2021g). Republic of Poland 2020 Article IV Consultation — Press Release; Staff Report; and Statement by the Executive Director for the Republic of Poland. *IMF Country Report No. 21/35, February 2021.*

IMF. (2021h). Republic of Slovenia 2021 Article IV Consultation — Press Release; Staff Report; and Statement by the Executive Director for the Republic of Slovenia. *IMF Country Report No. 21/94, May 2021.*

IMF. (2021i). Romania 2021 Article IV Consultation — Press Release and Staff Report. *IMF Country Report No. 21/190, August 2021.*

IMF. (2022a). Bulgaria 2022 Article IV Consultation — Press Release; and Staff Report for Bulgaria. *IMF Country Report No. 22/190, June 2022.*

IMF. (2022b). Czech Republic 2019 Article IV Consultation — Press Release; Staff Report; Supplementary Information; and Statement by the Executive Director for the Republic of Czech Republic. *IMF Country Report No. 22/23, January 2022.*

IMF. (2022c). Republic of Poland 2021 Article IV Consultation — Press Release; Staff Report; and Statement by the Executive Director for the Republic of Poland. *IMF Country Report No. 22/58, February 2022.*

IMF. (2022d). Romania 2022 Article IV Consultation — Press Release; Staff Report; and Statement by the Executive Director for Romania. *IMF Country Report No. 22/310, September 2022.*

IMF. (2022e). Slovak Republic 2022 Article IV Consultation — Press Release; and Staff Report. *IMF Country Report No. 22/202, June 2022.*

IMF. (2022). *World economic outlook database.* https://www.imf.org/en/Publications/WEO/weo-database/2022/October. (Accessed: 12-11-2023)

IMF. (2023). *Annual Report on Exchange Arrangements and Exchange Restrictions (AREAER) Database.* https://www.elibrary-areaer.imf.org/Pages/ChapterQuery.aspx. (Accessed: 12-09-2023)

IMF. (2023a). External Sector Report - External Rebalancing in Turbulent Times. *July 2023, International Monetary Fund.*

IMF. (2023b). Hungary 2022 Article IV Consultation — Press Release; Staff Report; and Statement by the Executive Director for Hungary. *IMF Country Report No. 23/70, February 2023.*

IMF. (2023a). *International Financial Statistics.* https://data.imf.org/?sk=4c514d48-b6ba-49ed-8ab9-52b0c1a0179b. (Accessed: 08-12-2023)

IMF. (2023b). *International investment position - quarterly and annual data (BPM6).* https://www.imf.org/external/datamapper/aradata.xlsx. (Accessed: 14-06-2023)

IMF. (2023a). Republic of Croatia 2017 Article IV Consultation — Press Release; Staff Report; and Statement by the Executive Director for the Republic of Croatia. *IMF Country Report No. 23/233, June 2023.*

IMF. (2023b). Republic of Estonia 2023 Article IV Consultation — Press Release; and Staff Report. *IMF Country Report No. 23/275, July 2023.*

IMF. (2023c). Republic of Latvia 2023 Article IV Consultation — Press Release; Staff Report; and Statement by the Executive Director for the Republic of Latvia. *IMF Country Report No. 23/330, September 2023.*

IMF. (2023d). Republic of Lithuania 2023 Article IV Consultation — Press Release; Staff Report; and Statement by the Executive Director for the Republic of Lithuania. *IMF Country Report No. 23/316, September 2023.*

IMF. (2023e). Republic of Poland 2023 Article IV Consultation — Press Release; and Staff Report. *IMF Country Report No. 23/189, June 2023.*

IMF. (2023f). Republic of Slovenia 2022 Article IV Consultation — Press Release; and Staff Report. *IMF Country Report No. 23/27, January 2023.*

IMF. (2023). *World economic outlook database.* https://www.imf.org/en/Publications/WEO/weo-database/2023/October. (Accessed: 12-11-2023)

Impavido, G., Rudolph, H. & Ruggerone, L. (2013). Bank Funding in Central, Eastern and South Eastern Europe Post Lehman: a “New Normal”? *IMF Working Paper 13/148.*

Jirasavetakul, L.-B. F. & Rahman, J. (2018). Foreign Direct Investment in New Member States of the EU and Western Balkans: Taking Stock and Assessing Prospects. *IMF Working Paper 18/187.*

Koroknai, P. & Lénárt-Odorán, R. (2011). The role of special purpose entities in the Hungarian economy and in statistics. *MNB Bulletin October 2011.*

Kuziemska-Pawlak, K. & Mućk, J. (2019). Structural current account benchmarks for the European Union countries: cross-section exploration. *NBP Working Paper No. 320.*

Lane, P. R. & Milesi-Ferretti, G. M. (2007). The external wealth of nations mark II: Revised and extended estimates of foreign assets and liabilities, 1970-2004. *Journal of International Economics 73 (2007) 223-250.*

Lane, P. R. & Milesi-Ferretti, G. M. (2011). External Adjustment and the Global Crisis. *IMF Working Paper 11/197.*

Lane, P. R. & Milesi-Ferretti, G. M. (2018). The External Wealth of Nations Revisited: International Financial Integration in the Aftermath of the Global Financial Crisis. *IMF Econ Rev (2018) 66:189–222.*

Lucas, R. (1990). Why Doesn’t Capital Flow from Rich to Poor Countries? *American Economic Review, Vol. 80 (May), pp. 92–96..*

Lízal, L. & Schwarz, J. (2013). Foreign exchange interventions as an (un)conventional monetary policy tool. *BIS Papers No 73..*

Mihaljek, D. & Klau, M. (2008). Catching-up and inflation in transition economies: the Balassa-Samuelson effect revisited. *BIS Working Papers No 270, December 2008.*

Milesi-Ferretti, Gian Maria. (2023). *How inflation, falling stock prices, and energy prices affected external balances in 2022 - External Wealth of Nations update.* October 19, 2023, Brookings, https://www.brookings.edu/articles/how-inflation-falling-stock-prices-and-energy-prices-affected-external-balances-in-2022/. (Accessed: 01-12-2023)

Milesi-Ferretti, G. M. (2022). *The External Wealth of Nations Database.* The Brookings Institution (based on Lane, Philip R. and Gian Maria Milesi-Ferretti, 2018, "The External Wealth of Nations Revisited: International Financial Integration in the Aftermath of the Global Financial Crisis," IMF Economic Review 66, 189-222, https://www.brookings.edu/wp-content/uploads/2022/12/EWN-dataset_12-2022.xlsx. (Accessed: 10-10-2023)

MNB. (2011). *Press release on the Monetary Council meeting of 29 November 2011.* https://www.mnb.hu/en/monetary-policy/the-monetary-council/press-releases/2011/press-release-on-the-monetary-council-meeting-of-29-november. (Accessed: 19-10-2023)

MNB. (2023a). *Press release on the Monetary Council meeting of 30 August 2022.* 30

August 2022, https://www.mnb.hu/en/monetary-policy/the-monetary-council/press-releases/2022/press-release-on-the-monetary-council-meeting-of-30-august-2022. (Accessed: 27-11-2023)

MNB. (2023b). *Press release on the Monetary Council's decision, effective from 8:45 a.m. On 14 October 2022.* 14 October 2022, https://www.mnb.hu/en/monetary-policy/the-monetary-council/press-releases/2022/press-release-on-the-monetary-council-s-decision-effective-from-8-45-a-m-on-14-october-2022. (Accessed: 27-11-2023)

NBP. (2012). *Information from the Meeting of the Monetary Policy Council held on 8-9 May 2012.* https://www.nbp.pl/en/aktualnosci/2012/mpc_2012_05_09.pdf. (Accessed: 19-10-2023)

NBR. (2023). Foreign Direct Investment in Romania in 2022. *September 2023, National Bank of Romania.*

NBS. (2023). *Balance of Payments, BPM6 methodology, 2022 (Q data) and 2021 (Q data).* https://nbs.sk/en/statistics/balance-of-payments-statistics/en-platobna-bilancia/. (Accessed: 25-02-2024)

Norton, L. & Zhao, W. (2022). Romania's Current Account Imbalance. *Romania: Selected Issues, IMF Country Report No. 22/311.*

Phillips, S., Catão, L., Ricci, L., Bems, R., Das, M., Di Giovanni, J., . . . Vargas, M. (2013). The External Balance Assessment (EBA) Methodology. *IMF Working Paper 13/272.*

Purfield, C. & Rosenberg, C. B. (2010). Adjustment under a Currency Peg: Estonia, Latvia and Lithuania during the Global Financial Crisis 2008-09. *IMF Working Paper 10/213.*

Rosenberg, C. B. & Tirpák, M. (2008). Determinants of Foreign Currency Borrowing in the New Member States of the EU. *IMF Working Paper 08/173.*

Roubini, N. & Wachtel, P. (1998). Current Account Sustainability in Transition Economies. *NBER Working Paper 6468.*

Summers, L. H. (1996). Commentary. *In Hausmann, Ricardo and Liliana Rojas-Suarez (Eds.), Volatile Capital Flows: Taming Their Impact on Latin America, pp 53–57. Washington, D.C.: . Inter-American Development Bank..*

United Nations. (2022). *File POP/02-1: Total population (both sexes combined) by five-year age group, region, subregion and country, annually for 1950-2100 (thousands).* Department of Economic and Social Affairs Population Division, World Population Prospects 2022, https://population.un.org/wpp/Download/Files/1_Indicators%20(Standard)/EXCEL_FILES/2_Population/WPP2022_POP_F02_1_POPULATION_5-YEAR_AGE_GROUPS_BOTH_SEXES.xlsx. (Accessed: 23-05-2023)

Vienna Initiative. (2022a). *Vienna Initiative 1.0 - Overview.* https://vienna-initiative.com/about/vienna-initiative-1-0/overview/. (Accessed: 08-12-2023)

Vienna Initiative. (2022b). *Vienna Initiative 2.0 - Mission Statement.* https://vienna-initiative.com/about/vienna-initiative-2-0/mission-statement/. (Accessed: 08-12-2023)

Vogel, U. & Winkler, A. (2016). Do Foreign Banks Stabilize Cross-Border Bank Flows and Domestic Lending in Emerging Markets? Evidence from the Global

Financial Crisis. *In: Brada, J.C., Wachtel, P. (eds) Global Banking Crises and Emerging Markets. Palgrave Macmillan, London.*

Wolff, G. B., Tagliapietra, S. & Lenaerts, K. (2023). How much investment do we need to reach net zero? *Bruegel blog, 25 August 2021.* https://www.bruegel.org/blog-post/how-much-investment-do-we-need-reach-net-zero#:~:text=Bloomberg%20New%20Energy%20Finance%20(BNEF,trillion%20per%20year%20until%202050.&text=In%20the%20EU%2C%20the%20European,billion%20on%20average%2C%20starting%20now.

Égert, B., Drine, I., Lommatzsch, K. & Rault, C. (2003). The Balassa–Samuelson effect in Central and Eastern Europe: myth or reality? *Journal of Comparative Economics 31 (2003) 552–572.*

Égert, B., Halpern, L. & MacDonald, R. (2005). Equilibrium Exchange Rates in Transition Economies: Taking Stock of the Issues. *Journal of Comparative Economics 31 (2003) 552–572.*

Żuk, P., Polgar, E. K., Savelin, L., del Hoyo, J. L. D. & König, P. (2018). Real convergence in Central, Eastern and South-Eastern Europe. *ECB Economic Bulletin, Issue 3 / 2018.*

Chapter 7
Trade, Deteriorating Terms of Trade and FDI

Zsóka Kóczán and Maxim Chupilkin

Abstract This chapter examines changes in trade patterns, terms of trade and foreign direct investment flows in Central and Eastern European Economies in the aftermath of the start of the war on Ukraine. Slower global trade growth and weaker demand from advanced economies weighed on the outlook for economies in Eastern Europe, closely integrated in European supply chains. The war in Ukraine also resulted in substantial reorientation in trade patterns between Central and Eastern European Economies, Ukraine and Russia. While the role of Ukraine as a trading partner was relatively modest before the start of the war, imports (in particular of food) from Ukraine and exports to Ukraine (driven by minerals and arms) rose sharply (though exports of machinery, chemicals and transport equipment, declined). Sharp initial increases in energy prices pushed up Central and Eastern European Economies' imports from Russia and worsened their terms of trade, though imported quantities of gas, and in some cases oil, declined, offsetting some of the price effect. Exports to Russia dropped for most goods, with the decline being most pronounced for machinery and transport equipment. Foreign direct investment inflows from Russia and Ukraine were modest before the start of the war. Flows from Russia, concentrated in coal, oil and gas, automotives, transportation and warehousing and metals, collapsed since the start of the war (though the decline started earlier). Inflows from Ukraine, in turn, increased substantially, predominantly in software and IT services, in line with significant movement of skilled Ukrainians to these economies.

Zsóka Kóczán ✉
European Bank for Reconstruction and Development, London, UK, e-mail: koczanz@ebrd.com
The views expressed in the chapter are those of the author and do not necessarily represent the views of the European Bank for Reconstruction and Development, its Executive Board, or EBRD management.

Maxim Chupilkin
European Bank for Reconstruction and Development, London, UK and University of Oxford, Oxford, UK, e-mail: chupilkm@ebrd.com
The views expressed in the chapter are those of the author and do not necessarily represent the views of the European Bank for Reconstruction and Development, its Executive Board, or EBRD management.

© The Author(s), under exclusive license to Springer Nature Switzerland AG 2024

L. Mátyás (ed.), *Central and Eastern European Economies and the War in Ukraine*,
Contributions to Economics, https://doi.org/10.1007/978-3-031-61561-0_7

7.1 Introduction

Russia's invasion of Ukraine in February 2022 has led to profound changes in trade patterns. This chapter examines trade, terms of trade and foreign direct investment in Central and Eastern European Economies after the start of the war.

The first part of the chapter looks at changes in trade patterns of Central and Eastern European Economies, focusing on changes in trading partners (export destinations and sources of imports), changes in exported and imported goods, zooming in specifically on trade with Ukraine and Russia. It also examines changes in trade patterns with Russia more broadly, including the role of 'intermediated trade' through the Caucasus and Central Asia, as well as changes in Central and Eastern European Economies' terms of trade. The analysis complements Chapter 1, which focuses on the economic impact of the economic sanctions introduced against Russia. The second part of the chapter mirrors this analysis for foreign direct investment inflows to Central and Eastern European Economies, focusing on investment inflows from Ukraine and Russia.

7.2 Changes in Trade Patterns

We provide an overview of the evolution of the exports and imports of Central and Eastern European Economies using disaggregated data on trade flows from the United Nations (2023). The analysis is conducted at the 4-digit Harmonised System (HS) level of analysis, in nominal US dollars, at monthly frequency. The HS4 level of disaggregation distinguishes, for example, between wheat (HS 1001), rye (HS 1002) and maize (HS 1005). We compare trade patterns in 2022 with trade in 2021, to provide a snapshot of changes shortly after the start of the war (but after the Covid-19 pandemic).

7.2.1 Global Trade

The growth rate of global trade (measured as the exported and imported volume of goods and services) was estimated to have declined from 5.1 percent in 2022 to 0.9 percent in 2023, before rising to 3.5 percent in 2024, well below the 2000-19 average of 4.9 percent (IMF, 2023; Figure 7.1). The slowdown was especially pronounced for imports of advanced economies, declining from 6.7 percent in 2022 to 0.1 percent in 2023.

The decline in 2023 reflected not only the path of global demand, but also shifts in its composition away from goods and towards services; lagged effects of dollar appreciation, which slows trade owing to the widespread invoicing of products in dollars; and rising trade barriers. In 2022, countries imposed almost 3,000 new restrictions on trade (for instance on agricultural goods in an attempt to keep domestic

Fig. 7.1: Slowdown in global trade
Data: International Monetary Fund (2023) and authors' calculations
Note: Trade volume of goods and services.

prices lower, or on strategic goods, such as critical minerals), up from fewer than 1,000 in 2019 (IMF, 2023).

Slow growth in Western Europe also weighed on growth prospects in Emerging Europe. Growth in advanced economies slowed sharply between 2022 and 2023, reflecting a broad slowdown in manufacturing activity as firms scaled back investments amid softening consumption of goods, continued uncertainty, weak productivity growth and more challenging financing conditions.

Central and Eastern European Economies are closely integrated with Western Europe through trade linkages (see Figure 7.2). The exports of Central European countries tend to strongly follow the export trends of Germany, with such correlations reaching 70-80 percent in Hungary, Slovakia and Slovenia (EBRD, 2023b).

Fig. 7.2: Slow growth in Germany weighed on Central and Eastern European Economies
Data: United Nations (2023) and authors' calculations

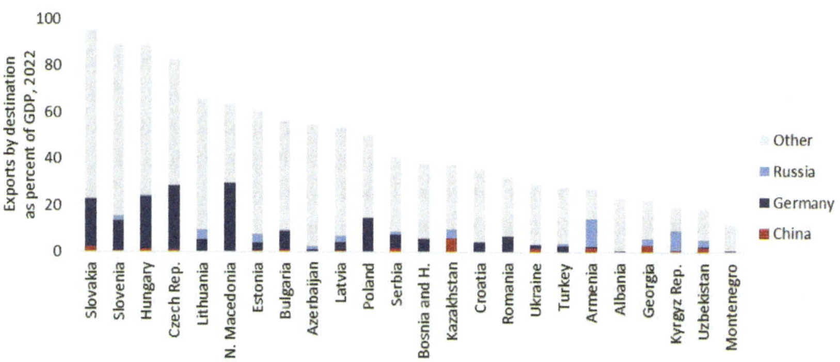

7.2.2 Trade with Ukraine

Imports from Ukraine accounted for a relatively small share of overall imports for Central and Eastern European Economies in 2021, however, increased substantially after the start of the war. Imports from Ukraine accounted for about 0.66 percent of GDP in the 11 Central and Eastern European Economies on average in 2021, increasing to 0.8 percent of GDP in 2022 (see Figure 7.3, left panel). This increase was most pronounced in economies in geographic proximity to Ukraine, in Central and South-Eastern Europe, with only relatively small changes in the Baltic states, Slovenia or Croatia.

Exports to Ukraine also increased on average, though again from low levels – from 0.84 percent of GDP on average in the Central and Eastern European Economies in 2021 to 0.96 percent in 2022 (see Figure 7.3, right panel). As for imports, increases in exports were particularly pronounced for Bulgaria, Poland and Slovakia (for Latvia exports increased more than imports from Ukraine, while for Hungary imports from Ukraine increased but exports to Ukraine declined).

Fig. 7.3: Changes in imports to and exports from Ukraine
Data: United Nations (2023) and authors' calculations

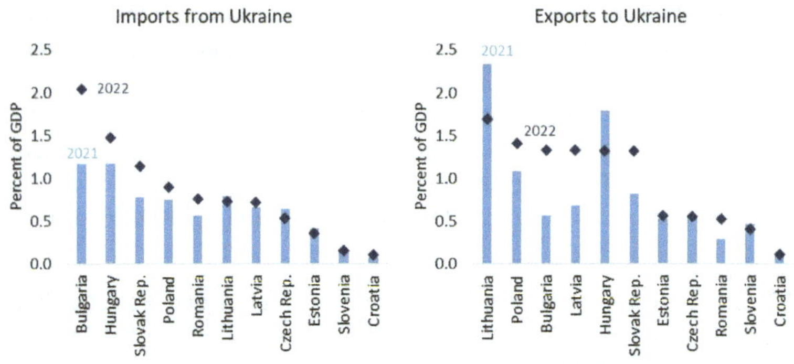

The increase in imports from Ukraine was to a large extent driven by food (see Figure 7.4). Overall food imports of the Central and Eastern European Economies also increased in 2022 relative to 2021, by about 20 percent, in part reflecting weak domestic harvests. However, Ukraine's share also increased sharply: food imports from Ukraine tripled between 2021 and 2022, accounting for about a fifth of Central and Eastern European Economies' increased food imports (see Figure 7.4).

Effects were particularly pronounced for Central and South-Eastern Europe, while patterns are similar, though more muted for the Baltic states (see Figure 7.5). The pick-up was driven by a very large increase in sunflower imports, but corn, wheat, rapeseed and other food imports from Ukraine also rose.

Fig. 7.4: Food imports
Data: United Nations (2023) and authors' calculations.
Note: Food imports to Bulgaria, Croatia, the Czechia, Estonia, Hungary, Latvia, Lithuania, Poland, Romania, Slovakia and Slovenia.

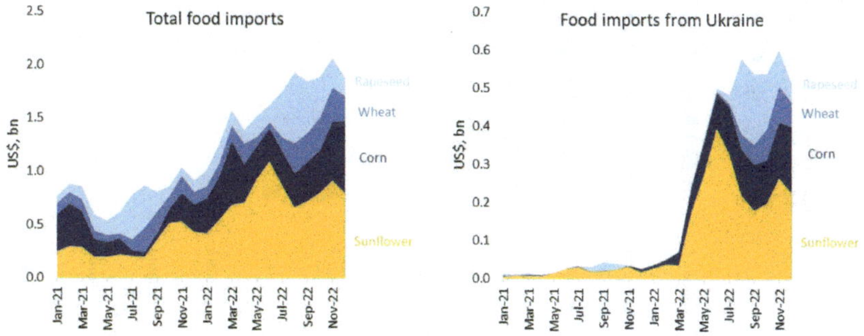

Fig. 7.5: Food imports from Ukraine
Data: United Nations (2023) and authors' calculations.
Note: Food imports to Bulgaria, Croatia, the Czechia, Estonia, Hungary, Latvia, Lithuania, Poland, Romania, Slovakia and Slovenia.

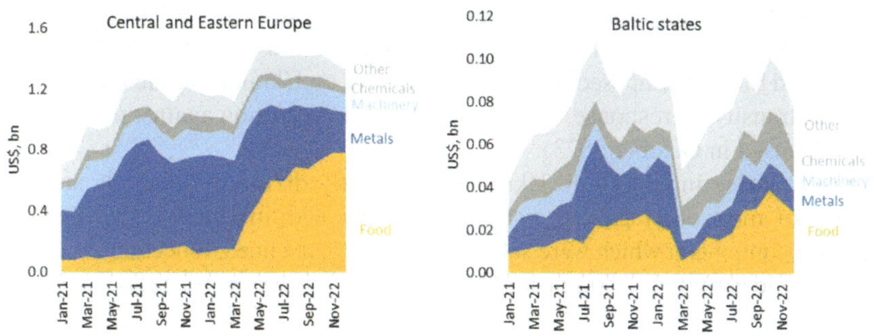

Overall food imports from Ukraine increased 7- to 10-fold in Bulgaria, Croatia, Hungary and Romania in March to December 2022 relative to the same period in 2021 (see Figure 7.6).

In part, the effects are driven by rerouting of food exports from Ukraine, with Central and Eastern European Economies becoming important transit routes. Danube river ports, together with the railroads and roads via neighbouring countries, became important routes for Ukrainian food exports. Using the Danube route, grain was transported to the Izmail and Reni ports by rail and trucks and onward by small coaster vessels directly to the ports of destination or to the Constanza port to be reloaded onto seagoing vessels. In June 2022, the EU and Moldova created alternative land routes, so-called Solidarity Lanes, for Ukraine to export its grains and oilseeds through

Fig. 7.6: Change in food imports from Ukraine
Data: United Nations (2023) and authors' calculations

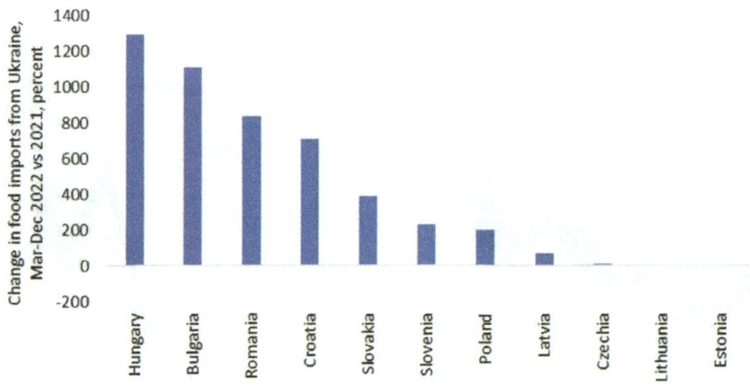

neighbouring economies. Hauliers could transit through the territories without the need for permits.

To mitigate the effects of increased supply on local prices and protect farmers in Bulgaria, Hungary, Poland, Romania and Slovakia, on 2 May 2023 the EU banned imports of Ukrainian grain into neighbouring countries while allowing trans-shipment to third countries. After this temporary ban expired in mid-September 2023, Hungary, Poland and Slovakia imposed their own restrictions on Ukrainian grain imports (other than for transit). In response, Ukraine launched legal action against the trio at the WTO (paused in October 2023).

The increase in exports to Ukraine was mostly driven by minerals and arms, exports of most other goods, including, for instance, machinery, chemicals and transport equipment, which were substantial in 2021, declined, reflecting the collapse of economic activity in Ukraine (see Figure 7.7).

7.2.3 Trade with Russia

While Ukraine's role as a trade partner for Central and Eastern European Economies was relatively modest on average, Russia was more important, in particular as a source of Central and Eastern European Economies' (energy) imports pre-war. As discussed in Chapter 1, Europe's pre-war trade ties with Russia had been dominated by energy-related products, with Europe's heavy reliance on imports of Russian energy dating back to the post-WW2 period and the construction of the Druzhba, Bratstvo and Yamal pipelines.

As energy prices spiked in the immediate aftermath of the start of the war (discussed in greater detail in Section 8.3 on terms of trade changes), Central and

Fig. 7.7: Exports to Ukraine
Data: United Nations (2023) and authors' calculations

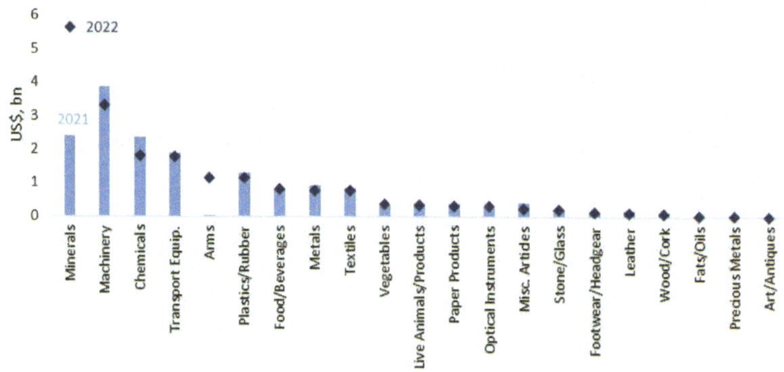

Eastern European Economies' imports from Russia increased from about 3.8 percent of GDP on average in 2021 to 4.2 percent in 2022 (see Figure 7.8).

Fig. 7.8: Changes in imports and exports to Russia
Data: United Nations (2023) and authors' calculations

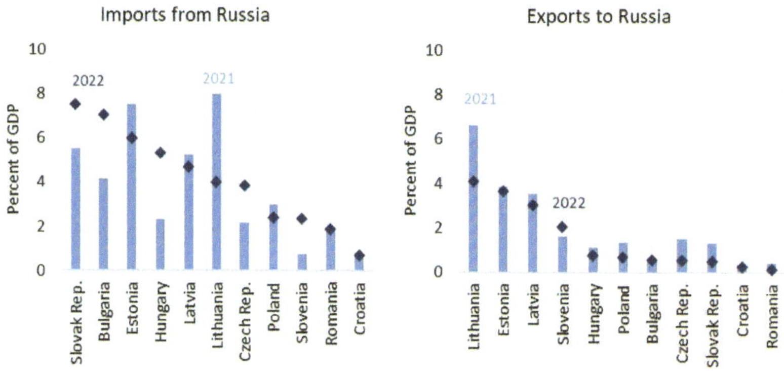

While energy-related sanctions were not imposed by the EU in the immediate aftermath of the Russian invasion of Ukraine, in early March 2022, the EU announced ambitious plans to reduce its reliance on imports of Russian energy, including an expedited reduction in reliance on fossil fuels and increasing role for renewables, the diversification of supplies and routes, the development of a hydrogen market, the improvement of the interconnection of European gas and electricity networks, as well as the improvement of energy efficiency.

Central and Eastern European Economies' oil and gas imports from Russia declined from a peak in March 2022, and this decline was particularly pronounced for the Baltic states (see Figure 7.9).

Fig. 7.9: Imports from Russia
Data: United Nations (2023) and authors' calculations.
Note: Imports to Bulgaria, Croatia, the Czechia, Estonia, Hungary, Latvia, Lithuania, Poland, Romania, Slovakia and Slovenia.

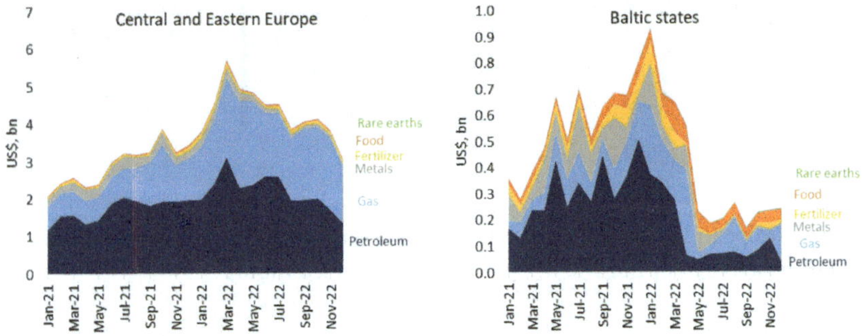

Examining quantities of oil and gas imports from Russia, measured in million tonnes in Figure 7.10, gas imports declined between 2021 and 2022 in all economies in Eastern Europe. Oil imports from Russia declined in the Baltic states, Poland, and Romania, and as a result in these economies the overall imports from Russia also declined between 2021 and 2022, as lower imported quantities offset the effects of higher prices.

Fig. 7.10: Oil and gas imports from Russia
Data: United Nations (2023) and authors' calculations

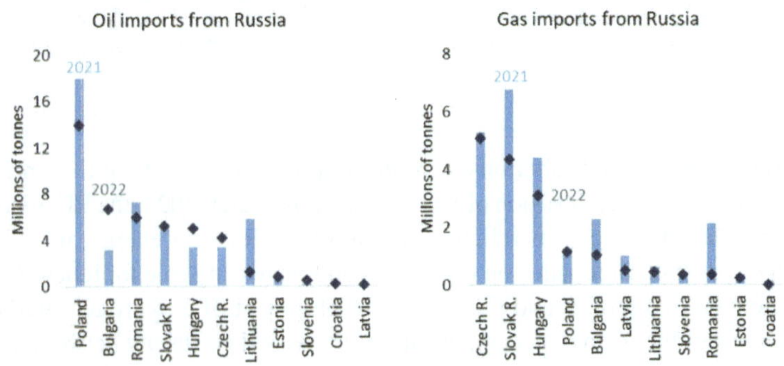

Consumption of gas in Europe fell by more than 20 percent during the winter of 2022-23 compared with the previous winter. However, this had a milder-than-expected impact on overall economic activity. Most of the adjustment to reduced supply of natural gas came from changes in the structure of industrial production—the shift away from gas-intensive industries, such as construction materials, chemicals and basic metals to less gas-intensive industries such as car manufacturing and pharmaceuticals (Plekhanov & Sassoon, 2023). In some economies, warmer weather and the shift to renewables in electricity generation also contributed. In a few cases, reliance on coal also increased. Total industrial output was also weaker than could be otherwise expected, contributing to slower economic growth. Large shifts in the structure of industrial production have, so far, by and large not been accompanied by reduced employment in industries with lower output, contributing to tight labour markets and high nominal wage growth amidst negative GDP growth numbers in 2023 (Plekhanov & Sassoon, 2023).

Fertilizer imports from Russia increased for a number of economies in Eastern Europe (possibly replacing fertilizer imports from Belarus). They doubled to tripled in Bulgaria, Croatia, the Czechia, Romania, Slovakia and Slovenia (declines in the Baltic states, Hungary and Poland were relatively more modest than in the other economies). In some economies, such as Bulgaria and Latvia, food imports from Russia also almost doubled.

In some economies, imports of metals, including rare earth elements from Russia also increased. Metals were not subject to sanctions and countries may have diversified suppliers to avoid supply chain disruptions. For instance, Russia's exports of rare earths, aluminium and ferro-alloys to Estonia more than doubled.

Exports to Russia dropped for most goods, with the decline being most pronounced for machinery and transport equipment, exports of which were substantial before the start of the war (see Figure 7.11).

Fig. 7.11: Exports to Russia
Data: United Nations (2023) and authors' calculations.
Note: Exports from Bulgaria, Croatia, the Czechia, Estonia, Hungary, Latvia, Lithuania, Poland, Romania, Slovakia and Slovenia.

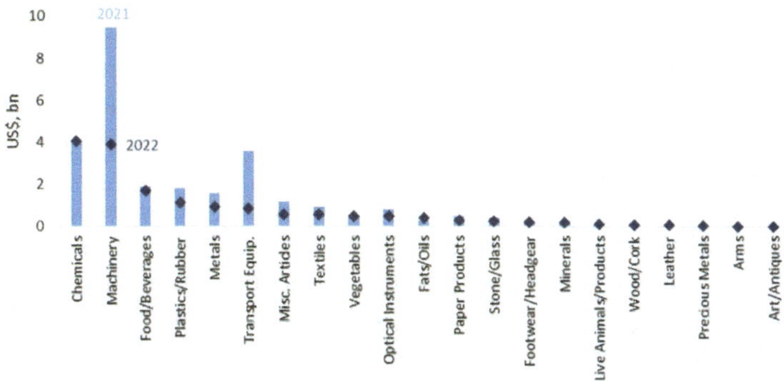

The war in Ukraine also resulted in the extension of sanctions in Russia and broader changes to its trade patterns. This section provides an overview of such changes in regional trade patterns, drawing on Chupilkin, Javorcik and Plekhanov (2023).

Prior to Russia's full-scale invasion of Ukraine in 2022, a narrower set of sanctions was already in place. These earlier sanctions were introduced in response to the annexation of Crimea in 2014 and the armed conflict in Eastern Ukraine that started in the same year. Those sanctions predominantly targeted specific companies and individuals. They were accompanied by counter-measures imposed by Russia, notably a ban on import of various food products from the EU, the US and the UK (see Peeva (2019) for an overview). Those sanctions and counter-sanctions were found to result in a broad-based reduction in Russia's trade with the sanctioning countries (Crozet & Hinz, 2020), an increase in prices of the affected goods (Hinz & Monastyrenko, 2022), weaker performance of sanctioned companies (Ahn & Ludema, 2020) and possibly an increased popular support for the government (Peeva, 2019).

On 23 February 2022, the EU expanded the sanctions in response to the recognition of the non-government controlled areas of the Donetsk and Luhansk oblasts of Ukraine and the ordering of Russian armed forces into those areas. The sanctions were expanded further in several waves, with most in place by the mid-March of 2022. Luxury goods, for instance, were added as part of the fourth package on 15 March 2022, while technology-related goods were added as part of earlier packages. Overall, export prohibitions have covered arms, advanced and dual-use technology, quantum computing, advanced semiconductors, sensitive machinery, transportation and chemicals, goods for use in the oil industry and maritime navigation and goods seen to enhance Russia's industrial production capacity as well as luxury products.

A total of 45 jurisdictions including Australia, Canada, members of the European Economic Area, Japan, Korea, New Zealand, Switzerland, Taipei China, UK and US adopted their own sanction packages. At the same time, China and Turkey are among Russia's main trading partners that did not impose economic sanctions on Russia.

Figure 7.12 depicts export values denominated in US dollars adjusted for US inflation. It traces trade in goods that subsequently were subject to sanctions, goods similar to sanctioned goods and other products. Starting with the top panel, the graphs depict a dramatic drop in the exports from the EU/UK to Russia, accompanied by a substantial increase in exports to Central Asia and the Caucasus (CCA4: Armenia, Georgia, Kazakhstan and the Kyrgyzstan). These changes are particularly pronounced for sanctioned goods, which accounted for the majority of exports prior to the war. A very similar pattern is visible for US exports, with the exports of sanctioned goods to Russia becoming negligible in terms of value after the Russian invasion of Ukraine and the exports to CCA4 being on the rise.

The picture is markedly different in the bottom part of the figure where exports from Turkey and China are depicted. After a temporary drop in Turkey's exports to Russia in March-April 2022, the trade flows resumed, reaching the record value during the period depicted in the graph (January 2017 – August 2022). Trade in all product categories went up. At the same time, Turkish exports to CCA4 saw a stratospheric increase, albeit from a small baseline in absolute terms. This increase

Fig. 7.12: Exports to Russia, by exporter and type of goods (A)
Data: United Nations (2023) and authors' calculations
Note: Based on trade reported by exporters. Trade in nominal US dollars is adjusted for US inflation. EU total includes the UK. Sanctioned refers to HS6 product lines where EU sanctions apply at least partially. Similar goods are those not sanctioned by the EU but within the same HS4 as sanctioned products. CCA4 refers to Armenia, Georgia, Kazakhstan and Kyrgyzstan.

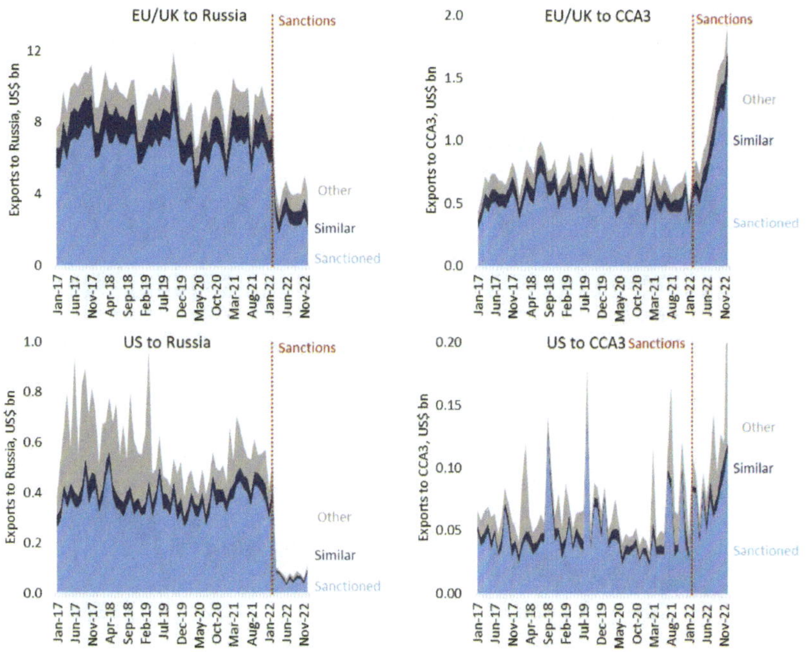

was most visible in sanctioned goods but is also visible in other goods. China's exports exhibited yet a different pattern – after a temporary drop in the aftermath of Russian invasion of Ukraine, they recovered to previous levels. Unlike flows from other countries, Chinese exports registered a steady and sizable increase in the 12 months prior to the war.

These patterns hold in relative terms as well. Figure 7.13 depicts EU/UK exports to Russia relative to aggregate EU/UK exports as well as EU/UK exports to CCA3 relative to aggregate flows. EU/UK exports to Russia dropped dramatically relative to the exports to the rest of the world, while the EU/UK exports to CCA3 went up in relative terms.

The right-hand side panel of Figure 7.13 repeats the same exercise for China. Normalizing exports to particular destinations by total exports may be particularly relevant in the Chinese context, given the disruptions caused in the country by the zero-Covid policy. However, even with this normalization, the broad patterns discussed earlier remain. After a temporary dip in Chinese exports to Russia immediately

Table 7.12 Cont.: Exports to Russia, by exporter and type of goods (B)
Data: General Administration of Customs of the People's Republic of China (2023); United Nations (2023) and authors' calculations
Note: Based on trade reported by exporters. Trade in nominal US dollars is adjusted for US inflation. EU total includes the UK. Sanctioned refers to HS6 product lines where EU sanctions apply at least partially. Similar goods are those not sanctioned by the EU but within the same HS4 as sanctioned products. CCA4 refers to Armenia, Georgia, Kazakhstan and Kyrgyzstan.

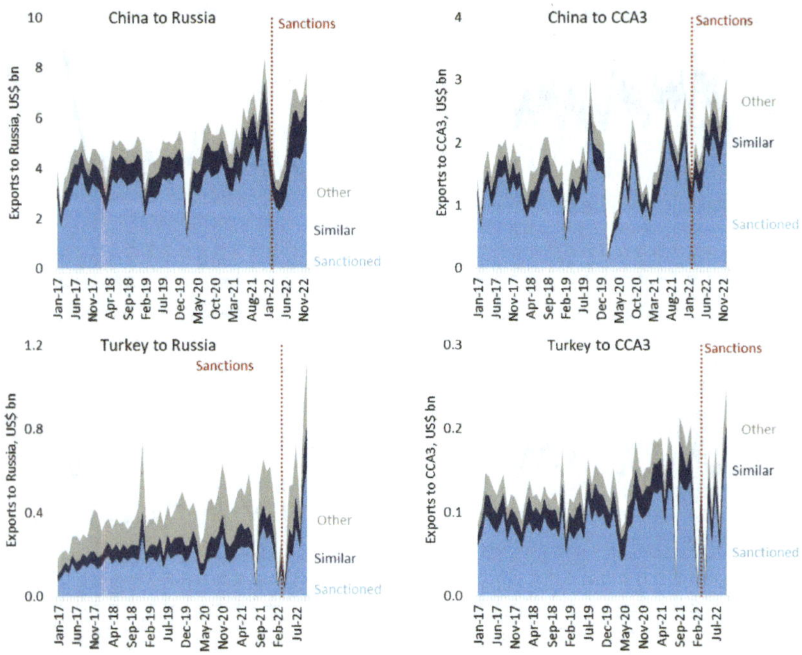

following the invasion of Ukraine, trade flows recovered and grew in importance as a share of total Chinese exports. Similarly, the importance of CCA3 as an export destination increased over time.

The pattern was broadly similar when examining export values adjusted for US inflation and normalizing the flows that took place during May-July 2022 by their value during the corresponding months in 2017-19. Again, this points to a drop in Western exports to Russia accompanied by an increase in exports to Central Asia and the Caucasus. More specifically, exports from the EU, UK and US to Armenia and Kyrgyzstan increased by 86 percent relative to the 2017-2019 average.

These striking trends suggest that a substantial part of additional exports to Central Asia and the Caucasus may have been re-routed to buyers in Russia. Indeed, Kyrgyzstan and Armenia recorded significant increases in exports to Russia (see Figure 7.10, though the records of trade within the EEU customs union are likely to

Fig. 7.13: Share of exports to Russia and CCA3 in total exports
Data: General Administration of Customs of the People's Republic of China (2023); United Nations (2023) and authors' calculations.
Note: The figure shows the log-difference between exports to Russia (or CCA3) and exports to the rest of the world in a given month. The 95 percent confidence intervals are based on the standard errors calculated for the entire period.

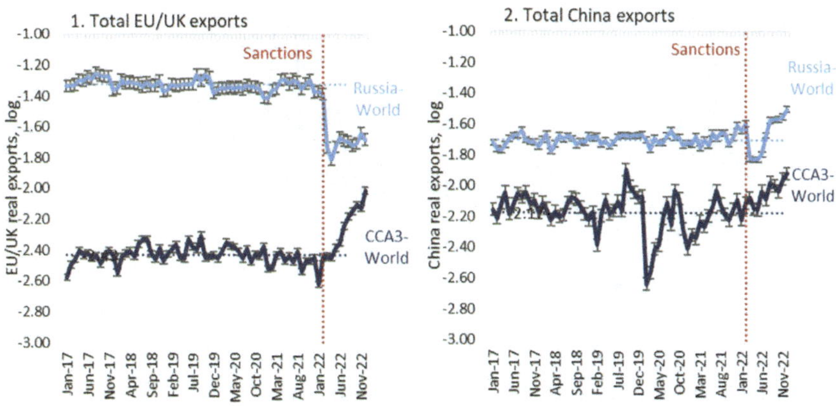

be incomplete), while Georgia recorded a significant increase in re-exports to Russia (see Figure 7.14).

Having said that, the rise in the (recorded) trade between the EU and CCA3 corresponds to a small fraction of the drop in direct EU exports to Russia (around 3-5 percent in the early months, rising over time). Nonetheless, the rerouted trade is important in case of specific product groups.

7.2.4 Trade with Belarus

Trade links with Belarus were strongest for the Baltic states, their imports from Belarus (consisting mostly of mineral products and wood) accounted for 1.4-2.2 percent of GDP in 2021. Such imports, however, declined substantially in 2022 (see Figure 7.14, left panel). Exports to Belarus were highest pre-war for Lithuania, accounting for 1.8 percent of GDP in 2021, consisting mostly of machinery and transport equipment and increased further in 2022 (see Figure 7.15, right panel).

Exports to Belarus also changed in terms of their composition – exports of machinery and metals dropped substantially, while exports of transport equipment, and to a lesser extent chemicals increased (see Figure 7.16).

Fig. 7.14: Exports to Russia from CCA4 increased substantially
Data: General Administration of Customs of the People's Republic of China (2023); United Nations (2023) and authors' calculations.
Note: Based on trade reported by exporters. Trade in nominal US dollars adjusted for US inflation.

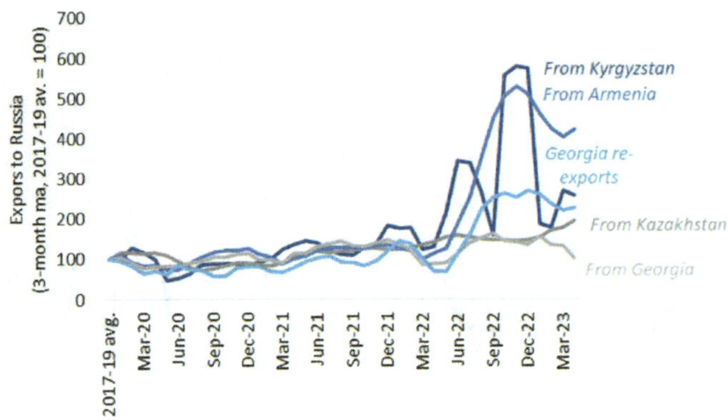

Fig. 7.15: Changes in imports and exports from Belarus
Data: United Nations (2023) and authors' calculations

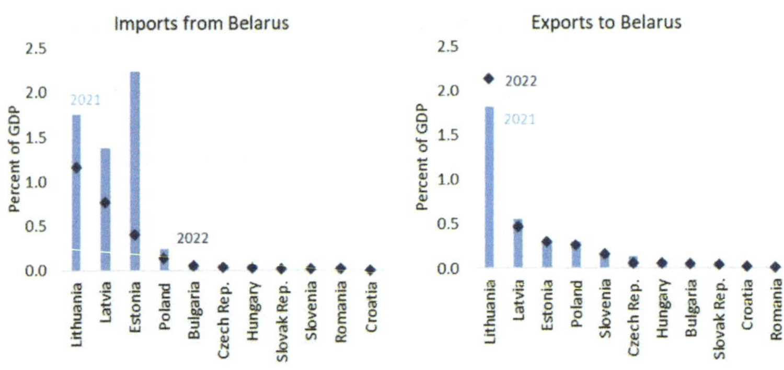

7.3 Changes in Terms of Trade

The terms of trade–the ratio of the price index for exports of goods and services to the price index for imports of goods and services–in general worsened for Central and Eastern European Economies in 2022 relative to 2021 (see Figure 7.17). This held across Central Europe, while the effect was less pronounced in South-Eastern Europe, Latvia and even showing a small improvement in Estonia (reflecting a milder initial decline).

This reflects to a large extent higher prices of imported energy. Brent oil averaged around USD 78 per barrel in 2021, increasing to USD 103 in 2022. Gas prices in

Fig. 7.16: Changes in exports to Belarus
Data: United Nations (2023) and authors' calculations.
Note: Exports from Bulgaria, Croatia, Czechia, Estonia, Hungary, Latvia, Lithuania, Poland, Romania, Slovakia and Slovenia.

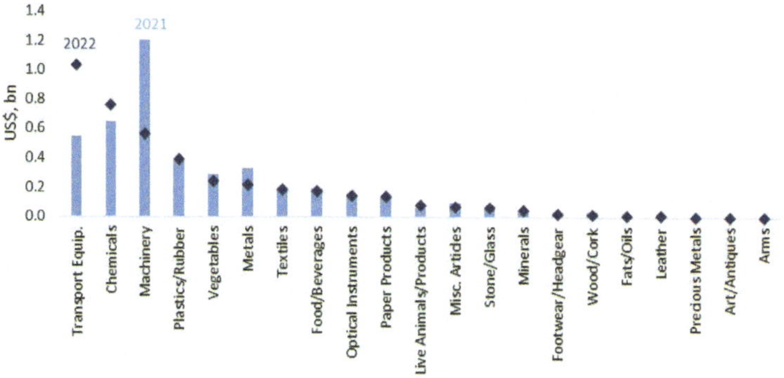

Fig. 7.17: Changes in terms of trade of Central and Eastern European Economies
Data: European Comission (2023) and authors' calculations

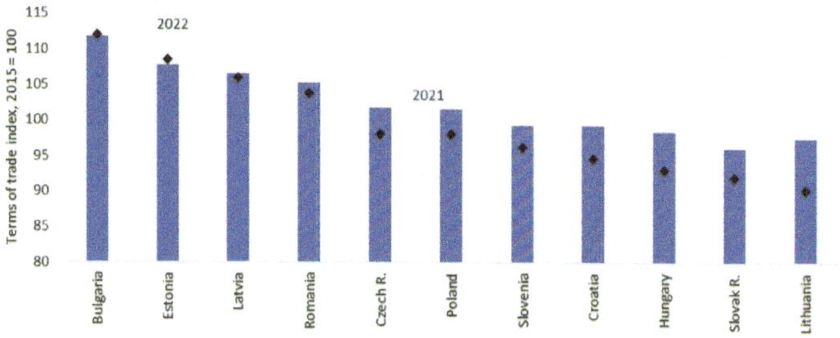

Europe more than doubled, from USD 61 per megawatt-hour in 2021 to USD 134 in 2022 (Figure 7.18).

As oil and gas prices in Europe came down from their peaks in the second half of 2022, the terms of trade of Central and Eastern European Economies also improved substantially (see Figure 7.19). As of late December 2023, oil and gas prices have fallen back to below their pre-war levels. However, gas prices in Europe remain significantly above their 2017-21 averages, almost 5 times the US price and are expected to pick up further later in the winter season.

The start of the war in Ukraine led to a sharp initial drop in maritime grain shipments from Ukraine, previously a major exporter via the Black Sea, and resulted in a sharp increase in prices (see Figure 7.20). To address the issue, in July 2022, the United Nations and Turkey brokered the Black Sea grain initiative which provided security guarantees to allow grain and other food exports from Ukraine (and Russia) to ease the tension on global markets. The deal covered 3 Ukrainian ports on the

Fig. 7.18: Oil and gas prices
Data: Bloomberg (2023); Refinitiv Eikon (2023) and authors' calculations.
Note: Prices adjusted for US inflation.

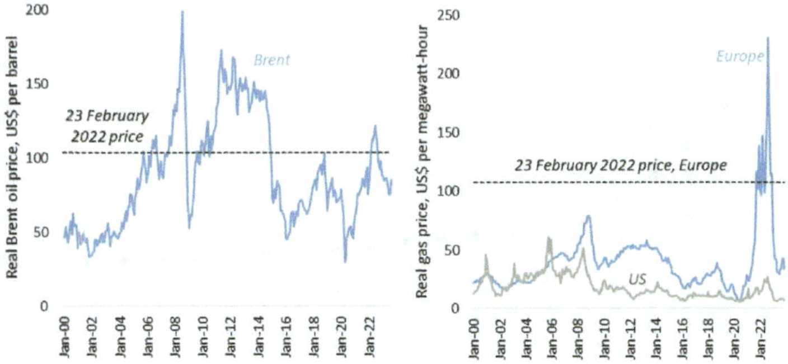

Fig. 7.19: Oil and gas prices and changes in the terms of trade
Data: Bloomberg (2023); European Comission (2023) and authors' calculations.
Note: Prices adjusted for US inflation. Terms of trade is a simple average across Czechia, Estonia, Hungary, Latvia and Poland.

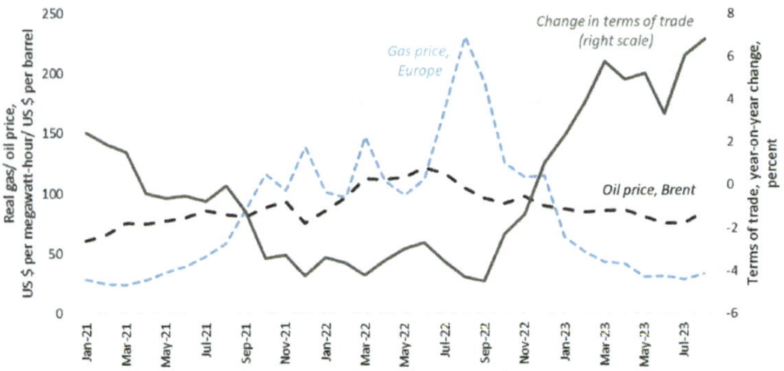

Black Sea – Odesa, Chornomorsk and Pivdennyi, otherwise blocked since the start of the war (in 2021 these ports accounted for 63 percent of Ukraine's grain exports).

For the period of its duration, the initiative ensured the safe passage of over 32 million metric tons of food commodities from Ukraine (40 percent of the country's food exports, with onward shipment to 42 countries) stabilising global grain prices. Key destinations included Turkey, Indonesia, Bangladesh, Italy, Spain, the Netherlands, China (for corn) and Egypt. Russia unilaterally terminated the deal in July 2023.

Wheat prices, however, largely continued to decline. Ukraine single-handedly announced on 10 August 2023 a temporary safe corridor along its own coast as well as the coasts of Romania and Bulgaria. Cargo shipments through this route have continued since, increasing sharply in November 2023. Wheat prices have fallen back

Fig. 7.20: Wheat prices
Data: Refinitiv Eikon (2023) and authors' calculations.
Note: Price adjusted for US consumer price inflation.

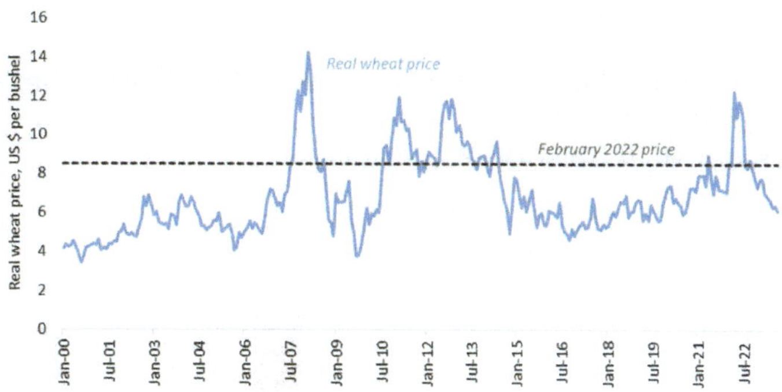

to below their 2017-21 average and, as of end-2023 futures markets expect a further decline in the price of wheat by spring 2024.

7.4 Changes in Foreign Direct Investment Patterns

This part of the chapter relies on project-level information on foreign direct investments (FDI) from the fDi Markets (2023). The fDi Markets (2023) covers new investments (greenfield FDI) rather than changes in ownership (brownfield FDI). It provides granular, project-level information, such as the investment's targeted sector and activity, source country, (estimated) capital expenditure and number of jobs created. The database tracks investments at their dates of announcement—this is in contrast with official data (for instance from UNCTAD), which tracks FDI at the date the capital effectively crosses borders.[1]

Foreign direct inflows to Central and Eastern European Economies are very large: they created almost 19,000 jobs per month on average over the period 2003-2019 (based on greenfield FDI inflows from the FT fDi Markets database). Inflows from Russia and Ukraine, however, accounted for only a very small fraction of these inflows on average in Central and Eastern European Economies even before the start of the war. Greenfield FDI inflows from Russia made up less than 1 percent of total

[1] fDi Markets data may thus at times reflect intentions rather than effectively carried out investments. Numbers referring to employment created in the following should thus be interpreted as referring to announcements over the given period, which may not all have been realized to date. Employment generated may also be estimates rather than actual values. While the database differentiates between announced, opened and closed projects, in practice, many announced projects are already in progress or may even be finished. All projects are thus included in the following analysis. This also provides the closest match with other aggregate sources, such as UNCTAD (see also Koczan, Paetzold & Vujic, 2021).

greenfield FDI related jobs generated in Central and Eastern European Economies; Ukraine only accounted for around 0.2 percent over the period 2003-2019 (Figure 7.21). Shares are higher in terms of capital expenditure, around 2.2 percent for Russia and 0.4 percent for Ukraine, as projects were relatively capital-intensive.

Fig. 7.21: Foreign direct investment inflows to Central and Eastern European Economies from Ukraine and Russia
Data: fDi Markets (2023) and authors' calculations.

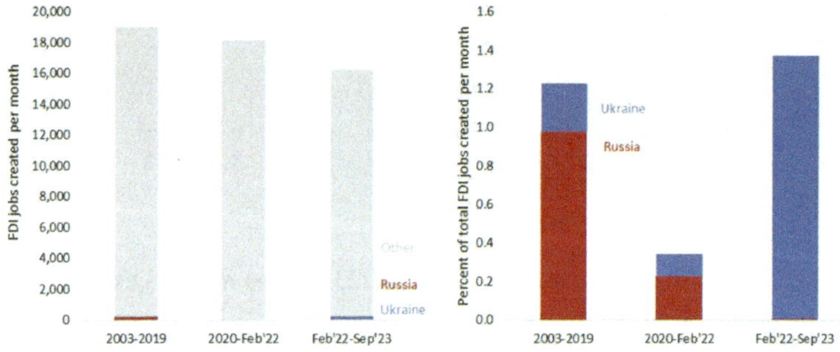

Greenfield FDI inflows from Russia to Central and Eastern European Economies over the period 2003-2019 created most jobs in coal, oil and gas, automotives, transportation and warehousing and metals (see Figure 7.22).

Overall greenfield FDI inflows declined somewhat over time, even before the start of the war in Ukraine. Greenfield FDI related jobs generated in Central and Eastern European Economies fell to around 18,000 jobs per month during the Covid pandemic, and around 16,000 since the start of the war in Ukraine. Russia's share in these inflows also declined sharply: already before the start of the war, in the period January 2020 to February 2022, its share fell from about 1 percent to just over 0.2 percent, and a negligible share since the start of the war. Inflows from Ukraine have, however, increased. Ukraine accounted for about 0.25 percent of greenfield FDI related employment creation in Central and Eastern European Economies in the period 2003-2019, 0.1 percent in 2020-February 2022, but rose to almost 1.4 percent since the start of the war, on average.

The patterns observed above hold across most Central and Eastern European Economies. Greenfield FDI inflows from Russia were largest in relative terms in the Baltic states, the only economies where Russia was among the 10 largest investors (accounting for around 3 to 6 percent of jobs generated) in the period 2003-2019, as well as in Bulgaria and Slovenia (making up around 2 percent). Its share declined to close to zero since the start of the war in Ukraine across the board (see Figure 7.23).

Ukraine's share in FDI-related job creation since the start of the war is largest in Estonia, accounting for about 5 percent of jobs generated on average, making it the 8th largest source country in terms of employment generated. It also accounts for

Fig. 7.22: Foreign direct investment inflows to Central and Eastern European Economies from Russia
Data: fDi Markets (2023) and authors' calculations.
Note: 2003-2019, total across all Central and Eastern European Economies.

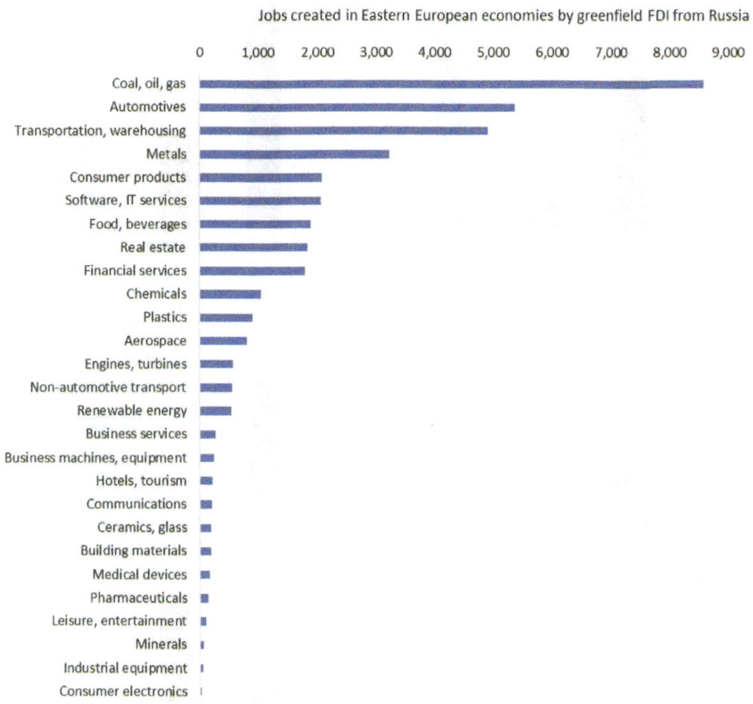

about 3 percent of jobs generated in Croatia, and around 2 percent in Poland and Slovakia.

Ukrainian greenfield FDI inflows created most jobs in Central and Eastern European Economies in software and IT services, in line with significant movement of skilled Ukrainians to these economies (and beyond) since the start of the war (see Figure 7.24). There was also some employment creation in Central and Eastern European Economies in business services, transportation and warehousing, food and beverages and space and defence.

Foreign direct investment inflows typically drop to countries engaged in wars and remain below the levels observed in similar economies thereafter (EBRD, 2023a). Net foreign direct investment was equivalent to 4.7 percent of GDP in Ukraine over the period 2003-13, that figure fell to 0.6 percent in 2014 (the year of the annexation of Crimea), with a net outflow being recorded in 2015. The associated uncertainty also weighed on future investment projects. For example, Chevron and Shell suspended their plans to develop the Olesska shale field in western Ukraine

Fig. 7.23: Foreign direct investment inflows to Central and Eastern European Economies from Ukraine and Russia (A)
Data: fDi Markets (2023) and authors' calculations.

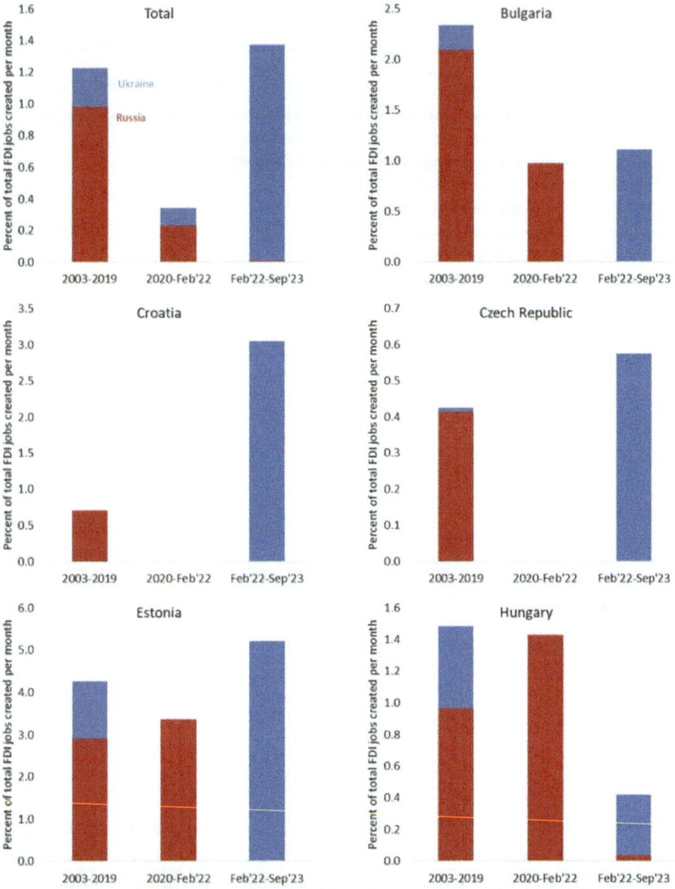

and the Yuzivska gas field in eastern Ukraine, respectively (EBRD, 2023a). The findings above highlight that the drop in net foreign direct investment inflows may, however, reflect a combination of both lower inflows (as expected, given disruptions to production processes and high uncertainty during war time) and higher outflows (capital flight, possibly following labour flows).

Fig. 7.23 Cont.: Foreign direct investment inflows to Central and Eastern European Economies from Ukraine and Russia (B)
Data: fDi Markets (2023) and authors' calculations.

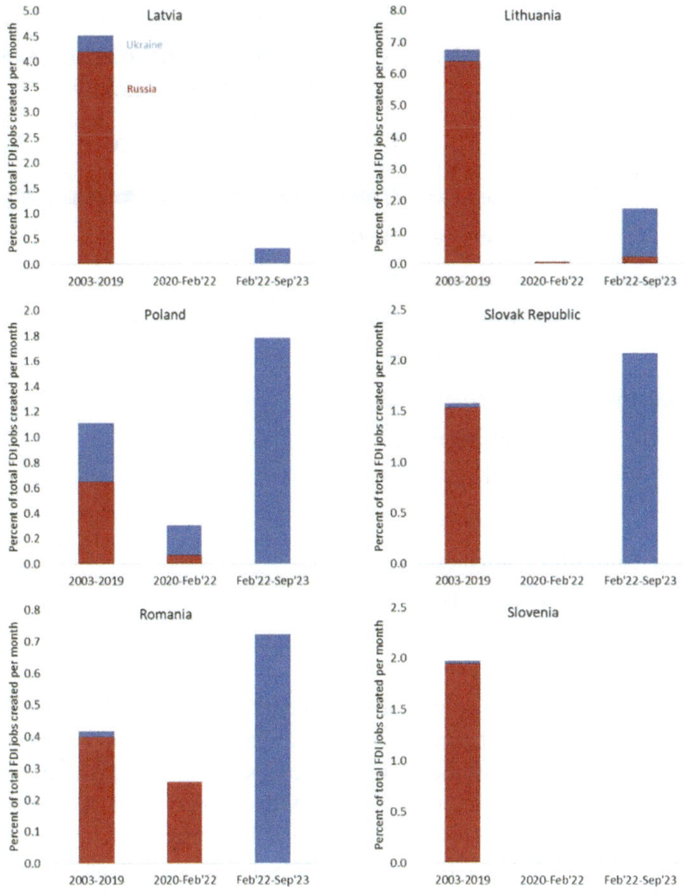

7.5 Policy Implications

In line with the findings presented in other chapters, this analysis has also highlighted that Central and Eastern European Economies remain exposed to external shocks—whether through changes in commodity prices, shifts in global market sentiment, or through value chains. Against this backdrop, Central and Eastern European Economies should enhance their resilience against such changes, including for instance by examining and tackling specific vulnerabilities across different stages of production and export and import linkages in supply chains, or in terms of energy needs (see also Chapter 2).

Fig. 7.24: Jobs created by foreign direct investment inflows to Central and Eastern European Economies from Ukraine
Data: fDi Markets (2023) and authors' calculations.
Note: 2003-2019, total across all Central and Eastern European Economies.

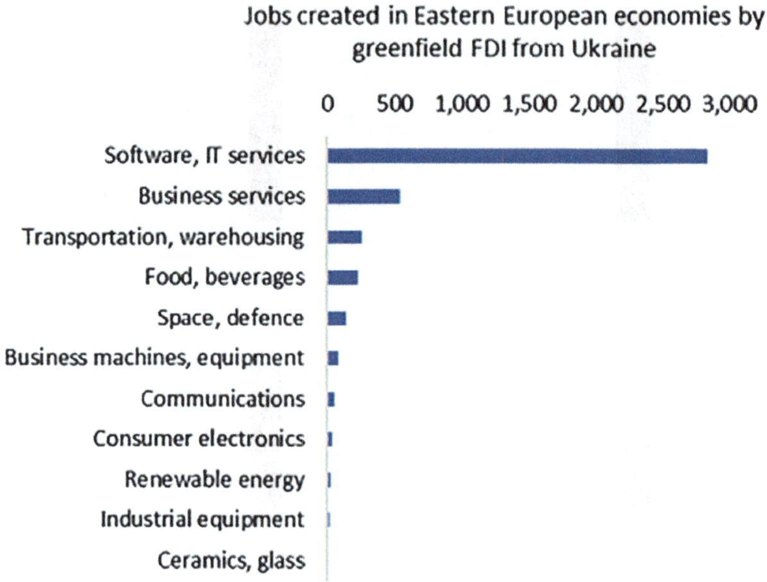

The chapter, however, also pointed to the benefits of Central and Eastern European Economies' high levels of integration. They have gained tremendously from foreign direct investment inflows over the past two decades. As this analysis suggests, they could also stand to benefit from the arrival of skilled workers and associated foreign direct investment inflows (see also Chapters 9 and 10). In general, a more conscious approach to managing foreign direct investments–to ensure matches with domestic production opportunities and available skill sets, and maximize spillovers in terms of technology and know-how–could help to increase such gains further.

On the flip side, a key takeaway for policymakers is that net foreign direct investment outflows during wars can not only consist of diminished inflows, but can also take the form of increased foreign direct investments abroad. While these are equivalent in terms of loss of funding and capital flight in the short run, in the longer term such outflows could enhance trade and other linkages between economies.

7.6 Conclusions

World trade growth slowed sharply between 2022 and 2023 as the composition of global demand shifted away from goods towards services, weighing on the outlook for economies in Eastern Europe, closely integrated in European supply chains.

The war in Ukraine has also resulted in substantial reorientation in trade patterns between Central and Eastern European Economies, Ukraine and Russia (and to a lesser extent Belarus). Imports from Ukraine accounted for a small share of overall imports for Central and Eastern European Economies before the war, however, increased substantially after the start of the war, driven by increased food imports (in particular sunflower, though corn, wheat, rapeseed and other food imports from Ukraine also increased). Exports to Ukraine also increased on average, though again from relatively low levels. The increase in exports to Ukraine was to a large extent driven by minerals and arms, exports of most other goods, including, for instance, machinery, chemicals and transport equipment, which were substantial in 2021, declined, reflecting the collapse of economic activity in Ukraine.

As the prices of oil and gas increased in the aftermath of the start of the war, Central and Eastern European Economies' imports from Russia also increased, though in some cases declines in quantities, in particular of gas, more than offset the price effect. However, for some economies, as for Ukraine, food and fertilizer imports from Russia also increased. In some economies, imports of metals, including rare earths from Russia also rose. Exports to Russia dropped for most goods, with the decline being most pronounced for machinery and transport equipment.

The terms of trade of Central and Eastern European Economies followed the path of energy prices: worsening after the start of the war, however as oil prices and European gas prices started coming down from their peaks in the second half of 2022, the terms of trade of Central and Eastern European Economies also improved substantially.

Foreign direct inflows to Central and Eastern European Economies created almost 19,000 jobs per month on average over the period 2003-2019. Inflows from Russia and Ukraine, however, accounted for only a very small fraction of these inflows, even before the start of the war. Greenfield FDI inflows from Russia made up less than 1 percent of total greenfield FDI related jobs generated in Central and Eastern European Economies over the period 2003-2019, and were concentrated in coal, oil and gas, automotives, transportation and warehousing and metals. Inflows from Russia fell to close to zero in most economies since the start of the war in Ukraine. Ukraine only accounted for around 0.2 percent of greenfield FDI-related job creation over the period 2003-2019, however, its share increased substantially since the start of the war, creating most jobs in Central and Eastern European Economies in software and IT services, in line with significant movement of skilled Ukrainians to these economies (and beyond) since the start of the war.

Acknowledgements The authors would like to thank Alexander Plekhanov, Laszlo Matyas, and Gyorgy Bogel for valuable comments and suggestions.

References

Ahn, D. P. & Ludema, R. D. (2020). The sword and the shield: The economics of targeted sanctions. *European Economic Review*, *130*, 103587. Retrieved from https://www.sciencedirect.com/science/article/abs/pii/S0014292120302178

Bloomberg. (2023). *Database.* (Accessed: 01-12-2023 through Bloomberg terminal)

Chupilkin, M., Javorcik, B. & Plekhanov, A. (2023). *The Eurasian roundabout: Trade flows into Russia through the Caucasus and Central Asia* (No. 276). EBRD. Retrieved from https://www.ebrd.com/publications/working-papers/the-eurasian-roundabout

Crozet, M. & Hinz, J. (2020). Friendly fire: The trade impact of the Russia sanctions and counter-sanctions. *Economic Policy*, *35*(101), 97–146. Retrieved from https://academic.oup.com/economicpolicy/article-abstract/35/101/97/5836299?redirectedFrom=fulltext

EBRD. (2023a). *The economics of war and peace* (Tech. Rep.). EBRD. Retrieved from https://www.ebrd.com/transition-report-2022-23

EBRD. (2023b). *Shifting gears* (Tech. Rep.). EBRD. Retrieved from https://www.ebrd.com/what-we-do/economic-research-and-data/rep.html

European Comission. (2023). *Annual macroeconomic database ameco.* https://data.europa.eu/data/datasets/ameco. (Accessed: 01-12-2023)

fDi Markets. (2023). *Database.* https://www.fdimarkets.com/. (Accessed: 01-12-2023 through subscription)

General Administration of Customs of the People's Republic of China. (2023). *Database.* http://stats.customs.gov.cn/indexEn. (Accessed: 01-12-2023)

Hinz, J. & Monastyrenko, E. (2022). Bearing the cost of politics: Consumer prices and welfare in Russia. *Journal of International Economics*, *137*, 103581. Retrieved from https://www.sciencedirect.com/science/article/abs/pii/S0022199622000137

IMF. (2023). *Navigating global divergences* (Tech. Rep.). IMF. Retrieved from https://www.imf.org/en/Publications/WEO/Issues/2023/10/10/world-economic-outlook-october-2023

International Monetary Fund. (2023). *October 2023 world economic outlook database.* https://www.imf.org/en/Publications/WEO/weo-database/2023/October. (Accessed: 01-12-2023)

Koczan, Z., Paetzold, P. & Vujic, N. (2021). *Those Were the Days? Greenfield FDI, Jobs and Inclusion in Emerging Markets* (No. 262). EBRD. Retrieved from https://www.ebrd.com/publications/working-papers/those-were-the-days

Peeva, A. (2019). *Did sanctions help Putin?* (Discussion Paper No. 2019/7). Free University Berlin, School of Business Economics. Retrieved from https://refubium.fu-berlin.de/handle/fub188/24769?locale-attribute=en

Plekhanov, A. & Sassoon, J. (2023). *Gas consumption in Europe during the winter of 2022-23* (No. 284). EBRD. Retrieved from https://www.ebrd.com/publications/working-papers/gas-consumption-in-europe-during-the-winter-of-2022-23

Refinitiv Eikon. (2023). *Database.* (Accessed: 01-12-2023 through subscription)

United Nations. (2023). *Comtrade database*. https://comtradeplus.un.org/. (Accessed: 01-12-2023 through premium API subscription)

Chapter 8
Refugees: Economic Costs and Eventual Benefits

György Bőgel, Jan Brzozowski, Karolina Czerska-Shaw, László Mátyás, and Katalin Tausz

Abstract The war between Ukraine and Russia resulted in Europe's largest refugee crisis since World War II. The chapter begins with a brief historic overview needed for a realistic assessment of the current situation. Then it deals with the problems of definitions and ambiguous, patchy, and sometimes contradictory statistics. The evolution of the international institutional and legal system for refugees is described, with its strengths and weaknesses analysed. Special attention is paid to the activities of the UNHCR. Recent trends and developments regarding attitudes and policies towards refugees are also discussed. The current Ukrainian refugee wave is compared with some earlier, and the most relevant data is presented on the magnitude and other dimensions of the refugee migration that the war has caused. The state of the refugees in CEE countries is described, focusing on Poland, where the number of Ukrainian refugees is the highest. Policies, field activities, costs and other expenditures are compared, especially those of accommodation, health, living conditions and education. A special section is devoted to the protection of children. The most important lessons learnt and policy recommendations are summarised at the end.

György Bőgel ✉
Central European University, Budapest, Hungary and Vienna, Austria, e-mail: bogelgy@ceu.edu

Jan Brzozowski
Jagiellonian University, Kraków, Poland, e-mail: jan.brzozowski@uj.edu.pl

Karolina Czerska-Shaw
Jagiellonian University, Kraków, Poland, e-mail: karolina.czerska@uj.edu.pl

László Mátyás,
Central European University, Budapest, Hungary and Vienna, Austria, e-mail: matyas@ceu.edu

Katalin Tausz,
Eötvös Loránd University, Budapest, Hungary, e-mail: tauszkati@gmail.com

© The Author(s), under exclusive license to Springer Nature Switzerland AG 2024
L. Mátyás (ed.), *Central and Eastern European Economies and the War in Ukraine*, Contributions to Economics, https://doi.org/10.1007/978-3-031-61561-0_8

8.1 Refugees and Migrants: Definitions, Data Sources, and the General Social and Political Context

According to the State Statistic Service of Ukraine (2021), the size of the country's population was 41.9 million in 2020, excluding the territory of the Autonomous Republic of Crimea and the city of Sevastopol occupied by Russia in 2014. The Russian army attacked Ukraine in February 2022. By the end of March, the same year, millions had fled the country, and millions had been displaced inside it. The conflict generated the largest flow of refugees in a single year since the end of the Cold War. The size and the speed of the refugee wave placed a huge strain on neighbouring countries.

For assessing the situation and for developing and implementing efficient and lasting solutions, we have to understand the economic, social, political, legal and institutional environment where this unprecedented wave of Ukrainian refugees arrived, considering similarities and differences between the host countries.

Analysis should always be supported with data, but in this case, it is not easy to meet that requirement. Ambiguity of definitions, differences in concepts and data collection methodologies between countries make the interpretation and comparison of international migration data very difficult. In some cases, people who have never undertaken migration are also referred to as 'migrants', e.g., 'second or third generation migrants'. Indicators change rapidly, statistics are frequently contradictory or confusing, and it is sometimes hard or impossible to identify the extent that different statistical populations overlap. Figures are often patchy and may understate the real number of uprooted people. In some countries, data published (or not published) may become 'political products' with the goal of influencing the public mood: the war is taking place not only on the battlefield, but also in the information space. The map of Central and Eastern Europe (CEE) has radically changed since 1990. The dissolution of the Yugoslav state started in 1991; the self-determined split of Czechoslovakia into the independent states of the Czech Republic and Slovakia took effect at the end of 1992; fifteen republics gained full independence after the dissolution of the Soviet Union in December 1991. As the borders have moved, some people might have become 'foreigners' officially or informally in the part of the world where they lived or could receive dual citizenship (Mikanowski, 2023). We try to use reliable information sources but are aware that even data coming from well-known organisations may sometimes be contradictory or confusing.

We have to be especially careful with using and comparing stock and flow figures (Shaver et al., 2022): within short periods, refugees may cross borders multiple times, they may look for asylum in different countries at the same time, many of them try to return home, several others are moving on to other countries, and all this may happen in a very short time. Refugees' movement from country to country inside the EU is not necessarily registered officially. When refugees enter a Schengen country, they are allowed to travel on to other Schengen countries without visa or border checks, consequently it is not precisely known where they are at any given time.

At the end of 2019 (the year before the Covid-19 epidemic struck) there were approximately 80 million uprooted or displaced people in the world for a variety of reasons (Loescher, 2021). According to the United Nations' 1951 Refugee Convention, refugees are persons who, 'owing to a well-founded fear of persecution, on the grounds of race, religion, nationality or membership of a social group', are displaced outside of their country of origin, and are unable or unwilling to enjoy the protection of that country. Their number was about 24 million at the end of 2019 (ibid.). Being a refugee is not only a formal status, but also a state of mind: refugees are abruptly and violently uprooted from their familiar world, may experience violence and discrimination, and may be perceived as an economic burden and cultural threat (Kurkov, 2023). They cross borders to receive protection and assistance, but many other displaced persons do not: they are called internally displaced persons or IDPs. Based on some estimates, in 2019 there were more than 45 million IDPs. Many refugees are asylum seekers who officially submit claims for asylum in their host country. We should add that there are also millions of stateless persons in the world, without citizenship or any official documentation.

Refugees, asylum seekers, and IDPs are collectively defined as forced migrants. Refugees are international migrants, but not all international migrants are refugees. The basis of the distinction is whether the movement is voluntary. The UN estimates that there were more than 250 million international migrants in 2019, and their number has grown by 49% since 2000 (Loescher, 2021). In many instances, it has become increasingly difficult to distinguish between refugees and migrants who often use the same routes. Governments are generally interested in keeping the definition of refugees narrow, concerned that otherwise, they may have obligations for a larger number of people.

Besides armed conflicts, war, massacres, genocides and other kinds of direct violence, there are several incentives for international migration: scarcity of land and water, poverty, differences in living standards, job opportunities, climate change and other environmental pressures, rapid population growth, degradation of human habitat, weak and failing states where governance capacity is collapsing and who are unwilling or unable to provide even basic human protection (Fiddian-Qasmiyeh, Loescher, Long & Sigona, 2014). According to some estimates, by the year 2050, 140 million people may be displaced due to climate change only (Betts, 2021). New opportunities for migration have also emerged: globalisation, improving transportation and telecommunications, the rapid spread of social media, growing and better-organised diaspora networks, the development of people smuggling as a business, and so on.

Before considering the costs and benefits of the international movement of refugees and forced migrants from Ukraine to CEE countries, we should explore the theoretical concepts of international migration. Although there is no single, unanimously accepted theory of international migration (Skeldon, 2012), there is a predominant understanding that most contemporary economic migrants are favourably self-selected in terms of their socio-economic and demographic characteristics (Chiquiar & Hanson, 2005). They tend to be younger (Mayda, 2022), healthier (Lu, 2008), better educated (Bernard & Bell, 2018), and have more work or business experience than the average individual in their home countries. This positive self-selection of economic migrants is further enhanced by selective migration policies in developed countries, where entry preferences are given to highly skilled individuals (Brücker & Defoort, 2009). Additionally, voluntary migration decisions are often made with at least some degree of rationality, involving planning and preparation, where future benefits and risks are considered (Brzozowski & Coniglio, 2021). Consequently, ex-post evidence shows that, upon settling in a new destination, economic migrants generally experience an improvement in their living conditions (Battisti, Peri & Romiti, 2022). Furthermore, international migration yields benefits beyond economic outcomes, as many individuals observe a significant increase in subjective well-being, measured by happiness or life satisfaction scores, compared to their situation before migration (Hendriks & Bartram, 2019).

However, these positive effects are valid mainly for economic migrants. In the case of individuals forced to leave their home countries due to military conflicts, persecution, or natural disasters, the selection process is not always positive. Studies indicate that refugees are positively selected for education in distant destinations, such as Iraqis or Syrians moving to Western Europe (Aksoy & Poutvaara, 2021), while those moving short distances, typically to neighbouring countries, are usually negatively selected in this aspect (Welker, 2022). Moreover, forced migrants move out of necessity, rather than choice, which may lead to ill-prepared migration projects, rushed departures without proper planning, and difficulty in obtaining essential documents certifying their educational and professional background. Additionally, they are more exposed to health hazards, physically and mentally, and are more likely to seek healthcare services at their destination than economic migrants. Consequently, welcoming refugees is primarily a humanitarian obligation and a moral principle rather than 'good business'. On average, the socio-economic integration of forced migrants and refugees is less successful than that of economic migrants (Brell, Dustmann & Preston, 2020).

Another crucial aspect requiring closer attention is distinguishing between voluntary and involuntary migration. While theoretical frameworks easily classify migrating individuals, real-life situations are often more complex (Erdal & Oeppen, 2018). Many economic migrants could be de facto refugees or forced migrants, as, even one individual may have diverse motives for moving. For example, during the 1980s political and economic crisis in Poland, some citizens were welcomed as refugees in Western Europe, the US, Canada, and Australia, while only a fraction of them had been active members of the Solidarity movement fighting the communist regime, which could result in political persecution (Pleskot, 2015). Similarly, in the Ukrainian diaspora's current situation, one should consider that for many Ukrainians, the military conflict began as early as February 2014, with the Russian annexation of Crimea and the Russian-sponsored separatist conflict in the Donbas region. Consequently, labelled as economic migrants, many Ukrainians who migrated to Central and Eastern Europe between February 2014 and January 2022, were at least partially internally displaced persons in Ukraine who later chose to emigrate from their home country. This continuity of economic and forced migration is a specific feature of the Ukrainian diaspora, resulting in unique patterns of social, cultural, and economic integration in major destinations.

Forced displacement and migration is not a new phenomenon in history. In the 1950s large groups of people fled the East European communist countries looking for resettlement in the West, where some 900,000 European refugees were absorbed, mainly by the USA. In the 1970s there was mass exodus from East Pakistan, Uganda, Cyprus, and Indochina. In the 1980s growing numbers of asylum seekers started to migrate from the Global South to the well-developed countries of the North. In the 1990s, brutal armed conflicts, genocides and ethnic cleansing in the Balkans, Afghanistan, Myanmar, and Central Africa forced many people to leave their countries and look for protection elsewhere. The early 21st century, the 'War on Terror' and the Western occupations of Iraq and Afghanistan opened a new chapter in the history of international migration. By the end of 2019, more than six million people had fled Syria, where millions more were internally displaced (Loescher, 2021).

In some countries of today's world, we notice a proliferation of complex emergencies, e.g., environmental degradation combined with ethnic and religious tensions generate political instability and armed conflicts, leading to economic collapse coupled with the disintegration of civil society. The average duration of refugee situations is getting longer, with increasing numbers of people spending decades outside their home countries. Millions of Palestinian have been in exile since 1948.

The vast majority of refugees do not travel far. They tend to stay in countries neighbouring their homelands, living in camps and urban areas (mainly slums). These days, 85% of them are in the Global South. At the end of 2019, the countries hosting the largest refugee groups were Turkey, Colombia, Pakistan, and Uganda. Since the refugee crisis in 2014-15, when more than a million people attempted to get into the EU (Pachocka, 2016), there has been a dramatic drop in the numbers of refugees and asylum seekers arriving in Europe from Africa and Asia, but even now many risk their lives crossing borders and the open seas.

The subject of migration is usually highly politicised. Immigration and refugee issues strike deep social, political, cultural, religious, and political chords in many countries. Several governments of developed countries set strict limits on migrants and use such control measures as tight pre-arrival screening, limiting access to social and health services, routine deportation to so-called 'safe third countries', forced separation of families, prolonged detention of asylum seekers, building walls and razor wire fences, and bilateral deals with transit countries. This attitude and behaviour are historically not new, e.g., the general consensus during the Great Depression in the first half of the 20th century was that national interest must be served by imposing limits on immigration, and the nations' own citizens must be prioritised when offering employment opportunities. Human rights principles frequently clash with the economic, security and political interests of certain groups of actors. Nationalist and populist leaders may use hatred and fear as political tools. Disinformation and prejudice spread very fast through online channels. Refugees and asylum seekers, mixed with other migrants who are looking for a better and safer life are frequently perceived as evidence of the risks and dangers of open societies and economic globalisation. In many people's eyes, refugees are 'economic migrants in disguise' who cause tensions and violence, and drain national resources.

Asylum practices differ from country to country, but asylum seekers are commonly asked to prove that they were persecuted at home, and if they have no proof, they may be deported or may only be granted temporary right to remain. The hidden goal of long and bureaucratic processes may be to deter others from seeking asylum. An emerging new refugee treatment model is based on prevention, containment, and fast repatriation.

Observing the high and growing numbers of forced displacements, it transpires that the international community must be mobilised to ensure protection and provide lasting solutions for refugees. The basic forms of lasting or 'durable' solutions are repatriation, resettlement in another country, or local integration in a receiving country, preferably a nearby one. It is not an easy job, because state sovereignty prevents the international community from intervening without the individual countries' approval, unless the UN Security Council authorizes such action under a specific chapter of the UN Charter. Unfortunately, the UN's Security Council is a rather inactive and sharply divided organisation.

Currently, the most important international organisation responsible for the protection of refugees is the United Nations High Commissioner for Refugees (UNHCR). It was created in 1950, a few years after World War II, and since then has undergone an impressive growth in the scope and scale of its work. According to data published on its website (UNHCR: The UN Refugee Agency, 2023), it works in 137 countries and territories, employing almost 19,000 people at the end of 2021, with their large majority based in the field. The UNHCR's budget increased to USD 9.15 billion in 2021, and in 2023 it planned to raise 10.211 billion USD, to support an expected 117.2 million displaced and stateless people (UNHCR, 2022f).

Officially the UNHCR works under the authority of the UN's General Assembly, but only its administrative costs are covered by the general budget of the UN, and for its operative work it needs voluntary contributions. The logic of the present international refugee system is built on the voluntary cooperation of states, with no binding obligation to share the costs of providing asylum. The UNHCR plays a vital role, but only with the approval and active contribution of states can it implement solutions. About 80% of its budget comes from a small group of donor states (Loescher, 2021). The organisation has to respond to the interests of the leading donor states, who frequently 'earmark' their contributions for specific countries and projects: in the recent past, mainly for Syria and Afghanistan. The consensus of states may be quickly eroded by the continuously changing global order and state interests.

Regarding the scope of the UNHCR's work, since 2005 it has also assumed formal responsibility for the protection of internally displaced persons.

The UNHCR is a major actor in the present 'refugee ecosystem', but only one of many. It has to compete for attention, resources and political support with other players like national and international offices, support organisations, religious and professional groups, and thousands of NGOs. There were relatively few international NGOs working on refugee issues until the late 1980s, but their numbers have recently exploded. After the European migration crisis in 2014-15, in most EU countries opposition to further inflows of refugees and asylum seekers increased quickly, nevertheless generosity towards refugees is still impressive in civil society. Some civil organisations, e.g., the IKEA Foundation have significant resources. Médecins Sans Frontières is a non-profit, self-governing, member-based, worldwide organisation that can mobilise more than 60,000 people, mainly doctors and nurses. Its activities are frequently coordinated with the Red Cross, a humanitarian organisation capable of mobilising about 100 million volunteers worldwide. In 2021, it raised EUR 1.94 billion from millions of individual donors and private institutions (Médecins Sans Frontières, 2023). Considering the size, diversity and complexity of the 'refugee ecosystem', assessing the total costs of specific operations is a complex task.

The 'refugee ecosystem' is a highly competitive 'marketplace' of many actors representing different and frequently clashing interests. The number of rich donor states is limited, and only a few of them run regular resettlement programs. In the emerging 'refugee regime complex' (Betts, 2010), issues of humanitarianism, security, labour migration, international travel, peace-building and economic development are mixed, and the same confusion and cacophony is observed in the media and common talk.

We have to note here that there is limited research available on the role of NGOs in contemporary refugee crises (Milner & Klassen, 2021), while the mechanisms and means of their influence, and the intended and unintended consequences of their work are frequently debated.

In 2016, the UN General Assembly adopted the New York Declaration for Refugees and Migrants. The document confirms that global approaches and solutions are required, and that closed refugee camps must be the exception, refugees should be included in the communities; they must be allowed to develop and use their skills and become self-reliant, to contribute to local economies, and support the development of the communities hosting them. On 17 December 2018, the United Nations General Assembly affirmed the Global Compact on Refugees, providing a framework and blueprint for governments and other actors to ensure that communities hosting refugees receive significant support and refugees can lead meaningful and productive lives.

In a nutshell, the general economic, social, political and institutional environment was hard hit by the war between Russia and Ukraine and the unprecedented refugee wave set in motion in February 2022.

8.2 Dimensions and Characteristics of the Ukrainian Refugee Flow

The number of international migrants has increased over the past decades. According to the statistics published in the United Nations' World Migration Report (United Nations, 2022, p. 23) the number of international migrants was 84 million in 1970. This number increased to 281 million by 2020, which means that about 3.6% of the world's population lived in a country other than where they were born. Although the impact of the Covid-19 epidemic on the population of migrants is difficult to assess, the UN estimates that it may have reduced the growth in the stock of international migrants by around two million, but that was only a temporary drop. According to EUROSTAT, 1.9 million immigrants entered the EU from non-EU countries in 2020, which is a decrease of almost 30% compared with 2019, but 2.3 million immigrants arrived in 2021 (Eurostat, 2023a). In 2020, the major region of residence (destination) for international migrants was Europe, currently hosting about 31% of migrant population (United Nations, 2022, p. 24). At that time, the majority of international migrants were of working age, and the male to female split was 52 to 48%.

Table 8.1 shows the size of foreign inflows in five former socialist countries of CEE, as registered by the OECD's migration database between 2008 and 2018 (Austria is added for comparison). Table 8.2 shows the percentage of foreign-born population in the same countries.

Table 8.1: Inflows of foreign population into selected OECD countries (thousand people)
Data: OECD (2023)

	2008	2009	2010	2011	2012	2013	2014	2015	2016	2017	2018
Czechia	76.2	38.2	28.0	20.7	28.6	27.8	38.5	31.6	34.8	43.5	55.9
Hungary	35.5	25.6	23.9	22.5	20.3	21.3	26.0	25.8	23.8	36.5	49.3
Poland	41.8	41.3	41.1	41.3	47.1	46.6	32.0	86.1	107.0	128.0	137.6
Slovakia	7.4	5.1	4.2	3.8	2.9	2.5	2.4	3.8	3.6	2.9	2.9
Slovenia	43.8	24.2	11.3	18.0	17.3	15.7	18.4	19.9	20.0	27.7	2.9
Austria	94.4	91.7	69.9	109.9	125.6	165.2	154.3	198.7	158.7	139.3	131.7

Table 8.2: Stocks of foreign-born population as a % of total population, 2019
Data: OECD (2023)

	%
Czechia	8.5
Hungary	5.8
Poland	2.0
Slovakia	3.6
Slovenia	12.8
Austria	19.3

As stated in the Introduction, not all migrants are refugees or asylum seekers. According to the UNHCR's 2022 Mid-year Trends report (UNHCR, 2022b), there were 32.5 million refugees in the middle of 2022 including 26.7 million under the organisation's mandate and 5.8 million Palestinian refugees who belong to the UNRWA.[1] The number of asylum seekers was 4.9 million, and there were 53.1 million internally displaced persons (ibid. p.2). More than three quarters of all refugees and other people in need of international protection came from just six countries (Table 8.3).

Table 8.3: Number of refugees by country of origin, middle of 2022
Data: UNHCR (2022b)

	Million
Syria	6.8
Venezuela	5.6
Ukraine	5.4
Afghanistan	2.8
South Sudan	2.4
Myanmar	1.2

Measured by today's standards, there were only three relatively large, forced displacement flows across borders within one specific year between 1981 and 2011, each well below three million persons. There was a sudden large outflow from Afghanistan in 1981, another one from Iraq in 1991 after the first Gulf War, and from Afghanistan again in 2000. Each extra wave was followed by smaller ones in the years after the large outflows. This trend has changed radically from 2012, when refugees started to flow out of war-ravaged Syria. Refugees from Syria, South Sudan and Myanmar ignited a large refugee wave of multiple years between 2012 and 2017. The Venezuelan refugee exodus, caused by power shifts in the country, pushed the yearly number above five million in 2018, then, after a short Covid-19 interval, came the war between Russia and Ukraine, igniting the largest and fastest cross-border refugee outflow in one year since the end of the Cold War.

Before the full-scale Russian invasion in 2022, the annexation of Crimea in 2014 and the war in the Donbas (both of which may in retrospect be interpreted as preludes to the frontal attack in 2022) had already resulted in more than two million refugees and internally displaced persons. According to some reports, their reception was rather cool in Europe with relatively low success rates in asylum claims and weak media interest (Mitchneck, Zavisca & Gerbe, 2016). Many of them were uprooted again when the war started in 2022.

[1] The war in Gaza which erupted in 2023 may change this number.

Due to a highly turbulent history and serious economic, social and political problems (Sakwa, 2014), in many parts of the world Ukraine had a large diaspora. At the end of 2021, 1.57 million Ukrainian citizens were officially authorised to stay in the EU, representing the third biggest non-EU citizen group. The largest groups lived in Poland, Italy (more than 230 thousand) and Czechia, and many had residence permits in Czechia, Poland, Lithuania, Estonia and Slovakia (Eurostat, 2023b). Before the war, Ukrainian citizens were the most numerous foreign workers in Poland, it is highly probable that in some periods demand far exceeded supply. After 2010, tens of thousands of Hungarians in Ukraine received Hungarian citizenship and passports, thus becoming dual citizens according to the Hungarian legal system. Double citizenship, although officially not penalised, is not legally recognised by the Ukrainian constitution. Under the present wartime conditions, it is extremely uncertain how this situation may change, how these travel documents can be used, where these people are, and what other international complications may arise from the system. Table 8.4 shows the number of Ukrainian citizens with a valid residence permit in the eight CEE countries at the end of 2021.

Table 8.4: Number of Ukrainian citizens holding a valid residence permit at the end of 2021
Data: UNHCR (2022b)

	Head
Bulgaria	9,149
Croatia	2,405
Czechia	193,547
Hungary	63,175
Poland	651,221
Romania	2,260
Slovakia	54,138
Slovenia	2,655

The war in Ukraine started on 24 February, 2022. By the end of February 2022, about 2.3 million Ukrainian refugees had entered neighbouring EU countries (The Economist, 2021), almost as many as in 2015 and 2016 combined, at a culmination period of the Syrian war. According to the data continuously collected and updated by the UNHCR (UNHCR, 2023b), 1,720,227 refugee arrivals were registered at the Polish border between 24 February and 13 March, plus 255,291 in Hungary, 204,862 in Slovakia, 84,671 in Romania, 131,365 in Russia, 106,994 in Moldova, 1,226 in Belarus, and 304,156 in other European countries. By the end of May, Poland alone had taken 3,5 million refugees.

Four million people fled war-ravaged Ukraine in just five weeks, and millions more were displaced at home. That number is far higher than any other since 1990, especially if we consider that, officially, men of fighting age were not allowed to leave Ukraine. The sentiments and intentions of uprooted people may fluctuate rapidly due to such after-shock psychological conditions as confusion, fear, panic, rage, euphoria, apathy, and depression. The Economist reported that in the two weeks to May 23, 2022 the number of Ukrainians travelling home from Poland (345,000) was well above of those entering the host country (253,000), and other countries also observed a similar trend (The Economist, 2022a). By the middle of June the same year, the cumulative number of border-crossings from Ukraine into neighbouring countries reached 7.7 million, while the flow in the opposite direction stood at 2.6 million, meaning that only about a third of those who fled the country may be going home (The Economist, 2022b). Some of the crossings may only be short trips to check what is happening, and how conditions are changing at home.

EU countries bordering Ukraine have allowed entry to all Ukrainian refugees, and the EU has invoked, with the unanimous approval of its Member States, the 2001 EU Temporary Protection Directive (TPD) providing temporary, but immediate protection for displaced persons arriving from outside the Union's borders. The directive was introduced in the aftermath of the Yugoslav wars, has been in effect since August 2001, but the first time it was invoked was in 2022. It is intended to be used in exceptional circumstances when the 'normal' EU asylum system cannot handle properly a sudden mass refugee influx. It requires Member States to host refugees according to their capacity and to behave by the principles of solidarity and balanced efforts.

Between May and September 2022, the UNHCR and its partners in some host countries conducted thousands of interviews with adult refugees from Ukraine about their profile, needs and intentions at the time of data collection (UNHCR, 2022d). According to that random sample survey, most adult refugees (85%) were women, many of them holding university or higher degrees (46%) or certificates of vocational training (29%). Since men aged 18 to 60 are not allowed to leave Ukraine, 87% of refugees were women with children, a ratio confirmed not only by official statistics but by numerous (sometimes shocking) photographs published in the media. The 'typical refugee' is a young woman with a small child. 13% were older persons. 23% of respondents had visited Ukraine at least once since their first arrival. The top three urgent needs were cash, employment, and accommodation. 63% of the respondents planned to stay in their present host country in the near future.

The unprecedented outflow of women and children may profoundly and permanently change Ukraine. The country's demographic decline may be accelerated to an unprecedented degree. The war with Russia has caused a large-scale demographic disruption with an unpredictable future (Aksyonova, 2022). Ukraine was a country in deep demographic crisis even before the war. The extremely low fertility rate (the lowest in Europe in 2021) is combined with a rapidly aging population, high mortality, poor health conditions, striking inequalities, intensive external and internal migration, a growing gap between rural and urban areas, and many other economic and social challenges. Most families have only one child. According to the Ukrainian data analytics website Opendatabot, the country's birth rate was 28% lower in the first six months of 2023 than in the same period in 2021, and that has been the highest decline since Ukraine gained its independence in 1991.

In March 2022, Andrey Kurkov, a prominent Ukrainian writer published an article in The Economist's 1843 Magazine (Kurkov, A., 2022) stating that although displacement on this scale is hard to grasp, in his opinion refugees fall into different 'tribes'. The largest group is that of 'first timers': people who had to flee their home for the first time, who are in panic, are disoriented and look into the future with horror. Another group is that of 'double refugees', persons who fled the war and the economic disaster in eastern Ukraine and resettled in the central and eastern parts of the country, mainly in cities. They are less scared but more fatalistic, and when having to flee again, they use their previous experience to decide what and what not to take along. Then, there are people who simply run for their life. Others plan their exit meticulously, collect information and try to assess the real situation before taking to the road. Groups and individuals have different choices and options. Although it is a mass exodus, each refugee has her/his own story. The confusion of refugees and of those receiving them, the complexity of life situations, the diversity of intentions and plans, and the general uncertainty are well reflected in the reports based on personal experiences on the spot (Hetényi, 2023).

In any serious conflict, the first to flee are people who can: individuals with cars, credit cards, family members or friends abroad, and language skills. Many refugees fleeing the invasion carry with them trauma and loss, and suffer the stress of family separation and living abroad. Politicians in host countries say refugees will return home once peace is restored, but that eventual return depends on several factors.

The UNHCR's Regional Bureau for Europe regularly publishes Flash Updates on the Ukrainian situation. In the 16 January, 2023 issue (UNHCR, 2023b, latest document), they reported that fluctuating pendular movements could be observed to and from Ukraine. Although there were some slight increases in exit numbers depending on the intensity of the war and the destruction taking place, no significant increase was reported.

As the war went on, the UNHCR's support shifted from an emergency project to a longer-term response. The UNHCR and the UNICEF established 39 Blue Dots (protection and support hubs) in eight countries. Using the country snapshots in the UNHCR's 16 January 2023 Flash Update, Table 8.5 gives the number of refugees registered for temporary protection and the numbers of those that received cash assistance. Temporary protection is a protection status for Ukrainian refugees, available in the EU. It provides residency rights such as access to shelter if one needs it, social welfare assistance, medical care, access to education for children under 18 and access to the labour market without a work permit.

Table 8.5: Ukrainian refugees, country updates as of January 11, 2023
Data: UNHCR (2022b)

	Refugees registered for temporary protection (head)	Refugees receiving cash assistance (head)
Bulgaria	150,510	5,060
Czechia	477,614	n.a.
Hungary	33,446	n.a.
Poland	1,563,386	293,073
Romania	103,825	43,000
Slovakia	105,533	29,458
Estonia	42,000	n.a.
Latvia	45,000	n.a.
Lithuania	73,000	n.a.

In March 2022, the UNHCR developed a Regional Refugee Response Plan (RRP) with the purpose of coordinating the efforts of 142 partners including the International Red Cross and Red Crescent, UN agencies, national and international NGOs, religious institutions, academic institutions and local civil societies. The plan was recalibrated in October the same year to be adapted to emerging priorities and winter-related needs. The UNHCR's continuously updated Operational Data Portal publishes data on the numbers of refugees from Ukraine recorded in the countries featured in the RRP (In February 2024 these were Bulgaria, Czechia, Estonia, Hungary, Latvia, Lithuania, Poland, the Republic of Moldova, Romania, and Slovakia), and in other countries. Table 8.6 shows the situation in the RRP countries and six others between January 2023 and February 2024.

Table 8.6: Number of refugees from Ukraine recorded in 16 selected countries, January–September 2023 (stock data, number of registered refugees present in a country on a given day)
Data: UNHCR (2023b)
Note: UNHCR's data table separates columns for 'refugees registered for temporary protection' (see Table 8.5 and the explanation above it) and 'refugees recorded in country' (used in this table), which is the estimated number of individual refugees who are currently present in a country. Some numbers may be rounded or not updated on time. Countries in italics are featured in the UNHCR's Refugee Response Plan (list downloaded on 22 Sept 2023).

Country	22 January	22 March	22 May	22 July	22 September
Bulgaria	50,325	49,610	50,576	162,935	61,150
Czechia	482,049	497,217	520,234	354,825	368,300
Estonia	66,074	67,601	71,215	48,590	50,450
Hungary	33,603	34,248	35,030	52,335	53,375
Latvia	35,212	35,243	31,769	38,145	32,470
Lithuania	73,040	75,197	77,444	48,425	49,970
Moldova	102,283	107,277	108,620	113,555	116,950
Poland	1,563,386	1,564,711	1,602,062	968,390	959,875
Romania	106,644	110,106	94,952	95,430	85,255
Slovakia	107,476	111,756	116,202	104,830	108,500
Austria	91,631	94,551	97,047	100,575	68,700
Croatia	20,164	21,232	22,382	22,760	23,430
Germany	1,021,667	1,021,667	1,061,623	1,079,815	1,094,155
Italy	167,925	171,739	175,107	163,750	167,525
Slovenia	9,081	9,075	9,312	9,935	10,195
United Kingdom	155,509	165,700	204,700	208,500	210,800

The total number of refugees from Ukraine recorded across Europe was 5,828,000 on 22 September 2023, and the global figure was 6,197,200. 24,882,825 border crossings were recorded from Ukraine since 24 February 2022, and 17,896,775 to Ukraine in the same period. The difference between the number of refugees recorded (stock) and border crossings (flow) is especially striking in the case of Poland where the high number of refugees is combined with intensive two-way border traffic (Duszczyk & Kaczmarczyk, 2022).

At the beginning of March 2023, The Economist, using multiple data sources (University of Warsaw, Destatis, Eurostat, IMF, ONS, UNHCR) published data on Ukrainian refugees living in selected countries as a percentage of the population

Table 8.6 Cont.: Number of refugees from Ukraine recorded in 16 selected countries, November 2023 – February 2024 (stock data, number of registered refugees present in a country on a given day)

Country	November 22nd 2023	January 23rd 2024	February 23rd 2024
Bulgaria	52,245	51,860	67,770
Czechia	368,685	375,590	381,400
Estonia	50,450	50,450	38,245
Hungary	53,375	63,775	65,558
Latvia	32,470	46,610	43,825
Lithuania	50,690	52,305	52,670
Moldova	113,185	120,695	116,195
Poland	958,939	956,635	956,635
Romania	83,280	85,710	78,745
Slovakia	111,860	114,270	115,875
Austria	106,215	83,185	84,135
Croatia	23,855	24,150	24,355
Germany	1,114,070	1,125,850	1,139,690
Italy	167,525	169,040	168,840
Slovenia	10,435	10,635	10,865
United Kingdom	246,760	250,360	253,160

(Fig. 8.1). It is evident from that chart, that the burden of supporting refugees is not spread evenly across countries.

At the end of 2023 and the beginning of 2024, Russia appeared to be determined to exhaust Ukraine and to wear out its partners turning the country into a dysfunctional and abandoned state whose refugees cause problems in Europe. Aware of the military situation, observers have increasingly expressed the opinion that both countries (and Europe) must be prepared for a long war and a prolonged refugee crisis. By UNHCR's Operational Data Portal (UNHCR, 2023b), 6,004,100 refugees from Ukraine were recorded in Europe in the middle of February 2024, and 6,479,700 were recorded globally.

Fig. 8.1: Ukrainian refugees living in selected countries, as % of population, Feb. 15, 2023 or latest available
Data: The Economist (2023a)

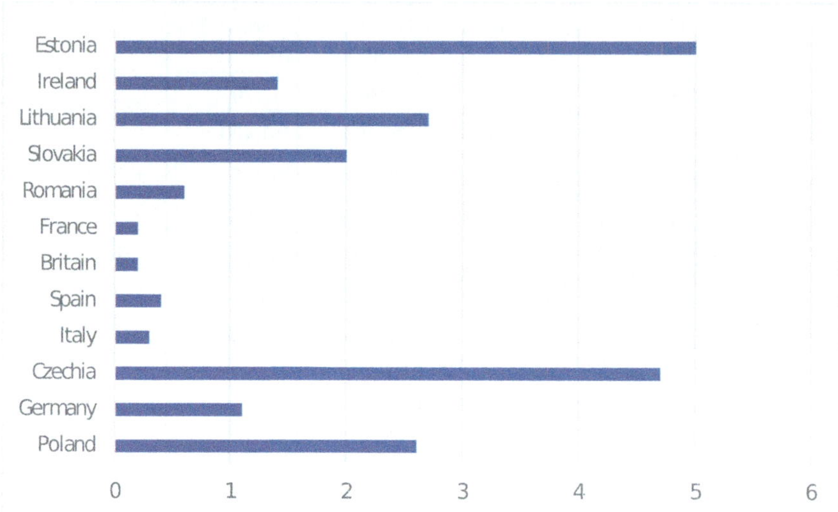

8.3 Assessing the Economic Costs of Refugee Protection in the CEE Region

As explained in the first section, navigating the distinction between economic migrants and refugees is a challenging task and, similarly, assessing the costs and benefits of migration – whether forced or voluntary – proves to be a complex endeavour. It largely depends on our units of analysis: we may consider the costs and benefits for people on the move, host communities, states, international institutions, local municipalities, or other actors. Additionally, the timeframe of assessment plays a crucial role – while short-term costs may appear substantial, benefits may unfold over time, or vice versa. In this section, we focus mainly on short-term demands on host society resources, such as public services, housing, infrastructure and social support programs. Before delving into the short-term costs of refugee protection in host societies of the CEE region, however, we should first consider the negotiation of burden-sharing between different actors in the 'refugee regime complex' (Betts, 2010) or 'refugee ecosystem'. In other words, the question is who bears the costs of refugee protection?

The answer to this question is not simple. We should remember that humanitarian relief is often interlinked with other sectors, particularly development aid and the security/peace complex. The actors involved in this space sometimes overlap, cooperate, run in parallel, or are in competition with one another (Betts, 2010). The Triple Nexus framework, which emerged from the 2016 UN Humanitarian Summit as a way of more effectively managing forced migration on a global scale, is based on the idea of increased cooperation and coordination between the humanitarian, development, and peace sectors (UNDP, 2023). In economic terms, we can trace commitments in humanitarian, financial and military expenditures. States, charities, private donors, civil society organisations, corporations, international organisations (IOs), multilateral institutions, such as UN institutions (UNHCR, International Organisation for Migration /IOM/), the World Bank and the IMF all form part of the Triple Nexus ecosystem.

Let us crunch some numbers to illustrate the scale of support to Ukraine, taking the Triple Nexus framework as our reference. According to the Kiel Institute for the World Economy, the EU Commission and Council have committed EUR 29.92 billion, in addition EUR 3.1 billion via the European Peace Facility, and EUR two billion through the European Investment Bank. Along with EUR 19.9 billion committed bilaterally by EU Member States, this brings the total EU commitments for the war effort to EUR 54.92 billion in the period between 24 January, 2022 and 15 January, 2023 (Trebesch et al., 2023). The authors of the report further note that "financial aid by multilateral organisations like the IMF, World Bank, UN and the European Bank of Reconstruction and Development add up to EUR 13.27 billion" (Trebesch et al., 2023). Zooming in on humanitarian aid, through Member State and donor support, the UNHCR distributed over USD 226 million in 2022 for the most urgent needs of displaced persons from Ukraine (UNHCR, 2022a). Since 24 February, 2022, the European Commission has spent EUR 685 million on humanitarian aid, up from EUR 350 million in the preceding period (European Commission, 2023a). Yet the burden of aiding refugees generally falls to individual hosting countries (Betts, 2010). According to data sourced in January-May 2023, Poland ranks highest in the world in terms of refugee costs in absolute numbers, totalling EUR 15.42 billion, followed by Germany with EUR 13.90 billion, and Czechia with EUR 3.85 billion (Kiel Institute for the World Economy, 2023b). CEE countries are the clear frontrunners if we calculate refugee costs as a percentage of the GDP: Poland (2.5%), Czechia (1.5%), Bulgaria (1.4%), and Slovakia (1.1%) rank in the first four places in the world as of 31 May, 2023 (Kiel Institute for the World Economy, 2023a). Bearing these numbers in mind, we should note that countries receive different forms of compensation for the costs incurred, including international donations, in-kind support, civil society mobilisation, and assistance by companies and private households. However, statistics on donations and costs undertaken by actors are notoriously difficult to track, as there is no standardised reporting or data, amounting to an unaccounted 'hidden aid' category (Trebesch et al., 2023). It is also worth considering where the costs are felt most acutely within the state structure. Research conducted by the Union of Polish Metropolises unequivocally points to local self-governments as bearing the burden of hosting refugees, including the provision of housing, access to public services, education and healthcare (Wojdat & Cywiński, 2022). It is also important to underscore the costs that have been absorbed by private citizens. In a series of surveys conducted by the Polish Centre for Public Opinion Research, in April 2022, 63% of Poles declared that they or someone from their household was offering free voluntarily support to Ukrainian refugees. This percentage dropped to 41% by January

2023, and a further steady decrease is expected, given people's limited resources and soaring inflation (Centre, 2023).

8.3.1 Immediate 'On the Spot' Emergency Assistance

In the first days, weeks and months after the full-scale Russian aggression on Ukraine, emergency assistance to people fleeing the war was delivered by a range of actors in the hosting countries. As emerging research suggests, the first responders and frontrunners of assistance were largely local civil societies, including NGOs, religious organisations, grassroots initiatives, and private individuals (Cullen Dunn & Kaliszewska, 2023; Grzymała-Kazłowska, Downarowicz & Wydra, 2023). With this in mind, it is important to underscore the role of Ukrainian organisations and private individuals already present in host societies in the mobilisation of assistance (Czerska-Shaw & Jacoby, 2023). Different levels of public authorities and self-governments were also involved, ranging from local public institutions, such as social services departments and cultural centres, to local and regional authorities, crisis management units, train station management teams, and others.

International charities and volunteers from Europe and beyond arrived on the scene within the first few months, bringing financial aid, often in cooperation with local NGOs, and crisis management know-how. However, more critical accounts of the humanitarian aid industry reveal major shortcomings in the collaboration and distribution of these resources (Cullen Dunn & Kaliszewska, 2023), alluding to important analyses such as the 'Crisis Caravan' (Polman, 2010), or the 'NGO game' (McMahon, 2017) that highlight the boom-and-bust economy of humanitarian aid and its neo-liberal underpinnings.

The on-the-spot aid ecosystem may be organised into six basic categories: (1) distribution of foodstuffs and basic material items, such as clothing, toiletries, off-the-counter medication and cleaning supplies, (2) provision of emergency shelters, (3) information and administrative points, sometimes with cash assistance programs, (4) support centres, including psychological aid, children's daycare zones, language classes and other cultural activities, (5) logistics hubs, including transport, relocation, warehouses for goods, and (6) coordination and communication networks (Czerska-Shaw, Krzyworzeka-Jelinowska & Mucha, 2022). As mentioned above, calculating the costs of these services is difficult due to the lack of standardisation and availability of data. We therefore focus on only a few examples for which there is reliable data.

Within the third category, the UNHCR set up 'Blue Dot' assistance points in collaboration with other UN agencies (IOM, UNICEF), as well as a host of local authorities and NGOs in major hubs of refugee arrivals in the region (UNHCR, 2022a). These Blue Dots serve as one-stop-shops where refugees from Ukraine can register their stay, obtain the information they require, as well sign up for cash assistance programmes. The UNHCR distributed over EUR 202 million through its cash assistance programme to refugees in surrounding states in 2022, of which EUR 79.3 million has been spent in Poland alone (UNHCR, 2022e). Some charities, such as Save the Children, have provided cash assistance and voucher aid, and measure their work through how many people they have reached.

Via the Temporary Protection Directive, triggered on 4 March, 2022, Member States have been able to formulate national resolutions to respond to and assist those escaping the war in Ukraine. TPD provides those with temporary protection free access to essential public services, including medical care, social and welfare assistance, some housing provision, and education for children under 18. Each of these services will be discussed below. Additionally, at the start of the full-scale invasion a number of states and transport companies provided free transport (trains and local public transportation) for a limited time. In Hungary, Ukrainian refugees could use 'solidarity tickets' to travel by train through the country; in Romania a similar 'ticket help Ukraine' scheme was introduced. In Poland, most municipalities offered free public transport to Ukrainian refugees for a period of three months (March-May 2022) (VisitUkraine, 2022).

8.3.2 Physical and Mental Health Services

Health care systems in receiving states undoubtedly face major strains with sudden influxes of patients in the system, particularly those who may have encountered trauma and mental health issues, the elderly, and those in need of specialised medical care. A study on Ukrainian refugees in Poland conducted by the World Health Organisation and Statistics Poland in 2022 found that 37.2% of respondents had health care needs in the 30 days prior to the interview, most often citing sudden illnesses (44%), chronic illnesses (40%), and dental needs (18%) (WHO & Statistics-Poland, 2023). Of those, 68% used a public health facility in Poland to deal with their needs. Another study estimates that nearly 10% of the refugee population in Poland, comprising of the elderly, have a significant disease burden, the most frequent of which are cardiovascular, gastrointestinal, and respiratory diseases (Piotrowicz et al., 2022). These health-related issues require immediate and systemic solutions. In the 2022 OECD International Outlook, costs associated with assisting Ukrainian nationals under temporary protection within national health care systems were estimated at a total of EUR 4.4 billion. The figures reveal that Germany incurred the highest costs among OECD countries, totalling EUR 1.361 billion, followed by Poland with EUR 664 million, and Czechia in the third place with EUR 341 million (OECD, 2022b).

Amongst the barriers to accessing health care services for refugees are long waiting times for specialised care, information on how to navigate often opaque health care systems that are different from those in their home countries, language and communication difficulties, and costs of medication (WHO & Statistics-Poland, 2023). One of the most acute problems is access to mental health services in welcoming states. This is in part because of disruptions to health care systems and rising mental health care needs in the wake of the Covid-19 global pandemic (Eurofound, 2021), gaps in provision as well as historically underdeveloped mental health care provision in Central and Eastern Europe (Winkler et al., 2017). The refugees' personal circumstances, for example, caring for children or elderly relatives, also severely limit the possibilities of accessing these services. It is also important to note that there is a cultural taboo on asking for psychological help (WHO & Statistics-Poland, 2023).

Nevertheless, there may be some benefits to the receiving states' health care systems. By the end of 2022, 1700 doctors and 860 nurses and midwives from Ukraine temporarily residing in Poland under the TPD applied for and received temporary medical licenses to work in Poland, thereby filling acute shortages in the medical profession (Jankowski et al., 2023). The critical situation has also engendered innovative solutions and inter-sectoral cooperation, such as the Health4Ukraine app, created by the Polish FinTech company Epruf in partnership with humanitarian donors providing funds for Ukrainian refugee-clients to cover the costs of their medicine purchases (Health4Ukraine, 2023). Other innovative solutions may trigger systemic changes to the receiving states' health care systems in general.

8.3.3 Social and Welfare Benefits

Under the TPD mechanism, receiving countries provide access to social and welfare benefits to those registered under this category with the same conditions as its own citizens. However, each EU Member State regulates the conditions under which benefits are given, which may account for differences between national systems. In Poland, Ukrainian nationals (as well as their spouses, regardless of their nationality) registered with the temporary protection status code 'UKR', have the same access as Polish nationals to the following: family benefits, child benefits, disability benefits, social assistance funds (unemployment insurance and crisis assistance, such as psychological help), as well as financial assistance for childcare for children up to three years of age (Stowarzyszenie Interwencji Prawnej, 2022). Additionally, before 1 March, 2023, the subsistence costs of those living in publicly run refugee shelters for Ukrainian nationals with temporary protection were fully covered. After 1 March, 2023, those living in shelters may need to cover up to 75% of these costs, although this is up to the discretion of public authorities (Ukrainian in Poland, 2023). Additionally, Ukrainians under the temporary protection mechanism in Poland were eligible for a one-off payment of PLN 300 (approx. EUR 65).

According to data provided by the Polish Ministry of Family and Social Policy, between 24 February, 2022 and July, 2023, the Polish state spent approximately EUR 540 million on child benefits alone (with the program 500+) for Ukrainians under the temporary protection mechanism (TVN24, 2023). Data from OECD statistics on social benefits falls in the 'living costs' category, which includes accommodation and other financial assistance (excluding education and health care), and is expected to amount to EUR 17.2 billion in OECD countries, as estimated for a 10-month period in 2022. The highest expected costs are estimated for Poland (EUR 6.2 billion), followed by Germany (EUR 4.42 billion), and Czechia (EUR 4.42 billion) (OECD, 2022b).

8.3.4 Housing and Accommodation

Access to affordable, liveable housing has been one of the most pressing needs for Ukrainian refugees in the CEE region since the full-scale invasion. According to research conducted by the UNHCR published in September 2022, Ukrainian refugees in Poland consistently rated housing as a top challenge, along with employment and cash assistance (UNHCR, 2022c). A study by the IOM published in April 2023 still highlighted the difficulty of finding affordable long-term accommodation (IOM, n.d.-a).

In January 2023, inflation in Poland skyrocketed to 17.2% and in Hungary to 21.9%, while the consensus forecast for 2023 had been 12.7% and 18.3% respectively, far above the eurozone projection (5.6%; Polish Economic Institute, 2023ab). Resulting high energy prices and hikes in interest rates meant that there were fewer buyers on the housing market, mortgage payments increased, and competition for rentals on the private market grew. The exorbitant rental prices on the housing market, especially in big cities such as Warsaw have been widely reported on by media outlets (e.g., Ciobanu, 2023). The influx of more than 1.1 million refugees from Ukraine, close to half of whom rented on the private market (UNHCR, 2022c), made this housing crisis acute. Additionally, systematic underinvestment and a dramatic shrinking of accessible social housing in the transition period of the 1990s remains a wider issue for the CEE region (Hegedüs, Horváth, Somogyi, Reháková & Sendi, 2017). As a point of comparison, the share of social housing in the CEE region hovers at around 2-3%, whilst it ranges from 14 to 20% in Western and Northern European regions (Hegedüs et al., 2017; OECD, 2022a).

Against this backdrop, societal and state responses to the inflow of refugees from Ukraine into the CEE region were undeniably unique. The first novelty was the urban nature of accommodation, largely bypassing regular asylum-seeker reception centres. This is due primarily to the nature of the Temporary Protection Directive (TPD), which allowed for semi-automatic residency rights and the concomitant wide-scale private hosting that spontaneously emerged as a result. It is estimated that around 18% of all refugees in Poland were hosted by private households as of September 2022 (UNHCR, 2022c), particularly through the strong social networks of Ukrainian nationals already residing in Poland. Another 44% were estimated to be renting privately (ibid.). Those living in collective accommodation, defined as assisted longer-term solutions (usually up to 12 months), ranges from 13% by some statistics (ibid.), to 35% in others (IOM, n.d.-a). As of October 2022, the Polish government estimated that 85,000 people were being housed in collective sites supported by the state, with a total of 386,000 since the beginning of the war (Kacprzak, 2022).

The public cost of supporting housing and subsistence for refugees, in particular the running and maintenance of collective sites and subsidies for private hosts, was estimated at 4,1 billion PLN in Poland by the third quarter of 2022 (Kacprzak, 2022). Other CEE states have also provided financial support to accommodating refugees, including to private hosting households, with Czechia and Slovakia among them (OECD, 2022b). Yet by 2023, states such as Poland started limiting housing support for Ukrainian refugees. As mentioned above, as of March 2023, a new law in Poland stipulates that Ukrainian refugees residing in publicly funded collective centres will be liable for up to 75% of their costs of accommodation. This has met with substantial criticism from civil society and migration experts, particularly because people accommodated in collective centres are amongst the most vulnerable (Jarosz & Klaus, 2023).

A second novelty in the housing sector has been the upsurge in private enterprise support, such as Airbnb's cooperation with IOM as well as with local NGOs. By November 2022, IOM's partnership with Airbnb had led to the provision of over 120,000 'safe nights' for over 5000 beneficiaries, which cost Airbnb approximately six million USD (IOM, n.d.-a). IOM's regional response plan foresees investments into repairs and renovations of collective centres and individual apartments, ongoing support for collective accommodation, as well as partnerships with social housing agencies.

Other costs also need to be considered, such as the emergency reception centres that were set up by civil society organisations and then closed, or ones set up by municipalities in association with NGOs or INGOs. While the response to the accommodation of refugees has been exceptionally agile, there are considerable hidden costs that are difficult to measure in the ad hoc, informal system in which they developed.

8.3.5 Local Services: the Case of Kraków

In 2022, it was estimated that 40,000 new residents from Ukraine with 'UKR' Temporary Protection status settled in Kraków and the surrounding areas. Before 24 February, 2022, there had been less than a hundred registered asylum seekers in the same geographical area (Pędziwiatr, Brzozowski & Stonawski, 2021). Kraków, just under 300 km from the Ukrainian border, was one of the main hubs for the transit of Ukrainian refugees, as well as a major destination point in Poland and the CEE region. The 'refugee regime complex' (Betts, 2010) began working on a local level from the first days of the full-scale Russian invasion on Ukraine, including a reception point at the main train station, operated by an ecosystem of municipal and regional authorities, train station management, informal groupings (like the grassroots 'Platform 4' volunteer group, or the 'Soup for Ukraine' group), the Polish scouting association, the Polish Red Cross, NGOs and countless private individuals offering their services (Czerska-Shaw et al., 2022).

In Kraków, the organisation of assistance has been largely decentralised, characterised by a high degree of informality and bottom-up structures with the support and participation of public institutions and municipal and regional authorities. A loose umbrella network named the 'Open Kraków Coalition', connecting over 70 social actors (NGOs, informal groupings, church organisations, INGOs, public authorities, private individuals, and academics) became a virtual communication hub particularly in the first stage of local assistance, mainly through Whatsapp and Slack channels (Czerska-Shaw et al., 2022). Services provided by the local refugee assistance ecosystem ranged from housing, distribution points, support centres and information hubs, education, health care, registration and administrative support, to logistics and relocation coordination. In short, the local level acted as a microcosm of the refugee assistance ecosystem in its full complexity.

While it is impossible to estimate the costs of the short-term emergency shelters, distribution points, support centres which were opened and closed, some examples may offer a brief look at the scale of the assistance provided. At the height of refugee arrivals in the spring of 2022, the regional and municipal authorities, who were responsible for coordinating a database of trusted sites for the accommodation of refugees (hotels, student residences, and temporary shelters such as schools, stadiums), counted 32,000 beds in their database. According to the regional authorities, by September 2022 there were around 17,000 refugees from Ukraine using the collective accommodation options accessible through the database (Pędziwiatr et al., 2021). From information provided by the spokesperson of the Lesser Poland Voivodship Office, the region spent PLN 507 million from 24 February 24, to September, 2022 on aid to Ukrainian refugees, of which PLN 215 million (41% of the total expenditure) was paid to host families (Pędziwiatr et al., 2021). The municipal government in Kraków, particularly the Social Welfare Centre, was responsible for running five collective accommodation sites housing up to 1,500 people, and the city authorities opened several stadium-style emergency shelters for newcomers, albeit for a very brief period.

We should consider that the rapid inflow of refugees implied a huge burden on the local educational services. From 24 February to October, 2022 almost 7,000 refugee children were enrolled in the public education system, including almost 2,000 in pre-schools and 4,000 in primary schools. Additionally, 98 preparatory classes were created in 58 schools in Kraków, providing educational services for 1,835 students. As for the 2022-2023 school year, the number of refugee children enrolled was smaller: slightly over six thousand, as some of the families decided to return home or migrate to other countries (Municipality of Kraków, 2023).

The bulk of the assistance in the first months of the war came in the form of the distribution of goods, such as clothing, off-the-counter medications, and household supplies, sometimes together with legal and psychological support. It is important to underscore the pivotal role of Ukrainian-led organisations in the provision of this support, along with the thousands of volunteers who helped in the daily running of reception and support centres. A case in point is the 'Live in Kraków' or 'R3 Aid Point' reception centre, operated jointly by two Ukrainian-led organisations, UA in Kraków and Zustricz, in conjunction with Salam Lab, with the support of the Jewish Community Centre, Internationaler Bund Polska, the Szlachetna Paczka organisation and the Juliusz Słowacki Theatre. The reception point gave shelter and assistance to over 3,500 people and replied to over 17,000 phone calls for assistance between 24 February and May 2022, aided by over 600 volunteers and 30 employees (Salam Lab, 2023; UA in Krakow, 2023). During the first seven months of functioning, the 'Goodwill Wardrobe' (Szafa Dobra), operated by the NGO Internationaler Bund Polska, served a total of 80,000 people, a daily average of 480 (Otwarty Kraków, 2022). The Warehouse operated by Internationaler Bund Polska at Daszyńskiego Street in Kraków provided refugees with basic food products and cosmetics: throughout 2022, more than 600,000 items were donated to 58,000 beneficiaries. Information points were located across the city, run in part by the municipality, such as the main registration point opened in Tauron Arena, the city's major mass event venue, or at the Information Point for Foreigners, a publicly-run project operated by Internationaler Bund Polska. The Information Point had served 18,000 people within 12 months (Internationaler Bund Polska, 2022). Local self-government support, international grants as well as partnerships with international non-governmental organisations have been key to the functioning of these centres.

8.3.6 Children and Schooling

In 2020, 19.6% of the Ukrainian population was 18 years old or younger, and 30.3% of households had one or more children under six years (State Statistic Service of Ukraine, 2021, p. 32).

Children either lived with their families or in some form of institutional care. In Ukraine, an extremely high number and proportion of children live in residential institutions (European Commission, 2022b, p. 13). A 10-year plan for 'deinstitutionalisation' was drawn up in 2007 and another in 2017, but not leading to much success. Contrary to the popular belief that orphans live in institutions, this is not the case in Ukraine, as about 90% of children living in institutions have at least one parent with parental rights who were unable to adequately care for their children due to the lack of financial resources or other family problems. Hope and Homes for Children, an international charity, published a comprehensive study of the Ukrainian child protection system based on qualitative and quantitative data collected in 2015-2016 (Hope and Homes for Children, 2023). According to the study, there were 99,915 children in institutional care in 663 children's homes in Ukraine, based on the data provided by the heads of the institutions, but only 9,291 children (9.3%) were orphans or deprived of parental care. The remaining 90,624 were placed in institutions by their parents or guardians mainly because of household poverty or other problems in the family.

As already highlighted above, the majority of Ukrainian refugees are women and children. According to a recent report by EUROCHILD, over 5.6 million children have been displaced since the war began. "While statistics are not comprehensive, there are significant numbers of children deprived of parental care, including unaccompanied and separated children, children who may have been trafficked, and Roma and stateless children, as well as groups of children evacuated from institutional care settings" (EUROCHILD, 2023).

The turmoil of the war has created a particularly precarious situation for displaced children, children living in institutions, and children with disabilities (UNICEF, 2023c).

Children fleeing Ukraine arrived in the host countries with relatives (mostly mothers) or unaccompanied. Especially in the first months of the war, emergency reception centres were set up, in several of which basic living conditions were lacking. Men, women, the elderly, and children were housed in cramped quarters.

In the case of unaccompanied children, identification is often challenging for authorities, increasing the risk of children remaining in emergency centres for an extended period or being trafficked and left without sufficient protection.

National child protection systems bear responsibility for the care of unaccompanied children separated from their families. However, national legal provisions, forms of care, guardianship, and custody responsibilities vary. The joint discussion paper by the UNICEF, EUROCHILD, and Child Circle, published in May 2022 (UNICEF, 2022), highlights the potential conflict and lack of consensus on the applicability of different legal instruments.

As noted above, the TPD lists, among other things, the rights of people enjoying temporary protection. The most important rights in relation to children are getting residence permits, access to suitable housing, social protection, medical care, education, and family reunification (European Commission, 2022a).

However, in several countries, there is a lack of capacity of service providers and availability of legal guardians. In addition, adjusting legal instruments to take in unaccompanied refugee children could be a time-consuming process.

To reduce the risks to which children in institutions are exposed, Ukrainian authorities decided to send 39,000 children home and make local authorities responsible for monitoring their situation. However, authorities do not always have the appropriate resources and personnel to carry out this task. Due to the high threat, authorities have repeatedly ordered the evacuation of groups of children and caregivers in groups several times, asking them to stay together abroad. The Ukrainian government had started negotiations with 23 European governments that accept Ukrainian children from residential care, but without much success, at least until March 2023, as only Poland and Lithuania responded positively (Human Rights Council, 2023b).

International law treaties prohibit the forcible transfer of children between countries, but evidence is mounting that Russia is setting up a child-deportation program. It is almost impossible to identify the exact number of children affected: data published in various announcements and in the press range between wide extremes, and there are spectacular differences between Ukrainian and Russian figures. Nevertheless, according to the official reports of the Ukrainian authorities as of 31 July 2023, 19,546 children had been deported from Ukraine to Russia since 24 February 2022, but these were only the officially documented cases, when a parent, a caretaker or a witness reported it to the National Information Bureau of Ukraine (Pohorilov, 2022).

In March 2023 the International Criminal Court issued arrest warrants for the 'unlawful transfer' of people (including children) from Ukrainian Russian-occupied territories into Russia and Russian-annexed Crimea (The Economist, 2023b). Researchers at Yale University published a report (Yale School of Public Health, 2023) about this in February 2023. Findings were based on the analysis of social media platforms, government announcements, local media reports, videos on camp websites, and satellite images. A network of 43 Russian facilities was uncovered where Ukrainian children had been moved since the beginning of the war. According to the researchers, at least 6,000 children had been transferred to those camps, but the figure is probably far underestimated. Among them, there were children with families, children considered orphans, children from institutions and children without a clear status. Many of the facilities are in Crimea and southern Russia, close to Ukraine but some others are far from the border.

The Yale study states that Russian officials would introduce the facilities as recreational camps to gain parents' consent. Parents and guardians may accept the offer because they wish to send their children out of the war zones, and in addition feel the pressure from occupying forces. Some children do return, but the camps may refuse to send them home citing 'safety problems'. The OHCHR reported that some children were sent to summer camps in the Russian Federation with the consent of their parents but were not returned home at the end of the vacation or were delayed (Human Rights Council, 2023a).

The camps present a Russia-centric worldview to their young inmates. 'Re-education' may contribute to the Kremlin's propaganda campaign. Russian officials (many of whom openly 'celebrate' their participation in the transfers and may possibly see the Russian invasion as a liberation of Ukrainians from a Western-backed fascist regime) say that many of the children are orphans – which Ukraine denies – and that they will receive proper care in Russian families.

Schools, kindergartens, and other educational institutions serve not only to cater for education and develop children's skills, but also to provide friendship, entertainment, and sports, and are the sites of secondary socialisation. When life in educational institutions becomes impossible, not only education but the entire process of socialisation is interrupted, which is especially important for children with disabilities or from disadvantaged families. The disruption of the education system has long-term effects on children's personal lives and chances in adulthood and, in addition, may lead to the underdevelopment of human resources for the economy. As Afshan Khan, the UNICEF's Regional Director for Europe and Central Asia formulated at the 2023 International Day of Education: "There is no pause button. It is not an option to simply postpone children's education and come back to it once other priorities have been addressed, without risking the future of an entire generation" (UNICEF, 2023a).

The Ukrainian Ministry of Education and Science reported that by February 2023, 441 educational institutions had been destroyed and 3,121 damaged, burdening the education of 5.3 million children, in addition to the two lost years caused by the Covid-19 pandemic (EUROCHILD, 2023).

Ukrainian education authorities have organised online learning opportunities to help not only children living in Ukraine but also refugee children. Unfortunately, military attacks and destruction of info-communication infrastructure have been blocking online education solutions, leaving millions of children without education. Lower family incomes, poverty, and the lack of appropriate electronic devices and Internet access also hinder children's participation in online learning. Ukrainian government agencies, UNICEF, the EU, and other official and charity organisations have helped by providing laptops and tablets (UNICEF, 2023b).

Adequate education for refugee children is extremely important but rather complicated to provide. According to UNICEF estimates, two-thirds of refugee children did not participate in education in their host country. According to the UNHCR's April 2023 report on the situation in Hungary, Poland, Moldova, Romania, and Slovakia, 44% of children were not formally enrolled at a school. The main reasons are language barriers, the hope of soon returning to their home country, differences in curricula and trying to use online education services from Ukraine. In several cases, children have participated in both Ukrainian online courses and the host country's face-to-face classes because attendance is mandatory for children of a certain age (UNHCR, 2023a).

In addition, guidelines for education in the occupied territories have changed significantly. "Restrictions on the exercise of the right to freedom of expression particularly affected teachers in Crimea. They were pressured to actively endorse the Russian armed attack on Ukraine, to cultivate a positive attitude among schoolchildren towards the military operations against Ukraine, and to generally refrain from criticizing the Russian authorities. Teaching staff who refused to follow these guidelines faced retaliation and sanctions" (United Nations Human Rights Office, 2023).

From the perspective of CEE countries, the massive influx of children resulted in an increased pressure on public education, including preschools, primary and secondary schools. Most young children were enrolled in schools poorly prepared for multicultural education. As seen in this interview with a war refugee from Nowy Sacz (city in Southern Poland):

"Only two schools are known to employ assistants to teach Ukrainian children. But these were not full assistants, but rather an attempt to hire Ukrainian teachers. They conducted extra classes in schools. During extracurricular activities. But there were no teaching assistants. The local authorities decided not to organize preparatory, integration classes, so that children could be faster included in the general educational process. Theoretically, there is such a program, but it does not work here." (Independent Research Team, 2023, interview with a war refugee from Ukraine)

Yet, due to the language and cultural similarity between Poles and Ukrainians, young refugee children usually integrated quite well in Polish schools:

"And these children are always with us, their parents assist them, so they integrate very well. Of course, they also have additional Polish language classes here several times a week, so they make up for it (...) they are getting better and better at learning. You know, they have no problems with math. Well, (some) with Polish, but I am already in constant cooperation with their parents. I say that they should read as much as possible in Polish, that they should try to speak Polish, considering that they simply want to stay here in Poland, continue their studies here from September. Parents have registered themselves here, they are very happy, so I am happy that children can stay here."(Independent Research Team, 2023, interview with a teacher of primary education)

Yet, Ukrainian teenagers' position is truly problematic. Many are still enrolled in online teaching conducted from Ukraine, which means that they do not socialise much with their Polish peers:

"There is a problem with teenagers. Many of them did not start their education in a Polish school because they studied online in Ukrainian school. Those who went to a Polish school were downgraded and [do not] feel comfortable. In life outside school, mom works hard, dad is away, and growing up is very hard. Children gather in large groups and go out all night. Those children who do not want to study make a negative impact on those who study with Ukrainian children. These children walk around the city like a herd." (Independent Research Team, 2023, interview with Ukrainian economic migrant)

This problem is likely to become much more pronounced in the future if the war does not end in the upcoming months, as these teenagers might be socially marginalised, with limited possibilities of further education (including also tertiary level) in Poland.

Since the invasion of Ukraine, there have been massive violations of children's rights, including guarantees of protection of children against all forms of physical or psychological violence, injury or abuse, neglect or negligent treatment, maltreatment or exploitation by caregivers, the right to identity, access to housing, medical and social services, and education, as defined in the UN Convention on the Rights of the Child. An entire generation of Ukrainian youths is deprived of a peaceful childhood. Their visible and invisible physical and mental injuries will have long-term effects on their adulthood and the future of Ukrainian society.

8.4 Economic Benefits

In this section potential or already observed benefits of the Ukrainian refugee wave are discussed, focusing on Poland where the number of Ukrainian refugees is the highest. The word 'benefits' may sound cynical in this dire war situation, but for the sake of accuracy we should consider them as well. Moral judgment is made more complicated by the fact that a disadvantage for some refugees may be advantageous from the hosts' point of view. There are some (sometimes mutual) benefits, but their legality or ethics may be questioned, while fortunately there are positive examples in all respects. The benefits may appear in several ways and forms: local companies may have access to skilled workers, refugees may start businesses independently or in association with locals, along with the refugees capital may flow into the country, consumption by refugees may generate demand for local products and services, thus, local people may be both suppliers and consumers of local and international support programs, and so on. It is very difficult to show the exact size of benefits, but there are many practical examples of their appearance. Some of them are presented below. Most examples cited in this section are related to work and employment, a topic discussed in detail in Chapter 9. Situations of decision-making and action are not easy for those involved, the utilisation of possible benefits may be hindered by several factors. The economic situation in the major countries receiving Ukrainian refugees in 2021, the year before the war started in February 2022, was mostly positive: the EU's economy was rebounding from the Covid-19 crisis and most CEE economies and the Baltic States showed healthy economic growth, while unemployment rates were relatively low (Table 8.7).

Table 8.7: Economic growth and unemployment in CEE countries (2021)
Data: World Bank (2023)

Coutry	GDP growth rate 2021 (%)	Unemployment rate 2021 (%)
Austria	4.6	6.5
Bulgaria	7.6	5.3
Czechia	3.6	2.8
Estonia	8.0	6.2
Hungary	7.2	4.1
Latvia	4.1	7.5
Lithuania	6.0	7.1
Poland	6.8	3.4
Romania	5.8	5.6
Slovakia	4.9	6.9
Slovenia	8.2	4.7

Another important characteristic of the CEE countries was the relatively large population of Ukrainian immigrants who arrived mostly as economic migrants.[2] Before 2022, the largest Ukrainian diaspora was located in Poland, followed by Czechia, Romania, Latvia and Hungary (Table 8.8). These pre-war immigrants were relatively well integrated into the host countries' societies and economy.

A representative survey carried out just before the Russian invasion for the FUME H2020 project (November 2021-January 2022) revealed that Ukrainian immigrants in Poland were predominantly young males (59%), relatively young individuals (the 18-29 age group comprised 37.7% of respondents, whilst the 30-39 group constituted an additional 31.8%), were employed full-time (78.2%), were satisfied with their economic situation (89.4%), and assessed their work-qualification match positively (64.7%). Moreover, many of them considered Poland as their 'new home' (87.8%), and most of them expressed a willingness to permanently stay in Poland (81%, Cf. Pędziwiatr, Brzozowski and Nahorniuk (2022)).

Naturally, many people changed their plans because of the outbreak of the full-scale war with Russia. Exact numbers are unknown, but it is estimated that about 200 to 300 thousand Ukrainian males returned from Poland to fight for their home country. Yet, a vast majority has remained, opting for family reunification: they simply brought their partners, children and even distant family members to Poland. On the other hand,

[2] Although, as mentioned before, many of these individuals had been internally displaced in Ukraine due to military conflict with Russia from 2014 onwards.

Table 8.8: Pre-war Ukrainian immigrant population in CEE countries
Data: FUME (2023)

Country	Ukrainian population (head)	Year
Austria	16,500	2021
Bulgaria	7,500	2019
Czechia	165,000	2020
Estonia	2,191	2020
Hungary	27,380	2021
Latvia	31,745	2021
Lithuania	6,224	2021
Poland	1,300,000	2020
Romania	37,600	2019
Slovakia	17,013	2021
Slovenia	222	2021

there were other types of forced migrants as well: displaced persons who fled the war at home and had few or no social contacts in Poland. As a result of this rapid inflow of forced migrants, the Ukrainian population in Poland reached 2.1 to 2.3 million persons by the end of 2022, including 1.1 to 1.2 million Ukrainians who arrived before 24 February 2022 (mostly economic migrants, but also internally displaced persons from Crimea and Donbas) and one to 1.1 million war refugees (Duszczyk, Górny, Kaczmarczyk & Kubisiak, 2023). In this second sub-population there were mostly mothers with children, sometimes accompanied by elderly parents.[3]

A survey carried out jointly in Vienna (Austria) and Kraków (Poland) between April and June 2022 reveals the phenomenon of refugees' self-selection, outlined at the beginning of this chapter: Vienna as a more distant location attracted a higher proportion of highly skilled individuals than Kraków. As for refugees surveyed in Vienna, 83% had tertiary education, and in Ukraine 61.5% performed skilled occupations,[4] whereas in Kraków this share was 66% and 45,2%, respectively (Kohlenberger et al., 2023). Consequently, the potential economic benefits stemming from a rapid inflow of Ukrainian refugees was not equally distributed in the EU: while some countries, such as Poland, Romania or Slovakia accepted forced migrants mostly due to humanitarian reasons, in the case of Western European countries humanitarian motivations were mixed with economic ones. For instance, even right-wing populist parties in Nordic countries welcomed Ukrainian refugees, and Ukrainians were

[3] It is important to mention that Ukrainian males aged 18-60 are not allowed to leave Ukrainian territory – some exceptions apply for fathers of 3+ children, single fathers, males with disability or fathers of children with disabilities.

[4] ISCO categories 1, 2 and 3 (managers, professionals, technicians, associate professionals).

"granted the right to work and participate in the receiving societies without having to endure year-long asylum processes" (Näre, Abdelhady & Irastorza, 2022).

Table 8.9: Ukrainian refugee population in Poland (July 2023)
Data: Gov.pl (2023)

Age	Male (head)	Female (head)	% Female
0-4	37,593	36,217	49.1%
5-9	60,758	59,310	49.4%
10-14	65,189	64,386	49.7%
15-18	48,413	42,847	47.0%
19-24	24,707	52,777	68.1%
25-34	31,517	95,680	75.2%
35-44	36,222	125,17	77.6%
45-54	16,637	72,600	81.4%
55-64	10,841	43,053	79.9%
65+	9,853	33,402	77.2%
Total	341,730	625,44	64.7%

When it comes to labour market issues,[5] it is important to mention that Ukrainian females who arrived in Poland after 24 February, 2022 (Table 8.9) frequently experience 'brain waste', i.e., they are usually forced to accept jobs below their qualifications. In spite of the fact that Polish and Ukrainian are similar, language competences are the main obstacles in the labour market, as illustrated by the following interview excerpt:

"Well, there was no choice here, I mean conversations with these people – there was no choice of the jobs they would like, but rather we tried to tell what jobs they could do. Bearing in mind some kind of limitations related to the language barrier. Paradoxically, it was easier for people without professional qualifications or those who performed those professions that were scarce on the labour market.." (Independent Research Team, 2023, interview with a worker in the Public Employment Service)

In this aspect, the Ukrainian refugees who were in highly skilled occupations at home were in a disadvantaged position in the host country:

"A big problem for Ukrainians is the lack of jobs corresponding to their level of education and profession. (. . .) It is usually difficult for Ukrainians to find a job. Usually, it is women with higher education that are not ready to work in a much lower position." (Independent Research Team, 2023, interview with a war refugee from Ukraine)

[5] For a more detailed analysis of the labour market, see Chapter 9.

For instance, a worker from public employment service describes the problem of a Ukrainian young female physician:

"... a client says that she graduated with honours, has a specialisation at the age of 27, is a general surgeon and is already experienced ... and nobody wants her! And now we... I'm thinking to myself, what's the problem. We call the hospital and only when we hear that the health service needs such specialists... She will probably be quickly absorbed by this market. It turns out that it's not that simple... The first barrier is language. Above all. She must have a qualification, knowledge of the language, and later, when it comes to the recognition of degrees ... There was also a matter ... Well, in fact, imagine that ... Well, we felt very sorry for this person ... And it worked out so that she went on an internship... Because wanted to do anything. (...) She was happy that she got such an internship offer from us. And she went into production... You could say she did... She sorted fruit. And what's even better, she proved herself in this and she later stayed at work after this internship." (Independent Research Team, 2023, interview with a worker in the Public Employment Service)

Naturally, this story does not imply that all Ukrainian doctors who come as refugees are bound to have the same fate. Yet, there are severe obstacles on the way: poor command of language skills, the procedure of diploma recognition ('nostrification'), work required at a Polish hospital under an experienced doctor's supervision, and finally the comprehensive medical exam ('Lekarski Egzamin Końcowy' in Polish), a public exam for physicians who wish to conduct an independent medical practice. These issues are manageable, but many refugees do not know whether they want to stay in Poland for long, although they lack financial resources and need some source of regular income.

Another issue is the precarity of work and the question of legality. Ukrainian refugees in Poland and other CEE countries are legally under the temporary protection regime, which implies that they have a legal status for residence until March 2024 (which might be prolonged in the future), and the full right to take any form of employment. Nevertheless, many females are in a disadvantaged position on the labour market not only due to a qualification mismatch, but also because of their family/childcare obligations. Thus, they often take part-time employment only, which in turn favours semi-legal employment and – in some instances – also the exploitations of workers' rights:

"Now it's very hard to work, it's hard in our district. First of all, a lot of work is done here without contracts, they don't want to give them, employers, Poles don't want to give them. (...) I don't know why they don't pay them. They don't want to pay taxes. He kept the Ukrainian woman for two or three weeks, and goodbye. (...) Why did they work here? Because they knew that they had to support themselves, because of the children, these little ones." (Independent Research Team, 2023, interview with a Ukrainian economic migrant)

Concerning the positive effects of the recent inflow of refugees, one definite advantage is that they can launch ventures. According to the aforementioned survey on Ukrainian refugees in Kraków, around 14% of respondents had been self-employed in Ukraine, and many of them expressed their willingness to start a business in Poland. This is a very positive phenomenon, as before the war the level of self-employment among Ukrainian immigrants was very low (3.6%), even compared with other foreigners in Poland (10.4%, Cf. Pędziwiatr et al. (2021)).

There are at least three factors that boost business creation. First, the legal framework has been amended: just like other foreign citizens, before 24 February 2022, only under certain conditions (for instance when being simultaneously a student of a local tertiary education institution) were Ukrainians in Poland allowed to be self-employed. This had been a requirement that greatly hindered business activity.[6] Since March 2022, by implementing a special law on Ukrainian refugees, self-employment has been allowed without any restrictions. Second, the large Ukrainian diaspora in Poland and smaller ones in Czechia, Romania and Slovakia provide a fertile ecosystem for the development of Ukrainian enterprises that may serve Ukrainian co-nationals. Finally, there is also a push factor towards entrepreneurship: many female refugees prefer to start a business to avoid working below their formal qualifications. In such cases, entrepreneurship could serve as a way to create better employment conditions for themselves. It is not surprising that recently the number of refugee enterprises has been growing in Poland: most of them are active in the field of services, including hairdressing and fitness training. As one of our respondents said:

"Talking about Ukrainian business in Nowy Sacz, there is a pizzeria, a massage parlour and a hairdresser. Many Ukrainians conduct unregistered activities within the limits of the tax-free amount." (Independent Research Team, 2023, interview with a Ukrainian economic migrant)

Indeed, numerous companies are in the early stages of their development, and Polish law allows unregistered small-scale business activity, provided monthly sales do not exceed 2,700 PLN (ca. EUR 450). In this case, formalities are minimal: accounting is simple, and taxes are paid according to a yearly tax declaration. Yet, based on our interviews with refugee entrepreneurs, even such formalities are not pursued by many small-scale or even 'ad hoc' entrepreneurs: for instance, many female refugees bake Ukrainian cakes and sell them online, promoting their products through their social networks. The activity is illegal, but the income is marginal, mostly just supplementing other earnings.

According to the analysis of the Polish Economic Institute, in the first nine months of 2022, 14,000 new ventures were established by Ukrainian refugees, most of whom registered their business as sole proprietors. This meant about 3,600 new companies and more than ten thousand sole proprietorships, plus significant Ukrainian capital investment in international companies (Notes from Poland, 2023).

Finally, we should address the problem of economic inactivity, which affects many refugees. This is not only due to the war trauma, but also to the traditional family role models in the home country. According to a survey conducted among the refugee population in Kraków between April and June 2022, prior to the Russian aggression, only 53% of female respondents had participated actively in the Ukrainian labour

[6] This was also connected to the legal framework of residence permits. Foreigners from third countries (i.e. outside the EU) could launch businesses, but only in the form of limited companies. However, this type of firm needed to exhibit a relatively high (taxed) income in order to provide legitimacy for the residence permit of a foreigner, which in the case of small firms in the early phases of development was extremely difficult.

market (Pędziwiatr et al., 2022). In many Ukrainian families, the husband earns the money, and the wife stays at home with the children and runs the household. At the moment of the survey, 20% of the females surveyed claimed that their plan for the nearest future was to wait for the war to end, while covering their daily expenses from savings, transfers from Ukraine and social benefits. The exact size of savings and transfers is unknown, moreover it is difficult to predict how safely they will arrive and how long they will last, but that money is spent in Poland where it increases demand for products and services. It is important to add that in Poland the social benefits granted to Ukrainian refugees are relatively modest: the monthly allowance after each child is PLN 500+ (EUR 110), supplemented by and additional three-month allowance from the UNHCR (maximum USD 600 per family), plus free accommodation in refugee shelters and hostels for the first months of stay (Pędziwiatr et al., 2022).

Case study: Influx of Russians to Georgia

The special problems of refugees, the complexity and contradictions of the economic, social and political situations are well illustrated by the example of Georgia.

In the middle of February 2023 (one year after the war in Ukraine had started) an International Monetary Fund (IMF) team visited Tbilisi, the capital of Georgia, a country with 3.7 million inhabitants, to discuss with government officials recent economic and financial developments and reform ideas. The end-of-mission press releases (IMF, 2023) reported that in 2022 the country's economic growth was strong at around 10%. That high figure reflected adverse spillovers from the war between Russia and Ukraine, a phenomenon influenced by such factors as growth in war-related migrant and financial inflows, buoyant tourism, and a rise in transit trade through the Caucasus country. These factors supported the local currency called *lari*, boosted fiscal revenues, and narrowed the current account deficit. In 2023 growth is expected to drop to around 4%.

The UNHCR Operational Data Portal reported 27,000 refugees from Ukraine at the end of July 2023 (UNHCR, 2023b). 1,145 applied for asylum or similar national protection schemes. Many had been forcibly deported by the Russian armed forces that were occupying territories in eastern Ukraine, did not have travel documents but received moral and material support from local people. For a period of three months, Ukrainians fleeing the war received social assistance from the Georgian government: 45 lari (around $16) per person per month with an additional one-time payment of 300 lari (approximately $108) per family. Accommodation was provided by the local authorities from July 2022 onwards as part of a special assistance program for Ukrainian refugees (Khasaia, 2023).

When the war broke out, refugees did not come to Georgia only from Ukraine: the invasion prompted tens of thousands, mainly middle-class Russians to leave their increasingly isolated homeland. Many Russian citizens went to countries where visas were not required, such as Armenia, Kyrgyzstan and Georgia. Turkey was a top destination not only because of its visa-free regime but also because of its large

Russian-speaking community. The exact number of Russian émigrés is unknown, but by some estimates at the beginning of the war it was approx. 200,000 (Najibullah, 2022). According to official data, about 1.5 million Russian citizens crossed the Russia-Georgia border in the first year of the war but reportedly many have left (Bolkvadze, 2023). The number of those who have stayed is not known, but their presence is evident. The fast rise of one-way airline tickets was a good indicator of people's movement.

The influx is worrying many Georgians. Georgia's position as a destination is unique: it is a post-Soviet country, but has introduced a series of economic and democratic reforms aimed at joining the European Union and NATO, an orientation which had worsened relations with Russia, a process leading to a war in 2008 and the Russian occupation of a part of the country. Many of its citizens, especially the older generation are connected to the Soviet regime, while many others, especially the young have strong pro-European sentiments. The government is trying to manoeuvre between the two conflicting orientations. Many Georgians watched the arrival of Russians with concern and anger, thinking that it could be the prelude to an invasion.

In the same way as their reception, Russians' motivations were fairly mixed. Some left their country in protest, others because of persecution, and many were afraid of the consequences of the international sanctions against Russia. It is highly probable that many of them are well-educated freelancers or 'digital nomads' who can set up shop anywhere with Internet access.

The Russian mass exodus caused an economic shock in Georgia. Locals and cab drivers sold bicycles and seats in cars to the escaping crowds. Prices of accommodation in Tbilisi increased to the extent that it was difficult to find a home or rent a room. The influx of Russian migrants, business people and tourists has in fact mobilised some sectors of the Georgian economy and helped balance the economic pressures generated by the war. At the same time, many refugees struggle for work or have to accept jobs and wages below their skill level. Most Georgians speak or at least understand Russian but a growing number of them refuse to speak it. As a consequence, many Russians have started to build their own communities, e.g., by opening their restaurants and cafés (Harlan, 2022). The average Russian is wealthier than the average Georgian, which explains the economic impact of the influx of foreign money, as observed by the IMF delegation referred to above.

8.5 The Main Policy Dilemma: Integration or Returning Home?

What are the general lessons to be learnt and suggestions regarding the management of the refugee crisis? Answering this question is a bold undertaking for several reasons. On the one hand, in early 2024, when this chapter was finalised, the Russian-Ukrainian war had not yet ended, and there were no signs of any kind of peace or agreement, so the refugee problem was still unresolved. On the other hand, the case of Ukrainian refugees cannot be discussed in complete isolation: apart from Ukrainians, members of other ethnic groups have been emerging in large numbers in many countries of the world. Considering these facts, following a short summary of the situation, we can only attempt to formulate some general requirements. We conclude the chapter with a sectoral case study, which shows how the fate and opportunities of refugees are influenced by business organisations and their resilience.

The war in Ukraine has generated the largest and fastest flow of refugees since the end of the Cold War. At the beginning of 2024, conditions were far from being ripe for a negotiated settlement. Instead, the most likely outcome was a bloody stalemate.

According to data collected and published regularly by the UNHCR, in the first year of the war, more than eight million people were displaced from Ukraine into other countries. This extremely large number corresponds to about one fifth of the Ukrainian population. Border crossing is frequent and intensive, many displaced persons are staying abroad while many others have returned home or commute between home and other countries. Data are often patchy and are likely to underestimate the true number of people affected. Anyway, as shown in Table 8.6 and Figure 8.1, it appears that the burden of hosting and supporting refugees is distributed unevenly and unfairly. Europe hosts more refugees now than any other region, and it is possible that forced displacement will be a fundamental challenge in many parts of the world in the 21st century. Europe as a whole cannot simply free ride on the generosity of some countries within it (Betts, 2022).

The progress of the war is unpredictable. However, more than two years after the immediate emergency situation caused by the military invasion, refugees, hosting governments, international support organisations and other stakeholders must think long term and compare their options. However, solving dilemmas and making long-term decisions is not easy in the fog of war.

In the first half of 2023, the International Organisation for Migration (IOM), a UN agency that provides advice and services to migrants and governments, conducted a series of surveys on the refugees' status, needs and intentions in some countries (see e.g., IOM, 2023 on Hungary, or IOM, n.d.-b). Although the study samples were small, the uncertainty of the refugees' plans is clear from the interviews. Humanly, it is completely understandable that many people do not want to return to war zones, but try to find a new homeland, but these intentions may quickly change if there is a turn in the course of the war, and there is a good chance of lasting peace and the reconstruction of their country.

The biggest dilemma for refugees is whether to build a new life in a foreign county and stay there, or to try to return home as soon as possible. The same question from the perspective of the host countries is whether to invest in the long-term integration of displaced persons or to provide only temporary protection, and help (and motivate) the refugees to return home. Ukrainian refugees are frequently surveyed and interviewed (see e. g. The Economist, 2023a) and it is obvious that many of them hope to go back, but it is impossible to predict when and how. Long term integration is expensive and arduous for both sides, and while it may be beneficial for the labour market of the host countries, it will destroy Ukraine's demographics and the country may lose a generation of young women with children and a major part of its workforce that is vital for the country's economic reconstruction and development.

It is absolutely understandable that in this situation many displaced persons feel caught between two basic options and two different worlds: they are unable to return home now or in the near future but are averse to building a new life in an unfamiliar environment. Calculations change over time as the war proceeds, and people are accustomed to new conditions, they adapt and learn, build contacts, or try to live double lives.

Beyond the peculiarities of the Ukrainian refugee situation, this cruel war raging at the borders of the EU, the dimensions of forced displacement, and the whole new reality have important implications for the EU's refugee policy: although it is impossible to predict the future of the war in Ukraine, the organisation must develop the capacity to receive large numbers of refugees and allocate the related costs and burden fairly, taking into account the differences between refugee groups.

The EU's New Pact on Migration and Asylum, adopted by the European Commission in September 2020, declares that no Member State should shoulder a disproportionate responsibility and that all Member States should contribute to solidarity on a constant basis (European Commission, 2023b). The uncontrolled arrival of migrants in 2015 exposed the weaknesses of the so-called Dublin System that allocates primary responsibility for refugees and asylum seekers to the first country they arrive in. In 2016, the European Parliament opened negotiations about replacing the criterion of first entry with an allocation system where the applicant would be allowed to choose to be allocated to some Member States with the fewest applications. After unsuccessful negotiations the process of introducing a new system was stalled, the Czech Republic, Hungary, Poland, and Slovakia blocked the reform (Betts, 2022).

At the start of the war in Ukraine, the EU temporarily provided a limited form of sanctuary allowing Ukrainian refugees to stay for at least three years. The new situation caused by the war, and the present acts of solidarity and humanitarian aid may provide a special opportunity for the EU to introduce fairer refugee regulations and its Members States to reconsider their position, while newly arriving refugee groups and their diasporas can lobby for more progressive solutions. Nevertheless, encouraging member countries to embrace a universal, non-discriminatory and cordial approach to refugees is a real challenge.

Reforming the EU's refugee system is not easy because of the obvious discrepancy in the treatment of refugee groups arriving from different regions, countries, ethnic, and religious background. Ukrainian refugees received a warm welcome in Poland and other European countries, but unlike the way African and Asian refugees have been received in recent years. When people speak about their experiences with Ukrainian refugees we frequently hear or read that 'they are European and civilised', 'they are white and Christian', 'they pray like us', 'they are middle class', and that 'they are dressed like us'. Psychologists know this phenomenon well and call it the 'racial-empathy gap', and 'identity economics' may also provide some explanations (Akerlof & Kranton, 2000). Cultural proximity and social cohesion between refugees and host communities are important factors in accepting and supporting refugees, but it is very difficult to separate natural human solidarity and neighbourhood help based on cultural proximity from nationalism, chauvinism and racism (Bayoumi, 2022).

Supporting refugees from allied countries may also feel comfortable especially when the leaders of a country provide moral clarity and guidance for the dilemmas.

The European response to the Ukrainian refugee crisis has been cordial and generous so far, but that might change if governments do not manage well the reception and integration of refugees, and disillusionment and fatigue take over. There is a real danger that the governments of slowing economies may fail to provide refugees jobs, housing and services. As a result, solidarity may exhaust itself and generate a backlash. In the recent past, Europe has seen instances of this phenomenon.

Humanitarian aid based on local people's willingness to help refugees may be essential in an emergency situation, but it may become problematic as economic, social and political costs are growing, if 'emergency' endures over a longer period or indefinitely. As refugee numbers grow, increasing stress is placed on healthcare, schooling, transport and other public services, more jobs are displaced, and social tensions may increase. The political situation in Europe and the U.S. is so sensitive now that even a minor shift in public mood may cause a landslide. Advocating ethically 'ideal' solutions which ignore the social and political reality and lack the support of main stakeholders may only increase the tension and drive the situation to a tipping point. The issue of migration obviously dominates politics, and people may easily put forcibly displaced refugees and economic migrants in one basket. In May 2023, the Polish Economic Institute reported that in Poland and elsewhere in the region the social acceptance of receiving and supporting Ukrainian refugees was still high, although decreasing over time, and Poland and Hungary were among the countries where the drop was the highest (Polish Economic Institute, 2023aa).

The ideal solution for migration problems in general and the Ukrainian refugee crisis in particular would be to address the underlying causes. If this does not work, sustainable long-term solutions must be found. The basic requirements of sustainability are that the model used should maintain political support at local, national, and international levels, and should be able to function at scale and endure over time (Betts, 2021, p. 6). An ideal model aids displaced people in helping themselves, provides opportunities for refugees to utilise their own capabilities and contribute to the local economy, considers the long-term interests of the country the refugees arrive from, and fulfil general ethical obligations. Providing protection, shelter, services, and jobs for refugees is expensive and requires massive investments. If political support is needed, investments should benefit both refugees and, importantly, host communities. Such 'ideal solutions' are easy to imagine but extremely difficult to implement. Literature sources are not of much help because of the absence of rigorous and interdisciplinary research on the economics of refugees, especially on what appears to work well and what does not.

Case study: the Ukrainian IT industry

The arrival of war shocked organisations, even the most prepared ones, but many of them adapted fast to the new reality. Obviously, technical, organisational and mental adaptation was needed. New workspaces had to be set up quickly equipped with generators and satellite internet when the Russian army started to attack Ukraine's energy infrastructure. Large numbers of employees had to be relocated, displaced persons needed work equipment, financial support, and various forms of personal help. Organisational resilience was a key issue, business recovery and continuity plans, kept in hidden drawers for a long time, had to be dusted off and implemented. People had to learn to work from anywhere, living with their children and the elderly. Managers had to learn new human skills e.g., treating burned-out workers, providing mental support, or simply listening to colleagues with empathy.

The war highlighted the importance of the tech sector and its potential role in such emergency situations. Coders and engineers of IT companies using distributed cloud-based systems can work anywhere at home or abroad where internet is available, while many 'physical' industries were disrupted by war damage. The Ukrainian technology sector grew by 36% in exports in 2021 (IT Ukraine Report, 2021), and the growth trend seems stable. It employs about 300 thousand professionals and generates more than 4% of Ukraine's GDP. Many large global tech companies have built centres of outsourced services, development and research organisations in the country, but it also has a vivid startup ecosystem with some high-flying unicorns. The largest foreign customer is the United States. Ukraine is one of the largest exporters of IT services in Europe, maintaining constant growth despite the Russian invasion. Thanks to high-quality formal and informal education and personal motivation, the Ukrainian IT talent pool is truly unique.

There are about 5000 IT companies in Ukraine. According to the report cited above, most ventures provide services in fintech, banking and e-commerce. The number of professionals working on cutting-edge technologies like artificial intelligence, machine learning, blockchain and robotics is growing continuously.

For Ukrainian IT professionals, remote work was common long before the Covid-19 pandemic. By 2021, the large majority of companies had decided to switch completely to a hybrid work mode. Working remotely for foreign companies is widespread. Remote experience allows IT personnel to provide continuous quality services and maintain productivity. The size of the export market and regular cooperation with foreign customers helps to stabilize the market. In the 2014-2016 period, after the Russian occupation of Crimea, the sector proved that it can adapt and recover very fast.

For many international IT companies recruiting from Ukraine was simply smart practice. The positive legacy of the decades in the Soviet Union is strong science and tech education. When the war started in February 2022, the IT talent pool proved to be highly mobile. Men of military age had to stay at home, but many others crossed the borders and the country's tech diaspora exploded: tens of thousands moved to the West, mainly to Poland, Germany, Spain, Czechia, and the Netherlands and continued servicing their clients remotely.

One of the large IT internationals directly hit by the war in Ukraine was EPAM Systems, an American company, founded in the USA and Belarus, traded on the NYSE now, currently headquartered in Pennsylvania. Its portfolio consists of software engineering services, digital product design, and digital platform engineering. When the military invasion began, EPAM had 14,000 staff in Ukraine and 18,000 more in Belarus and Russia. The company was facing a real existential risk; its stock dropped by 50% in a few days. The question was how fast it would execute personnel relocation, replace many employees with new ones hired in India, Central Europe, and Asia-Pacific.

At the end of February 2022, the company reported to the SEC that its business continuity plan was executed, and it was actively monitoring the security of its people and equipment. EPAM started to reallocate work to other geographies within its global footprint. It issued a press release announcing that it was withdrawing its financial outlook due to heightened uncertainties. On 4 March it announced that it would discontinue services to Russia-based customers. The transition was accelerated by active employee relocation. Many Russia-based employees were moved to delivery locations outside the country. It was also announced that EPAM would continue to support its Ukrainian employees and their families, offering assistance and mobility as needed, backed with a $100 million humanitarian commitment. In April 2023, EPAM's recruitment website advertised more than 2,000 job openings all over the world. (For the EPAM story, only publicly available sources were used including the company's SEC reports from the beginning of 2022. SEC filings can be accessed on the website of the company.)

8.6 Conclusion

Before making any proposals regarding refugees from Ukraine, we should have a stand on how to measure success.

The number of refugees is several million, but EU countries are struggling with demographic problems and labour shortages in many areas and could take in a large number of people from Ukraine without major difficulties. Most Ukrainian refugees are young, relatively well-educated, want to work, have experience abroad, many have acquaintances in host countries, and have no particular communication and cultural problems with the locals. It is considered short-term success if their integration is successful during the war, they have access to work, learning and entrepreneurship opportunities, live under safe and acceptable conditions. Long-term success, however, mostly means a safe return home, and participation in the reconstruction and the development of Ukraine. Refugee policies and projects should support these two simultaneous goals (short-term and long-term success), maintaining a balance between them. This political dilemma will become extremely hot as we get closer to March 2025 when the three-year protection afforded to Ukrainian refugees will expire. Governments of host countries have to consider the humanitarian, social, political, and economic aspects of this complex issue, while the Ukrainians also know that their refugees deserve safety, but their nation needs workers, brains, customers, taxpayers and families to rebuild and revitalize the country (The Economist, 2024).

Overall, one of the most important lessons of this migration wave is that to be able to successfully deal with it, we should get local communities on board. They should be given financial, administrative, psychological, moral, logistical and other support.

They should feel that they are making a positive impact in a crisis situation and that they receive wide ranging support. The positive attitude of local migrant-receiving communities is the key to success. Effective, sustainable solutions require mutual benefits: refugees should be supported and helped, but the supporting communities should also experience that they are gaining something, be it in terms of financial benefits (e.g., labour, business partners, services, or state support) or a moral feeling (we helped someone, we did something good). Therefore, policies and projects should be based on comprehensive stakeholder analysis.

Positive government attitude, the conscious and methodical development of business relations, the search for mutually beneficial solutions, and the establishment of a supportive advisory and administrative system may yield fruit. Facilitating the support of refugees which provides benefits to the host country, to professional and to local communities seems the best approach.

It also seems important to ease communication for migrants, to get in touch with their families and friends at home, and to obtain reliable first-hand information about their situation. Access to the digital infrastructure (network and personal devices) is required. This, on the one hand, may decrease the stress and anxiety of migrants, and on the other may help them make informed decisions about their future. In addition, this may assist local authorities in guiding migrants in the administrative maze. It is also important to provide the local and broader community with reliable, continuously updated information so they feel that they worries and anxiety are addressed as well.

The lack of reliable, continuously updated data, using consistently the same definitions and methodology may hamper quick and efficient action. Currently conflicting data just add to the confusion and makes the realistic evaluation of the current situation harder.

Due the special demographic structure of Ukrainian refugee communities, and because men between the ages of 18 and 60 can only leave the country with a permit, in the host countries new businesses or new corporate shared support units have been started mostly by Ukrainian women. These women-led ventures may need special attention, unbiased venture investors and focused accelerator programs.

To deal with children is also of paramount importance. Their schooling is a must, as neither Ukraine (if eventually the children return home) nor the hosting countries (if these children stay) can afford to lose a generation. Schooling is crucial in building a sense of perspective and future for teenagers who should not get disillusioned and depressed. In addition, studying keeps them occupied and out of trouble. These efforts should be balanced: on the one hand, young people should not feel detached from home, on the other, they should get to know their new host, the language and the culture.

In the given situation, it seems evident that advanced online education solutions are needed at all levels of training. This can give a new impetus to the development of online education, and the emergence of new solutions and businesses. Experience shows that blended learning, which includes both online and offline components, is more effective than online education. It requires the cooperation of local schools, which should be motivated and supported to participate.

All the above requires coordination among different actors: state administration, NGOs, the private sector and international organisations. It must be made clear, however, that the main coordinators should be the hosting state and local authorities, otherwise unnecessary and unhelpful conflicts will arise. International aid should also be distributed more evenly within the EU. Here as well, coordination is vital. Different donors should not act separately, creating states-in-the-state, as this will inevitably result in a loss of efficiency and serious conflicts. The extreme wave of refugees is the problem not only of specific affected countries, but of the entire European Union. To such a European problem, a coordinated European response must be given. The management of the refugee crisis is an instructive test of the cooperation, decision-making and action system of the European countries.

***

At the end of the chapter, we must say a few words about the data we relied upon. Finding reliable data in times of an ongoing violent war is a daunting task. As already pointed out at the beginning of the chapter, some factors of uncertainty in addition to the war, are also at play, such as the ethnic, linguistic and political diversity in the Central and Eastern European region, the twists and turns of recent history, the potential political intentions behind the publication (or non-publication) of data, the deliberately deployed toolbox of disinformation warfare, the travel and residence rules within the Schengen area that allows the free movement of citizens, the characteristics of the EU labour market, the presence and dimensions of the grey economy, the uncertainty around the interpretation of definitions regarding the status of refugees and guest workers, the sheer dimensions of the rapid movement of masses of people, and the high degree of uncertainty of refugees' motivations and intentions.

When collecting the data, we tried to use primarily reliable sources (e.g., EUROSTAT, OECD, UNICEF, and mainly the UNHCR), international databases that were collected on the basis of a uniform methodology as far as possible, and where metadata and necessary explanations are available. Due to the given chaotic situation, however, the accuracy and up-to-datedness of all information cannot be fully guaranteed. Since it takes time to publish peer-reviewed articles and peer-reviewed studies, we have also used numerous online 'on the fly' sources, more than usual in academic circles. Those sources contain important, interesting and fresh data, but their reliability is not perfect. Thus, in some cases we had to choose between freshness and reliability, and more than once we went for the former. In the course of events, it was sometimes difficult to decide whether we should include in the text individual sentences or paragraphs in the present or past tense.

Being a refugee is not only an official status, but also a state of mind. Photos and the words of those involved can be telling, sometimes even more telling than statistics. We could not include photographs in the volume (although by following the links, the reader will find abundant material); instead, for personal touch, we have included a few statements and short interview excerpts.

References

Akerlof, G. A. & Kranton, R. E. (2000). Economics and Identity. *The Quarterly Journal of Economics, 115*(3), 715–753.

Aksoy, C. G. & Poutvaara, P. (2021). Refugees' and irregular migrants' self-selection into Europe. *Journal of Development Economics, 152*, 102681.

Aksyonova, S. (2022, Dec.). Rebound in Fertility in Ukraine: Expectations, Factors, Obstcles. *Demography and social economy, 50*(4), 3–22. Retrieved from https://ojs.dse.org.ua/index.php/dse/article/view/119 doi: 10.15407/dse2022.04.003

Battisti, M., Peri, G. & Romiti, A. (2022). Dynamic effects of co-ethnic networks on immigrants' economic success. *The Economic Journal, 132*(641), 58–88.

Bayoumi, M. (2022). *They are "civilised", "European" and "look like us": The racist coverage of Ukraine | Moustafa Bayoumi.* The Guardian, March 2. Retrieved from https://www.theguardian.com/commentisfree/2022/mar/02/civilised-european-look-like-us-racist-coverage-ukraine

Bernard, A. & Bell, M. (2018). Educational selectivity of internal migrants: A global assessment. *Demographic research, 39*, 835–854.

Betts, A. (2010). The Refugee Regime Complex. *Refugee Survey Quarterly, 29*(1), 12–37.

Betts, A. (2021). *The Wealth of Refugees: How Displaced People can Build Economies.* Oxford University Press.

Betts, A. (2022, Apr). The Ukrainian Exodus. Europe Must Reckon with Its Selective Treatment of Refugees. *Foreign Affairs.* Retrieved from https://www.foreignaffairs.com/europe/ukrainian-exodus (Accessed: 27-3-2023)

Bolkvadze, G. (2023). *Georgia becomes a hub for anti-war russians. euronews, 23 february.* https://www.euronews.com/2023/02/18/georgia-becomes-a-hub-for-anti-war-russians. (Accessed: 18-08-2023)

Brell, C., Dustmann, C. & Preston, I. (2020). The labor market integration of refugee migrants in high-income countries. *Journal of Economic Perspectives, 34*(1), 94–121.

Brücker, H. & Defoort, C. (2009). Inequality and the self-selection of international migrants: theory and new evidence. *International journal of manpower, 30*(7), 742–764.

Brzozowski, J. & Coniglio, N. (2021). International migration and the (un) happiness push: Evidence from polish longitudinal data. *International Migration Review, 55*(4), 1089–1120.

Centre, P. O. R. (2023). *Polish public opinion 1/2023.* https://www.cbos.pl/PL/publikacje/public_opinion/2023/01_2023.pdf. (Accessed: 1-10-2023)

Chiquiar, D. & Hanson, G. H. (2005). International migration, self-selection, and the distribution of wages: Evidence from Mexico and the United States. *Journal of political Economy, 113*(2), 239–281.

Ciobanu, C. (2023). *Desperate measures as housing crisis grips poland.* https://balkaninsight.com/2023/03/21/desperate-measures-as-housing-crisis-grips-poland/. March 21, 2023. Balkan Insight. (Accessed: 29-09-2023)

Cullen Dunn, E. & Kaliszewska, I. (2023). Distributed humanitarianism. Volunteerism and aid to refugees during the Russian invasion of Ukraine. *American Ethnologist*, *50*(1), 19–29. (Accessed: 27-09-2023) doi: \url{https://doi.org/10.1111/amet.13138}

Czerska-Shaw, K. & Jacoby, T. (2023). *Mapping Ukrainian Civicness Abroad in the War Effort: A Case Study of Poland.* Conflict and Civicness Research Group, London School of Economics.

Czerska-Shaw, K., Krzyworzeka-Jelinowska, A. & Mucha, J. (2022). *Mobilizacja pomocy uchodźczyniom i uchodźcom ukraińskim w Krakowie Wyzwania i szanse zarzędzania niepewnością. Multiculturalism and Migration Observatory.* Cracow University of Economics.

Duszczyk, M., Górny, A., Kaczmarczyk, P. & Kubisiak, A. (2023). War refugees from Ukraine in Poland–one year after the Russian aggression. Socioeconomic consequences and challenges. *Regional Science Policy & Practice*, *15*(1), 181–199.

Duszczyk, M. & Kaczmarczyk, P. (2022). The war in Ukraine and migration to Poland: outlook and challenges. *Intereconomics*, *57*(3), 164–170.

Erdal, M. B. & Oeppen, C. (2018). Forced to leave? The discursive and analytical significance of describing migration as forced and voluntary. *Journal of Ethnic and Migration Studies*, *44*(6), 981–998.

EUROCHILD. (2023). *Ukraine 2023: What are the challenges to uphold children's rights during the conflict in Ukraine?* https://www.eurochild.org/news/ukraine-2023-what-are-the-challenges-to-uphold-childrens-rights-during-the-conflict-in-ukraine/. (Accessed: 09-08-2023)

Eurofound. (2021). *Living, working and COVID-19 (Update April 2021): Mental health and trust decline across EU as pandemic enters another year.* https://www.eurofound.europa.eu/en/publications/2021/living-working-and-covid-19-update-april-2021-mental-health-and-trust-decline. Publications Office of the European Union, Luxembourg. (Accessed: 01-10-2023)

European Commission. (2022a). *Commission Opinion on Ukraine's application for membership of the European Union.* https://neighbourhood-enlargement.ec.europa.eu/system/files/2022-06/Ukraine%20Opinion%20and%20Annex.pdf. (Accessed: 31-08-2023)

European Commission. (2022b). *Temporary protection.* https://home-affairs.ec.europa.eu/policies/migration-and-asylum/common-european-asylum-system/temporary-protection_en. (Accessed: 07-08-2023)

European Commission. (2023a). *European Civil Protection and Humanitarian Aid Operations.* https://civil-protection-humanitarian-aid.ec.europa.eu/where/europe/ukraine_en. The European Commission. (Accessed: 27-09-2023)

European Commission. (2023b). *Migration and Home Affairs.* The European Commission. https://home-affairs.ec.europa.eu/policies/migration-and-asylum/common-european-asylum-system/country-responsible-asylum-application-dublin-regulation_en.

Eurostat. (2023a). *Migration and migrant population statistics. highlights.* https://ec.europa.eu/eurostat/statistics-explained/index.php?title=

Migration_and_migrant_population_statistics. (Accessed: 02-02-2023)

Eurostat. (2023b). *Ukrainian citizens in the EU.* https://ec.europa.eu/eurostat/statistics-explained/index.php?title=Migration_and_migrant_population_statistics. (Accessed: 02-02-2023)

Fiddian-Qasmiyeh, E., Loescher, G., Long, K. & Sigona, N. (2014). *The Oxford handbook of refugee and forced migration studies.* OUP Oxford.

FUME. (2023). *Future Migration Scenarios for Europe. Ukraine.* https://futuremigration.eu/case-study-areas/ukraine/. (Accessed: 27-09-2023)

Gov.pl. (2023). Poland's data portal, Registered applications for UKR status, 18 July 2023, data for available at: https://dane.gov.pl/en. (Accessed: 27-09-2023)

Grzymała-Kazłowska, A., Downarowicz, P. & Wydra, A. (2023). *Private assistance for Ukrainian refugees and attitudes towards refugee sponsorship in Poland.* https://www.migracje.uw.edu.pl/wp-content/uploads/2023/03/Spotlight-MARCH-2023-1.pdf. Centre for Migration Studies Spotlight 3(49). University of Warsaw. (Accessed: 27-09-2023)

Harlan, C. (2022). *Russians fleeing to georgia face resentment, graffiti, loyalty tests at bars.* The Washington Post, 2 November. (Accessed: 15-09-2023)

Health4Ukraine. (2023). *About the programme health4ukraine.* Retrieved from https://health4ukraine.com/en/

Hegedüs, J., Horváth, V., Somogyi, E., Reháková, V. & Sendi, R. (2017). Affordable housing in Central and Eastern Europe: Identifying and overcoming constrains in new member states. *Budapest: Metropolitan Research Institute.*

Hendriks, M. & Bartram, D. (2019). Bringing happiness into the study of migration and its consequences: What, why, and how? *Journal of Immigrant & Refugee Studies, 17*(3), 279–298.

Hetényi, Z. (2023). *Nyugati, keleti: Ogyesszától Odesszáig, 1973-2023.* Kalligram.

Hope and Homes for Children. (2023). *The illusion of protection.* http://hopeandhomes.org.ua/blog/the-illusion-of-protection-an-analytical-report-based-on-the-findings-of-a-comprehensive-study-of-the-child-protection-system-in-ukraine/. (Accessed: 09-08-2023)

Human Rights Council. (2023a). *Report of the Independent International Commission of Inquiry on Ukraine.* Available at: https://www.ohchr.org/sites/default/files/documents/hrbodies/hrcouncil/coiukraine/A_HRC_52_62_AUV_EN.pdf. (Accessed: 07-08-2023)

Human Rights Council. (2023b). *We Must Provide a Family, Not Rebuild Orphanages.* https://www.hrw.org/report/2023/03/13/we-must-provide-family-not-rebuild-orphanages/consequences-russias-invasion. (Accessed: 09-08-2023)

IMF. (2023). *IMF Staff Concludes Visit to Georgia. Press release no, 23/45.* https://www.imf.org/en/News/Articles/2023/02/17/pr2345-georgia-imf-staff-concludes-visit#:~:text=%E2%80%9CThe%20Georgian%20economy%20grew%20strongly,in%20transit%20trade%20through%20Georgia. (Accessed: 17-08-2023)

Independent Research Team. (2023). *Interviews conducted by a research team in July 2023 in Nowy Sacz, Southern Poland* . (Interviews conducted within the project nr 12/14-2022/OG-FAMI Open Małopolska, funded by Asylum,

Migration and Integration Fund (FAMI),)

Internationaler Bund Polska. (2022). *Annual Report.* 2022. Available at: https://ib-polska.pl/wp-content/uploads/2023/02/IB-Polska-2022-Raport-roczny-Annual-Report.pdf. (Accessed: 27-09-2023)

IOM. (n.d.-a). *Poland - surveys with refugees from Ukraine: Needs, intentions, and Integration Challenges (Jan-Mar 2023).* https://dtm.iom.int/reports/poland-surveys-refugees-ukraine-needs-intentions-and-integration-challenges-jan-mar-2023.

IOM. (n.d.-b). *Romania - surveys with refugees from Ukraine: Needs, intentions, and Integration Challenges (Jan-Mar 2023).* https://reliefweb.int/report/romania/romania-surveys-refugees-ukraine-needs-intentions-and-integration-challenges-jan-mar-2023.

IOM. (2023). *Hungary - surveys with refugees from Ukraine: Needs, intentions, and Integration Challenges (Jan-Mar 2023).* https://dtm.iom.int/reports/hungary-surveys-refugees-ukraine-needs-intentions-and-integration-challenges-jan-mar-2023.

IT Ukraine Report. (2021). *Ukraine IT Report 2021.* https://reports.itukraine.org.ua/en.

Jankowski, M., Lazarus, J. V., Kuchyn, I., Zemskov, S., Gałązkowski, R. & Gujski, M. (2023). One year on: Poland's public health initiatives and national response to millions of refugees from ukraine. *Medical Science Monitor: International Medical Journal of Experimental and Clinical Research*, *29*, e940223–1.

Jarosz, S. & Klaus, W. (2023). *W punkcie wyjścia. monitoring zbiorowego zakwaterowania uchodźczyń z ukrainy.* https://konsorcjum.org.pl/w-punkcie-wyjscia-monitoring-zbiorowego-zakwaterowania-uchodzczyn-z-ukrainy/.

Kacprzak, I. (2022). *Polska wydała na pomoc uchodźcom z ukrainy 5, 5 mld zł.* https://www.rp.pl/polityka/art37286771-polska-wydala-na-pomoc-uchodzcom-z-ukrainy-5-5-mld-zl. Rzeczpospolita. (Accessed: 29-09-2023)

Khasaia, K. (2023). No papers, little support - Ukrainian refugees in Georgia. *IPS, 16 November.* https://reliefweb.int/report/hungary/hungary-surveys-refugees-ukraine-needs-intentions-and-integration-challenges-jan-mar-2023. (Accessed: 12-08-2023)

Kiel Institute for the World Economy. (2023a). *Government support to Ukraine: By donor GDP incl. refugee costs.* Government support to Ukraine: by donor GDP, incl. refugee costs (23degrees.io). (Interactive table).

Kiel Institute for the World Economy. (2023b). *Government support to Ukraine: Total aid with refugee costs.* Total Aid with Refugee Costs (23degrees.io). (Interactive table).

Kohlenberger, J., Buber-Ennser, I., Pędziwiatr, K., Rengs, B., Setz, I., Brzozowski, B., J. Riederer, ... Pronizius, E. (2023). High self-selection of Ukrainian refugees into Europe: Evidence from Kraków and Vienna. *Plos One*, *18(12).* https://doi.org/10.1371/journal.pone.0279783.

Kurkov, A. (2023). *Diary of an invasion.* Deep Vellum Publishing.

Kurkov, A. (2022). *Exodus: the four kinds of Ukrainian refugee.* The Economist, 1843 Magazine, Mar. 17.

Loescher, G. (2021). *Refugees: a very short introduction* (Vol. 673). Oxford University Press.

Lu, Y. (2008). Test of the 'healthy migrant hypothesis': a longitudinal analysis of health selectivity of internal migration in indonesia. *Social science & medicine, 67*(8), 1331–1339.

Mayda, A. M. (2022). International migration: A panel data analysis of the determinants of bilateral flows. In *Global labour in distress, volume i: Globalization, technology and labour resilience* (pp. 33–65). Springer.

McMahon, P. C. (2017). *The NGO game: Post-conflict peacebuilding in the Balkans and beyond.* Cornell University Press.

Médecins Sans Frontières. (2023). *Financial Independence and Accountability.* Retrieved from https://www.msf.org/reports-and-finances

Mikanowski, J. (2023). *Goodbye, Eastern Europe.* Pantheon Books.

Milner, J. & Klassen, A. (2021). *Civil Society and the Politics of the Global Refugee Regime.* https://www.unhcr.org/people-forced-to-flee-book/wp-content/uploads/sites/137/2021/10/James-Milner-and-Amanda-Klassen_-Civil-Society-and-the-Politics-of-the-Global-Refugee-Regime.pdf.

Mitchneck, B., Zavisca, J. & Gerbe, T. (2016). Europe's Forgotten Refugees. The Humanitarian Crisis in Ukraine. *Foreign Affairs, 24.*

Municipality of Kraków. (2023). *Raport o stanie gminy 2022.* Avaliable at https://www.bip.krakow.pl/plik.php?zid=400279&wer=0&new=t&mode=shw (Interactive table). Kraków. (Accessed: 27-09-2023)

Najibullah, F. (2022). Fearing Fallout From Putin's War, Russians Flee Abroad. *Radio Free Europe, 14 March.* https://www.rferl.org/a/russians-flee-fearing-war-fallout/31752961.html. (Accessed: 15-08-2023)

Notes from Poland. (2023). *Almost 14,000 Ukrainian businesses created in Poland in the first nine months of 2022.* https://notesfrompoland.com/2023/01/12/almost-14000-ukrainian-businesses-created-in-poland-in-the-first-nine-months-of-2022/. (Accessed: 20-08-2023)

Näre, L., Abdelhady, D. & Irastorza, N. (2022). What can we learn from the reception of Ukrainian refugees? *Nordic Journal of Migration Research, 12*(3), 255–258.

OECD. (2022a). *Housing support for ukrainian refugees in receiving countries.* Retrieved from https://www.oecd.org/ukraine-hub/policy-responses/housing-support-for-ukrainian-refugees-in-receiving-countries-9c2b4404/ (Accessed: 01-10-2023) doi: https://doi.org/https://doi.org/10.1787/30fe16d2-en

OECD. (2022b). *International migration outlook 2022.* Retrieved from https://www.oecd-ilibrary.org/content/publication/30fe16d2-en doi: https://doi.org/https://doi.org/10.1787/30fe16d2-en

OECD. (2023). *International Migration Database and Labour Market Outcomes of Immigrants.* https://www.oecd.org/els/mig/keystat.htm. (Accessed: 01-02-2023)

Otwarty Kraków. (2022). *Szafa Dobra ponownie otwarta w nowej lokalizacji!* https://otwarty.krakow.pl/aktualnosci/264292,1992,komunikat,szafa_dobra_ponownie_otwarta_w_nowej_lokalizacji_.html. (Accessed: 27-09-2023)

Pachocka, M. (2016). Understanding the Visegrad Group States' Response to the Migrant and Refugee Crisis 2014+ in the European Union. *Yearbook of Polish European Studies*(19), 101–132.

Pędziwiatr, K., Brzozowski, J. & Nahorniuk, O. (2022). *Refugees from Ukraine in Kraków*. Centre for Advanced Studies of Population and Religion, Krakow University of Economics. (Accessed: 27-09-2023)

Pędziwiatr, K., Brzozowski, J. & Stonawski, M. (2021). *Integracja imigrantów w krakowie i województwie małopolskim*. Obserwatorium Wielokulturowości i Migracji: Kraków.

Piotrowicz, K., Semeniv, S., Kupis, R., Ryś, I., M.and Perera, Gryglewska, B. & Gąsowski, J. (2022). Disease burden in older ukrainian refugees of war: a synthetic reanalysis of public records data. *The Lancet. Healthy Longevity*, *10*(3). https://doi.org/10.1016/S2666-7568(22)00187-8. (Accessed: 27-09-2023)

Pleskot, P. (2015). Polish political emigration in the 1980s: Current research, perspectives, and challenges. *Polish American Studies*, *72*(2), 49–64.

Pohorilov, S. (2022). *Russian ombudswoman reports about deporting over 700,000 Ukrainian children to Russia*. Ukrainska Pravda, 31 July. (Accessed: 29-08-2023)

Polish Economic Institute. (2023aa). *80% of refugees from Ukraine see a positive attitude towards them among Poles*. https://pie.net.pl/en/80-of-refugees-from-ukraine-see-a-positive-attitude-towards-them-among-poles/#. (Accessed: 08-08-2023)

Polish Economic Institute. (2023ab). *CEE Economic Monthly*. https://pie.net.pl/wp-content/uploads/2023/05/Miesiecznik-Makro_5-23_EN.pdf. (Accessed: 29-09-2023)

Polman, L. (2010). *The crisis caravan: what's wrong with humanitarian aid?* Metropolitan Books.

Sakwa, R. (2014). *Frontline Ukraine: Crisis in the borderlands*. I.B. Tauris.

Salam Lab. (2023). *On the first day of Russia's invasion of Ukraine, Salam Lab organized an Aid Point at 3 Radziwiłłowska Street*. https://salamlab.pl/en/r3-aid-point/. (Accessed: 29-09-2023)

Shaver, A., Krick, B., Blancaflor, J., Yein Ku, S., Liu, X., Samara, G., ... Zuo, Z. (2022). *The Causes and Consequences of Refugee Flows: A Contemporary Re-Analysis* (Tech. Rep.). Princeton: Princeton University. https://esoc.princeton.edu/WP29.

Skeldon, R. (2012). Migration transitions revisited: Their continued relevance for the development of migration theory. *Population, Space and place*, *18*(2), 154–166.

State Statistic Service of Ukraine. (2021). *Statistical Yearbook of Ukraine*. https://ukrstat.gov.ua/druk/publicat/kat_u/2021/zb/11/Yearbook_2020_e.pdf. (Accessed: 06-08-2023)

Stowarzyszenie Interwencji Prawnej. (2022). *Are the fleeing Ukrainian citizens entitled to family benefits and when, according to the Special Act? What conditions must be met? What kind of help can you count on?* Retrieved from https://ukraina.interwencjaprawna.pl/are-the-fleeing-ukrainian-citizens

-entitled-to-family-benefits-and-when-according-to-the-special-act-what -conditions-must-be-met-what-kind-of-help-can-you-count-on%ef%bf%bc/

The Economist. (2021). *Almost 3m people have fled Ukraine.* The Economist, March 3.

The Economist. (2022a). *As Russia's invasion stalls, Ukraine's refugees return home.* The Economist, May 24.

The Economist. (2022b). *Ukrainian refugees are beginning to return home.* The Economist, June 21.

The Economist. (2023a). *Lives in limbo.* The Economist; February 25: 62-64.

The Economist. (2023b). *Why Russia is deporting Ukrainian children.* The Economist, April 14.

The Economist. (2024). *Homeward bound, one day.* The Economist, February 24.

Trebesch, C., Antezza, A., Bushnell, K., Frank, A., Frank, P., Franz, L., . . . Schramm, S. (2023). *The ukraine support tracker: which countries help ukraine and how?* (Tech. Rep.). Kiel: KIEL working paper.

TVN24. (2023, July). *Ilu obywateli ukrainy pobiera 500 plus? podano koszt.* TVN24 Biznes. Retrieved from https://tvn24.pl/biznes/pieniadze/500-plus-dobry-start-ilu-obywateli-ukrainy-pobiera-swiadczenia-w-polsce -ministerstwo-rodziny-i-polityki-spolecznej-podalo-dane-7224664

UA in Krakow. (2023). https://uainkrakow.pl/who-we-are/. Ukrainska Pravda, 31 July. (Accessed: 01-10-2023)

Ukrainian in Poland. (2023). *Specjalna ustawa: zmiany dla Ukraińców w latach 2023-2024 w Polsce - czy azyl zostanie rzedłużony?* https://www.ukrainianinpoland.pl/amendments-to-the-special-law-what -awaits-ukrainians-in-poland-in-2023-pl/#:~:text=M%C3%B3wi%C4%85c% 20dok%C5%82adniej%2C%20od%201%20marca,wi%C4%99cej%20ni% C5%BC%2040%20z%C5%82%20dziennie. Centre for Advanced Studies of Population and Religion, Krakow University of Economics. (Accessed: 29-09-2023)

UNDP. (2023). *Humanitarian, development and peace nexus.* https://www.undp.org/crisis/humanitarian-development-and-peace-nexus. (Accessed: 27-09-2023)

UNHCR. (2022a). *Global report.* https://reporting.unhcr.org/global-report-2022. (Accessed: 26-09-2023)

UNHCR. (2022b). *Mid-year Trends.* https://www.unhcr.org/mid-year-trends. (Accessed: 02-06-2023)

UNHCR. (2022c). *Refugees from Ukraine in Poland - Profiling Update (September 2022).* https://data.unhcr.org/en/documents/details/97157. (Accessed: 01-10-2023)

UNHCR. (2022d). *Ukraine situation: Regional protection profiling and monitoring factsheet.* https://data.unhcr.org/en/documents/details/97720. (Accessed: 02-02-2023)

UNHCR. (2022e). *UNHCR Poland Factsheet July 29, 2022.* https://data.unhcr.org/en/documents/details/94749. (Accessed: 26-09-2023)

UNHCR. (2022f). *UNHCR receives record support for forcibly displaced people as they face a daunting year.* https://www.unhcr.org/news/press/2022/12/

638f5efe4/unhcr-receives-record-support-forcibly-displaced-people-face-daunting-year.html?query=10,211%20billion. (Accessed: 05-01-2021)
UNHCR. (2023a). *Displacement Patterns, Protection Risks and Needs of Refugees from Ukraine.* https://data2.unhcr.org/en/documents/details/100191. (Accessed: 09-08-2023)
UNHCR. (2023b). *Ukraine Refugee Situation. Operational Data Portal.* https://data.unhcr.org/en/situations/ukraine. (Accessed: 03-02-2023)
UNHCR: The UN Refugee Agency. (2023). *UNHCR web site.* https://www.unhcr.org/. (Accessed: 02-01-2023)
UNICEF. (2022). *Concept Note: Children without parental care, including unaccompanied, separated and children evacuated from institutions, fleeing Ukraine.* https://www.unicef.org/eca/sites/unicef.org.eca/files/2022-07/Concept%20note%20legal%20study.pdf. (Accessed: 11-08-2023)
UNICEF. (2023a). *11 months of war in Ukraine have disrupted education for more than five million children.* https://www.unicef.org/romania/press-releases/11-months-war-ukraine-have-disrupted-education-more-five-million-children-unicef. (Accessed: 06-08-2023)
UNICEF. (2023b). *UNICEF reboots online learning for Ukrainian school children.* https://www.unicef.org/ukraine/en/stories/online-learning-for-schoolchildren. (Accessed: 10-08-2023)
UNICEF. (2023c). *War in Ukraine: Support for children and families.* https://www.unicef.org/emergencies/war-ukraine-pose-immediate-threat-children#latest-updates. (Accessed: 05-08-2023)
United Nations. (2022). *World Migration Report.* Available at: https://publications.iom.int/books/world-migration-report-2022. (Accessed: 01-02-2023)
United Nations Human Rights Office. (2023). *Report on the Human Rights Situation in Ukraine.* https://www.ohchr.org/sites/default/files/documents/countries/ukraine/2023/23-03-24-Ukraine-35th-periodic-report-ENG.pdf. (Accessed: 04-08-2023)
VisitUkraine. (2022). https://visitukraine.today/blog/841/vengriya-umensaet-kolicestvo-besplatnyx-poezdov-dlya-ukrainskix-bezencev. (Accessed: 1-10-2023)
Welker, J. (2022). Relative education of recent refugees in Germany and the Middle East: Is selectivity reflected in migration and destination decisions? *International Migration*, *60*(2), 65–80.
WHO & Statistics-Poland. (2023). *Health of refugees from Ukraine in Poland 2022. Household survey and behavioural insights research.* Report, February 2023. e-ISBN 978-83-67087-39-1.
Winkler, P., Krupchanka, D., Roberts, T., Kondratova, L., Machů, V., Höschl, C., ... others (2017). A blind spot on the global mental health map: a scoping review of 25 Years' development of mental health care for people with severe mental illnesses in Central and Eastern Europe. *The Lancet Psychiatry*, *4*(8), 634–642.
Wojdat, M. & Cywiński, P. (2022). Urban hospitality: unprecedented growth, challenges and opportunities. A report on Ukrainian refugees in the largest

Polish cities. *Research and Analysis Centre. Union of Polish Metropolises.*

World Bank. (2023). *World development indicators database.* Available at: https://databank.worldbank.org/source/world-development-indicators. (Accessed: 27-09-2023)

Yale School of Public Health. (2023). *Russia's Systematic Program for the Re-education & Adoption of Ukraine's Children.* Available at: https://hub.conflictobservatory.org/portal/sharing/rest/content/items/97f919ccfe524d31a241b53ca44076b8/data. (Accessed: 09-08-2023)

Chapter 9
Pathways to Inclusion: Labour Market Perspectives on Ukrainian Refugees

Martin Guzi, Maciej Duszczyk, Peter Huber, Ulrike Huemer and Marcela Veselková

Abstract The chapter provides an overview of the situation of Ukrainian refugees in the labour markets of Austria, Czechia, Poland, and Slovakia, emphasizing the initiatives aimed at facilitating their integration. Refugees face challenges in securing employment adequate to their skills due to language barriers, limited capacity in childcare services, strict entry conditions for skilled occupations, and uncertainty surrounding their refugee status. The chapter concludes with recommendations for enhancing the labour market integration of refugees.

9.1 Introduction

This chapter provides an overview of the situation of Ukrainian refugees in the labour markets of Central and Eastern European economies. The situation is presented through the window of four main destination countries: Austria, Czechia, Poland, and Slovakia, which collectively received over two million refugees in 2022 (for details, see Chapter 8).

Martin Guzi ✉
Masaryk University, Brno, Czech Republic and Central European Labour Studies Institute (CELSI), Bratislava, Slovakia, e-mail: Martin.Guzi@econ.muni.cz

Maciej Duszczyk
University of Warsaw, Warsaw, Poland, e-mail: m.duszczyk@uw.edu.pl

Peter Huber
WIFO, Austrian Institute of Economic Research, Vienna, Austria, e-mail: peter.huber@wifo.ac.at

Ulrike Huemer
WIFO, Austrian Institute of Economic Research, Vienna, Austria, e-mail: ulrike.huemer@wifo.ac.at

Marcela Veselková
Social Policy Institute, Ministry of Labour, Social Affairs and Family of the Slovak Republic, Bratislava, Slovakia, e-mail: Marcela.Veselkova@employment.gov.sk

© The Author(s), under exclusive license to Springer Nature Switzerland AG 2024
L. Mátyás (ed.), *Central and Eastern European Economies and the War in Ukraine*,
Contributions to Economics, https://doi.org/10.1007/978-3-031-61561-0_9

The Russian invasion of Ukraine has elicited a huge wave of sympathy in many countries. Numerous initiatives have been launched to provide support to displaced individuals arriving from Ukraine (for more details, see Chapter 8). Platforms dedicated to the integration of foreigners have been established to streamline the registration process for refugees. Public institutions have set up hotlines and websites containing valuable information to assist them. Non-governmental organizations have played a vital role by offering counselling services and actively searching for suitable accommodation and employment opportunities. Special attention has been given to children, ensuring their access to education, while families have been granted access to various social benefits and services. Notably, in the initial days after crossing the border, refugees were able to utilize train transportation free of charge. Additionally, several cities also provided free public transportation. Universities have shown support by creating temporary academic positions for researchers and establishing funding programs specifically for Ph.D. students arriving from Ukraine. These collective efforts reflect a widespread commitment to providing comprehensive assistance and support to those affected by the conflict.

Ukrainians with temporary protection, in accordance with the Temporary Protection Directive, are not restricted regarding housing, social benefits, health insurance, or entry into the labour market or educational system. Many countries have taken measures to facilitate the entry and stay of Ukrainian refugees, such as the provision of language courses and childcare services.

This chapter outlines the migration context of receiving countries, examines the acceptance of refugees through opinion polls, discusses the demographic profile of arriving refugees, explores their access to social assistance upon arrival, and analyses the employment patterns and barriers encountered by refugees. It concludes by offering recommendations for enhancing the labour market integration of refugees.

9.2 Arrival of Ukrainian Refugees

Countries in Central and Eastern Europe have had different experience with migration. Over the last two decades, Poland and Slovakia have seen more extensive emigration, while Austria and the Czech Republic are traditionally immigration countries. Austria experienced a large inflow of refugees during the 2015–2016 refugee migration. The presence of a large Ukrainian community in the Czech Republic and Poland facilitated the arrival of war refugees in 2022–2023. In contrast, the Ukrainian communities in Austria and Slovakia before 2022 were relatively small.

9.2.1 Austria

Austria has recent experience with large refugee inflows. Between 2014 and 2016, during the Syrian war, Austria witnessed one of the highest refugee arrivals per capita in the European Union (EU). The Ukrainian migrant community in Austria was relatively small. According to official statistics, in 2021, only 12,673 Ukrainians resided in Austria, constituting approximately 0.1% of the total Austrian population. This percentage contrasted with the overall foreign national population of 1.6 million, making up 17.6% of the resident population.

The large surge in refugee numbers from Ukraine came as a surprise. By March 2022, 14,500 Ukrainians had already registered in Austria, and throughout 2022, the official migration statistics reported a total of 78,439 Ukrainians moving to Austria. Of these, approximately 11,086 refugees later moved to other countries, resulting in a net increase in migration from Ukraine of over 67,000 individuals. According to UNHCR (2024), the total number of registrations in 2022 exceeded 111,000. This figure, however, includes double applications as well as persons who have returned or moved on since their registration. Geographically, nearly half of the Ukrainian nationals (43%) reside in Vienna, with an additional fifth in Lower Austria (18%), followed by Upper Austria (11%). On the other hand, the Ukrainians are less concentrated in Burgenland (3%) and Vorarlberg (3%, OIF, 2023).

The relatively large number of Ukrainians arriving in Austria may be attributed to the fact that, before 2022, many seasonal workers in agriculture came from Ukraine. Many of these workers were students, engaging in summer employment to finance their studies. Consequently, as some Ukrainians had previous work experiences in Austria, it was easier for them to arrive in Austria. However, this hypothesis was not confirmed, as Bock-Schappelwein and Huber (2022) discovered that only around 3% of the displaced Ukrainians registered in 2022 had previously been in employment in Austria before the outbreak of war.

9.2.2 Czech Republic

Over the last two decades, the Czech Republic has become a favourite destination for immigrants. The inflow of immigrants largely accelerated in economically successful years preceding the Great Recession in 2009. The number of immigrants residing in the country decreased temporarily after 2009 and increased again in 2015. At the end of 2021, the number of legally residing immigrants reached a historic high of 660,849 representing 6.3% of the Czech population. The immigrants are attracted to the Czech Republic because of favourable economic conditions, a shortage of skilled workers in the labour market, and a pro-labour immigration policy. Most immigrants originate from countries outside the EU, and the top five source countries in 2021 included Ukraine, Vietnam, Russia, Mongolia and the United States. The migration motives are primarily work-related (Guzi, Macková & Čech Valentová, 2021).

In contrast to the labour immigration policy, granting asylum or international protection is highly restrictive. Over the last two decades less than 3% of the applicants for international protection were approved asylum. Most immigrants residing in the Czech Republic are of working age (15-64 years old) and their employment rates are higher than those of native-born Czechs. Migrants mostly work in manual, low-paid, low-quality positions that are less attractive to the Czech labour force. The Czech population is ageing, and the participation of older people in the labour market is rather limited. The inflow of the migrant workforce is therefore supported by employers to at least partly alleviate the acute shortage of workers.

Before the outbreak of the war, the Ukrainian community numbered almost 200,000 people, making it the largest migrant community in the Czech Republic. In 2022, the country accepted 433,071 Ukrainian refugees (MVCR, 2024). The majority of these refugees chose to settle in the Central Bohemia region, particularly near Prague. However, the high concentration of refugees in certain areas posed challenges, particularly in finding suitable housing and securing school placements for children.

In the Czech Republic, temporary protection for refugees was initially provided for a period of one year until 31 March 2023. Ukrainians had to prolong their temporary protection by registering at the website of the Ministry of Interior Affairs, otherwise the residence rights could be lost. The compulsory electronic registration showed that roughly a third of refugees left the Czech Republic and did not extend the temporary protection. After registration, temporary protection was prolonged by one additional year (i.e., until 31 March 2024). The protection could also be prolonged by applying for the single work permit, EU Blue Card, seasonal worker and family reunification.

9.2.3 Poland

Poland has traditionally been known as an emigration country. The EU enlargement in 2004 triggered a substantial emigration wave, with over one million people leaving Poland between 2004 and 2010 (CSO, 2021). The inflow of migrants to Poland began to rise in 2008 when the liberalization of immigrants' access to the Polish labour market was introduced. The year 2014 marked the beginning of Russia's aggression against Ukraine, including the annexation of Crimea and significant parts of the Donetsk and Lugansk regions, further escalating the flow of Ukrainians to Poland. According to estimates by the Central Statistical Office, the number of immigrants in Poland increased from around 100,000 in 2011 to over two million in 2019 (CSO, 2020). Before the war in 2022, the number of Ukrainians residing in Poland was estimated at one million. In 2022, the country transformed into both a destination and a transit country for war refugees from Ukraine.

Poland decided to open its border crossings with Ukraine immediately upon learning of the entry of Russian troops into Ukraine. The war in Ukraine triggered an unprecedented influx of refugees. In two months, over three million people crossed the Polish border, with over 95% being Ukrainian citizens. After the initial surge in the first three weeks, the migration movement stabilized (Duszczyk, Górny, Kaczmarczyk & Kubisiak, 2023). Approximately two million refugees stayed in Poland for at least a few weeks. Since 5 April 2022, displaced persons from Ukraine have had the opportunity to obtain special identification numbers (PESEL), analogous to Polish citizens and foreigners, with the only difference being that the number has the extension 'UKR'. The number of refugees in Poland reached the highest level of

1.4 million in July 2022 (based on the number of active PESEL UKR). The PESEL UKR database serves as the most reliable source of information on war refugees from Ukraine residing in Poland. Two years after the outbreak of the war, there are 952,000 active registrations (as of February 2024). The total number of Ukrainian citizens (including refugees) staying in Poland for more than 12 months is estimated at about two million, constituting the largest Ukrainian community in the EU.

Refugees from Ukraine are concentrated in large cities, with the Warsaw agglomeration being of particular importance. Initially, after the outbreak of the war, a relatively large number of Ukrainians remained in regions near the border with Ukraine. Over time, they began to move inland, especially to regions with favourable labour market conditions.

9.2.4 Slovakia

Historically, Slovakia has been a country whose residents used to migrate abroad for work. Emigration of young and highly educated Slovaks intensified after Slovakia joined the EU (Kahanec & Kureková, 2016). It is estimated that approximately 300,000 individuals (5.5% of the population) left Slovakia between 2002 and 2012 (Haluš, Hlaváč, Harvan & Hidas, 2017). Slovakia is not a typical destination for immigrants, largely due to its cumbersome immigration policy. The country remained largely unaffected by humanitarian migration flows in 2015 and 2016. The number of granted asylums has remained low, typically not exceeding ten per year. The inflow of the foreign population to Slovakia accelerated only in economically successful years shortly before the Covid-19 pandemic, driven by the shortage of low-skilled workers in some sectors. According to statistics collected from the Bureau of Border and Foreign Police, the number of foreign citizens with valid residence permits doubled from 71,649 in 2013 to 143,075 in 2019 (Guzi & Fabo, 2021).

Slovakia allowed all persons fleeing the war in Ukraine to enter the country. Before 2022, Slovakia had limited experience with managing the large inflow of migrants also because the country hosted the lowest number of migrants in the EU. In 2021, there were 167,519 individuals with foreign citizenship in Slovakia, constituting 3% of the population. About two-thirds of foreigners were from outside the EU and Ukrainians were the largest group, accounting for up to 50% of third-country nationals. However, by the end of 2022, the number of foreigners in Slovakia had surged to 278,595. Almost half of the refugees reside in the capital district of Bratislava and nearby regions.

The unprecedented mass migration of refugees from Ukraine presented a unique challenge for Slovak institutions, as it was the first time they had to manage such a situation. Within the first month following the onset of the conflict, over 269,111 refugees crossed the Slovak border, and the total number of displaced people passing through Slovakia surpassed one million in 2022. It is noteworthy that 90% of Ukrainian refugees subsequently moved on to other countries. In 2022, a total of 104,704 refugees were registered in Slovakia, of which a third were children. Most registrations (70%) occurred within the first two months after the conflict began. Veselková and Hábel (2024) estimate that a third of refugees who were granted temporary refuge had returned back home by the end of 2022. In Slovakia, the temporary protection was initially valid for one year until 4 March 2023, and then it was automatically extended.

9.3 Acceptance of Refugees Measured by Public Opinion Polls

Many citizens in Central and Eastern European countries have personally contributed to helping Ukrainian refugees. For example, numerous households have offered shared housing or provided material support. While Austria had recent experience in assisting Syrian refugees, the Czech Republic, Poland, and Slovakia showed solidarity with refugees for the first time.

Public opinion polls provide insights into attitudes towards refugees from Ukraine. For example, the majority of Czech society initially supported the short-term acceptance of a smaller number of Ukrainian refugees (79% of respondents agreed to accept up to 150,000 refugees). Additionally, over half of the Czech public agreed to accept a larger number of war refugees (52% agreed with the short-term acceptance of 300 to 500 thousand refugees). The high acceptance of Ukrainian refugees is significant, considering that the Czech Republic received one of the highest numbers of refugees relative to its population by the end of 2022. Specifically, the Czech Republic accepted 45 refugees per thousand inhabitants in 2022, while Poland had 41, Slovakia had 20, and Austria had 10 (see also Figure 2.13). However, by the end of November 2022, the acceptance of Ukrainian refugees in Czech society had declined by approximately one-quarter or 15 percentage points (Münich & Protivínský, 2023).

At the end of 2022, GLOBSEC, a non-governmental organisation based in Bratislava, conducted a representative survey (including 1,000 respondents in each country) to measure opinions about refugees (Szicherle & Kazaz, 2022). The survey covered Visegrad countries but not Austria. Overall the acceptance of refugees was high, with nearly 90% of citizens holding a favourable view of Ukrainian refugees. However in Slovakia acceptance was lower at 65% (Figure 9.1). Similarly, the support for the presence of Ukrainian refugees is strong, apart from Slovakia, where the majority had negative feelings about hosting refugees (60%).

The level of agreement varies among countries regarding whether displaced people should receive support. While the majority of Poles opposed reducing benefits for Ukrainian refugees, Czechs (46%) and Slovaks (68%) leaned towards decreasing social assistance provided to Ukrainians. Furthermore, the majority of Slovaks expressed the opinion that refugees should not be granted access to free healthcare.

Respondents also reported how their lives had been affected by the influx of refugees. Slovaks were most likely to indicate negative impacts on their lives. Conversely, Czechs reported the highest incidence of experiencing inappropriate behaviour from Ukrainian refugees.

Income level influences perceptions of Ukrainian refugees. Respondents from average and lower-income households show less support for providing welfare to refugees and express more negative views towards them. Notably, individuals who rely on social media as their main source of news are more likely to hold negative views on refugees. Additionally, perceptions and experiences are shaped by anti-migrant narratives promoted by political party leaders favoured by respondents.

Fig. 9.1: Opinions on Ukrainian refugees at the end of 2022
Data: Szicherle and Kazaz (2022)
Note: Questions asked: "Would you agree to allow Ukrainians to enter (the country)?","How do you feel about your country hosting Ukrainian refugees?", "Have there been any changes to your life because of Ukrainian refugees coming to (country)? If yes, is this change positive or negative?", "Support for reducing benefits to Ukrainian refugees". The proportion of respondents answering 'strongly agree'/'agree' and 'very'/'rather' positive are presented.

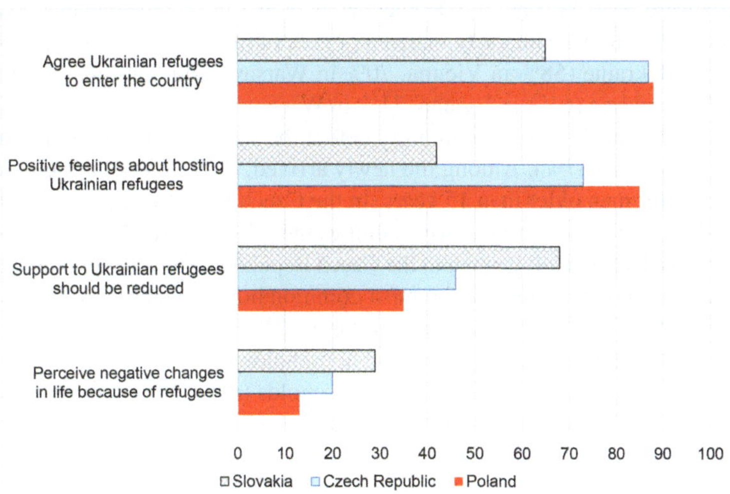

9.4 Demographic Characteristics of Ukrainian Refugees

9.4.1 Gender and Age Structure of Refugees

The incoming population of displaced persons from Ukraine was significantly different from the previous Ukrainian minority residing abroad in terms of its demographic structure. This is because men aged 18–60 were prohibited from leaving Ukraine. However some Ukrainian men in economically productive age may want to join their families in the future. In Poland, there were 505,000 refugees over the age of 18 (adults) and 387,000 children, of whom 288,000 were of school age (Table 9.1). Half of the refugees were of working age, while pensioners accounted for 6%. The vast majority of refugees were women (63%), but gender differences among children were minimal. A similar gender structure of Ukrainian refugees is observed in other countries as well.

The arriving refugees could be compared to the Ukrainian community residing in the country since before 2022. In Austria, the Ukrainian community comprised a high number of women (70%) mostly between 15 and 44 years old, and 10% of Ukrainians were children younger than 15. In 2022 around two-thirds of the Ukrainians who moved to Austria were women, and 28% were children. Most women refugees arriving in Austria were 30 to 44 years-old. Kohlenberger et al. (2023) illustrate that displaced Ukrainians were in their majority married or cohabiting women with a spouse who remained in Ukraine (58% in Vienna, 70% in Warsaw) and that most immigrants moved with children (61% in Vienna, 71% in Warsaw).

In contrast, the Ukrainian community before the war in the Czech Republic was dominated by men (57%). Among the newly arrived, only 37% were men but only 24% were adult men older than 15 years. In the Czech Republic, a third of refugees were children, and half of refugees were adult women (Klimešová, Šatava & Ondruška, 2022). Almost half of adult women in the Czech Republic were younger than 35 years. It is therefore not surprising that the most common households were a mother with one child (21%) and a mother with two children (13%). Around 14% of households with a single adult have three children, and households with more children constitute less than 5%. A significant proportion of households (43%) have children under the age of 5. Many of them thus require assistance in finding daycare for their children.

9.4.2 Education Structure of Refugees

The incoming displaced persons typically have education above the Ukrainian average. In the Czech Republic, a third of incoming refugees have tertiary education (Klimešová et al., 2022). Hence, among refugees, university graduates represent twice as many as in the Czech population. In general, the education level of the population in Ukraine is high also because university education includes a two-year professional junior bachelor's degree that does not exist in the Czech Republic.

Table 9.1: Demographic characteristics of Ukrainian refugees in hosting countries
Data: Own elaboration
Note: Figures refer to the number of registrations in Austria, Czechia, and Slovakia at the end of 2022 and to the number of active refugees (UKR PESEL) in Poland on 13 February 2024. Age brackets are 0-14, 15-29 and 60+ for Austria.

	Austria	Czechia	Poland	Slovakia
Refugee (people)	78,439	433,049	952,000	110,114
Refugee (%)				
Children 0-18 years	28	26	41	29
Adults 18-64	59	70	53	62
Pensioners 65+	12	4	6	9
Refugee males (%)				
Children 0-18 years	14	13	21	14
Adults 18-64	15	23	15	16
Pensioners 65+	4	1	1	3
Refugee females (%)				
Children 0-18 years	14	13	20	14
Adults 18-64	44	47	38	46
Pensioners 65+	9	3	5	6

In Austria, arriving Ukrainian refugees are better educated than residing migrants. Over 80% of refugees had completed tertiary education, 15% spoke German, and 62% spoke at least some English. Interestingly relative to displaced Ukrainians in Warsaw those moving to Vienna are more highly educated and more often speak German and English. The favourable educational structure and language proficiency of displaced Ukrainians will facilitate their labour market integration.

In Poland, half of the refugees had a university education (Dudek, Panuciak & Strzelecki, 2023) and the same result is confirmed by Chmielewska-Kalińska, Dudek and Strzelecki (2023). The study by the Centre for Migration Research shows a higher percentage of refugees with higher education of 55% (Górny & van der Zwan, 2024).

9.5 Social Assistance and Access to Social Benefits

9.5.1 Austria

Ukrainian refugees are entitled to housing, food, clothing, cost for transportation, long-term care, medical treatment, and mandatory health insurance. Displaced persons in Austria are included in the subsistence scheme *Grundversorgung* that temporarily supports foreigners who need help and protection. Typically, it is paid during an asylum procedure and up to four months after asylum is granted. In contrast to asylum seekers, displaced Ukrainians have no access to procedures that lead to a residence permit. Their legal presence in the country depends on the EU mass-influx directive when they want to prolong their stay in Austria. This adds to the uncertainty relating to the length of stay of displaced Ukrainians in Austria and may represent an obstacle to labour market integration.

In Austria, Ukrainian refugees are entitled to a daily fee of EUR 25 to cover residence and food costs (usually paid to the providing institution) and monthly 'pocket money' of EUR 40 in case they reside in officially organized accommodation. Any income from employment that exceeds the income threshold (EUR 110 per month, plus EUR 80 for each family member) results in a deduction from the financial support granted under the subsistence scheme for asylum seekers. The income from employment that exceeds the social security minimum (EUR 486 in 2022) results in a complete loss of this support, including housing support (ELA, 2023). In 2023, the subsistence scheme changed in six out of nine federal states (not in Carinthia, Salzburg, and Lower Austria) and for every euro earned above the allowance of EUR 110, the benefit is reduced proportionately. The new system turns out to be complicated for displaced persons to understand how much they can earn without losing access to income support.

9.5.2 Czech Republic

In the Czech Republic and Slovakia, persons with temporary protection who are employed or residing in the country are entitled to social welfare benefits under the same conditions as nationals. Children who are granted temporary protection or asylum can attend schools according to their level of education. People with temporary protection status are entitled to full health care just like local citizens.

In the Czech Republic, Ukrainian refugees were eligible for the *humanitarian benefit* of CZK 5,000 (EUR 200) paid on a regular monthly basis. The benefit was means-tested paid to persons whose income, social and material situation does not allow them to cover their basic living needs. After six months, the amount of benefit was decreased to CZK 4,620 (EUR 185) for adults and CZK 3,320 (EUR 130) for children under 18 years of age. Full coverage by the public health insurance system was granted free to Ukrainian refugees for 150 days. After this period, it remained free for children and the elderly (older than 65 years) and the working-age population had to cover health insurance themselves.

In the Czech Republic, refugees found accommodation in shared households (44%), in rental accommodation (commercial rentals or council housing, 24%) or stayed in non-residential housing (hostels or hotels). The government introduced the *solidary household benefit* that was paid to local households who were hosting Ukrainian refugees. Over 70% of hosting households were Czech, and 28% were Ukrainian. Housing benefits helped half of the refugees who have accommodation provided entirely for free. Some refugees paid partial costs of accommodation, and about a third of refugees paid their housing costs fully (Klimešová et al., 2022). The housing benefit was paid directly to owners and the amount was tied to the size of the hosting family (CZK 5,000 for one person and up to CZK 12,000 for three people). It may occur that housing conditions for some families were substandard also because Ukrainian families were larger but 75% of refugees report to be satisfied with their housing conditions and the highest satisfaction was reported by refugees living in hosting households (Klimešová et al., 2022). It can be concluded that access to housing was successfully managed in 2022. The close contact of refugees with Czech households was beneficial to the language and school integration of children and the labour market participation of Ukrainian families.

In July 2023, the Czech government imposed restrictions on social benefits, impacting approximately 70% of refugees. Own income earned by displaced Ukrainians deducted from the financial support provided. This means that for every euro earned, the allowance is decreased by one euro. This setup could discourage refugees from earning legal income, potentially leading to an increase in informal payments. Consequently, the state may experience a loss in tax collections and social contributions. Additionally, as of July 2023, the solidarity housing benefit was discontinued, requiring refugees to pay for rented accommodation. Only the most vulnerable groups, including children, individuals caring for a child up to the age of six and seniors aged 65 and above (23,662 people in July 2023), can continue living in subsidized housing.

Ukrainian refugees experience material hardship, although their circumstances have improved over time. As of June 2023, seven out of ten refugees still faced material deprivation, a decrease from 85% in August 2022. Additionally, approximately half of the refugees have incurred debts as they had to borrow money to flee their country. Consequently, refugees struggle to save money. Seven out of ten refugees have enough resources to cover their expenses for one month without income. By comparison, about 30% of the Czech population finds themselves in similar circumstances (PAQ Research, 2023).

9.5.3 Slovakia

Similarly, in Slovakia the government introduced a compensation scheme to local households who provide accommodation free of charge to displaced persons. Owners were compensated EUR 10 for an adult and EUR 5 for a child younger than 15 years per night of accommodation. The maximum allowance amount depended on the number of habitable rooms provided (maximum allowance EUR 710 per month for one room, EUR 1,080 for two rooms, EUR 1,430 for three rooms). The provision of allowances was granted until 31 March 2024.

9.5.4 Poland

According to the Law on Assistance to Ukrainian Citizens in Connection with the Armed Conflict on the Territory of Ukraine, war refugees are entitled to social benefits under the same terms as Polish citizens. The most common family benefits available to Ukrainian citizens included:

- *Child benefit 800+* is available for parents and guardians of children younger than 18. The amount of PLN 800 (EUR 186) is paid monthly (tax-free) for each child, regardless of family income. The family programme was launched in 2016 as "500+ Family". Starting from January 1, 2024 the benefit was increased from PLN 500 to PLN 800.
- Benefit *Good Start*, EUR 70 benefit granted to children at the beginning of each school year, regardless of their parents' income.
- *Family Care Capital* is granted for the second and subsequent children between 12 and 36 months. The monthly amount is chosen by the parent, i.e., it may be either PLN 500 per month for two years or PLN 1,000 per month for one year. The benefit is paid regardless of family income.
- *Nursing benefit* is paid to people looking after a child up to the age of three.
- *Family allowance* is granted to families or individuals who are studying and whose income per capita is below a certain threshold.

The most popular and costly benefit is the 800+ family benefit. At the end of 2023, almost 210,000 children of war refugees from Ukraine were receiving it, at a cost of almost PLN 1.5 billion (approximately EUR 310 million, based on our own calculation). The other child benefits were less popular and consequently less costly.

In addition, war refugees are entitled to benefits specifically dedicated to them. One-off financial support is a benefit of EUR 70, which can be used to cover living expenses, particularly expenditure on food, clothing, footwear, personal hygiene products, and housing fees. Financing or subsidising accommodation and meals in private residences (EUR 9 per person per day) or in collective accommodation (up to EUR 16 per person per day). Refugees have the right to free access to healthcare and enrolment of their children in the Polish school system.

Table 9.2: Number of Ukrainian children supported and estimated related costs in 2023
Data: own calculations based on data from Social Insurance Institution (ZUS)

Type of benefit	Number of children	Amount in EUR
Child benefit 800+	209,682	338,421,947
Good start	124,626	8,694,421
Family Care Capital	3,132	13,299,765
Nursing benefit	967	1,181,293
Family alowance	39,422	54,021,364
Total		415,618,790

9.6 Employment of Ukrainian Refugees

All displaced persons from Ukraine gain access to the labour market upon registration for temporary protection. Their population is specific as it includes mainly female working-age individuals with tertiary level education and with high integration prospects in the labour market. These are more likely to learn the language and find a job quickly in their destinations, provided, they receive adequate childcare services and access to public schools .

9.6.1 Poland

Poland liberalised access of Ukrainians to the Polish labour market to a very large extent after the first aggression against Ukraine in 2014. Before the outbreak of full-scale war in 2022, approximately 1.3 million Ukrainians were residing in Poland, more than 90% of whom were active in the labour market. The study by Deloitte (2022) estimates that Ukrainians contributed an annual increase of 0.5 percentage points to the GDP growth of the Polish economy from 2013 to 2018. The well-established Ukrainian diaspora helped war refugees find employment. In addition, a favourable economic situation and low unemployment (remaining below 5% in large cities) indicated good labour market prospects for refugees. The estimated potential increase in Poland's GDP associated with the refugees inflow is positive and ranges from 0.2% to 3.5% (Deloitte, 2022).

Polish employers have to submit a notification on the work assignment to a Ukrainian citizen that allows monitoring their economic activities. The notification is submitted within 14 days of the foreigner taking up employment. It entitles a refugee to work without the requirement of a work permit or declaration. In 2022, more than

786,000 permits were registered with labour offices, and the number of registrations in 2023 was even higher (1,080 million permits).

The economic activity of refugees was exceptionally high, reaching 65% by the end of 2022 (Zyzik, Baszczak, Rozbicka & Wielechowski, 2024). The latest data confirm that economic activity remained high throughout 2023. Notably, this represents the highest level of economic activity among Ukrainian refugees in the OECD countries (OECD, 2023). The Social Insurance Institution (ZUS) records also confirm the high economic activity of refugees. In February 2024, there were 1,124 million foreigners employed, including 755,000 Ukrainians. Although some employed foreigners may not be registered in the ZUS database, Ukrainians' high professional activity can be well-documented.

Several studies have documented the characteristics of Ukrainian refugees in the Polish labour market (Górny & van der Zwan, 2024; Duszczyk et al., 2023; Kaczmarczyk, 2023). Approximately 50% of refugees in Poland are employed in positions that align with their acquired qualifications. The employment chances are higher for refugees with a good command of the Polish language. The employment rate for refugees with proficient language skills was 82%, while for those without good language skills it was only 50%. A high share of refugees (around 45%) engage in simple jobs, while approximately 25% of refugees hold positions requiring high qualifications, such as lawyers, doctors, or teachers.

The labour market integration of refugees can be contrasted with that of Ukrainian migrants who arrived before 2022. Fewer refugees have full-time employment than Ukrainian migrants (40% vs. 80%). Male refugees are less likely to be employed in professions requiring manual skills than Ukrainian male migrants (20% vs. 40%). Less than 10% of refugees have part-time employment, and another 10% take on occasional work. Around 20% of refugees are neither employed nor seeking work, primarily due to childcare responsibilities. Another 20% of refugees actively seek employment while temporarily unemployed. Some refugees telework as they continue their work for Ukrainian employers. The International Centre for Migration Policy Development results indicate that 24% of those registered at labour offices work remotely for Ukrainian companies (Katsiaficas, Segeš Frelak & Castelanelli, 2023).

In 2023, nearly two-thirds of Ukrainian citizens (including war refugees) worked with civil-law contracts, and around one-third with employment contracts. They are mostly employed in manufacturing, transport and storage, administrative and support services (including temporary work agencies), and construction. Based on officially declared amounts, the average salary of employed Ukrainian citizens is slightly above the minimum wage.

Many Ukrainian refugees have ventured into entrepreneurship in Poland. Data from the Central Register and Information on Economic Activity reveals that between 2022 and 2023, nearly 45,000 businesses were established with Ukrainian citizens as their founders (Dębkowska, Kłosiewicz-Górecka, Szymańska, Wejt-Knyżewska & Zybertowicz, 2022). This implies that one in ten businesses established in Poland during these two years was founded by Ukrainians.

Under Polish legislation, Ukrainian citizens can register at a labour office as unemployed or job seekers on equal terms with Polish citizens. The number of registrations of Ukrainian citizens at labour offices peaked during the first months after the Russian invasion of Ukraine, reaching its highest point in April 2022 when 15,700 people, mostly war refugees, were registered. 128,700 Ukrainian citizens registered from February 24, 2022, until the end of January 2024.

Individuals registered at labour offices as unemployed or job seekers can participate in training courses. Around 43,000 foreigners, the majority being war refugees from Ukraine, have benefited from various assistance measures organized by Polish labour offices. In 2022, language courses were introduced for unemployed and job-seeking foreigners to facilitate their entry into employment. From 2022 to February 2024, almost 6,700 Ukrainian citizens (5,378 persons in 2022 and 1,302 persons in 2023) benefited from training courses, primarily in the Polish language. The cost of language training for Ukrainian citizens specializing in the medical profession was supported by the Labour Fund. Between 2022 and 2023, 20 agreements were signed with district chambers of doctors and district chambers of nurses and midwives, covering the training costs for 704 participants.

9.6.2 Czech Republic

In the Czech Republic, half of the refugees were economically active in the summer of 2022, and this figure increased to 72% of refugees by the end of 2023 (Figure 9.2). Around 7-9% of Ukrainians kept their employment in Ukraine and teleworked (mostly those with more specialized jobs). Economists predict that the economic activity of refugees could increase to 85% (PAQ Research, 2023).

Research studies show that the major difference between refugees who are employed and those who are not lies in the knowledge of the Czech language. The participation rate in families with children depended largely on the children's enrolment in the school system. Interestingly, Ukrainians residing in Prague worked less, possibly because they could rely more on the support of the Ukrainian diaspora, but also due to worse access to kindergarten in large cities. The families staying in standard-quality housing were more likely to work. It is estimated that around 40% of refugees face barriers that prevent them from finding a job in the long term.

The many refugees who are working in the Czech Republic have unstable employment. Some refugees take occasional jobs and one-time work contracts. The survey shows that every third refugee who was employed either changed jobs (24%) or lost their job (10%) between December 2022 and March 2023 (PAQ Research, 2023).

The majority of refugees (80%) are employed in low-skilled professions, and they mostly work for large employers with more than 200 employees. Although most refugees work in specialized, technical, or managerial positions in Ukraine, they are often in unqualified positions (two-thirds of workers). Half of those employed perform manual and low-skilled work. Overqualification is more common among women, older individuals, and those who do not speak Czech.

The wages of Ukrainian workers are generally lower than those of Czech workers in most occupations. More than a third (35%) of refugees earn less than CZK 100

Fig. 9.2: Employment of refugees in the Czech Republic between August 2022 and November 2023
Data: PAQ Research

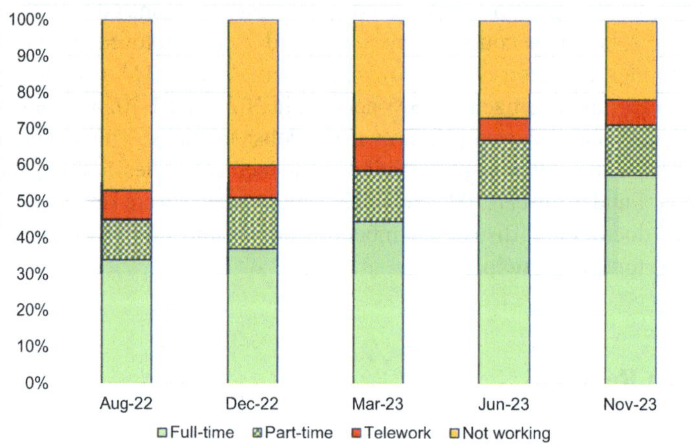

(EUR 4) net per hour, while only 11% earn above CZK 200 (EUR 8) net per hour. Approximately one-fifth of Ukrainian refugees have found employment through a work agency or informal intermediary, which typically offer low-paying jobs (PAQ Research, 2022).

9.6.3 Austria

Ukrainian refugees, despite being highly qualified, have been slow to integrate into the Austrian labour market. Administrative records from December 2023 indicate that about 44% were economically active (i.e., employed or unemployed), with 3% participating in active labour market policy measures. The majority (about 56%) were neither employed nor unemployed. The employment rate stood at 30%, which is one of the lowest among EU countries (Arbeitsmarktdatenbank, 2024).

Limited integration could be attributed to administrative obstacles in obtaining residence and work permits. Thränhardt (2023) shows that refugees had greater success in entering the labour market in European countries where access was streamlined as a 'one-stop shop'. In contrast, countries like Austria maintain a separate system for residence and work permits for third-country nationals. Despite

Ukrainians having free access to the labour market in Austria, many displaced persons are not registered with the Austrian public employment service, and the reasons for this lack of registration remain unclear.

Analysing Austrian social security records, Bock-Schappelwein and Huber (2022) show that Ukrainians entering the labour market after 2022 worked fewer days and received lower wages than those who arrived before 2022 during their first year of stay. Similarly, Thränhardt (2023) finds significant variations in the employment rates of displaced Ukrainians across several European countries. Austria, Belgium, Germany, and Switzerland all had employment rates for Ukrainian displaced persons below 30%. This contrasts with the high employment levels of Ukrainians who arrived in Austria before 2022. Current Ukrainian refugees are more concentrated in low-skill segments of the labour market, mainly working in low-paid temporary jobs. The average monthly wage of employed Ukrainians was EUR 948, largely below the nationwide average of EUR 2,900 (Bock-Schappelwein & Huber, 2022).

As of January 2024, over 50% of Ukrainian employees were concentrated in three sectors: 1) accommodation and food service activities, 2) wholesale and retail trade, and 3) manufacturing. The particularly high employment rates of Ukrainians in accommodation and food service activities are surprising. Traditionally, this sector has served as a low-skilled 'port of entry' for many migrant groups in Austria, providing low-skilled temporary (seasonal) employment to migrant workers. This sector is experiencing a severe labour shortage in the post-Covid boom of 2023, which may have additionally fostered employment opportunities for Ukrainian displaced persons.

9.6.4 Slovakia

Ukrainian refugees entered Slovakia during the post-Covid boom when the labour market was suffering from a shortage of workers. There were 25,638 refugees who were employed during the first year, and 28,464 refugees were employed during the second year after the outbreak of war. During the first year of Russia's aggression against Ukraine, 110,114 refugees from Ukraine registered for temporary protection in Slovakia.

The calculation of employment rates is complicated because the exact number of working-age refugees is not recorded in the official statistics. It is estimated that the employment rate was between 22% and 37% (Veselková & Hábel, 2024). Characteristics of employed refugees could be observed. Over 70% of employed were women, and half of the employed were refugees younger than 40 years. In contrast to other countries, the population of refugees in Slovakia included relatively more older persons and a lower proportion of tertiary-educated refugees. A quarter of employed refugees have a university education, but a third have found employment in elementary occupations that require only primary education.

Ukrainian refugees can be compared to Ukrainian labour migrants who entered Slovakia in 2021, i.e., one year before Russia's invasion of Ukraine. Veselková and Hábel (2024) compare 4,373 Ukrainian labour migrants and 24,295 refugees in the labour market during 2022. The findings reveal that refugees face greater challenges in the Slovak labour market compared to Ukrainian labour migrants. They are often overeducated for their initial jobs and more likely to be employed in elementary occupations. Both groups struggle to advance their careers within the first year of arrival, leading to underutilization of human capital and reduced economic contribution. Urgent policy interventions are required to facilitate the integration of migrants and refugees into the labour market in Slovakia.

9.7 Barriers to Employment

Migrants often lack specific skills relevant to their host country, such as language proficiency and knowledge of local labour regulations. Consequently, they may end up accepting jobs that require lower levels of education than they possess, leading to overqualification (Guzi & Kahanec, 2015; Guzi, Kahanec & Kureková, 2021; Guzi, Kahanec & Mýtna Kureková, 2023). This risk is particularly considerable for highly educated migrants, as many professions demand additional certifications. Employers often prioritize proficiency in the host country's language over other qualifications, making it challenging for migrants to secure jobs that match their education or experience.

The labour market prospects of refugees are generally disadvantageous. Refugees tend to have lower employment rates and are more likely to experience occupational downgrading compared to other migrants. While a 'work-first' policy may accelerate entry into the job market, the jobs available are often precarious with limited hours. Additionally, refugees who begin working immediately upon arrival may invest less in language learning and skill acquisition, which may hinder their long-term employment prospects. This pattern is evident in the recent influx of Ukrainian refugees, who have been permitted to seek employment promptly but are often employed in low-skilled positions.

In many countries, the arriving displaced persons are not obligated to participate in language courses before entering the job market. The insufficient proficiency in the local language forces refugees to accept non-qualified and low-skilled positions with lower wages. As of February 2023, only 31% of refugees attended Czech language courses, while 55% pursued individual language study, and 13% did not engage in language learning at all. The primary barriers to attending language courses include job priority (50%), the costs associated with language courses (41%), and childcare responsibilities (24%) (PAQ Research, 2023). According to several studies, refugees primarily need assistance with learning the local language. Strong language proficiency is particularly requested by employers seeking highly qualified workers. In the Czech Republic, the Czech and English language competencies of refugees in 2022 were generally low, although almost one-third of refugees had some command of Czech (Klimešová et al., 2022). It is likely that in Slavic countries refugees have improved their language proficiency quickly over time. In June 2023, nearly half of the Ukrainian refugees reported that they could communicate in Czech in daily situations.

The survey of 621 employers who have experience with employing Ukrainian refugees was organized in the summer of 2022 in the Czech Republic to understand the major limitations to the employment of refugees (Coufalová, Fumarco & Mikula, 2022). Employers report the knowledge of the Czech language as the major barrier to employment, especially for qualified positions. Language proficiency is considered more important for high-skilled than for low-skilled positions.

Another limitation for highly qualified refugees is the lack of work experience acquired in the Czech Republic and recognition of their qualifications. The process of acquiring and recognizing qualifications for foreign workers is known to be administratively demanding in the Czech Republic. Employers state that employer testing must be accepted as a sufficient demonstration of qualifications for both medium- and highly skilled professions.

Employers consider the potential return of refugees to Ukraine a risk factor when employing them in more qualified positions. These positions require greater investment in employee training. Such investments are lost when refugees decide to return home. Moreover, return migration is difficult for employers to foresee, so they may prefer to avoid hiring refugees for qualified positions. On the other hand, the health risks and administration burden related to the employment of refugees are rarely reported by employers as a barrier to refugee employment.

Since most refugee families have children, the active participation of children in the education system is crucial for their families' employment prospects, as it contributes to higher overall refugee employment rates. In the Czech Republic, 57% of Ukrainian refugee children attended Czech primary and secondary school in 2022. The reasons of low enrolment include a rejection by schools due to capacity limits as well as a lack of information about where and how to enrol children (PAQ Research, 2023).

9.8 Conclusion and Suggestions for the Successful Integration of Refugees

After the outbreak of the war, Ukrainians were granted temporary protection, including humanitarian assistance, housing, social and health insurance, and unrestricted access to the labour market and all educational levels. They have received broad acceptance from the public, regional authorities, and non-governmental organizations. Nevertheless, despite these provisions, they continue to face challenges in their daily lives in both the Czech Republic and Germany, primarily due to less effective integration policies. Frequently, they find employment in low-skilled positions due to limited language proficiency impeding their overall adaptation. Consequently, many of them end up in precarious situations.

Language proficiency is an important factor in the integration of refugees into the labour market. The government will increase the availability of language courses and support refugees to learn the language. Germany primarily focuses on teaching the German language and ensuring high-quality integration before involving Ukrainians in the labour market. In March 2023, 65% of adult Ukrainians attended German language courses, and an additional 10% had already completed the courses. This is significantly higher than in the Czech Republic, where only a third of the refugees attend Czech language courses. In Germany, attending a language course is free up to level B2, and it is a requirement to receive financial support if the refugee is not working or caring for a family member (PAQ Research, 2023).

The demographic structure of refugees is important. Among those of working age, there is a prevalence of single women with children whose spouses have stayed in Ukraine. Refugee women encounter various challenges, as they must secure employment and affordable housing and often arrange for childcare or school placement. The accessibility of childcare facilities presents a particular difficulty, often incurring additional costs.

At the outset, most refugees anticipated a short war and expressed intentions to return to Ukraine promptly once the conflict was over. Especially married Ukrainian women were anticipated to return home to their families after the war's conclusion. However, survey data indicate a shift in intentions. In Austria, one-third of working-age Ukrainian women expressed the intention to return home in 2022, but by April 2023, the return intentions had decreased to 13% (Mazal, Dörfler-Bolt & Kaindl, 2023). Refugees' current residence is temporary and depends on the extension of temporary protection. It therefore diminishes their likelihood of accepting long-term job offers. Employers, in turn, perceive the uncertainty associated with refugee status as a major limitation. Clearly defining the rules regarding the long-term status of Ukrainian refugees with temporary protection would greatly benefit their situation. Refugees need a clear perspective on the possibility of obtaining permanent residency in host countries. This would (a) enable them to maintain their current status in the job market, (b) incentivize refugees to invest in integration efforts, such as language learning, and (c) reduce the risk of return to Ukraine, which may discourage employers from hiring refugees for skilled positions that typically require expensive training.

Entry conditions for some occupations are excessively stringent. Governments could simplify the qualification recognition system, facilitating refugees' access to the necessary qualifications for positions in high demand. Poland, for instance, has relaxed entry qualification requirements for Ukrainians seeking employment in education, healthcare, veterinary services, and social work. Consequently, Ukrainians with the requisite qualifications have successfully secured employment in these sectors.

The 'inactivity trap' can potentially emerge in the welfare systems of the Czech Republic and Austria. In this scenario, refugees integrated into the subsistence scheme may face a complete reduction (100%) of their benefit allowance when they earn income, resulting in the loss of their benefits. Such a system can potentially discourage refugees from seeking legal employment, possibly leading to a rise in informal payments.

The large inflow of Ukrainian refugees in Central and Eastern European economies offers an opportunity for researchers to study the role of structural characteristics and institutional regulations on pathways to inclusion. Further research should uncover the mechanisms that facilitate or hinder the successful integration of refugees, paving the way for more informed and effective policy interventions in the future.

Acknowledgements Martin Guzi acknowledges support by the NPO 'Systemic Risk Institute' no. LX22NPO5101, funded by the European Union – Next Generation EU (Ministry of Education, Youth and Sports, NPO: EXCELES). The authors thank Ivan Fursin (Masaryk University) for technical assistance.

References

Arbeitsmarktdatenbank. (2024). *Arbeitsmarktdatenbank table mon_erwerb_uni_epi.* https://arbeitsmarktdatenbank.at/. (Accessed:19-03-2024)

Bock-Schappelwein, J. & Huber, P. (2022). *Flüchtlinge aus der Ukraine. Erwartete Entwicklung und Herausforderungen.* WIFO.

Chmielewska-Kalińska, I., Dudek, B. & Strzelecki, P. (2023). *The living and economic situation of Ukrainian migrants in Poland - the impact of the pandemic and the war on the nature of migration in Poland.* Narodowy Bank Polski.

Coufalová, L., Fumarco, L. & Mikula, S. (2022). *Ukrajinští uprchlíci očima zaměstnavatelů.* SYRI Narodni Institut.

CSO. (2020). *Population of foreigners in Poland at the time of Covid-19.* Central Statistical Office.

CSO. (2021). *Information on the size and directions of temporary emigration from Poland in 2004-2020.* Central Statistical Office.

Deloitte. (2022). *Refugees from Ukraine in Poland Challenges and Potential for Integration.* Deloitte.

Dudek, B., Panuciak, A. & Strzelecki, P. (2023). *Sytuacja życiowa i ekonomiczna migrantów z Ukrainy w Polsce w 2023 roku.* Narodowy Bank Polski.

Duszczyk, M., Górny, A., Kaczmarczyk, P. & Kubisiak, A. (2023). War refugees from Ukraine in Poland – one year after the Russian aggression. Socioeconomic consequences and challenges. *Regional Science Policy & Practice*, *15*(1), 181–199. doi: 10.1111/rsp3.12642

Dębkowska, K., Kłosiewicz-Górecka, U., Szymańska, A., Wejt-Knyżewska, A. & Zybertowicz, K. (2022). *Ukraińskie firmy w Polsce po wybuchu wojny w 2022.* https://pie.net.pl/wp-content/uploads/2023/01/PIE-Raport_Ukrainskie_firmy_2022-1.pdf. Polski Instytut Ekonomiczny. (Accessed: 24-03-2024)

ELA. (2023). *Overview of national measures regarding employment and social security of displaced persons coming from Ukraine.* European Labour Authority.

Guzi, M. & Fabo, B. (2021). *Geography of new employment dynamics in Slovakia.* ESPON.

Guzi, M. & Kahanec, M. (2015). Socioeconomic Cleavages between Workers from New Member States and Host-country Labour Forces in the EU during the Great Recession. In *Market Expansion and Social Dumping in Europe* (pp. 97–122). Routledge. doi: https://doi.org/10.4324/9781315766607

Guzi, M., Kahanec, M. & Kureková, L. M. (2021, December). What explains immigrant–native gaps in European labor markets: The role of institutions. *Migration Studies*, *9*(4), 1823–1856. doi: 10.1093/migration/mnab044

Guzi, M., Kahanec, M. & Mýtna Kureková, L. (2023, October). The impact of immigration and integration policies on immigrant-native labour market hierarchies. *Journal of Ethnic and Migration Studies*, *49*(16), 4169–4187. doi: 10.1080/1369183X.2023.2207339

Guzi, M., Macková, L. & Čech Valentová, E. (2021). *Governance of Migrant Integration in the Czech Republic.* Diaconia ECCB Center of Relief and Development.

Górny, A. & van der Zwan, R. (2024). Mobility and labor market trajectories of Ukrainian migrants to Poland in the context of the 2014 Russian invasion of Ukraine. *European Societies*, 1–31. doi: 10.1080/14616696.2023.2298425

Haluš, M., Hlaváč, M., Harvan, P. & Hidas, S. (2017). *Odliv mozgov po slovensky.* Institute of Financial Policy.

Kaczmarczyk, P. (2023). Ukraińscy migranci w Polsce w czasie wojny: stan wiedzy i kluczowe wyzwania. *Ubezpieczenia Społeczne. Teoria i praktyka*, *154*(3), 1–22. doi: 10.5604/01.3001.0016.2359

Kahanec, M. & Kureková, L. M. (2016). Did Post-Enlargement Labor Mobility Help the EU to Adjust During the Great Recession? The Case of Slovakia. In *Labor Migration, EU Enlargement, and the Great Recession* (pp. 189–218). Berlin: Springer.

Katsiaficas, C., Segeš Frelak, J. & Castelanelli, C. (2023). *Displacement, integration and return: What remote work possibilities for Ukrainians.* International Centre for Migration Policy Development.

Klimešová, M., Šatava, J. & Ondruška, M. (2022). *Situace uprchlíků z Ukrajiny.* Ministerstva práce a sociálních věcí.

Kohlenberger, J., Buber-Ennser, I., Pędziwiatr, K., Rengs, B., Setz, I., Brzozowski, J., . . . Pronizius, E. (2023). High self-selection of Ukrainian refugees into Europe: Evidence from Kraków and Vienna. *PloS One*, *18*(12), 1–24. doi: 10.1371/journal.pone.0279783

Mazal, W., Dörfler-Bolt, S. & Kaindl, M. (2023). *Ukraine-Vertriebene in Österreich ein Jahr nach Kriegsbeginn.* ÖIF.

MVCR. (2024). *Statistika v souvislosti s válkou na Ukrajině - archiv [Statistics Related to the War in Ukraine - Archive].* Ministry of the Interior of the Czech Republic.

Münich, D. & Protivínský, T. (2023). *Vývoj postojů české veřejnosti k válečným uprchlíkům z Ukrajiny.* IDEA - Institute for Democracy and Economic Analysis.

OECD. (2023). *What we know about the skills and early labour market outcomes of refugees from Ukraine.* https://www.oecd.org/ukraine-hub/policy-responses/what-we-know-about-the-skills-and-early-labour-market-outcomes-of-refugees-from-ukraine-c7e694aa/. (Series: OECD Policy Responses on the Impacts of the War in Ukraine)

OIF. (2023). *Ukrainische Bevölkerung in Österreich.* OIF.

PAQ Research. (2022). *Voice of Ukrainians: Refugee jobs, skills and qual-*

ifications. https://migrant-integration.ec.europa.eu/library-document/voice-ukrainians-refugee-jobs-skills-and-qualifications_en. PAQ Research.

PAQ Research. (2023). *Ukrainian refugee integration: one year on.* PAQ Research.

Szicherle, P. & Kazaz, J. (2022). *Perception of Ukrainian refugees in the V4.* Center for Democracy & Resilience.

Thränhardt, D. (2023). *Mit offenen Armen – die kooperative Aufnahme von Kriegsflüchtlingen aus der Ukraine in Europa. Eine Alternative zum Asylregime?* Friedrich-Ebert-Stiftung.

UNHCR. (2024). *Refugees fleeing Ukraine (since 24 February 2022). Operational Data Portal, Ukraine Refugee Situation.* https://data.unhcr.org/en/situations/ukraine. (Accessed: 01-03-2024)

Veselková, M. & Hábel, B. (2024). *Refugees and labor migrants from Ukraine in Slovakia.* Social policy institute, Ministry of Labour, Social Affairs and Family of the Slovak Republic.

Zyzik, R., Baszczak, L., Rozbicka, I. & Wielechowski, M. (2024). *Refugees from Ukraine in the Polish labour market: opportunities and obstacles.* Polish Economic Institute.

Chapter 10
Economic Reconstruction of Ukraine

Michael Landesmann, Olga Pindyuk, Maryna Tverdostup, and Artem Kochnev

Abstract The chapter analyses characteristics of Ukraine's economic reconstruction following the intensive phase of the war. We first cover the demographic situation, which is indeed very problematic given a long-run population decline and the significant shock of war-induced migration and displacement of persons. Then, we analyse patterns of the comparative (specialisation) advantages of Ukraine's economy, identifying the potentials Ukraine will have in order to attract FDI and integrate into cross-border production linkages. Next, we cover the varying situation across Ukraine's regions, their highly uneven potential for recovery, and evaluate their future possibilities for production and trade specialisation. We discuss Ukraine's position in the context of its accession to the EU: this covers how Ukraine compares in terms of a multitude of indicators with other Central and Eastern European countries before they acceded to the EU, as well as with candidate countries in Southeast Europe. Finally, we discuss how Ukraine's accession will impact existing member countries – with an emphasis on countries in Central and Eastern Europe – in macroeconomic and structural terms, and also with respect to implications regarding Ukraine's participation in EU budgetary programs.

Michael Landesmann ✉
WIIW, Vienna Institute for International Economic Studies, Vienna, Austria, e-mail: landesmann@wiiw.ac.at

Olga Pindyuk
WIIW, Vienna Institute for International Economic Studies, Vienna, Austria, e-mail: OlgaPindyuk

Maryna Tverdostup
WIIW, Vienna Institute for International Economic Studies, Vienna, Austria, e-mail: tverdostup@wiiw.ac.at

Artem Kochnev
WIIW, Vienna Institute for International Economic Studies, Vienna, Austria, e-mail: kochnev@wiiw.ac.at

© The Author(s), under exclusive license to Springer Nature Switzerland AG 2024

L. Mátyás (ed.), *Central and Eastern European Economies and the War in Ukraine*, Contributions to Economics, https://doi.org/10.1007/978-3-031-61561-0_10

10.1 Introduction

At the time when this manuscript is closed (March 2024), the war is still raging, and it is very unclear when its intensive phase will be over. Any analysis of the possible developmental perspectives of Ukraine's economy will depend on assumptions made regarding the scenario in which a 'reconstruction' is likely to take place. From today's standpoint it seems the most likely situation is one in which full-scale war will continue throughout 2024, possibly even longer. What scenario will emerge after that when a cease-fire might take place remains unclear. Short of an overthrow of the Putin regime, it seems that a cease-fire will not put an end to the conflict as such, as neither side can afford to withdraw from mutually incompatible demands: the Ukrainian side will formally keep the demand of a full withdrawal of Russian troops from the territory they have occupied since 2014, i.e., including Crimea and the Donbas region; anything else would be politically unfeasible. On the Russian side, anything less than keeping further territory in the Donbas region beyond what was already occupied after the invasion of 2014 would be seen as defeat, i.e., not having achieved any of the aims of the 'special military operation'; this would endanger the stability of the regime. This does not mean that an armistice would not take place, along the separation lines which the trench warfare will have carved out between the warring parties by the time battle-exhaustion (on both sides) has set in. But any stop to the intense phase of the conflict is unlikely to lead to a proper peace agreement. Hence a 'frozen conflict' scenario which time and again might 'unfreeze' with local eruptions of military clashes, seems the most likely outcome. We take this as our base scenario and in Section 10.2, we also specify a number of more specific scenarios, depending on the timing of a possible cease-fire and the intensity of the conflict before that. Around this base scenario, we sketch out possible demographic trajectories which are highly sensitive to the extent of return migration.

What are the outlines of an 'economic reconstruction' of Ukraine in the context of such a base scenario, and what aspects are we going to cover in this chapter?

In Section 10.2, we cover Ukraine's demographic trajectory, which had been problematic already before the current intense phase of the war but has further deteriorated due to the war. We see demographic developments as a vital issue and constraint for economic recovery and the future successful economic development of Ukraine. As economic reconstruction will go along with deepening trade and production linkages with the countries of the EU, Section 10.3 will cover trade specialisation prospects, as well as the issue of attractiveness for foreign investors. Section 10.4 analyses the rather momentous challenge of the within-country regional reallocation of economic activity in Ukraine, as the continued conflict with Russia as well as the prospect of close integration with the EU opens up differentiated challenges and prospects for Ukraine's different regions. Section 10.5 will return to issues related to EU accession and how current members of the EU — and Central, Eastern and South-Eastern European (CESEE) members in particular — might be affected by Ukraine's prospects of economic reconstruction and development. Section 10.6 presents concluding remarks.

10.2 Demographic Challenges in the Wake of the Refugee Shock

10.2.1 Pre-war Demographic Trends

Ukraine faced very grim demographic prospects long before the full-scale Russian invasion due to a combination of factors, such as low fertility, high mortality, and steadily high outmigration. Over the past three decades, Ukraine's population has decreased by almost 20%, from around 52 million in 1990 to 42 million in 2021 (Eurostat, 2023). Since the early 1990s, the population growth rate has turned negative (see panel (ii) of Figure 10.1). The population decline following the collapse of the Soviet Union was expected, as the fall of the 'Iron Curtain' and the transition to an open economy facilitated cross-border mobility and emigration, including permanent relocation. In addition, extreme economic fluctuations and the emergence of immigration opportunities faced by post-Soviet countries in the first years of independence further fuelled emigration, with the majority of emigrants being those with foreign roots (e.g., of German or Polish ancestry, Kaucher, Deckert, Becher & Winkler, 2017) and regular labour migrants (Mansoor & Quillin, 2006). A steep decline was followed by a meagre improvement in the early 2010s mainly due to a slowdown in emigration and increasing fertility[1] (see panel (iii) of Figure 10.1). The population growth rate was falling again steeply from 2015 onwards, reaching an annual 1% decline by 2021.

The fluctuation in fertility rates over the last few decades has signalled an inevitable population decline. In 1990, the average number of children per woman was 1.8, which dropped to almost 1.1 in 2011, followed by a recovery to approximately 1.5 in 2012,[2] and a major subsequent drop to 1.2 in 2021. In comparison, the EU-27 average stood at 1.5 in 2021 (Eurostat, 2023). Therefore, even before the war, birth projections were pessimistic, and no population growth was realistically foreseen.

While low fertility is the primary factor of population decline and aging in the EU member states, in Ukraine, low life expectancy and resulting high mortality have been additional drivers of the declining population. Despite substantial advances in the healthcare sector, improved income levels, and technological advancements, life expectancy has only marginally improved from 75 to 77 for women, and from 65 to 67 for men between 1990 and 2021 (panel (iv) of Figure 10.1). A low life expectancy, particularly for men, largely stems from common health issues, as well as poor access to and quality of medical care.[3]

---

[1] During the early 2010s, Ukraine implemented a series of maternity leave and family benefits reforms aimed at increasing birth rates. However, the effect of these reforms proved to be limited, and the increase in fertility was short-lived.

[2] The temporarily spike in fertility in 2012 and several years afterwards stems from childbirth support reform, which increased financial support for families, with the largest increase for families having two and more children.

[3] Including cardiovascular disease and health failure caused from tobacco and alcohol use, see Lisenkova (2015).

Fig. 10.1: Ukraine key demographic indicators, 1990-2021
Note: panels (i) and (ii): mid-year population (as of 1 July). Population growth rate is computed as the difference between the population in the current year and in the previous year, divided by the population in the previous year, and multiplied by 100.
Source:United Nations (2023); own calculations

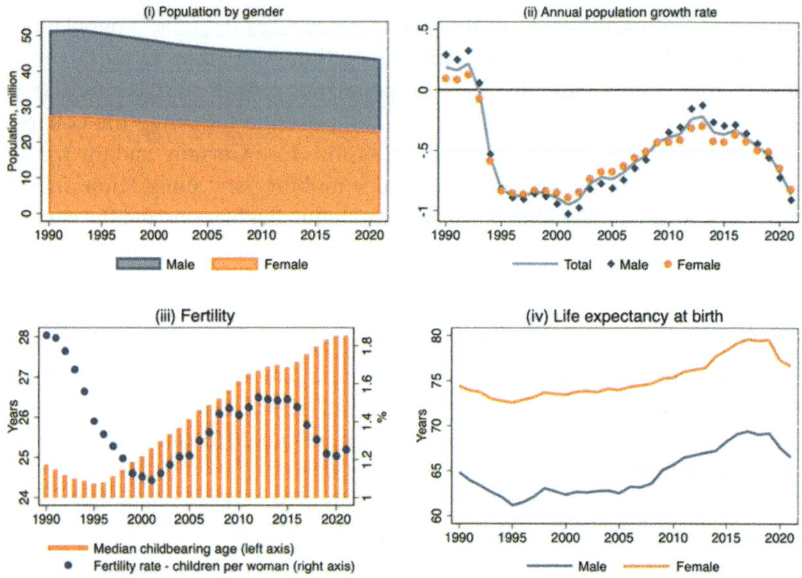

In addition to low fertility and high mortality, the negative net migration flow was another persistent factor contributing to population decline in Ukraine. In the early 1990s, millions of Ukrainians left the country due to economic hardship in the first years of independence and migration opportunities that emerged after the collapse of the Soviet Union. People migrated both to other post-Soviet states and beyond. However, massive outward mobility, especially of younger labour migrants, continued until the early 2000s (Lapshyna, 2022). Notably, mass emigration was not an issue from the early 2000s until the Russian invasion in 2014. Moreover, net migration was positive for several years preceding the Russian occupation of Crimea and parts of the Donetsk and Luhansk regions. However, since 2014, net migration has either been negative or fluctuated around zero, putting further pressure on demographic prospects.

Over the past three decades, the Ukrainian population has been aging rapidly. The under 35 population declined significantly between 1990 and 2021 for both men and women (Figure 10.2). The share of over-65s in the total population increased from 12% in 1990 to almost 18% in 2021, whereas the share of the population aged under 14 dropped from 21% in 1990 to 15% in 2021. The rising median age of the Ukrainian

Fig. 10.2: Ukrainian population by age and gender, 1990 (left panel) and 2021 (right panel)
Note: Mid-year population (as of 1 July).
Source:United Nations (2023)

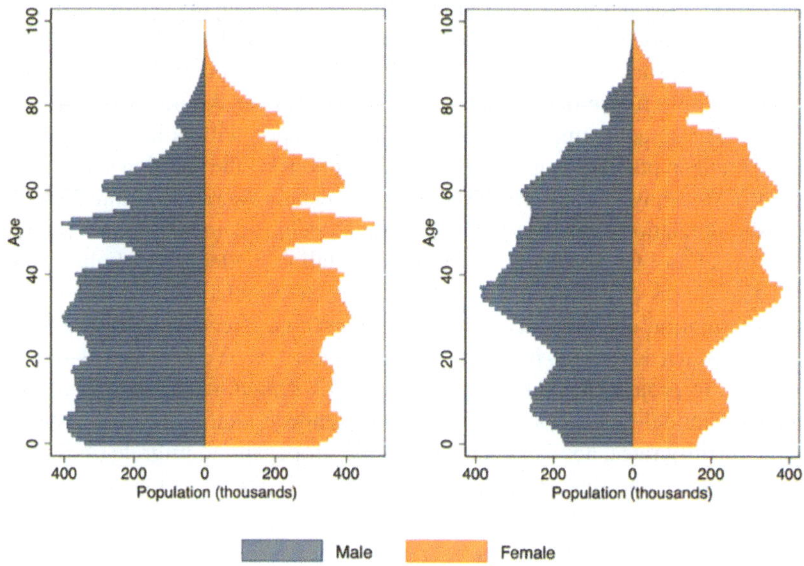

population from 34 years in 1990 to almost 41 years in 2021 also reflects rapid aging (Lapshyna, 2022).These trends are the outcome of decades-long stagnation in fertility rates and steadily high outward migration, which is especially considerable among the youth. These trends have inevitably led to a massively shrinking working-age population, which is even more pronounced than the overall population decline.

The decades-long drop in Ukraine's population has had a lasting negative impact on the country's economic development. The steadily shrinking working-age population strained the labour market long before the war and the outflow of workers, especially highly skilled youth, hampered human capital development, and limited economic growth in many promising sectors, including high-tech industries. However, not only skill-intensive sectors faced a restrained growth potential due to the demographic decline. Labour-intensive sectors, including manufacturing, construction, and agriculture, could not achieve their full potential due to, among other reasons, the increasing shortage of a qualified workforce, especially in remote, rural regions.

The war has had a significant impact on Ukraine's already challenged demographic situation. A massive outflow of war refugees, primarily consisting of working-age women and children, has irreversibly undermined Ukraine's demography.

10.2.2 (Potential) Demographic Future of Ukraine

To develop a feasible reconstruction plan, despite significant uncertainty, it is crucial to have a rough idea of Ukraine's potential demographic future. This involves understanding the number of individuals that Ukraine may have lost permanently (or for an extended period) due to the invasion, as well as their demographic characteristics, such as age and gender, under various scenarios. To this end, we explore possible future demographic developments over the next two decades by running a demographic microsimulation. This simulation will replicate the evolution of the Ukrainian population under several assumptions on the duration and escalation of the war. We apply a microsimulation technique and run a series of Monte Carlo (MC) stochastic simulations, which is widely used for modelling demographic developments and is a vital tool for analysing structured population models[4](Van Imhoff & Post, 1998; Mielczarek & Zabawa, 2021). The stochastic population sub-model utilized in our simulation exercise incorporates demographic uncertainty, as the primary parameters, such as fertility, mortality, and migration, can be considered as stochastic processes. To project the demographic future of Ukraine, we employ an elaborate population model that accounts for age- and gender-specific mortality rates, age-specific fertility rates, age- and gender-specific propensity to migrate (as a refugee fleeing the war), and time-varying return propensity. The model also incorporates population aging.[5]

We simulate the demographic projections across four macro-scenarios, varying the duration of the war (whether the war ends in 2024 or 2025) and further military escalation while the war lasts (further escalation of the military conflict occurs or not). Our findings indicate that Ukraine will suffer a long-term population loss as a result of the war under any feasible scenario. However, the range of outcomes in our different scenarios is very wide, meaning that the future path and duration of the war will be extremely important in determining the magnitude of the demographic shock and its impact on the reconstruction process.

Table 10.1 provides an overview of simulated population size across four scenarios, focusing on the maximum population size achieved in the post-war years and the total population at the end of the simulation horizon, in 2040. In the best-case scenario, assuming that the war ends in 2024 without further military escalation, Ukraine's population would start to increase again in 2025 and reach its post-war maximum of 36.1 million by 2032. However, the population will never return to pre-war levels (i.e., the level of 2021) and will be around 35.2 million by 2040, which is 17% lower than before the war. In the worst-case scenario, assuming that the war escalates and continues until 2025, the total population size will fall below 32 million by the end of

---

[4] Microsimulation has a number of major advantages when projecting future demographic developments, as it allows (i) to capture a very broad range of factors, including age- and gender-specific mortality and migration patterns related to military service, moving abroad and subsequent return; (ii) to easily vary the sets of interrelated assumptions; (iii) to incorporate randomness in the crucial demographic indicators, such as fertility, mortality, outflow and return of refugees.

[5] Details on the simulation model and procedure can be obtained from the authors, see also Tverdostup (2023).

Table 10.1: Simulated population size across four scenarios – maximum total and working-age population size achieved in 2022-2040 and population size in 2040
Source: Own calculations with our simulation model. Model description available from the authors

Scenario	Maximum population size achieved			Population in 2040	
	Year	Population thsd.	Growth rate vs 2021, %	Population thsd.	Growth rate vs 2021,%
I. Total population					
(i) 2024 and no escalation	2032	36,089.51	-14.5	35,184.17	-16.5
(ii) 2025 and no escalation	2033	35,386.39	-16.0	34,777.76	-17.8
(iii) 2024 and escalation	2033	34,531.09	-18.1	33,976.88	-19.4
(iv) 2025 and escalation	2035	33,849.58	-19.7	33,562.77	-20.4
II. Working-age population (18-59 years)					
(i) 2024 and no escalation	2032	20,370.65	-16.1	19,065.42	-21.5
(ii) 2025 and no escalation	2033	19,969.81	-17.8	18,888.97	-22.2
(iii) 2024 and escalation	2033	19,654.67	-19.1	18,580.39	-23.5
(iv) 2025 and escalation	2034	19,316.06	-20.4	18,494.05	-23.8

the war. The post-war population maximum of 33.8 million will be achieved in 2035, yet the population will start declining again and range at 33.6 million by 2040, which is 20% below the pre-war level and 1.5 million below the best-case scenario (panel (i) of Figure 10.3).

Under all scenarios, the working-age population is projected to shrink even more than the total population, which is largely driven by the age-gender profile of refugees. While the working-age population dynamic improves drastically in the post-war years, it starts falling steadily by the end of the simulation horizon, with the speed of the decline exceeding that of the total population. In 2040, the working-age population is projected to range between 19.1 million in the best-case scenario and 18.5 million in the worst case, which is 21.5% to 23.8% below the pre-war level, respectively. Hence, the working-age population will be disproportionately affected by the war, which will have significant implications for the labour market, social security, and post-war economic recovery of Ukraine.

The outflow of refugees throughout the war and their subsequent return appears to be the most decisive factor behind future demographic developments. In the best-case scenario, the cumulative number of people fleeing the war could reach 8.8 million by the end of 2024, while in the worst-case scenario, it could be as high as 11 million by the end of 2025. Hence, military escalation in the foreseeable future may deprive Ukraine of another 2 million individuals. However, a longer war and further escalation

Fig. 10.3: Simulated population projections under four macro scenarios, 2022-2040, thousands
Note: The panels depict population dynamics as an average of 10,000 MC simulation rounds. The trajectories depict yearly (non-cumulative) simulated projections. Working-age population includes individuals aged 18 to 59 in a current year.

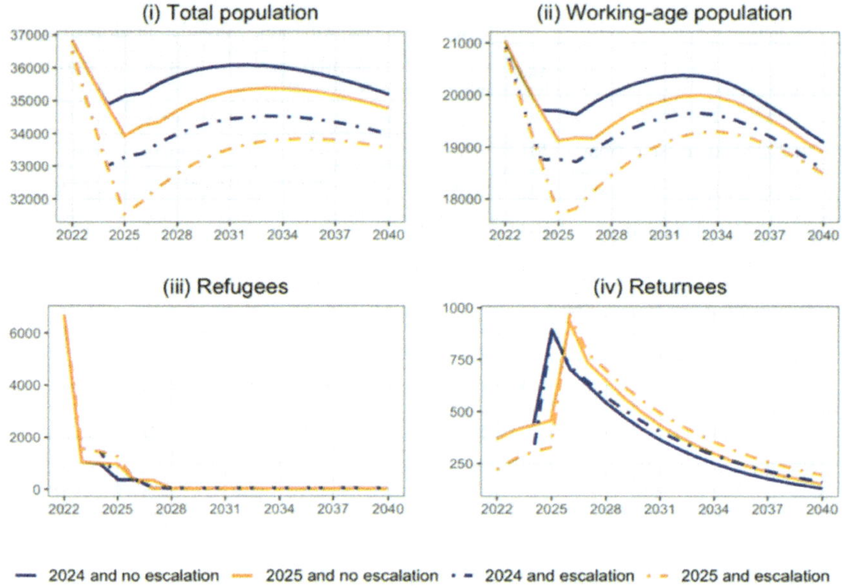

would also mean fewer people coming back when the war is over. Under different scenarios, the number of people returning in the first ten years of the end of the war ranges between 5.1 and 5.9 million, whereas between 3.7 million (best-case scenario) and 5.1 million (worst-case scenario) refugees may never return to Ukraine.

Under all scenarios, the absolute majority of refugees are female, which leads to a significant narrowing of the gap between the male and female population (Figure 10.4). The female population will reach its minimum in the last year of the war, and will be the lowest under the scenarios assuming the war to be over in 2025. Furthermore, under the 'escalation' assumption, the female population drops below the male population, something that is unprecedented in the recent history of Ukraine. In the post-war years, the female population will increase steadily driven by return migration, while the male population will see no major improvement and keep declining, as some men will likely leave Ukraine to join their families abroad once the martial law is lifted.

Although our simulation does not account for the immense geographical disparities in the scale of demographic decline, with the Eastern and South-Eastern regions being most severely depopulated, it is important to acknowledge the highly differentiated demographic prospects that Ukraine faces. The territories currently occupied and the regions neighbouring the frontline will take years for their infrastructure and housing

Fig. 10.4: Simulated population by gender under four macro scenarios, 2022-2040, thousands
Note: The panels depict population dynamics by age as an average of 10000 MC simulation rounds. The trajectories depict yearly (non-cumulative) simulated projections of total male and female population.

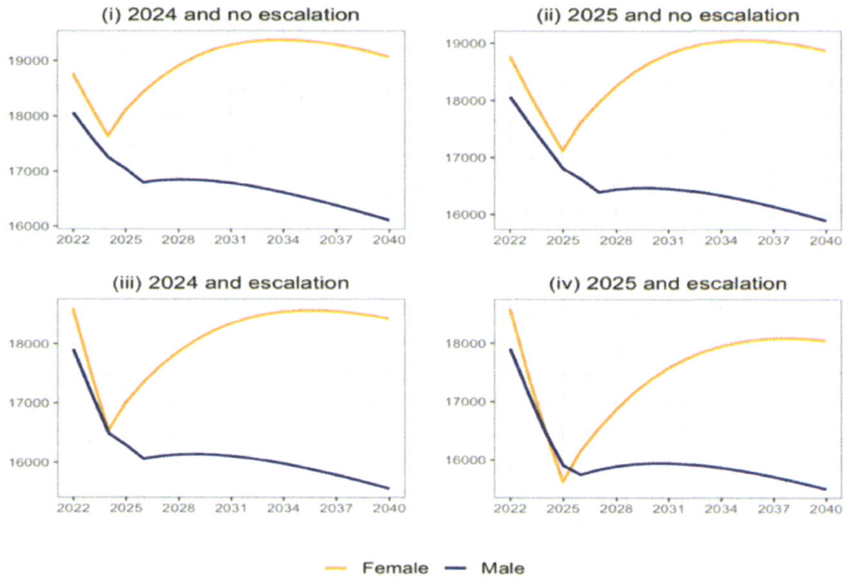

to be rebuilt, hampering the return of refugees and internally displaced persons. Thus, the population, especially working-age population, and fertility will likely decline in the regions most affected by the war even more severely than our simulation results suggest. In contrast, the central and western regions, as well as the city of Kyiv, are likely to face the most positive demographic prospects, as the majority of internally displaced persons have settled there, and many may decide to stay permanently (IOM, 2023b).

Our simulation results highlight that a lack of workers is going to be one of the central challenges of Ukraine's reconstruction. Immense population decline, uncertain return intentions of refugees, and relatively low involvement of the diaspora hamper the availability, capacity, and quality of human resources essential for Ukraine's reconstruction. To overcome this challenge, Ukraine will need to adopt measures that facilitate the return, relocation, and inclusion of displaced people, the reconstruction and improvement of infrastructure and services, the revival and expansion of the economy, and the provision of mental and physical health care for the impacted population. Policy action in the demographic domain is not only about attracting as many working-age people as possible back to Ukraine after the war, but also about attracting those with the right skills to the areas where they are needed more, to reduce regional disparities in the population dynamic.

10.3 Trade and FDI

10.3.1 Introduction

Ukraine had established itself as a competitive global supplier of agricultural products and IT (information technologies) services before the full-scale invasion by Russia in 2022. The country had generally liberalized its trade regime, with free trade agreements covering over half of its trade in 2021. The full-scale invasion caused significant human loss and physical capital destruction, resulting in severe economic disruptions. The relocation of production facilities and changes in the transportation routes that followed forced a substantial re-orientation of trade flows and changes in the country's foreign trade structure.

In the following, we take an up-beat view of the potential areas of Ukraine's future competitiveness, where we assume that the reconstruction of the economy after the end of the war, which is expected to be based on the principle of 'build back better' and a green transition will allow it to 'leapfrog' and develop more technologically advanced sectors with higher value added. Moreover, the reconstruction will occur in the framework of broad-based legal alignment with the EU and advancing fundamental political reforms (particularly anti-corruption and legal and judicial reform) that will further reduce barriers to trade and barriers to the entry of foreign investors, an area of important reform to which the AA/DCFTA (Association Agreement/Deep and Comprehensive Free Trade Area) already contributed.

For reconstruction to be successful and for EU integration benefits to be maximised, Ukraine needs to have an internationally competitive economy that can withstand the competition in the EU market (Copenhagen criteria) and globally. Apart from an abundance of (skilled) labour and capital and modern infrastructure, a central part of modern global competitiveness is successful integration into global value chains (GVCs) that allow technological transfer and functional upgrading. We analyse in what sectors Ukraine already has a competitive advantage, and in what sectors it is expected to strengthen its competitive edge by estimating the degree of participation in GVCs and its potential in terms of technology up-grading.

Especially six industries can be identified where a combination of industrial policy, an FDI attraction strategy and institutional and education reforms should allow to maximise the post-war recovery potential: agro-food, IT, as well as renewable energy, critical minerals and the manufacture of machines and equipment. Furthermore, manufacture of metals has been deeply affected by destruction during the war but might become important again in the longer run after considerable modernisation efforts. These sectors are expected to play a crucial role in Ukraine's recovery and reconstruction and help integrate Ukraine into the EU economy. However, Ukraine's growing competitiveness in agriculture might be an issue for Ukraine's EU accession due to the most likely resistance of the strong EU agricultural lobby, as the 2023 agricultural imports crisis revealed.

10.3.2 Structural Shifts in External Trade Between 2014 and 2021

Ukraine has undergone a significant structural shift in its sector and geographic trade structure since Russia's annexation of Crimea and the onset of the military conflict in the Donbas in 2014.[6] Ukraine's trade structure changed because of the occupation, the loss of industrial capacity in the east, and deepened relations with the EU as the AA/DCFTA was signed and partially applied starting in 2014.[7] The agreement envisaged the nullification of import duties for all industrial and most agricultural products within up to ten years, though the EU abolished most duties already in April 2014. Nonetheless, TRQs (tariff rate quotas) within zero import duties were imposed by both the EU and Ukraine for politically sensitive goods. Moreover, the AA/DCFTA envisaged a gradual reduction of non-tariff measures.

Figure 10.5 shows that the share of CIS (Commonwealth of Independent States, predominantly Russia) decreased over 2014-2021 in Ukraine's exports and imports of goods and services. In goods trade, CIS was replaced by the EU, Asia (primarily China) and Turkey,[8] which became the main destinations of Ukraine's merchandise exports and the primary sources of its imports (accounting for 73% of goods exports and 64% of goods imports in 2021). The most striking development in services trade was an increase in the EU and the US shares in Ukraine's exports.

Analysis of the changes in the goods trade structure reveals a striking increase in the share of agriculture and food products in Ukraine's exports - from 29% in 2013 to 44% in 2021 (Figure 10.6). This is related to two main factors. On the one hand, industrial exports were reduced because Ukraine lost a big chunk of its industrial base in the Donbas region and sharply lowered its exports to Russia, mainly machinery and transport equipment shipments. On the other, growing crop yields and market openings contributed to expanding agricultural production and exports.[9]

---

[6] See also Chapter 7 for details on external trade.

[7] The DCFTA has been provisionally applied since January 1, 2016. However, the EU opened its market unilaterally for Ukraine already in April 2014 with autonomous trade measures replicating the first year of the DCFTA tariff schedule.

[8] In Ukraine's foreign trade statistics, Turkey is classified as a country in Asia.

[9] According to Ukrstat (2022), the average yield of cereal and leguminous crops was 5.4 tons per hectare (ha) of the harvested area in 2021, doubling compared to 1991. Ukraine has come close to Poland in wheat yields and surpassed it for corn (maise). The growing yields should be primarily attributed to changes in Ukraine's sector structure, with the development of agricultural holdings controlling large land banks and benefiting from extensive economies of scale. The holdings accumulated sufficient resources to invest in new technologies and equipment, boosting production capacity.

Fig. 10.5: Geographic orientation of Ukraine's international trade, 2013 and 2021
Source: National Bank of Ukraine (2023b); own calculations

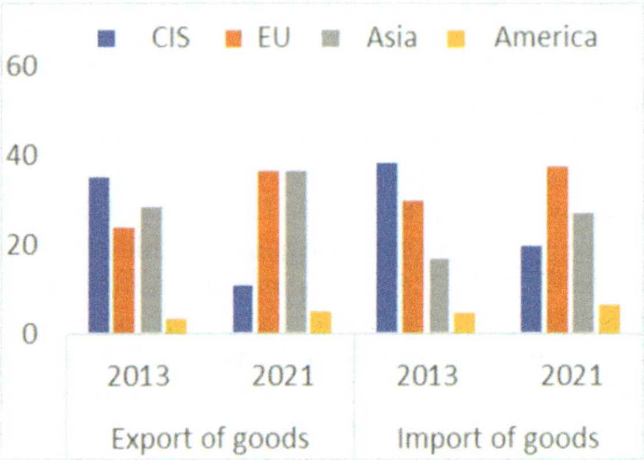

(a) Geographic structure of Ukraine's goods trade, %

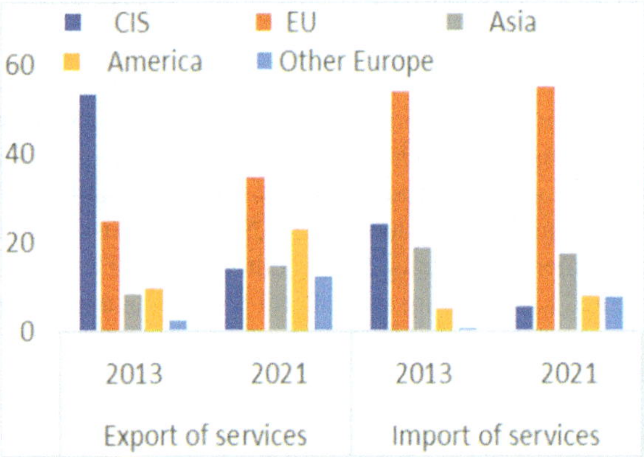

(b) Geographic structure of Ukraine's services trade, %

Fig. 10.6: Product structure of Ukraine's foreign trade, 2013 and 2021
Source: National Bank of Ukraine (2023b); own calculations

Although the aggregated commodity structure of Ukraine's trade with the EU did not change much between 2013 and 2021, the qualitative characteristics of Ukraine's exports to the EU changed. Ukraine's exports to the EU moved away from raw materials and semi-processed/semi-finished products to processed/finished products, with the share of the latter increasing from 32% in 2013 to 42% in 2021 (Figure 10.7). Most of Ukraine's exports aim at EU industrial consumption, with the share of intermediate exports at 81% in 2021, four percentage points down from 2013.

Furthermore, the share of new products and products with a higher degree of processing in exports to the EU was increasing (Giucci, Movchan & Kirchner, 2019). Ukraine's exports to the EU were almost as diversified as its total exports in terms of product variety, with Ukraine shipping to the EU about 75% of its entire export nomenclature or ca. 2900 tariff lines at HS (Harmonized System) 6-digits. For comparison, Ukraine's exports to China at their peak included only ca. 300 tariff lines. These percentage points were distributed between consumer exports, whose share grew to 16% (+3 p.p.), and capital goods exports (3%, +1 p.p.).

The service trade structure had also been evolving since 2014 (Figure 10.8). In exports, the most pronounced change was the boom in computer (IT) services exports that moved the ICT (information and communication technologies) sector to first place in total services exports, accounting for 39% of the total in 2021. The ICT sector boom is explained by several factors, including solid education in math and IT, favourable taxation for private entrepreneurs, and strong personal links with the US diaspora, including in Silicon Valley.

Fig. 10.8: Ukraine's structure of service trade, 2013 and 2021
Source: National Bank of Ukraine (2023a)

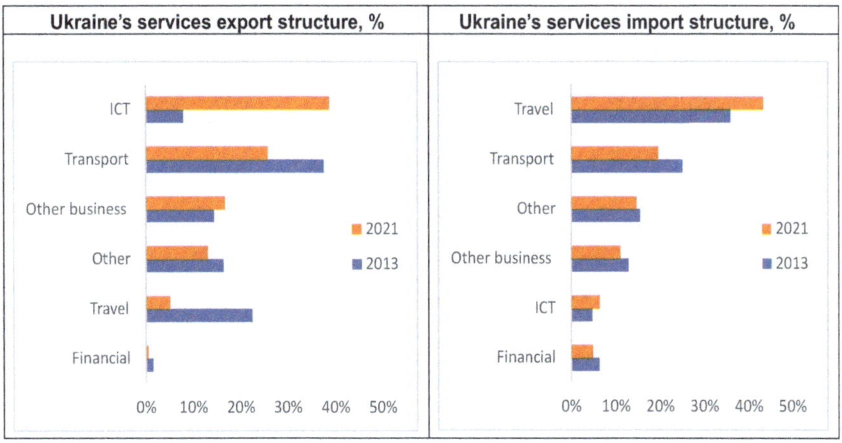

Fig. 10.7: Composition of goods exported, 2013 and 2021
Source: World Bank (2023a); own calculations
Note: * Based on MTN nomenclature. ** Based on BEC Rev 5, aggregated as follows: capital goods include capital/consumer and capital/intermediate goods; consumer goods include consumer/capital and consumer/intermediate goods; intermediate goods include intermediate/capital and intermediate/consumer goods.

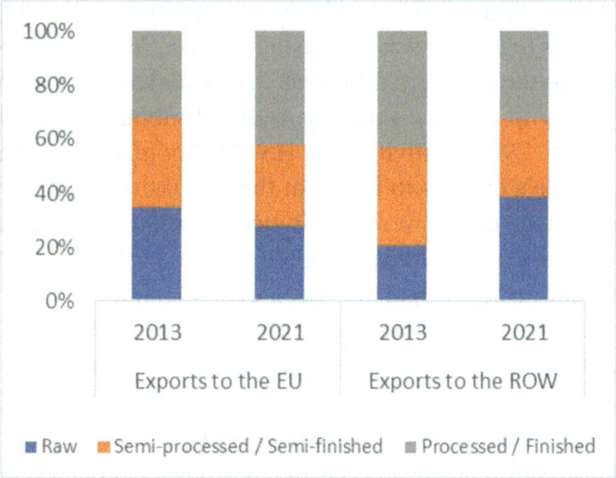

(a) Goods exports to the EU and ROW by the level of processing*, %

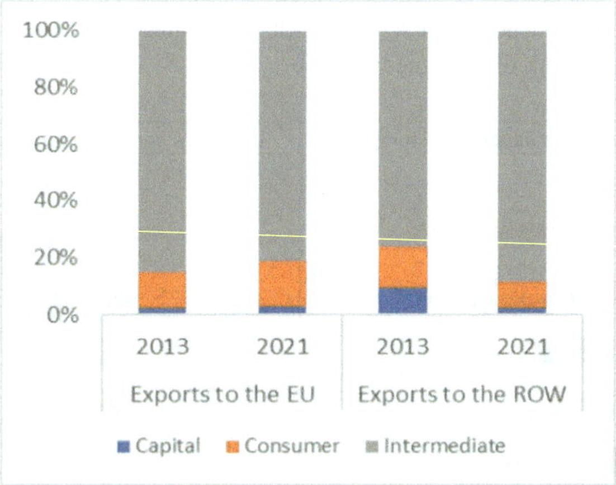

(b) Goods exports to the EU and ROW by the end-use**, %

10.3.3 War-induced Shifts in Ukraine's Trade Structure

The impact of the full-scale aggression amplified the trends introduced above regarding the product structure of merchandise exports (Figure 10.9). On the one hand, owing to the global efforts to bring Ukraine's grain to the world market, the export share of the agro-food sector rose to 57% in 2022, thirteen percentage points higher than a year before, and further expanded to 63% in 2023. At the same time, the share of metals in exports dropped to 11% of the total in 2023 compared to 25% in 2021, as the sector lost its factories in occupied territories, primarily in Mariupol, and faced significant logistical problems.

Fig. 10.9: Structure of goods exports and imports, 2021, 2022 and 2023
Source: National Bank of Ukraine (2023a)
Note: *based on January – November 2023

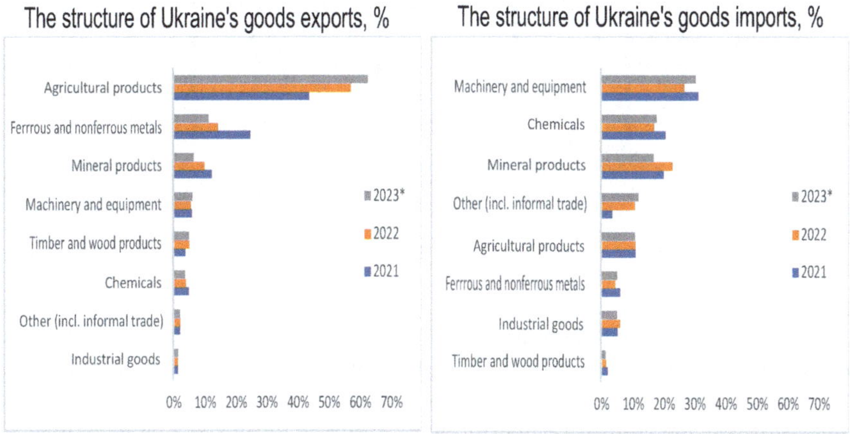

As a result of the negative stimulus of war-induced logistic bottlenecks and the positive stimulus of the EU unilateral liberalisation, the EU share increased to 61% of the total in Ukraine's goods exports and 44% in imports in 2022 (Figure 10.10). It expanded to 63% and 47% in 2023, respectively . China's share dropped to about 5% in 2022 due to the lack of transportation options, although somewhat revived in 2023, while trade with Russia has been completely banned.

10.3.4 Potential Areas of International Competitiveness

The in-depth integration into global value chains has been considered a central part of Ukraine's successful reconstruction and preparedness to join the EU. That will enable stabilising Ukraine's trade flows and fostering technological transfers and can also help mitigate attitudes towards protectionism within the EU regarding Ukraine's accession.

Fig. 10.10: Geographic orientation of goods and services exports, 2021, 2022 and 2023
Source: National Bank of Ukraine (2023a)
Note: *based on January – November 2023

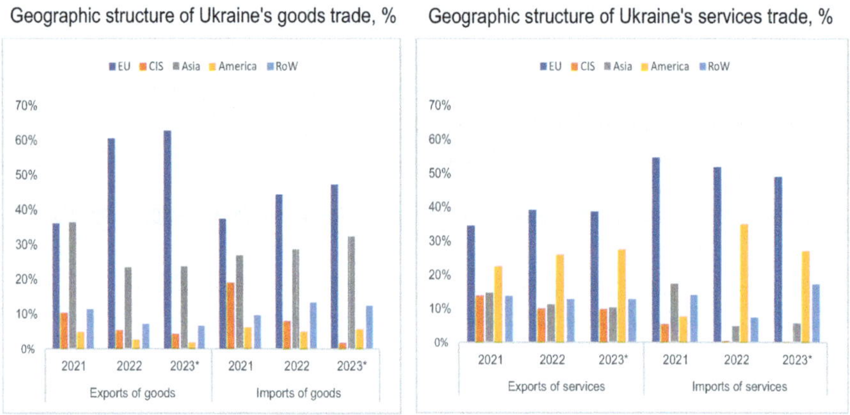

Compared to its regional peers, Ukraine remains relatively little integrated into global value chains (Figure 10.11). Only Azerbaijan, Georgia, Russia, and Armenia had lower values of the global value chain integration indicator in 2019. At the same time, Slovakia and Hungary outperformed Ukraine in this respect by more than 20 percentage points. That suggests an important potential for higher integration of Ukraine into global production chains in the post-war period, especially given the recent friend-shoring and near-shoring trends, as well as Ukraine's largely untapped potential in green energy and critical mineral resources.

On the plus side, Ukraine has a strong comparative advantage in ICT-related sectors, which can be further developed in the post-war period. The country has achieved remarkable progress in exporting digitally delivered services, the share of which in exports was the highest in the CESEE region in 2021, lagging slightly behind the EU average level (Figure 10.12). In the eight years between 2013 and 2021, the share of digitally delivered services in services exports more than doubled from 25% to 56%.

Ukraine is technologically quite developed for a non-EU member state – according to the frontier technology readiness index[10] developed by UNCTAD, it occupies a better position in this respect than many of its peers in the Western Balkans and CIS (Figure 10.13). However, the digitalisation of the economy is not uniform, and there are many areas where there is a need for technological modernisation - here, the

[10] The frontier technology readiness index can take values between 0 and 1, with values closer to 1 indicating that a country is ready for the use and adoption of frontier technologies. The index consists of five building blocks that measure the capacity to use, adopt and adapt frontier technologies.

Fig. 10.11: Global value chain integration in 2019
Note: Global value chain integration indicator (GVA) in 2019.
Source: UNCTAD (2023c)

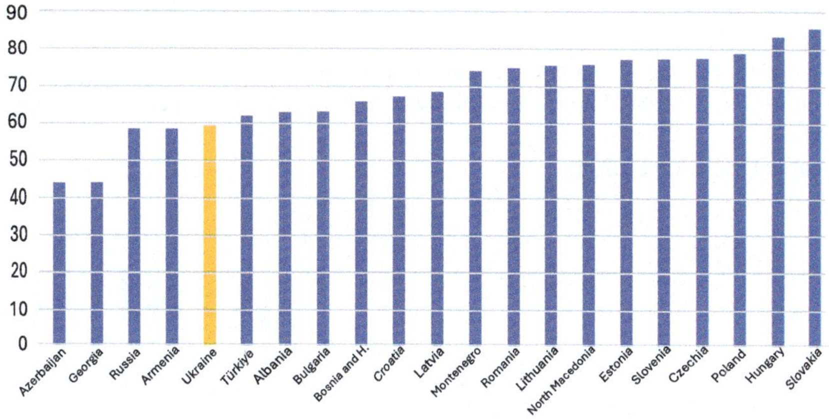

Fig. 10.12: Digitally delivered services in total services exports, 2013 and 2021
Note: Digitally delivered services as a share of total services exports, %
Source:UNCTAD (2023b)

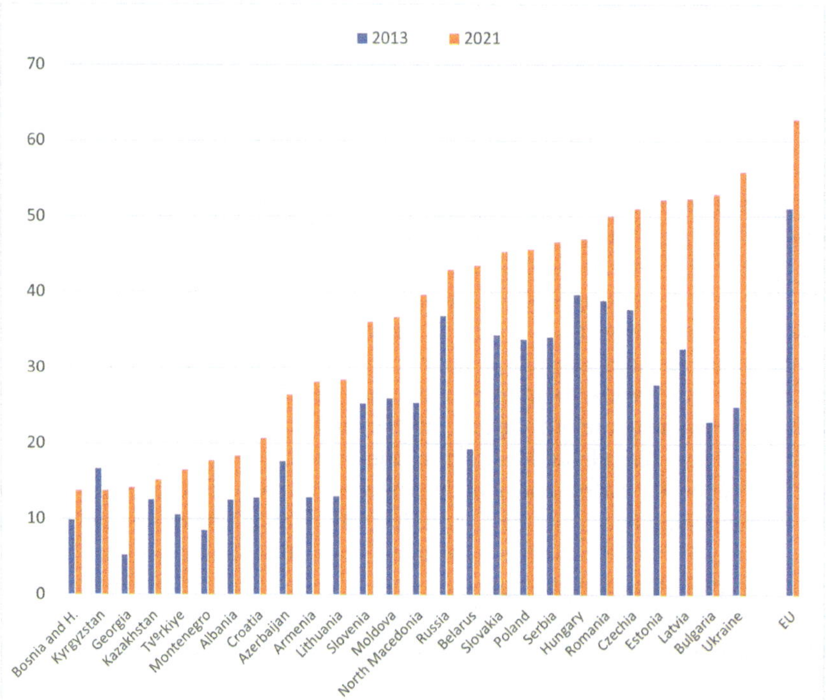

country still lags far behind many of the countries in Central Europe. Although the country still has a relatively strong position among its peers in the CESEE concerning skills and R&D (research and development) - 11th and 7th best out of 26, respectively - it has been losing its competitiveness in these areas over the last 11 years.

Fig. 10.13: Frontier technology readiness index, 2019
Note: Frontier technology readiness index in Ukraine and its peers in the region, 2019.
Source:UNCTAD (2023a)

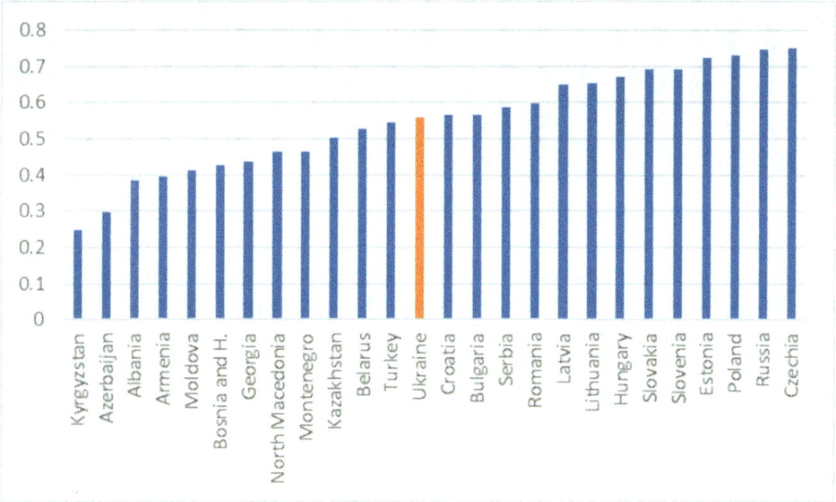

Ukraine's areas of relative strength and potential highlighted above hint at where policy in the post-war years should focus in maximising the recovery potential. Overall, the economy invaded in 2022 was very different from the one invaded in 2014 – more reliant on agriculture and services, less on the extractive industry and metallurgy, and somewhat modernised. The widespread deregulation, the switch to digital public services, opened public registers and fiscal data, reforms in public procurement, the switch to up-to-date international standards and clean-up of the banking system, major reforms in gas and electricity markets based on the EU Third Energy Package, agricultural land reform, administrative reform and comprehensive decentralisation, the establishment of the new anti-corruption institutional framework, and ongoing alignment with the EU product safety requirements are the abridged list of changes that Ukraine has undergone since 2014. Based on this, industrial policy, an FDI attraction strategy and institutional and education reforms should focus on maximising the post-war recovery potential. Particularly, identified sectors are expected to play a critical role in Ukraine's recovery and reconstruction and help integrate Ukraine into the EU economy.

10.4 Regional Restructuring as an Essential Element of Postwar Reconstruction

10.4.1 Introduction

Ukraine's regions will have dramatically different needs under post-war reconstruction.[11] These will depend on their strengths and weaknesses (both domestically and as regards their integration into the wider European and global context) as well as on how they have been impacted by the war. Since the occupation of parts of the Donbas in 2014, regions have been affected in very different ways that have changed the state of their infrastructure, impacted the dynamic of their economic activity, and produced dramatic shifts in their population profile. The ongoing war and subsequent reconstruction process are shrouded in uncertainty, notably about outcomes. This creates tremendous challenges regarding funding ability and institutional capacities. The danger of wide disparities in regional development patterns getting entrenched in the post-war pattern of economic development is great.

To increase the chances of cohesive post-war economic development, policymakers need to prioritize support based on regional economic strengths and potential. Ukrainian regions share some common features in output structure but differ remarkably overall. Hence, a one-size-fits-all policy is unlikely to foster cohesive long-term growth. The goal in the following is to pinpoint the most promising structure for economic activities in Ukraine's regions, with a focus on the tradable sector, to support the potential of post-war growth of its regions. We first document medium-term patterns of regional and industrial differentiation among those regions by examining the composition of GVA (gross value added) and individual regions' export profiles (Section 10.2). We then analyse the geographical and industrial exposure of the Ukrainian economy to armed hostilities and how this uneven impact may have altered pre-war growth trends (Section 10.3). On the basis of this analysis, we suggest adopting an active regional and industrial policy that is tailored to the different conditions in which post-war Ukrainian regions will find themselves regarding infrastructure, housing and demography, as well as their geographic position with respect to potential further conflict and distance to EU neighbours. Reconstruction will have to orientate itself towards the potential for industrial specialisation and integration with the European economy at large, thereby taking into account, on the one hand, past trends but also, on the other hand, forward-looking potential for a changing composition of industrial activity.

With war damage disproportionately affecting some Ukrainian regions, industrial policies must inevitably take on board spatial differentiation in refining their support for structural change. Hence, identifying regional specialisation patterns is the cornerstone of our analysis.

---

[11] Section 10.4 relies heavily on the report by Kochnev, Landesmann, Maucorps and Moshammer (2023).

10.4.2 Strong Regional Heterogeneities

Regional growth rates post-2014 (but pre-2020) show strong geographical divergence (Figure 10.14).[12] Regions of the West (with the exception of Volyn and Zakarpattia), the South-West, and Kyiv constitute the ‘emerging core’ with above-average growth. In contrast, regions in the East and the South-East have stagnated.

Fig. 10.14: GRP (gross regional product) average growth rates 2016–2021, constant prices
Source:Ukrstat (2023), own calculations

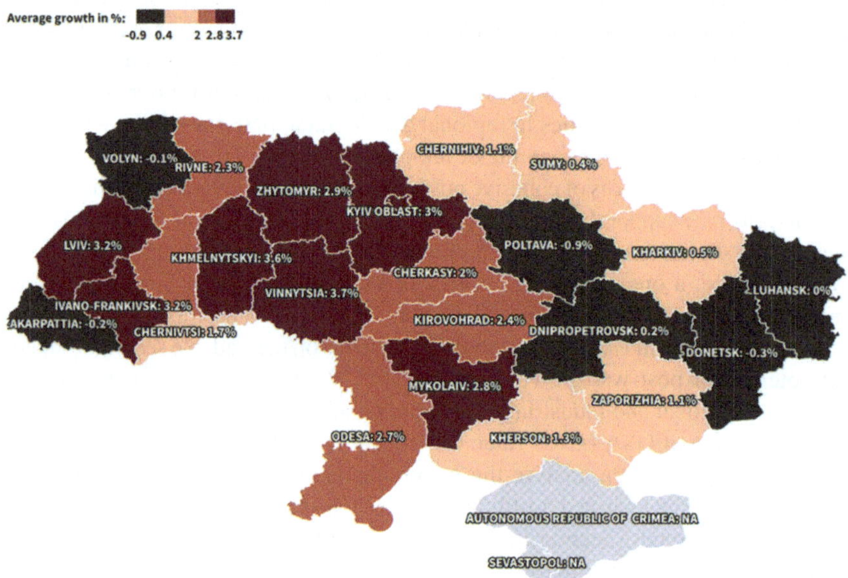

Many regions lack the capacity to manufacture advanced products in many industries. Albeit there are exceptions, many exports are concentrated either at the raw material, less processed or lower value-added end of the product spectrum or in legacy industries such as metals and minerals. This implies that there is a lot of scope for upgrading and foreign direct investment while integration into pan-European

[12] If at the time of writing data were available only until 2020, we trim the sample to the 2016-2019 period to avoid the impact of the Covid pandemic. However, when following export activity, we aim to capture developments up to 2021, stopping just short of the year in which the current war started.

production networks will be key to such up-grading. Furthermore, there is a tendency towards 'tertiarization' which pervades the Ukrainian economy as a whole.[13]

Cases of IT and telecom industries, which were growing rapidly from 2014 to 2021 in Kyiv and other big cities such as Lviv and Kharkiv, show that Ukraine does have the capacity for quick product development in certain niches. But a single industry is unlikely to be the basis for growth in all regions due to differences in endowments. As an important step to evaluate potentials for regional specialisation we start with an analysis of historical data to identify industry portfolios for each individual Ukrainian region.

10.4.3 Patterns of Regional Production Specialisation

We attempt to identify the growth potential of Ukrainian regions through the lens of patterns of the most recent pre-war trends in domestic output and exports. We use the concept of revealed specialisation as a starting point, according to which competitive industries in a particular region manifest themselves through a greater share of production or export volumes compared to other regions.

Timewise, we restrict our analysis to the 2016 – 2019 (and/or 2021) period. Albeit comparatively short, we find this sample useful as it approximates most closely to three main features of the post-war environment: fragile macroeconomic stability, regional reorientation of economic activity (linked to the deterioration of productive capacities in some regions), persistent security risk/threat of hostilities with Russia.

In the following we focus on three dimensions when analysing the patterns of geographical and industrial structures:

- The share of regional production in each industry within nationwide production of that industry. This metric reveals the region's importance in nationwide production of that industry. Plus, we look at how this share evolved during the pre-war period.
- Industry's absolute growth rate. An industry located in a particular region might be important from a national point-of-view, but nonetheless growth may be low – or vice versa.
- Share of a given industry in the regional economy. From a regional economy perspective, it matters little if a region accounts for a relatively large share of the national industry and even enjoyed rapid growth when, in the end, it represents only a small slice of that regional economy. Larger industries are more likely to serve as an engine of regional economic growth.

For the sake of simplicity, we bundle Ukrainian regions into groups called 'macro-regions' following the definitions used by the International Organisation for Migration

[13] Tertiarization involves the service ('tertiary') sector coming to comprise the biggest element of the economy.

based on Ukrainian Law (Figure 10.15).[14] This classification would correspond to EU NUTS1 level, which reflects 'major socio-economic regions'.[15]

These groupings combine multiple NUTS2 regions (oblasts) based on their similarity in socio-economic characteristics. This classification would correspond to EU NUTS1 level, which reflects 'major socio-economic regions'. This reduces complexity albeit at the cost of masking variation at sub-regional level. Where this occurs, we discuss these individual sub-regions separately or provide a more detailed exposition on the graphs.

Fig. 10.15: Classification of Ukrainian macro-regions
Source: Ukrstat (2022): own illustration

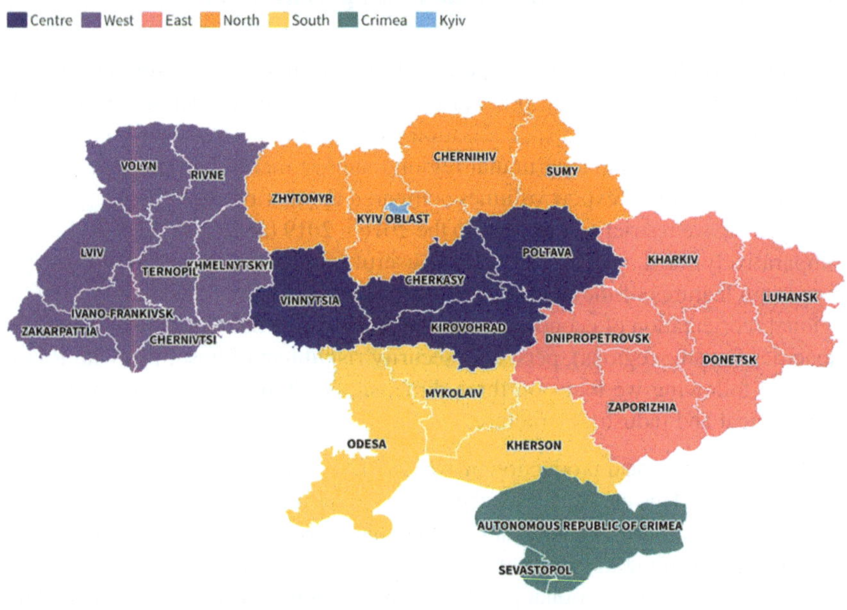

Figure 10.16 presents an overview of the main patterns of industrial specialisation across Ukrainian macro-regions, encompassing tradable and non-tradable industries.

The *East macro-region* historically specialized in mining and manufacturing, especially metals. Over a decade of war has changed this. If there is some pacification of this macro-region, then more services activities are expected to emerge in the

[14] The Law of Ukraine "On the Principles of State Regional Policy" (Article 1, item 2) defines a 'macro-region' as a geographical unit comprised of multiple oblasts (regions, Legislation of Ukraine, 2024). We are not aware of any formal subdivision, therefore we follow the classification used by the International Organisation of Migration in their regular reports (IOM, 2023a).

[15] Nomenclature of Territorial Units for Statistics is a geocode standard for referencing the administrative divisions of countries for statistical purposes.

reconstruction phase and beyond. The East region accounted in 2016 for 60 percent of the mining industry and 40 percent of manufacturing output (in value added terms) of Ukraine while overall only accounting for about 28 percent of Ukraine's GVA (gross value added). Looking at the more detailed profile within manufacturing (Table 10.2) we see the pre-war dominance of iron and steel, metal products and mechanical engineering, but also – to some extent – pharmaceuticals and various food processing industries. Due to exposure to war damage occurring, this has and will seriously affect the potential for the future, though. The war has dramatically changed the position of this region with regard to the industries in which it has historically specialised. Even before the current intensive phase of the war, infrastructure (water supply, waste management, electricity and gas distribution/supply) as well declined strongly over the 2016-19 period. As a mirror-development, the share of service industries increased significantly.

The *South macro-region* shows a specialisation profile blessed by its location on the Black Sea and its temperate weather conducive to agricultural production. This region accounted for just below 10 percent of Ukraine's GVA pre-war. Two sectors stick out as occupying strong positions within Ukraine's overall economy: agriculture and transport, the latter largely due to its maritime links. Otherwise, this region is heavily oriented towards services, both private sector but also public services (public administration and naval defence facilities; education; healthcare). Over the 2016-19 period, the highest growth rates were achieved in professional services, information and telecommunications, but also in public administration and defence. When looking at manufacturing (Table 10.2, we can observe the region's distinctive focus on shipbuilding as well as agricultural products requiring a temperate climate (wine, sunflower oil, various food products). Given the complete destruction of the large steel works in Mariupol during the war, the data on metals production refers to these former facilities. The macro-region South has been significantly affected by the war, the region has become a focus of the military conflict, with agricultural production severely affected, grain storage and port facilities having been destroyed and grain exports curtailed. During the reconstruction phase, demining of land and the reopening of shipping ports will have to become a priority so that agricultural production can move quickly towards its pre-war potential.

The *Centre macro-region* has some strengths in manufacturing and, given that it has been less impacted by the war than the Donbas region that was traditionally home to heavy industry, it could take on further related capacities during the reconstruction phase and beyond. It encompasses central micro-regions ('oblasts) around the capital city Kyiv. The region accounted for about 13 percent of national GVA and it was home to around a quarter of Ukraine's agriculture and mining. While mining declined in importance over the period 2016-19, agriculture slightly improved its share in national production. Manufacturing here accounted persistently for about 15 percent of the national sector. Given that the old industrial heartland in the Donbas has and will be severely affected by the war and occupation, the Centre might – together with some of the Northern and Western regions – take over as a location for manufacturing, albeit with a rather different sectoral profile (see below in the section on trends in export composition). The shift towards services is also a feature. As regards manufacturing

Fig. 10.16: Shares of regional industries in the national economy (GVA) and growth rates 2016-19
Source: Ukrstat (2020), own illustration
Note: Size of the circle represents the share of the industry's regional production (gross value added; GVA) in the nationwide industry; the growth rates refer to average annual growth of GVA (at constant prices) over the period 2016-19.

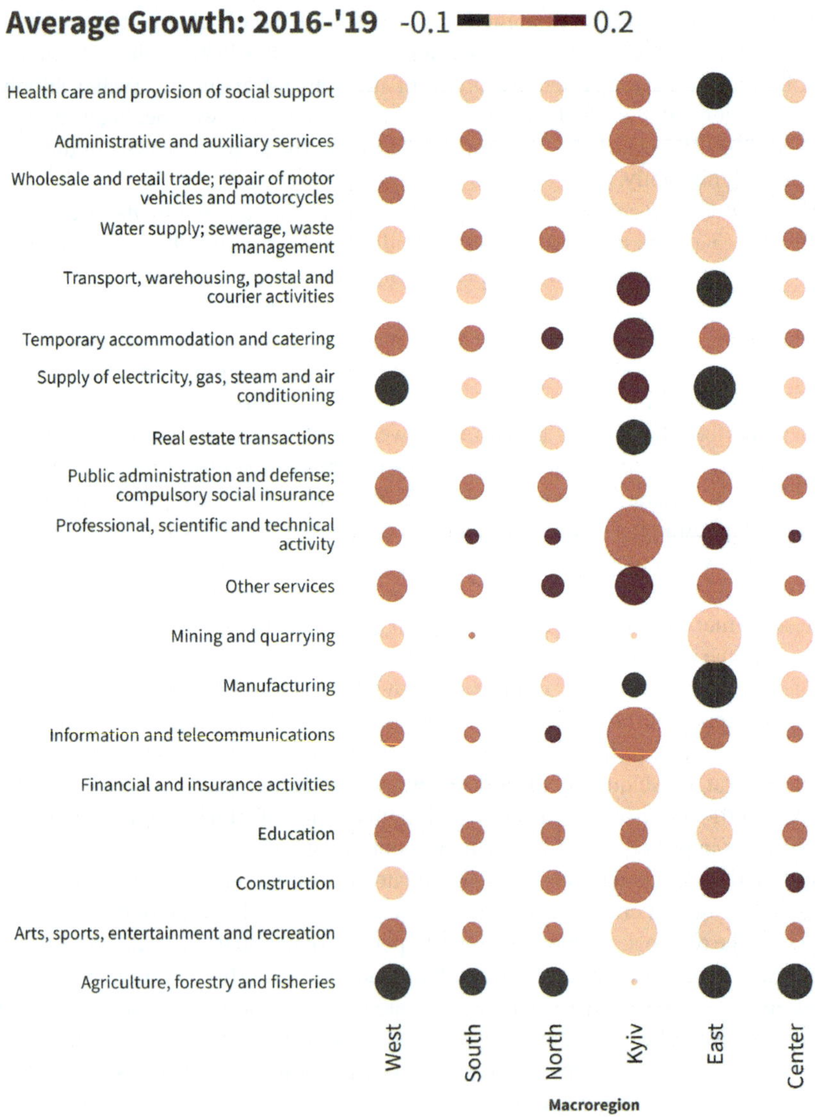

Table 10.2: Dominant industries in regional manufacturing 2019 (industries with highest shares in regional value added)
Source: Ukrstat (2023), own calculations
Note: Growth is nominal. Only the top six largest industries (in terms of value-added shares) are reported plus a specialisation indicator (i.e., comparison with shares of these industries in the national economy), as well as average (nominal) annual growth rates over the period 2016-2019.

NACE2 code	Industry description	Share in region's Manufaturing 2019, %	Spec. Index: 2019	Growth 2016-2019
Centre				
10.41	Manufacture of oils and fats	17.71	6.46	0.97
10.51	Operation of dairies and cheese making	14.50	9.01	1.66
10.82	Manufacture of cocoa, chocolate and sugar confectionery	6.50	5.58	1.01
28.30	Manufacture of agricultural and forestry machinery	4.72	3.32	1.02
23.61	Manufacture of concrete products for construction purposes	4.62	1.11	2.83
10.39	Other processing and preserving of fruit and vegetables	3.74	4.10	–
East				
24.10	Manufacture of basic iron and steel and of ferro-alloys	20.81	2.86	0.43
33.12	Repair of machinery	9.57	1.75	2.90
24.20	Manufacture of tubes, pipes, hollow profiles and related fittings, of steel	3.04	2.86	0.93
22.22	Manufacture of plastic packing goods	2.65	1.38	1.03
10.13	Production of meat and poultry meat products	2.65	1.38	1.64
21.20	Manufacture of pharmaceutical preparations	2.56	0.43	1.27
Kyiv				
21.20	Manufacture of pharmaceutical preparations	17.48	2.92	1.48
23.61	Manufacture of concrete products for construction purposes	5.78	1.39	1.44
18.12	Other printing	4.73	2.06	1.02
33.20	Installation of industrial machinery and equipment	4.70	2.36	4.07
10.71	Manufacture of bread; manufacture of fresh pastry goods and cakes	4.16	1.29	1.60
33.12	Repair of machinery	3.81	0.70	2.62

Table 10.2 Cont.: Dominant industries in regional manufacturing 2019 (industries with highest shares in regional value added)

NACE2 code	Industry description	Share in region's Manufaturing 2019, %	Spec. Index: 2019	Growth 2016-2019
North				
17.21	Manufacture of corrugated paper and paperboard and of containers of paper and paperboard	9.79	4.43	1.55
23.61	Manufacture of concrete products for construction purposes	7.64	1.84	1.70
10.13	Production of meat and poultry meat products	6.00	3.13	5.52
28.13	Manufacture of other pumps and compressors	5.69	7.08	0.96
16.10	Sawmilling and planing of wood 4.80 2.12 2.22			
10.71	Manufacture of bread; manufacture of fresh pastry goods and cakes	3.52	1.09	0.83
South				
10.41	Manufacture of oils and fats	20.17	7.36	0.35
33.15	Repair and maintenance of ships and boats	9.52	23.98	1.01
11.02	Manufacture of wine from grape	6.00	23.98	0.50
10.61	Manufacture of grain mill products	5.28	6.44	2.62
33.12	Repair of machinery	4.72	0.86	1.08
25.11	Manufacture of metal structures and parts of structures	3.35	1.44	0.89
West				
29.31	Manufacture of electrical and electronic equipment for motor vehicles	11.90	7.25	1.88
16.21	Manufacture of veneer sheets and wood-based panels	8.16	5.27	0.84
16.10	Sawmilling and planing of wood	6.52	2.88	1.88
31.09	Manufacture of other furniture	6.44	3.92	1.75
23.61	Manufacture of concrete products for construction purposes	4.83	1.16	1.46
10.71	Manufacture of bread; manufacture of fresh pastry goods and cakes	3.83	1.19	0.96

(Table 10.1), the Central macro-region shows a prevalence of a wide variety of food products (dairy, fruit and vegetables, confectionary, juice, etc.), but also machinery and equipment linked to agriculture and the food industry, plus automotive parts and components.

The *North macro-region* holds a strong position in public administration and defence (18 percent share of national industry) and in agriculture (16 percent of national output). Other industries for the most part fall below a 10 percent share. Many of the services industries, like financial and insurance services, professional services and information and telecommunications, arts, sports, and entertainment, displayed high real growth between 2016 and 2021. Their positions in the respective national industries sectors improved. This shows a tendency to 'deagglomeration' from Kyiv City. Within manufacturing, the North enjoys quite a diversified profile covering the paper and paperboard industry, various metal and machinery products, construction materials, wood products and–again–a wide range of food products. Given the loss of manufacturing production capacities in the East, the evidence would suggest a shift into this region and scope for further development.[16]

The *West macro-region* has won and will gain prominence in Ukraine's economy as it has been much less affected by the war. It accounted on average for about 17 percent of Ukraine's GVA overall, and quite a few of the industries have already, over the 2016-19 period, increased their shares in the national industry. This is true for agriculture, manufacturing, wholesale and retail trade, repair of motor vehicles etc. Growth was also quite high in a range of services activities – public and private. Our projection is that this will further accelerate because of the war and the related internal migration/displacement. Never before has the centre of manufacturing activity in Ukraine, the West gained ground in this sector. It benefits from its geographic location far from the conflict zones in the East and South of the country, but also from its proximity to EU countries and the potential this provides for cross-border production networks. The composition of manufacturing industries covers by now a wide spectrum, from advanced segments such as electrical and electronic equipment via wood-based products and furniture to clothing and textiles plus various food products.

As a city with at least three million inhabitants, Kyiv shows a typical capital city profile: it accounts for about 45-70 percent of national value added in a variety of private sector and public services (professional services, information and telecommunications, financial services and telecoms but also administrative and auxiliary services, plus arts, sports, entertainment). This compares with Kyiv's share of about 23 percent of Ukraine's GVA. Because of some degree of 'de-agglomeration' of such services provision, Kyiv's share of these industries fell over the period 2016-19. Furthermore, one has to bear in mind the so-called 'headquarter' effect, that companies declare their revenues at their headquarter (HQ) location (more often than not the capital city) rather than at production sites per se. We can observe Kyiv's greater importance in some areas, such as transport services which is likely due to

[16] The Ukrainian government operates a programme supporting the relocation of enterprises under which, by end-September 2022, 558 businesses had relocated to safer parts of the country, see Ministry of Economy (2022).

the national airport, and also in utilities (such as electricity, water, postal services, etc.). Nonetheless, as regards manufacturing, we wish to highlight pharmaceuticals. Furthermore, HQ functions, including product development and marketing, are key contributions emanating from Kyiv for a range of manufacturing industries (though not captured by our analysis of manufacturing activities in Table 10.1).

10.4.4 Patterns of Regional Export Specialisation

To account for export profile, recent pre-war developments and the importance of export activity for the different regional economies, we construct a competitiveness index from individual components (these are depicted in Figure 10.17).[17][18] The index then integrates three variables in a single measure: the share of the industry's exports within a region's overall exports, its share in national exports of that industry and the industry's export growth performance in the recent (pre-war) past. In general, higher values reflect a better performance of the industry in the recent past. After constructing the index, we select the top 20 percent industry-region pairs to focus on the best-performers.

When focusing on the best-performing industries, we see that each region has a more diverse industry mix than appears at first glance. Figure 10.18 highlights the fact that each region - note that the figure refers to individual 'oblasts' - has typically around three to four industries that score highly in the contributing factors which account for the overall score an industry gets (see Table 10.3 below for the labels and contributing factors).

Based on Figure 10.18 we come to the following conclusions as far as export specialisation is concerned:

- The areas of advanced processing and manufacturing have started to be distributed more widely geographically. A notable case is machinery/electrical products. While it was common to associate the main production and exports of these products with sites in the East, we identify sizeable (Volyn, Ternopil, Zakarpattia) - and in some cases rapidly growing (Chernivtsi, Zhytomyr) - production in the West as well.
- Minerals output experienced some shift in regional production and exports and is one of the most promising industries. Lviv (West), Poltava (Centre), and Dnipropetrovsk (East) regions have been rapidly growing albeit the growth is partly driven by rising global prices.
- Services industries are not just concentrated in Kyiv. Lviv, Vinnytsia in the West and Kharkiv in the East show a sizeable and dynamic - this restricted to the western regions - IT sector, whereas Odesa dominates transport services.

[17] Note that the comparatively high performance for metals and minerals is at least in part artificially driven by high global commodity prices.

[18] Note that Kyiv accounts for a big share of agricultural exports, which cannot be cultivated in an urban area. This reflects the fact that most of the exporting companies are registered in Kyiv, while their production is located elsewhere.

Fig. 10.17: Export specialisation of the Ukrainian macro-regions

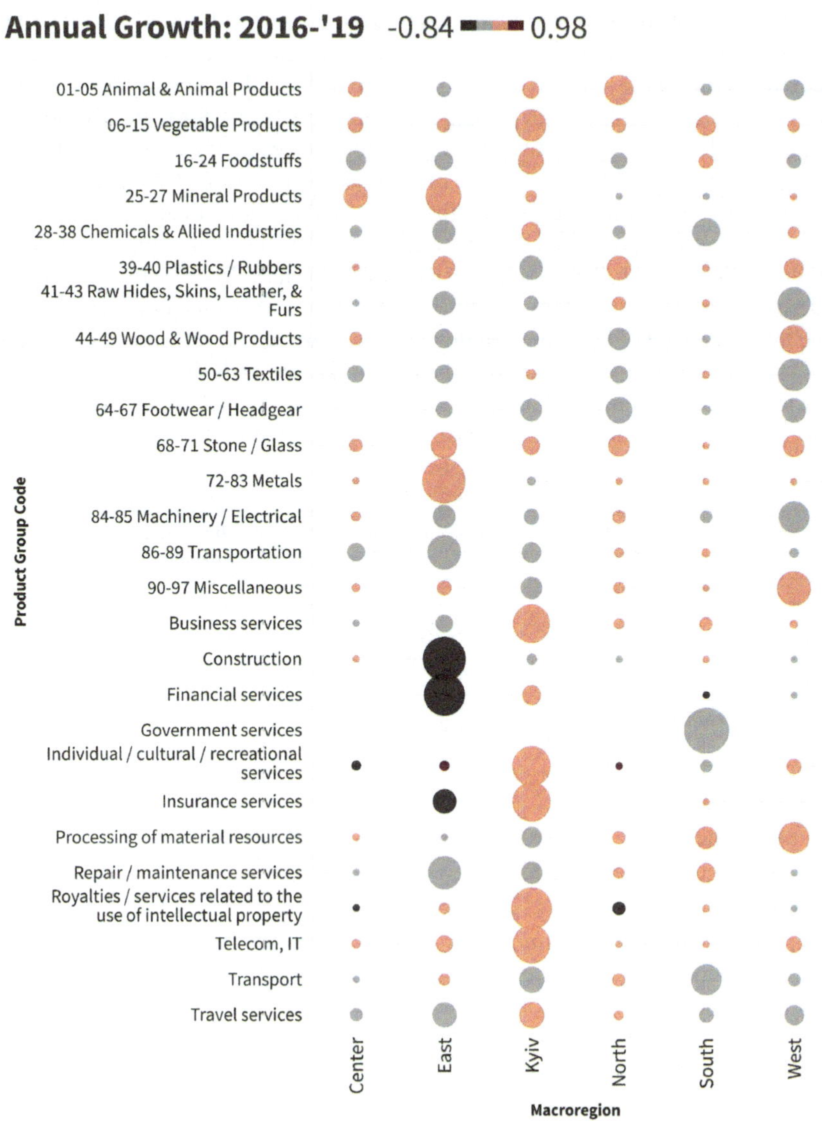

Table 10.3: Types of the top-performing industries
Note: An industry in a particular region classifies with an (x) if the value of a particular considered variable belongs to the top 33 percent of the selected sample; growth rates are calculated for the 2016–2021 period. The classification labels are constructed modularly to reflect the strength of individual components. For industry-region pairs, names with comparatively high growth are defined as 'stars' for their outstanding performance. For pairs with a high share in the regional economy we use a 'regional' postfix, and for pairs with a high share in the national economy we use 'market' in the label. Therefore, if the industry-region pair had a high growth and a big share in national exports - but not regional - it has a strong positioning on the "market" and is a 'star' due to high growth. This results in a label 'Market star'. There are two exceptions: 'Underdogs' and 'National star'. 'Underdogs' are industry-region pairs which belong to the top 20 percent of the index but do not have a strong individual position in any of its subcomponents. Therefore, they belong to the best industry-region pairs but show less potential compared to their peers. 'National star' is the opposite of that. Their excellence at all three subcomponents - high growth, high shares nationally and regionally - might be considered as the best of the best.

Label	High export growth	High share in total regional exports	High share in nationwide industry exports
National star	X	X	X
Regional cluster		X	X
Rising star	X		
Market dominator			X
Market star	X		X
Regional star	X	X	
Regional staple		X	

- Agricultural industry, prominent in Ukrainian exports, has a different nature and role depending on the region. For non-West regions, the industry typically occupies a large share of regional international exports, but it is only the western and northern regions that display high growth.
- Wood-based production is the most frequent underdog industry. It shows potential in several regions of the West and Centre, but not the rapid export growth dynamic of other industries.

An important general take-away is that the portfolio of industries suitable for (domestic and international) investment is not restricted to the industries traditionally associated with Ukraine. With each region having at least three industries within the top 20 percent according to the competitiveness index, a favourable investment portfolio should be differentiated by region. At the same time, the sources of relative competitiveness vary, which allows for multiple strategies for policy intervention. This is particularly helpful under multiple financing scenarios. Under extremely limited finance, a conservative

Fig. 10.18: Export specialisation of the Ukrainian macro-regions

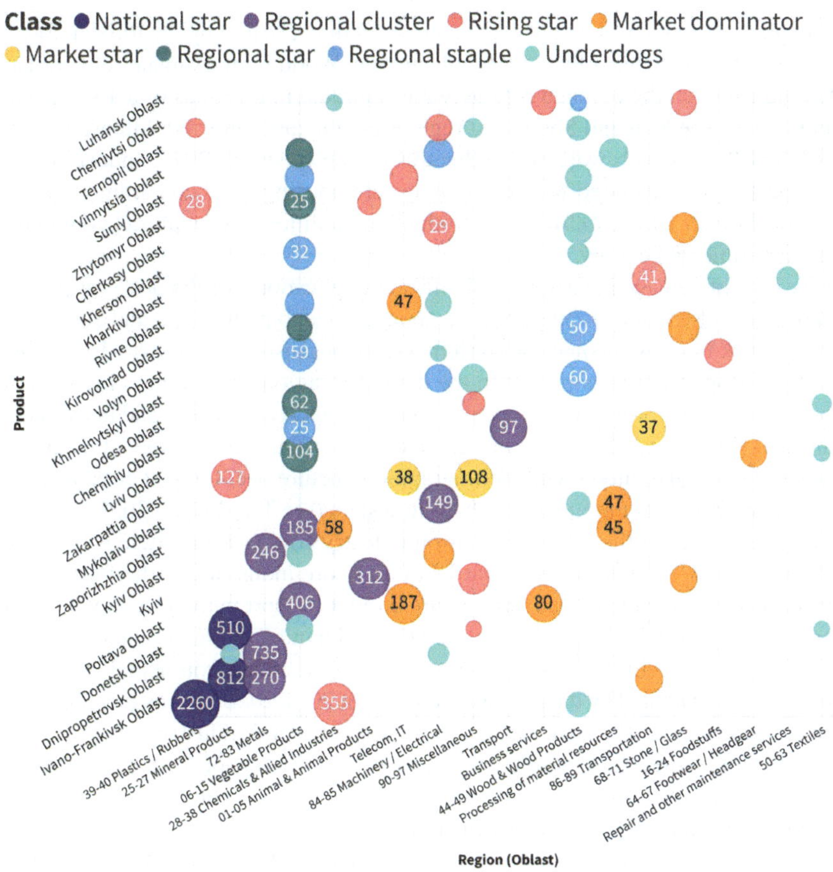

investment strategy focused on the top/most competitive industries (regional or national stars) is most likely to be the one that guarantees the highest return on investment. If, however, reconstruction is implemented across the board and funding it will meet its targets, a more progressive strategy that targets 'rising stars' and 'underdogs' is likely to be more successful when it comes to achieving the qualitative and technological advance in Ukraine's economic structure that will be sought. The analysis can be further deepened, e.g., by using more detailed product-level trade statistics, which, however, are not available at the regional level.

10.4.5 How have Different Regions been Affected by War Damage?

Although each region of Ukraine has experienced direct strikes by the Russian forces, the extent of the damage inflicted is highly uneven. World Bank estimates of February 2023 indicate that the damage is largely concentrated in the areas of active ground operations.[19] The East and South-east regions are the most affected, followed by the North and Kyiv, which were active theatres of war in spring 2022. Industry-wise, the largest costs associated with war damage are housing, land contamination, and transport infrastructure, followed by production facilities in agriculture, commerce, manufacturing, and energy.

The type of damage incurred has significant implications for the post-war production structure of Ukraine. From a macroeconomic standpoint, the East- and South-East may get stuck in a low-income equilibrium with poor prospects of growth. Even when hostilities stop, security concerns in the damaged regions will remain high due to geographical proximity to the aggressor country, wrecked housing, and unexploded ordnance. This implies that return migration of the most productive population groups is anything but guaranteed, with demographic structure becoming skewed towards the elderly who are net recipients of fiscal transfers (see Tverdostup, 2023).

When it comes to the impact of war on industry composition, there is both bad and good news: The bad news is that Ukraine's core industries of the East region have been severely affected and will require prompt support in the recovery phase to ensure growth. Even in the pre-2014 period the coal mining and metals industrial core showed signs of declining productivity and deteriorating environmental spoliation, which were exacerbated by the partial occupation of 2014-2022 and ensuing hostilities (Havlik, Kochnev & Pindyuk, 2020). With the cities and industrial sites severely impaired by the direct and indirect impact of the war, we do not see the potential for the region to recover on its own and this calls for active government intervention in the region to avoid perpetual impoverishment.

The good news is that such a policy intervention is unlikely to face much resistance from the industrial lobby, including oligarchs, inherited from Soviet-era industries (such as coal mining). This in turn creates an opportunity for rapid intervention—at least in the early stages of the reconstruction process—focused on promoting a more advanced industrial mix.

10.4.6 Policies to Accompany a Regional Shift in Economic Activity

The Ukrainian economy faces a high risk that wartime damage will lead to a deep and long-lasting division between the Eastern/Southern regions and the rest. While the East will require significant net fiscal transfers for years to come, the government

[19] The estimation does not reflect needs to recover from damage that occurred after February 2023. Note that needs are different from losses and damage. Needs reflect the costs for restoration of sustainable economic growth in the long term. Losses reflect foregone revenues or benefits of the wartime. Damage stands for destroyed asset value due to the direct impact of war.

also needs to actively support investments that will help to rebuild local production capabilities in the drive for long-term economic growth. Our analysis found that, even within a short timeframe (2016–2021) and despite an unstable environment, some regions have experienced the advent and development of advanced industries. This implies that further development is possible even amidst instability.

The allocation of reconstruction funds needs to take account of both regional economic and social inequalities and demographic disparities and the territorial distribution of war damage. Ukraine's reconstruction plan(s) should address these aspects by combining overarching national objectives with centralised fund management and regional and municipal level reconstruction programmes with devolved fund management. The balance between the two depends on the type and extent of the reconstruction needs observed at local and regional level, as well as the capacity of national, regional and local authorities to manage the volume of reconstruction funding.

Ukraine's recent decentralisation reforms brought its local government structures closer to EU benchmarks. The reconstruction governance model(s) should thus be aligned with (consolidated) decentralisation reforms and ensure that local government bodies are empowered, both politically and financially, especially in regions and municipalities hardest hit by the war.

To ensure the efficient absorption of funds from the EU and other key actors, administrative capacity in Ukraine's authorities across all governance levels needs to be boosted, especially at local level where authorities only recently saw their competences considerably increased. At this stage, Ukraine still lacks the administrative capacity and experience to absorb large-scale funds (European Commission, 2023a). To that end, the implementation of Ukraine's reconstruction plan could also lean on the experience of the EU's Instrument for Pre-accession Assistance (IPA), much like Pillar III of the Ukraine Facility (European Commission, 2023b) which addresses the issue of administrative capacity by providing technical assistance and support to Ukraine in a way comparable to the support EU currently proposes to pre-accession countries. Even though the IPA has become less focused on compliance with the EU acquis (a requirement for formal accession), it is still praised as a useful means to promote the (capacitated) decentralised management of funds by the beneficiary (Koeth, 2014). Between 1990 and 2006 overall EU commitments for Ukraine were (obviously) much less than what the EU members in the CESEE received. While Ukraine received EUR 35 per capita in that period, Poland received EUR 159 per capita (Wolczuk & Žeruolis, 2018). In parallel, Ukraine's reconstruction at regional level could be (partly) co-managed by an EU institution and Ukraine's relevant national and regional authorities. We favour an activist regional and industrial policy, which would be critical when major changes in economic structure and in regional development are necessary within a longer-term timeframe. This requires front-loaded and regionally differentiated public investment in infrastructure, in training facilities and labour market institutions which support return migration, internal mobility and jobs-labour force matching. Special attention should also be given to support start-ups (also as a tool to encourage return migration) and a strong hand of competition policy to control the market power of dominating enterprises which can stifle the sustained growth of the SME sector. Encouragement of FDI and the stimulus it can give to local firms will be essential (Movchan & Pindyuk, 2024, forthcoming). The effectiveness of schemes in this area will have different time-horizons in different regions, because of the highly uneven regional impact of the war.

10.5 Economic Reconstruction and EU Accession

The starting point to embark on economic reconstruction and a possible take-off towards a catching-up process similar to the one which had taken place in the Central and East European economies since about the mid-1990s, does not look very feasible at the moment. One reason is the precarious security situation pointed out above, but let us briefly mention also a few economic and institutional factors.[20]

Figure 10.19 shows that while the level of GDP per capita in Ukraine in 1990 at the start of the so-called 'transition' (to a market economy) was at a similar level with countries such as Hungary and Slovakia, it fell dramatically behind even before the current phase of the war. It is now in a league with Moldova and Albania, the poorest countries in Europe. Many writers have addressed the problems which led to this situation (see e.g., the Poland Ukraine comparison by Gylfason, Hochreiter & Kowalski, 2022).

Fig. 10.19: GDP per capita in 1990 and 2021
Sources: wiiw (2023a), own calculations
Note: Data show per capita GDP in EUR at purchasing power parity

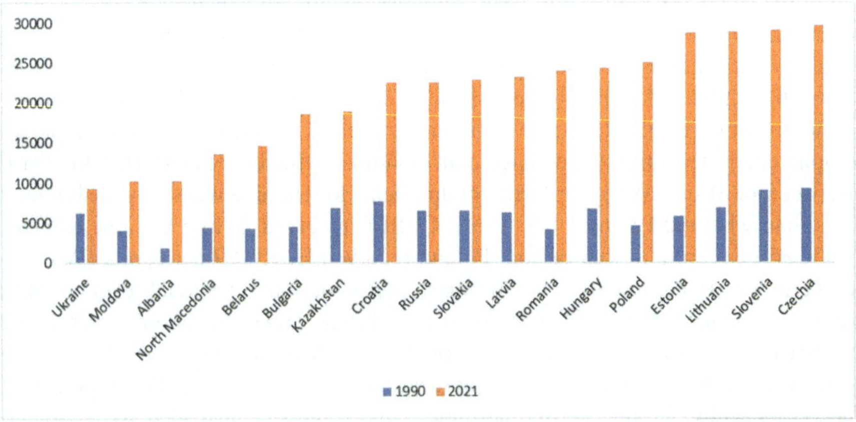

Before going into more detail in the following sections of the paper, let us refer to two factors in the introduction which can be seen as important to understand

[20] This section draws on detailed material from Grieveson et al. (2023).

the situation of Ukraine in comparison with other countries of Central-Eastern and Southeastern Europe (CEE-SEE). In order to make a comparison with CEE-SEE countries we take as the phase of comparison for those countries which are already members of the EU the period before they acceded to the European Union and for the countries which are currently candidate countries of the EU we look at the recent 5 year period.[21] The first factor we want to mention is foreign direct investment (FDI) which played a very important role in the catching-up process of the CEE countries and supported their re-industrialisation and through strengthening their export performance also their macroeconomic stability. Sticking to the period before the current war Figure 10.20 shows that Ukraine's FDI stock (as a share of GDP) was the lowest amongst the comparator groups of countries.

Fig. 10.20: FDI stock (% of GDP) – five-year averages
Sources: wiiw (2023b). own calculations.
Note: Data show inward FDI stock, as a percentage of GDP, on a five-year average. For EU-CEE countries, the five years are those before (but not including) the accession year, and the EU comparison is for the EU-15 over the same period. For non-EU member states, the five years are 2017–2021, and the EU comparison is for the EU-27 over the same period.

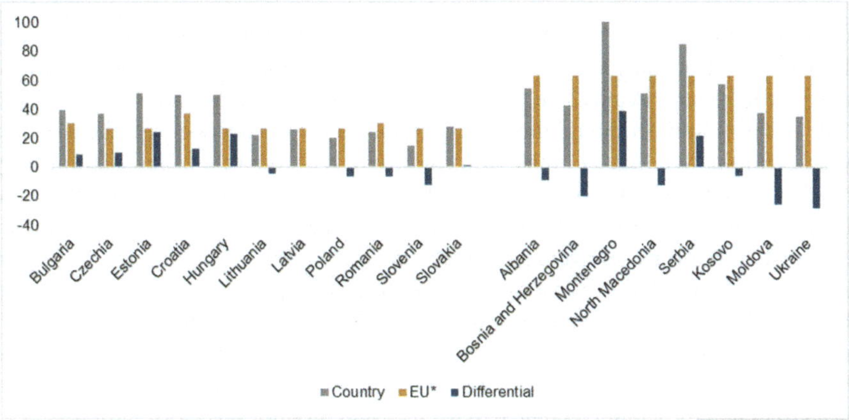

The second factor, often used also as an explanatory factor for the (dis)interest of foreign investors to get engaged in a country refers to the quality of institutions. Figure 10.21 shows the position of Ukraine – again in comparison with the group of CEE and SEE countries – in relation to a number of governance indicators compiled by the World Bank.

What we see in Figure 10.21 is that Ukraine in terms of institutional quality according to a number of indicators is judged to be at a level similar to the weakest

[21] We refer the reader to Grieveson et al. (2023) where this comparison is more extensively undertaken and from where some of the following figures have been taken.

Fig. 10.21: Governance indicators – relative to average Germany, France and Italy
Source: World Bank (2023b) Own calculations
Note: World Bank Worldwide Governance Indicators relative to the average of France, Germany and Italy at the time of each CESEE country's application to join the EU. For those that applied in 2022, 2021 data are used (latest available).

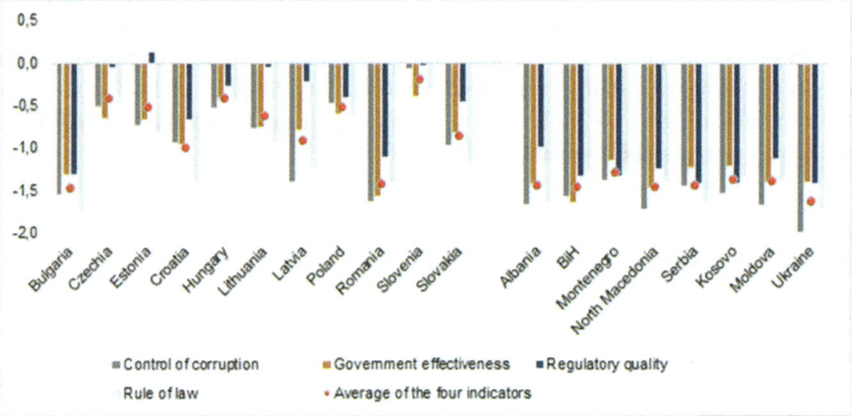

countries amongst the CEE-EU countries prior to their accession to the EU, i.e., Bulgaria and Romania, and more or less at the level of the other countries which are now in the group of candidate countries; it scores the weakest in 'corruption' and 'rule of law'. To meet the minimum requirements for EU accession in the next few years, Ukraine will have to make reform progress on the rule of law significantly quicker than its EU-CEE peers did. The EU's 2007 and 2013 joiners, plus the three institutionally weakest 2004 joiners (Latvia, Lithuania, Slovakia), improved their rule-of-law score by an average of 0.05 per year in the four years leading up to accession. At the start of those years, they were at a significantly higher level than Ukraine. Assuming a similar rate of progress, Ukraine will not reach the theoretically minimal level (i.e., that of Romania in 2007) until 2032. This indicates that Ukraine has a lot of work ahead, but it also underlines the strong role that EU institutions will need to play in providing technical assistance and monitoring reform progress. The above quick review indicates that Ukraine has to overcome big challenges to start on a trajectory of catching-up which has characterised the group of Central-Eastern European economies that have become members of the EU. However, the experience of the countries in this comparative group indicates that EU accession can be a major driving force of such a process. It does lead to institutional convergence (given the obligation to implement the Acquis Communautaire), although we have seen that backlashes in institutional developments have taken place (such as in the judicial system) in some countries. Both through institutional convergence and the integration into the Single Market, trade and production linkages get intensified and a process of productivity and wage (level) convergence is set in motion. However, there are also issues specific to Ukraine's case and also the specific historical context in which the next 'round of enlargement' of the EU might take place; some of these might create frictions along the path towards accession. Ukraine is a large country with a very sizeable agricultural sector, with - as we have seen – a particularly low level of income plus very strong challenges of uneven regional developments (which will be covered in Section 4 of this chapter) which will need to be addressed during its economic reconstruction. Hence it will, under current policy-making structures, absorb a significant share of the two large EU budgetary programs, the CAP and the Cohesion Funds. This will not be an easy issue for the existing members of the EU to adjust to. Furthermore, Ukraine's accession process will move in parallel with that of a wider range of countries – the Western Balkan countries as well as Georgia and Moldova - also aspiring to joining the European Union over the coming decade. As regards the number of countries involved – although not regarding the size of their economies and populations where Ukraine is an exception – this amounts to a very sizeable next wave of 'enlargement' which the current constitution and internal decision-making structures of the EU will find difficult to cope with. Many commentators have stated that this will require major adaptations in the ways how the EU operates, up to the point of having to move towards a new Treaty or series of Treaties. This, as we know, is an arduous (if not impossible) task to carry through, especially in the current internal political dynamic in which the EU finds itself in which disparate political trajectories characterise a range of member countries. We shall come back to these issues in the following sections of the chapter.

There has been a consensus that Ukraine should be offered a 'European perspective' (European Council, 2022), as can be seen by the decision taken in December 2023 to make it a candidate country and the opening of accession negotiations in 2024. The EU's most successful instrument for stabilising its so-called 'near abroad' as well as for driving economic, social and political progress has been its enlargement policy, and this will apply more than ever in the case of Ukraine.

While the war and the desire to support Ukraine have catalysed the accession process, doubts about enlargement have crystalised more concretely in the case of Ukraine owing to the supposedly unique challenges of taking in a large, poor, corrupt country with a big agricultural sector. Ukraine has a long-standing reputation as something of an economic basket case, having posted a uniquely disastrous post-Communist economic convergence performance, with the comparison to the success of neighbouring Poland being particularly stark (Gylfason et al., 2022). Ukraine is seen as having unique economic challenges even in the CESEE context, linked to factors such as weak institutions, high levels of corruption, and the prevalence of the oligarchic class. Moreover, many feel that the EU itself is not ready for Ukrainian membership; that reforming the EU's current budget allocation, its institutional set-up and its decision-making processes is already long overdue; and that it simply could not cope with new members, especially a country like Ukraine (Toyguer & Bergmann, 2023). If and when Ukraine joins the EU, there is a fear that it will suck away all the EU funds from the EU's poorest regions and turn the EU-CEE countries into net contributors to the EU budget. In the following we shall first examine how Ukraine is placed in comparison with other EU-CEE countries before they acceded to the EU and also in relation to other current candidate countries. Then we examine the challenges and potential benefits which current EU member countries might face in light of a future accession of Ukraine.

10.5.1 Ukraine Accession to the EU: Would it Really be a Game-changer for the EU to Absorb Ukraine?

In terms of the sizes of both its economy and population, Ukraine is comparable with some of the EU-CEE countries when they joined the EU.[22] Ukraine's economy is about 1 percent of the size of the EU-27 economy, which is roughly the equivalent of Hungary's or Romania's economy relative to the then-EU-15 before they joined the EU in 2004 (Figure 10.22). Meanwhile Ukraine's population is about 9 percent of the EU-27, whereas Poland's population was 10 percent of the EU-15 on the eve of its accession. The idea of taking in another Poland in population terms is certainly not insignificant. Yet this is manageable and, given EU labour shortages, could even be highly advantageous from an EU perspective.

Fig. 10.22: Ukraine's GDP and population in comparison to EU accession and candidate countries
Source:wiiw (2023a) Own calculations
Note: Data show nominal GDP as a percentage of the EU's GDP (left) and population as a percentage of the EU's population (right). For EU-CEE countries, the comparison for both membership application and accession years is the EU-15. For non-member states, the comparison for both membership application and accession years is the EU-27 and the accession year is the latest available data, meaning 2022 for economic size and 2021 for population size.

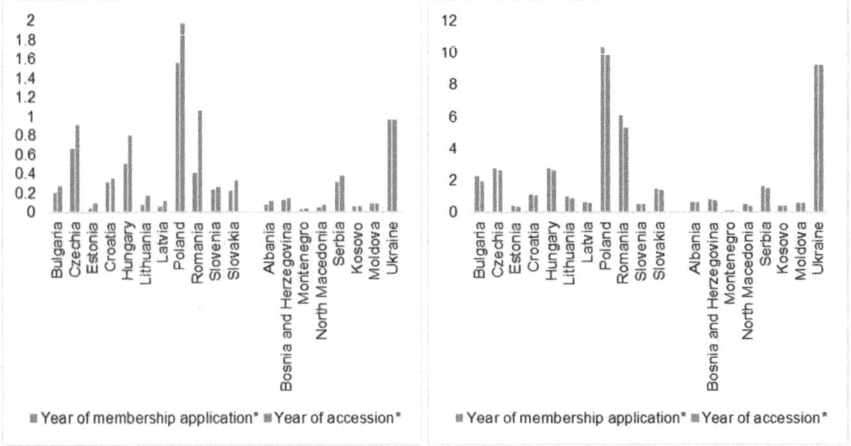

[22] We draw in this section on material presented in the report by Grieveson et al. (2023).

In terms of income levels (measured in per capita GDP at purchasing power parity), Ukraine at the time of its membership application is at the level of the very poorest previous CESEE joiners (e.g., Latvia and Romania) when they applied to join in the mid-1990s relative to the then-EU (Figure 10.23). However, Ukraine is much poorer than any country at the time of its accession thus far, and it is also much poorer than any other current accession hopefuls aside from Kosovo and Moldova. Nevertheless, given sufficient external support as part of reconstruction and Ukraine's potential in various areas (see discussion in Sections 10.3 and 10.4 above), Ukraine has a good chance of closing a large part of the development gap relatively quickly in the coming years and ahead of EU accession. The indicators suggest that Ukraine is in several ways comparable with Romania before its accession, which is a positive sign. From a low starting point, Romania has been one of the success stories of economic convergence in the EU (Figure 10.24). This naturally does not guarantee anything for Ukraine, but it does suggest one possible positive future. For a country at a low level of economic development relative to the EU (as Romania was in 2007), the catch-up potential due to a large initial income differential combined with access to EU resources and technical assistance can be a very powerful one.

Fig. 10.23: Ukraine's GDP per capita in comparison to EU accession and candidate countries
Source:wiiw (2023a)
Note: Data show per capita GDP at PPP, as a percentage of the EU's GDP. For EU-CEE countries, the comparison for both membership application and accession years is the EU-15. For non-member states, the comparison for both membership application and accession years is the EU-27, and the accession year is the latest available data (i.e., 2022).

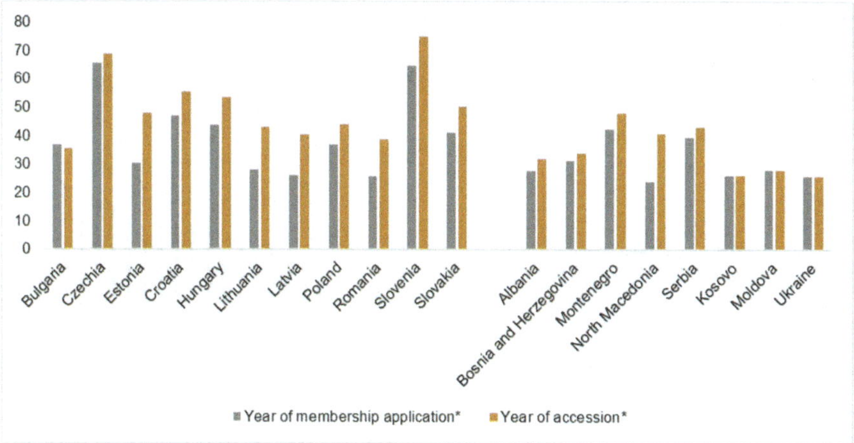

Ukraine starts its economic reconstruction from a position of very low wage levels and low productivity (see Figures 10.25 and 10.26). This could in principle give it

Fig. 10.24: Romania's GDP per capita in 2007 and in 2022
Source:wiiw (2023a) Own calculations
Note: Romanian per capita GDP at PPP, as a percentage of Germany's GDP and the EU-CEE average in 2007 and 2022. EU-CEE average = simple average.

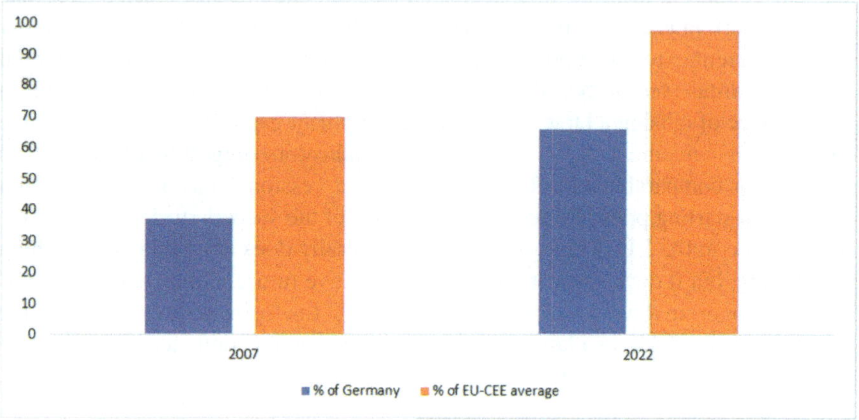

also an advantage as a low wage destination for FDI (and location of labour-intensive stages in cross-border production networks) if such FDI flows at the same time allow the country to follow a path of productivity catching-up.

Fig. 10.25: Wage rates in Ukraine and comparator countries
Source:wiiw (2023a); own calculations
Note: Average monthly gross wages, total economy, in EUR. Data in the right-hand figure are for 2022.

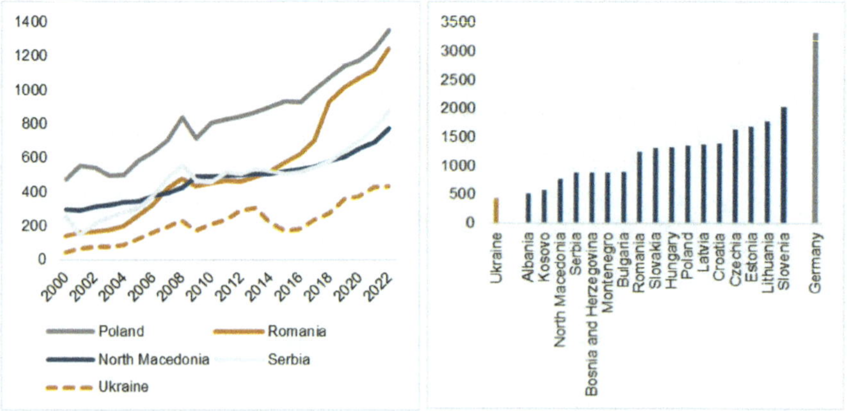

Fig. 10.26: Labour productivity in Ukraine and comparator countries
Source:wiiw (2023a); own calculations
Note: Labour productivity, in million EUR. Real GDP based on EUR 2019 prices, divided by LFS employment.

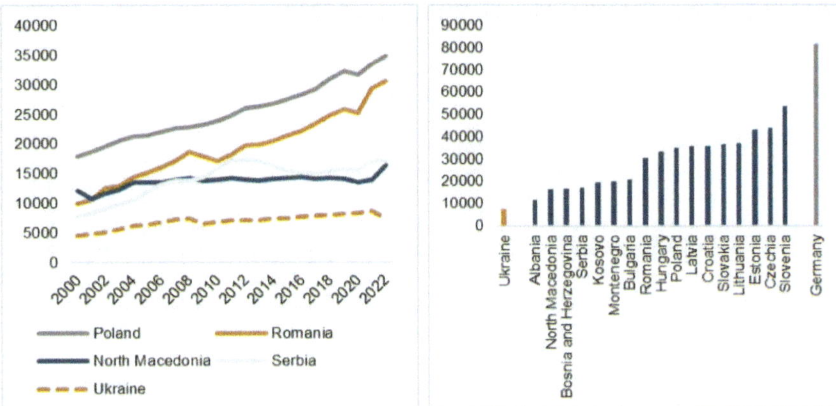

Furthermore, Ukraine seems to be relatively well placed in terms of the quality of education. As of 2022, Ukraine's PISA score was actually higher than that of some EU member states (Figure 10.27, right). According to the European Centre for the Development of Vocational Training (CEDEFOP), Ukraine is comparable on the PISA metric, depending on the subject, with EU member states Croatia, Greece, Italy, Luxembourg, Malta and Slovakia, which is a very healthy position for a country that is just starting its EU accession process (Cedefop, 2022).

Lastly, we should point out that the strong position of its IT industry as well as the rather strong comparative advantage position of some of its sectors (see Section 3) would potentially make Ukraine a promising addition to the Single Market in terms of trade integration, emerging specialisation and size of its own domestic market. The two areas which we see as important constraints on a successful catching-up process are the ones already mentioned: overcoming important weaknesses in institutional quality also in the light of the great uncertainty how the post-war political economy might evolve, and secondly, the severe issue of shortages in the employable labour force due to the demographic calamity that has befallen the country (analysed in Section 2).

Fig. 10.27: Pisa scores in Ukraine and comparator countries
Source:World Intellectual Property Organisation (WIPO) (2023) Own calculations
Note: Data on the left show PISA scales in reading, maths and science, calculated by the WIPO, as of 2013 (Croatia) and 2022 (all other countries), and the difference versus the EU for the relevant year. Data on the right show PISA scales in reading, maths and science, calculated by the WIPO, as of 2022.

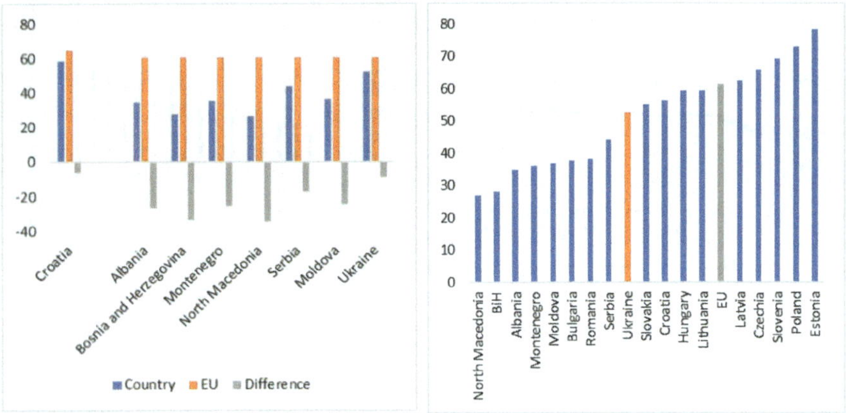

10.5.2 What are the Challenges and Potential for Existing EU Member States, Particularly for the EU-CEEC?

Integrating a rather large country such as Ukraine with distinct comparative advantages and with a very low starting level in terms of GDP per capita into the EU will not be an easy process. We highlight in this section some of the challenges but also the advantages which a successful process of accession to the EU will bring to the table for the existing members of the European Union.

A proper quantitative evaluation of the impacts of Ukraine's accession to the EU and for its individual member states would require simulations on a fully specified multi-country general equilibrium model which we do not possess in order to undertake such an evaluation. But even if we had such a model (for previous modelling exercises evaluating the effects of previous rounds of enlargement, see Baldwin, Francois, Portes, Rodrik & Székely, 1997, Breuss, 2002, (Commission, 2022), Baas & Brücker, 2010, Caliendo, Opromolla, Parro & Sforza, 2021), such models still remain partial regarding the many paths and inter-dependencies by which economies and their structures might be affected. In the following we shall therefore limit ourselves to discussing the various channels through which incumbent countries of the EU and also some of the candidate countries (specifically those of the Western Balkans) might be affected by Ukraine's accession to the EU. A proper evaluation would also have to take into account the time horizon of an accession process which is far from clear at this stage; we shall assume in the following that it will not be fully accomplished before the end of the current decade. There will, furthermore, be likely changes in the way how the accession process will be handled in the case of Ukraine, given that the security dimension will remain important and one can expect that rather large additional financial flows are likely to be mobilised to support Ukraine's reconstruction process (in which important allies and institutions will participate beyond the EU). Changes in the accession process were already introduced under the Revised Enlargement Methodology (REM)[23] to accompany the planned accession of the Western Balkan countries and it is likely that further changes will take place in the context of the wider enlargement process that would include Ukraine, Moldova and Georgia. An area that will be particularly important – given past and current experiences with countries that became members of the EU – would be to be more effective in imposing a tighter regime of conditionalities especially regarding rule of law and governance issues. However, there are also various proposals regarding a stage-managed process of integration which would allow Ukraine to become a 'quasi-full member' of various policy areas (such as in research, student mobility etc.) before becoming a full member of the EU and as various chapters of the Acquis Communitaire are concluded (see e.g., Grieveson et al., 2023).

We now come to discussing the various channels through which economies of the current EU member countries might be affected by Ukraine's accession to the EU. We shall thereby focus particularly on the potential impact on the countries in Central and Eastern Europe (CEECs). The following areas will be covered:

- Trade and FDI
- Mobility of labour
- Energy
- Reconstruction of infrastructure, transport etc.
- EU budget and EU governance issues
- Macroeconomic considerations
- Military and strategic issues

Trade and FDI: Regarding this channel, there is general agreement amongst economists (also borne out by the model simulations that analysed the impacts of previous rounds of enlargement referred to earlier) that any accession of a new – especially neighbouring - country such as Ukraine would lead to an intensification of trade and FDI linkages and would thereby have an overall positive macroeconomic welfare effect. In the case of Ukraine there is already an AA/DCFTA (Association Agreement / Deep and Comprehensive Free Trade Agreement) (Szyszczak & Disney,

---

[23] The Revised Enlargement Methodology (REM) was endorsed by the General Affairs Council in March 2020. It was titled 'Enhancing the accession process – A credible EU perspective for the Western Balkans' and its aim was to set out "concrete proposals for strengthening the accession process, by making it more predictable, more credible, more dynamic and subject to stronger political steering" – see European Commission (2020). Already earlier, in the context of the accession process of Bulgaria and Romania, the EU had tightened conditionality requirements in the context of passing the 'Cooperation and Verification Mechanism' (CVM), which attempted to more tightly monitor the countries' progress especially in the areas of rule of law and governance (European Commission, 2022).

2022) in place which has liberalised a significant share of commodity trade. However, some tariff quota restrictions are still in place particularly in the all-important agricultural sector, although these were temporarily lifted during the course of the war, leading to sharp reactions by some of the member states. The AA/DCFTA also already committed Ukraine to a gradual adoption of the Acquis. Nonetheless, embarking on full accession means a much fuller adoption of common standards and participation in EU programs. Furthermore, one can confidently predict that without the prospect of EU membership it is unlikely that the institutional and governance issues would be seriously tackled which strongly impact on the interest of foreign investors and trading partners to engage in the country's economic reconstruction.

The prospect of EU accession will intensify trade and FDI links through three channels: (i) a direct effect of reduction of trade barriers and convergence of standards (ii) the impact on institutional and governance issues given various conditionality clauses in the accession process and the institutional anchorage in the EU (iii) the impact on growth and qualitative up-grading of Ukraine's economy through factors (i) and (ii) as well as the increased participation in EU policy-programmes and increased EU budgetary flows. These themselves generate feed-back loops by stimulating growth in EU member states through increased trade, FDI and financial linkages.

Despite this overall positive picture, we should not forget structural adjustment issues which are often a crucial element in the political perception of whether countries gain or lose from trade and FDI liberalisation. As discussed in Section 10.2, agriculture and potentially food products are an important sector of Ukraine's economy and they have a significant comparative advantage in these areas. Hence, in this sector Ukraine will become an important supplier to the EU market as a whole, but also an important competitor in both quantity and quality to existing EU producers; this has already led to strong reactions by farmers (and – in response to this – by governments) in neighbouring countries during the war period when tariff-quota restrictions were lifted by the EU. Such reactions are likely to increase as Ukraine's accession process is unfolding and the prospects of it being able to draw on CAP support become more real (although initially transitory arrangements will mean only a phased-in disbursement of CAP money even after accession). International investors will furthermore play an important role in the qualitative up-grading of the food-producing sector and this will strengthen Ukraine's competitive position. There will also be other areas (see Section 10.3) in which competitive pressure will be exerted by Ukraine on existing member countries; these countries will be differentially affected given their geographic location (gravity factor) and the extent to which their current comparative advantage position overlaps with that of Ukraine. Hence, structural adjustment will definitely take place in the incumbent EU member countries as a result of Ukraine's accession to the EU and these will cause a certain amount of political resistance even though over time the overall welfare benefits will become apparent – as they have in previous rounds of Enlargement.

Mobility of labour: We have covered the precarious demographic situation of Ukraine in Section 10.2 and pointed out that despite the already experienced decline in population and, even more so, of its labour force, there will be a further fall in both when the intense phase of the war ends. The reasons for continued net emigration also after the war is that income level gaps will remain very high, labour markets and employment prospects in Ukraine will take time to recover and - while family reunion could go either way - husbands/partners whose outward migration was prevented through martial law during the war are more likely to join their spouses/partners abroad rather than the other way round. Hence the simulations presented in Section 2 indicate that further net emigration will take place after the war ends. While the contraction of the available labour force will be detrimental for the reconstruction of Ukraine after the war, it will be a benefit to EU incumbent countries who can count on a net inflow of persons in workable age, together with a beneficial skill/qualification composition of such immigrants. Also here, the main beneficiaries will be countries in relative geographic proximity, with already existing migrant network connections, and depending on the attractiveness of their labour markets, as well as of schools and universities, and – of course - income prospects. From a policy point-of-view it will be important to make sure to find arrangements that encourage return migration or circular migration schemes so that Ukraine's economic recovery is not hit very badly by labour force and skill supply constraints.

Energy: Ukraine can potentially be an important actor in the energy field for the EU as a whole and CEE economies might be able to benefit specifically from Ukraine becoming an important supplier of more traditional sources of energy (gas, nuclear, water) but also of renewables (solar, hydrogen). This has been pointed out in a number of studies (see e.g., Darvas et al., 2024, Movchan & Pindyuk, 2024, forthcoming; also the extensive discussion in Chapter 2).

Reconstruction of physical infrastructure, transport, social infrastructure, etc.: This is another area where neighbouring countries will benefit from Ukraine's economic reconstruction. Given the enormous destruction of physical infrastructure during the war there will be a strong demand for contractors, specialists in different areas but also general work forces in the building and transport sector, to support this reconstruction effort which also has a declared goal of 'build back better', i.e., to better efficiency, environmental and quality standards. There will also be demand to support the recovery of the social infrastructure (schools, hospitals, dealing with war invalidity, etc.) which will draw on resources and expertise from other (especially neighbouring) countries.

EU budget and EU governance issues: This is likely to be an area which will attract special (and controversial) attention. As in previous episodes of EU Enlargement, the discussion of the impact on 'net receivers' and 'net payers' plays a central role in countries' assessment whether they 'gain' or 'lose' from new members. This is, of course, a narrow (and partial) Finance Minister's view on gains and losses from Enlargement, abstracting from the more far-reaching growth and structural impacts of a process of deeper integration with new members which can only be captured by a fully specified economic model as referred to above. Nonetheless, given that EU budgetary implications play such an important role in accession negotiations and even in the public's perception of the gains/losses of Enlargement, it is important to analyse the details of the potential impact of Ukraine's accession on the EU budget allocation as a whole and its main components. The latter refer specifically to the

Cohesion Funds on the one hand and the Common Agricultural Policy (CAP) on the other hand.

In the following we shall refer to an exercise by Darvas et al. (2024) which estimates the allocations from these two spending programs to the Ukraine. His exercise was set up to analyse the implications of what the allocations would have looked like if Ukraine had already been a full member of the EU over the MFF (Multi-year Financial Framework) spending programme over the years 2021-2027. This is a useful exercise as the key to allocations for this MFF over this period are completely clear, while the situation regarding the budget structure and allocations of a future MFF when Ukraine would actually enter the EU are not known at this stage. We shall therefore refer to the estimates in this study.

As regards *Ukraine's participation in the EU's Cohesion Policy*, Darvas et al. calculate a scenario in which Ukraine's agricultural land would be reduced by 20 percent (either because of Russian occupation or being mined and not yet available for cultivation) and Ukraine would also have suffered a long-term decline of its prewar GDP and population in the same order of magnitude due to the war. In this case, Ukraine would have received EUR 27 bn cohesion support over the 2021-27 period from a total EU Cohesion budget of EUR 400 bn (all at current prices). As the overall EU budget would have increased as a result of Ukraine's accession (from 393 bn to 400 bn), the other EU 27 members would have received EUR 19 bn less. The reason for a relatively limited redistribution to the Ukraine from the cohesion budge, is that most cohesion policy payments are capped at 2.3 percent of GDP for countries with less than 55 percent of EU average GNI per capita (at PPS). Without this cap, Ukraine would – given the allocation criteria of the MFF 2021-27 – have received around Eur 170 bn!

As to the implications for the EU incumbent countries who will receive less cohesion policy funding, the main impact would fall on regions transiting from formerly being classified as 'less developed regions' to becoming 'transition regions' and some of those formerly classified as 'transition regions' graduating to become 'more developed regions'. This will affect the poorer regions in the CEECs the most since many regions fall into those categories, and we can expect negotiations coming up with a phasing-in scenario during the relevant MFF period, so that transiting regions in EU incumbent countries would only gradually lose the support; this has precedent as it was the case with transiting regions in Southern Europe, i.e., Portugal, Spain and Greece, when Eastern enlargement took place.

A significantly bigger sum would be allocated (by the rules in place for the MFF 2021-27) to Ukraine from the *CAP budget*. Ukraine would in this scenario receive Eur 68 bn out of a total EU CAP budget of EUR 446 bn. Again, a phasing-in process is likely as incumbent EU member countries would argue that their farming sector would suffer too strong dislocation effects.

Ukraine's participation in *other EU programs* (innovation, border management and migration, security, defence, etc.) would lead to an allocation to Ukraine of another EUR 6 bn. Given that Ukraine would no longer be eligible to receive money under the 'neighbourhood' policy programs (minus EUR 2 bn) and would itself contribute to the EU budget EUR 14 bn, the total net flow to Ukraine over the 2021-27 period would have amounted to 27+68+6-14 = EUR 87 bn, and the net budgetary costs to the incumbent EU27 countries would amount to EUR 110 bn over that period, which amounts to about 0.10 percent of EU27 GDP. Hence, while EU budgetary issues and negotiations are always in the limelight, the macro-picture is one where even from a narrow budgetary point-of-view Ukraine's accession should be affordable, and it also should be set in the context of the considerable additional funds that would be necessary to support the reconstruction of the Ukraine after the end of the war.[24]

We should also keep in mind that the above estimated (re)allocations to Ukraine and from incumbent EU member countries refer to only direct budgetary payments and do not include fiscal benefits which these countries would receive from the growth (GDP and employment) impulses which EU member countries would receive from Ukraine's accession; these, in turn, would lead to more tax and social security contributions, plus profits from contracts which firms in incumbent countries would receive from participating in Ukraine's reconstruction effort; and this in turn would lead to corporate tax receipts for the treasuries.

EU governance: Another important topic refers to the impact that Ukraine and other candidate countries (from the Western Balkans plus Georgia and Moldova) joining the EU would have on EU governance and decision-making structures. These could indeed pose considerable challenges. This is an unsolved issue as having another eight countries joining the EU within the current governance structure of the EU (size of the Commission, size of European Parliament, limited qualified majority voting in various EU policy domains) can raise significant problems for the functioning of the EU. The problems can be particularly acute – as we have seen with the cases of Hungary and Poland – when countries' political developments diverge from a consensus regarding constitutional issues (rule of law, media control), the state's involvement in the economy (clientelism in public procurement and oligarchic control of crucial sectors) and foreign policy orientation (currently especially attitudes towards Putin's Russia). Some (though not all) of these issues can become problematic in the case of Ukraine's accession to the EU. We do not know at this stage in what shape Ukraine will emerge politically. Given its role during the war, it is likely that the office of the president will have a strong position in post-war Ukraine and hence the above areas will be strongly influenced by how the president will use his power. Potentially the position of Ukraine's oligarchs will have been significantly weakened as many of the assets they had originally were located in the heavily war-affected eastern and southern regions. Furthermore, Ukraine has already experienced a strong mobilisation of civil society before the current intensive phase of the war on issues such as corruption, and this might be further strengthened due to a post-war climate in which society demands clean behaviour from its elite and rulers given the enormous sacrifices made. On Ukraine's position regarding foreign policy there can be no doubt of its strong commitment to the Western alliance and its willingness to significantly contribute to it militarily. Finally, in the likely reduced territory of Ukraine, there are unlikely to be any inter-ethnic conflicts – which still strongly affects some of the Western Balkan countries – and, as a society, Ukraine will appear relatively united

[24] An updated estimate by the World Bank over a 10 year reconstruction period was in the region of USD 490 bn; see World Bank (2024).

and determined on its path towards economic reconstruction. Thus, while political developments in post-war Ukraine are unpredictable, it looks as if the accession of a large number of small Western Balkan economies where the enthusiasm for EU membership has long gone and inter-ethnic and inter-state disputes remain unresolved might generate more problems for EU governance and coordinated policy decisions than Ukraine's accession.

Further macroeconomic considerations: There are some important macroeconomic issues which can create hazards for Ukraine's economic reconstruction. The large inflow of international financial support which is expected to accompany Ukraine's reconstruction together with the significant inflow of remittances of the grown diaspora of Ukraine's migrants abroad (many of them young who will have a strong motivation to support those left in Ukraine), can generate a significant pressure on the real exchange rate and thus generate a type of 'Dutch disease'[25]. We have seen such developments also in some of the Western Balkan countries which received substantial aid after the Yugoslav-wars and were also beneficiaries of large inflows of remittances. Such pressure on the real exchange rate might cause serious problems for the tradable sector, impinging upon a recovery of the industrial sector and the building up of strong export capacities which would allow Ukraine to avoid balance-of-payments disequilibria in the longer-term.

The other macroeconomic issue could be instabilities in the financial/banking sector which will have to cope with the financial inflows, mediate their allocation to the domestic economy, and this might lead to phases of 'exuberance' by international lenders followed by reversals of capital flows. This can generate volatility in exchange rates and pose severe problems for monetary policy management, which many 'transition economies' amongst the CEECs experienced in the past. The volatility of international capital flows and instability of exchange rates, in turn, poses problems for the banking system with potential currency mismatches generating survival problems for the domestic banking system – as experienced by CEECs as well. It is important that monetary policy and supervision of the financial system is prepared for these challenges and lessons have been learnt from past experiences of transition and emerging economies in this respect. A sustained attempt should be made to use financial supervision and industrial policies to make sure financial inflows make their way into the build-up of productive capacities, particularly in the export sector, thereby avoiding the Dutch disease phenomenon.

Military and strategic issues: Finally, the issue which will be of benefit to the European Union and the neighbouring CEE countries in particular concerns the significant contribution that the Ukraine will make to the defence capabilities of the EU and the Western Alliance. This will be particularly welcome in the current phase in which the EU is trying to build a stronger position in military capabilities in the wake of the Russia-Ukraine war, other conflicts in its neighbourhood and the tensions which have been flaring up in transatlantic relationships (particularly with the prospects of a second Trump presidency). Ukraine will no doubt be able to draw on its current war experience, a sizeable army, and the build-up of a potent domestic

---

[25] For an early reference to the Dutch disease, see Corden (1984).

military industry. All of this will strengthen the defence capabilities of Europe as a whole.

10.6 Concluding Remarks

It is possible to take both an up-beat as well as a pessimistic position with respect to the possibility and potential of economic reconstruction of Ukraine.[26] We outline both these two angles with respect to the outlook on Ukraine's economic development.

In any case, the current military situation is such that it is impossible to predict the length or intensity of the war over the coming years, and any outlook on Ukraine's economy will heavily depend on this.

About the upside: EU candidate status, catching-up potential and restructuring progress already achieved.

Let us start with the up-beat assessment: Firstly, the war has brought about a change in perspective regarding the possibility of EU accession. It will not happen overnight, but Ukraine has now been officially recognised as a candidate country for EU membership. This means that Ukraine's economic reconstruction will take place in the context of such an EU accession perspective, bringing with it pre-accession support both in financial terms but also technical assistance to gradually align Ukraine's regulatory framework with the Acquis Communautaire as well as (at least partial) inclusion already in EU programs such as the European Green Deal and an intensified involvement in EU's energy systems and in the trans-European (TRANS) network programs. All of these are likely to give coherence to any plans for Ukraine's economic reconstruction and also involve significant support to improve institutional capacity to implement such plans. The focus on EU accession and convergence in institutional/legal terms should provide a basis for economic stabilisation and focus efforts from the main actors (internal and external) towards this goal.

Secondly, the adaptation of economic structures to the new geo-political reality already started in the aftermath of the 2014/15 events: Russian annexation of Crimea and its intervention in the Donbas region, leading to substantial trade reorientation as well as the economic decline of what was once the industrial heartland of Ukraine's economy. In that sense the impact of the 2022/24 war is further speeding up the structural and regional realignment of Ukraine's economy. It means a much weaker position of some of the traditional industrial sectors, specifically the iron&steel and metals industries which used to account for a major part of the country's exports. On the other hand, it led to a much greater reliance on agriculture and the agro-food industry which will likely have further scope to strengthen its position through up-grading into processing and higher value-added segments. Furthermore, the IT industry has expanded strongly and is now a major contributor to export earnings; this industry (but also other service industries) opens up employment opportunities for highly skilled persons and plays therefore an important role to cater for this segment

[26] This section draws on the contribution by Landesmann, M. (2023).

of the labour force and thereby slow down the brain drain. Also those who emigrated keep in touch with domestic activities of this industry and they thereby contribute towards its international reach.

Thirdly, pre-war Ukraine was plagued by very problematic governance structures (in particular in the areas of rule of law and corruption) as well as entrenched oligarchic power structures. There are a number of reasons why one could expect a positive break in political and economic governance structures: the shock of the war weakened specifically oligarchic economic interests based in the East of the country and strengthened the position of the presidency through its leadership role during the war. Further, there is going to be a rather strong involvement of international agencies (European Commission, IFIs, donor countries) in monitoring the use of the significant funds that are likely to flow into Ukraine to support its reconstruction after the war. It is difficult to make confident forecasts in this respect, but it is likely that both civil society and international donors will exert strong pressures to improve the situation with respect to transparency, rule of law and control of corruption. At least for some time, the spirit of mobilising national efforts to successfully move towards a path of economic, political and social renewal is likely to prevail.

Fourthly, we have the track record of those Central and Eastern European countries which moved towards EU accession and are examples of successful international catching-up processes in income terms. There was also improved institutional development, even though there are also examples of back-sliding in a number of countries (most notably in Hungary). It can be expected that Ukraine could follow these experiences in that there is plenty of scope to gain from intensified trade and production integration with the European economy, and from the role which international investors can play in modernising production facilities and access to markets. Given the legacies of the war (destroyed infrastructure, loss of people through emigration, risk of continued military conflict) it is likely that such a catching-up process will face big hurdles especially in the initial phases, but – in comparison to the previous 'transition countries' – there is also the advantage that the institutional and systemic changes associated with transition have already taken place to an important extent. Ukraine, after all, starts to embark on its accession process well after the shift away from a planned economy system. The adoption of the AA/DCFTA furthermore speeded up regulatory convergence with the EU. The pre-accession phase – if well handled – has the potential to encourage reforms as it focuses society's interests towards achieving this aim.

On the downside: very high costs of reconstruction, demographic decline and questions over investment attractiveness

We now move to the other side of the coin which leads one to a more sober assessment of the scenario of a fast and successful recovery (and restructuring) of the Ukrainian economy and polity:

Firstly, what we consider the most important factor which might hold back economic recovery is the dramatic 'demographic shock' which Ukraine has experienced: the estimates are about 6 million internally displaced persons plus about 5 million persons having emigrated abroad, mostly women and children (September 2023 estimates). This comes on top of the demographic decline which was also apparent before the start of the current war: Ukraine had a population of over 50 million in the mid-1990s, which fell to about 42 million at the start of the war and – accounting for recent emigration – stands now at about 35 million. This decline has been due to a long-term low fertility rate (about 1.3 children per woman) and emigration due to a widening income gap with neighbouring CEE countries (Poland in particular) also before the war. Furthermore, the conflict since 2014 has led to depopulation in regions in which military conflict was most acute and in regions close to these. The age profile of the population has deteriorated strongly, putting strong pressures on the social security (pension and health) system long into the future. Furthermore, as is common in most migration flows, the composition of migrants is biased towards the young and the more highly skilled, which is likely to have a significant impact on the (size and quality) of the domestic labour force. Of course, there can be 'return migration' of a significant share of those who migrated, but the longer the military conflict lasts (and hence the integration of young families and children in host countries proceeds), this becomes less likely. It will therefore be extremely important to initiate effective policy initiatives to attract especially the more highly qualified to return to the country as well as to keep in close contact with the sizeable and growing diaspora.

Secondly, given the experiences of other catching-up economies – we consider the role of foreign investors as very important in the task of restructuring and modernisation of Ukraine's economy. However, there are a number of reasons why it might be difficult to attract foreign investors at least over the medium-term: first, there is the 'risk' of continued military conflict that will deter foreign investors. In this respect there is a strong case to advocate internationally funded 'risk insurance' schemes which cover some of the risks which international investors and traders will encounter in Ukraine even when a cessation of the most intense phase of the conflict has taken place. Then, Ukraine will start its recovery with a lot of destruction of its infrastructure, major damage to the housing stock, and potentially a strong mismatch between regional labour needs and the availability of adequately trained work forces (see Giacomo, Tito, Kudlyak & Zholud, 2022). Thirdly, there is the issue of those institutional factors which also deterred foreign investment in the past (rule of law, corruption, market structures and political influence skewed towards oligarchs) and these will take time to rectify. Lastly, the regions which will need economic reconstruction and modernisation the most will be the regions in (or close to) those regions that were heavily affected by the military conflict, with the most destruction of its infrastructure, most displaced persons and the most risk of continued conflict, hence the least attractive for international investors. These regions will have to rely mostly on public investment, public support for training and education, special schemes to incentivise return migration, and they need to be covered most heavily by 'risk insurance' schemes.

Thirdly, quite a few studies (see Becker et al., 2022; Bogdan, Landesmann & Grieveson, 2022; Kirkegaard, Kleine-Brockhoff, Stokes & Ganster, 2022; World Bank, 2024) have calculated the necessary funds for the economic reconstruction of the Ukraine which will be very high: the estimates range from 400 bn – 1 tn USD over about a ten-year period. The finance of these funds is far from clear at this stage, as the international community (US, EU, G7) is mostly concerned with still covering the most urgent budgetary needs to support current vital social and administrative services apart from military needs. However, major pieces of analysis have already discussed detailed sectoral plans as well as priority areas of economic restructuring of Ukraine (see Gorodnichenko, Sologoub & Weder, 2022; Bogdan & Jovanivič, 2023). There are also suggestions regarding the institutional set-up of such a reconstruction effort and how to deal with coordination of the multiplicity of donor countries and institutions. It is fair to say that we are still far away from having a clear idea where the finance for the massive funding needs will come from and how problems of coordination, but also Ukrainian 'ownership' of such programs will proceed given institutional deficiencies in the country which might still persist after the war (there are institutional initiatives in this direction as well sets of detailed proposals (see e.g., Commission, 2022).

Fourthly, there is another issue which we learnt from the experiences of the 'transition countries' and this refers to macroeconomic imbalances which emerge in the process of economic restructuring and catching-up. The economic reconstruction of the Ukraine will – over a considerable period – be likely accompanied by persistent trade deficits as – initially – there will be very strong import demand and domestic production (and export) capacities will have taken a hit and will take time to recover. On top of that, the considerable inward financial flows which will support the reconstruction effort together with significant remittances of a sizeable Ukrainian diaspora may exert an upward pressure on the Ukrainian hryvnia exchange rate which can be detrimental for competitiveness and the build-up of export capacities. We have seen such developments in a range of transition countries, particularly in the Balkans which have experienced long-term balance-of-payments problems. It will be difficult to counter these pressures unless there is a special focus on supporting the tradable sector (such as focussed efforts to support integration into cross-border production networks through regionally differentiated industrial policy measures including infrastructure, training, FDI supports, etc.), measures to avoid domestic real estate booms and channelling remittance flows at least in part towards investment and business start-ups.

Finally, the speed and indeed the very commitment to Ukraine's EU accession are far from settled. The example of the terribly protracted process of EU integration of the Western Balkans (let alone Turkey) should be a warning sign, also with respect to the political repercussion such long delays and indecision of EU partners can cause in candidate countries. The pre-accession phase can (as the track record of previous accessions shows) be a successful period of institutional reform and economic catching-up if credible milestones are set and consistency in conditionalities and timelines is maintained. It will also be important that - already in the pre-accession phase - new schemes of fast integration into major EU programs (EU regional and industrial policy, educational exchange and research collaboration, transborder infrastructure development, Green Deal) are developed and offered so that Ukraine (and other candidate countries) can – from the point-of-view of integration into such schemes – be considered already a 'quasi-EU member' country even when it still has candidate status.

References

Baas, T. & Brücker, H. (2010). Foreign-born scientists: mobility patterns for 16 countries. *Applied Economics Letters*, *17*(2), 125–128.

Baldwin, R. E., Francois, J. F., Portes, R., Rodrik, D. & Székely, I. P. (1997). Foreign-born scientists: mobility patterns for 16 countries. *Economic Policy*, *12*(24), 125–176.

Becker, T., Eichengreen, B., Gorodnichenko, Y., Guriev, S., Johnson, S., Mylovanov, T., . . . Beatrice Weder, d. M. (2022). A Blueprint for the Reconstruction of Ukraine. *CEPR Rapid Response Economics*, *April 07*(1).

Bogdan, T. & Jovanivič, B. (2023). Public Expenditure Policy for Post-War Reconstruction of Ukraine. *wiiw Policy Notes and Reports*, *June*(69).

Bogdan, T., Landesmann, M. & Grieveson, R. (2022). *Evaluation of Ukraine's National Recovery Draft Plan* (Tech. Rep.). Vienna: Vienna Institute for International Economic Studies.

Breuss, F. (2002). Benefits and Dangers of EU Enlargement. *Empirica*, *29*(3), 245-274.

Caliendo, L., Opromolla, L. D., Parro, F. & Sforza, A. (2021). Goods and Factor Market Integration: A Quantitative Assessment of the EU Enlargement. *Journal of Political Economy*, *129*(12), 3491-3545.

Cedefop. (2022). *Annual Report 2022.* https://www.cedefop.europa.eu/en/content/annual-report-2022.

Commission, E. (2022). Five years of an enlarged EU: Economic achievements and challenges. In *How to organise aid* (Vol. European Economy 1, pp. 515–563). European Commission, Directorate General for Economic and Financial Affairs.

Corden, W. (1984). Booming Sector and Dutch Disease Economics: Survey and Consolidation. *Oxford Economic Papers*, *36*(3), 359-380.

Darvas, Z., Dabrowski, M., Grabbe, H., Moffat, L. L., Sapir, A. & Zachmann, G. (2024). *Impact of a potential future EU accession of Ukraine on Austria and the European Union.* https://www.bruegel.org/policy-brief/ukraines-path-european-union-membership-and-its-long-term-implications.

European Commission. (2020). *Remarks by Commissioner Olivér Várhelyi at the press conference on the revised enlargement methodology.* https://ec.europa.eu/commission/presscorner/detail/el/statement_20_208.

European Commission. (2022). *Cooperation and Verification Mechanism for Bulgaria and Romania* . https://commission.europa.eu/strategy-and-policy/policies/justice-and-fundamental-rights/upholding-rule-law/rule-law/assistance-bulgaria-and-romania-under-cvm/cooperation-and-verification-mechanism-bulgaria-and-romania_en.

European Commission. (2023a). *Analytical Report following the Communication from the Commission to the European Parliament, the European Council and the Council Commission Opinion on Ukraine's application for membership of the European Union.* https://ec.europa.eu/transparency/documents-register/api/files/SWD(2023)30_0/de00000001046221?rendition=false.

European Commission. (2023b). *Proposal for a regulation of the European Parliament and of the Council on establishing the Ukraine Facility.* https://www.eumonitor.eu/9353000/1/j9vvik7m1c3gyxp/vm44h4mcvhwn.

European Council. (2022). *European Council conclusions on Ukraine, the membership applications of Ukraine, the Republic of Moldova and Georgia, Western Balkans and external relations.* www.consilium.europa.eu/en/press/press-releases/2022/06/23/european-council-conclusions-on-ukraine-the-membership-applications-of-ukraine-the-republic-of-moldova-and-georgia-western-balkans-and-external-relations-23-june-2022/.

Eurostat. (2023). *Fertility Statistics.* https://ec.europa.eu/eurostat/statistics-explained/index.php?title=Fertility_statistics.

Giacomo, A., Tito, B., Kudlyak, M. & Zholud, O. (2022). The labor market in Ukraine: rebuild better. In Y. Gorodnichenko, I. Sologoub & B. W. di Mauro (Eds.), *Rebuilding ukraine: principles and policies* (pp. 283–321). CEPR Press.

Giucci, R., Movchan, V. & Kirchner, R. (2019). Positive effect of the DCFTA on Ukraine's exports to the EU. *GET Ukraine*.

Gorodnichenko, Y., Sologoub, I. & Weder, B. (2022). *Rebuilding Ukraine: Principles and Policies* (Vol. 7). CEPR Press.

Grieveson, R., Jovanovic, B., Kosmehl, M., Landesmann, M., Pidnyuk, O., Tverdostup, M. & Weiss, S. (2023). *Outlier or not? Assessing the Ukrainian economy's preparedness for the EU accession process in the context of previous joiners and current candidates).* https://www.bertelsmann-stiftung.de/en/publications/publication/did/outlier-or-not-the-ukrainian-economys-preparedness-for-eu-accession.

Gylfason, T., Hochreiter, E. & Kowalski, T. (2022). Different Choices, Divergent Paths: Poland and Ukraine. *wiiw Research Report, December*(465).

Havlik, P., Kochnev, A. & Pindyuk, O. (2020). Economic Challenges and Costs of Reintegrating the Donbas Region in Ukraine. *wiiw Research Report, June*(447).

IOM. (2023a). *Ukraine — Internal Displacement Report — General Population Survey Round 12 (16 - 23 January 2023).* https://dtm.iom.int/reports/ukraine-internal-displacement-report-general-population-survey-round-12-16-23-january-2023.

IOM. (2023b). *Ukraine — Internal Displacement Report — General Population Survey Round 13 (11 May - 14 June 2023).* https://dtm.iom.int/reports/ukraine-internal-displacement-report-general-population-survey-round-13-11-may-14-june-2023.

Kaucher, S., Deckert, A., Becher, H. & Winkler, V. (2017). Migration pattern and mortality of ethnic German migrants from the former Soviet Union: a cohort study in Germany. *BMJ open*, *7*(12), e019213.

Kirkegaard, J., Kleine-Brockhoff, T., Stokes, B. & Ganster, R. (2022). Designing Ukraine's Recovery in the Spirit of the Marshall Plan. *Washington, DC: The German Marshall Fund*.

Kochnev, A., Landesmann, M., Maucorps, A. & Moshammer, B. (2023). *Ukraine's economic reconstruction: addressing territorial inequalities, consolidating regional policy and reaping the benefits of EU integration.* https://www.bertelsmann-stiftung.de/en/publications/publication/did/ukraines-economic-reconstruction.

Koeth, W. (2014). *The New Instrument for Pre-Accession Assistance (IPA II): Less Accession, More Assistance?* https://www.eipa.eu/wp-content/uploads/2022/01/20160318134447_WorkingPaper_2014_W_01.pdf. European Institute of Public Administration.

Landesmann, M. (2023). What future for the economic reconstruction of Ukraine? In L. Andor & U. Optenhögel (Eds.), *Europe and the war in Ukraine* (p. 242-250). FEPS - Foundation for European Progressive Studies. https://feps-europe.eu/wp-content/uploads/2023/06/Europe-and-the-war-in-Ukraine.pdf.

Lapshyna, I. (2022, Jul). *Ukraine – emigration and displacement in past and present.* Bundeszentrale für politische Bildung. Retrieved from https://www.bpb.de/themen/migration-integration/laenderprofile/english-version-country-profiles/510002/ukraine-emigration-and-displacement-in-past-and-present/#node-content-title-2

Legislation of Ukraine. (2024). *On the Principles of State Regional Policy.* https://zakon.rada.gov.ua/laws/show/156-19?lang=en#Text.

Lisenkova, K. (2015). *Life expectancy in Ukraine: Why is it so low.* Vox Ukraine. Retrieved from https://voxukraine.org/en/life-expectancy-in-ukraine-why-is-it-so-low/

Mansoor, A. & Quillin, B. R. (2006). Migration and Remittances: Eastern Europe and the Former Soviet Union. *World Bank Publications*, 1-236.

Mielczarek, B. & Zabawa, J. (2021). Modelling demographic changes using simulation: Supportive analyses for socioeconomic studies. *Socio-Economic Planning Sciences*, *74*, 100938.

Ministry of Economy. (2022). *Ministry of Economy: 558 relocated enterprises have resumed work in safe regions of the country.* Author. Retrieved from https://www.kmu.gov.ua/en/news/minekonomiky-558-relokovanykh-pidpryiemstv-vzhe-vidnovyly-robotu-u-bezpechnykh-rehionakh-krainy

Movchan, V. & Pindyuk, O. (2024, forthcoming). *What we know about the skills and early labour market outcomes of refugees from Ukraine.*

National Bank of Ukraine. (2023a). *External Sector Statistics.* https://bank.gov.ua/en/statistic/sector-external.

National Bank of Ukraine. (2023b). *Trade Statisics.* https://ukrstat.gov.ua/operativ/menu/menu_e/zed.htm.

Szyszczak, E. & Disney, R. (2022, Jun). *Ukraine's accession to the European Union: What difference would it make?* Retrieved from https://www.economicsobservatory.com/ukraines-accession-to-the-european-union-what-difference-would-it-make

Toyguer, I. & Bergmann, M. (2023). The EU Isn't Ready for Ukraine to Join. *Foreign Policy, June.*

Tverdostup, M. (2023). The Demographic Challenges to Ukraine's Economic Reconstruction. *wiiw Policy Notes and Reports, July*(71).

Ukrstat. (2020). *Value added at factor costs of enterprises by type of economic activity by region in 2014-2020.* https://ukrstat.gov.ua/operativ/operativ2021/fin/pdp_roz_reg/dvvvh_ved_14-20.xlsx.

Ukrstat. (2022). *Regions of Ukraine.* https://ukrstat.gov.ua/druk/publicat/kat_u/2022/zb/12/Regionu_21_pdf.zip.

Ukrstat. (2023). *Gross regional product (2004-2021) with revised balance of payments data.* https://ukrstat.gov.ua/operativ/operativ2021/vvp/kvartal_new/vrp/VRP_%20reg_04_20_II_ue.xls.

UNCTAD. (2023a). *Frontier Technology Readiness Index.* https://unctad.org/system/files/official-document/tir2023ch7annex_en.pdf.

UNCTAD. (2023b). *International Trade in Services.* https://unctadstat.unctad.org/datacentre/.

UNCTAD. (2023c). *UNCTAD-EORA Global Value Chain Database.* https://worldmrio.com/unctadgvc/.

United Nations. (2023). *UN Population Division Data Portal.* https://population.un.org/dataportal/.

Van Imhoff, E. & Post, W. (1998). Microsimulation methods for population projection. *Population: An English Selection*, *10*(1), 97-138.

wiiw. (2023a). *Annual database.* https://data.wiiw.ac.at/annual-database.html.

wiiw. (2023b). *FDI database.* https://data.wiiw.ac.at/foreign-direct-investment.html.

Wolczuk, K. & Žeruolis, D. (2018). Rebuilding Ukraine – An Assessment of EU Assistance. *Chatham House Research Paper*, *August.*

World Bank. (2023a). *World Integrated Trade Solution (WITS) database.* https://wits.worldbank.org/.

World Bank. (2023b). *Worldwide Governance Indicators.* https://www.worldbank.org/en/publication/worldwide-governance-indicators.

World Bank. (2024). *Updated Ukraine Recovery and Reconstruction Needs Assessment Released.* https://www.worldbank.org/en/news/press-release/2024/02/15/updated-ukraine-recovery-and-reconstruction-needs-assessment-released.

World Intellectual Property Organisation (WIPO). (2023). *Webpage.* https://www.wipo.int/portal/en/index.html.

Correction to: Economic Growth & Resilience

Péter Benczúr and István Kónya

Correction to:
Chapter 2 in: L. Mátyás (ed.), *Central and Eastern European Economies and the War in Ukraine*, Contributions to Economics, https://doi.org/10.1007/978-3-031-61561-0_2

The chapter "Economic Growth & Resilience", written by Péter Benczúr and István Kónya, was originally published without open access due to typesetter's mistake. The copyright of the chapter changed on 11-Sep-2023 to © European Commission 2024 and the chapter is now distributed under the terms of the Creative Commons Attribution 4.0 International License (https://creativecommons.org/licenses/by/4.0/), which permits use, sharing, adaptation, distribution and reproduction in any medium or format, as long as you give appropriate credit to the original author(s) and the source, provide a link to the Creative Commons licence and indicate if changes were made.

The images or other third party material in this chapter are included in the chapter's Creative Commons licence, unless indicated otherwise in a credit line to the material. If material is not included in the chapter's Creative Commons licence and your intended use is not permitted by statutory regulation or exceeds the permitted use, you will need to obtain permission directly from the copyright holder.

The updated version of this chapter can be found at
https://doi.org/10.1007/978-3-031-61561-0_2

© The Author(s) 2024

L. Mátyás (ed.), *Central and Eastern European Economies and the War in Ukraine*,
Contributions to Economics, https://doi.org/10.1007/978-3-031-61561-0_11

Open Access This chapter is licensed under the terms of the Creative Commons Attribution 4.0 International License (http://creativecommons.org/licenses/by/4.0/), which permits use, sharing, adaptation, distribution and reproduction in any medium or format, as long as you give appropriate credit to the original author(s) and the source, provide a link to the Creative Commons license and indicate if changes were made.

The images or other third party material in this chapter are included in the chapter's Creative Commons license, unless indicated otherwise in a credit line to the material. If material is not included in the chapter's Creative Commons license and your intended use is not permitted by statutory regulation or exceeds the permitted use, you will need to obtain permission directly from the copyright holder.

Index

© The Author(s), under exclusive license to Springer Nature Switzerland AG 2024

L. Mátyás (ed.), *Central and Eastern European Economies and the War in Ukraine*, Contributions to Economics, https://doi.org/10.1007/978-3-031-61561-0

SPRINGER NATURE

GPSR Compliance

The European Union's (EU) General Product Safety Regulation (GPSR) is a set of rules that requires consumer products to be safe and our obligations to ensure this.

If you have any concerns about our products, you can contact us on ProductSafety@springernature.com

In case Publisher is established outside the EU, the EU authorized representative is:

Springer Nature Customer Service Center GmbH
Europaplatz 3
69115 Heidelberg, Germany

The manufacturer's authorised representative in the EU is Springer Nature Customer Service Centre GmbH, Europaplatz 3, 69115 Heidelberg, Germany. If you have any concerns regarding our products, please contact ProductSafety@springernature.com

Printed and bound by CPI Group (UK) Ltd, Croydon, CR0 4YY

28/09/2026

02224062-0005